Improving
Student
Learning

Published by
THE OXFORD CENTRE FOR STAFF DEVELOPMENT
Oxford Brookes University
Gipsy Lane
Headington
Oxford
OX3 0BP

Improving Student Learning –
Through Assessment and Evaluation
ISBN 1 873576 43 9
British Library Cataloguing-in-Publication Data.
A catalogue record for this book is available from the
British Library.

Designed and Typeset in Palatino by Thomas Nicolaou

Printed in Great Britain by
Oxonian Rewley Press Ltd
Oxford

Printed on paper produced from sustainable forests.

The Oxford Centre for Staff Development

Improving Student Learning

Through Assessment and Evaluation

Editor Graham Gibbs

Contents

Preface

This book contains 40 chapters developed from papers presented at the 2nd International Improving Student Learning Symposium held in Oxford in 1994. They provide evidence of an exciting new movement in attempts to improve the quality of teaching and learning in higher education. This movement is scholarly rather than wholly pragmatic, but 'applied' rather than 'pure', and uses theory and research tools to understand and intervene in student learning. Those undertaking the research are often those directly involved in making decisions about course design, teaching methods and, especially, assessment methods: the lecturers themselves. In some cases students are involved too and examples of both collaborative course design and student research are to be found amongst these pages.

The extent to which research into student learning is being brought to centre stage is well illustrated by Noel Entwistle's paper. He applies key findings from the literature to the way Quality Assessment has operated in Scotland by scouring Assessment reports. Perhaps unsurprisingly he finds little evidence of judgments of the quality of teaching being informed by what is known about what fosters quality in learning: a damming indictment of the lack scholarship underpinning Quality Assessment.

Chris Knapper's paper takes student learning research developed in the context of conventional undergraduate education and applies it to students' approach to learning in a different context - the workplace. This imaginative work demonstrates the diverse ways in which researcher practitioners are extending and adapting the research tools, concepts and theories developed by pure researchers. The vigour and excitement of the Improving Student Learning Symposium could hardly be illustrated more vividly or effectively. Those developing the concepts and research tools encounter those who are using them to practical and impressive effect and those using tools to improve practice develop in the rigour and vision of vision of their applied research practice.

Meyer and Scriverer's work illustrates how research in very practical contexts (in this case the diagnosis of students at risk and likely to benefit from student learning skills intervention) has itself developed and extended both the concepts and the research tools involved.

The symbiosis between research and practice is the raison d'etre of the Improving Student Learning Symposium. This collection of papers is a vivid testimony to this symbiosis in action and of a movement of growing influence and significance. Both researchers and practitioners should pay attention!

Graham Gibbs

1   Approaches to study and lifelong learning: some Canadian initiatives

Christopher Knapper (Queen's University, Kingston, Ontario)

Introduction

Although Canada has one of the most advanced education systems in the world , its educational problems and achievements are relatively unknown to most academics elsewhere, probably because we live under the shadow if our bigger and more flamboyant neighbour to the south. Yet Canadian universities are not so very different from universities in Britain or Australia. Indeed there is a lively exchange of faculty and students between Canada, Europe and many of the countries of the old commonwealth. Canadian academics are concerned with many of the same issues as our colleagues elsewhere – from finding a balance between teaching and research to the problems of plagiarism and grade inflation. In particular, the theme of this book – understanding student learning – would strike a chord with many Canadian university teachers, even though they would be quite unfamiliar with most of the research that is being discussed here.

The purpose of this chapter is to explore some important characteristics of Canadian higher education in relation to two themes. The first theme examines the links between students' learning approaches and acquisition of lifelong learning skills, while the second theme considers what teaching methods night best encourage learning approaches and skills that can be transferred readily to the workplace. Although most of the seminal research in these fields was done outside Canada, I will also describe some modest Canadian initiatives that are largely unknown elsewhere.

Some Characteristics of Canadian Higher Education

Origins and structure

Although the origins if Canadian Higher Education can be traced back to British and French roots, contemporary Canadian universities are now much closer to US institutions in philosophy and organization. To cite a few randomly chosen indicators, our institutions use a credit system with continuing assessment; we allow quite easy transfer from one institution to another; favour broadly-based (liberal arts) general education for most undergraduates, and make no use of external examiners for assessing undergraduate degrees.

Canada has about 50 universities, all of them public institutions, and most offer a wide range of programmes up to the doctorate. The Canadian university system is much more homogeneous than that of the USA, although individual institutions enjoy considerable autonomy with respect to policy matters and academic programmes, as well as setting salary scales and conditions of employment. Until now there has been a fairly rigid demarcation between the university and college sectors with only universities allowed to award degrees. The comments in this chapter primarily reflect the experience of teachers and students in the university sector.

As in many other jurisdictions, university policies multiple roles for academic staff, including involvement in teaching, research and service to the institution and wider community. These policies, increasingly enforced through collective agreements, give highest – and equal – priority to teaching and scholarship. However, it is widely perceived by Canadian academics that current reward systems over-emphasize research accomplishments at the expense of teaching (Piccinin, 1990; University of Toronto, 1994a). This is a perception shared by many colleagues in the USA, Australia and perhaps beyond (see Knapper, 1990).

Pressures for change

Funding for universities is channelled through the ten provincial governments, and indeed there is no federal ministry of education in Canada. Due in part to the way universities are funded, there has traditionally been very little government leverage exerted on universities compared to institutions in the United Kingdom, Australia, Europe and the United States. However, the recent Canadian debt crisis, and consequent cutbacks affecting the public sector (especially health services and education) have bought increased government pressure on universities to be more accountable for the quality of their teaching and research endeavours. For example, the Ontario Council on University Affairs, which has responsibility for distributing funds to universities in that province, is currently contemplating a new funding arrangement, and one of the options it has put forward for debate is the notion of contractual arrangements whereby universities would bid for funds to offer specific teaching programmes or undertake mission-oriented research (see Ontario Council on University Affairs, 1994). This proposal has already been flatly rejected by the Ontario university presidents, and is likely to incur a storm of protest from academic staff. At the same time, government calls for accountability have received public support from any politicians and the media.

A particular focus of attention has been quality of teaching – judged both on its own terms and as a preparation for employment. (In August 1994 Canadian unemployment was around 11%, though less for university graduates.) 1991 saw the publication of the report of Canada's first commission of inquiry to deal with the quality of university education (the 'Smith Commission' – see Smith, 1991). The report was extremely critical of many aspects of university teaching and, among other things, recommended:

- more tangible rewards for teaching and instructional innovation;
- a redefinition of 'scholarship' to encompass more than publication of research articles;
- different career paths that would allow staff to emphasize teaching;
- increased teaching hours for academic staff;
- compulsory training in teaching methods for those entering the academic profession;
- earmarked funding for educational development;
- regular evaluation of teaching competence, including the use of teaching portfolios;

- regular surveys of graduates to enquire how well their studies prepared them for work; and
- the establishment of a nation-wide system for developing performance indicators for quality control (Smith, 1991).

Reaction to Smith in the academic community has been mixed, but although many university presidents believe the report to have been buried, its recommendations continue to be used as a set of benchmarks by those who control university funding.

Another source of pressure to change teaching methods has come from students, who are increasingly vocal in their criticisms of universities, caused no doubt in part by the sharp rise in tuition fees over the past decade. At Queen's, for example, the Queen's Alma Mater Society raised no less then $750,000 to support the establishment of an instructional development centre to improve the quality of teaching. It also lobbied successfully for introduction of university-wide student evaluation of courses.

Teaching and Learning

Canada has had a system of 'mass education' much longer than most European or Australian universities. Currently about one-quarter of all 18 – 21 year-olds are enrolled in university, a proportion exceeded only by the USA, and about double the percentage enrolled in Britain. Hence Canadians have long been concerned with the problems of teaching a diverse student population comprising learners of different ages, ethnic backgrounds, and abilities. A recent University of Toronto survey, for example, showed that over 50per cent of the student body were non-Caucasian, and 49per cent came from a home where English was not the preferred language of discourse (University of Toronto, 1994b).

Traditional teaching methods still predominate in Canadian universities, and the amount of formal teaching is larger than in many other countries. A typical Canadian student in the arts and humanities takes fine classes a term, each of which meets for three hours (usually lectures) each week. In the sciences and professional schools additional time is spent in laboratories. Students are also tested with great frequency. For examples, each one of the typical five courses entails at least a mid-term and final examination, in addition to occasional essays and assignments. Credits are accumulated, often leading to fierce competitive for marks to enhance the 'curriculative grade-point average', and there are no final (end-of-programme) examinations as in Britain and Australia. Classes can be very large, especially in the first year, since many departments offer huge introductory lecture courses in order to offer smaller, more specialized courses in the upper years. At Queen's, a medium-sized university, introductory classes of 200 students are quite common and more than 400 is not unknown. There is widespread use of graduate teaching assistants (post-graduate students) who run tutorials, act as laboratory demonstrators, and undertake most of the marking of assignments and exams in introductory courses. For the most part the assistants receive no preparation for their teaching responsibilities, although there is increased pressure to provide training and evaluation of TAs, and a number of universities have training programmes, generally organized by the in structural development centre (Piccinin, Farquharson and Mihu, 1993).

Despite this somewhat gloomy picture, there are some well-known pockets of innovation in Canadian universities. For example, many institutions offer very successful co-operative education programmes (similar to British sandwich courses), and the University of Waterloo has the largest such programme in the world (McCallum and Wilson, 1987). Problem-based learning in professional schools was pioneered in Canada, and the McMaster medical curriculum has been imitated in many countries (Neufeld and barrows, 1974). And long before the creation of the British Open University many Canadian institutions offered innovative distance education programmes using an variety of technologies, from print to radio (see Mugridge and Kaufman, 1986).

Research on Student Learning

There has been relatively little Canadian research on higher education, partly because there are very few departments of higher education in Canadian universities, and educational researchers have preferred to concentrate on school age populations. There is even less research on teaching and learning in higher education, with the exception of a considerable body of scholarship on student evaluation of instruction (see Knapper, 1981, for a review of Canadian research on university teaching and learning).

On the whole, the findings of this research have done little to inform or change teaching practices in Canadian universities. Although many Canadian academics do have learning goals for their students, they are largely unaware of any empirical research on study processes that might shed light on appropriate methods to produce desired learning outcomes (Knapper, 1990). In common with academics in other countries, most Canadian teachers have had no preparatory training in instructional methods, and they rarely read educational literature dealing with teaching and learning issues. It is only recently, with the establishment of instructional development centres, that university teachers have started to attend workshops, seminars, and courses that deal with pedagogical issues, and as a consequence become areas of literature on teaching and learning in higher education. Hence it is not surprising that choice of teaching methods is based largely on traditions or models derived from other contexts – such as instructors' own undergraduate studies or experiences at academic conferences.

Lifelong Learning and University Teaching

The main purpose of undergraduate education is presumably to acquire knowledge, values, and skills that will transfer to situations beyond the university – in particular the workplace. At a time of turbulent change, both social and technological, and rapid obsolescence of knowledge, it is not surprising that many educators have argued for a model of university education that stresses not just a short-term demonstration of expertise, but rather the acquisition of generic cognitive skills and values, such as the ability to make decisions and solve problems in an ethically responsible manner and to communicate such decisions effectively. Hence it has been argued that an overriding educational goal of the university is to have student 'learn how to learn'. Commentators such as Edgar Faure (1972), have used the term 'lifelong learning', implying that students should leave higher education with the ability and motivation to continue learning through the rest of their lives and from a wide variety of sources – not just formal educational institutions. Indeed, in Canada, the term lifelong learning has become something of a cliche, and is mentioned as an overriding educational objective in many university mission statements and public reports.

Knapper and Cropley (1991) described an 'idealized' lifelong learner as someone with the following competencies:

- the capacity to set personal and realistic learning goals;
- the ability to apply existing knowledge and skills effectively;
- the ability to evaluate one's own learning;
- skill at locating information from different sources; and
- the capacity to use different learning strategies in different situations.

Lifelong learning is seen by Knapper and Cropley as a guiding principle for education and, as such, is a much broader concept than the notion of learning style and learning approach. None the less, the attributes of the lifelong learner as described above are certainly consistent with many of the learning characteristics being discussed in this volume. More specifically, an effective lifelong learner would undoubtedly be capable of a deep approach to learning, especially the ability to interpret material being studies and forge links between such material and other sources of information. (Note the emphasis on the word 'effective'. It is possible to envisage a lifelong surface learner, but such an individual would have trouble rising to the challenges of change listed by Knapper and Cropley -- though they might perform well in television quiz shows.) Hence it is not surprising that Knapper and Cropley devote a part of their book to research on learning approaches developed by many of the contributors to those proceedings.

As explained above, many Canadian faculty seem to accept the principles of lifelong learning as providing appropriate goals for their students (see Knapper, 1990). however they often teach in ways that discourage the types of learning proposed by Knapper and Cropley. One disincentive to change is the lack of a perceived link between teaching methods and learning outcomes, especially outcomes that translate into cognitive skills for real-world application. In this context the work of Ramsden and Entwistle (1981) is of particular importance in showing how teaching methods and learning climate are related to student learning approaches.

In fact there is considerable evidence from many different studies that quality of teaching is related to effective learning and cognitive development. For example, Astin (1993) in a massive project that involved 20,000 students, 25,000 academic staff, and 200 institutions in the USA, showed that the characteristics and behaviour of teaching staff had major implications for student development. In particular, opportunities for student–staff interaction had 'positive correlations with every self-reported area of intellectual and personal growth' (p. 383), and there were similar positive effects associated with opportunities for interactions among students themselves. In contrast, sheer number of hours devoted to teaching was unrelated to cognitive development, suggesting that it is the quality of staff–student contact, not the quality, that is of critical importance.

Pascarella and Terenzini (1991) analysed the results of over 2,600 empirical studies dealing with the impact of higher education on student learning and development. They concluded that student learning is 'unambiguously linked to effective teaching, and we know much about what effective teachers do and how they behave in the classroom' (p. 619). Such behaviours include the instructor's ability to establish rapport with students, interpersonal accessibility, feedback to students, active learning strategies, opportunities for students to interact with their peers, and 'a curricular experience in which students are required to integrate learning from separate courses around a central theme' (p. 619). Writing about the implications of their research for policy and practice, Pascarella and Terenzini conclude that academic departments should strive to 'create environments that attract and engage students in both intellectual and interpersonal learning' (p. 653).

These recommendations echo the conclusions of Paul Ramsden (1991) in a paper about the use of the Course experience Questionnaire as a performance indicator of teaching quality. Ramsden and Entwistle (1981) had earlier shown links between a deep approach to learning, as measured by the Approaches to Study Questionnaire, and the characteristics of academic departments. For example, a deeper approach was associated with departments that demonstrated 'concern for and availability to students; enthusiasm and interest of teachers; clear organisation and goals; feedback on learning; the encouragement of student independence and active learning; an appropriate workload and relevant assessment methods; the provision of a suitably challenging academic environment' (Ramsden, 1991, p.129). More recently, Kember and Gow (1994) have shown that learning approaches are affected by the orientations of individual teachers, and that interactive teaching methods seem especially important for fostering a deep learning orientation. Although neither Astin nor Pascarella and Terenzini were specifically concerned with deep learning approaches, as defined by Ramsden and others, all these researchers' conclusions about the links between learning and teaching approaches are surprisingly consistent.

The data cited by Astin and by Pascarella and Terenzini were derived almost entirely from sources in the USA. Indeed, what is remarkable about their review of the literature, is that of the 2,600 references cited in their bibliography, there is no mention of the key European and Australian researchers who have examined student approaches to learning -- people such as Ramsden, Entwistle, Marton, Biggs, etc. It is interesting to speculate why the European/Australian research on deep and surface learning approaches has been largely disregarded in North America. It may be partly because of a suspicion of qualitative methods, partly due to ethnocentrism, and partly because the research is seen as more 'value-laden' than the typical US work on learning styles, where it is common to imply that all styles have their own merits. In introducing the idea of learning approaches in workshops in the USA I have frequently found that many participants will argue for the merit of surface approaches for some types of learning situations. It is interesting too that although the present conference attracted many delegates from outside Britain, there were virtually none from North America.

Probably none of this matters in Canada, where most academics remain ignorant of both lines of research. However, there has been some Canadian interest in studying student approaches to learning. For example, Kirby and his students, in a series of projects using the Biggs SOLO taxonomy, investigated the way in which undergraduates process textual material, and explored relationships between depth of processing, verbal ability and available working memory (Kirby and Woodhouse, 1994). Hilliard (1994) and Garrison, Andrews and Magnusson (1994) used Biggs' Study Process Questionnaire to measure learning approaches of student in medicine, science and social science. And Wong (1992) investigated approaches to study of mature students studying at a distance, based on responses to Ramsden's Approaches to Study Questionnaire.

I have also gathered data on student learning approaches from undergraduates at two Canadian universities, using the Approaches to Study Questionnaire and a shortened version of the Course Experience Questionnaire. For example, Bertrand and Knapper (1991) found significant difference between three academic departments on the ASQ, and these difference were related to scores on the CEQ in ways very similar to the relationships described by Ramsden and Entwistle (1981). Specifically, the departments where students adopted a deeper approach to learning were characterized by better teaching, more freedom in learning, greater openness to students, more reasonable workload, and less formal teaching methods (Knapper, in press).

Other studies by my students have replicated these findings, and it seems clear that the constructs investigated in Europe, Australasia, and Asia are equally valid for North American students, and the learning approaches are influenced in similar ways by the institutional learning climate.

Lifelong Learning: Links Between University and the Workplace

An underlying assumption of university education is that the skills and values learnt there will transfer to other situations -- in particular the workplace. Without debating the relative merits of a broad liberal education versus more specialised preparation for the professions, it would be fair to say that attitudes and competencies learned in university should be useful in other walks of life. This is why proponents of lifelong learning, such as Knapper and Cropley (1991) place such stress on "learning to learn" skills that individuals will carry with them into many situations beyond school and college. The idea here is that people will be able to direct their own learning endeavours on a continuing basis without the need for formal instruction at an educational institution -- in other words, lifelong learning does not mean lifelong schooling.

Of particular interest is the individual's approach to learning new things. Specifically, do students who adopt sophisticated learning approaches in university transfer such approaches to the workplace? I am assuming here that learning at work is both desirable and inevitable, and indeed there has been considerable recent interest in the concept of the workplace as a learning environment. For example, Watkins and Marsick (1993) define the learning organisation as one "that learns continuously and transforms itself" (p. 8). Naturally, such learning involves individuals within the organisation, "integrated with, and running parallel to, work" (p. 8). (4) It seems plausible that the type of lifelong learner who would contribute most effectively to the learning organisation would be capable of adopting a deep learning approach so as to integrate knowledge from different fields to solve unforeseen or novel problems (see Botkin, Elmandjra, and Malitza, 1979; Senge, 1990).

However, there is surprising little evidence about the transfer of learning approaches from school to other situations. Pascarella and Terenzini (1991) refer to the motion that attending university"provides the basic intellectual, analytical and interpersonal competencies that permit one to effectively learn new occupationally relevant skills on the job" (p. 432). However, their exhaustive review revealed very little empirical research bearing on this link, in contrast to the large number of studies that have demonstrated relationships between attending university and salary or career success.

Measuring Approaches to Learning in the Workplace

The University of Waterloo provided a unique opportunity to study links between learning in university and learning at work, since a majority of undergraduates are enrolled in cooperative (sandwich) programmes which alternate study with paid employment. With the help of a colleague, Robin Banks, I therefore attempted to devise a measure of learning in the workplace by adapting the Approaches to Studying Questionnaire. This was done rather crudely by simply taking the items on the short form of the instrument and changing individual items to make them suitable for description of experiences at work. This proved to be relatively easy to do. For example, "I find it easy to organise my study time effectively" was changed to "At work, I find it easy to organise my study time effectively", "I like to be told precisely what to do in essays and other set work" was changed to "When I am given a job to at work, I like to be told precisely what is expected", etc.

We made a similar adaptation of the Course Experience Questionnaire. Once again, it was possible to construct many of the items with only minor changes in wording. For example, "The workload is too heavy in this department" simply became "The workload is too heavy", "It's always easy here to know the standard of work expected of you" was the same for both questionnaires, and so on.

A total of 256 students from six academic departments at the University of Waterloo completed the Approaches to Work Questionnaire (AWQ) shortly after completing a four-month work placement. Of this group, 114 also completed the Work Experience Questionnaire (WEQ) and 118 completed the Approaches to Study Questionnaire at the end of the following term when they were immersed in their university studies in the major discipline. Most of the students were in the third year of their academic programme, with a few in the second year. The job placement settings varied greatly, depending upon the discipline concerned (eg. Accounting vs. Engineering), but all worked for the four moths and received a salary from the employer.

For the Approaches to Study and the Approaches to Work Questionnaire, scores on achieving orientation, reproducing orientation (surface approaches to learning) and meaning orientation (deep approach to learning) were calculated using the weighings suggested by Ramsden (1983). Scale reliabilities were estimated and found to be satisfactory, though low. Fortunately, they were highest for the scale measuring meaning orientation, and I shall devote most attention in the following discussion to results from that scale.

Correlations between scale scores on the two questionnaires were all significant, and were highest for the scales measuring meaning orientation at university and in the workplace (r = .45, p < .001). Mean scores were compared for the subscales on the two instruments. Although they were comparable for achieving orientation, in the case of reproducing orientation scores were significantly higher on the Approaches to Study Questionnaire than on the Approaches to Work Questionnaire (t = 4.35, p < .001). Conversely, scores on meaning orientation were significantly higher for the AWQ than the ASQ (t = 6.5, p < .001). Although it is dangerous to generalise from such a small sample, there is a hint here that students in the workplace encounter more scope for deep approaches to learning than they do at university. Of course it is possible that this was because the workplace was, at least for these students, a novel environment which offered more opportunities for quickly learning new things. If so, it is nonetheless interesting that students met this challenge by increasing their meaning orientation and reducing their reproducing orientation.

There were very few significant differences between scale scores for the six academic departments, although numbers in some groups were so small that this is not entirely surprising. There was also only one significant difference between respondents of different gender: on the AWQ females scored significantly higher than males on achievement orientation (t = 2.56, p < .01).

In the cases of the Work Experience Questionnaire, it had proved more difficult to find exact equivalences for some of the items in the Course perceptions instrument, and hence responses to the WEQ were subjected to principal-components analysis in an attempt to determine the underlying structure of items, and identify scales that most appropriately described the work environment. Three principal factors emerged, accounting for 33% of the variance. I have tentatively labelled Factor I Good Supervision and Concern for staff - - characterised by such items as "Managers/Supervisors are extremely good at explaining things to us" and "Managers/Supervisors here normally give helpful feedback on how you are going". Factor II was labelled Consultation/Openness, loading highly (and negatively) on such items as "In this job you have very little say in the way your performance is evaluated" and "The managers/supervisors frequently give the impression they haven't anything to learn from staff". Factor III, labelled Work Climate and Motivation, was characterised by such items as "The managers/supervisors motivate staff to do their best work" and "This firm really tries to get the best out of all its staff".

Factor scores on these dimensions were calculated for each respondent, and these scores were correlated to their scores on the three sub-scales of the ASQ and the AWQ. Only one of the three factors yielded significant correlations. Scores on Factor III, Work Climate and Motivation, were positively related to both achievement orientation and meaning orientation, and negatively related to reproducing orientation. In other words, this very tentative finding indicates that a deeper approach to learning at work and in university is associated in the work setting with managers and supervisors who motivate their employees and provide a supportive work environment.

Learning at University and in the Workplace: Next Steps

This preliminary study permits some cautious conclusions. Firstly, it does seem to be meaningful to measure learning approaches in the work setting. Employees -- albeit highly educated employees -- do not apparently find it strange to be asked about the workplace as a learning environment, nor are they reluctant to describe their own learning approaches to work. Secondly, it appears that people's approaches to study in an academic setting partly determine the way they learn at work (indicated by the significant correlations between scale scores on the ASQ and the AWQ). Thirdly, the work settings in the present study appear to demand deeper approaches to learning than the same students demonstrated at university, although this may not be true for all work settings.

Based upon the results from the Work Experience Questionnaire, it is possible to measure employees' perceptions of what might be termed "learning climate in the workplace". However, the dimensions that I found descriptive of the work environment are not entirely consistent with those typically used to describe academic environments, as measured on the Course perceptions Questionnaire. The three dimensions that emerged all involved attitudes of supervisors to employees, indicating that the role of managers in the work setting is just as important as the role of teachers in university. Clearly much more research has to be done to develop a valid instrument, using a larger sample of respondents and introducing more controls over the type of work situation studied.

There is only tentative evidence from the present study of a relationship between work environment and learning approach. Perceptions of a positive, motivating work climate were related to greater achievement and meaning orientation, but the pattern of correlations here was much weaker than those described by Ramsden and Entwistle (1986) linking approaches to study and characteristics of academic departments in British universities. Further investigation might clarify how different work environments and experiences are linked to different learning approaches.

Implications for Educators

Despite a lot of rhetoric about lifelong learning and learning organisations, there is rather little empirical study of how and what people learn in their day-to-day lives, both as employees and in other situations outside formal educational institutions. Moore (1986) has discussed the need for a "pedagogy of work experience" that would help identify what factors in the work environment contribute to learning, and has offered a number of learning narratives and case studies that describe how individuals learn new work tasks. Candy and Crebert (1991) catalogue the differences between university and workplace learning and call for increased attention to the way in which graduates adapt to the new learning environment they face as employees. They point out that though there has been increased attention to the interface between university and the world of work, the focus has been mainly on the "technical competencies of workers, rather than more generic skills or predispositions" (p. 589).

Few researchers have asked employees to describe the workplace in terms of its encouragement of learning or have tried to describe and measure employees' approaches to learning at work. As Anderson and Gonczi (1992, p. 98) say, "By far the least understood and researched area of skills formation is learning on the job". This is perhaps somewhat surprising, given the importance of work in most people's lives and the widespread belief that a principal function of higher education is to equip students with skills (including learning skills) they will be able to use in work situations. The present investigation gives some support for the idea that research on approaches to study developed by Marton, Biggs, Ramsden, Entwistle, and their colleagues might provide a paradigm for investigating workplace learning. This in turn could provide some empirical underpinnings for the current discussions on how to change business into learning organisations.

A next step would be to show how learning approaches in the workplace are linked to other variables, such as employees' sense of control over the work environment, their capacity for innovation, productivity, or work satisfaction. Establishment of such connections would allow universities – at least in principal – to demonstrate that their teaching programmes not only can produce students with deep approaches to academic problems, but that such orientations foster learning effectiveness at work – providing the work environment itself encourages ongoing learning efforts.

I do not wish to imply here that preparation for employment is the only purpose of higher education. However, I do believe that the capacity to learn how to learn and adopt a deep, integrative approach to learning tasks is a desirable component of citizenship that embraces people's social and family lives. Transfer of learning approaches such situations could also be studied, although this would probably be more difficult than studying learning in business or industrial settings.

I am arguing, then, that study of how learning transfers to the work situation is an important means of demonstrating accountability for higher education. It builds upon the notion of using teaching effectiveness as a performance indicator as suggested by Ramsden (1991). It goes a step further, however, by suggesting that acquisition of learning skills at university is not sufficient unless we can demonstrate that they have been transferred effectively to the world outside.

Mention of performance indicators will be a provocation to many of my colleagues, especially in Canada, where we lag behind Britain and Australia in developing such, indices, and in particular when it comes to providing evidence for learning accomplishments and teaching effectiveness. This was one of the strongest criticisms of the Smith Commission, and perhaps the one that provoked most defensiveness on the part of Canadian universities (Smith, 1991). Following path from teaching evaluation to learning outcomes and perhaps to learning transfer might show that some institutions or academic departments actually discourage effective learning approaches and that they prepare students inadequately for the learning challenges they will face once they have graduated.

Conversely, it may be found that institutions or departments do indeed equip students with appropriate learning approaches and skills, but that these are discouraged or negated by inappropriate workplace practices, especially the attitudes and action of management. If research along the present lines were to promote a more sophisticated dialogue between employers and academics, then it should be possible to demonstrate empirically what is intuitively obvious – that the preparation and sustenance of a sophisticated workforce requires a partnership between higher education and business.

Our task as knowledgeable educators is to try and change institutions by introducing teaching that we know – thanks to the work of many present at this conference -- will enhance sophisticated learning approaches. For their part, business and industry must ensure that our graduates entering the workplace receive rewards and encouragement for the ongoing development of their lifelong learning skills, not only for their own self-fulfilment, but also for the benefit of employers and the wider community.

References

Anderson, G., & Gonczi, A. (1992). Human resource development for the global economy. *Studies in Continuing Education*, **14**, 97-103.

Astin, A. W. (1993). *What matters in College? Four critical years revisited.* San Francisco: Jossey-Bass.

Bertrand, D., & Knapper, C.K. (1991). Contextual influences on students' approaches to learning in three academic departments. Unpublished honours thesis, University of Waterloo, Ontario.

Botkin, J. W., Elmandjra, M., & Malitza, M. (1979). *No limits to learning.* Oxford: Pergamon.

Candy, P. C., & Crebert, R. G. (1991). Ivory tower to concrete jungle: The difficult transition from the academy to the workplace as learning environments. *Journal of Higher Education*, **62,**570-592.

Faure, E. (with others). (1972). *Learning to be: The world of education today and tomorrow.* Paris and London: Unesco and Harrap.

Garrison, D. R., Andrews, J. & Magnusson, K. (1994). In A. G. Konrad & K. M. Grieve (Eds.), *Proceedings of the Annual Conference of the Canadian Society for the Study of Higher Education* (pp. 160-163). Calgary, Alberta: University of Calgary.

Hilliard, r. (1994). Learning styles of undergraduate medical students [Summary]. In J. Falconer (Ed), *Proceedings to the Sixth Ottawa Conference on Medical Education* (p. 30). Hamilton, Ontario: McMaster University, Faculty of Health Sciences.

Kember, D. & Gow, L. (1994). Orientations to teaching and their effect on the quality of student learning. *Journal of Higher Education*, **65**, 58-74.

Kirby, J. R. & Woodhouse, R. A. (1994). Measuring and predicting depth of processing in learning. *Alberta Journal of Educational Research*, **40**, 147-161.

Knapper, C. K. (1981). A decade review of college teaching research: 1970-1980. *Canadian Psychology*, **22**, 129-145.

Knapper, C. K. (1990). Lifelong learning and university teaching. In I. Moses (Ed), *Higher education in the late twentieth century: Reflections on a changing system* (pp. 202-214). Kensington, New South Wales: Higher Education Research and development Society of Australasia.

Knapper, C. K. (in press). Understanding student learning: Implications for instructional practice. In W. A. Wright (Ed), *Successful Faculty Development: Strategies to improve university teaching.* Bolton, MA: Anker.

Knapper, C. K. & Cropley, A. J. (1991). *Lifelong learning and higher education* (2nd ed.). London: Kogan Page.

Marshall, H. H. (1988). Work or learning: Implications of classroom metaphors. *Educational Researcher*, **17**(9), 9-16.

McCallum, B. A. & Wilson, J. C. (1987). They said it wouldn't work (a history of cooperative education in Canada). *Journal of Cooperative Education*, **24**(2-3), 61-67.

Moore, D. T. (1986). Learning at work: Case studies in non-school education. *Anthropology and Education Quarterly*, **17**, 166-184.

Mugridge, I. & Kaufman, D. (Eds.). (1986). *Distance education in Canada*. London: Croom Helm.

Neufeld, V. R. & Barrows, H. S. (1974). The 'McMaster philosophy': An approach to medical education. *Journal of Medical Education*, **49**, 1040-1050.

Ontario Council on University Affairs. (1994). *Sustaining quality in changing times: Funding Ontario universities*. Toronto: Author.

Pascarella, E. T. & Terenzini, P. T. (1991). *How college affects students: Findings and insights from twenty years of research*. San Francisco: Jossey-Bass.

Piccinin, S. J. (1990). *Summary of the results of the survey on teaching*. Unpublished internal report, University of Ottawa, Centre for University Teaching, Ottawa.

Piccinin, S. J., Farquharson, A. & Mihu, E. (1993). Teaching assistants in Canadian universities: An unknown resource. *Canadian Journal of Higher Education*, **23**(2), 104-117.

Ramsden, P. (1993). *The Lancaster Approaches to Study and Course Perceptions Questionnaire: Lecturers' handbook*. Oxford: Oxford Polytechnic, Educational Methods Unit.

Ramsden, P. (1991). A performance indicator of teaching quality in higher education: The Course Experience Questionnaire. *Studies in Higher Education*, **16**, 129-150.

Ramsden, P. & Entwistle, N. J. (1981). Effects of academic departments on students' approaches to studying. *British Journal of educational Psychology*, **51**, 368-383.

Senge, P. M. (1990). *The fifth discipline: The art and practice of the learning organisation*. New York: Doubleday.

Smith, S. L. (1991). *Report of the Commission of Inquiry on Canadian Higher Education*. Ottawa: Association of Universities and Colleges of Canada.

University of Toronto. (1994a). *On the balance between research and undergraduate teaching: Faculty perceptions at the University of Toronto*. Unpublished internal paper, University of Toronto, Office of the Provost, Toronto.

University of Toronto. (1994b). *Questions on surveys: Partial answers*. Unpublished internal paper, University of Toronto, Office of the Provost, Toronto.

Watkins, K. E. & Marsick, V. J. (1993). *Sculpting the learning organisation: Lessons in the art and science system change*. San Francisco: Jossey-Bass.

Wong, S. (1992, July). Approaches to study of distance education students. *Research in Distance Education*, pp. 11-17.

2   The use of research on student learning in quality assessment

Noel Entwistle (Centre for Research on Learning and Instruction University of Edinburgh)

Introduction

This chapter explores what research on student learning has to offer to quality assessment of teaching and more generally to the theme of this book Improving Student Learning. The chapter draws on different sets of experience: as a researcher into student learning; as a reviewer of work on the effects of teaching on learning outcomes; as a member of the Quality Assessment Committee of the Scottish Higher Education Funding Council (SHEFC); as the Head of an education department; and as a university teacher. All of these experiences affect my views on how research on student learning can be used to improve student learning.

    Underlying the title of this chapter is an assumption that quality assessment can be used to improve the quality of student learning, and that quality assessment itself can be improved if findings from research on student learning are taken more actively into account. The starting point will be the perceived need for improvements in the quality of teaching and the function of quality assessment in encouraging such improvements. That will lead to a brief description of how the quality of teaching in departments is currently being judged in Britain, drawing specifically on experiences from SHEFC. The criteria on which quality of teaching is judged will be described, as well as the outcomes of those judgements and, in particular, comments on the teaching found in departments rated as 'excellent'. There do seem to be problems in the way quality in teaching is currently being judged, and these will be examined in the light of research on student learning. Some recent research is used to develop an argument about the way teaching needs to support the development of conceptual understanding, and that leads on to a consideration of staff development activities, and their effectiveness in changing the conceptions staff have about the nature of teaching and learning in higher education.

The Need for Improvement in the Quality of Teaching

Over the years, there have been repeated complaints about the quality of teaching in higher education. These complaints have come partly from educationists, who have pointed to the lack of formal training given to teachers in higher education, but also from students who have felt that their experience of higher education left a good deal to be desired. What criticisms, in particular, have been made? An analysis of more than 600 feedback questionnaires at the University of Teesside (Pennington,1994) revealed three specific weaknesses in teaching. Students identified the need for more effective teaching delivery (50%), greater coherence in assessment methods (23%), and better course management and design (16%), with other factors mentioned by a further 11% of the students.

Another survey (Williams and Loader, 1993), this time including teaching staff and administrators as well as students, allows us to see in more detail which particular aspects of teaching provision are generally perceived to be weak (see Table 1).

Table 1 Criticisms of teaching in higher education made by administrators, lecturers and students

Academic staff are not showing sufficient:

- enthusiasm for their subject
- good presentational skills
- encouragement of active participation by students
- provision of detailed and prompt feedback to students
- putting knowledge of learning principles into practice (students only)

Institutions are not providing sufficient:

- collective discussion by staff of good teaching practice
- recognition of teaching skills
- active encouragement of teaching innovations

Source: adapted from Williams and Loader, 1993.

Official concern about the quality of teaching in higher education was noted in the 1987 White Paper *Higher Education: Meeting the Challenge*, which asked for improvements in both quality and efficiency in teaching (Nightingale and O'Neil,1994), and again in the 1991 White Paper on *Higher Education: a New Framework* which also laid down the procedures for improving quality. Of course, the current political climate has meant that economy and efficiency have been the main targets, although the rhetoric has continued to stress the improvement in quality. The funding councils for higher education have each set up their own procedures for assessing quality in teaching, but the general procedures are fairly similar. Here we shall look at the operation of the SHEFC quality assessment procedure.

The SHEFC Quality Framework

Initial ideas on the definition of quality in Scottish higher education were set out in a consultation paper issued in August 1992, based on the experience of a pilot quality assessment exercise carried out earlier that year. The paper described a 'systems model' based on inputs (such as staffing and the curriculum), processes (such as teaching and assessment), and outputs (such as learning outcomes, and student and employer satisfaction), and argued that certain criteria of quality could be established about which there would be a general consensus.

Quality in education is dependent on many factors, which may be incorporated in an operational quality framework ... For example, curriculum aims and objectives should be explicit and known to staff and students; courses should be periodically reviewed to assess their suitability; the learning and teaching environment should be generally conducive to learning; accommodation should be appropriate for the curriculum on offer; lectures should be well planned and prepared, and effectively performed; and learning should be enriched by appropriate reference to cross-curricular links, current research, industrial applications and the development of generic skills such as communication and teamwork. (para. 8)

The current Quality Framework had its origins in this analysis, with modifications introduced on the basis of the consultation exercise and subsequent experience in its use over the last two years. It should also be remembered that, in Scotland, the development of this framework was led by HMIs whose experience was in the visits and the reporting procedures developed within the Scottish Office Education Department. Their remit was broad with a concern essentially for what has since been described as 'total quality management'. The framework established reflected that breadth. The thinking behind the framework was certainly informed by research on teaching and learning, but the criteria included were derived from the experience of HMIs. Consultation with institutions led to modifications in the procedure, but there was less concern among institutions about the details of the framework.

Table 2   Aspects and reporting headings within the SHEFC Quality Framework

Curriculum	Aims and curricula Curriculum design and review
Environment and resources	The teaching and learning environment Staff resources Learning resources
Teaching and assessment	Course organization Teaching and learning practice Assessment and monitoring
Student guidance and support	Student support
Outcomes and quality control	Students' work Output, outcomes and quality control

The Quality Framework is now used by departments in making their self-evaluations, and also by the panels of assessors both in judging the self-assessments and in discussing their impressions after visiting the department. (In Scotland, all departments being assessed are visited.) Self-evaluations are based on eleven aspects, but the framework for reporting has only five categories. Table 2 shows the 11 aspects, within the five reporting areas, while Table 3 shows examples of the 63 elements within the framework.

Table 3   A quality framework for assessing teaching

Curriculum

Departmental aims are consistent with the institutional 'mission'

Aims are appropriate for students, society and the economy

Curricula are up-to-date in terms of both content and delivery

Appropriate balance of specialist content and transferable skills

Courses are effectively organized, managed, and reviewed

Environment and resources

The teaching environment is conducive to learning

Equipment is adequate and up-to-date

There are sufficient library, computer and other learning resources

Staff numbers, qualifications and experience are appropriate

Arrangements for staff development are adequate

Teaching and assessment

Teaching methods are linked to course objectives

Teaching is well-planned, efficiently carried out and varied

Teaching encourages links with other courses and applications

Teaching develops generic skills and independent learning

Assessment is varied and appropriate

Student guidance and support

Concern is shown for the well-being of students

Formal advice systems are in place within the department

Institution-wide support is provided for counselling and guidance

Outcomes and quality control

The quality of student work is comparable to courses elsewhere

The department operates effective internal quality control

The institution has implemented quality assurance procedures

Source: adapted from the Scottish Higher Education Funding Council Quality Framework,
October, 1992.

We shall come back to the Quality Framework, but let us look first at the results of using this framework in assessing the quality of Scottish departments over the first two years of its operation. In the first year, departments were graded as 'excellent', 'satisfactory' and 'unsatisfactory', while assessments in the second year sub-divided the 'satisfactory' category into 'highly satisfactory' and 'satisfactory'. The intention was that the other two categories would continue to carry their original meanings. Table 4 shows the distribution of grades awarded so far, by cognate area and university type.

The distributions of grades differ markedly between cognate areas, with Chemistry finding half of the departments 'excellent' compared with 15% in Computer Studies, while 90% of departments of civil engineering were considered 'highly satisfactory' with the remaining department being considered 'unsatisfactory'. So far, 62% of the 'excellent' departments are in the ancient universities, while 59% of those described as 'satisfactory' are in the newly established universities.

Table 4   Distribution of assessment categories in Scotland by cognate area and university type

Cognate area		Excellent N	(%)	Highly satis. N	(%)	Satisfactory N	%)	Unsatisfactory N	(%)
Chemistry		6	(50)	5	(45)	1	(5)	0	
Computer Studies		2	(15)	3	(23)	7	(54)	1	(8)
Economics		4	(36)	3*	(27)	4*	(36)	0	
Engineering – civil		0		9	(90)	0		1	(10)
Engineering – electrical		3	(27)	4*	(36)	4*	(36)	0	
Engineering – mechanical		1	(10)	6	(60)	3	(30)	0	
Environmental Science		1		1		0		0	
Geology		2		2		0		0	
Geography		4	(67)	1	(17)	1	(17)	0	
Mathematics		2	(15)	11	(85)	0	0		
Physics		4	(40)	4	(40)	2	(20)	0	
Ancient	(N = 4)	18	(50)	14	(39)	4	(11)	0	
1960s New	(N = 4)	8	(27)	16	(53)	5	(17)	1	(3)
1990s New	(N = 5)	3	(8)	19	(53)	13	(36)	1	(3)
Totals (%)		29	(28)	49 *	(48)	22 *	(22)	2	(2)

Note: Numbers for 'Highly satisfactory' and 'Satisfactory' are estimated in the 1992/93   session by dividing those in the original category equally between the two new categories.

Source: SHEFC (1994).

The assessors visiting each institution write two reports, one which is published and another which is sent in confidence to the institution. Looking at the published reports, what impressions are obtained about what counts as 'good teaching'?

The Teaching Methods Found in 'Excellent' Departments

The first impression, which comes both from the distributions and the comments in the reports, is that either there are major differences in teaching quality between the cognate areas or, alternatively, 'excellence' and 'highly' satisfactory' are being interpreted in different ways by assessors in different cognate areas. The second impression is that 'high quality teaching', as judged by peers, must differ from what staff developers or researchers into student learning would mean by that term.

Looking, as an illustration, at reports from the two cognate areas published in July 1994 (Chemistry and Physics), what did the assessors say about staff development arrangements, and the methods of teaching used, in the ten 'excellent' departments? In three departments, the assessors found 'significant', 'some', or 'clear evidence of' staff development activity related to teaching, learning and assessment, but in the remaining seven departments, such activity was either 'low', 'little', 'limited' or not mentioned at all. The complete set of extracts from the reports are shown in the Appendix, but the following comments illustrate the range, with variants of the second comment being the most typical:

1990s University

'There was a significant amount of staff development activity, notably in the area of teaching ... (with) regular one-day "School conferences" which were held away from the University ... There was (also) a structured ... scheme which successfully identified individual training needs'.

Ancient University

Beyond initial training, 'there appeared to be little staff development activity in the area of teaching, learning and assessment'.

Comments on teaching methods showed a heavy reliance on traditional methods, with reports on only two departments from 'old' universities mentioning the use of any innovative methods. The two departments in the 'new' universities had both used a mix of methods, but in one of them the assessors considered the methods to be 'of variable quality'. It is more difficult to give a flavour of the more varied comments on teaching, but the following probably give the right impression.

Ancient University

'Lectures observed were well delivered using mainly traditional methods and appeared to be adequately prepared. However, there was, in general, little interaction with the students. Overhead projectors were not always properly used ... In the first year ... there was poor attendance at the tutorials.'

1990s University

'A wide range of teaching and learning methods was employed ... appropriate to course aims. Lectures observed were generally well prepared, carefully planned and effectively delivered with good use of overhead projector and, in some cases, of handouts.'

Ancient University

Great emphasis was placed on 'small group tutorial teaching based on exercises ... which were clearly a valuable learning experience... Lecturing observed was traditional in style and used principally as a vehicle for conveying factual information'.

1960s University

'Lectures tended to be traditional: there was scope for more variety in presentation and activity ... [as] in some cases [they] were not particularly imaginative. A great reliance was placed on the use of [overheads] and little student participation was evident. However, other more innovative teaching methods were also used.'

Looking back at the criticizms of teaching made by students and staff, we find that several of these 'excellent' departments are criticized for very similar failings – unimaginative or ineffective presentation and a failure to encourage active learning. Of course, there were many complementary remarks made about these 'excellent' departments, and it was clear that describing the teaching as 'traditional' was not intended by the assessors as a criticism. However, there were a surprising number of criticisms, either implied or actual, of the teaching practice observed in these departments. The more complementary remarks generally referred to the organizational arrangements for teaching, rather than the teaching itself.

It may seem surprising that these 'excellent' departments attracted so few enthusiastic comments on staff development and teaching practice. There are perhaps two main reasons for this. First, we have focused on just one element within each of two of the 11 aspects of the Quality Framework. Judgements of excellence were presumably being based on other aspects. And yet it is evident that the assessors' observations on low levels of staff development activity and unimaginative teaching did not prevent the award of 'excellent'. These judgements may reflect the existing norms and cultures of these particular cognate areas, but there may be other reasons which are more pragmatic and political. Although the instructions to assessors do not rule out the use of differential weightings in reaching their decisions, the difficulty in coping with 11 aspects of quality may mean that, in practice, they are forced to rely on equal weightings and looking at how many aspects have been found to be 'excellent'. And, in reviewing the work of their peers, perhaps some panels of assessors have been more ready to stress the positive indications of quality and find reasons to excuse negative indications, thus producing a substantial skew towards high ratings. However, without being involved in either the observations or the decision-making, these possibilities remain speculative.

As the Quality Framework is currently being used, at least in the two cognate areas considered here, it seems unlikely that the assessments would lead to much reconsideration of traditional approaches to teaching and learning. If anything, they would seem to reinforce the status quo. If we want to use quality assessment to encourage more imaginative approaches, there would need to be a substantial change in the emphasis given within the Quality Framework to teaching practice and staff development, and assessors would have to use more of the indicators of 'high quality teaching' . Additional indicators could readily be based on research on student learning

Encouraging and Supporting High Quality Learning

Research on student learning has been identifying a variety of teaching approaches which encourage students to adopt a deep approach to learning and studying, in other words to seek personal understanding rather than being satisfied with simply reproducing course content. Biggs (1989) identified four broad aspects of the learning environment which he believed would encourage a deep approach.

1 **Motivational context** which depends on students experiencing 'ownership' of course content and establishing a positive emotional climate associated with learning.

2 **Learner activity** which not only involves 'doing', but also reflecting on the activity and developing abstract conceptions.

3 **Interaction with others** which allows the negotiation of meaning with peers, either in tutorial contexts or in autonomous student groups.

4 **A well-structured knowledge base** to promote the integration of content into broad inter-related wholes rather than concentrating on pieces of information in isolation.

In a recent paper for SHEFC assessors, Entwistle (1994a) has suggested additional indicators of quality in teaching which have been derived from the literature on student learning. The influences on the quality of learning shown in Table 5 can be justified in terms of research findings and derive mainly from an earlier review of the effects of teaching on learning outcomes (Entwistle,1992).

Table 5   Influences on the quality of learning

- ensuring students have adequate prior knowledge and understanding;

- matching content to the intellectual stage of development students have reached;

- helping students to perceive relevance and to develop interest in the syllabus;

- encouraging in students more independent, purposive, and reflective ways of studying;

- offering choice in both courses or topics studied and assignments;

- providing a syllabus which encourages depth and avoids an excessive workload;

- teaching in ways which explain concepts fully, with enthusiasm and empathy;

- emphasizing and modelling the ways of thinking characteristic of the discipline;

- choosing textbooks and providing learning resources which provoke thinking;

- providing opportunities for discussion and collaborative working on realistic problems;

- designing assignments which encourage active questioning and discussion; and

- assessing and providing feedback in ways which directly reward understanding.

Commenting on other recent reviews of the effects of teaching on learning, Nightingale and O'Neil (1994) come to similar conclusions about how best to promote a deep approach and to encourage the development of personal understanding.

A deep approach to learning is best fostered by teaching and assessment methods that promote active and long-term engagement with learning tasks. Stimulating and considerate teaching which demonstrates the lecturer's personal commitment to the subject matter and stresses its meaning and relevance to students also shapes deep learning. Opportunities to exercise responsible choice in the method and content of study, including opportunities for independence in studying, play a major role in promoting meaningful learning too. (p. 80)

It is tempting to move from this analysis to pick out particular methods of teaching which will support a deep approach and there have been many suggestions about the particular methods which promote high quality learning (e.g. Gibbs,1992a; Ramsden,1992; Entwistle *et al.*,1992). However, a review of the literature on the differing teaching methods suggested strongly that research had demonstrated few **consistent** beneficial effects from any specific teaching method (Entwistle,1992). And this conclusion has also been reached at school level (Dahllof,1991).

There are at least two reasons why we should not expect strong or consistent effects from any specific teaching method in higher education. First, the outcomes of learning in any course depend **not** on a single teaching method, but on a set of interacting features of the whole learning environment. In the traditional context, for example, it is impossible to isolate the effects of lecturing from the influences of tutorials, conversations with staff and fellow students, carrying out assignments, and a whole range of independent activities such as reading and reflecting on course content. Even where a method is more likely to encourage high-quality learning, its effectiveness will be crucially dependent on the way it is implemented. Much of the staff development literature concentrates on the activities of both staff and students. It is much more difficult to explain how particular aspects of those activities come to influence the quality of learning. That requires a much more fundamental grasp of how teaching influences learning. But only if staff grasp the essence of the innovation will they be able to adapt the method effectively to the particular context within which they are working.

Rather than looking for particular innovations, a more subtle and complex analysis is necessary. A form of 'systems thinking' is necessary (Entwistle,1987, 1994b). There is a whole armoury of methods available for presenting information and encouraging learning. We have to ask which particular combination should this member of staff use on this course, with these students, at this level, and with these aims? And what combination of assessment methods will match those teaching arrangements? As Dahllof (1991) has said:

Too much attention is directed towards finding ... 'the best method', even though fifty years of educational research has not been able to support such generalisations. Instead we should ask which method – or which combination of methods – is best ... for which goals, for which students, and under which conditions (p. 148)

If staff are to grasp the essence of innovatory methods, and also be able to develop learning environments which support high quality learning, they will need to understand much more about how these methods and environments influence learning. And what is often currently lacking in descriptions of innovative methods is any discussion of the content, as opposed to the process, of learning. Research on student learning has looked at both content and process, but difficulties in generalizing about the learning of content has led to greater emphasis on process. So, we find extensive discussions of the importance of encouraging a deep approach, but much less is written about what a deep approach involves in specific subject areas. Academic staff are, naturally, more interested in their own discipline than in concepts introduced by educationists or social scientists, unless direct connections can be shown between those concepts and their own experience. That is what some of the recent research in student learning is beginning to do.

Developing Conceptual Understanding

In higher education, students are expected to learn how to think and use evidence in ways which are characteristic of the discipline they are studying. The essence of understanding is the connection between new ideas and what a person already knows (Entwistle, Entwistle and Tait, 1992). It is thus, necessarily, individually constructed. In developing effective conceptual understanding, students have to construct their own frameworks of interpretation from the evidence, arguments and explanations they have heard and read. The extent to which students will be able to construct fully independent frameworks will depend, to some extent, on the discipline. In the humanities and social sciences, these constructions can incorporate personal experience to a greater extent than in the sciences. But even in studying science, students necessarily come to understand concepts in somewhat idiosyncratic ways. They use the available representations of the abstractions in contrasting ways – some more visual and some more mathematical, for example.

Diana Laurillard (1987, 1993) has argued that academic learning has to be distinguished from everyday learning – it involves a difference between acquiring 'percepts' and 'precepts'. Much of academic learning is not just abstract, but it depends on thinking in 'approved' ways. Laurillard argues that the task of the teacher involves mediating learning. It is essentially a rhetorical activity in which the teacher seeks to persuade students to change their ways of making sense of various kinds of phenomena, using the concepts and ways of thinking characteristic of their discipline. The independent frameworks that students develop are thus constrained by the history of the discipline, and yet retain elements of individuality. To make this discussion more concrete, let us look at some recent research being done in Edinburgh.

We have been investigating how students develop interpretative frameworks. We have done this by interviewing students in their final undergraduate year and asking them how they go about integrating complex material, both in preparing for coursework essays and in revising for Finals (Entwistle & Entwistle,1991; Entwistle,1995). Initial analyses produced descriptions of common experiences of understanding during revision, and distinctive differences in the **forms of understanding** students were seeking. Here, we will look just at these differences (see Table 6).

Table 6   Contrasting forms of understanding during revision for finals

- Absorbing facts, details, and procedures related to exams without consideration of structure

- Accepting and using only the knowledge and logical structures provided in the lecture notes

- Relying mainly on notes to develop summary structures solely to control exam answers

- Developing structures of understanding from strategic reading geared to exam requirements

- Developing structures from wide reading relating understanding to the nature of the discipline

In analysing the interview transcripts, it became clear that students were using the word 'understanding' in quite different ways. Their descriptions differed in terms of **breadth** (how much material was being brought together to create an understanding), **depth** (the variety and strength of the connections made within the material and to related ideas), and **structure** (the principles of organization used to provide a scaffolding for those connections). The forms represent a hierarchy with increasing levels of conceptual sophistication.

The study was not large enough to indicate what proportion of students would predominantly aim for which form of understanding, but there was a worrying suggestion that the second category might prove the most common, and indeed that some exam questions might well require no more than that. This category implies that the student is accepting the lecturer's understanding without developing it into the **personal** framework which creates deeper meaning. Relying too much on the lecturer's framework leads to explanations which 'parrot' the lecturers' arguments and borrow their examples and evidence. The result is superficial knowledge mimicking conceptual understanding, although it can be difficult for an examiner to detect.

The first category was used, in the sample, only by medical students in referring to their experience in pre-clinical exams, which again was worrying. The only first-class degrees were awarded to students in the penultimate category, who combined a deep approach with a strategic awareness of the demands of the examination system.

The final category described students who were predominantly concerned with their own conceptual understanding of the content, but as a result they seemed to lack an equivalently clear awareness of examination requirements. As one student said:

> Well, there were cases where I knew too much ... I had to go through all the stages of working through [the topic] and showing that I had understood it. I couldn't gloss over the surface. And once I started writing, it all just 'welled up'. I felt that I couldn't interrupt the argument half-way, as it was developing ... [because] it ties together as a whole. It's very difficult to pick something like that apart, when you understand the theory like that. Half an understanding doesn't make sense!

Are you saying that you have to explain it in the way you understand it for yourself?

Yes. It's essential to demonstrate your understanding of the whole, and its implications and limitations ... You could say I shouldn't be (doing) that in an exam, but basically I have to do it that way, because that's me. Anyway, gearing your learning too closely just to previous exam papers seems a bit like a form of cheating.

Discussions of the transcripts with Ference Marton – triggered by one particular extract – led to a reanalysis of certain sections of the transcripts (Entwistle and Marton, 1994). The extract which suggested this particular re-analysis came from a student who was able to reflect particularly clearly on how she used her revision notes and brought them to mind on demand. Her general strategy in revising each topic involved 'concising' voluminous notes, step by step, down to a simple framework which she then used to rehearse her own understanding. Her experience of using these frameworks involved something like visualization, and yet not quite. She experienced her understanding in a quasi-sensory way, knew what was there, could 'see' the main points in her final summary notes, and was confident that more details were linked to the main points and could be retrieved when required.

The subsequent analysis of the whole set of interviews suggested that this experience was not uncommon, although the majority of students found more difficulty in articulating their experiences. Piecing together the range of incomplete descriptions, we concluded that students were experiencing their understandings as having some internal form and structure – almost as entities in their own right and these came to control their thinking paths in some way (Entwistle and Marton, 1994). The term **knowledge object** has been used to describe the essence of these quasi-sensory experiences of aspects of understanding. Focusing on key points within their knowledge object would 'pull up' additional information which they had memorized separately. In the words of one student, describing his ability to visualize a diagram he had been revising,

> I can see that virtually as a picture, and I can review it, and bring in more facts about each part ... Looking at a particular part of the diagram sort of triggers off other thoughts. I find schematics, in flow diagrams and the like, very useful because a schematic acts a bit like a syllabus; it tells you what you should know, without actually telling you what it is. I think the facts are stored separately, ... and the schematic is like an index, I suppose.

The knowledge object also seems to be used to provide flexible control of an examination answer as it develops. There is a dynamic interplay between the knowledge object and the demands of the question which creates essentially a unique answer, but the knowledge object creates a generic structure for a topic which is likely to remain consistent. Some students seem also to use the knowledge object to monitor the adequacy of their explanations, and in some comments it was even given an independent existence – at least metaphorically.

> Following that logic through, it pulls in pictures and facts as it needs them ... Each time I describe [a particular topic], it's likely to be different ... Well, you start with evolution, say, ... and suddenly you know where you're going next. Then, you might have a choice ... to go in that direction or that direction ... and follow it through various options it's offering ... Hopefully, you'll make the right choice, and so this goes to this, goes to this – and you've

explained it to the level you've got to. Then, it says 'Okay, you can go on to talk about further criticisms in the time you've got left.'

The term 'knowledge object' is used to describe an experience. It is **not** intended to suggest that knowledge is a commodity which can be transferred from teacher to student. Quite the opposite. The whole essence of the knowledge object is that it is a personal construction which provides a mnemonic structure to summarize complex interconnections that have developed in the process of developing conceptual understanding.

We are currently analysing interviews with students about coursework essays to see to what extent similarly tight bundles of knowledge are developed. Our preliminary conclusion is that the knowledge objects formed in essay writing are much less firmly established than through extensive revision and occur only when the students engage personally with the topic. In our sample, most of the students interviewed seemed to be far too strategic in their approaches to essay writing for this to occur. But, of course, many of the students revising for finals were being equally strategic, and relied heavily on reproducing the understandings of their lecturers. Only those students fully committed to a deep approach created clearly defined knowledge objects.

One of the strengths of this type of qualitative research which describes students' experiences of learning is that the results should describe a 'recognizable reality'. The idea of a knowledge object should tally with experiences of both students and staff. Whether it will also prove a useful way of encouraging improvement in the quality of learning remains to be seen. At the moment, we have to rely on more fully developed concepts and ideas.

Changing Conceptions of Teaching

So far, we have argued that improvements in the quality of student learning cannot come from recommending specific methods of teaching. Encouraging student activity is important, but the form that activity takes is crucial. And the 'right' activity comes not from any single teaching method, but from a careful arrangement of the whole learning environment, including above all assessment which provides reward for deep, active ways of studying. It is by no means clear that the most effective learning environments **necessarily** involve innovative methods, but there is a strong probability that they will. It is clear that they **will** have involved the member of staff, or course team, in considerable thought about which teaching arrangements are most likely to support the type of learning required. But components of that environment could certainly involve traditional approaches carried out thoughtfully and imaginatively.

There is often a problem in the published reports describing innovations in teaching. They are often presented in unqualified and over-enthusiastic terms, without making clear how dependent success will be on the context and the individuals concerned. I am reminded of a comment made by Friedlander (1975) in describing 'open', or progressive, elementary education in the USA:

> It is a gross oversight of available knowledge in psychology to asume that looser structure in the environment of the classroom is of some benefit for **all** children, just because it is of great benefit for **some** children. It is predictable that children who have a low tolerance for

ambiguity and uncertainty would find an open classroom, which operates very successfully for some children, extremely threatening and anxiety provoking. It is also predictable that personality configurations of administrators and teachers who seek out the challenge of innovation in developing the open classroom would tend to be unmindful of the valid needs for order, predictability, and specificity for persons unlike themselves. (p467)

Traditional, as well as innovative, methods of teaching have been very effective in helping students to master the ways of thinking characteristic of the discipline. For example, another on-going study at Edinburgh is looking at how tutors encourage their students to develop conceptual understanding in conventional social science tutorials (Anderson, 1995). What is particularly interesting is the way that the best tutors seem to **challenge** the students to think critically and independently, and do so in a vigorous and direct way. And yet at the same time the tutors provide the encouragement and support necessary for the difficult process of developing more complex and abstract conceptions of topics and of the discipline as a whole. They create a climate in which misunderstanding is accepted as a necessary step along the path towards understanding. And in some of the best innovatory teaching involving collaborative work, students are encouraged to develop similar climates of acceptance in which alternative conceptions of the problem or task can be freely discussed without individuals feeling threatened, or their ideas devalued (Nightingale and O'Neil,1994).

One of the challenges for quality assessment, institutions and staff developers is to create a similar climate for academic staff. If more imaginative teaching is to be introduced into higher education it must be seen to be rewarded, both within the quality frameworks, to provide incentives for departments to reconsider existing courses and methods of teaching, and within promotion criteria, to ensure that individual staff benefit from the efforts they put into teaching. But the task of staff developers is more complex. It is by no means sufficient to draw attention to alternative methods of teaching and learning. They have to act, like the staff themselves, as mediators in the task of changing conceptions.

Currently, many staff have conceptions of learning which allow traditional, and ineffective, methods of teaching to go unchallenged, and some seem to have a 'deficit model' of student behaviour. They see teaching largely as a matter of covering the syllabus (Trigwell and Prosser,1994), believing that what is in the lecture course will then be known, and what is not covered is necessarily either unknown or misunderstood. And they seem to believe that many students are inherently lazy or confused, without appreciating that their motivation and clarity of thinking is, in part, a function of their experiences on the course (Entwistle,1984). Changing such conceptions is, however, no simple task. The psychological literature is replete with examples of how difficult it is to change firmly entrenched attitudes and conceptions. How, then, should we proceed?

Evidence on conceptual change suggests that, first, the individual has to perceive a reason for change. If the existing conception still feels adequate and comfortable, change is unlikely. A variety of experiences have to be provided which both challenge existing conceptions and suggest interesting alternative conceptions. But these experiences have to be carefully managed within an encouraging and supportive climate. The experiences also have to be designed to fit the previous knowledge and learning habits of the learners involved. Unfortunately, there seems to be a developing orthodoxy in staff development circles that learning must necessarily take place in workshops in which the participants negotiate both content and learning activity. Yet this seems totally to disregard how most academic staff learn. They learn by reading, by attending conference papers, as well as through discussions with colleagues. They are quite capable of taking from presentations what interests them and may be useful, and are quite unused to situations in which they are expected to negotiate what is to happen. Why is it believed that this is the best way to run staff development? Presumably because there is a belief that there is a 'best' method for encouraging deep approaches to learning and that this should be exemplified in learning about teaching. But, just as there is no evidence of a 'best method' existing anywhere else in education, it seems reasonable to doubt whether a 'best method' exists for staff development. What is more likely to work is to arrange a variety of experiences which provide information, challenges and support, and which above all allow staff to decide for themselves what methods suit them, as individuals, best. Choice, yes. But not choice within the constraints of a single format, surely.

Trigwell and Prosser (1994) have been exploring university teachers' conceptions of teaching. Their research has led them to conclude that

> improvements in teaching ... [depend on] a conceptual change on the part of some teachers. ... Such changes are difficult to bring about, and are unlikely to occur through the attendance at, and participation in, the occasional three-hour professional development workshop. A much more sustained and systematic approach is required, built upon teachers examining, and critically reflecting on, their own practices.

Such approaches are likely to work best where departments collectively agree to be involved in reappraising their teaching – perhaps as part of quality assessment or quality assurance procedures. Then the focus can be on that particular area of study. There is an understandable suspicion of methods of teaching which are presented as being 'best' for any discipline. Effective teaching, particularly in higher education, depends critically on the content and traditions of the individual discipline or profession. And examples of good teaching will be most influential if they come from a similar area of study.

Unfortunately, many of the innovations in teaching are not only advocated by social scientists, but the evidence of effectiveness has come solely from the same area. Not surprisingly, staff from other disciplines are unimpressed. We need good exemplars from different subject areas, and not just as written descriptions (see Cryer, 1992), but also as videos. And, in whatever format, they need to be supported by thorough discussions of the underlying rationale and of both practical utility and practicality. In the current situation facing colleagues, descriptions of methods which depend on greater staff input may understandably create anger and incredulity. Whatever is suggested must be within the constraints of existing time and resources, and those constraints are currently oppressive.

Conclusion

The introduction of quality assessment has created a climate in which discussion of more imaginative combinations of teaching methods can be encouraged. To have any marked effect, however, there will have to be substantial changes in the current situation. There will have to be changed emphases in the criteria used to assess teaching quality, changed institutional policies which give teaching excellence equal prominence in promotion decisions as research productivity and, finally, a changed ethos in staff development to provide a variety of approaches which cater for differing backgrounds and contrasting learning styles, and which also also capitalize more effectively on the particular strengths of academic staff as learners.

References

Anderson, C.D.B. (1995). Personal communication.

Biggs, J.B. (1989). Does learning about learning help teachers with teaching? Psychology and the tertiary teacher. *The Gazette* (supplement), 26 (1). Hong Kong:University of Hong Kong.

Cryer, P. (1992). (ed.) *Effective Learning and Teaching in Higher Education*. Sheffield: Universities' and Colleges' Staff Development Unit

Dahllof, U. (1991) Towards a new model for the evaluation of teaching. In U. Dahllof et al. (Eds.) *Discussions of Education in Higher Education*. London: Jessica Kingsley.

Entwistle, N.J. (1984). Contrasting perspectives on learning. In F. Marton, D.J. Hounsell, and N.J. Entwistle (eds) *The Experience of Learning*. Edinburgh: Scottish Academic Press.

Entwistle, N.J. (1987). A model of the teaching-learning process. In J.T.E. Richardson, M.W. Eysenck, and D. Warren Piper (eds). *Student Learning: Research in Education and Cognitive Psychology*. Milton Keynes: S.R.H.E./ Open University Press.

Entwistle, N.J. (1992). *The Impact of Teaching on Learning Outcomes in Higher Education*. Sheffield: Universities' and Colleges Staff Development Unit.

Entwistle, N.J. (1994a). Defining quality in teaching: evidence from research. Paper prepared for training sessions of SHEFC assessors. Edinburgh: SHEFC.

Entwistle, N.J. (1994b). *Teaching and the Quality of Learning in Higher Education*. London: Committee of Vice-Chancellors and Principals, 29 Tavistock Square, London, WC1 9EZ.

Entwistle, N.J. (1995). Frameworks for understanding as experienced in essay writing and in revising for examinations. *Educational Psychologist*, 30, 47-54.

Entwistle N.J. and Entwistle, A.C. (1991). Contrasting forms of understanding for degree examinations: the student experience and its implications. *Higher Education*, **22**, 205–27.

Entwistle, N.J., Entwistle, A.C. and Tait, H. (1992). Academic understanding and contexts to enhance it: a perspective from research on student learning. In T. Duffy and D. Jonassen (eds).*The Design of Constructivist Learning Environments*. Berlin: Springer-Verlag

Entwistle, N.J. and Marton, F. (1994). Knowledge objects: understandings constituted through intensive academic study. *British Journal of Educational Psychology*, **64**, 161–78.

Entwistle, N.J., Thompson, S. and Tait, H. (1992). *Guidelines for Promoting Effective Learning in Higher Education*. University of Edinburgh: Centre for Research on Learning and Instruction.

Friedlander; B.Z. (1975). Some remarks on open education. *American Educational Research Journal*, 12, 465-68.

Gibbs, G. (1992a). Improving the quality of student learning through course design. In R. Barnett (Ed.). *Learning to Effect*. Buckingham: SRHE/Open University Press.

Gibbs, G. (1992b). *Improving the Quality of Student Learning.* Bristol: Technical and Educational Services.

Laurillard, D. (1987). The different forms of learning in psychology and education. In J.T.E. Richardson, M.W. Eysenck, and D. Warren-Piper (eds) *Student Learning: Research in Education and Cognitive Psychology.* Milton Keynes: SRHE/Open University Press.

Laurillard, D. (1993). *Rethinking University Teaching.* London: Routledge.

Nightingale, P. and O'Neil, M. (1994). *Achieving Quality Learning in Higher Education.* London: Kogan Page.

Pennington, G. (1994). Developing learning agents. In P. Nightingale and M. O'Neil (eds) *Achieving Quality Learning in Higher Education.* London: Kogan Page.

Ramsden, P. (1992). *Learning to Teach in Higher Education.* London: Routledge.

SHEFC (1992). *Quality Framework.* Edinburgh: SHEFC.

SHEFC (1994). SHEFC Annual Report, 1993-4. Edinburgh: SHEFC.

Trigwell, K. and Prosser, M. (1994). Congruence between intention and strategy in university science teachers' approaches to teaching. *Higher Education* (in press).

Williams, G. and Loader, C. (1993). Identifying priorities. Newsletter 3 of the project *Identifying and Developing a Quality Ethos for Teaching in Higher Education.* Institute of Education, University of London: Centre for Higher Education Studies.

Appendix

Comments by Assessors on Staff Development and Teaching Methods in 'Excellent' Chemistry and Physics Departments

1 Staff development arrangements

CHEMISTRY
Old University A
Beyond initial training, 'there appeared to be little staff development activity in the area of teaching, learning and assessment'.
Old University B
'The low level of participation of staff in the University's programme of staff development in relation to teaching, learning and assessment caused assessors some concern.'
New University C
'The University had adopted a policy of mandatory teaching training for all new academic staff. However the involvement of established staff in teaching and learning development was somewhat limited.'
New University D
'There was a significant amount of staff development activity, notably in the area of teaching ... [with] regular one-day "School conferences" which were held away from the University ... There was [also] a structured ... scheme which successfully identified individual training needs.'
Old University E
Beyond initial training, 'there appeared to be little staff development activity in the area of teaching, learning and assessment'.
Old University F
'Each lecturer was allowed three days per year for self development. Courses were provided ... to assist with teaching and learning ... [and] there was clear evidence that staff were availing themselves of these opportunities.'

PHYSICS
Old University A
'There was no formal mechanism for the systematic identification of staff development needs.'
Old University B
'Development needs were identified ... and there was evidence that staff members engaged in training to up-date their teaching skills. However, the emphasis seemed to be ... on research.'
Old University C
(No staff development activities mentioned)
Old University D
Excellent facilities for staff development in teaching were provided, but 'take-up of centrally provided staff-development courses by members of the Department was low'.

2 Teaching methods

CHEMISTRY
Ancient University A

'The standard of lecturing observed was high and in some cases outstanding.' Small-group tutorials were provided for first-year students, but for subsequent years 'only larger group problem classes (~20) were provided'. 'The Department stated that these classes were intended to develop students' self-learning and self-awareness: however, there was no evidence that this was achieved in practice. '

Ancient University B

'Teaching practice ... was generally traditional in manner with limited use of audio-visual aids. Even in the later years of courses ... little attempt was made to interact with the students in the delivery of lectures. All lectures were, however, delivered in a highly competent manner.'

1990s University C

'Teaching methods ... [showed] an adequate mix of traditional and modern approaches, ... [but] the planning and delivery of teaching was somewhat variable in quality.'

1990s University D

'A wide range of teaching and learning methods was employed... appropriate to course aims. Lectures observed were generally well prepared, carefully planned and effectively delivered with good use of overhead projector and, in some cases, of handouts.'

Ancient University E

Great emphasis was placed on 'small group tutorial teaching based on exercises... which were clearly a valuable learning experience ... Lecturing observed was traditional in style and used principally as a vehicle for conveying factual information'.

1960s University F

'The lecturing observed was traditional and ... of a high standard. There were no formal tutorials in the first year ... and a limited number ... in the fourth year ... (although) the tutorial is generally accepted to be one of the best learning opportunities available to students.'

PHYSICS

Ancient University A

'Lectures observed were well delivered using mainly traditional methods and appeared to be adequately prepared. However, there was, in general, little interaction with the students. Overhead projectors were not always properly used ... In the first year ... there was poor attendance at the tutorials.'

Ancient University B

'The lectures delivered were, in the main, well-prepared, ... and often enthusiastically delivered to attentive student audiences ... A mainly conventional approach to lecturing was adopted with use of blackboard and overhead projector the chief means of delivery ... There were also interesting teaching development projects in hand, but not yet implemented.'

Ancient University C

'The lectures were all clearly delivered, though occasionally in a rather mundane manner, and more student participation would have been desirable. There were a few notable exceptions in which interesting lecture demonstrations were observed.'

1960s University D

'Lectures tended to be traditional: there was scope for more variety in presentation and activity ... [as] in some cases [they] were not particularly imaginative. A great reliance was placed on the use of (overheads) and little student participation was evident. However, other more innovative teaching methods were also used.'

3   A framework for evaluating and improving the quality of student learning

J. H. F. Meyer (University of Cape Town) and K. Scrivener (Imperial College)

Introduction

Student learning is a complex multivariate phenomenon. There are many sources of variation, some of them unobserved and uncontrollable, that contribute to manifestations of learning behaviour and of learning outcome. Practitioners are often confused by the layered complexity found in competing conceptual models of student learning; they generally fail to appreciate the penalties that are incurred as the genuine complexity of student learning is approximated for modelling purposes. From a practitioner perspective there is thus an inherent tension in adopting a model that is conceptually simple and 'user friendly', and actually using that model in practice for the very serious business of evaluating and improving student learning. The simpler the model, the fewer the number of variables in it, and the more limited the sources of contributory (or explanatory) variation for the observed phenomenon. Part of the art of modelling lies in deciding what it is that needs to be understood or explained, and then using some common sense in selecting and using a model that is sufficiently detailed for that purpose. This is basically what this chapter is about; the application of a model to evaluate both static and dynamic aspects of student learning.

Individual Differences

At the most basic level it is recognized that students engage learning with differing intentions and motives (Biggs, 1979). This is not surprising, as intention and motive are two powerful forces that plausibly explain much observable human endeavour. This is especially so when the **intention** to do something is supported by a congruent **motive**; the intention to understand something, for example, is congruent with a motivation based on intrinsic interest. The intention could equally well be based on ambition; a desire to compete and excel. It could also be motivated by fear of failure. Alternatively, the intention to understand could be motivated by a combination of motives. Looked at in this way it is already apparent that some combinations of motive and strategy are more likely to realize the stated intention than others. There is thus a first layer of variation in student learning based on intention and motive.

The motive on its own, however, is no guarantee that the intention will be realized. At the very least, some method and process is involved, and these are likely to be further shaped to some degree by personal preference or habit (Entwistle and Ramsden, 1983). In short, it follows that the acquisition of conceptual understanding is also dependant on additional cognitive processes. Some of these processes address the manner in which students interact with the content of what they are learning; how they appraise, organize and reflect upon information in relation to what they already know. Contrasting intentions are clearly likely to be associated with different processes. For example, an intention to **understand** may invoke an iterative process of reflection and critical conceptual interaction, while an **intention** to memorize information for subsequent reproduction in an examination may simply be realized by a process of repeated rehearsal. Some students are also predisposed to do certain things (like solve problems) in a characteristic manner; such preferences introduce a 'style' distinction between divergent and convergent approaches (to solving problems), and they represent a further important source of inter-individual variation. There is thus a second layer of multivariate complexity in student learning **that can substantively alter a perception that two individuals with the same declared intention and motive are similar.**

A third layer of variation recognizes that learning cannot be decontextualized; it is purposefully shaped by perceptions of the learning environment, and especially by the demands that are perceived to regulate academic success and failure. From what has already been said, it is self-evident that substantial **inter-individual variation** can occur in the manner in which perceived learning demands are responded to. There are other perceptions of the learning environment that can contribute further to an explanation of individual differences; perceptions of the content of what is being learned, of learning materials, of the learning space, perceptions of self, and perceptions of causal attribution (Meyer, 1991; Lefcourt et al., 1979).

Decompositions of a Deep-Level Structure

There is considerable empirical evidence that the 'dimensionality' of variation in student learning is relatively stable across different studies in respect of what might be called a 'deep-level' structure, but that it is less stable in terms of other posited 'strategic-' or 'surface-level' ones. This evidence has accumulated from numerous group-level exploratory factor analyses of undifferentiated datasets based on models of varying layered complexity as outlined. A review of these quantitative studies by Richardson (1994) provides an excellent contemporary summary of this research (circa 1993).

Empirically, additional (factor analytic) dimensions of variation emerge when the fundamental assumption that a group adequately represents its constituent members is relaxed, and many of these dimensions **do not conform to stereotyped conceptions of variation in learning behaviour.** Under this relaxed assumption it can very easily be demonstrated that contemporary conceptual models of student learning, or admissible aspects of them, do not 'fit' some individual-similarity data structures, even at a relatively coarse level of individual similarity constituted on the basis of gender (Meyer, Dunne and Richardson, 1994; Meyer, 1995)

This observation is equally true in respect of analyses of student learning based on an individual-difference statistical model that is independent of correlational assumptions (Meyer and Muller, 1990). **Conceptual stereotypes are, in fact, of very limited value in attempting to interpret individual differences.** This observation has led to the exploratory modelling of conceptual differences in **observed** data (as opposed to empirically manifested differences), and has presented a promising framework for addressing the manifestation and consequentiality of inter-individual variation in learning behaviour (Meyer, 1993)

Categorisation

In essence, this approach admits the **categorization** of discrete conceptual decompositions of an 'ideal' deep-level learning behaviour structure. At an individual level, or in analyses of **individual-similarity** subgroups, stereotyped dimensions of variation in learning behaviour, or their admissible conceptual variants, are simply admitted as special cases. At the same time full justice is done to manifestations of aberrant or atypical 'high risk' patterns of learning behaviour that are associated with academic failure. The categorization, furthermore, carries with it an assignment of **risk** that is, in this case, informed by conceptual argument and the results of previous empirical modelling. (It should be noted that the concept of 'risk' is inherent in the **definition** of learning if students themselves define it in qualitatively contrasting terms.)

The instrument used as a (data yielding) basis for the categorization procedure is one that has proved useful in previous individual-difference studies. It is a modified and Extended version of the Approaches to Studying Inventory (EASI), further supplemented by a set of contextual perception, and causal attribution, variables. A subset of EASI variables that are relevant to this study are introduced further on.

Each individual student response is quantified in respect of the variables embedded in the Inventory, and the assigned values then determine a (symbolic) **profile** based on a ranking of the individually averaged item values. This profile is then treated as a **preference structure** (for analytical purposes) and is examined for distinguishing conceptual features that determine the categorization. This somewhat complicated procedure is fully explained elsewhere (Meyer, 1993; Meyer and Parsons, 1994), and the technical details are not further discussed here.

The categorisation procedure produces a **risk category**; this is simply a number (that presently ranges from 1 to 13) that is regarded for exploratory purposes as possessing conceptually ordinal properties. Notwithstanding the dangers inherent in the presumption of strict conceptual ordinality in the 13-way categorization, it remains true that, under ideal conditions, each category isolates a unique set of features in the individual response. It is these categories in a collapsed form (on a scale of 1 to 5) that have been used with some success in modelling learning outcomes, especially the relationship between 'high risk' learning behaviour and academic failure. The categorization thus provides a direct method, subject always to error variation, but amenable to independent verification (via interviews), of distinguishing between self-reported individual student responses.

Background to this Study

At the commencement of the 1993 academic year, students in the Department of Materials at Imperial College were asked to describe how they had previously engaged the studying of Science in their final secondary school year. Data thus obtained were used as a basis for initial risk assessment, and as a comparative base for establishing subsequent changes that would be presumed to be essentially attributable to the effects of the course. Three months later students were again requested to self-report their learning behaviour in the context of the Materials Science and Engineering course.

The 13-way risk distributions obtained prior to the commencement of undergraduate studies, and within the course, are shown in Table1. Discrepancies in sample size are due to missing data. (There were 53 students in the course at the time of completing the second Inventory.)

Table 1   Risk distributions

Category	1	2	3	4	5	6	7	8	9	10	11	12	13	
Before-course	0	4	3	0	0	2	10	3	1	13	7	4	1	(n=48)
Within-course	4	3	5	0	0	17	2	1	2	10	3	3	1	(n=51)

Note: '1' =highest risk category, '13' =lowest risk category.

The data in Table 1 indicate that the within-course risk distribution is worse than the before-course risk distribution, notwithstanding the fact that the two distributions are derived from all complete (but not necessarily matched) data obtained on the two successive administrations of the Inventory. These categorical data form part of the framework of this study, the purpose of which is to demonstrate how Inventory data can be used to inform an evaluation of student learning in a static, dynamic and diagnostic sense.

Some Group-Level Learning Behaviour Dynamics

The first part of the framework illustrates some dynamic aspects of learning behaviour via empirical results that require conceptual interpretation.

A subgroup of individuals (n = 45) completed both Inventories and these matched sets of individual-response data are now considered. Table 2 contains the results of an analysis of differences in mean scores for the paired comparison data on the full variable set. Only differences that are significantly non-zero are tabulated, and they are listed in decreasing order of statistical significance. The sign of the mean (difference) indicates whether the shift is positive or negative relative to the before-course value on that variable. It is thus clear from Table 2 that an overall significant deterioration has occurred; all the positive shifts represent increases on the mean scores of theoretically undesirable variables, while all the negative shifts represent decreases on theoretically desirable variables.

Table 2. Statistically significant differences

Variable		mean	err.	t	p val.
Disorganized studying	DS	0.68	0.14	4.89	0.0001
Fragmentation	FA	0.56	0.13	4.37	0.0001
Workload	WL	0.60	0.14	4.36	0.0001
Learning space surface	LS	0.43	0.11	3.96	0.0003
Improvidence	IP	0.31	0.08	3.69	0.0006
Fear of failure	FF	0.44	0.12	3.67	0.0007
Intrinsic motivation	IM	-0.41	0.12	-3.52	0.0010
Deep approach	DA	-0.27	0.08	-3.18	0.0027
Success: favourable context	COS	0.38	0.13	2.87	0.0063
Failure: lack of ability	ABF	0.39	0.14	2.84	0.0068
Syllabus boundness	SB	0.31	0.11	2.76	0.0084
Use of evidence	UE	-0.23	0.08	-2.75	0.0087
Failure: lack of effort	EFF	0.28	0.11	2.59	0.0129

Note: mean = mean difference, err. = standard error (dispersion of the mean), t = t statistic, p val. = significance level.

Table 3. Oblique factor pattern

Variable		F1	F2	F3
Fragmentation	FA	70	.	-20
Success: favourable context	COS	58	.	.
Disorganized studying	DS	44	32	.
Workload	WL	35	.	31
Deep approach	DA	-41	-28	22
Intrinsic motivation	IM	-51	.	.
Learning space surface	LS	.	47	.
Failure: lack of effort	EFF	.	43	.
Syllabus boundness	SB	.	40	36
Use of evidence	UE	.	-38	22
Fear of failure	FF	.	.	61
Improvidence	IP	23	.	26
Failure: lack of ability	ABF	.	.	-32
Inter-factor correlations				
F1			27	21
F2				13

Note: All values multiplied by 100 and rounded to two places. Factor loadings with an absolute value less that 20 are printed as a period.

Of further interest is whether there is an underlying **empirical structure** that can be used to interpret the shifts indicated in Table 2 in a conceptually coherent manner. To this end an exploratory (principal) common factor solution is presented in Table 3 under oblique rotation. The factors represent unobserved, and empirical, **dimensions of variation** across which all students contributing to the analysis can be expected to vary. While acknowledging the influence that the relatively small sample size may have on the stability of the factor structure, the challenge here is nevertheless whether these dimensions **make sense conceptually**, and whether they can contribute to an evaluation of the **dynamic effect** that the course is presumed to be having on the students.

The loadings on Factor 1 suggests a dimension of variation that is conceptually quite coherent; in the **absence** of both a deep approach (DA) and intrinsic motivation (IM), there is a manifestation of perceptions of a heavy workload (WL) and disorganized studying (DS) in the absence of an organizing principle with which to deal with new information (fragmentation: FA), with an added weak qualification in terms of over reliance on factual detail (improvidence: IP). This dimension of variation in learning behaviour is furthermore associated with an (external) attribution for academic success in terms of favourable circumstances (COS).

Factor 2 captures a contrasting, but complementary, dimension of variation compared to Factor 1. The narrow focus here, in the **absence** of both a deep intention to understand (DA) and making use of evidence (UE), is on relational aspects of learning that is disorganized (DS); perceptions of the learning environment that facilitate the efficient transfer of information (LS) and a reluctance to expend intellectual effort beyond stated requirements (syllabus boundness: SB). This factor is associated with an (internal) attribution for academic failure in terms of a lack of effort (EFF).

The emphasis in Factor 3 is essentially motivational; fear of failure (FF), is linked to an **absence** of (internal) attribution for academic failure in terms of a lack of ability (ABF), to syllabus boundness (SB), and workload (WL). This dimension of variation is further weakly qualified by deep intention (DA), use of evidence (UE), and improvidence (IP).

Interim Discussion

Most first-year students come from a school environment where they were generally taught one broad subject (such as Physics) by one teacher, where homework requirements were clearly laid out, and where there was very little necessity for them to find out information for themselves (for example, from books). In their first year of university study they may have ten different lecture courses taught by different people. In each of these courses they are set work, often with complete disregard for the workload imposed by other courses. The whole style of information delivery is also very different to their previous experience. Compared to school, it thus appears reasonable to **expect** changes in the learning behaviour of first-year students to occur.

The practitioner's reaction to the shifts depicted in Table 2 is that they are consistent with common sense expectations. Students find it more difficult to organize their time (a problem exacerbated by being away from home and taking advantage of many new social opportunities); the subject appears fragmented without an overall structure, and they are overwhelmed with the amount of work that needs to be done. They don't really know how to take notes and tend to focus on the minutia of legibility and delivery of lectures, resulting in improvidence. All these pressures lead to an increased fear of failure and decrease their internal motivation. Attempts to understand (deep approach) are undermined, and their perception of the course content is superficial.

From a research perspective, one cannot infer causal relationships from the temporal proximity of events captured in a factor structure. However, interpreted against the findings of other studies, and within the underlying theory, the dimension of variation captured in Factor 1 is symptomatic of a classic syndrome: perceptions of a heavy workload, and an inability to cope with it in an organized manner signal the start of what can become a destructive cycle of deterioration in learning behaviour that is demotivating and is not directed towards conceptual understanding (Meyer and Sass, 1993). A broader interpretation of Factor 2, seen in relation to Factor 1, signals what may be the beginning of a strategic readjustment, or coping strategy within the course, while Factor 3 adds the motivational influence of fear of failure.

Some Individual-Level Learning Behaviour Dynamics

The analyses presented thus far essentially capture some of the group-level dynamics of changed, or changing, learning behaviour that may be attributed to the effects of the course (and the university environment in general). It now remains to address the dynamics of learning behaviour **at an individual level**. One way of doing this is to construct a frequency table of before- versus within-course categories as in Table 4 (based on a collapsed 5-way categorization of self-reported learning behaviour; 1 = high risk, 5 = low risk).

The contents of Table 4 communicate a wealth of information. The totals at the bottom, and on right hand side, of Table 4 indicate the before- and within-course **risk distributions** respectively. The diagonal cell entries represent subgroups of individuals manifesting apparently stable (categorical) patterns of learning behaviour; for example, five individuals self-reportedly appear to be in the 'high-risk' category, while none of the five individuals coming into the course with a 'low-risk' categorization maintained that categorization.

The upper triangle of cell entries (those that lie to the right of the diagonal) indicate subgroups of individuals who have apparently **deteriorated** relative to their initially self-reported learning behaviour, while the cell entries in the lower triangle indicate subgroups that have apparently **improved** upon their initial categorizations.

It is self-evident that the frequency table is asymmetric about the diagonal (and significantly so in terms of the McNemar statistic); there is, as expected, more deterioration than improvement. In addition, there is moderate association between the two sets of categories as evidenced by the various summary statistics. **The ultimate value of Table 4, however, lies in the fact that the cell entries represent subgroups of individuals whose identities (in this case) are known on a voluntary basis.**

Table 4 Contingency table of before- versus within-course categories

Within categories	Before categories: 1	2	3	4	5	Total
Freq.	1	2	3	4	5	Total
1	5	0	3	4	0	12
2	2	2	6	5	0	15
3	0	0	0	3	1	4
4	0	0	3	5	4	12
5	0	0	0	2	0	2
Total	7	2	12	19	5	45

Note: McNemar chi-squared statistic = 21.67, df = 10, (p = 0.025); Gamma = 0.612 (ASE = 0.109); Somers' D C | R = 0.448 (ASE = 0.096); Somers' D R | C = 0.463 (ASE = 0.090); Pearson correlation = 0.537 (ASE = 0.085); Spearman correlation = 0.530 (ASE = 0.104).

The Evaluation of Learning

There are now two complementary sets of data that are amenable to evaluation; one represents the dynamics of learning at an aggregate level, the other represents intra- and inter-individual learning dynamics. The former data can be used to compare patterns of evolving learning behaviour across different courses, or within the same course over time, or across successive versions of the same course.

An interest here is in individual differences and their consequentiality. The presentation that follows is based on one set of examination results, relating to one fifth of the first-year course. The association of these results with the categorizations of self-reported learning behaviour are good, but no better than the association with the performance at 'A-level' before entry. However, the data on which the categorizations are based have diagnostic as well as predictive properties; the point is that, at an individual level, these data can inform a variety of counselling and intervention activities. In both cases there are some pronounced exceptions to the general trend, although these exceptions are generally different students in the two cases.

The academic progress of students who self-reportedly had either remained in, or had shifted to, a 'high-risk' category of learning behaviour is of particular interest here. The before-course categorizations identified seven students with 'high-risk' learning behaviour patterns (see Table 4); five of them maintained a relatively stable condition, and two of them manifested some improvement. These seven students were informally observed more closely during the course of their studies.

Subjectively, two of these students were clearly problematic. They appeared to have little, if any, grasp of the basis of 'scientific method' and, when questioned, could recall little (if any) material delivered in lectures only hours previously. Both students, however, managed to scrape along by transferring segments of information from lecture notes and text books into laboratory write-ups with sufficient editorial skill to obtain adequate marks. Many of the staff independently identified these students as having bizarre learning strategies which emerged clearly from this study. Both of these students maintained a 'high-risk' pattern of learning behaviour in terms of the within-course categorization, and performed poorly in the examination, obtaining 37per cent and 43per cent respectively.

A second initially identified 'high-risk' subgroup consisted of four students who were clearly weak, and who were observed to be having difficulty in understanding things at a conceptual level. However these students had clearly evolved strategies which allowed them to cope. All were able to provide good answers to questions of a type previously encountered, and performed comparatively well in the examination.

The remaining initially identified 'high-risk' student is the most interesting case; this student had good entry qualifications and performed very well (72per cent) in the examination. This student was interviewed (as part of a separate study aimed at designing teaching software) in order to establish how some of the essential course concepts were being understood. The interview data clearly indicated that this student had developed a successful coping strategy. The basis of this strategy rested on an almost perfect ability to recall key definitions and explanations given in lectures. However, when questioned further about the meaning of some of these, this student commented along the lines of 'You don't want to try and understand things too deeply or you will just get confused; some things should just be accepted without question.'

The general pattern of within-course shifts was viewed by the practitioner as being rather depressing; the learning behaviour of the majority of students appeared to have deteriorated. Of particular concern was the subgroup of seven students who initially had not manifested 'high-risk' patterns of learning behaviour, but who subsequently did so within the course. The categorizations associated with this subgroup dropped to 1 from a previous 3 or 4. Three of these students had independently been perceived to be having some difficulties with the course, and two of them did badly in the examination. Of the remaining four students, one had a very poor attendance record for the course, but the other three appeared to be doing well and also performed well in the examination. It was felt by the practitioner that some of these students' learning behaviour may have deteriorated only temporarily, or that their within-course responses may have been biased by particular sections of the course with which they were having difficulty at the time, but not to the extent of affecting their overall performance.

Improving Learning

The framework that has been outlined produces a wealth of diagnostic data, some of which can clearly be used to 'improve' learning in a number of respects; the choice however depends on whether the students, the course, or both, require attention. For example, a similar exercise carried out within the same framework on a first-year engineering course has been reported by Meyer and Sass (1993) and has contributed to a major revision of that course. The focus here, however, is on the students.

There are, firstly, static 'snapshots' of individual patterns of learning behaviour before students enter the course, and when they are in the course. The frequency of within-course snapshots can obviously be increased and can be used for monitoring purposes. The value of the first snapshot lies in being able to identify individuals potentially manifesting 'high-risk' forms of self-reported learning behaviour **before they even commence their undergraduate studies**. The danger is that, without assistance, these individuals may fail to adjust, or may fail to adjust quickly enough, or may adjust inappropriately, to the demands of undergraduate study. In some individuals, 'high-risk' patterns of learning behaviour appear to endure, with a consequent expectation of academic underachievement or failure. There is some evidence that early detection of this condition, and explicit forms of intervention intended to improve it, can meet with limited success if attempted at an intensive individual level, but not on a large impersonal scale (Meyer, Cliff and Dunne, 1994).

Of equal concern are the individuals who deteriorate to 'high-risk', or nearly so, patterns of learning behaviour **within the course**. In another similar study to this one, but carried out on a larger scale, it has been observed that some previously 'good' students will 'recover'; this 'recovery' may take the form of a strategic readjustment to course demands (Meyer and Sass, 1993). However, the 'worse' the previous learning history, the less likely the 'recovery'. The problem of intervention here for students who fail to 'recover' (or readjust) is that when the deterioration has been detected, it may be too late to do anything about it. However, the major sources of variation associated with the condition (at an aggregate level of analysis), as exemplified in the interpretation of the data in Table 2 and Table 3, represent 'early warning signals' that can be of strategic value in forestalling the condition for at least some individuals.

Such an intervention has recently been attempted in the form of a learning 'Hot Seat' (Meyer and Kaschula, 1994). This is basically a walk-in learning counselling service on student learning that operates within a specific course. Students are informed at various points in the course of what the 'early warning signals' are, and are asked to seek counselling assistance if they feel that they are, for example, being overwhelmed by the workload, are experiencing difficulty in organizing their studying, are working hard and not doing very well, and so on. In the context of this study a suitably paraphrased description of the data contained in Table 2 substantively constitutes such a set of 'early warning signals'.

The practitioner's overall reaction to the analyses presented is that it has confirmed and illuminated what should have been known; that a major cause of the deterioration in learning behaviour is the difficulty in adjusting from the highly regulated school environment to the less highly regulated working environment of the university. It is also conceded that the coursework component in this particular course is too high. Another contributing factor to what has been observed is that first-year courses in general concentrate on providing the basic tools of a discipline that will only be integrated at a later stage. Students may thus experience difficulty in seeing the relevance of what they are attempting to learn in the overall context of the subject. This is, in fact, frequently the reason given for disillusionment by students who consider leaving the course around the end of the first year.

Concluding Discussion

The framework for evaluating student learning that has been outlined is a versatile one that has been used in a number of different contexts. It produces data that is both diagnostic and strategic, and that can directly inform academic practice and learning counselling.

The question of whether a knowledge of school-leaving learning behaviour can be used for selection purposes also arises. From the limited data available there appears to be no prospective benefit in selection based on self-reported learning behaviour versus selection based on A-level results as at present. However there might be some potential benefit in terms of selecting students with a comparatively poor at A-level performance but who nevertheless manifest learning behaviours that are likely to enable them to succeed at university.

References

Biggs, J.B. (1979). Individual differences in study processes and the quality of learning outcomes. *Higher Education*, **8**, 381–94.

Entwistle, N.J. and Ramsden, P. (1983). *Understanding Student Learning* (London, Croom Helm).

Lefcourt, H.M., Von Baeyer, C.L., Ware, E.E. and Cox, D.J. (1979). The Multidimensional-Multiattributional Causality Scale: the development of a goal specific locus of control scale, *Canadian Journal of Behavioral Science*, **11**, 286–304.

Meyer, J.H.F. (1991). Study Orchestration: the manifestation, interpretation and consequences of contextualised approaches to studying. *Higher Education*, **22**, 297–316.

Meyer, J.H.F. (1993). The individual-difference modelling of student learning: I – Static and dynamic aspects of causal attribution. Paper presented at the *Fifth European Association for Research on Learning and Instruction Conference*, Universite de Provence, Aix-en-Provence, France, 31 Aug – Sept 5.

Meyer, J.H.F. (1995). Gender-group differences in the learning behaviour of entering first-year university students. *Higher Education*, **29**, 201–215.

Meyer, J.H.F., Cliff, A. and Dunne, T.T. (1994). Impressions of disadvantage. II – monitoring and assisting the student at risk, *Higher Education*, **27**, 95–117.

Meyer, J.H.F., Dunne, T.T. and Richardson, J.T.E. (1994). A gender comparison of contextualised study behaviour in higher education, *Higher Education*, **27**, 469–85.

Meyer, J.H.F. and Kaschula, W. (1994). Helping engineering students to learn better: the concept and creation of a learning 'hot seat'. In Smith, A.J. (ed.) *Engineering Education, Increasing Student Participation*, Sheffield Hallam University, Sheffield, 294–300.

Meyer, J.H.F. and Muller, M.W. (1990). Evaluating the quality of student learning. I – an unfolding analysis of the association between perceptions of learning context and approaches to studying at an individual level, *Studies in Higher Education*, **15**, 131–54.

Meyer, J.H.F. and Parsons, P. (1994). Conceptually at risk students: diagnostic and intervention strategies based on individual differences. In Gibbs, G. (ed.), *Improving Student Learning: Theory and Practice*, OCSD, Oxford.

Meyer, J.H.F. and Sass, A.R. (1993). The impact of the first year on the learning behaviour of engineering students, *International Journal of Engineering Education*, **8**, 328–35.

Richardson, J.T.E (1994). Cultural specificity of approaches to studying in higher education: A literature survey. *Higher Education*, **27**, 449–468.

4   Qualitative changes in learning and teaching brought about by using records of student achievement

Valerie A. Potterton (School of Life Sciences, Cape Technikon) and Phillip G. Parsons (Teaching Development Unit, Cape Technikon)

Introduction

Assessment of student achievement has become rather a delicate issue in that it is a combination of a number of distinct but related roles within the educational process. 'It performs different functions and needs to be regarded in light of the educational functions it is intended to perform' (Eisner, 1993, p. 224). Rowntree views assessment as 'an attempt to get to know about the student and find out the nature and quality of his learning – his strengths and weaknesses, or his interests or aversions, or his style of learning' and he lists the six main roles of assessment:

- to aid in selection

- to maintain standards

- to motivate students

- to give feedback to students

- to give feedback to teachers

- to prepare students for 'real life' (Rowntree, 1981, pp. 178–9).

Given the vital and varied roles played by assessment in the educational process it is highly desirable that the methods of reporting the results of assessment enhance and inform these roles. Traditionally, in higher education, study/learning is prescribed for a specified time period, at the end of which, written and/or practical examinations are undertaken in order that a single mark or symbol can be allocated. This single mark is intended to indicate the extent to which the learned material was mastered or understood, the level at which certain skills were performed and the degree to which certain attitudes were displayed.

Although used extensively, the method of reporting an assessment as a single mark, grade or symbol does not appear to be as good an indicator of a student's individual achievement as would be desired by students, teachers and society in general. In relation to selection, Gibbs is of the opinion that the conventionally established assessment methods do not achieve their aims. 'If we are assessing students primarily to provide employers with useful information then we are making a bad job of it' (Gibbs, 1991, p.1). Indeed he goes so far as to allege that prospective employers interviewing graduates judge them on 'their presentation of self, articulacy, quick–wittedness and work experience' (Gibbs, 1991, p.1), rather than on the reported assessment results of their formal education. If one of the roles of assessment in the educational process is to provide a means of being able to distinguish comparative differences in diverse students' capabilities, and this is not being accomplished, then possibly it is the way in which the assessment is reported that is at fault.

An additional problem of traditional assessment and assessment reporting techniques is that these reinforce for many students the perception that learning entails 'a process of accumulating bits of knowledge, like bricks in a wall' (Entwistle, 1992, p.597) which will need to be repeated (regurgitated) in an examination. This, in turn, has a 'backwash effect on teaching methods and on students' study and learning habits' (Boyce, 1987, p.1). Students may be encouraged to adopt this approach because they know that their learning outcome will be reported by means of a single quantitative measure. This leads Kirsch to ask the question: 'when will we design examinations that will encourage deep, retentive learning and a system of marking that rewards those that have understood what they have learnt more than those who simply regurgitate facts?' (Kirsch, 1992, p.587).

If, in higher education, the shortcomings of traditional assessment and assessment reporting techniques are evident, then there appears to be a strong rationale for devising a more comprehensive method of **reporting** the results of student assessment. This could be achieved by supplementing the traditional procedure with additional information derived from the variety of discrete types of achievement that are subsumed in current assessment methods. This, in turn, might have the effect of increasing motivation (through improved feedback) and producing positive changes in teaching methods and in the quality of student learning. It was considered to be a non–threatening approach, since the changes envisaged would initially be to the reporting methods only. The potential benefits of such a system are well summarized by Garforth and Macintosh when they suggest that a well designed assessment reporting system 'can substantially improve the quality of the whole teaching/learning experience for everyone' (Garforth and Macintosh, 1986, p.135).

Alternative Assessment Reporting Systems

The widespread dissatisfaction with the present reporting system which fails to reflect, in an adequate manner, a record of the student's achievement during his period of formal education has, according to Harrison, led to various methods that 'could provide more explicit information on the skills mastered, and the level of understanding reached, by candidates who have obtained a given grade' (Harrison, 1983, p.7). In the United Kingdom, at the secondary level, and in further education, a number of schemes have been developed which attempt to provide a more adequate reflection of students' achievements by means of profiles or records of achievement: 'documents, which may include the results of a variety of examinations, graded tests and other assessments, and other information about a student, as well as internal records compiled by teachers and/or students covering the total educational progress of the student' (Broadfoot, 1986, p.238).

Such a record is **not** a method of assessment to replace or compete with traditional examinations, it is merely a logical and informative system of **recording** the assessed achievement. The record may be presented in such a way that it could be of value in the formative process, as a means of feedback to the student, as well as being a summative record as a possible predictor of future success. The reason for this is that it could provide different information about a students' capabilities over a varied range of abilities which have in fact been tested and assessed but which are not currently reported on by traditional assessment reporting methods. Indeed, such records would go a long way to fulfilling more adequately the six roles of assessment outlined by Rowntree.

Within the further education sector, it was the vocational and pre–vocational education initiatives of the Manpower Services Commission which, according to Garforth and Macintosh (1986), made the most use of profiling. The application by some of the vocational training schemes 'led to a rather different set of developments', where the courses had profiling as an integral and core element, and it was no longer considered 'an appendage to conventional arrangements but had a key role to play in both the curriculum and communication aspects of the new courses' (Broadfoot, 1987, p. 15). This was supported by the fact that a number of further education examination boards such as City and Guilds of London Institute (CGLI), the Royal Society of Arts (RSA) and the Business and Technical Council (BTEC) had concurrently begun to incorporate records of achievement as part of their certification process. It is in this context that profiling became 'a part of everyday life for managers, lecturers and tutors in Colleges of Further Education' (Garforth and Macintosh, 1986, p. x). Most of the schemes that identify with profiling fall within the parameters of what are loosely known as 'course–related profiles', which are those profiles developed for certificate courses such as the Certificate of Pre–Vocational Education (CPVE), the Technical and Vocational Education Initiative (TVEI) or the RSA Certificate of Vocational Preparation. These profiles pertain to specific further education courses and the resultant 'Profile Certificates' consist of a series of statements of what the student is able to do as a consequence of following the particular course.

The range of items included in such profiles or records is varied and comprehensive (for their historical development see, for example, Broadfoot, 1986). These profiles vary from those that include comments about attitudes, educational experiences, interests and character based on personal judgement, to those that aim to increase students' understanding of assessment and permit them to gain insight into their shortcomings by involving them in their own assessment profile (Engel Clough, Davis and Sumner, 1984, p. 202), to those that merely report the results of examination assessment in greater detail than was previously traditional. Despite the differences, all summative (as distinct from purely formative) profiles have two basic purposes in common. They:

1 **acknowledge achievement**, whereby the record encompasses a whole range of activities, experiences, achievements and qualities that the student has shown throughout his/her period of education; is it generally regarded that such a record of achievement is a way of improving a student's motivation and self–respect;

2 form the basis of **a report for all interested parties**, that is potential employers and other tertiary educational institutions, whereby a different emphasis is given to the record such that it provides a comprehensive picture of the student's total achievements (Broadfoot, 1987, pp. 17–18).

As Rowntree has plainly said, whatever 'the span encompassed, a profile and especially one that includes narrative analysis, helps **humanise** the reporting response. Even the simplest of profiles differentiates the student from other students who share the "same" total but "add up differently" from him' (Rowntree, 1987, p. 236). It is this ability to differentiate one student from another that makes the concept of providing individual records of achievement particularly attractive to higher education, where large numbers, relatively impersonal teaching methods and a more pronounced gap between staff and students militate against the availability of qualitative information concerning individual student differences.

On the basis of existing profile schemes it appears that there are three basic components that should be addressed regardless of the format/style of the profile:

1. A 'list of items forming the basis of the assessment. These may be called "criteria" and may be in the form of a list of skills or qualities or may be embodied within a course description' (Garforth and Macintosh, 1986, p.2). This requirement is echoed by recent developments in 'criterion–referencing to emphasize actual levels of achievement rather than "order of merit"' (Dockrell, 1989, p. 478).

2. The profile should have some 'means of indicating the level and/or nature of performance reached for each item in this list' (Garforth and Macintosh, 1986, p. 2). The method used to depict the level can be entirely arbitrary and is often peculiar to the particular profile and its intent.

3. In order to vindicate the criteria and levels shown in the profile there must be must be an 'indication of the evidence used to arrive at the description provided ... to indicate the context in which a particular skill is assessed' (Garforth and Macintosh, 1986, p. 2).

Perceived Benefits for Higher Education of an Alternative Assessment Reporting System

The United Kingdom Department of Education and Science envisaged that the introduction of records of achievement would have at least the following benefits and implications for secondary education:

- improve student motivation;

- prompt schools to change the curricula;

- be a positive statement of achievement, not a prediction;

- provide a more rounded picture than is offered by a list of examination results;

- provide records which are valued and recognized;

- involve students in the production of the records;

- ensure the record becomes the property of the student.

(Evans, 1986, pp.172–3; Hargreaves, 1986, p.205; Hitchcock, 1986, p.150).

When the question of introducing an alternative assessment reporting system into the Horticulture course at the Cape Technikon was considered, it was envisaged that at least these benefits would be evident. At the same time the main consideration was to ensure the provision of more useful information on the results of student assessment to potential users in the horticulture and allied industries in South Africa.

For staff the anticipated benefits were associated with the fact that with the introduction of more comprehensive assessment reporting methods the assessment itself becomes a more detailed and constructive activity (Broadfoot, 1987, p.17). These more detailed results can more clearly indicate to each teacher the extent to which their teaching has been effective and in which areas of the curriculum more or possibly less detail may be required. It is this diagnostic benefit to teachers that marks what is in the authors' opinion the greatest benefit to teaching staff.

It is perhaps significant, with hindsight, that the most important benefits and implications were not envisaged at the outset, namely a change to the quality of assessment and, consequently, a marked change in the quality of learning on the part of the students who participated in the scheme.

The Introduction of Records of Student Achievement (ROSA)

The pilot programme envisaged the introduction of Records of Student Achievement (ROSA) in the Department of Horticulture within the School of Biological Sciences at the Cape Technikon. The type and format/style of ROSA had to take into account the constraints that this context imposed.

In reviewing the basic types of records of achievement that were currently in use in the United Kingdom, Mortimore and Keane (1986, p.69) make mention of five possibilities:

- open reporting sheet – both teachers and pupils enter comments on the basis of agreed criteria;

- **a matrix grid of skills and subjects** – assessors (teachers) tick the appropriate box(es);

- **the use of 'comment banks'** – assessors select suitable comments from a 'bank' of possible responses;

- **the use of a checklist of items** – assessors tick the appropriate series of items;

- **the use of a hierarchically designed grid** – assessors select and tick a particular 'step' on the grid.

It was decided, for the purposes of the project which forms the basis of this report, to exclude personal information from the proposed ROSA. This was necessitated by the fact that typically, a large number of lecturers are normally associated with the student over the standard four semesters with a relatively short period of time and hence association (six months) for each subject. Employers surveyed expressed concern that personal qualities, if included, might not be valid and could be potentially harmful. Therefore, it was decided that for this project it would be outside the proposed parameters to include valid and reliable information on personal qualities. This decision was taken, even though it had been clearly established that in the United Kingdom and South Africa this type of personal information was in fact 'part and parcel' of what was desired by prospective employers. Although most existing schemes surveyed in the United Kingdom report on a wide range of aspects, the usefulness of reporting primarily the results of examinations has been recognized, especially with those schemes developed within the further education sector.

Unlike many of the various profiles and records of personal achievement reported, this project would include only the results of existing assessment exercises. However, it was felt that even with these restrictions ROSA would benefit staff, students, and prospective employers (for whom the system was intentionally devised). Consequently ROSA was designed to include:

- general skills required in the particular subject / discipline;

- specific skills acquired in the particular subject / discipline;

- specific abilities accumulated as a result of the above skills;

- examination results on the subject / discipline;

- content elements of the subject.

Finally it was planned that two central factors would constitute the proposed records of achievement: previously **defined elements within each of the subject–specific topics** which would be related to one or more of three specified levels of achievement. The intention was to obtain the relevant raw data for ROSA by analysing the results attained by each student in each of the elements, at each level of achievement for the topics that had been assessed by the usual tests and the final examination.

The fact that profiled examination results should not stand alone but should form a part of summative records of achievement is corroborated by Hitchcock who states that 'the incorporation of existing assessment and reporting procedures offers the opportunity for both school and pupil to benefit from the keeping of fuller, more accurate records. This in turn leads to a more complete summative report' (Hitchcock, 1986, p.153). ROSA would thus contain a formative component by providing the individual student with his or her performance on each of the three levels of achievement for the discrete elements defined from topics within the course by way of test and examination results. These formative Records of Achievement would be given to final fourth semester students, together with a summative Record of Achievement upon the completion of their diploma. This would be in the form of a simple computer–generated histogram which could be easily inserted into a personal portfolio. This, in turn, could be expanded by the student to record particulars of extra–mural activities and / or sporting and other achievements as well as final examination results to make the portfolio a more complete report of their personal achievement. The Record would be given to the student in conjunction with his / her traditional end–of–semester final examination results, and he or she would retain the right to decide whether or not to show it to prospective employers and others.

To obtain ROSA marks would be allocated to different levels of achievement within pre-determined elements of the specific topics within the subject. This is consistent with Crooks' suggestion that it is often 'useful to classify assessment items on two different dimensions: the topic or section of the course to which the item relates, and the type of skill which the student is asked to display' (Crooks, 1988, p.18). Crooks suggests that the traditional six levels of intellectual achievement (Bloom, 1956) can be compressed from six to three but warns that this should only apply to assessment of intellectual skills as **additional** categories would be required, for example, for interpersonal and physical skills (Crooks, 1988, p.18). The three levels of achievement decided upon below approximate to those proposed by Crooks (1988):

Level 1   Knowledge

Level 2   Application (of that knowledge gained from level 1)

Level 3   Evaluation (which was deemed to subsume analysis and synthesis).

The proposal was for the first author to systematically grade as levels 1, 2 or 3 all assessment topics with regard to the intellectual skills that were being assessed, also taking into account how each topic was related to the course contents. This meant that the levels of the learning skills could not be graded in isolation when setting the assessments. Rather the levels would have to be selected so that they adequately represented the desired learning outcomes within the teaching–learning environment. Logically, then, if the assessment was to be 'graded' in this way the teaching would have to **reflect** these desired levels, and not as is often the case, simply level 1 (knowledge).

It was also decided that the summative ROSA would only display the respective student's performance at the three levels of achievement and that these would **not** be related directly to the individual elements of each topic as this would be too detailed for assimilation by prospective employers, parents or sponsors. However, this detailed information **would** be provided to the students and teaching staff as part of the proposed **formative** (feedback) Report.

The proposed introduction of such a system was wholeheartedly supported by prospective employers who were canvassed by way of a questionnaire. Of the 93 returns 88 felt that traditional assessment reporting methods were inadequate and 92 agreed that a record of achievement would be of assistance. Of 24 final semester students questioned, 23 expressed a desire for the introduction of Records of Achievement, with 21 of these feeling that both they and the employer would benefit directly: **'I feel that for myself I could work in the areas that I underachieved in. For the future employer they would have a better idea of what they are getting.'**

When asked if the introduction of Records of Achievement would have affected their studying in any way, students provided comments which displayed considerable insight into the current educational process:

'I would have worked harder and not just worked to pass the exams and tests which mean nothing anyway.'

'I would have worked harder because at the moment everybody gets the same certificate on completion of the National Diploma, regardless of personal achievement.'

The first step in introducing Records of Student Achievement was to classify the assessment questions in terms of their applicable elements and their appropriate level of achievement. This resulted in an assessment programme for the semester with the characteristics shown in Table 1.

Table 1	**Assessment programme**		
	Knowledge	Application	Evaluation
Test 1	80%	20%	0%
Test 2	40%	40%	20%
Test 3	10%	50%	40%
Examination	10%	40%	50%

The above allocation was to ensure that a progression through the prescribed levels of achievement occurred with time, with the final examination being in this sense nothing more than a fourth test. For each test the students received their total mark, as is customary, but they were also provided with three other marks which indicated their current achievement at the three prescribed levels. These marks were **in addition** to their normal average which, together with marks attained in assignments and projects, formed their semester mark which afforded them entry to the final examination at the end of the course.

The set of nine marks was **not** totalled at this stage because the examination was considered to be a fourth test. However, it was noted that the students themselves added the marks representing each of the three levels of achievement. In this way they were able to assess for themselves how they had progressed in the three areas of knowledge, application and evaluation up to that point.

Once the examination had been written and marked, a fourth set of marks was then available for each student in respect of all three achievement levels. The summative Record of Achievement was then compiled and made available to the student (Table 1).

Table 2   Summative record of achievement

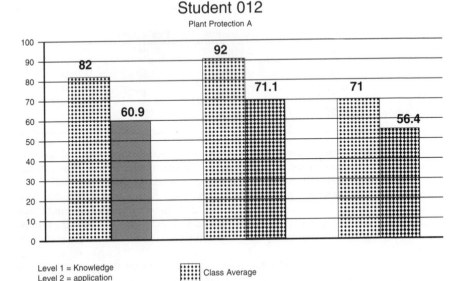

Student 012
Plant Protection A

Level 1 = Knowledge
Level 2 = application
Level 3 = evauation

Class Average

The effects of introducing Records of Student Achievement

A number of significant effects were evident when ROSA was introduced. These were primarily related to changes in teaching method and consequent changes in the quality of student learning.

Changes in teaching methods were necessitated as a result of the new focus on learning quality. It became clear as the course progressed that classifying questions into levels of achievement would not be of any significant value unless the first author **taught** the students in a manner which reflected these levels. As a result, the author had to modify her usual method of teaching and initially teach the students not only to think conceptually at the three levels but also how to interpret and answer questions set at these levels.

The changes that were made to the method of teaching evolved spontaneously between the author and the students. Initially the author covered the prescribed course material by way of formal lectures which were reflected in the structure of the notes provided to students. (It is noteworthy that the author had received a prestigious award for good teaching in 1989 on the basis of peer and student evaluation.) However, after the first test it was clear that this traditional method would not suffice and would have to be drastically revised if any of the students were to have a chance of answering questions set at levels higher than 'knowledge'.

The change that was necessitated meant that the author dispensed with the lecture notes (the students still retained theirs) and replaced the usual lecture with co–operative problem–solving exercises. These required of students a high level of perceptual comprehension and developed in them an ability to think critically and evaluate situations against certain predetermined criteria.

In terms of assessment activities the author stressed from the outset that obtaining the correct answer was of less significance than the choice of the methods that were employed. Consequently, for the first month students were awarded no marks for the correct answer, only for their methodology. Initially this produced some indignant outbursts. However it was not long before this was replaced by a sense of **pure** achievement. This 'sensation' appeared to be heightened by the fact that each student was now fully aware of **how** he or she had arrived at a particular answer. In other words, students' conception and experience of learning had moved beyond the view that learning consists of devoting a period of time to committing one's notes to memory. Students who maintained this view failed to obtain any recognition for the reproduction of their notes.

For the duration of this 'initiation' period all of the students were at liberty to question the 'new' method and were informed that, if at any time anything should occur during the implementation of this pilot project that, in their opinion, could jeopardize their final results, the project would be abandoned. After approximately one month an informal classroom survey was conducted by means of a secret ballot to determine student opinion as to the new method. The result was unequivocally positive with all students (32) voting to retain the method.

This gradual acceptance of the usefulness of providing supplementary information to students on their assessment performance by way of a formative Record of Achievement and the consequent changes in teaching method paralleled a new awareness of the purpose and the process of learning. Entwistle states that 'understanding depends on transforming the knowledge presented by relating it to what is already known and making sense of it in personal terms' (Entwistle, 1992, p.597). However it is seldom that students **entering** higher education would perceive learning in these terms; rather the situation is that students 'study with blinkers, paying attention only to what might be examinable' (Pastoll, 1992, p.3). Making explicit distinctions between levels of achievement within the existing forms of assessment might encourage a deeper level of learning, as well as providing a better means of reporting the results of assessment.

One of the most significant and pleasing results to come from the introduction of ROSA was the positive change in student satisfaction with the course. This was partly due to the provision of detailed feedback as to their levels of achievement on the specific course elements, which enabled the students to monitor their own achievement, but partly due to the change in the teaching methods, which seemed to them to allow more scope in their learning. One student described the effect in these terms: 'I no longer have to swot, I just read through my work and arrive at the test the following morning.'

Perceived qualitative changes were evident in many of the students' attitudes to:

- themselves as people;

- their specific course and the subject in that course;

- their projected aims on completion of their studies

- their view of education 'as a necessary evil' in order to obtain a licence to practice;

- their traditional view of the lecturer–student relationship.

It was unfortunately not possible to validate the usefulness of Records of Student Achievement for prospective employers as the majority of the students who participated in the pilot scheme, on leaving the Cape Technikon, either went straight into private practice and started their own businesses, or they were already under contract to previous employers and did not have an opportunity to use their ROSA.

Table 3   A comparison between selected records of student achievement

Student	Level 1 knowledge	Level 2 application	Level 3 evaluation	Mean
Class mean	*60,8*	*71,1*	*58,4*	
001	57	71	41	56,3
006	49	69	51	56,3
031	61	71	37	56,3
022	70	59	64	64,3
017	61	77	56	64,6
004	68	70	66	68,0
025	60	78	69	69,0
013	75	66	67	69,3

Notes: 1.   All marks are given as percentages, rounded to the nearest whole number.
        2.   Means are calculated on the basis that the three levels are weighted equally.

However, one of the main objectives of ROSA, that of distinguishing between the achievements of individual students who might obtain a similar final mark, could be evaluated. By reporting traditional assessment results differently, as three levels of achievement instead of a single global mark, it is possible immediately to perceive more detail and this inevitably gives a better indication of a candidates' potential abilities. The usefulness of ROSA in this regard is evidenced by the examples given in Table 3, where the supplementary information provided regarding performance on the three levels of achievement would potentially assist employers in selecting students on the basis of their evident strengths.

Conclusion

Records of Student Achievement in higher education have begun to attract considerable interest (Assiter and Shaw, 1993). Whereas the emphasis has tended to be on providing feedback and information on aspects of student achievement not currently assessed, this pilot project has demonstrated that there is much value in providing supplementary information to students, staff and employers on aspects that already form part of the assessment programme. What has also been evident is that this non–threatening method of looking at the assessment programme of any course has the potential to have a positive impact on teaching and assessment. In turn, there are indications of positive benefits to students in terms of qualitative changes in their perceptions of the nature of learning in higher education as a consequence of the changes in assessment and teaching methods.

Because all parties to the changes experience a perceived benefit with no perceived threat or incurred risk, it is contended that the introduction of Records of Student Achievement in higher education should be considered seriously by those who are concerned with effecting qualitative changes to learning and to teaching. Considerable work still needs to be done in refining the methods of reporting and extending the range of achievement that is included, as well as in determining methods to record more rigorously the qualitative changes that are experienced by those involved. However, the results to date indicate that this is an enterprise that would repay the effort required.

Acknowledgement

The financial assistance of the Centre for Science Development towards this research and the presentation of this chapter is hereby acknowledged. Opinions expressed in this chapter, and conclusions arrived at, are those of the authors and are not necessarily to be attributed to the Centre for Science Development.

References

Assiter, A. and Shaw, E. (eds) (1993) *Using Records of Achievement in Higher Education*. London, Kogan Page.

Bloom, B.S. (1956) *A Taxonomy of Educational Objectives: Handbook I, The Cognitive Domain*. New York, Longmans.

Boyce, A.N. (1987) Integrating assessment into teaching and learning. *Technikon Natal Forum*, 3(1), 1 –15.

Broadfoot, P.M. (ed.) (1986) *Profiles and Records of Achievement – A Review of Issues and Practice*. London, Holt, Rhinehart & Winston Ltd.

Broadfoot, P.M. (1987) *Introducing Profiling – A Practical Manual*. London, Macmillan Education Ltd.

Crooks, T.J. (1988) *Assessing Student Performance*. Kensington, Higher Education Research and Development Society of Australasia.

Dockrell, W.B. (1989) The changing face of educational assessment. *Journal of Curriculum Studies*, 21(5), 478–80.

Eisner E. W. (1993) Reshaping assessment in education: some criteria in search of practice. *Journal of Curriculum Studies*, 25(3), 219–33.

Engel Clough, E., Davis, P. and Sumner, R. (1984) Pupil assessment – an Interim Report on the findings of the NFER 'Assessment procedures in schools project'. *Journal of Curriculum Studies*, 16(2), 200–2.

Entwistle, N.J. (1992) Influences on the quality of student learning – implications for medical education. *South African Medical Journal*, 81, 596–606.

Evans, A. (1986) Pupil Profiles and Records of Achievement: an NUT perspective. In Broadfoot, P.M. (ed.) *Profiles and Records of Achievement – A Review of Issues and Practice*. London, Holt, Rhinehart & Winston Ltd, 169–82.

Garforth, D. and Macintosh, H.G. (1986) *Profiling: A User's Manual*. Cheltenham, Stanley Thornes Ltd.

Gibbs, G. (1991) Eight myths about assessment. *The New Academic*, 1(1), 1–4.

Hargreaves, A. (1986) Record Breakers? In Broadfoot, P.M. (ed.) *Profiles and Records of Achievement – A Review of Issues and Practice*. London, Holt, Rhinehart & Winston Ltd, 203–27.

Harrison, A.W. (1983) *Profile reporting of examination results*. Schools Council Examinations Bulletin 43. London, Metheun Educational.

Hitchcock, G. (1986) Instituting Profiling Within a School. In Broadfoot, P.M. (ed.) *Profiles and Records of Achievement – A Review of Issues and Practice*. London, Holt, Rhinehart & Winston Ltd, 146–65.

Kirsch, R. (1992) They know enough who know how to learn. *South African Medical Journal*, 81, 587.

Mortimore, P. and Keane, A. (1986) Records of Achievement. In Broadfoot, P.M. (ed.) *Profiles and Records of Achievement – A Review of Issues and Practice.* London, Holt, Rhinehart & Winston Ltd, 65–75.

Pastoll, G. (1992) *Students and Standards: How Written Examinations Hold Us All Back.* University of Cape Town.

Rowntree, D. (1981) *Developing Courses for Students.* Maidenhead, McGraw–Hill.

Rowntree, D. (1987) *Assessing Students: How shall we know them?* London, Kogan Page, Ltd.

5   Using a Record of Professional Development to Improve Student Learning

Glynis Wood and Madeline Campbell (St Martin's College)

Introduction

The focus of this chapter is the development and critical analysis of a professional profile used by both postgraduate and undergraduate students in Initial Teacher Education over the last five years. The chapter is offered as a stimulus for discussion in this challenging field.

The structure of the profile itself has been informed by the work of Elliott, Winter and Calderhead with specific reference to Elliott's revised version of Lewin's action research model. The profile attempts to develop the students' awareness of professional competence and, through moving towards the integration of a personal profile, acknowledges the value of transferable skills. The chapter also addresses the value of using research within the working context as a tool in the professional development of tutors and in course enrichment.

Background

In 1988 the first Record of Professional Development (RoPD)for Year One B.Ed. students was introduced at St Martin's College, Lancaster. It sought to give students and tutors a clear understanding of the expectations of the course. At that time the shared, working understanding of competence was skill orientated. The RoPD reflected the structure and aims of the existing B. Ed course and had no subdivisions or clusters of competences. It soon became clear that we needed to make evident our belief, through the RoPD, that teaching could not be construed as a behaviourist model . We were determined that attention should not merely be given to the execution of individual tasks, skills, acts or procedures which could be reducible to the ticking of a competence. We wanted it to be much more. The Dreyfus (1979) linear model of competence from novice to expert caused many worries, not the least of which was the assumption that absolute competence, in any context , was attainable. For example, one of the management competences

the effective management of pupil behaviour,

which was in the original RoPD, caused both tutors and students concern and, had the novice to expert model been adopted, would have caused even more angst for students and tutors. This was kept clearly in mind when the opportunity really to develop the profile further came with the introduction of an Early years PGCE programme in 1989. The programme was structured into subject specific phases including Science and Humanities, and focused on professional progression through specific subjects. This was translated directly into the RoPD. Also included were additional skills required of the trainee teacher and not previously included such as

> Recognise the value of teacher expectation in developing confidence and relationships in the classroom

The subject specific and professional competences required at each phase were broken down and clearly stated, for examplein the Science phase:

> To what extent can you:

> Make use of a variety of resources in Science related activities in school?

and in the Humanities phase with an emphasis on planning and record keeping:

> To what extent can you:

> Plan activities to secure clear progression in children's competence in either history or geography?

The RoPD was used as an integral aspect of the tutorial and teaching studies element of the course. Students, in conjunction with their tutors, used the RoPD to focus on evidence of their progress, but it was not used as a specific assessment tool. Areas of progression could be highlighted as could areas requiring further support or opportunity for practice. The document enabled the student to revisit competences and record their relative progress by marking on a continuum. The use of a continuum avoided the problem of level or capacity, so often a cause of angst with students. In fact they took advantage of being able to move themselves back on the continuum, displaying a growing understanding of the complexities of competence.. Tutors clearly wanted to emphasize the necessity of developing the student teachers' skills in becoming and continuing to be reflective practitioners and built aspects of this into the document at an early stage.

A new four-year BA/BSc + QTS degree was introduced the following year which, again, provided the opportunity for development of the RoPD. A revised RoPD document was more detailed and acknowledged both the cognitive and affective dimensions of teaching. The document has been modified to reflect and accommodate the continuing updating of the course. Refer to Appendix 1 showing the developmental cycle within Lewin's revised model (Elliott, 1991).

The need for acknowledging the strong link between professional and personal development became evident through the tutorial system, especially in the area of transferable skills. The use of the profile encouraged the students to be reflective of their practice and their development but the tutorials soon explored the additional aspects of developing as a teacher beyond the stated competences in the Record. So often areas which students identified from the RoPD as a focus for future action were reliant upon developing a particular transferable skill. For example:

> To what extent can you:

> Establish good working relationships with colleagues

frequently depended on the level of competence in using communication skills.

It was also recognized that little account was taken of what students brought with them to college in terms of experience and skill, such as, a student with previous experience in the travel business came with highly developed interpersonal skills and there appeared to be nowhere to recognize or document these competences.

Funding provided by the Pegasus Initiative was used to facilitate the development of a Record of Personal Development. (RoPED). This was to be generic across the ITT, Christian Ministry and the Combined Studies BA Programmes within college. A working group was established and the document produced. The RoPED was introduced last year and, on the ITT programme, has been effectively used by some students and tutors in conjunction with the RoPD but ineffectively by others.

Throughout the development of the RoPD profiling system certain issues have arisen through tutor monitoring as befits Elliott's notion of 'reconnaissance' in a developmental cycle (1991). These recurring issues are as follows.

1. Ownership, where the belief that the document should remain the property of the student where open and honest argument and debate could take place on the student's terms, does not sit happily with a college-owned record which could be utilized for assessment purposes.

2. The growing size of the RoPD and the possible slimming down of each document as they became increasingly detailed and voluminous.

3. The value placed on this method of working, both by course leaders, tutors, teachers and students.

4. The overall effectiveness of working with profiles.

5. A shared definition and understanding of the term competence.

The Research

As practitioners working on the courses involved in the use of the RoPD it seemed a sensible step to use an action research framework to improve the quality of our teaching and evaluation, modifications and future developments of the document. A constant team of tutors enabled an action research approach to the continued development of the RoPD through regular course meetings where issues arising from tutorials were discussed, ideas revised and the document updated. The issues included: what constitutes evidence of competence; how valid is self assessment and should tutors be involved in the moderating of students' perception of their own competence? The discussions and written evaluations from both students and course tutors informed the developmental process.

Cohen and Manion (1994) define one context for action research as being

concerned with innovation and change and the ways in which these may be implemented in ongoing systems, (p. 188)

This relates directly to our situation. Adelman (1993) supports the Lewin model of action research as the discussion of problems followed by group decisions on how to succeed. Action research must include the active participation by those who carry out the work in the exploration of problems that they identify and anticipate. (p. 8)

Staff development was certainly a priority in the field of profiling and, at this time in college, all tutors were involved in evaluating the effectiveness of different methods of learning and teaching. The combination of these two areas benefited the development of the profile, giving tutors the official backing required in trying and evaluating innovations on the course. The appropriateness of the RoPD in supporting methods of teaching and assessment used on the first-year course was directly relevant as all tutors responsible for the development of the RoPD taught on the course. In doing this the tutors were continually evaluating their role and influencing change which improved their effectiveness. Cohen and Manion (1994) identify a context for action research as:

focussing on job analysis and [which] aims at improving professional functioning and efficiency. (p. 187)

This gave status and value to the combined expertise of the team of experienced primary teachers and college tutors, many of whom would not consider themselves in the role of the researcher. The team have faith in what they are doing in terms of profile development through what many call as ' gut reaction', probably more correctly described as 'informed professional expertise'. They are able to develop and monitor the effectiveness of this innovation from a sound pedagogical framework.

Time was also an important factor in the style of research utilized. Although Adelman (1993) and Cohen and Manion (1994) agree that a step-by-step process requires monitoring over a period of time and by a variety of mechanisms, it still appeared to be the most conducive approach to the necessary on-going evaluations and modifications, giving the dynamic feel to the research, that was demanded by the tutors and the students involved. In essence

giving credence to the development of powers of reflective thought, discussion, decision and action by ordinary people participating in collective research. (Adelman, 1993, p. 8)

The research tools include questionnaires, semi-structured interviews administered by course leaders and case study materials from students and tutors on a range of teacher training courses between 1989 and 1994 which focused on the competences required of trainee teachers. The qualitative data from semi-structured interviews and questionnaires over the research period continues to support the view that the profile is only effective when both tutor and student see its potential and give specific time to address it.

Data relating to the recurring issues stated below support our decision to continue to develop the RoPD.

Ownership

Students who worked with their tutor on their RoPD found it easier to identify expectations, strengths, gaps in experience and future targets. Those students who were not supported in its use rarely returned to it and often saw it as a waste of time and effort (Year 1 student)

Students generally wished to have the opportunity to share the RoPD with tutors and some expressed the wish for specific time allocated for peer sharing.

My tutor has been great, she's gone through it with me and around half way through my placement we looked at the bits I really felt I needed to work on. (Y 3 BEd student)

I worked on it with her and she straightened me out when I underestimated myself. (Y1 BA QTS student)

I shared it with my tutor and it enabled me to get constructive feedback and targeted areas for development. (Year 1 BA QTS student)

I'm sure it would be very useful if it's used properly but I've never really got into it and my tutor doesn't seem to mind.It's a bit late to start on it now I'm leaving and have got a job (Year 4 B.Ed student)

I found the first entry really difficult so my friend and I filled it in over coffee. That was useful and I felt I must be doing alright. (Year 1 BA QTS student)

There appears to be little evidence of the tutors' assumption of the need for total privacy, invoking the control through student ownership, although confidentiality is seen as essential.

The growing size of the RoPD
Both tutors and students were aware of this problem and comments from students reinforced our conviction that if the document increased in volume so the students' motivation to use it would decrease.

The value placed on this method of working
The tutor team regularly discuss the pros and cons of this way of working and have decided, at each stage, to continue to try to improve the document as the benefits in terms of students' learning is tremendous. This is evidence of continued support for this approach which places the focus on the learner as opposed to the course. Students have recently expressed their support for the use of a profile and are now included in the development group on profiling across the programmes of Initial Teacher Training.

Effectiveness of the profiling system
With the continued use of the profiling system students are more able to develop responsibility for their own learning and are able to take a more active role in tutorials, this qualitative evidence is drawn from many discussions with tutors and teachers that students encounter throughout their college career.

Shared definitions
These have evolved through staff development seminars, general discussions, readings and external forum. Although the team are not, and probably never will be, in total agreement in defining the term 'competence', the team do agree that it is progressive, it is

developmental and it is the ability to do, it is contextual and dynamic and that it is very difficult to quantify effectively as it must contain attitudes and other qualitative domains and ability to adapt using higher order teaching skills.

The Present

Evaluations to date show the essential ingredient for success of the RoPD to be the value placed on it by the students and the tutors participating. All parties need to have a clear, shared understanding of its purpose and benefit in terms of students developing a metacognitive awareness and control over their own development and hence a greater self-efficacy.

The trailing of a student's career path identifies three strands: (1) professional development, (2) personal development and (3) subject knowledge. Strands (1) and (2) were catered for in the RoPD but the subjects followed by the student were seen as a separate entity. Following the rationale that all three interact with and feed from each other it seems a logical development to incorporate this third strand in the profile. The RoPD has been refined yet again and its present form sees it as a document that is held by a student throughout his or her college career. Its component parts are as follows.

Section 1: An introduction to the Programme

An overview/summary of

(a)   Educational and Professional Studies courses

(b)   Core skills

(c)   Subject Studies

Section 2: Extended competences
(a)   Professional Years 1–4 including when addressed

(b)   Core skills

(c)   Subject Expertise

Section 3: Review of progress by course

(a)   Educational and Professional Studies

(b)   Subject Studies

(c)   Personal including annual review with Prof.and Acad. tutor

Section 4: Additional Information

This may include extra curricular activities, information on learning styles or achievements.

The main document will be shared by tutor and student and only the final section may be totally owned and kept by the student alone, should he/she wish.

The issue of ownership is closely linked to the assessment dilemma. In order to raise its status the team were aware of the need to link the profile to assessment but avoiding its becoming the actual item of assessment. The very fact that students know it is not assessed ideally gives them the freedom to use it purposefully and openly, whereas, given an assessment tag could essentially close it down and induce a tendency to 'the right answer approach'. However it is recognized that linking it to assessment not only raises its importance and status in the eyes of the students and the tutors but also utilizes the extremely valuable information which is collated in the document in terms of the students' experience and their reflections on that experience, this information may otherwise remain untapped. To this end a link will be made between the desired learning outcomes of the course, the core skills required and assessment through an action plan and report, thus ensuring the use of the RoPD in the item of assessment while not assessing the profile itself.

The profile is an attempt to integrate the three main strands. It is being piloted this academic year '94/'95 with the first year BA QTS course and includes the link to assessment. It will continue to be monitored and evaluated and developed through the students and tutors on the course. It is envisaged that separate information will be worked on and added to Section 4 throughout a student's time in college. If the pilot is successful the RoPD could be introduced across college, initially through other courses within the ITT remit.

The Future

The shared understanding of what is meant by 'competence' needs to be continually explored and discussed. The understanding of a broad definition of competence which essentially relates to a specific context is held by course members; it recognizes the complexity in teaching which transcends a categorized list. This is not moving away from the traditional meaning of competence as capacity to achieve purpose, but it does take it beyond the reductionist and behaviourist view. The profile will need to reflect this view. Staff development through discussion is crucial if the profile is to be embedded in the courses offered to trainee teachers and not be a 'bolt on'.

Staff development is paramount and issues raised by tutors – including: relevance of profiling to academic learning; more useful in vocational training; transferability; another load of papers to fill in and encouraging others to give it value – must be addressed if profiling is to be successful. These issues will be continually discussed with different groups of tutors and, we hope, as the message spreads, understanding will follow in its wake. However if the RoPD is to be an integral part of a student's learning it is essential that a recognition of its importance is accepted and supported both in principle and in practical terms by senior management of the institution. This should include the provision for staff development opportunities through external conference and more sharply focused in-house workshops.

The more we move to school-based training the more essential it is to give students clear targets of achievement and explicit evidence of their progress. Head teachers, class teachers, mentors, college tutors and students all need a common, shared understanding of both college and placement based expectations and, something which can get lost, the means by which students are able to attain these targets. A competence-based approach, even in its broadest sense, cannot be effective if students are not given the opportunity to work towards the competence stated. This is not only true for placements but also for college-based courses and it is to this end that desired learning outcomes should be analysed by each course team.

Issues Still to be Addressed

1. Continually increase status of the RoPD

2. More links to assessment

3. College-wide introduction

4. Monitoring and evaluating

5. Response to Government Directive (Circular 14/93)

   - identical terminology

   - incongruence-lack of contextualization

   - remains essentially mechanistic

Summary

We have moved a long way since our first RoPD and we realize we still have a way to go but we hang onto the belief in its purpose: to develop each student's awareness and control over his/her learning and to support the student throughout this learning and through his/her college course. This document is offered as a stimulus for discussion.

Bibliography:

Adelman (1993). *Kurt Lewin and the Origins of Action Research* from *Educational Action Research*, Volume 1, No. 1.Triangle.

Burke, J.W. (1989). *Competency Based Education and Training*. The Falmer Press.

Cohen, L. and Manion, L. (1994). *Research Methods in Education*. Routledge.

Dreyfus, H. (1979). *What Computers Can't Do*. New York, Harper & Row.

Elliott, J. (1991). *Action Research for Educational Change*. Oxford University Press.

Jessup, G. (1991). *Out-Comes, NVQs and the Emerging Model of Education and Training*. The Falmer Press.

Schön, D.A. (1987). *Educating the Reflective Practitioner*. Jossey-Bass. San Francisco.

Whitty,G. and Willmott,E.(1991). Competence-based Teacher Education: Approaches and Issues, *Cambridge Journal of Education* 21(3).

Winter, R. (1991). *The ASSET Programme Conference Papers*. Essex Social Services Department.

6   The use of a portfolio in assessing professional education

Melanie Jasper (University of Portsmouth)

Introduction

A portfolio is often regarded as a retrospective collection of artifacts which represents the work of an individual. However, the introduction of a portfolio process into educational strategies has involved the broadening of this definition to encompass the act of portfolio compilation, the learning activities and processes which can be incorporated within it, and the means by which it can be assessed against course outcomes (Knapp, 1975, Brown, 1992). As such it represents an exciting strategy for professional education of all types, albeit one that presents a number of challenges.

This chapter examines the features of the portfolio, and its potential for assessing professional education by setting its development within the theories of student-centred learning, and by examining the structure, process and outcomes of portfolio compilation. Reference will be made to the author's own area of practice in nursing education. Finally, the issues of assessment will be examined in relation to the role of the personal tutor, objectivity and subjectivity, and quality control. However, the first task is to review the nature of professional education.

The Nature of Professional Education

Professional education has the purpose of not only enabling the student to acquire the appropriate knowledge and skills but also to achieve the socialization necessary for the neophyte professional to be acceptable to the profession and to function within it (Jarvis, 1985, Becker et al., 1961). This latter process involves the transformation of 'lay' imagery to the 'institutionally approved' imagery whereby the student has acquired the approved attitudes, beliefs and values of the chosen profession.

While the knowledge and skills may be adequately taught within the educational setting, the socialization processes are only achieved by exposure to the culture of the professionals in the workplace (Merton et al., 1957, Melia, 1987). This dichotomy poses problems for teachers in that some mechanism needs to be created for bridging the inevitable theory–practice gap if the student is to be successfully employed following qualification, and is not to be subjected to reality shock (Kramer, 1974).

To some extent the purposes of higher education, to develop the individual qualities of the student such as critical analytical abilities and the capacity for rationalized decision-making, are contrary to the purposes of professional education where there is a deliberate attempt to produce a practitioner in a professional mould.

Professional education is additionally constrained by regulating bodies in terms of syllabus content, and prescriptive outcomes and standards of competence that the student must achieve if they are to be awarded a licence to practise (Rolfe, 1993).

In the past, nurse education has subscribed to a pedagogic model (Knowles, 1975) where the teachers had total control of the content and nature of the educational process. Outcomes of a nursing programme were measured against behavioural objectives in practice, and the assessment system often bore no relationship to the skills and knowledge needed for either competent practice or autonomy as a practitioner. A revolution hit nursing education in 1986 in the form of 'Project 2000 – a new preparation for practice' (UKCC, 1986). It proposed fundamental changes to initial nurse preparation which included full student status, the award of both a professional qualification and an academic award, and students entering clinical placements as supernumerary to the staff numbers. The concurrent move of Schools of Nursing into institutes of higher education provided the opportunities and challenges to nurse teachers to explore innovative and exciting methods of teaching and learning in order to educate, rather than train, the practitioner of the future. This led to the adoption of more student-centred methodologies (Rogers, 1984, Knowles, 1980) and in turn this facilitated interesting ways of assessment, such as the portfolio, in both initial and post-registration education.

The Educational Portfolio

An educational portfolio is a dynamic piece of work, which contains both the recorded achievements of the student and their reflections upon the concurrent learning (Glen and Hight, 1992, Gerrish, 1993). Knapp, (1975, p. 2) defines the portfolio as

> a file or folder of information which has been accumulated about a student's past experiences and accomplishments . . . [it] can be the vehicle for organising and distilling raw experiences into a manageable form for assessment . . . a process by which prior experiences can be translated into educational outcomes or competencies, documented, and assessed for academic credit or recognition

The underlying basis for the portfolio method can be attributed to Knowles (1975) four assumptions about the adult learner.

1 The student is self-directed.

2 The student's past experiences are a rich resource for learning.

3 The readiness to learn develops from life tasks and problems.

4 The student demonstrates curiosity and is self-motivated to grow and achieve. The self-directed learner is therefore seen as one who diagnoses her/his learning needs, identifies resources for learning, and evaluates learning outcomes. Learning is conceptualized as a self-initiated, participatory, lifelong process resulting in an increase in perception and/or change in behaviour.

Glen and Hight (1992) warn against the notion that student-centred methodologies equate with a lack of learning structure for the student. In the author's opinion, the teacher has a moral responsibility to create a framework for the student, comprising the parameters and rules for learning. Without these the student is likely to flounder in an overwhelming sea of learning outcomes without sufficient knowledge of the subject to plan a way through the course. The author, together with her colleague Gary Rolfe, created a shortened common foundation programme for graduates, based on student-centred methodology, which uses the portfolio workbook as a pivotal feature. The philosophical foundations of this course are:

1. a philosophy of student-centred teaching and learning strategies which recognize the students as equal partners in the learning process, and involves them actively in decisions about the content, structure and learning methods of the course (Rolfe, 1993, Jasper, 1994);

2. the integration of nursing theory and practice into a meaningful whole through the philosophy and techniques of reflective practice;

3. and an on-going programme of course evaluation owned and directed by the students, in which recommendations can be swiftly implemented during the lifetime of the course intake of which they are members (Rolfe, 1994).

The portfolio provides the documentation not only for the outcomes of learning itself, but for the whole process of achieving that learning.

The theories of experiential learning (Kolb, 1984) and reflective practice (Schon, 1984) provide the framework for portfolio creation which will help the student to acquire the cognitive and affective elements of learning, while ensuring that this learning is applied to practice. The portfolio process described here is grounded in the reflective cycle, with the structures of the process outlined in a workbook. The content is provided by the student, thus ensuring that individual learning needs are met. This process is described below. The portfolio provides the documentation for not only the outcomes of learning itself, but for the whole process of achieving that learning. This can be divided into the features of outcome, structure and process.

Outcome

The starting point for the portfolio is a clear identification of the outcomes expected by the student. These relate to the professional competencies required by the regulating body, but are transformed into 'student-friendly' language so that the student can see exactly what they have to achieve within the specified timescale. They relate to theory skills, and practical competence.

Structure

In order for the student to negotiate a way through the course, the learning outcomes are broken down into a manageable series of themes, which continually build upon each other. The students receive, at the beginning of the course, a sufficient number of workbook frameworks to last for the whole of the course. The format of each is the same, the content differs with the weekly theme. The student builds upon this framework by adding their own material in the form of reading, care plans, notes etc. Thus the portfolio becomes a comprehensive record of their training, individualized to their particular needs.

The individual work by the student is supplemented by a regular planned tutorial with the academic tutor, group work and clinical supervision in the workplace.

Process

This makes use of Kolb's learning cycle developed into a spiral curriculum (Rolfe, 1993) to enable the student to develop their understanding of a theme from first principles to developing theory from practice. The components of the workbook are structured so as to guide the student through this process each week.

Components of the Workbook

These can be summarized as:

1   essential reading, clinical and theoretical objectives relating to the week's theme;

2   identification of prior learning and experiences;

3   identification of additional learning needed to achieve objectives;

4   strategies to achieve these, with checklist;

5   critical incident analysis;

6   reflective journal detailing the week's achievements and experiences;

Essential Reading, Clinical and Theoretical Objectives

These are identified for the student by the teacher leading the theme. Students are guided to key texts and expected to pre-read these prior to the start of the week's theme. The theoretical objectives provide the level of the knowledge to be achieved, and thus enable the student to gauge their own workload needs. The clinical objectives relate to competencies expected by the end of the course. (To enable the student to gain an overview of the clinical competencies they are given all of these in a separate document.) By attaching these objectives to the weekly theme they become manageable for the student and practice supervisor, and assist the bridging of the theory – practice gap.

Identification of Prior Learning and Experiences

The first task for the student, in using the portfolio, is to evaluate their previous learning and accomplishments relating to that theme (Lyte and Thompson 1990, Lambeth et al 1989). This enables the student to assess their own levels of knowledge, and plan to remedy any deficits identified. The students write their own objectives for meeting these, both theoretical and practical.

This process is important in terms of enabling the students to recognise and document their experiences, and to use these as building blocks. They have to achieve the same course outcomes in six months that other students have 18 months to complete, thus it is vital that maximum use is made of skills and knowledge already acquired.

Identification of Additional Learning Needed to Achieve the Objectives

In turn the students make most effective use of this prior knowledge by identifying areas of the course where they need to concentrate their time and energy in order to meet the outcomes.

Strategies to Achieve Learning Objectives

The student turns the objectives into a learning plan, which is reviewed with the academic tutor. The individual components of this are entered into a grid which documents their acquisition on an incremental basis (Table 1).

Table 1   An example of an action plan

competence		A	B	C	D	E	F	G	signed
1)	measurement of blood pressure								
2)	measurement of oral temperature								
3)	measurement of axillary temperature								

where A - not yet encountered

B - observed

C - undertaken under supervision

D - undertaken alone

E - competent at level zero

F - competent at level one

G - competent at level two

Critical Incident Analysis

Each week the student analyses a critical incident relating to the week's theme. This is subsequently used at the weekly portfolio workshop. The emphasis for this component is placed on an incident that is significant for the student in terms of their learning, and which provides the material for examining the relationship between theory and practice. It also serves the important purpose of identifying the areas that the student finds stressful, providing the indication for extra work related to the theme, or increased tutorial support.

Reflective Journal

This is the culmination of the week's work and focuses the students on the learning outcomes of the course in general. The students are asked to review their week and identify the objectives that have been achieved, and those that are yet to be acquired. By reviewing their progress on a regular basis the students gain the satisfaction of monitoring and controlling their own learning.

The latter two components of the workbook draw together the educational theories of critical incident analysis (Flanagan, 1954, Smith and Russell 1991) and reflective practice (Schon, 1984) currently in fashion. These have their roots in the theories of experiential learning (Kolb, 1984) suggesting that a valid way of learning is by systematically examining experiences through deconstruction and subsequent reconstruction in terms of what we have learnt in order to develop strategies for future use. By the end of each week the student has a clear picture of the learning that has occurred, and what more needs to be done to achieve the objectives.

Assessment of the Portfolio

Due to the individual nature of the portfolio the strategy for assessment has to be criterion referenced. However, the portfolio is a continuous piece of work, is seen as both formative and summative, and in which the student demonstrates the accomplishment of the specified components. This provides the opportunity for the assessment, on an on-going basis, of knowledge, skill and attitude development. This can be achieved by using the following approaches:

Formative assessment

- **Monthly tutorial** – in this the student is facilitated to self-assess their professional development and acquisition of competencies. The portfolio provides the evidence of the work in progress, and any problems can be identified at an early stage. This enables the student and tutor to constantly monitor progress throughout the course.
- **Portfolio workshop** – students work in small groups with their academic tutor facilitating experiential learning. During this time the students are invited to explore and share incidents which have helped them to develop their practice. This enables the students to learn from each other, and to test their own development against that of others.
- **Clinical supervision** – the acquisition of practical skills can be assessed by the placement supervisor by using the action plan. As an incremental process, this reduces the tension of the end of placement summative assessment as the student can identify areas that need further work in time to achieve the necessary standard.

Summative assessment

This is criterion-referenced according to student guidelines for the portfolio (Table 2) and the portfolio marking criteria (Table 3). The strategy of providing the student with clear guidelines for the assessment at the beginning of the course enables the student to plan their work to meet these criteria.

The marking criteria are sufficiently broad to encompass the individuality of the student while ensuring a uniform standard is met.

Table 2   An example of student guidelines for the portfolio

Objectives of the portfolio

In compiling the portfolio you will:

a) study in detail at least one aspect of care in relation to one patient that you have nursed each week.

b) if appropriate, i.e if an area of care is being examined, write a care plan for that client with reference to that aspect of care, and supported by researched material.

c) critique and evaluate the care being received by the client.

d) reflect on your own actions and contribution to nursing care, with the aim of identifying knowledge and skill deficits, and planning to remedy these.

Each week's work should be clearly delineated in order to facilitate the marking of the portfolio.

Table 3   Portfolio marking criteria at level two

Criteria

1) There is a clear focus on an aspect of care for each entry.

2) Evidence is provided of integration of subjects which inform nursing practice.

3) There is evidence of reflective practice through a systematic and logical evaluation of the aspect of care.

4) The student demonstrates the ability to assess, plan and evaluate nursing care.

5) The portfolio incorporates relevant usage of literature in an attempt to rationalise and support conclusions reached.

6) There is evidence of professional development by justifying conclusions reached.

7) There is evidence of ability to self-direct personal and professional development.

8) The portfolio demonstrates an ability to identify own learning and learning needs demonstrated by critical incident analysis.

9) The portfolio demonstrates acquisition of nursing knowledge through the integration of course components.

10) It is a logical and sequential portfolio, referenced, where necessary to an accepted format.

Each criterion is awarded marks according to the following scale:

0-3 little or no evidence of satisfying any aspect of the criterion.

4 some evidence of satisfying at least one aspect of the criterion.

5 evidence of more aspects of the criterion being satisfied.

6 evidence of nearly all aspects of the criterion being satisfied.

7-10 evidence of the criterion being met in all its aspects.

Issues Arising from the Assessment Process

Most previous studies relate to portfolios being used in a formative capacity (Oechsle and Volden, 1990, Lambeth *et al* 1989), and for evaluation for the award of credit accumulation and transfer (CATS), the accreditation of prior experiential learning (APEL) or prior learning (APL)(Budnick and Beaver, 1984). The summative use for assessment raises many issues in terms of objectivity, reliability and standardization in comparison to more traditional methods of assessment.

It can be argued that the only objectivity required in relation to the portfolio is that of the marker in assessing its content as evidence of the required acquisition of competence. The relationship between the tutor and student during the portfolio process is necessarily close, involving the development of trust to enable the student to share their experiences honestly and to facilitate learning from those experiences. There is a potential dilemma for the tutor in that relationship, if the student does not achieve the required standard. This can be overcome by the internal moderation of all portfolios.

How can the reliability of portfolios be assessed? While the portfolio cannot test the knowledge possessed by the student, it can provide evidence of the application of it to practice. Similarly, the cognitive and affective elements of the educational process can be documented, providing some evidence of the acquisition of 'institutionally approved' attitudes and movement towards a professional ethos. However, the value of the portfolio lies in the nature of the process, rather than the end product *per se*. The portfolio itself merely documents the process, rather than supplying any measure of quality. Quality and standards of practice need to be verified in another way, namely in this case, by a practice assessment document. The sufficiency of the knowledge base can be tested via an examination.

Despite the nature of the supportive tutorial role of the teacher, the marking of portfolios has the potential to be time-consuming and arduous. This can, to some extent, be overcome by the use of the formative process during tutorials during which the tutor becomes familiar with the standard of the portfolio. Thus an assessment is being made as the course progresses. As a result the most thorough reading for marking only occurs in the last few entries which have not already been read by the teacher. At this stage the teacher will be assessing the course outcomes rather then the process itself.

Similar arguments can be applied to the issue of standardization – as a unique document pertaining to its author the portfolio can only record the process of outcome achievement, it is irrelevant to make comparisons between students. The use of standardized marking criteria to assess the portfolio overcomes the problem of the idiosyncratic nature of students' experience.

While the description above relates to a specific course in initial nurse education, it contains many features that are applicable to professional education of any type. These are the capacity of the portfolio:

1 to bridge the theory–practice gap by a cyclical process of acquiring theory, testing it in practice, reflecting on that practice, generating theory about practice and relating back to a known knowledge base;

2 to provide a prospective account of the student's progress in acquiring the knowledge, skills and attitudes required for professional practice;

3 to monitor the development of the student in the application of theory to practice through the use of objectives and competencies.

These make it a valuable addition to the assessment strategies available for any type of professional education

References

Bloom, B., Krathwohl, D. and Masia, B. (eds.) (1964). *Taxonomy of Educational objectives*. vol. 2, Longman, London.

Budnick, D. and Beaver, S. (1984). A student perspective on the portfolio. *Nursing Outlook*, **32**(5), 268–9.

Burnard, P. (1988). The journal as an assessment and evaluation tool in nurse education. *Nurse Education Today*, **8**, 105–7.

Flanagan, J. C. (1954). The critical incident technique. *Psychological Bulletin*, **51**, 327–58.

Gerrish, K. (1993). An evaluation of a portfolio as an assessment tool for teaching practice placements. *Nurse Education Today*, **13**, 172–9.

Glen, S. and Hight, N. F. (1992). Portfolios: an 'affective' assessment strategy? *Nurse Education Today*, **12**, 416–23.

Jarvis, P. (1985). *The Sociology of Adult and Continuing Education*. Croom Helm, London.

Knapp, J. (1975). *A Guide for Assessing Prior Eperience through Portfolios*. Educational Testing Service, Co-operative Assessment of Experiential Learning (CAEL Working Paper no.2).

Knowles, M. (1975). *Self-directed Learning: A Guide for Learners and Teachers*. Follett Publishing Company, Chicago.

Kolb, D. A. (1984). *Experiential Learning: Experience as the Source of Learning and Development*. Prentice Hall New Jersey.

Lambeth, S. Volden, C. and Oeschele LH (1989). Portfolios: they work for RNs. *Journal of Nursing Education*, **28**(1) 42–4.

Lyte, V. J. and Thompson, I. G. (1990). The diary as a formative teaching and learning aid incorporating means of evaluation and re-negotiation of clinical learning objectives. *Nurse Education Today*, **10**, 228–32.

Oechsle, L. Volden, C and Lambeth SO (1990). Portfolios and RNs: an evaluation. *Journal of Nursing Education*, **29**(2) 54-59.

Rogers, C. and Lambeth, S. (1983). *Freedom to Learn for the 80s*. Charles E Merrill, Columbus, Ohio.

Rolfe, G. (1993). Towards a theory of student-centred nurse education. *Nurse Education Today*, **13**, 149–54.

Schon, D. (1984). *The Reflective Practitioner: How Professionals Think in Action*. Temple Smith, London.

7

Critical Theory and Practice in Evaluation and Assessment: Enhancing quality while using evaluation and assessment to improve thinking and learning skills in higher education

Professor Diane Montgomery (Middlesex University, London)

Introduction

In the last half-decade of the twentieth century the whole of higher education in Britain is faced with the challenge of large increases in the number of students but with the number of teaching staff held at former levels or in decline. Such changes are not new but occur in cycles. This present one repeats on a wider scale that which took place in teacher education in the late 1970s when after a period of rapid expansion the birth rate figures showed a rapid plunge in the numbers of children about to enter primary then secondary schools. In some institutions 50 per cent of the teaching staff were retired, redeployed or made redundant. In the wake of these changes, ratios of 90 students to 1 member of teaching staff were not uncommon in some areas, particularly the educational disciplines while ratios of 8 to 1 or even 4 to 1 might be retained in subject areas.

One of the results of extreme pressures on staffing such as these can be a retreat to traditional methods and an increase in formal methods such as large-scale lectures, the doubling of size of seminar groups and a decline in individual tutorials. Pressures also arise in the assessment areas, decreasing more interpretive activity and they can increase the numbers of formal summative examination assessment papers, an increase in machine-marked factual recall and recognition test items and a decline in double marking, assignment comments and interpretive and real problem solving activities. Experience from the 1980s showed that responses to mass education by moving further into didactic 'schooling' and summative assessment strategies did lead to an increase in '*anomie*' in the students and an alienation from the educative process from more than the marginalized students. In fact many more felt and became marginalized and this was recorded many times in the evaluation strategies such as questionnaire returns, nominal group techniques (NGTs), objectives based rating scales and self-reports which we were using at the time as part of course and institutional evaluation. Such results need not however be the consequences of mass higher education. Decisions have to be taken in principle by course leaders about how they will organize and manage a transfer period. Students cannot without training magically convert to independent, self-regulating, intrinsically motivated learners as they enter higher education.

In our case it was decided that the innovations in methods and strategies geared to learning would have to be stepped up. The course content on 'Learning Difficulties' provided us with both the theory, the research backing and the applications evidence which the students were not slow to point out. Comparisons and monitoring of effectiveness could be made with parallel programmes which simply increased lecturing groups and seminar size. In what was considered a 'crisis' period there was *carte blanche* to deal with the problem and hold on for as long as possible until some means of additional support or transfer of staff might be identified.

In periods of upheaval and change positive innovation can occur. This phenomenon has not gone unnoticed in the literature. Periods of gradual innovation in fact have rarely been recorded. In periods of funded expansion there tends to be a focus on traditional ways of doing things. Doing them as they were always done, there is no imperative for change. In expansion, with funding declining, the pressures are so great that change and innovation are more easily accepted, especially where changes promise to offer some resolution of the problems.

Defining Quality

It is extraordinary to find that there has been so little accessible research about quality in learning in higher education particularly in this country until recently. McClelland (1958) whose work was widely influential in education in the 1960s and 1970s argued that intelligence was a much more widespread characteristic than was then believed, transformed into talented performance by the 'right sorts of education'. He said we should concentrate upon learning environments which link learning opportunities with identification rather than rely on intelligence tests and school attainments to predict who would benefit most from advanced education. A wide range of researchers had at that stage come to the conclusion that a large number of able and gifted individuals were never identified and encouraged to enter higher education. Lowering the threshold for entry into higher education may have assisted somewhat in giving these individuals opportunities but once in it the progress hoped for had not been achieved.

The result was that some of those concerned with higher education regarded the broadening of opportunities as leading to a lowering of standards. If they had realized that so few of the able were really with them in higher education and that the methods which they were using were leaving others – perhaps two-thirds and often the most able – unmoved and unmotivated, they might have reconsidered their methods even then.

Goldberg (1965), for example, having reviewed 176 research studies on gifted education, came to the conclusion that there were two great research needs, to find:

- what would stimulate a love of learning among able students;and
- what kinds of assignment would most effectively develop independence of thinking and independence of effort.

Twenty-five years later Passow (1990) in his review of research on gifted education was still able to conclude that the two major areas for research and development were:

- what kinds of educational and social opportunities are needed to promote high ability?; and
- how can we identify and nurture high ability in disadvantaged populations?

These questions are still preoccupying us as we broaden and deepen access to higher education, especially when we must also challenge the basis of our selection system founded as it is upon A levels, GCSEs and NVQs. Grades at A levels and IQ scores are rarely more than 30% predictively accurate with later achievement leaving us to determine which 30%. Some types of A-level programme for example can offer high levels of success to those with very good memorizing capacities and lead to predictably good results in degree programmes loaded with hierarchies of information. Other programmes requiring the ability to think and use knowledge to gain more information to solve real problems and to communicate ideas in a variety of modes find many students ill equipped to do this. Various MSC surveys have shown these 'cognitive skills' to be what employers really need and value. Cognitive skills and abilities can be found in a range of highly successful individuals both in and outside higher education but may never be directly assessed and only indirectly 'taught'. Most often these attributes appear to be acquired incidentally in the learning process. Strangely they have been observed in programmes where no attempt is made to teach the students at all and the students becoming concerned have thought it wise to do something about it for themselves. Poor lecturers, absentee professors and self-help educational groups often illustrate the fact that the results obtained are no worse, whatever is done to the students. What is required appears to be an appropriate environment in which to learn. Mass education environments, however, do not appear to be appropriate.

These conclusions have not been arrived at easily but seem to be confirmed when academic results after three years in higher education demonstrate the pattern of the normal distribution curve or that which might have been achieved albeit by different individuals by a process deriving marks whose sum results from a random distribution of errors.

A recent survey by HMI (1992) examined the provision for able pupils in maintained schools and confirmed a number of recent research studies that the National Curriculum geared to meet the needs of average learners in schools was not extending the development of able learners. As early as 1972 Thomas and Harri-Augstein had found that more than 50 per cent of students in a range of degree programmes did not have the necessary higher order reading skills to deal with the demands of the subjects and the texts which they were reading for their degrees. Students arrived from a wide range of schools without these skills (Meek and Thomson, 1987) and yet later study skills programmes and the pursuit of their subject studies for their degrees did not necessarily inculcate them.

We found so often that the learning experiences of the student were in a cycle of disconnections from the earliest years in school into higher education.

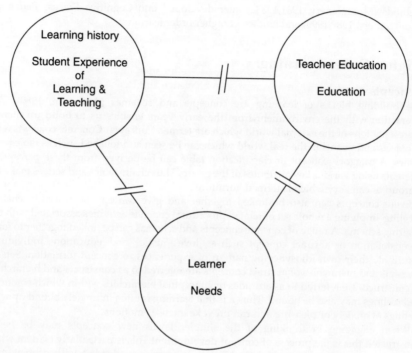

Figure 1 "A cycle of disconnections"

They also lacked many of the sub skills which would make them autonomous learners. Repetition and rote learning were the most frequently used strategies for difficult material. Rereading notes, summarizing, key words listing and mnemonics were the approaches in which they engaged at revision times. The more successful adopted the more advanced strategies. Connections between their own understanding and the disciplinary contents were rarely made except by the 'better' students. What needed to be done was to enable all our students to become better learners. This was clearly not being achieved by the didactic methods which we were using. When we offered revision sessions and exemplified revision strategies, students were more successful.

When they were encouraged to establish small revision groups this was a further support to many. What was of continuing concern was that they were not learning for its own sake. If the threat of the examination was removed there was little doubt that many students would not put in the effort required to learn the material the team considered essential if they were to function as competent professionals. A system of teaching and learning had to be envisaged which would cause the students to learn, motivate them intrinsically and enable them to sit the examination without requiring the drudgery of revision. Many of the most intelligent and creative students were failing to achieve high degree classes because of the stultifying boredom of the revision process however well organized they might have been. Attention was increasingly directed therefore to Process Methods (Montgomery, 1981,1983a) later developed into Cognitive Process Pedagogy (Montgomery, 1989,1990) and studies of higher order learning.

Higher Order Learning:

Concepts
The building blocks of learning are concepts and schemas (Anderson, 1980). The interaction with the environment from the early years enables us to build up mental representations of the external world which are termed 'concepts'. Concrete concepts refer to objects and events in the real world which can be seen and touched such as tables and chairs. A category concept or classification table can be derived from these perceptual referents using various key attributes of the group. Thus chairs,tables and settees make up a group or category which is termed 'furniture'.

Event concepts can also be linked together and give concepts such as to ' chair a meeting' implying a whole set of related procedural concrete activities associated with the chairing schema. A range of concrete concepts and schemas can be linked together to form a constellation or abstract concept such as 'love', 'justice' and 'education'. Individuals contribute their own idiosyncratic pattern of experiences to concept formation. Sets of concepts and hierarchies of abstract concepts are referred to as **constructs** and hierarchies of constructs are referred to as attitudes or conceptual hierarchies within which emotions and feelings may also be bound, Thus it is that learning is often intimately bound up with feelings of anxiety or pleasure and can provoke intense emotions.

When engaging in thinking at the simpler levels new concepts may be being constructed this is the process of **concept development**.This is particularly evident when learning new subject contents and skills. Programmes overloaded with content may occupy all of student learning time in the area of concept development so that on entering employment there is little competency and capability to do the work for which they are employed. Balancing the demands of learning new content with the needs to link it in a meaningful way with student understanding and real-life problem-solving and experience can be a difficult problem to resolve. It requires a change from monological thinking to higher order, critical or multilogical, thinking on the part of both tutors and students.

Cognitive skills
Sophisticated thinking involves the manipulation of various levels of concepts by what we call **cognitive processes**. These may involve searching through concepts and constructs in sequential order, ranging through hierarchies of concepts for critical features, probing deeply into a construct, focusing on 'key' concepts with similar tags of reference, re-ordering and reconstructing to develop new constructs scanning data and schema, missing key attributes and using personal or idiosyncratic attributes. It may also include re-rieving old, well-tried strategies to solve a new problem or using part of an old strategy to help in the process. On appropriate occasions analogies may be used to solve old problems in an entirely different context in an imaginative and new way. Broad reading

and broadening experiences can facilitate creative modelling and analogous thinking where there is flexibility in thinking and time for reflection. Deep study, narrowing down on a topic, can extend the complexity of conceptual hierarchies but may not achieve the desired resolution of problems unless there is time for reflective thought and opportunity to integrate the new material and then use it in cognitive processing. Many processes occurring simultaneously, drawing on many conceptual hierarchies, are typical of multilogical thinking.

The different hemispheres of the brain are set up to engage in different forms of data processing. The sequential ordering processes are thought to be typical of the left or language orientated hemisphere. Imaginative, inductive and appositional thought processes (Gazzaniga, 1967, and Bogen, 1969) are found to be characteristic of right hemisphere activities. The most creative of our scientists and artists appear to have had great facility in the use of both hemispheres. Regrettably Western Education has been accused of only valuing and educating the left hemisphere linguistic functions (Ornstein, 1982). To this can be added that there is a world-wide tendency to develop monological, single-track, context defined thinking through the overuse of didactic teaching methods.

Critical Thinking Theory and Multilogical Thinking

Critical thinking is:

- the art of thinking about your thinking while you are thinking so as to make it more precise, accurate, relevant, consistent and fair;
- the art of constructive scepticism;
- the art of identifying and reversing bias, prejudice and one-sidedness of thought;
- the art of self-directed, in-depth, rational learning;
- thinking that rationally certifies what we know and makes clear where we are ignorant Paul (1990, p. 32).

The skills of accomplished critical thinkers are sophisticated and they are in command of the elements of thought. These include an ability to formulate, analyse and assess those elements. Paul described these elements as follows:

- the problem or question at issue;
- the purpose or the goal of the thinking;
- the frame of reference or points of view involved;
- the assumptions made;
- the central concepts involved;
- the principles or theories used;
- the evidence, data or reasons advanced;
- the interpretations and claims made;
- the inferences, reasoning and lines of formulated thought;
- the implications and consequences involved.

In our programmes it was essential to shift students to higher order critical thinking and to design the appropriate teaching and learning strategies for doing this. Even in monlogical mathematical problem-solving students needed to think their way non-algorithmically into mathematical systems just as we expected them to work with schoolchildren.

Teaching for critical thinking was considered to be essential in our programmes. Students entering the teaching profession hoping to help pupils with learning difficulties in mainstream education would be beset by complex multilogical issues for which they needed to be prepared. These issues would, at the outset, be more complex than subject-based disciplinary problems and some would have no resolution. Didactic theory had nothing to offer in such a context, although the declining unit of resource made didactics a popular solution. It was determined that critical theory would be the organizing principle for the teaching programmes although at that stage it was known by other titles such as 'cognitive theory of learning', 'cognitive process pedagogy', 'higher order thinking' and 'cognitive process study skills'. It had to be achievable with increased numbers of students and decreased assessment times.

Teaching for the Critical Thinking

Thomas and Harri-Augstein at the Brunel Centre for Studies of Human Learning had undertaken a number of research studies of students' abilities to engage in higher order reading and study skills. They focused on the students' abilities in learning to learn, how they learned factual material their ability to summarize principles, main ideas and overall structure of technical and literary material.

They found that many strategies could be taught and situations could be set up where other higher order reading strategies could be practised and learned. In other words, aspects of critical thinking could be taught. The process by which this was achieved was for the students to be taught or helped to 'hold learning conversations' with themselves. In a related research project the performance of trained teachers was enhanced by enabling them to hold learning conversations with themselves about their teaching (Montgomery, 1984, Montgomery and Hadfield, 1989).

Self-monitoring and self-regulatory activities according to Wang and Lindvall (1984) not only contributed to improved acquisition in their researches with students but also to improved generalization and transfer of knowledge and skills as well as a sense of personal agency. Self-regulatory activities have been defined by Brown, Bransford, Ferrara and Campione (1983) as including planning, predicting outcomes and scheduling time and resources. Monitoring included testing, revising and rescheduling with checking to evaluate outcomes obviously using criteria developed by the individual and those which were externally defined also formed part of a matrix of self-regulatory activities engaged in by the autonomous and capable learner.

In a previous decade Flavell (1979) had established that metacognition was a highly important contribution to higher order learning:

> Metacognition is the process by which we think about our cognitive machinery and processing mechanisms (Flavell, 1979 , p. 907)

These metacognitive activities underpinned the development of the self-regulatory and self-management skills already referred to as well as the sense of personal agency. Metacognition has in recent years become a powerful theoretical tool in the explanation of many aspects of cognitive processing including the learning of language and in becoming literate. Learning conversations may be a term with similar meaning and power. Failure to develop learning conversations or metacognitions left the learner in 'robot mode' according to Thomas (1976). This was a state of learned helplessness where the response to problems was to use old well-worn strategies even if they had little hope of success and to profit little from experience. It was estimated that some 80 per cent of the population were in robot mode.

Failure to develop higher order cognitive skills in schools and colleges was according to Resnick (1989) not surprising. It had, he postulated, never been the goal of mass education to do more than develop basic skills of literacy and numeracy and core subject knowledge. He defined higher order cognitive skills as follows:

- non-algorithmic;
- complex;
- has multiple solutions;
- nuanced judgement and interpretation;
- involves the use of multiple criteria which sometimes conflict;
- involves uncertainty and ambiguity;
- involves self-regulation;
- imposes meaning and structure on apparent disorder;
- is effortful.

Lower order thinking was illustrated in the opposite of these processes and prevented the person from developing into an autonomous and independent learner.

Researches have begun to show that there are strategies which tutors can use to develop critical thinking but these have not always rested within the domain of knowledge under study but as part of study skills and learning strategies programmes. In some courses critical thinking has been an integral part of the programme but has never been the subject of research and development or made explicit to the learners. It became imperative for our course design to make explicit the critical thinking goals and purposes and to develop strategies by which they might be realized despite the declining resource base and institutional counter pressures.

Teaching for Critical Thinking and Linking Assessment and Cognitive Process Strategies.

With the cuts in teacher education we were faced with a set of problems or dilemmas. On the one hand we had increased number of students per member of staff. The students typically had insufficiently developed cognitive skills and skills for independent learning all of which they needed if 'education' in the mass was to be undertaken. Seminar discussion, small group work and more open systems of assessment which we had found to develop higher order cognitive skills were in retreat. Research quoted by Race (1992) now supports what we knew we needed to introduce to student learning programmes if we were to achieve higher order learning. For example it was found that the extent of undergraduate learning through different methods and materials was as follows:

Lecture	5%
Books	10%
Audiovisual presentation	20%
Dramatic lecture with AV presentation	30%
Discussing	50%
Explaining	75%
Teaching	90%
Assessing	95%

We have found that a programme of 'dramatic' lectures followed by discussing and explaining had enabled students to move from surface to deep learning. When we set up situations where they taught us and assessed various models of work and learning outcomes we found new material was fully accommodated or achieved deep levels. These processes of explaining, teaching and assessing involved the student in the higher order cognitive processing activities of planning and self-regulation. It was first difficult but not insuperable to resolve the problem of how similar results might be achieved with large groups and lower tutor input. This tutor input had still relied to some extent upon 'judicious questioning' which HMI (1992) had found crucial to the needs of able and highly able students of schools. The model developed was the Cognitive Process Learning Spiral.

COGNITIVE - PROCESS

LEARNING SPIRAL

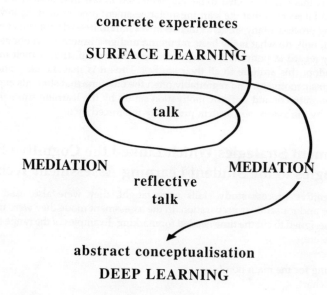

concrete experiences

SURFACE LEARNING

talk

MEDIATION   MEDIATION

reflective
talk

abstract conceptualisation

DEEP LEARNING

(accommodation)

Figure 2 Cognitive Process Learning Spiral

This was used as a model for teacher education in schools and on degree programmes. Material to be learned was presented through a variety of what were called Cognitive Process Strategies or Pedagogies as follows:

- investigative and problem-solving and resolving approaches;
- cognitive study skills;
- language experience methods;
- experimental learning;
- collaborative learning;
- games and simulations.

These strategies have been found through grounded research to be effective in moving students from surface to deep learning and had to be applicable to all subjects in the school and higher education curriculum.

In the first cycle the students most frequently discussed subject, content, skills and applications and explained them in ways which fostered understanding. Understanding by which they ordered and tried to make structured patters and sense of the incoming information. The second cycle of talk was reflective thought and talk induced to enable them to examine the process by which they planned and executed the learning and then evaluated the outcomes, thus tapping into their metacognitive processes. This was often as can be seen from the diagram to be 'mediated' by the judicious questioning from the tutor. It was this which needed to be supplemented in our new system for large group teaching and it seemed that the learning and assessment process held the key rather than the teaching process. Many students then as now (Terrell, 1993) despite what tutors would believe will only do what is the basic minimum and go through the motions in modules which they regard as peripheral to their main programme of studies, their majors. Many students adopt this attitude to all their studies. Thus it is that the assessment tool is a prime extrinsic motivator and regrettably often the only one that students experience. We wanted commitment and intrinsic motivation set up by the learning strategies used and supported by the assessment system preferably reinforced by it.

Assessment Strategies Which Linked the Cognitive Process Pedagogies to the Student Learning Assessment Techniques

When cognitive process study skills were taught, they were also used in learning workshops and for seminar preparation. In the assessment mode they were used again as tools but designed to cut the time needed for marking. Examples of the range of skills/tool available were:-

- reading for the main point;
- flow chart;
- concept mapping;
- sequencing;
- deletions;
- diagramming;
- classifying;
- summarizing;
- evaluating in relation to internal and external criteria;
- comparing and contrasting;
- critical comprehension in its various aspects.

Reading for the Main Point

In formative and summative assessment it was possible to present textual abstracts, research articles and chapters from course and recommended texts and to ask that the students identify, e.g.

1. the six main points;

2. the main point and subordinate points;

3. the main issue and its three causes and effect consequences.

When the **reasons** for these choices and decisions were also required the responses would fit into a 200 – 500 word format and could substitute for a course essay or assignment. They could be written in examination conditions or as course work and coherent expression of ideas and argument with reference to relevant research could be required. It could enable an exam paper or course work to be tailored to fit a tight marking schedule and cut student irrelevant wordage. The quantity of pages for the exam question papers increased but answer books were reduced in size.

Flow Charting

Giving students an article, research paper or book to read or research within or outside an examination setting could cut the final response to a one-page summary for the marker but levels of understanding could be clearly marked in pass/fail or on a sliding scale of 1 to 5, 1 to 12 or 1 to 20, depending on whether justifications for the structure were required at each point and whether pros and cons and requests for similarities and differences were required or consequences of particular patterns were hypothesized.

Essay Test Papers, Case Studies and Scenarios

The cognitive process techniques are similar to essay answers in most subjects which demand cognitive processing as opposed to straightforward stimulus–recall responses required by short answer papers or recognition responses in multiple-choice machine-marked test papers. Essay examination papers in various disciplines have their own structures for acceptable responses which elicit coverage of most aspects relevant to the question. Education, psychology and special needs areas have common structures which facilitate student response and speed up marking capacity. For example such essays contain in appropriate measure according to the focus of the question:

- critical examination of the key concepts in the question;
- examination of relevant theoretical positions and frameworks;
- critical review of relevant research;
- relevance to application of the above in the 'real' situation with test examples;
- a presentation of the writer's own views and a summing up of the main points in a conclusion.

Students can revise to this format and write to it which keeps them working to the point, enables comparisons to be made between 'good' and 'better' answers with some basis in fact and enable a criterion referenced scale for marking to be used which improves consistency between markers. The C-R scale refers directly to the essay structure required (Montgomery, 1983b). Accuracy is also considerably enhanced when as the questions for the exam paper are proposed the answer plan acceptable is roughed out by the tutors and agreed. Variations on the theme can be accepted as appropriate and relevant as well as reasoned variations in approaches to theory and evidence.

Case studies and scenario papers can be presented in the exam for analysis with reference to the same structure or a focus can be required on critical theories; conceptual analysis; or intervention strategies with reference to research.

Summarizing

Students often do not read sufficiently widely and in any depth although recommended to do so. One of the assessments used was to provide guidelines on how to prepare, construct and pattern a book review. Two examples were given and the students were asked to select from a specified range of texts or another text was agreed where relevant and a 600-word book review was required. Not only have student found the task interesting and stimulating but it was also a valuable learning experience both in terms of the content of the text and the process of mastery learning the content.

Other summarizing strategies used were to condense a short story, a book, a presentation into a minisaga or a marketing message of 50 words no more no less. At other times a 250 word abstract, a 600 word review and a 1500 word article were required of the same content area. On other occasions they were asked to produce a chronology with annotations or as visual display in pictures or cartoons. Sometimes 5 overhead transparencies were required to summarize key points for a target audience. Instead of project work annotated bibliographies for particular audiences were requested or the production of a staff handbook on a particular problem area had to be designed.

Reversibility of Assessment Roles

Frequently reversing the assessment roles was employed so that students were asked to read text, pursue investigations but instead of writing a report were asked:-

- to design a flow chart (plus the answers) for other students;
- to design a short answer examination paper based upon material from three research papers;
- to design an examination paper with answer plans in a given area;
- to use a set of assessment criteria and mark two essays, a good and a poor essay (anonymous) from a previous cohort giving constructive comments to the writer about how the essay could be improved;
- to evolve a set of marketing criteria for a particular project or piece of creative work with a group of colleagues. Each individual then applied the criteria to 2 or 3 pieces of work justifying the grades given.

In each example it was important to be able to define the work of the individual and assess it in about half the time or less then the usual assessment activities. These are only examples of a wide range of strategies which can be used. They can be taught to large groups of students and may be set as collaborative activities in the large group settings to ensure understanding and stimulate judicious questioning. Used later as assessment devices they can help to halve the time spent on assessment activities.

At the time we did not see any evidence that it was diminishing the quality of much of what we would normally have done. Complaints were from the administration over the thickness of the exam paper. Dyslexic students were given half an hour extra reading time or opportunities to have papers read to them.

Multiple Criteria Assessments

Several frameworks were used as illustrative material for this aspect of the work and on some occasions students were asked to work in groups to evolve their own criteria. Here 'pyramiding' and snowballing strategies might be used to focus gradually on and evolve relevant dimensions.

External criteria such as Bloom's (1956) taxonomy of educational objectives were used to help students define the level of their own and their pupil's learning.

Higher levels	Lower levels
6 Evaluation	3 Application
5 Synthesis	2 Comprehension
4 Analysis	1 Recall

In particular it was stressed that analysis needed to include not just a breaking down into component parts but it must include an identification of the relationship between those parts to be 'proper' analysis. Synthesis had to include not just the building of something from component parts which was not the same as previously but the new whole had to be different and innovative, not just the sum of the original parts.

Evaluation should include the application of either internal or externally defined multiple criteria and would include several or all of the lower levels of functioning in the taxonomy.

When essays or performance were to be required then criteria to be used for marketing them were given in advance or evolved with the learners as in the examples already given.

Peer Assessment

When work was to be peer marked then it was crucial for the criteria for the marks to be awarded to be evolved or discussed and understood. This would for example mean a drawing up of a set of constructs which would enable the marker to identify the A qualities in an A answer and have these agreed by other expert markers. Similarly B, C, D and E grades would be criterion-referenced (Montgomery, 1983b) and practice examples given. From this students grew in confidence that the judgements made were rational and they could with considerable accuracy arrive at similar conclusions about grades.

The New Work Pattern

The course was scheduled to occupy four hours contact time per week for the final year students. The new pattern was as follows:

- 1 hour lecture to the whole cohort with audio-visual input, advance organizers to show structure of the lecture and a summary given at the end with a short reading list. Attendance by students optional.
- 1.5 hours workshop in large lecture space or several rooms. Introduced by tutor(s) circulating or organized by work sheets and schedules in student leaderless groups. Compulsory attendance.

- 1.5 hours seminar on alternative weeks in 15 person groups of students. Seminars were never permitted to be larger and 8–12 person groups were preferred.

(a)   student led but leaders primed and prepared;

(b)   leaderless groups and tutor monitored;

(c)   tutor led on three-week cycle with groups A and B for 45 minutes each;

(d)   tutor led with two other part-time colleagues not specialist in the field but primed and prepared.

All students who had not read the papers were asked to go and do so.

The first 15 – 30 minutes of the seminar session contained a debriefing/reflective session on the workshop. In the final term groups of students opted for specialist areas which they then organized for the whole day and taught the rest of the students and the staff.

Summary and Conclusions

A whole range of options such as the above and others besides were used as staffing levels changed and student feedback indicated different areas of need. 'What was significant throughout this period however was that the commitment of the students to learning and to the subject was growing stronger and stronger. The course evaluations which were an essential part of the development, quality control and monitoring showed they felt involved with the whole process of planning, learning, teaching and assessing. These were roles which every teacher has to play in a major way and so they felt they were being prepared for them. In addition they were learning about the learning needs of themselves and their pupils. They were also learning in a very effective way about a content area, namely psychology and special needs which was highly relevant to their mainstream teaching. At the time there was insufficient connection in the literature between theory, research and application and this had to be constructed to justify the programme to the students. With it there developed a notion and strong sense of quality in teaching and learning which did enhance performance. It also made the students critical of other programmes with which they were involved and they used their new found strategies to organize change and enhance them. It was clear to us from the results which began to emerge from the regular cohorts that the students' standards of achievement had at least been maintained and in fact were improving. The numbers of those gaining grades which would put them in the 2.1 and first-class range had markedly increased over the period. The new skewed distribution with a large hump at the upper end began to preoccupy examiners and auditors but it could not be adjusted.

The students' attitudes to the programme became very positive and many wished to spend all their time working in this way and some even wished to spend all their time working in this subject area when they had started by thinking it might not be central to their interests or needs as teachers.

The teaching strategies incorporated what was thought to be significant quality learning experiences in which students were involved:

- critical thinking;
- real problem-solving;
- research and development activities;
- explaining and teaching;
- evaluation and assessment.

These activities caused them to engage in all the aspects of higher order multilogical thinking such as those described. In particular tolerance of ambiguity and uncertainty, nuanced judgement and effort carried with them emotional qualities and feelings which needed to be discussed during and after the process of learning both with the students and the tutors (Montgomery, 1993). Finding multiple solutions was also worrying to many individuals who were used to finding the one solution required by the 'teacher'. Imposing meaning and patterns on the material to be learned they found strenuous and tiring and using multiple criteria difficult though not impossible.

The students appeared to go through a cycle of affective change in addition to the cognitive one. This began with anxiety at not being given lectures and seminars weekly and having to cope with independent workshops and other autonomous activities. At first they failed to complete the workshops satisfactorily as they did not have the appropriate strategies and even when the lecture gave them the required tools and strategies they failed at the 'applications' level. For this they blamed the tutor, the lack of clarity of the instructions, the materials, anything or anyone but themselves. At their request the whole event was repeated and they all achieved success. Suddenly they became very much more alert and better adapted to listening in lectures and then applying the knowledge later. After a period of adjustment to the new strategies and format which they did find difficult there was a period of stability and then in the second semester there was an increase in mastery observed. The students challenged the tutors and brought along new and different and more up-to-date papers, questioned and intervened in lectures and seminars to bring in different perspectives.

It was an exciting partnership in learning we had entered into and one we decided we could not retreat from. It was a balance between a totally directed and tutor-led programme and a completely autonomous student tutorless programme. When the staffing ratios were finally readjusted from 90 to 30 to 1 there was no return to the old methods. The staff used the independent study group times for their own research and development planning meetings.

The cognitive process strategies pedagogies have been linked to student learning and assessment strategies in a challenging way for tutor and student so that both achieved higher levels of critical thinking and professional competence and capability. These achievements corresponded very closely to those mapped out by Stephenson and Weil (1988) in *Facing the Challenge of Higher Education for Capability*. Education for Capability, a project of the RSA, is pledged to work with institutions and teachers to create more and varied opportunities for learners to manage their own learning and to explore and account for its relevance to their own needs and those of the society of which they are a part. The networks have been established and the challenges have been issued and in 1994 the first *Journal of Education for Capability* has been published. Critical theory and cognitive process pedagogies can be seen as a major vehicle for the realization of capability goals for an education for the twenty-first century.

References

Brown, A. L., Bransford, J.D., Ferrara, R. A. and Campione, J. C. (1983). Learning, remembering and understanding. In Flavell, J. and Markman, E., (eds.) *Carmichael's Manual of Child Psychology* Vol. 1 ,New York, Wiley.

Flavell, J. H. (1979). Metacognition and cognitive monitoring. *American Psychologist*, **34**, p.906 – 11.

Freeman, J. (ed.) (1985). *Psychology of Giftedness* ,London, Wiley.

Gazzaniga, M. S. (1967). The split brain in man. *Scientific American*, **217**(2) 24 – 29.

Gibbs, G. (1990). In Gibbs (1992). *Improving the Quality of Student Learning*. Bristol Technical Education Services.

Goldberg, M. L. (1965). *Research on the Talented*. New York Teachers College Press.

Hirst, P. (1968). The contribution of philosophy to the study of the curriculum. In Kerr, J. F.(ed.) *Changing the Curriculum*. London, University London Press.

HMI (1992). *Provision for Highly Able Pupils in Maintained Schools*. London, HMSO.

McClelland, D. C. (1958). In, (eds.) *Talent in Society: New perspectives in the Identification of Talent*. (Princetown, N. J., Van Nostrand) McClelland, D. C., Bronfenbrenner, U., Strodtbeck, F. L.

Meek, M. and Thompson, B. (1987). *Study Skills in the Secondary School*. London, Routledge.

Montgomery, D. (1981). The nature of modern teaching: education comes of age, *School Psychol. Internat.* **1**(6).

Montgomery, D. (1983b). *Learning and Teaching Strategies: Study Skills*. Maldon, Learning Difficulties Research Project.

Montgomery, D. (1984). *Evaluation and Enhancement of Teaching Performance*. Maldon, Learning Difficulties Research Project.

Montgomery, D. (1989). *Managing Behaviour Problems*. London, Hodder & Stoughton.

Montgomery, D. (1990). *Children with Learning Difficulties*. London, Cassell.

Montgomery, D. (1993). Learner Managed Learning in Teacher education, *Learner Managed Learning Proceedings of 34th International Conference of the World Education Fellowship*. London, WEF.

Montgomery, D. (1994). Enhancing student learning in higher education through the development and use of cognitive process strategies. In Gibbs, G. (ed.) *Managing Student Learning* (In press).

Ornstein, R. (1982). *The Psychology of Consciousness* 2nd. eds,. San Francisco, W.H. Freeman.

Passow, A. H. (1990). Needed research and development in educating high ability children. *European Journal of High Ability*. **1**. 15 – 24.

Paul, R.W. (1991). Critical thinking: what every person needs to survive in a rapidly changing world. Chapter 3. In Binker, A. J. A. (ed.). *Critical Thinking in North America.* Centre for Critical Thinking and Moral Critique. Sonoma State University, USA, 17 – 41.

Race, P. (1992). Developing competence. *Professional Inaugural Lectures.* Glamorgan, University of Glam Wales, 112 – 185.

Resnick, L. B. (ed.). (1989). *Knowing Learning and Instruction: Essay in Honour of Robert Glaser,* Hillsdale, N. J., Erlbaum, 1 – 24.

Span, P. (1988). Intelligence and high ability, Keynote presentation at Plovdiv conference. *9th Bulgarian International Education Seminar.*

Terrell, I. (1993). *Distance Learning: Pump Priming Project.* Discussion paper, Middlesex University.

Thomas, L. F. and Harri-Augstein, E. S. (1972). *Reading to Learn: Research Project Report.* Centre for Study of Human Learning, Brunel University Public.

Thomas, L. F. and Harri-Augstein, E. S. (1984). The self organised learner: a conversational science for teaching and learning. Paper presented at *SCEDSIP/COPOL Conference Kingston.* Centre for Study of Human Learning Brunel University Public.

Wang, M. C. and Lindvall, C. M. (1984). Individual differences and school learning environments. In Gordon, E. W. (ed.). *Review of Research Education,* Vol 2. Washington DC, Amer. Educ. Res. Assoc.

8   Hierarchical Teams: action research project

Ann Latham and Jenny Gilbert School of Computing and Information Technology, University of Wolverhampton.

Abstract

The focus of our action research project is to produce students who can easily and quickly adapt from university life to working life. In the field of computing, and information systems in particular, the ability to work in teams is becoming increasingly important. Different methods of team working have been investigated and the result has been the development of hierarchical teams.

A hierarchical team is a group of 15 or more students working together as a simulated company. A structured approach is adopted, with one student acting as manager, and two or three others as project leaders. Students' prior experience is recognized and employed, the structured peer support giving students confidence and motivation.

Management of change is central to the research. Firstly there is the increasing pressure on education to adapt to changing circumstances. Secondly the project gives an opportunity to consider curriculum innovation as an example of learning by doing. Thirdly, the change from student life to working life needs to be managed, and this project helps students in that transition.

Background

The concept of the hierarchical team has been developed at the University of Wolverhampton over the last five years, using two final year Information Systems modules. Students operate in simulated consultancy companies comprising 15 or more students. They undertake a live project, visiting local secondary schools in order to investigate the schools' Information Technology (IT) facilities and usage and to devise an IT strategy for the schools.

This research has been ongoing for five years. The focus of the research is to improve the employability of students, helping to prepare them for the world of work. In computing working in teams is usually considered essential, and negotiation skills are highly valued. With this in mind our aim is to enhance these skills in students. Different methods of team-working have been investigated and the result has been the development of hierarchical teams.

The Concept

The hierarchical team concept focuses on the allocation of responsibility and the requirement to work together in one large unit, this being broken down into smaller units as appropriate. We aim to empower students and to improve the learning experience by providing a challenge, a support mechanism and concrete experience to illuminate the theory that is presented to them.

How does the hierarchical team concept operate? Firstly, depending on the number of students, we agree how many simulated companies must be established. For each company a manager is then selected together with two or three project leaders. In order to accomplish this, advertisements are posted and students are invited to apply for the positions. The actual selection process varies from year to year. Following selection, managers negotiate with each other and with tutors to agree which project leaders and which team members should be allocated to their company.

The Three-Cycle Approach

A three-cycle approach is used to prepare students to work effectively with their peers and to enable them to carry out the live project with the minimum of supervision. The first cycle, the 'nursery slope', comprises tutorials dedicated to developing group work techniques. Students solve a variety of simple and complex problems which require communication skills, organizational skills, logical reasoning and the application of ethical considerations. Students are expected to reflect upon these experiences, consider adjusting their behaviour and draw out guidelines for effective team work.

The second cycle requires students to complete an assessment based upon a case study. This allows them the opportunity to work as a hierarchical team in a safe environment.

Finally, students embark on the third cycle. Students visit secondary schools to carry out the IT investigation and make recommendations for the future.

Action Research

Cohen and Manion (1994) define one context for action research as being 'concerned with innovation and change and the ways in which these may be implemented in ongoing systems'. This definition is appropriate for the project being carried out. Innovation and change have certainly been evident during the five years of research. The research is ongoing and is carried out primarily to feed into our teaching.

Action research is a form of research carried out by practitioners into their own practice. It is a form of self-reflective enquiry undertaken in order to improve practice. The essentially practical, problem-solving nature of action research makes this approach attractive to the practitioner, the researcher identifying a problem during the course of his or her work, seeing the merit of investigating it and if possible of improving practice. Galliers (1992) believes that the role of researchers carrying out action research is to associate themselves actively with the practical outcomes of the research. As practitioners in education we have seen the merit of investigating our teaching, reflecting upon the process in order to improve the practice. It is our intention that the research has practical and helpful outcomes.

Action research needs a focus and should then be based on a cyclical process of planning – acting – observing – evaluating – planning etc., where evaluation involves reflecting upon the observations of previous practice.

The focus of the project is the employability of students. The aims are to help students develop team skills and to take control of their own learning.

Each year changes in mechanism have been introduced as the experiences are fed back: students and tutors making suggestions for improvements. Over a period of five years we have evaluated the modules using various mechanisms: observation, vivas, questionnaires, student diaries etc. Our evaluation has primarily been used to influence the future direction of the modules.

Breakwell (1990) acknowledges that action research is designed to initiate change in people, organizations or procedures. The aim is to improve,not simply describe, what already happens. This research aims to change people, organizations and procedures. Within the educational process, students' team-working skills are certainly enhanced and the procedures used during the modules are constantly changing with the overall aim of improving the employability of the students. At this stage it cannot be said that the university as an organization has changed because of our research, although our 'part' in the change process is acknowledged. Within the schools it is our intention to improve the IT provision. Students have acted as catalysts on many occasions, and we have seen evidence of change in teachers, IT within the schools (organizations.) and the procedures adapted.

Management of Change

A number of authors have focused on the management of curriculum change and this is a timely issue when there is increasing pressure on education to adapt to rapidly changing circumstances. Quality Assurance demands accountability; there are increasing numbers of students, improved access to higher education, demands for more effective teaching modes and the need to prepare students to work in a technologically changing society. We felt the project gave an opportunity to consider curriculum innovation as an example of learning by doing. Both lecturers and the students were synthesizing theory and practice. Our premise was that being involved in a practical exercise with potential effects would facilitate learning to a greater degree than the normal teaching mode.

By using an example of small-scale change our aim was to identify the factors that influence effective learning through change, whether the learners be lecturers, the teachers in the schools or the students.

This project examines the response of students to the situation where they must form an effective working team, undertake a project and report within tight time scales. The accent is on speedy implementation, effective group interaction and rapid response to external change.

This is a very similar scenario to that facing the education professional. The interpretation of teaching as a management activity further reinforces the importance of considering the management of change as an essential part of teaching in HE.

> Teaching and learning are inseparable: teaching involves the whole management and promotion of student learning by a variety of methods, including student access to a wide range of learning resources. Quality can and should be assessed both in terms of student achievement and in terms of the totality of the learning experience. (HEFCE, 1993)

The adoption of secondary schools as the client/collaborator in this project enabled another perspective on the management of educational change to be available. With the advent of the National Curriculum, there is a requirement for IT skills to be taught and assessed across the curriculum and the provision and application of IT has to be managed.

Both Fullan (1991) and Brighouse et al. (1991) identify a number of critical factors and key themes which are necessary to ensure successful implementation of curriculum change.

The necessary factors are as follows

- purpose;
- encouragement;
- vision;
- struggling through ambivalence;
- evolutionary planning;
- a fixer.

Our research confirmed a number of their findings. Firstly there is the importance of purpose and encouragement. Our aim was to produce employable graduates by enabling them to work on a real project in simulated companies. The students are motivated by a live project. After their first visit to the school they realize the worth-while nature of advising the school. However, in one of the schools where the head teacher was not personally prepared to be interviewed by the students, they became very demotivated. It was clear to them that the school management did not value their input. (In the other schools where staff took the students seriously, motivation was maintained.)

maintains that there should be clarity about goals and the means to attain those goals. This group must share vision and ownership of the project. Our research confirms this: one company lost motivation as a result of confusion over devising a questionnaire, and this stemmed from a lack of clear guidelines and poor communication.

Fullan raises the issue of simplicity versus complexity. Complexity creates problems for implementation but may result in greater change because more is being attempted. By imposing a hierarchical structure on the student groups we attempt to deal with this issue. Individuals are at different starting points and we recognize this by giving management responsibilities to those who are better able to deal with complexity. Nevertheless we do find that the intractable problem for the lecturer is deciding when to give structure and guidance and when to let students learn through the struggle. Fullan's proposition holds that it is not always possible to tell people what to do. In order to learn and accomplish change they must often struggle through ambivalence.

Both Fullan and Brighouse stress the need for evolutionary planning, that is having a plan but being prepared to adapt it in line with local circumstances. Have a plan but learn by doing must be the watchword of action research and curriculum innovation. All students realized the need to adapt in interview situations. Where adaption seemed easier, interviews were well planned. The strategy of evolutionary planning applies also to lecturers planning the modules. The more thoroughly we have planned, the more readily we can adapt when necessary.

Brighouse specifies that each project should have a 'fixer'. This is a key person, who is accorded status by the others and can ensure that communication is facilitated, time for development is negotiated and people are provided with resources and moral support. We have found that where there is a fixer in a group, who might not always be the manager, the group performance improves. It is also beneficial where there is a recognized fixer based in the school to link with the student group.

Our small-scale student curriculum project did confirm Fullan's work and in focusing on the secondary school as the domain for the investigation of curriculum change we also found that external agents can be effective catalysts for change, partly because they are outside of the organizational politics.

A task force, brought together to accomplish a task and then disbanded, is unlikely to suffer from internal politics. In order to function effectively it must be structured and organized and must quickly develop trust so the members can operate in a collegial fashion.

Although in this chapter we have not dwelt on the learning process or the underpinning theories of experiential learning we did find that the formal structure did provide students with peer support and motivation.

Benefits

Students learn from being active and involved and find it very difficult to hide. There is a great improvement in student motivation and response and the contribution from all members is increased. The formally imposed structure is beneficial providing the company does not try to operate too bureaucratically. Students frequently find it a better experience than small group work. As one student said

> The hierarchical structure helps to speed an organization's passage through problems, thus avoiding the time-consuming issues of leader emergence. Leaders break deadlocks and move stagnating problems on.

For those students who bring personal 'baggage' with them the structured peer support helps them to cope, motivates them and gives them more confidence in themselves and thus facilitates learning. An effective learning environment should provide contingent support as we learn best when given support at key points. Creating a formal structure helps to provide the contingent support that cannot always be provided by tutors.

The structure gives the support required to enable the students to accept the challenge of dealing with ambiguity. The hierarchical structure provides the key factors needed to manage change effectively.

> The encouragement and helpfulness of the team led me to believe if I let myself down I let the company down!

Students take on different responsibilities and have the opportunity to develop skills which are appropriate to their present development. This does raise problems in terms of assessment but it allows all students to be challenged. When writing references for any of these students, we find that we know a great deal more about their real capabilities than we would after teaching them on a conventional module.

The hierarchical-team approach significantly reduces the number of students consulting about problems, instead they use the formal structure of the company. It is essential that we organize all the initial material and contacts for the live project so that the students can be allowed to take control. The lesson is Trust the students!.

Hierarchical teams have allowed us to operate group work without the usual problems of bickering, students who do not pull their weight, or groups which fall apart. There are still some interpersonal problems but these can be dealt with more easily. The technique has made the introduction of live projects valuable to the students and in addition they have been catalysts in the schools, acting as external agents for change.

A number of students have contacted us some time after graduation. They have often found the experience provided by the hierarchical-team approach a significant factor in the successful transition from student life to working life. In employment, it is necessary to be able to work with others and to continue to acquire new skills and knowledge. This approach helps students to manage this.

Curriculum Change as Action Research

There are parallels between action research and curriculum change, whether we are focusing on small- or large-scale change. The need for a focus encompasses the factors of purpose, motivation and common goals. We then need to develop a clear vision of what it is we are trying to do. During the phases of acting and observing we need peer support, good lines of communication and we need to build our own reality. In the evaluation stage we undertake evolutionary planning, we revise what is to be done and proceed through the plan, act, observe and evaluate steps of the cycle again (Table 1)

Table 1	Action research phases, reflective questions and Fullan and Brighouse's criteria

Action research phases	*Reflective questions*	*Fullan and Brighouse's criteria*
Focus	Why am I doing this?	Purpose
Plan	What am I trying to do	Vision
Act	Who will help me? Can I do this?	Peer support, fixer Confidence
Observe	What is happening	Struggling through ambivalence
Evaluate	What have I learnt? What needs to be changed?	Evolutionary planning

When curriculum developers and students are pitched into change situations they often do not consider each of the five phases. If we consider each question in turn we can learn from reflection, and implementation is far more likely to be successful.

If we fail to address the early phases change may not be permanent or effective.

Although our research involved the use of hierarchical teams we believe the model applies to any learning situation.

We have successfully used the model with groups of students and with students undertaking individual assessments. In both cases their performance improved.

References

Breakwell G. (1990). *Interviewing* The British Psychological Society, Leicester and Routledge.

Brighouse T.R.P., Brown, C., Gleeson, D., Glover, D. (1991). *How to Manage Change in Colleges, Polytechnics and Universities: An Illustrative Study.* Centre for Social research in Education, University of Keele.

Cohen, L. and Manion, L. (1994). *Research Methods in Education.* Routledge.

Fullan M.G. (1991). *The Meaning of Educational Change.* Teachers College, Columbia University.

Galliers, R.D. (1992). Choosing information systems research approaches. In R.D. Galliers (ed.) *Information Systems: Research: Issues, Methods and Practical Guidelines.* Blackwell Scientific Publications Ltd.

HEFCE (1993). Circular 3/93. *Assessment of the Quality of Education*, Higher Education Funding Council England, Feb 1993.

9   Evaluating a deep approach to assessment

Allan Davies (Worcester College of Higher Education)

The Project

The purpose of this ongoing project is to evaluate the impact of a self- and peer assessment programme on students' approaches to their learning

The Case Study

The student group which is taking part in this study are in their second year of a BEd Primary Art programme.

The particular focus of this part of the research is the final assessment of a 120-hour project in Creative Textile Design.

What I wish to know, in this particular study, is whether involving students in the assessment of their own work and that of others promotes a deep approach to learning.

For this study I used two contrasting instruments to gather information. One was a 'fly-on-the-wall' video recording of one of the assessment groups participating in an assessment. The other was a questionnaire given to the whole year group.

Background to the Project

The framework for the self- and peer assessment programme now used at Worcester was first devised and introduced, three years ago, while I was course leader of the BA(Hons) Graphic Information Design course at Falmouth School of Art and Design. A commitment to student-centred learning and an involvement in the Improving Student Learning Project led by Graham Gibbs confirmed my belief that assessment, as it is normally practised in art and design education, is the major contributor to students taking a surface approach to their work.

The task at the time was to develop learning objectives and assessment criteria that would make explicit what a student was expected to know, understand and be able to do as a result of the project work given to them and also enable them to know how well they had performed at the end of the project. This explicitness would then enable students to be reflective about their work in a more structured way. In order to promote reflectiveness the course team established learning teams which had the express purpose of enabling students to identify and comment on what they had learned over a given period (usually a week). The focus on their learning rather than on the subject was crucial to the exercise for this became the site where students were able to articulate the approach (deep/surface) that they were taking to the project.

The learning team as a curriculum component aspired to the four key elements, identified by Biggs (1989), as associated with good teaching. By focusing on learning, each member of the group was able to explain and test out their ideas and modify them in the light of supportive comments. This supportive climate provided both the **motivational context** and **interaction with others**. Although much of art and design work involves active rather than passive work, the opportunity for **learner activity** of planning, reflecting and relating abstract conceptions through the learning teams is greatly enhanced. It is also through the learning teams that students can test how **well structured their knowledge base** is in relation to the tasks they have set themselves.

The assessment criteria were designed to cover the main domains of art and design practice. Each domain contained at least one set of four descriptions. The four descriptions were progressive in their sophistication, each one intended to be compatible with Saljo's SOLO taxonomy (Marton F and Säljö R, 1984); unistructural, multistructural, relational and extended abstract.

It was through the conception of the learning team that the self/peer assessment programme emerged. As the learning team was a well-informed group in respect to the achievements of its members it made sense that it should also be the site of the assessment of those achievements. It also made sense that if we were truly to tackle the problem of assessment and surface approaches then we should take the obvious step and hand as much responsibility as we could for assessment to those who would directly benefit from it.

One of the difficulties in assessment in art and design is in being able to differentiate between the quality of a student's product of a particular project and the quality of learning as an outcome of the making of that product. There is no inconsistency in a student producing an aesthetically elegant design solution but having learned little or nothing as a result. Equally, a student may well have learned a substantial amount and taken a deep approach in a project but the material outcome in itself does not reflect the learning. What we can say is that the material outcome, the art or design work, is part of the evidence of student learning and not the learning itself. It is my belief that confusion over this issue by both students and teachers has contributed to a misunderstanding of the purpose of assessment and its impact on student performance (see Gibbs, 1992, pp. 80–1).

In September 1993 I joined the art department at Worcester College of Higher Education. My task has been to introduce innovations into the curriculum which promote a deep approach. The most significant innovation, and possibly the most challenging, has been to establish a self/peer assessment programme for the art and design modular programme which begins in September 1994. During the year I involved 1st-year BEd students in a pilot self/peer assessment to enable them to judge for themselves the worthwhileness of the practice. However, the 2nd-year students heard about it and asked if they could also field test this form of assessment. From my previous experience of introducing innovations into a context of established practice I felt reluctant but what was different and interesting about this is that they were the prime movers rather than me as the teacher. It is this group which is the subject of this case study.

The Problematic

The following pertinent issues have emerged since the curriculum changes, to promote a deep approach to student learning through assessment, were made on the Graphic Information Design course.

There is little point in having a programme of study which is intended to promote a deep approach to student learning if the assessment of that programme encourages a surface approach. Whether we as teachers intend it or not, many students organize their learning around the assessment. That is where they start. 'How do I get the best marks in this project?' and not 'How do I make sense of/improve my understanding of . . .?', is the first question asked by a student taking a strategic approach to learning. In the absence of any explicit criteria the student will always default to the teacher's implicit suggested criteria. In art and design students learn fairly quickly what their teacher approves and disapproves of and, if they are strategists, take appropriate action. Satisfying or impressing the teacher, not the enhancement of their learning, becomes the goal of these students.

On the Graphic Information Design course the approaches to learning questionnaire identified over two-thirds of the students in one year group as having either an achieving or reproducing orientation towards their learning. Students who display these orientations in their approaches to learning often hold a 'clcsed' conception of teaching and learning (Gibbs, 1992, p. 7). A characteristic of this conception is that students expect, even if they don't like it, to be assessed by their teacher or some other institutional representative. Being assessed by themselves and/or their peers conflicts so profoundly with their expectations that some students find it difficult to cope with, even when the procedure is demonstrated to be more rigorous, more open, more objective, more democratic and so on than they have previously experienced. The question is therefore: how do you convince over two-thirds of any group that they should adopt an approach to learning and assessment which conflicts so strongly with their established expectations? My experience on the Graphic Information Design course was that unless students reoriented themselves towards a deep approach to their learning by 'owning' all the issues related to their reconceptualization (and this includes the politics of their educational experience) then they gradually returned to their previous expectations despite the nature of the curriculum and the assessment process.

Another feature, related to this last point, which has made evaluating the effectiveness of promoting a deep approach, through both curriculum and assessment change', more difficult, is that phenomenon that involves the concepts of 'variation' and 'reorientation' (House, 1974). While reorientation of student approaches to learning is what we wanted to achieve, there was a surprising number of students who were willing to vary their behaviour to satisfy the requirements of the innovations. It took some time to recognize that there were students who were willingly participating in the learning teams and self/peer assessments and displaying behaviour appropriate to a deep approach and who subsequently returned to the original closed conception of teaching and learning as the final examinations drew near. Differentiating, during the course or a project, between those students who have genuinely reoriented themselves and those who only vary their behaviour is not as straightforward as I first believed. This realization emerged during the final degree interviews with students who had experienced at least a year of peer review. The questionnaire is useful in determining at the outset what approach students take to their learning and enables us to make informative comparisons across time and groups but it requires fairly close questioning of students over a period of time about their learning to determine whether they are genuinely taking a consistently deep approach.

Part of the difficulty is that, for self/peer assessment purposes, it is necessary not only to enable students to recognize what approach they are taking but also to enculture them into the institutional and educational superstructures which foster the approaches. Committed strategists, particularly achievers, are therefore fully briefed to continue their surface approach albeit in the guise of a deep approach. They are effectively taking a surface approach rather than a deep approach to learning. They are continuing to ask the question, 'What do I have to do to get the best marks?'

Finally, one feature which is presently insurmountable also seems to be the one that lets the strategist off the hook. The assessment procedure I have been using is criterion referenced. To all intents and purposes the BA(Hons) is norm referenced. How can we convince our students to accept an assessment procedure that is designed to promote learning through the negotiation of explicit criteria when the final award is focused on a distribution curve that has more to do with elitism than understanding?

The Study

Introduction

Prior to the project I spoke to the year group about their expressed wish to participate in self/peer assessment. I outlined some of the differences to their previous assessment experience and alerted them to my concern that the anxiety on their part might be greater than those experienced by the 1st year since they have already established their expectations about what assessment should be on their course. I assured them that, as this was a test run, we could return to the previous practice of tutor assessment if they so wished.

Reflective journals are an established element of the course, although they are not used solely to identify the particular approach to learning that each student has taken. Nevertheless, I pointed out to them that reflective journals have proven to be very useful in evidencing a deep approach that has been taken to a project, particularly when the product is not a source of that evidence. Students on the course also have to write out a rationale of what they intend doing in the project. Again I pointed out that being able to relate original intentions to final outcomes can support reflectiveness and so provide evidence of the approach that a student has taken.

I introduced them to the assessment criteria (see Appendix) and we had a session when they could ask questions about criteria and the assessment procedure.

They were grouped into learning teams of five or six and met regularly throughout the project. At the end of the project we asked for a team to volunteer to be videoed during a self/peer assessment session for the benefit of this study.

The research instruments

One of the difficulties in determining whether a student is taking a deep or surface approach is actually capturing, in a reliable form, a student reflecting on a task specific activity. In interviews with students, I have found that it can quite often take a while for them to begin to take a relational or extended abstract approach to the particular task that they have been involved with. Many students, in formal interview conditions, seem to prefer to adopt a distanced, descriptive approach when questioned about how they went about their work, despite the evidence of previous encounters with them (e.g. learning teams), which suggested that they were taking a deep approach. Eliciting evidence in this way can be a lengthy and expensive task. Also the interview format requires that students are having to talk about learning that has already happened. I wanted to know if there was any qualitative difference between task specific events as they happen and students reports of these events.

Another difficulty with interviews is that students may feel inclined to provide me, who has an instrumental role in their lives, with answers of a particular nature.

As the assessment teams were small in number, sited in a particular room, and participating in an activity which was designed to promote a deep approach to learning, a video recording of the event seemed obvious. It would satisfy some of the concerns expressed above and be a visual, as well as oral, testament.

In order to enable the students to reflect on both their experiences and views of the assessment and to provide me with another source of information, I designed a simple questionnaire. I decided to make it an anonymous questionnaire to overcome the concerns I have of students' perceptions of my role in the exercise.

The video

It was obvious from the video that the students were keen for the procedure, at least, to be successful. They were well organized, polite to each other and patient on those occasions when required. Their self-consciousness in front of the camera, if it existed, was not evident and it seemed that its presence was soon forgotten about. Their methodological approach and commitment to the task surprised me somewhat as the novelty of the circumstances had the potential for creating anxiety. This may be explained by the fact that they are trainee teachers and have a vested interest in assessment.

In order to provide a critical perspective appropriate to the concerns of the conference, I looked at the video from the viewpoint of the strategies that foster a deep approach; the motivational context, learner activity, interaction with others and a well-structured knowledge base.

Was there evidence that it was a motivational context? Although the session lasted for over four hours the concentration of this particular group of students was maintained. There was no evidence to show that the student being assessed last was being rushed or dealt with in a less rigorous way. It was clear, as the assessment proceeded, that the students were becoming more familiar with the criteria and developing more confidence in applying it but that did not diminish the concern they had for each other. One specific instance in the early part of the session was their concern to make sense of the apparent subtleties of the criteria. They spent some time discussing meanings and interpretations of different expressions. There were many instances where they related the comments in the learning journals to the artwork displayed on the wall in an attempt to determine what level the assessed student had achieved. What is clear from the video is that most of the discussions centred around the specifities of the criteria and whether the fit between criteria and project work was accurate, rather than attempting to use the criteria as a guide for determining what SOLO level the student had been operating on.

Was the learner activity successful? Although the nature of the session meant that all the students would be active, what they were learning as a result of the activity was less easy to determine. Apart from the debate about interpretations, the only other obstacle that they were faced with was making a commitment about the level of learning that each had achieved. It might be significant that many of their judgements fell on the borderlines of the levels.

Was the interaction successful? Throughout the session each student had the opportunity to participate. However, two students had much more to say than the other four. They tended to take the lead. They were more willingly assertive and articulate than the others and were able to manage the direction of the session. There was no evidence of anyone feeling uncomfortable about this arrangement and no one appeared to be excluded from the debate. There demeanour, on the contrary, was inclusive. No one gravitated towards the fringe.

A well-structured knowledge base? One of the consequences of this innovation is that their prior experiences and expectations of assessment will be challenged. Their concern about the meaning of expressions in the criteria seemed to be evidence that they were attempting to relate the new conceptual scheme to their own. Following the session the group met and produced a short report with recommendations for modifications to the procedure.

The questionnaire

The self/peer questionnaire was administered a few weeks after the assessment. Sixteen out of 22 students responded. The following questions were asked:

THE PURPOSE
1   What do you think the purpose of the self- and peer-assessment was?

2   Was the purpose satisfied in this particular assessment? If so, why and how? If not, why not?

THE PROCESS
3   Was the process of the assessment clear to you? If not why not?

4   How could the process be improved?

THE EXPERIENCE
5   How did you feel about assessing yourself?

6   What were the difficulties in assessing yourself?

7   How did you feel about assessing your colleagues?

8   What were the difficulties in assessing your colleagues?

9   How did your experience of this assessment differ from your previous experiences of assessment?

10   Has the experience of this kind of assessment changed your approach to learning? What do you now do that is different?

11   If you were to be assessed in the same way for your next project would you approach your work differently? If so, what would you do that was different?

Below I have provided a selection of student responses to each question (the letter relates to each questionnaire);

1 WHAT DO YOU THINK THE PURPOSE OF THE SELF AND PEER ASSESSMENT WAS?
    b   By assessing each others' work, it makes us look more closely at each piece and study the thought process behind it instead of judging work on initial impressions of the final

piece. Having assessment criteria as a guideline to marking work allows us to become familiar with what examiners look for and what we should concentrate on when working on a project. Assessing college work is good practice for marking pupils' work in schools and develops our abilities to judge. The self assessment is an important par' in developing techniques and processes, as we can study where we lost marks and correct that in our next project.

o   Self assessment helps you to become more analytical and critical of one's own development. Making judgements about your work creates a basis for future improvements not only of end products but also of working procedures which should lead to greater depth of knowledge and self satisfaction. Peer assessment is beneficial in becoming experienced in the whole process of assessment. Making impartial and objective judgements and then relaying these findings to peers requires skills in many areas ie communication, diplomacy critical awareness etc.

f   To show students exactly how marks are allocated so that they know why they are given their allocated grade. This then shows students exactly what their strong and weak points are and where they can improve.

The experience of self assessment also gives valuable experience which is useful for marking work in school.

It gives students a chance to look back over the term and concentrate upon their performance during it, students are 'forced' to consider how they've worked.

2 WAS THE PURPOSE SATISFIED IN THIS PARTICULAR ASSESSMENT? IF SO, WHY AND HOW? IF NOT, WHY NOT?
n   Yes, I was actively involved in the self and peer assessment through the decision-making process, i.e. discussion. Yes, I think the experience has developed my skills in assessment. In particular my skills of analysis ie through examining the aesthetic qualities in a piece of work. In addition my communication skills and ability to articulate ie through discussions with peers. Finally my skills of judgement, through practice at assessing a project 'fairly', and in relation to that of others.

b   I think all the above purposes were fulfilled in the assessment and personally, I found it crucial to take a professional approach to the whole exercise, which means thinking about why we are doing this, what the criteria is looking at and most importantly putting aside personal opinions about the work or the artist. It is important to cover all angles of the work, i.e. techniques, media, presentation etc. and mark the elements separately as each may have a different weight on the overall mark.

j   I didn't feel it was an overall success because within each group you tended to get an 'average' mark, and between all the groups – those marks varied. Who's to say which group marked the work most accurately.

l   I am not sure that the purpose was satisfied in this particular assessment because I did not quite understand the assessment procedure, and each of us had different ideas about what the assessing meant.

3 WAS THE PROCESS OF THE ASSESSMENT CLEAR TO YOU? IF NOT WHY NOT?
a   I feel certain parts of the criteria lacked clarity of precision in some areas and even with a high degree of intellect a significant difference between each point couldn't be

deciphered. The underlying meaning of each point became confused and lost in several places. I therefore feel that a lack of clear justification within the assessment makes the marking of each individual difficult.

b   At first the process was confusing, particularly the media/material questions that I found hard to distinguish between, but after a while I found it fairly easy if time-consuming.

4 HOW COULD THE PROCESS BE IMPROVED?

c   It was felt, within our group, that it would be valuable to have an objective 'outsider' present to pose questions without leading the groups opinions but perhaps 'opening' them further. I think, also, that the number of persons in each assessment group needs to be carefully decided – six appeared to be too many as the views were often so diverse. However, with only 3/4 people decisions could be lead by an 'influential' member.

k   . . . and, surely, something which is the major piece of work of the whole course, deserves to be assessed by people who are qualified, practised and know what they are talking about, i.e. Tutors external examiners, not students, who are, after all, still learning. Would the Government allow learner drivers to be tested by other learner drivers?

l   Making the marking criteria a lot simpler to understand would hopefully improve the process.

5 HOW DID YOU FEEL ABOUT ASSESSING YOURSELF?

b   I had no qualms about assessing my own work and I deliberately adopted the approach of marking what I saw as if it was not my own work. I found it easier to do this after I had closely studied other peer members work then gone back to mine.

e   I felt quite uncomfortable assessing myself as I don't feel, have the confidence to 'blow my own trumpet' as it were, although the marks I generally give myself are usually spot on.

f   I quite enjoyed assessing myself. I found that I tended to work myself harder than the group marked me. I think that was something that we found happened quite frequently.

p   I found this quite difficult as I didn't want to mark myself too high, but also wanted to make sure I got a good mark due to the amount of effort I knew I put into my work.

6 WHAT WERE THE DIFFICULTIES IN ASSESSING YOURSELF?

b   It is difficult to be entirely honest in your mark and there is a temptation to mark in the extremes, usually marking yourself down to avoid embarrassment or disappointment when your peer group gives you a lower mark than you gave yourself. It is important to judge your work on what is presented rather than to think of all the hard work you have done and reward yourself for that.

d   It is difficult to step outside of your own work, as obviously you become very involved. You have sometimes to admit to your own lack of research etc. You have to be constructively critical about your own work throughout to realise where you could have improved, for assessment.

f   Being honest.

j   Making the marks appropriate to all the hours of hard work, and setting aside how hard I knew I had worked – to marking what I had actually achieved. But because I knew I had to do this anyway I tended to over compensate – when deciding what grade to give myself.

o Being completely honest and distinguishing between the amount of effort I had put into it and the quality of that effort. i.e. in some areas I felt that I worked flat out and that might lead me to make a biased, subjective judgement.

7 HOW DID YOU FEEL ABOUT ASSESSING YOUR COLLEAGUES?

b As long as I kept my views and opinions totally professional and marked the work as if I didn't know the colleague, I felt it relatively easy. I feel that as long as I can justify my marks and give reasons for each mark, then I don't mind being totally honest and I don't feel embarrassed or awkward about discussing marks with the colleague.

e I felt quite comfortable assessing colleagues as I knew I wasn't solely responsible for the grade given and there was several opinions of the work given. It also gave me more of an insight to their work which I normally wouldn't have been aware of.

f It felt a bit awkward assessing the others because you build up a supportive relationship as you work through the term, then this changes and becomes critical.

g I am more comfortable assessing others' work than my own. It's also made easier by doing it in a group, especially when assessing a friend.

k Worried about friendships, friction, confidences and personalities. Not wanting to upset people, and possibly wanting to upset people. (professional eh? - but true).

p Nobody really wants to give a peer a low mark, even if they think its what they deserve. Once or twice our group said 'Go on give them a 3, we gave them a 4 last time' simply because we didn't feel we could mark them too low and offend.

8 WHAT WERE THE DIFFICULTIES IN ASSESSING YOUR COLLEAGUES?

c It is often difficult to be completely honest and objective when assessing colleagues – especially when they are good friends! Again, this is where the stress lies, in trying to be diplomatic, in not offending or hurting people – how do you give a low mark, even when able to justify why, without 'flattening' someone?

o Putting personal feelings aside. Giving a completely objective and impartial judgement. This proved extremely difficult on this occasion as the group had given each other support throughout the project. Having given support and guidance, and if peers had taken it, it was then hard not to feel some responsibility for it therefore even harder to admit failure in some cases.

9 HOW DID YOUR EXPERIENCE OF THIS ASSESSMENT DIFFER FROM YOUR PREVIOUS EXPERIENCES OF ASSESSMENT?

b This assessment was much more in depth than any I had experienced. It was possible to argue your case or justify your marks given instead of just providing a final mark – no questions asked.

d Previously assessment was by a tutor. This should have been more fair as tutors have no bias. Peer assessment can be coloured by individual likes and dislikes. However peer assessment can give more opportunity for justifying work – this should be in the diary anyway, but may not be read in depth.

h   We all took it more seriously as we knew what to expect. Throughout the term we were taking assessment into consideration at our peer group meetings.

m   Previous experience of assessment has involved a tutor/teacher marking or grading work and justifying this by giving a short comment – this method of assessment involves the combination of many people's opinions – and clear reasons for the final grade.

n   This assessment offered active involvement, peer group discussion and an important role in the decision making process. Whereas my previous experiences of assessment failed to offer any of the above.

10 HAS THE EXPERIENCE OF THIS KIND OF ASSESSMENT CHANGED YOUR APPROACH TO LEARNING? WHAT DO YOU NOW DO THAT IS DIFFERENT?

a   I now look at the criteria first to see what type of project will reap me the best marks. I would usually work the other way around but I no longer feel this is a beneficial way to work.

d   I am more self aware. It has made me take on other people's constructive criticism about my work more easily. I analyse work more, and ensure I am attaining the aims of the work/assessment. The discussions with others can enable you to get an objective opinion on your work, and to give others wider thoughts about how they can work.

e   I think beforehand about some of the criteria needed when thinking of a project but when I think about it is this expressing myself or expressing myself within a given structured form? I think my basic approach is different to what it was.

g   I feel a lot more relaxed about my work now.

For me the emphasis has switched from concentrating on a final piece to taking time to experiment more, take time to find a theme that interests me. I feel more comfortable with a series of pieces as long as I feel I am progressing and learning from it. I think this is due to my involvement in the assessment being able to discuss what I've done and why.

I feel my ideas, reasoning, effort and presentation are being assessed together, not just what I pin up on the wall at the end of term.

h   Since experiencing this kind of assessment my reflective diary has improved, it has made me think more clearly about my aims – discussions with peer group members was also helpful.

j   Firstly I look at the way in which I'm going to be assessed – and then I think about which statements I need to meet, with my work – before I went with an idea and followed its natural progression – now I try to satisfy the marking criteria.

l   Yes, this assessment has changed my approach to learning. It has made me look a lot closer and deeper at people's work and it has guided me in what is needed in my own work. It also let me see that there is a lot more to assessing than I previously thought.

p   This form of assessment has brought more discussion into our work, which is beneficial. Working on your own you never know if something looks 'right' to other people, and works as a piece of art.

Having the ideas of others to work with as well as your own is very useful.

11. If you were to be assessed in the same way for your next project would you approach your work differently? If so, what would you do that was different?

b I think I would probably provide more evidence of my experiments instead of just talking about them or drawing sketches and plans in my journal.

c Yes, and this, I feel, is the biggest downfall of the process. Having such a full/wide criteria for marking it seems that the obvious way of making sure each element of the criteria is fulfilled – to ensure a good mark – is to follow it rigorously. I feel that this would inhibit one's natural flow of creativity or influence ones choice of which lines/styles to follow and thus work would be produced only to fulfil criteria and would not be truly individual work – this is what I understood our 3rd year project to be about. I hope this assessment process won't cull individuality and originality.

e I probably would as I know what's expected. I try and be more confident with my ideas and in group discussions contribute more and believe my opinions are as important as anyone else's. I also know what analysing, not describing work in my diary, is so I feel next time I can improve on that.

f I would concentrate more on areas where my marks were lower.

g Next term I want to apply the same made of working as last term. To explore different materials and exploit them as much as possible. Even if I'm told not to think of grades constantly. It's very difficult not to. In actual fact I have found that if I'm enjoying what I'm doing like last term I don't think of what mark I'll get. Is this solely down to the self/peer assessment? I don't know but I feel it has contributed.

j I'd try to satisfy marking criteria, and then try to work upon my idea to that particular system.

l Yes, I would change my approach to the next project. I would spend more time developing the process and noting every step I take. I will also look into more ideas before starting a project.

n Yes, I would analyse what I was learning through the project, why I was learning it, and how the end product shows evidence that learning has taken place.

p I changed my way of working last term due to the assessment style. Making sure I included each of the assessment requirements, so I get a good mark.

I do find it quite sad that our working should be changed simply to get a good grade, rather than because it's how we want to do it.

From the selected responses above it is clear that some students found this form of assessment difficult. Some of the statements could well provide evidence of students taking a surface approach to the assessment. The issue of using the criteria to work out how to get the best marks is a worrying one in so far as those students have misconceived the role of the criteria in the process. The purpose of the criteria is to provide a guide within a domain for determining which SOLO level has been achieved. The question, nevertheless, remains as to whether the procedures should be even more clear, as some students suggest, or whether we should look a little more closely at those students who are having difficulties to see whether they are committed surface learners.

Also what is evident from the statements is that some students feel confident with the procedure and claim to have altered their approach to learning as a result.

Conclusion

Has using these two methods of information gathering helped me to determine whether involving students in the assessment of their own work and that of others promotes a deep approach to learning? The video was a recording of what turned out to be the most successful group. In permitting the students to formulate their own assessment groups it seems that, in several cases, friendships have determined the make-up of the group. As this was a pilot study for the students themselves I agreed that the students should determine the group membership, This they did by picking names from a hat (literally). Despite the randomness of selection by this method some of the groups were constituted of well-established friends. These friendship groups turned out to be either entirely motivated towards a deep approach or entirely motivated towards (as one comment from the questionnaire suggests) the students' bar.

The video group was clearly the former. Those students who expressed concern in the questionnaire about assessing friends clearly did not recognize the importance of the lifeskill of giving and receiving feedback with sensitivity. This exercise has confirmed to me that self/peer exercises if they are to be successful in promoting a deep approach to learning must be introduced at the beginning of a student's programme of study – before the basis of friendships is established. This is not to suggest that friendships should not be a part of the learning experience but that they should be recognized as a potential threat to objectivity in the context of assessment.

For it to be successful, students need to understand what counts as the difference between a deep and surface approach – simply telling them is not enough. Those students who took a surface approach to their project work also took a surface approach to their assessment and, in several instances, did not realize it.

The questionnaire was illuminating in many respects. It confirmed the friendship issue. It alerted me to the need to revise the assessment criteria in relation to the students' understanding of them, It has demonstrated that surface learners can happily convince themselves that they can continue to be surface learners by using the criteria strategically,

There were several comments made about feeling stressed at having to assess other students yet the process is intended to avoid the stress caused by other, less negotiable, forms of assessment.

What this evidence supports is the view that self/peer assessment as constructed in this project does support a deep approach to learning for those who recognize what counts as a deep approach. It does not seem to enable those who take a surface approach either to change their approach or, in some cases, to recognize that they are taking a surface approach.

References

Biggs, J.B. (1989). Does learning about learning help teachers with teaching? Psychology and the tertiary teacher. Supplement to *The Gazette*, 26, (1). University of Hong Kong.

Gibbs, G. (1992). *Improving the quality of student learning*, TES.

House, E.R. (1974). *The Politics of Educational Innovation*,

Marton, F. and Saljo, R. (1984). *Approaches to Learning* in Marton. F et al (eds), The Experience of Learning, Scottish Academic Press.

Appendix 1

1 Assessment Criteria

1.1 Introduction

1.1.1 The assessment criteria are descriptions of grades which apply to particular levels of achievement. They are intended to make more explicit the grades that are achieved at the end of each project.

1.1.2 The learning which students may achieve on the course can be classified under four different headings, or domains. Three of these domains are sub-divided;

A the conceptual
    1 ideas
    2 information
B the productive
    1 design and form
    2 materials
    3 media
C the contextual/ critical
D lifeskills
    1 personal skills
    2 interpersonal skills

1.1.3 The descriptions within these domains identify four levels of achievement. These levels progress from a basic competence (surface learning) to a mature competence (deep learning). These levels should enable the students to understand what each grade means and what they need to do in order to improve their grades. It is intended that there is a uniformity of progression in the descriptions from a surface learning approach to a deep learning approach

A *surface approach* to learning is essentially learning by rote. It depends on memory rather than understanding and it can only usually be reapplied in a situation identical to the one initially encountered. Surface learning does not last.

A *deep approach* to learning, on the other hand, leads to understanding, to the ability to determine interrelationships and to apply underlying principles. This implies a capacity to transfer thinking and performance to other situations. Deep learning is long lasting.

1.1.4 These assessment descriptions should form the basis of self-, peer- and tutor assessment programme. They are designed to apply in art and design but can have a universal application because they are all based on the following model;

Level 1   This is learning that students perceive is done to them by teachers rather than something they do. Learning is memorising. The student has an active role in memorising, but the information being memorised is not transformed in any way.

Level 2   This is learning that is acquiring facts, skills or procedures which are to be used. What is learning is soon as needed in order to do things at a later date, but there is still no transformation of what is learnt by the learner.

Level 3   This is learning that makes sense. The student makes active attempts to abstract meaning in the process of learning.

Level 4   This is learning as understanding reality. Learning enables the student to perceive the world differently. the student see her work in a world context and recognises its value.

1.2 Project Assessment Criteria

The criteria are divided into four discrete domains
A the conceptual
    1 ideas
    2 information
B the productive
    1 design and form
    2 materials
    3 media
C the contextual/criteria
D lifeskills
    1 personal skills
    2 interpersonal skills

A Conceptual

A1 IDEAS
1   Generated only one or two ideas for selection.
    Demonstrated limited judgment in selection
    Developed the ideas to an obvious conclusion

2   Deliberately generated several ideas for selection
    Some of the ideas were of good quality
    Demonstrated judgment in selection
    Developed the ideas beyond the obvious

3   Generated a substantial number of ideas
    Many of the ideas were imaginative
    Demonstrated a clear understanding of appropriateness of ideas in selection
    Developed the ideas to a sound and imaginative conclusion within the set deadline

4   Demonstrated a broad range of mature ideas
    Most of the ideas demonstrated a developed imagination
    Demonstrated sound understanding in selecting ideas to progress
    Demonstrated imagination and innovation in the development of the ideas and concluded the task within the time set

A2 INFORMATION

1   Researched and used only readily available material
Showed ability to select and analyse some of the information available
Managed an answer to the requirements of the task with the material

2   Extended the research beyond the immediate
Showed thought in analysing the material
Modified and adapted information to fit the requirements of the task

3   Showed imagination in the research of information
Demonstrated care and attention in selecting and analysing information
Transformed information intelligently

4   Showed sound ability in researching and exploiting a broad range of information sources
Demonstrated an accomplished ability in analysing and selecting
Demonstrated an intelligent and mature imagination in transforming information intomeaningful patterns

B Productive

B1 DESIGN AND FORM

1   Understood the basic language of art and / or design
Demonstrated adequate skills in arrangement and layout

2   Showed judgment in selecting from a fair knowledge of the language
Demonstrated good skills in arrangement and layout

3   Showed good judgment in selecting from a sound knowledge of the language
Demonstrated a good degree of care and thought in the presentation and arrangement of the layout

4   Showed a well developed judgment in selecting from a broad understanding of the language
Demonstrated a high degree of care, attention and imagination in the presentation and arrangement of the layout

B2 MATERIALS

1   Chose appropriate materials with guidance
Used materials with guidance

2   Chose appropriate materials
Used materials with care

3   Demonstrated thought and care in the selection of materials
     Used materials with confidence

4   Demonstrated an accomplished approach in selecting materials
     Used materials professionally

B3 MEDIA
1   Selected media with guidance
     Used media with guidance

2   Showed ability in selecting media
     Used media with care

3   Showed good judgment in selecting media
     Used the media with confidence

4   Demonstrated an accomplished approach to the selection of media
     Used the media professionally

C Contextual/ critical

C1 CONTEXTUAL/CRITICAL
1   Showed some evidence of having considered aspects of his/her own work in
     relation to that of others
     Written work was generally descriptive

2   Provided description and analysis of his/her own work and that of others in the
     contexts in which the work was produced

3   Provided description, interpretation and analysis of his/her own practice and that
     of others across time and cultures

4   Provided a clear recognition and understanding of the importance of his/her own
     work in art/design in relation to cultural production across times and cultures

D Lifeskills

D1 PERSONAL SKILLS
1   Demonstrated adequate skills in time management
     Met some goals
     Managed some projects adequately
     Showed signs of responsibility in some projects

2   Demonstrated good skills in time management
     Met several goals
     Managed several projects well
     Showed responsibility in several projects

3   Demonstrated very good skills in time management
     Met all goals
     Managed most projects very well
     Showed mature responsibility in most projects

4   Demonstrated excellent skills in time management
     Met all goals
     Managed all projects professionally
     Showed mature responsibility in all projects

D2   INTERPERSONAL SKILLS

1   Demonstrated some skills in communication
     Was a member of a team
     Gave and received feedback on occasions
     Gave help occasionally

2   Demonstrated good skills in communication
     Was an active team member
     Gave and received feedback
     Was helpful

3   Demonstrated very good skills in communication
     Was a committed member of the team
     Demonstrated sensitivity in giving and receiving feedback
     Gave help willingly

4   Demonstrated excellent skills in communication
     Demonstrated full commitment to the success of the team
     Actively gave and received feedback with sensitivity
     Gave help willingly and on all occasions

10   Innovative assessment: its impact on students

Liz Mcdowell and Graham Mowl (Educational Development Service, University of Northumbria at Newcastle)

Introduction

Assessment is potentially a powerful tool for shaping student behaviour, and influencing both students' approaches to learning and the outcomes of that learning. However, a number of studies have demonstrated that in some contexts assessment can have a negative impact on learning. Assessment methods which are perceived as threatening and anxiety-provoking may push students towards a surface approach which does not lead to the development of depth in understanding (Gibbs, 1992; Ramsden, 1992). Some examination systems result in students engaging in last minute cramming and rote learning followed by rapid forgetting (Entwistle and Entwistle, 1991). According to Boud (1990, p. 104):

> Despite the good intentions of staff, assessment tasks are set which encourage a narrow, instrumental approach to learning that emphasises the reproduction of what is presented, at the expense of critical thinking, deep understanding and independent activity.

Earlier research in student learning has therefore been critical of some applications of traditional assessment methods and has provided the basis for innovation in assessment. The academic case for a more innovative approach to assessment has been strongly made (Heron, 1981; Boud, 1990; Ramsden, 1992; Brown and Knight, 1994) . The pattern of assessment in higher education is now much more varied than was the case even five or ten years ago. This change can be attributed only in part to the strong arguments put forward on educational grounds for a restructuring of the assessment system. Another influence has been the rapid expansion of the higher-education sector over the last few years, which has meant increasing student numbers against a fixed or diminishing unit of resource and even greater pressures on staff time. Other incentives for innovation and change have been provided by initiatives such as the United Kingdom Enterprise in Higher Education initiative (Wright, 1992).

The majority of the research to date on the impacts of innovative assessment practices has focused on the relative reliabilities of student, staff and peer assessments (Boud and Falchikov, 1989; Boyd and Cowan, 1985; Falchikov and Boud, 1989; Orpen, 1982; Stefani, 1994;) and there has been very little systematic research in relation to innovative assessment methods which examines the impact they have on students, their perceptions of their courses and their views on whether these assessment methods enhance or hinder their learning.

The Impact of Assessment project based at the University of Northumbria at Newcastle (UNN) aims to illuminate the ways in which innovative assessment methods influence

131

student perceptions, behaviour and learning. In order to do this a case-study approach has been adopted, with data being gathered intensively on specific pieces of assessment using observation and interviews with the staff and students involved. In this chapter, we report on some of the preliminary findings of this research, drawing on three case studies involving self and peer assessment and group and individual assignments. These pilot case studies were undertaken in order to test and refine the approach and methods to be used but a significant amount of rich data was collected and we are able to report on that here.

The Impact of Assessment Project

Literally defined, innovative assessment could be any form of assessment which involves the application of a new or different technique or method regardless of the purpose or underlying educational philosophy. Innovators may, therefore, adopt the same techniques or tools of assessment but have very different motives for innovation: some may be committed to improving the quality of student learning via assessment, while others may simply be responding to extrinsic forces, such as increasing student numbers, decreasing staff-student contact time, or pressures to introduce more work-based learning into the curriculum. For the purpose of our pilot research, innovators were identified as any teaching staff who were known to be using new or non-traditional methods to assess their students. Their motives for innovation were not considered when we asked them to participate. The research project was designed to be collaborative, with findings reported back to the relevant course teams so that they would be able to review their assessment practice in light of our observations.

The findings presented here are based on research conducted as part of the pilot stage of the project. Informal semi-structured interviews were conducted before and after the assessments with the members of staff concerned and with a sample of the students involved in the assessments. Where possible, the researcher observed the actual assessment taking place and also attended briefing and debriefing sessions.

The three case studies described in this chapter are based in different subject areas: one is a social science course, the other two are more vocational courses in Built Environment and Business Studies subjects. Furthermore, the cases involve assessing students at different levels, namely, first-year undergraduate, final-year undergraduate and postgraduate. The nature of the assessments was also different. Two involved forms of self- and peer-assessment of coursework and the third an extended group project assessed via a group presentation and written reports.

Case Study 1 A BA (Hons) Course in the Social Science faculty (year 1), Applied Statistics

The innovative assessment took place towards the end of a first-year Applied Statistics compulsory course. Students must pass this course although the grade obtained is not carried forward from Year 1. Normally in this subject all assessment is carried out by staff, and students are required to submit course work exercises and take termly phase tests.

The course tutor decided to require students to self-mark one of their course work exercises. His main purpose was to provide a valuable learning experience for the students which would encourage them to think about what they were doing rather than being the recipients of marked work, noted only for the mark given rather than for any formative feedback. Most of the students had already completed the exercise and handed it in. He then explained to them that he was going to hand back their work and ask them to mark it themselves using his model answer. He also explained to them his reasons for doing this. The students were given a week to mark their work after which they had to hand their marked exercises back in. To ensure that the students did this reliably, the lecturer explained that he would pick about half a dozen students at random who would then have to justify to him the marks they had given themselves.

Two contextual and organizational issues affected the way that this exercise worked. Some students at this point had already accumulated enough marks to pass the course and therefore there was little incentive for them to take the exercise seriously at least from the point of view of gaining marks. In addition, the lecturer did not keep records of who initially handed in the exercise which gave scope for some students to do the work after the model answer had been handed out.

Case Study 2 A vocational BSc (Hons) course in Built Environment, year 4 compulsory module

This case study involved a compulsory module in the final year of the course. The course tutors decided to change the form of the assessment from 60 per cent coursework and 40 per cent final examination to 100 per cent coursework and to include self- and peer-assessment. This was therefore a rather significant change in the final year of a course where students had little experience of self- and peer-assessment.

The lecturers wished to abandon the exam because they felt 'realistic' course work assignments were a better indicator of students' professional capabilities than an exam. They hoped that self- and peer-assessment would reduce staff time spent on marking assignments but also that students assessing their own and each other's work would be exposed to several different ways of approaching the problems set and in doing so they would hopefully learn more about the process. The students on this course were involved in the self- and peer-assessment of two separate coursework assignments both of which simulated the kinds of tasks which they would be expected to undertake in professional practice.

In both cases students marked their own and other students' work using model answers provided by lecturers. There were criteria such as neatness, accuracy, use of industry regulations, completeness and referencing. The actual marking was done under exam-type conditions and steps were taken to ensure anonymity of work being marked. However these were only partially successful. Some students recognized whose work they were marking and some communication between students did take place. In the first exercise students did not know that they would be self- and peer-assessing their work until they arrived on the day.

The lecturers decided that if there was less than a 15 per cent gap between the self- and peer-mark then the self mark would stand. If, however, the difference between the two was greater, then the lecturers would also mark the work and the lecturer mark would be used. In the first exercise, 13 courseworks out of a possible 67 had self- and peer-marks with more than a 15% difference and had to be remarked by the lecturer. Since this was part of a final-year compulsory module, the marks were significant to students in terms of contributing towards their final degree classification.

Case Study 3 A post-graduate/MA course in Business Studies, compulsory integrative module

This case study focused on a compulsory module on a vocational postgraduate Diploma/Masters course. As the title suggests, one of the principal aims of this module is to enable students to demonstrate their ability to synthesize a broad range of skills and knowledge from the course. It is also designed to encourage students to apply their skills and knowledge and to devise solutions to practical, realistic problems. Finally, the students are expected to demonstrate their communication skills and ability to work effectively as a member of a team. The module which counts for about 15 per cent of the final course marks, was originally assessed via a final examination and has been running in its present group project form for about three years. The course team decided to change the form of the assessment to make the module more vocationally relevant and to encourage the development of transferable skills.

Students are allocated to teams of 5 or 6. Each team is given a case study folder containing background information about a particular organization and setting out their task, e.g. 'Devise an information technology strategy for your organization', 'devise a customer case policy for your organization'. Students have 13 weeks (including the Easter vacation) to prepare for a presentation of their proposals (50 per cent of the marks) and a further week to complete a written report. Teams make their presentation to two members of staff who act as representatives of the organization concerned. An element of role play is therefore involved. The team's written documentation consists of the case study report (40 per cent) and a team performance report (10 per cent). The criteria for the assessment of the presentation and reports are given to students at the initial briefing for the project.

Teams are not allowed to contact the lecturers running the module for advice on their projects. Lecturers feel that at this stage of their course students should be able to work independently. However they can make appointments to see lecturers, or external people, as 'experts' who may answer questions or provide information on specific aspects of their projects. After the presentations and reports have been assessed, each team has the opportunity to attend a debriefing session at which the course tutor tells them what mark they have gained together with written and verbal feedback on their performance. All members of the team receive the same mark regardless of their relative contributions to the team's presentation and report.

The Impact on Students: Positive Outcomes

Students in both groups had positive things to say in general about the benefits of innovative forms of assessment. All students felt that they learnt more from coursework based assessments, such as these, especially where they were related to realistic situations, than they did from traditional examination based assessments or essays.

> We prefer it to an exam . . . this is a good step forward (Built Environment)

Students reported many of the outcomes which the lecturers had hoped these forms of assessments would achieve. They also experienced problems and had a number of criticisms. These were related at least as much to the ways in which the assessments were conducted and the organizational details as to innovative forms of assessment per se. Most students remained in favour of such innovations.

> I think all of this [criticisms of the process] is probably quite true but I don't think that's a reason to stop that particular process being done. . . . at least we should have the opportunity to do more of this sort of thing. (Applied Statistics)

The major positive outcomes from the student perspective are outlined below.

Opportunities for self-assessment

Two of the case studies involved students in self- or peer-assessment or, more accurately, self- and peer-marking, of assignments. In general they saw this as a positive opportunity although there was some divergence of opinion. Some students wanted to be given more responsibility for their own assessment, whereas others were strongly of the view that assessment was the lecturers' responsibility. Students did recognize that being able to assess their own or another student's performance was a valuable skill which could help them in their studies and be useful in their later careers.

From the students' point of view an advantage of self-assessment was that they were able to award themselves a mark not just on the basis of what they had submitted but also in relation to the effort they had put into the work. Lecturers may well disagree on the value of awarding marks for effort and might argue that it does not matter how much effort a student puts into the work if the end product is not up to standard. However, if students put a lot of effort into a piece of work and then do not feel adequately rewarded by their marks, they can be left feeling dissatisfied, alienated and demoralized by the experience. This is particularly the case when students do not receive adequate feedback about their work. Even if self-marking does not explicitly allow marks to be awarded for effort, it is virtually impossible for the student not to consider the amount of effort they have put into a piece of work when they come to mark it.

One thing that influenced me when I was marking it which wouldn't influence a lecturer when they're marking someone's notes was the fact that I knew how long it had taken me and for six hours work and a splitting migraine the next day, I thought, well I'm going to have decent marks out of this. (Applied Statistics)

An increase in reflection and self-evaluation

In the self- and peer-marking examples, the lecturers hoped that students would consider their own performance more carefully and be more reflective, rather than just note the mark received. Student comments showed that this did indeed happen in many cases:

I found it interesting for me to have to sit down and think about it all from another point of view and it didn't actually solve any of my problems but it did certainly help me think about how to approach answering something like that in the future. (Applied Statistics)

This kind of outcome is illustrated most strongly by one of the students in Applied Statistics who marked himself down because he knew he did not fully understand the concepts covered by the assignment, even though he thought a lecturer would have awarded him higher marks:

I did all the graphs and I seemed to have got most of it right but I knew myself that I didn't understand what I was doing all of the time and consequently, I probably could have given myself high marks, if I'd simply gone through it and ticked the bits that were right, but I knew I didn't understand what I was doing. The graphs were no problem and I was quite happy with using the computer but it was just the actual data and principles of what it all means and I knew I hadn't got the full gist of it and I'm aware of that and I marked it accordingly. I gave myself ten out of fifteen but some of the five that I lost was because I didn't understand, It's one thing getting the graphs right but it's another thing understanding what you're doing. I don't think that would have made any difference if someone else had marked it because they would have assumed I knew. (Applied Statistics)

By having to assess his own work, this student became more aware of his own limitations; consequently he knew where he should direct his efforts and in what specific areas he needed the lecturer's help.

In the group project example, reflection on the teamwork element of the project was required as a section of the report submitted. Student comments showed that they were genuinely engaged in reflection on their individual learning and their role within the group. There were many examples and just two are given below:

I wish we had tried to communicate more with Joe. I feel both Anne and I probably brought a negative attitude about him into the group and influenced the other two members' attitude and approach to him. I also wish we had tried to analyse the actual task of the assignment more (Business Studies)

On reflection, I realised that I should have more confidence in my ideas. I should have been more forceful (Business Studies)

Development of transferable skills and work-related competencies

Students were aware that these assignments and marking exercises provided them with the opportunity to acquire knowledge and develop skills which would be relevant in their future careers. The ability to be self-critical and to give and receive criticism came out most clearly from the self- and peer-marking exercises:

> I do think it's good to be critical of your own work and other people's because, let's face it, when you go out into industry you have to be able to accept criticism and be able to give criticism in a professional way (Built Environment)

Students particularly valued the learning they derived from the two assignments which were based on simulations of the kinds of activities or problems they would face in professional practice:

> I do think that you get more out of the exercise. I used to dread the exams because you go in and it's a completely false environment. This method has had its problems but I've learned an awful lot more from it (Built Environment)

A wide range of skills and abilities emerged from student comments as having been developed or enhanced as a result of these assignments. A number of abilities connected with team work were cited including interpersonal and leadership skills and the personal qualities of patience and persistence. Students also felt that they learned something about coping under pressure and about evaluating their own strengths and weaknesses. In terms of organizational skills, students valued project planning, time management and problem-solving skills. Students also felt that their communication skills in oral presentations, report writing and the presentation of technical data were enhanced.

> Some insights as follows: difficulties in effective communication, sense of personal responsibility, shift of project control from a personal individual level to a group one (Business Studies)

> ... in any job you should be able to communicate by what you've put down in a logical way (Built Environment)

> If you're stuck on something you don't just sit there ... you go and find out how you can solve it by using other people's experience (Built Environment)

> I got out of this [the need to] practise patience and teamwork. How to cope under stress and other adverse conditions (Business Studies)

Although students did feel that they had learned a lot it is worth noting that they were not always convinced that this was recognized in the marks they achieved.

> I do think you get more out of the exercise but that isn't reflected by the marks (Built Environment)

It became clear to the researcher when following the progress of some Business Studies groups that some became engrossed in the problem-solving and the development of solutions required by the assignment but failed to consider how they would be assessed.

Hence they felt that they had achieved and learned a lot but, since this did not always match closely with the assessment requirements and criteria, it was not recognized by the marks they were eventually awarded.

Motivation and a sense of achievement

We noted that most students worked hard and conscientiously. Some commented that they spent more time on these assignments than could really be justified by their weighting in the overall assessment. Part of the motivation seemed to derive from tasks which could be seen as relevant to their future careers and to developing their own professional knowledge and skills. Many of the Applied Statistics students, who were in a rather different position, were motivated by the wish to improve their own performance within the course by better understanding of what was required and of the shortcomings and strengths of their own work.

However working with other students, in informal or formal groups was a key motivator for many students and also helped them to develop and clarify their ideas and understanding.

We shared the worry and the workload (Business Studies)

Often others came up with ideas I had not thought of (Business Studies)

At the end of the day if somebody said 'Have you learned more by it?' I would have to say yes, because I have. You learn a lot from other people. (Built Environment)

At the end of the assignments, despite the hard work, problems and setbacks involved, or perhaps because of the need to overcome these difficulties, students expressed satisfaction about what they had achieved in ways which, we suspect, they would not have done with more traditional forms of assessment.

After experiencing several problems during the preceding weeks, it felt like an achievement! (Business Studies)

We finally produced a document outlining our plan which covered the points as briefly and concisely as possible. I was pleased with it. (Business Studies)

Tailoring to individual interests and skills

None of the three assignments we studied involved a great deal of student choice or flexibility. The tasks and topics were set by the lecturers. However within the group project there was evidence that some student groups divided up the tasks according to the interests and abilities of group members, thus the individual activities were to an extent tailored to suit personal requirements.

The strengths and weaknesses of individuals could be utilised (Business Studies)

We shared the responsibility and the workload and made use of people's talents in key areas (Business Studies)

The Impact on Students: Common Concerns

Students were in general positive about the possibilities of innovative assessment particularly in comparison with the traditional forms of assessment which they had experienced. However, a number of concerns and problems arose from their experience of innovative assessment in the three examples discussed here. Some of these problems were almost certainly due to technical and organizational problems which could be rectified in future, but others do cast doubt on the extent to which innovative forms of assessment can fulfil all of the claims made for it in terms of enhancing student learning

Fairness

The first concerns raised by all students were to do with 'fairness'. Did the assessment system reward them fairly for their work and achievements? Were all students given the same opportunities – here the students were looking for 'a level playing field'.

In the cases of self- and peer-assessment, students were concerned about the potential both contexts gave for other students to cheat. In the Applied Statistics example, several of the students believed that there were not sufficient controls to prevent some students doing no work but awarding themselves a reasonable mark. In the Built Environment case study, despite the careful controls introduced in an attempt to make the peer-marking process anonymous, most of the students expressed concerns about the way the exercise was conducted and particularly the lack of anonymity. Several students felt that the exercise still provided an opportunity for some students to mark themselves up or for students to make pacts with friends to secure good peer marks. These worries were lessened somewhat when the assessment exercise was repeated and tighter controls were placed on the students' behaviour during the assessment. As well as expressing worries about other students cheating some of those interviewed confessed that they had tried to manipulate their self-assessed marks to get the grade they wanted.

> I think the system is open to a lot of abuse because I don't mind admitting yesterday I went in and knew what mark I needed to get to get what I wanted for my coursework so I spent the first 20 minutes juggling figures to get it right. (Built Environment)

> We had a break in between the self marking of the coursework and second marker and . . . when we got them back, there was a number of people who knew who [was] their second marker and were saying, I've given myself such a mark, you know, give me around about that. (Built Environment)

> I also think that people might have actually tampered, changed, altered their things once they had got the answer sheet. (Applied Statistics)

A number of students were concerned about varying information and guidance given by lecturers while they were working on their assignments:

> I went to see him before the assignment had to be in and I asked him if it needed an abstract which he said no, definitely there is no need for an abstract and also I said, do I have to hand in my drawings, and he said, no definitely not. And in the criteria for marking it said, there was work required . . . it had a list of submissions that should have been included, abstracts and drawings were two of them! (Built Environment)

In the case of the Business Studies group project, concerns about equitable treatment arose because case-study problems were assigned at random to groups and some felt they were disadvantaged by having a difficult case-study or a topic about which they knew very little or had little interest, while other groups had 'easy' topics or ones which directly related to areas where their levels of knowledge and interest were high:

Other groups' projects are more straightforward. They've got more idea of what they've got to do. Theirs are more a matter of common sense. It's because it's IT [Information Technology] that it's a problem (Business Studies)

It was not fair because I had to develop new abilities and understanding (Business Studies)

The subject was unknown to all of us so it took longer to understand (Business Studies)

Since this was a group project concerns inevitably arose because of the inter-personal problems which some groups experienced including the occasional 'non-contributing' member. In this case all group members received the same mark and so there was no opportunity to differentiate between different levels of contribution at the marking stage.

I do not feel that my abilities can be tested fairly when other people's abilities and motivation levels ultimately affected the quality of the work handed in (Business Studies)

Some of the concerns students raised about fairness could be resolved by changing the detailed procedures for assessment. For example, stricter controls could virtually eliminate 'cheating' by completing work after a model answer had been provided or by making pacts with peer markers. Guidance given by staff could be more strictly controlled so that all students received the same, accurate information. Marks could be allocated to individual group members to resolve the issue of their differing contributions, although this is likely to lead to a different set of problems, such as who can fairly assess the contribution made by each group member? It is less easy to see how a 'level playing field' can be created when students are engaged in project-type work with different scenarios. In this situation some projects are bound to be seen as easier or more difficult depending on the characteristics and knowledge of the groups working on them and as the project continues different problems will be encountered. The assessment situation cannot be controlled as in an exam room.

Lack of feedback

In general students were concerned about the feedback they received on their work. They felt strongly that feedback was important so that they could improve on their work and learn from their mistakes and successes. They commented that the timeliness, quality and quantity of feedback they normally received on assessed work varied considerably between subjects and individual lecturers.

In the two examples of self- and peer-marking, the emphasis was on awarding marks rather then giving feedback and some students felt that this was a missed opportunity. However, they realized that even if the work had been marked by their lecturers they might have got very little more in the way of feedback. Many students believed that, in the ideal situation, self- and peer-marking should be complemented by feedback from lecturers. They thought that it was essential to get feedback from 'an expert', and someone better qualified to assess the work than themselves. They lacked confidence in their own ability and that of fellow students to judge academic work and give feedback on it:

> that exercise was quite complex and really hard and I'd have liked to have handed it in so I knew exactly where I'd gone wrong so I think it would have been a better idea if the lecturers marked them. (Applied Statistics)

In contrast, one of the students in the Applied Statistics course felt that the most informative and useful feedback was actually derived from self-assessment and realizing one's own limitations and lack of understanding and that this was something on which lecturers were less able to give feedback.

> . . . when people actually put a piece of work in, that is all that is there for the lecturer to look at when he is marking, and he doesn't really know (a) how many hours were put into it or (b) whether you understand it or not, and that can only really come from the person who is self assessing it (Applied Statistics)

For the Business Studies group project the situation was rather different. Students were notified of the assessment criteria but marking was entirely in the hands of the lecturers. Careful attention was paid to feedback at the end of the project with timetabled debriefing sessions for each group after their presentations and reports had been assessed. In this case the kind of feedback that students perceived that they lacked was formative feedback during the course of a lengthy project undertaken over a period of about 15 weeks. However the lecturer perspective was that by this stage of the course the students ought to be able to work independently without guidance from their lecturers. Typical student comments were:

> There was minimal constructive feedback on the work as it was being completed. The stress affected my health (Business Studies)

> A supervisor would enable the assignment to be a more positive learning process (Business Studies)

This lack of feedback on the ways in which they were tackling the task and the progress they were making made students feel that they were 'working in the dark'. Although many enjoyed the tasks and became very involved in the problem area they were studying, they still felt unsure about how their work would be judged and whether their efforts would be rewarded in terms of a good mark.

Subjectivity and expertise in marking

Most of the students involved in self- and peer-assessment seemed to doubt their ability to mark their own work. They had very little experience of self- and peer-assessment and felt unprepared for the process. They has not been consulted about its introduction. A number of the Built Environment students were strongly of the view that it was the lecturers' job to mark their work since they were paid to do that. They believed that the lecturers were the experts, and only they could be objective in the marking of the work:

> I think that if the lecturers set course work that we've spent a long time doing and put a lot

of effort into then I think that it's their duty to mark them and give them full justification by looking at them themselves. I don't see how they can justify having our opinion at our level of experience especially when we're still learning. (Built Environment)

Students were concerned about what they felt to be the subjectivity of their own marking. They believed that marking would vary considerably between different individuals and considered lecturer marking to be more reliable:

. . . people have got different levels, you know, some people are quite a harsh marker on themselves and on other people, whereas some people . . . (Built Environment)

the lecturer marking [is] much fairer because you've got one person marking all the papers, so it is a standard. (Built Environment)

Some commented on how 'irrelevant' characteristics of the work submitted such as presentation could sway their judgments:

I was looking at the second one that I got to mark and thinking, well this person has bound them, it's got the joins in the back, you know, it's really nicely written out, . . . that was just my first initial reaction. (Built Environment)

The ambiguities in the model answers provided and the different ways in which assessment criteria could be interpreted even in two subjects which were relatively 'right or wrong' highlighted this subjectivity for students:

. . . a lot of people . . . didn't agree with certain parts of his table but in that kind of situation you can't really argue, you've just got to try and mark from it. (Built Environment)

you've got to try and relate ... what you have written down compared to what is written on that sheet [the model answer]. I think that is a very grey area because some people think 'well it's nothing like the same' and others think ' well it's not much different really' (Applied Statistics)

Most students seemed to be concerned about variability and subjectivity in marking only in the case of self- and peer-assessment. In the main they retained confidence in the ability and expertise of their lecturers to mark fairly and reliably. Only a minority of students believed that marking by lecturers was also subject to variability and subjectivity in individual judgments to any great extent.

Stress and lack of control

One of the reasons why assessment systems are changed is to reduce unnecessary stress on students which is thought to arise particularly from a system heavily weighted towards traditional unseen exams. This stress is thought to induce a 'fear of failure' in many students and a tendency towards taking a surface approach to learning. However the examples of innovative assessment which we studied were certainly not stress-free for students. This came out most clearly from the Business Studies students who undertook a lengthy group project:

. . . it was so demanding, a constant pressure (Business Studies)

This assignment seemed to hang over us constantly and took up too much time, emotionally and physically (Business Studies)

In these examples students did not have very much scope to negotiate the form of the assessment or the way in which it would be assessed. Business Studies students were given written information about assessment requirements and criteria but were not able to seek guidance from their lecturers during the project. They were not able to choose their own topic or determine group membership. The students involved in self- and-peer marking had to mark according to model answers provided by their lecturers. It seems that much of the stress felt by students was due to their lack of control in relation to the assignments and a lack of clarity about how they would be judged:

I didn't like the exercise that much to start off with because we had no idea, from the exercise book, what the marks were going to be given for . The thing was in three sections and you found the section which had the most writing which you thought would have the most work involved in it was in fact the bit which only gave you three marks out of a possible fifteen. (Applied Statistics)

It wasn't clearly explained. We weren't sure what was expected or how much we could ask. (Business Studies)

There was no solid information on the presentation so it involved a lot of guesswork. (Business Studies)

Some of these students did in fact make the wrong guesses about what was required or misinterpreted assessment criteria so that the marks they eventually gained were lower than they might otherwise have been.

Lack of interest and motivation

We have already mentioned that most students found these assessment tasks motivating and worked hard. Nevertheless the degree of interest and motivation varied. Some of the Applied Statistics students said that they lacked motivation to undertake the self-marking exercise, even though they could see its potential benefits, because it did not 'count' for anything – they had already accumulated enough marks to pass the course, and they suspected that the lecturer had only tried it out because this was the case.

Motivation for the Business Studies students varied according to the nature of the project they had been allocated in relation to their own interests and to the functioning of their project group.

I'm not interested in banking and finance and very unsure about information technology – hence nil interest!

I didn't want to do this topic because in my job 'customer care' is used cynically to undermine staff

The lack of interest [from group members] meant that I was not prepared to take on as much work as I probably would have under different circumstances. I had no enthusiasm for the assignment at all

However, interest and motivation could also vary throughout the life of the project and it is encouraging that at least some students overcame their initial reluctance and lack of interest:

> IT strategies are, as I see it, quite complicated and not having the time or the inclination to look it up, it wasn't interesting. Once I understood a bit more it became more interesting – but still financial companies are not my interest!

Purpose of innovation

Lecturers explained to students their reasons for each of the innovations in assessment described here. The Business Studies and Built Environment students had no concerns about the general purpose of the assignments they undertook which was to simulate the kinds of tasks they might be required to undertake in professional practice and to help them to develop skills and knowledge.

The self- and peer-assessment exercises did cause more concerns about purpose even though students could see some positive outcomes for example, being able to look more critically at their own work. In Applied Statistics, students felt that the exercise had been devalued because of the stage of the course at which the assignment was set. Some students did not take the exercise seriously because they knew they had already passed this element of the course. They suspected that perhaps the lecturer had introduced self-marking at this stage because it did not really have any impact.

> Do we presume that they only go to the self-marking exercise because everybody's already passed the course? (Applied Statistics)

In contrast, in the Built Environment the students felt that it was inappropriate and unfair to be introducing 'new', 'experimental' methods of assessment at such a crucial stage of their degree course. Some of the students also doubted the value of the exercise in terms of learning, believing that the exercise had been introduced chiefly for the benefit of the lecturers so that they could save time on marking student work:

> If they tried this system with the first years and got feedback from them, then fair enough it's not that important, but for to us, to try it now! (Built Environment)

> I mean has this marking system, been designed for the convenience of the lecturers? I don't know, but I certainly don't feel that it's in any way beneficial to us. (Built Environment)

Conclusions

Our case studies represent examples of innovative assessment techniques, that is, assessment methods which were new or non-traditional in the subject area. Our research aimed to investigate whether these techniques were innovative in educational terms and resulted in the benefits which earlier research and development has suggested should be achievable through such assessment methods. This earlier research suggests that innovative assessment may: encourage students to take a deep approach to learning; increase students' motivation and intrinsic interest; contribute to the development of skills or competencies and the development needs of individuals; and allow students to enjoy a more powerful position within the assessment process. We also needed to consider, as students in these examples forcibly reminded us, whether the assessment methods were fair and valid, since without this basis any supposed educational advantages would be of doubtful benefit. In the three cases we studied, innovative assessment did have a number of positive impacts on the learning experiences of students but some very problematic issues remained to be resolved. Students were, unsurprisingly, very concerned about assessment and were keen to talk about it and reflect on it with the researchers. It was encouraging that despite a number of problems and concerns, students in the main supported the ideas of innovative assessment.

A key benefit of the forms of innovative assessment which we studied was that they gave students opportunities to develop skills and knowledge which they believed would be useful to them at a later stage in their academic or employment careers. Students placed a high value on such skills and welcomed assessment methods where they were, to an extent, rewarded by the marks received. In each of these examples, students were encouraged to be more reflective and evaluative about their own learning and achievements. This is a desirable academic goal and was also recognized as valuable by the students themselves. Most students found their motivation and level of interest enhanced by the forms of assessment used in the case studies. They worked hard, they reviewed and reflected on their learning, they expressed an interest in the topics they were studying and, in two cases, in the processes of self- and peer-marking.

Assessment in these cases encouraged intrinsic motivation and interest among students and enhanced the development of skills and competences. Students were also, to an extent, allowed a more powerful position in the assessment process, though even in the cases of self- and peer-marking this was limited. It would perhaps be better to say that students were in a more informed position rather than a more powerful position. Some of these educational benefits would have been unlikely to have arisen with more traditional forms of assessment, if, for example, the Business Studies Integrative Module has been assessed by a formal exam as it was in the past, rather than by the group project.

A major negative issue from the student perspective was a concern about the fairness or otherwise of innovative assessment. A related issue is subjectivity in marking which students in these cases raised in relation to their own marking though not to marking carried out by their lecturers. In the case of peer- and self-marking, there is scope to tighten up on procedures but with many forms of innovative assessment students need to work in uncertain or variable contexts. These may be simulated or real world contexts; they may be different for each individual or group. In such situations we cannot replicate the apparent 'level playing field' of the exam room. Unseen, closed-book assessments taking place in time-constrained isolation represent for many people, including many lecturers and students, fair and rigorous assessment. However, approaches which are high in rigour and reliability are often low in validity, that is, in their ability to assess the knowledge and skills regarded as most significant within the course (Brown and Knight, 1994, p. 14–21).

It seems likely that the way forward in situations which cannot be closely controlled is increased openness and clarity within the assessment setting. If all those involved, mainly students and lecturers, can understand and have some ownership of assessment tasks and the ways in which marks will be awarded, there is a good opportunity to build systems which can be seen to be fair to those most directly concerned. Trust in the judgment abilities of all those involved also has to be built up through discussion and collaboration. This goes alongside the current emphasis on quality assurance in assessment by which the course or department is accountable for assessment procedures which are reliable and rigorous. As Brown and Knight (1994, p. 15) suggest, it may be more feasible, under new circumstances with varied assessment, to demonstrate reliable procedures rather than reliable tests.

A second very significant point to note was that stress was certainly not removed from the assessment process because it took a different form than the nerve-wracking (for some) unseen three-hour written paper. We need to be aware that a certain amount of stress is necessary as a stimulus to performance, but in many assessment situations and, we believe, in these examples too, students did suffer from unnecessary stress. This was largely due to students being disempowered by not having sufficient information to manage the situation in which they were placed. Students often suffered from the lack of formative and summative feedback and had not in the main developed sufficient confidence in their own abilities to judge their learning and achievements in an academic context. Students were very unclear about the ways in which marks were to be awarded and what was really required by the assessments studied. Not only did this cause unnecessary stress but it also meant that in some cases students' achievements were less than they might have been as they made the wrong guesses about what was required.

The lack of student choice in relation to the content and nature of these assessments had the disadvantage of reducing motivation and interest. (Although we have said that motivation and interest were generally high they could have been more consistently high across the student groups.) The lack of choice and individuality within the assessments also meant that the potential to meet the developmental and learning needs of individual students was reduced.

Student concerns about the purpose of changes to assessment practices were also uncovered. Although educational grounds for innovation were espoused by lecturers in each of these cases and explained to students, there was still some feeling that perhaps there were other unstated purposes, the main one being to save staff time. More discussion between lecturers and students would be needed to reach a consensus about the ways in which the benefits of self- and peer-assessment in particular could outweigh the perceived disadvantage of potentially less feedback from lecturers.

This preliminary investigation indicates that new assessment techniques, perhaps not surprisingly, do not necessarily solve all assessment problems and enhance student learning in every respect. In fact, they may bring to the surface issues which were previously taken for granted and these then come to be seen as problematic. However the research is encouraging because it revealed support for innovation from students and a number of positive outcomes, most clearly here the enhancement of motivation, intrinsic interest, reflection and skills development. The more negative outcomes suggest some ways forward. Firstly, there are practical or technical issues which need to be carefully considered to make any assessment process as reliable as possible. However notions about rigour and reliability may need to be adjusted to take into account newer methods of assessment. A reliance on close control needs to be replaced by the notion of openness, fair procedures and the building of shared understandings to validate tasks, criteria and judgments. Secondly it is clear that the empowerment of students within the assessment process does not necessarily result from the application of new techniques yet is essential if innovative assessment is to live up to its potential to enhance student learning.

References

Boud, D. J. (1990). Assessment and the promotion of academic values, *Studies in Higher Education*, **15**(1), 101–111.

Boud, D. and Falchikov, N. (1989). Quantitative studies of student self-assessment in higher education: a critical analysis of findings. *Higher Education*, **18**, 529–49.

Boyd, H. and Cowan, J. (1985). A case for self-assessment based on recent studies of student learning. *Assessment and Evaluation in Higher Education*, **10**(3), 225–35.

Brown, S. and Knight, P. (1994). *Assessing Learners in Higher Education*, Kogan Page, London.

Entwistle, N. J. and Entwistle, A. (1991). Contrasting forms of understanding for degree examinations: the student experience and its implications. *Higher Education*, **22**, 205–27.

Falchikov, N and Boud, D (1989). Student self assessment in higher education: a meta-analysis. *Review of Educational Research*, **59**(4), 395–430.

Gibbs, G. (1992). Improving the quality of student learning through course design. In Barnett, R. (ed.) *Learning to Effect*, SRHE and Open University Press, Milton Keynes.

Harris, D. and Bell, C. (1990). *Evaluating and Assessing for Learning*, Kogan Page, London.

Heron, J. (1981). Assessment revisited. In D. Boud (ed.) *Developing Student Autonomy in Learning*. Kogan Page, London.

Orpen, C (1982). Student versus lecturer assessment of learning: a research note. *Higher Education*. **11**, 567–72.

Ramsden, P (1992). *Learning to Teach in Higher Education*. Routledge, London.

Stefani, L. (1994). Peer, self and tutor assessment: relative reliabilities. *Studies in Higher Education*. **19**(1), 69–75.

11   Arenas of representation within experimental learning

Tony Wailey (University of East London)

Introduction

In the use of assessment to promote student learning this chapter seeks to ask two questions. The first is simply **What is the role of reflection?** The second is to ask **To what purpose do students reflect?** In many ways a conservative position is presented here in that it seeks to maintain that until some form of sustained analysis (an essay) is completed there is no great evidence of critical reflection within a students portfolio.To this end assessment in relation to reflection is used in both a formative and summative way.

The chapter would propose to identify shifts in the learning process experienced by this cohort of nursery nurses, as they approached the different frameworks of reflection via a linked scheme of assessment processes.

If the participants had more than four years post-qualifying experience they were able to claim a semester's credit, i.e. 60 credits at level one. As part of this process they had to complete a portfolio of their professional experience. The **model was based upon time and learning outcomes** in that the production of relevant learning outcomes within the portfolio was the benchmark for credit. Apart from attendance at the university to complete their concurrent study at level one, the participants met at the local In Service Centre one evening each week over the semester to complete their portfolios. **This formed an important link between work-based and university learning.**

It is important to remember the past experience of the group. These were a cohort of extremely experienced nursery nurses, some with a second qualification, who worked with teachers in local schools and were frustrated in terms of professional advancement and who in many cases not only aspired to be teachers themselves but felt in many ways they were already fulfilling a teaching position. There was both a disdain and an attraction of the academic. This combined with an eagerness to claim credit from their work experience **revealed a constant question** in what the academic would come to mean in terms of anxiety, threat or promise.

If the group's attitude (to the academic) was influenced by work history, life cycle and the social setting, it was important to establish at which point did **biography and social setting connect** with strategies for the assessment of prior learning and turn it into relevant learning outcomes. Drawing loosely from frameworks and taxonomies proposed by such diverse thinkers as Carl Rogers, R.S. Carter and David Kolb, it was to enquire **how the processes of assessment** affected the outcome.

For many of the group, the problem of socialization to a new role, that of scrutinizing their own experiences for academic credit was problematic enough, fraught with contrasts, paradoxes and contradiction. Power also entered the arena. Many studies in the sociology of education have alluded to this in projects concerning mature students (Locke, 1991). Power, in this instance related to academic language and conceptual processes, was counterpoised by the power of the participants self and professional identity. It was this tension that the assessment exercises tried to explore.

Assessment Exercises

The first three exercises within the portfolio construction dealt with the following.

- The self as central to the learning process: a position paper based upon where the participants had come from, where they were at present, where they hoped to arrive and what means were they going to utilize to achieve this. In many ways an abbreviated version of a Learning Contract associated with a humanist cognitive perspective (Rogers, 1983; O'Reilly, 1993).

- The second asked them to analyse by means of an extended curriculum vitae what skills, knowledge and personal qualities they possessed in relation to their work experience. This was based upon taxonomies of skills and knowledge and focused very much on behaviourist philosophy of trying to identify systematic educational objectives which included affective learning (Carter, 1985).

- A switch in focus took them to the third assignment which was based more upon a social constructivist approach to learning to describe the outcomes of specific work situations (Kolb, 1984). This model needed to be more prescriptive before the participants started to use assessment to negotiate their own learning situations.

The stages of this process took around six weeks and was vaguely successful within its own terms of reference. For anyone engaged in the assessment of prior learning, the difficulties of identifying learning outcomes with the learner at the centre, the categorizing of knowledge, skills and personal qualities, the different attributes of extracting learning from experience in precise statements, are all well categorized. When the programme moved to the stage of re–assembling these learning outcomes into a reflective learning essay **which shadowed generic outcomes of level one academic study** rebellion was loud and bitter.

What was being asked of the participants was extremely difficult. It was asking them to identify the **assessment processes** by which they categorized their learning at the same time as they were also engaged with the pain of assimilation to academic learning within a concurrent degree programme. The assessment of prior learning as an admissions process to a particular point within a degree programme often poses problems, the assessment of that learning being integrated with concurrent study adds another dimension. Studies in work-based learning have alluded to this problem as a constrictive force (Sharp and Land, 1994) while others have seen within it a mirroring process which reflects both institutional and personal conflicts (Smith and Turner, 1993). It echoes issues raised in the *Captive Triangle* (1989) in that participants claiming experiential learning are often expected to jump through more hoops than is necessary.

Yet in a strange way that has everything to do with process and nothing with product, the actual engaging with an academic essay, i.e. the attempting to link work based learning outcomes based upon practical experience already collected within the portfolio to a more theoretical exposition of learning provided the creative link for the participants in the **arenas of representation** of their past learning experiences.

What appeared to take place was a shift in power in the ownership of learning. This had taken most of the semester at the Inset Centre. No amount of persuasive language on the part of the tutor could convey ownership until it was felt by the participants. At a discipline level we could label this a paradigm shift, at the more personal level, transformative learning in that the participants became more aware and critical of the assumptions they made not only of the academic but, and more crucially, of their own capacity for bringing critical judgement to bear on problems which originate in the actual construction of their portfolio.

The essay simply asked them to relate how they had arrived at the documentation of their learning – the different reflective practices – contained within their portfolio and to try and make sense of it against a more theoretical exposition of learning (instrumental, communicative, critically reflective).

After the period of rebellion what was perceptible was the changed culture of the group. What had been a dominant ethos of 'practice' versus the 'academic' had been replaced by a vocabulary of engagement. The vehicle of this change in terms of the re–assessment of the portfolio, itself, was the essay.

This is not to suggest that the move from technical to hermeneutic to emancipatory learning was in any way fulfilled **but a certain cycle of learning seemed to have been concluded** with the learner firmly at the centre. As the participants now move through their degree programme, learning outcomes from their formal assessments within the unitized degree scheme are added to their portfolio. Further evaluation suggests that they are monitoring their academic performance against their personal performance embodied within their experiential learning. It is within such a creative tension that Mezirow and Kolb, (1990) suggests that the movement to foster critical learning within adults **needs such specific frameworks to validate meaning,** if assessment is to improve student learning and provide deeper insights in the way adults reflect on their own learning processes.

What is being suggested here is that the essay provided the **critical bridge** after a number of other assessments had pointed the way. It could easily have been some other artifice but its centre needed to relate the academic and the workplace and provide a **conception** of them both. In an age when the essay itself is coming under scrutiny as a method of assessment (Gibbs, 1992) it is worth making the case for the context of its validity. This is important given the issues of **overassessment** which feature in the debate on competence with **work-based** qualifications.

Discussion

In terms of **arenas of representation** the point was made about the different ways according to different learning styles, the participants were coming to terms with seeing learning as presenting different strategies and problems. Discussion ranged around the validation of meaning and the precise terms of students' sense of epistemological perspectives.

What also became evident in discussion was the possibility of feedback loops from the conceptual essay to the more practical exercises, which some participants, after completing both, sought to revisit again within their own specific contexts.

The gradual shifting of perspectives on the nature of knowledge was evident in the depth of response to the way in which the reflective essay was constructed in the first instance. This echoes an important study of the learning development of first-year students (Hyland, 1994) in that the relationship between this and their specific concepts of learning requires a longer study. A tentative conclusion however might be that some of the difficulties in learning experienced at this stage are part of the broader intellectual problem posed by coming to terms with multiple interpretative paradigms.

Fundamental to this process of critical activity was that it should be cumulative, something often omitted in the drive for accreditation,in that learning should proceed in line with perceptions of tasks or, as Robb (1994) suggests, 'slowly, in terms of content, in order to gain mastery over concepts'. It should be emphasized however that **speed and depth are not mutually exclusive** but depend upon the different terms of reference in assessment.

For the critical reflection which, at its best within experiential learning, coheres and embraces academic and non-academic education, the assessment requirements must more closely **reflect the transparency of the overall purposes**. These need to be clarified not just for students but **with** students,in the way that deeper approaches to learning separate qualitative from quantitative research.

Conclusion

Reflection takes place across a number of cognate discipline areas. The discourse it explores often relates to specific purpose but it would be wise not to reify those purposes (Race, 1994). As a tool of assessment in the above context its central component in promoting student learning has been to link the learning outside of the institution with that which takes place inside. If, as Boud suggests (1991) assessment should be based on three principles:

- to help students become self-determining;
- to be like real research or real work; and
- to focus on 'deep learning' processes;

this has major implications for the curriculum both in terms of formative and summative feedback. If reflection provides the coherence in what would otherwise be a **babble of different discourse**, a sense of context rather than 'students repeatedly expressing disappointment over what they regarded as a denial of the voice of their experience' (Metcalf, 1993), exploring the different arenas of representation helps re–define the autonomy of the learner, at the level of the personal, the professional and the academic.

What has been attempted here is to illustrate how reflection is utilized in different arenas of representation that go into the making of a portfolio. Each of these arenas depends upon an assessment framework of its own. It is not sufficient to say to students simply **reflect upon the process**, it is also to suggest, in keeping within cycles of learning:

- why do they reflect?
- what do they reflect upon?
- how do they reflect?
- what if they reflected a different way?

Specific frameworks have to be provided for participants at each stage in the establishing of reflective practices and these stages can come from examples of differing theories of learning that again are not mutually exclusive. It is not until the linkage takes place, bringing together **these different arenas** that assessment informs **critical reflection** and all that sense of development that forms a student's own sense of learning.

In the use of assessment to promote that learning we return to the two questions this chapter originally sought to address, **What is the role of reflection?** and, **To what purpose do students reflect?** It is simply to register that for more and more mature students taking degree-level programmes there is an involvement with a sense of a realization of the self, that goes beyond rational reconstruction of learning associated with vocational or professional qualifications. As Habermas (1974) suggested, 'Rational reconstructions deal with anonymous rule systems, which any subjects whatsoever can comply with in so far as they have acquired the corresponding competence with respect to these rules. Reconstructions thus do not encompass subjectivity, within the horizon of which alone the experience of reflection is possible'.

References

Atkins, M., Beattie, J. and Dockrell, W.B. (1993). *Assessment Issues in Higher Education.* University of Newcastle.

Boud, D. (1991). Three principles for good assessment practices. *New Academic.* 1(1). See also Gibbs G. *Eight Myths About Assessment* (19). Op Cit (1991)

Bryan, I. and Usher, R. (1989). *The Captive Triangle: Adult Learning as Theory, Practice and Research.* Routledge.

Carter, R. (1985). A taxonomy of objectives for professional education. *Studies in Higher Education.* 10(2).

Dritchell, B.H. (1991). Autobiographical memory in natural discourse. *Applied Cognitive Psychology,* Vol. 5.

Gibbs, G. (1992). *Down with Essays.* New Academic. Vol 1(2).

Habermas, J. (1974). *Theory and Practice.* Heinemann.

Hyland, R. (1994). Know the formula and hit the jackpot. *Improving Student Learning,* OCSD.

Kolb, D. (1984). *Experiential Learning.* Prentice Hall, Englewood Cliffs.

Locke, M. (1991). *Mature Students: Exploring Good Practice,* CIS, No. 39.

Metcalf, H. (1993). *Non Traditional Students' Experience of Higher Education.* CVCP.

Mezirow, J. and Kolb, D. (ed.) (1990). *Fostering Critical Reflection in Adulthood: A Guide to Transformative and Emancipatory Learning.* Oxford, Jossey Bass

O'Reilly, D. (1993). Negotiating in an institutional context. In Stephenson, J. and Laycock, M. (eds.) *Using Learning Contracts in Higher Education.* Kogan Page.

Race, P. (1994). *Principles of Assessment.* Open Learning Foundation.

Robb, J. (1994). Learning in the process of learning. *Improving Student Learning, Theory and Practice,* OCSD.

Rogers, C. (1983).*Freedom to Learn.* Ohio, Bell & Howell Co.

Russo, J. and Schoemake, P. (1989). *Decision Traps.* Piatkus.

Sharp, N. and Land, R. Negotiating Work Based Learning. *Conference on Work Based Learning.* CBI University of Middlesex, May 1994.

Smith, P. and Turner, I. (1994). Jude Comes to Christminster. *SEEC News,* Issues 8, 9 and 10.

12 Assessment practices in art and design: a contribution to student learning?

Barry Jackson, (Middlesex University)

Introduction

This chapter reports the background, intentions and methodology of a three year research project recently launched by the author at Middlesex University. Using theoretical frameworks derived from the work of Säljö, Biggs, Marton, Entwhistle and others it explores the problematic issues surrounding approaches to learning in art and design. Although the focus of the research project is in a design context initially, there are many areas of commonality with fine art. Later work will seek to explore these more fully.

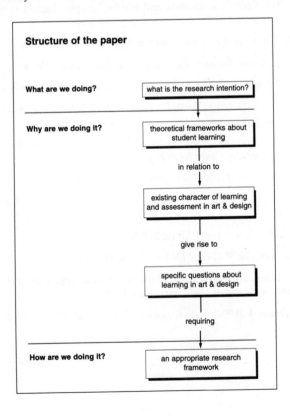

Figure 1

What are we Doing?

What is the research intention?

The principal aim of the research is to help to improve the quality of student learning in design. It is intended to be practically helpful to teachers and course designers, and the research itself will be largely carried out by teachers as action researchers.

It is hoped that the understanding gained from the project will be of more than local value, and will be transferable to other sites and subjects.

The central research question can be summarized as:

'Are we currently using the best assessment methods to improve the quality of students' learning on design courses?'

In answering this we will throw light on several questions:

- How are we currently assessing learning in design?
- To what extent do the existing methods encourage a deep approach to learning?
- Can better methods be found?
- How will we know they are better?

Each of these questions will itself require other questions to be investigated. For example in order to answer the question. 'How are we currently assessing', we will have to find out what is happening according to course documentation and staff, and what students say is happening.

In order to clarify further the objectives of the project, it is necessary to consider why we are doing the research. And to understand this we need to know:

- something about the research and theoretical frameworks which inform the project, and
- something of the character of learning and assessment in design as it currently exists.

Why are we Doing it?

Relevant theoretical frameworks about student learning

There exists a good research and theory base regarding the nature of learning in higher education. This research suggests that it cannot be taken for granted that existing teaching and assessment practices are working as well as practitioners believe.

The research has collected data about learning from a broad range of academic subjects in a number of different countries. A broadly consistent picture has emerged and it has been assumed that the concepts and structures which have been constructed on this research basis are therefore universally transferable. However, the implications for art and design subjects remain relatively unexplored.

While there is no reason to doubt that the frameworks are also relevant for art and design, there are some interesting problematics in translating some of the concepts into an art and design context in a way which can be easily accessed by teachers in those subject areas.

Of particular interest are theoretical structures and research instruments associated with the concepts of levels of learning outcome, and approaches to learning, which offer potentially valuable insights. Associated with these, and linking them are **conceptions of learning**. These three interrelated concepts form the theoretical framework in which the learning and assessment of students will be evaluated (see Figure 2).

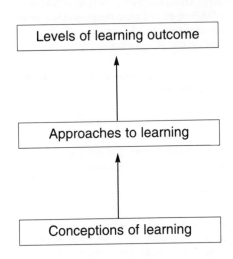

Figure 2

These have begun to be applied to art and design in a case study undertaken by myself and a colleague at another institution. The outcomes were promising (Davies, 1993). However, the studies raised more questions than they answered, and left a good starting point for a more focused research programme.

Levels of learning outcome

Students show qualitatively different levels of understanding of what they have learned. They are described as showing different levels of learning outcome.

The work of Marton, Säljö, Dahlgren, Svenson and others on learning outcomes provides a framework for thinking about the level of students' learning as demonstrated by the outcomes, and relates those levels to the approach that students take.

There are several ways of categorizing and analysing learning outcomes. Work has been done to investigate content specific outcomes in a number of subjects (e.g. Dahlgren, 1978), but work is just beginning on content-specific analyses of art and design subjects.

Biggs and Collis (1982) offer an empirically derived **general** taxonomy of levels of learning outcome, called SOLO (Structure of the Observed Learning Outcome). The categories Biggs and Collis describe are intended to be generally valid, independent of the kind of questions asked, or the subject matter contained in them. Subsequent use of the taxonomy in research seems to confirm the transferability of the taxonomy across a number of disciplines (see for example some of the case studies in Gibbs,1993).

In the SOLO taxonomy five levels of learning outcome can be distinguished, of increasing complexity:

1   **Prestructural**   no evidence of anything learned.

2   **Unistructural**   one correct and relevant element is present.

3   **Multistructural**   several relevant elements are present but in an unrelated way, often in list form.

4   **Relational**   the relevant elements are integrated into a generalised structure; there is evidence of induction.

5   **Extended-abstract**   The structure of elements is related to other relevant domains of knowledge; answers are not bounded by the question.

Although the SOLO taxonomy is intended to be a generally applicable categorization, and was used in the design case study reported in Gibbs (1993), it is not formulated in a helpful way for analysing outcomes of learning in design. The taxonomy has been constructed using written or verbal evidence for analysis, and this is clearly not a usual outcome of design learning. Current use of the taxonomy in a design learning context therefore requires that interviews, reports or other written evidence be produced specifically for analysis. The identification of what, in design terms, constitute the various levels of outcome in the SOLO taxonomy remains to be done and is one of the objectives of the current research project.

John Biggs has also suggested a system of qualitative grading for assessment, based on the five conventional letter grades (A–F) linked to the levels of the SOLO taxonomy (Biggs, 1992 quoted in Brown, Rust and Gibbs, 1994). A similar attempt to use the SOLO levels as the basis for qualitative grading was an important feature of the earlier project in design carried out by the author and colleagues at Falmouth School of Art and Design (see Davies, 1994). The potential of this system has not yet been fully explored and the current research project seeks to develop that work in a new context.

Approaches to learning

Approaches to learning are the strategies which learners adopt in order to succeed at learning. The term 'approach' is used to signify both the learner's intention and the way in which s/he processes information.

The quality of outcome of students' learning has been shown to be closely correlated to the level of approach they take to learning.

The concepts of approaches to learning have been developed in some detail and described elsewhere (Marton and Säljö in Marton, Hounsell and Entwhistle, 1984). Broadly speaking a student may take a 'surface' approach, in which material is learned superficially without evidence of understanding, or they make take a 'deep' approach in which the learning changes the way in which the student understands or perceives the subject and its context.

A deep approach is one which would involve the learner in constructing a personally meaningful and well-formed knowledge base. It will be a significant feature in the development of the designer's tacit 'theory of design' .

The approaches are highly context-sensitive. An individual student may adopt quite different approaches in different classes. In seeking the reasons for this, research has postulated and tested a number of features of course design and delivery which encourage a deep approach, and a number of factors which are associated with students taking a surface approach.

Features encouraging a deep approach

Four features associated with encouraging a deep approach were identified originally by Biggs (1989):

MOTIVATIONAL CONTEXT
Students are more likely to take a deep approach to learning when the motivation to learn is internal, coming from the student's own needs and desires. A positive climate, in which students 'own' their learning, can be established by involving students in the selection and planning of what is learned and how learning takes place. A good motivational context may be a necessary condition for deep learning. Motivational context is profoundly sensitive to the assessment strategies used.

LEARNER ACTIVITY
Deep learning is associated with activity. Students are more likely to make connections between what is being learned and past learning if they are active rather than passive.

INTERACTION WITH OTHERS
Talking and discussing ideas and concepts with others is a powerful way of reflecting on and testing learning. It provides a means of negotiating and structuring meaning which is more effective than solitary reflection alone.

WELL-STRUCTURED KNOWLEDGE BASE
New learning can only be approached deeply if the student can relate it to their existing knowledge and experience. The growing sense of a visible structure, which the subject matter acquires if it is presented in an integrated way, provides the student with a model of the knowledge they are acquiring, which can then be more easily manipulated and related to other knowledge. Interdisciplinary approaches can encourage a well-structured knowledge base.

Features associated with a surface approach

Research has similarly identified a number of features of course design and delivery which are associated with students taking a surface approach.

HEAVY WORKLOAD
A heavy workload allows no time for reflection and discussion: there is limited opportunity to consolidate the structure of knowledge or to relate it to existing knowledge. The actual workload which is imposed on students may often be heavier than

lecturers think. The expectations of various lecturers associated with a course or programme may mean that students have to commit substantial extra time to work on assignments, reading set texts and preparing presentations.

RELATIVELY HIGH LEVELS OF CONTACT TIME

Students need to be independent and active in their learning, and to have opportunities to discuss their learning with peers. A high level of contact time may not leave sufficient time for these important activities. It may also encourage the view that learning is passive, which is likely to encourage a surface approach.

EXCESSIVE AMOUNTS OF COURSE MATERIAL

In addition to contributing to a heavy workload, excessive amounts of course material reduce the student's chances of being able to relate the various components of their learning meaningfully, and to build a well-structured knowledge base.

LACK OF OPPORTUNITY TO STUDY SUBJECTS IN DEPTH

If students have no opportunity to develop their learning in depth in any particular area, their 'ownership' and their ability to make personally meaningful sense of it are likely to be diminished.

LACK OF CHOICE IN WHAT IS STUDIED, AND HOW

Lack of choice may reduce the positive emotional climate associated with good motivation.

ANXIETY-PROVOKING ASSESSMENT METHODS

A sense of anxiety or threat may be conditions which are in themselves sufficient for surface learning. Assessment is the main source of anxiety in any educational experience.

To this list can be added one further feature:

ASSESSMENT METHODS WHICH REWARD SURFACE APPROACHES

The power of assessment to determine students approach to learning has been recognized in several research projects. Assessment methods which permit or even encourage surface approaches to be rewarded can be a strong influence on how students learn.

Work in other disciplines has found a clear correlation between a deep approach and the higher levels of learning outcome. There is some evidence that the same correlation exists in design learning.

Evidence suggests that many, if not most, learners are able to take a surface or deep approach in different circumstances. That is to say that approaches, unlike 'learning styles', described for example in the work of Kolb or Honey and Mumford, are not personal unchanging characteristics. They are, by contrast, very dependent on context.

However, there does seem to be evidence of a small proportion of learners who find difficulty in employing a deep approach, even in favourable contexts.

Work by Entwhistle and Ramsden has demonstrated the significance of looking at students' approaches to learning in relation to their orientation. The Approaches to Study Inventory (ASI) identifies three possible orientations:

1 **meaning orientation**, which correlates with a deep approach;

2 **reproducing orientation**, which correlates with a surface approach;

3 **achievement or strategic orientation**, in which a student will be oriented primarily towards being successful, and will therefore readily adopt whichever learning strategy is most likely to gain success.

There is some evidence that a relatively high proportion of design students may enter higher education with an achievement orientation. This will be of interest to the current research project, since it would have significance for the kinds of strategies which might be successful in improving student learning in the subject.

The nature of the connection between the two approaches and the level of outcomes may be illustrated in the Figure 3

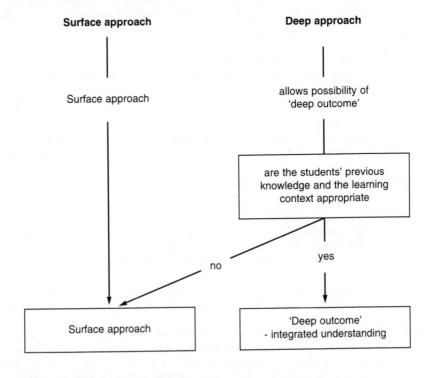

Fig 3: The relationship between approaches, context and outcomes

Two possible avenues of improvement thus suggest themselves:

1 to design and provide learning contexts which encourage 'achievement orientated' students to take deep approaches, and which reward their appropriate outcomes in assessment situations;

2 to find ways to encourage 'chronic' surface learners to understand and apply deep approaches to their learning.

Conceptions of learning

The approach to learning that a student takes is very sensitive to the context in which learning is done. The features outlined above are examples of this. For some students, however, the ability to take a deep approach appears to be limited by the conception they hold of learning.

This conception will to a large extent determine the student's expectation of what the learning process entails: and of what teaching entails.

From research Van Rossum and Schenk (1984) developed a set of categories of conceptions of learning held by students which is a helpful framework for further work. Learning can be conceived of as:

1 a passive increase in knowledge;

2 memorization of all apparently relevant facts;

3 acquisition of usable facts;

4 abstraction of meaning;

5 understanding reality.

Of these categories, levels 4 and 5 are qualitatively different from the first three, since they involve an active construction of personal meaning on the part of the learner.

The same authors demonstrated a correlation between these more advanced conceptions of learning and a deep approach to learning.

The relationship is illustrated in Table 1. Preliminary work suggests that the descriptions of the various levels of conception are meaningful to students of design, even though they have to translate the descriptions into statements more related to conceptions of learning in a design context.

The three related concepts of conceptions of learning, approaches to learning and levels of learning outcomes provide the structures within which the research project is framed. In order to consider the particular ways in which design learning relates to these, it will be necessary to explore the current character of design education.

The existing character of learning and assessment in design

Design practice requires the exercise of a complex interrelationship of skills, knowledge and understanding. In acquiring the competences that mark the path from novice towards expert, the developing designer also learns a body of knowledge. Some of this knowledge is explicit and factual; it is usually acquired, in the way of most factual knowledge, from sources of information such as lectures, reading and observation.

Table 1: Relationship of conception of learning to approach

| | Approach to learning | | |
Conceptions	Surface	Deep	Sub-totals
1. Increase in knowledge	6	0	6
2. Memorization	19	4	23
3. Acquisition of usable facts	8	7	15
4. Abstraction of meaning	1	11	12
5. Understanding reality	1	12	13
sub-totals	35	34	69

(from van Rossum and Schenik, 1984 quoted in Marton, Hounsell and Entwhistle, 1984)

A more significant part of the designer's knowledge and understanding has more problematic origins: the understanding of what design itself is, and the ability to choose and apply appropriate methodologies, for example. These are learned through the practice itself, in which the reflective designer constructs a personal knowledge-base. This knowledge base, although individually formulated, shares common conceptions with others in the design community and amounts to a tacit theory of designing and design values.

Unlike other academic subjects, design has only a small body of factual knowledge which a student has to acquire and which can be assessed. There are an infinite number of right answers to any problem, but not all answers are right. The theoretical understanding has to be gained by practice and reflection.

The learning process in which designers acquire, formulate and construct theories of designing during the progress of their formal education is not well understood. The teaching of the subject has evolved a set of practices based on assumptions and shared values. These values have certainly contributed to the successful education of many designers – the British design education system is well regarded, particularly by its own practitioners, and, with some reservations, by the industry it mostly serves.

However, these values are not necessarily helpful in encouraging students' development of learning, and while this may not ultimately be harmful to some students, there are many students who do not perform as well as they might. This fact in itself is associated with one of the concepts underlying design education, that of intrinsic talent. Students who do not perform well, it is argued, are either lazy, or simply lack the necessary talent.

The research project aims to question the validity of such assumptions and to test the hypothesis that the differential between students' performance can be at least partly attributed to the differences in their understanding, and that that in turn can be helped or hindered by the teaching and assessment which the students experience.

There are other features of design education which are relevant. Some of these might be expected to encourage a deep approach to learning, others not.

- Learning is focused on skills, and therefore students are involved in active learning for most of their time.
- Within the culture of design education there is a resistance to the use of verbal language.
- There is a celebration of the individual achievement within the culture which discourages collaborative work.
- There is a high level of intrinsic motivation in students studying design.
- Accomplished professional performers are valued highly as 'masters'.
- Students are expected, and expect, to personally invest a great deal of their own time in their learning, outside of class hours.

The assessment practices in art and design education also have a weight of tradition behind them, but there is little evidence that they are appropriate to encouraging a deep approach. Assessment usually centres on the quality of the design artifact, and this is exactly the area in which connoisseurship plays such an important part. There is an increasing emphasis on using clear assessment criteria and this has helped overcome problems of subjectivity. However there remains an overriding concern with the quality of 'creativity', a notoriously slippery concept, and one subject to considerable variations in personal interpretations.

In the context of this chapter it may be useful to draw attention to some features of assessment in design which seem to me to be important.

For simplicity's sake the description of art and design assessment will be generalized, not to say caricatured, in a way which I am aware does not do justice to the variety of practice which exists now, and has existed to a lesser degree in the past; it does, however, give insight into the cultural context in which innovations are taking place.

When does assessment happen?

Assessment in art and design higher education begins before the students start the course. It starts at admission, when students, typically having spent a year on a Foundation course, are interviewed and assessed in order to predict the probability of their success on the course they are about to enter.

Assessment continues throughout the course, culminating in a grand summative assessment at the end, on the basis of which an appropriate level of award is recommended. This practice continues even on some modular courses.

Many, if not all, projects which students undertake as part of their studies may be assessed, with a formative and/or summative intention. The results of these assessments may contribute to a summative assessment of the student's ability to progress to another level or another module, or to the final award.

There are often stage or interim assessments, points at which students must achieve a specified level before being allowed to progress into the next stage of the course. On modular schemes these are formal end-of-semester assessments.

How does it happen?

Often summative assessment and formative assessment are combined: students are given feedback intended to be helpful to them, in addition to being marked or graded.

Formative assessment often takes place informally in the studio or as part of a tutorial;

this practice was until recently almost always one-to-one, and is now more often undertaken in groups. The crit has been a site for critical comment and formative assessment of a kind, although the quality of crits is very variable and the practices vary considerably, both within and between courses.

Summative assessment occurs at the end of projects, at the end of semesters or at stage assessment points, and of course at the exit point. The dominant form of assessment in all of these has been the assessment of the appropriate visual work, usually in exhibition, and usually led and dominated by tutors.

Assumptions and values underlying 'traditional' assessment in art and design

There are several assumptions to be noted underlying 'traditional' assessment practices.

Underlying the 'traditional' practice of the end of course, or end of semester, assessment by exhibition there are several assumptions:

- that students' achievement of course objectives can be judged adequately from looking at the physical artwork products;
- that students develop progressively towards their best work, and that their 'exit velocity' is the best and fairest measure of their ability;
- that students are novice designers, who, on graduation become qualified, if somewhat junior, experts;
- that the judgement of student' readiness to join the fraternity of designers rests most properly in the hands of proven experts – that is, designers working in education;
- that the concept of 'final assessment' is a useful and valid one.

Although student involvement in project assessment has grown substantially it is still not uncommon to encounter situations in which students participate in critical comment about each others' work, but the work is then taken away by tutors to be marked.

Behind this practice are assumptions that only tutors are adequately informed, experienced and 'reliable' to make these important judgements. Of course this is not the case only in design; in many other disciplines the marking is wholly in the hands of lecturers. But for art and design it is both less understandable and at the same time more difficult to break out of.

It is less understandable because the individual nature of much of the project work being assessed makes it almost certain that the person with the best understanding of the objectives is likely to be the student herself.

It is more difficult to break with because art and design has a hero culture which privileges the judgements and opinions of individual practitioners/teachers. There are few other disciplines which pride themselves so much on the eminence or on the level of professional practice (by which I mean practice as artist or designer) of their staff teaching at undergraduate level.

Specific questions about learning and assessment in design

Attempts to think about learning and assessment in design programmes, in the context of the theoretical frameworks outlined above, very quickly encounter difficulties.

The concepts of 'deep' and 'surface' approach were originally defined in terms of texts

– whether a reader seeks for meaning below the surface of a text, or instead tries to memorize the information in the form in which it appears in the text. The concepts were quickly extended to other learning situations where their validity was confirmed. They are now taken to be valid in any area of learning.

However, translating these concepts into a form which can usefully be applied to design is not unproblematic. There are teachers within design education who would assert that the study of design is synonymous with a deep approach, arguing that the intensely personal motivation, the active learning by project and the group critiques of work which characterize design education necessitate a deep approach. They also argue that in design learning there is no place for an equivalent of the simple factual learning which is a feature of a surface approach. There are similar problematics about describing learning outcomes. We are led to a series of questions:

- what does a deep or surface approach look like in design?
- can the SOLO taxonomy be applied to the normal products of design learning?
- if so, how?
- if not, what evidence or framework may be used to distinguish levels of outcome?
- do current assessment methods permit low-level learning outcomes?
- do current assessment methods encourage a deep approach?
- how might assessment methods be improved?

These are the questions the research project attempts to address.

How are we Doing it?

An appropriate research framework

The research takes the form of an investigation and case study in the first stage, alongside proposals for innovations and action research into their effectiveness.

The action research paradigm is very appropriate for this kind of study. The research is intended to have practical and helpful outcomes, and to be carried out by staff who are closely concerned with putting the outcomes into practice. It is this lack of division between practitioner and researcher which characterizes action research.

It is in the nature of action research that the specific research aims, the hypotheses underlying the research, emerge more clearly as a part of the research process itself. In this it reflects a characteristic of the phenomenographic research process used by Marton and others. In this research method the categories of data are not prejudged but emerge directly as the result of rigorous qualitative analysis of the data. Both methodologies will be used in the current study.

The action research elements of the project will be grounded in the theoretical frameworks outlined earlier in the chapter. This body of work also provides a useful methodology and valuable research tools.

By using the methods of data collection familiar to readers of the research literature, that is the questionnaire inventory, and analysis of student interviews, it is hoped that insights into the impact of assessment on learning in design can be gained. At the same time the appropriateness, in this context, of the research tools and theoretical frameworks themselves will be tested, and this may lead to the development of more sophisticated instruments.

Action research is based on a cyclical process of action–observation – reflection–planning – action – etc. The project plans, as reported here, are the outcome of reflection on observations of previous practice. The detailed planning of the first stage is now underway and will lead to activities to take place in the new academic year, 1994–95. The outcomes of the project will be reported when appropriate.

References

Biggs, J. B. and Collis, K. F. (1982). *Evaluating the Quality of Learning*. New York and Sydney: Academic Press.

Biggs, J. B. (1992). A qualitative approach to grading students, *HERDSA News*, **14**(3).

Brown, S., Rust C. and Gibbs G. (1994). *Strategies for Diversifying Assessment in Higher Education*. Oxford: Oxford Centre for Staff Development.

Davies, A. (1993). *Improving student learning in design: a case study*. In Gibbs (1993).

Davies, A. (1994). *Identifying and working with student expectations of learning*. In Gibbs (1994)

Davies, A. (1994). *Self and peer assessment in design*. In Gibbs (1994).

Gibbs, G. (1993). *Improving the Quality of Student Learning*. Bristol:TES.

Gibbs, G. (1994). *Improving Student Learning - Theory and Practice*. Oxford: Oxford Centre for Staff Development.

Marton, F., Hounsell, D. and Entwhistle, N. (1984). *The Experience of Learning*. Edinburgh: Scottish Academic Press.

Marton, F. and Säljö, R.(1984). *Approaches to Learning* in Marton, Hounsell and Entwhistle (1984).

Dahlgren, L. O. and Marton, F. Students' conceptions of subject matter: an aspect of learning and teaching in higher education. Studies in Higher Education, (1978) 3, 25-35.

Van Rossum, E. J. and Schenk, S. M. (1984). The relationship between learning conception, study strategy and learning outcome. *British Journal of Educational Psychology*, **54**, 73–83.

13 Usability and beyond: Evaluating Educational effectiveness of computer-based learning

Cathy Gunn (Heriot-Watt University)

Abstract

The starting point for design of effective evaluation studies for CBL is a detailed statement of original development objectives. This provides focus for evaluation in two respects; whather the implementation actually meets the stated objectives, and if the objectives have proved to be valid, measureable by the stated criteria and appropriate to the learning outcomes required. This is a general and simplistic statement about objectives that, by nature of the systems they seek to describe, are likely to be both highly complex and specific. Educational effectiveness of CBL systems cannot realistically be measured in isolation from other factors, for example, quality of implementation, instructional strategy employed and relevance of content and presentation. From the perspective of measuring educational impact, these issues become potential confounding variables. Their effects must be identified and measured, before degrees of success or failure can be considered truly reflective of educational value. This chapter analyses some typical problems encountered with traditional methods, and offers a model for design and evaluation of educationally effective CBL. A specific application of the model is described, using the TLTP (1) CLASS (Courseware for Learning and Study Skills), software environment as a case study. The model is based on a contemporary approach which has evolved from recognition of the inadequacies of commonly 'borrowed' methodologies in the field of educational research. It is characterized by a purposeful move away from reliance on quantitative data gleaned from scientific experimental studies to more in depth research based and quanlitative measures. This shift is necessary if researchers hope to identify casual factors relating to the use of CBL in real educational settings.

Introduction : definitions

Three definitions are required to give the correct perspective to this chapter.

CBL : Adopting a broadly based definition, CBL is used to include all types of computer-based learning systems. This is not due to ignorance of the significant differences among system types, e.g. knowledge-based systems vs content-free frameworks and tools. The proposal is that the design and evaluation frameworks described can be successfully applied to all implementation types by appropriate weighting of the various system components.

Evaluation : Another broadly based definition is used for evaluation. This covers

168

formative study of existing practice and all phenomena which contribute to the design process, as well as summative measures used to gauge various aspects of use and effectiveness of the finished product.

Educational effectiveness : The third definition is that of educational effectiveness, a less tangible concept which varies according to the objectives a system is designed to achieve. For this study, educational effectiveness mainly refers to students acquiring deep level understanding of an academic subject domain, so an example of appropriate objectives might include :

- specification of a desired level of understanding of concepts and principles involved in the subject domain;
- ability to demonstrate transfer of acquired knowledge to other relevant contexts

However, it is also recognized that perceived adequacy of the ability to repeat facts or describe concepts is largely driven by current teaching and assessment requirements and consequently may render other learning objectives more difficult to promote.

The Current Situation: an overview

Prolific development of CBL in recent years has resulted in products which can claim varying degrees of educational success and failure. To date, there is no universally accepted theoretical basis or effective model for design and evaluation of CBL. Laurillard (1993) offers perhaps the best contemporary statement on design while Draper et al. (1994) offer the best empirically based work on evaluation. Both are too recent to have been subjected to extensive validation and testing at this stage.

Many different approaches to implementation of instructional materials have evolved and evaluation studies designed to prove their worth. It is argued here that even where developers have based their systems on sound theoretical work and proven instructional strategies, the adopted approach to evaluation has often been at best inappropriate, at worst irrelevant and ineffective.

Popular Misconceptions

One major misconception is the belief that evaluation is something that should take place only after a product has been developed. Another common problem is that in summative studies, assessment of effectiveness has frequently taken second place to evaluation of usability factors which are relatively easy to measure. It is no easy task to identify and measure the complex interaction of effects of the many variables, (including usability issues), which determine outcomes and thus allow the researcher to arrive at valid conclusions regarding the quality of the learning experience for users. This is particularly true where inappropriate evaluation methodologies have been 'borrowed' and adapted from other disciplines as with the scientific experimental approach taken from the behavioural and physical sciences. The scientific approach offers a useful, though extremely resource intensive methodology for some aspects of summative evaluation but is quite inadequate as a formative measure (Kulik and Kulik, 1986, 1991).

Multiple Perspectives of Users

Students approach learning tasks from widely different individual perspectives, involving e.g.

- perceptions of task and situation;
- levels of prior knowledge / education;
- conceptions of the subject domain;
- preferred study styles;
- personal preference in interaction style;
- personal objectives.

Adding the context of an innovative delivery platform, the problem of measuring educational effectiveness of CBL remains an extremely complex one. It is considered quite inappropriate to employ methods which examine only the learning outcomes and not the processes by which they are achieved. There is a growing acceptance of the need for an innovative approach to CBL design for effective instruction. The implications are that an appropriate model would rely heavily on a research-based formative evaluation component. It is suggested that a useful basis for such formative evaluation is found in the qualitative approach traditionally applied to anthropology research (Säljö, 1988). However, 'borrowed' methodologies should always be treated with caution.

Problem Definition in Context: Meta-analysis

Meta-analytic reviews express outcomes of all evaluation studies in standard deviation units and statistically investigate relationships between outcomes and study features. Kulik and Kulik (1991) conducted a meta-analysis of results from 55 evaluation studies designed to measure effectiveness of computer-aided learning material by examination of learning outcomes. The results of most studies reported increased educational effectiveness measured by :

- examination results;
- follow up testing;
- user attitudes to academic work.

Most showed only modest positive effects, though some in the domains of education and psychology, showed exceptionally large improvement effects. Comparison with results of earlier meta-analyses reported by Kulik and Kulik (1986) showed an increased effect for all systems over time. This may be partly due to concurrent improvements in hardware and instructional software design. Another overall positive effect was a reduction in instruction time. Results of these studies clearly identified two important issues for future research :

- that insufficient detail was made available to identify what specific factors contributed to success or failure of the systems under study;
- they provided evidence that scientific experimental studies were inadequate as a

means of effectiveness evaluation where the required outcomes were anything other than repetition of facts or examination passes, two measures that are now recognized as mere indicators of short-term memory capacity.

Kulik and Kulik suggest that much more specifically focused research is necessary to translate the generally positive phenomena identified by the meta-analysis into detailed design and implementation issues. After the meta-analysis must come the micro-analysis, if indeed the meta-analysis is other than a luxury the researcher cannot afford. Starting with assumptions which are empirically supported by the meta-analysis, i.e. that CBL can be designed to teach satisfactorily, while also reducing instruction time, it is now necessary to identify the specific features that cause these positive effects and consider how to include them in a model of effective CBL design. Similar meta-analytical research was conducted from 1974–84 and later reported by Kulik and Kulik (1991). Around the same time, it was reported that many educationalists believed detailed research should try to identify more specific areas where educational technology could be used most effectively. The issues then arising would be how to gear design to the needs of these areas and by what standards effectiveness could be measured. These claims were made in the belief that too much reliance had been placed on evaluation methodologies demanding a level of proof which, in the majority of cases of educational technology, could not be satisfied. In the case of formative evaluations such methodologies could not even be considered appropriate. The scientific experimental approach thus came to be regarded as the wrong kind of research using inappropriate methods to achieve the type of results required.

A traditional approach and a novel situation

The current need is for studies to ascertain under what conditions and with what objectives CBL can be most effective (Schramm, 1977).

Unlike the history of science, where systematic observation led to development of theories on which subsequent experiments were based, there is currently no adequate theory of instructional media to provide a satisfactory basis for evaluation studies. As a result, a common practice has been to adopt established methods of evaluation, regardless of whether or not they are truly suitable to the area of study.

The scientific laboratory experimental approach to evaluation attempts to control all variables except those in focus for the study. Effects of confounding factors such as different levels of existing knowledge or interest in the subject were assumed to be balanced by random assignation of subjects to experimental groups. A typical hypothesis would be that comparison of one group using CBL with another using books or other media would show results which reliably favoured one medium over the other. It is now recognized that difficulty in identifying and controlling all variables in an experiment involving human subjects is only one of many potential pitfalls of this approach.

Cronbach and Snow (1977) identified development of CBL as an area where individual differences do matter and should provide a focus for study rather than being randomized and subsequently ignored. Their suggestion was for a model incorporating interactions between form and content of media and learner skills with the specific media employed.

Studies designed to produce comparative data for different media-based systems have often come under serious criticism too, as conclusions have sometimes been based on what is actually an attempt to compare two unlike systems. In this respect, it is argued that too many other differences exist to be able to attribute cause and effect reliably to the delivery media alone.

A final criticism of the scientific experimental approach is recognition of the importance of measuring the effects of the particular media implementation in the real educational setting it is designed to function in rather than in a contrived experimental environment as was previously the norm. The artificial nature of experimental environments therefore represents another confounding factor, and the high resource requirements involved in such studies often renders them inaccessible to the average researcher.

However, the argument against experimental evaluation does not aver that it has little worth in any aspect of CBL research. It does provide a useful means of meta level analysis where quantitative data can identify areas of focus for subsequent qualitative analysis, albeit it a very expensive means of obtaining such data. It is also appropriate as a method of performing large-scale summative evaluation of finished products, and as a means of producing quantitative data over time for comparative or cumulative purposes.

Building a theoretical foundation

Without accurate observation of the nature of learning and instruction through the use of different media, and without a carefully developed set of assumptions about the conditions which are likely to influence learning through different media, it is difficult to see how satisfactory experiments can be designed (Bates, 1981).

A set of assumptions representing a sound basis for design of CBL evaluations would necessarily be quite different from those applied to classical experimental research. For example, attempts at randomizing the effects of individual differences within study populations to achieve generalizable results, even if effective, are not particularly relevant where CBL evaluation is concerned. This is particularly true of formative evaluation, where a top-level requirement might be to identify the possible range of individual differences and define the design requirements that would accommodate all types of learners. However, it is also true where summative evaluation is required to determine the level of success a design has achieved with different approaches to and styles of learning.

Problem Definition in Context: Micro-analysis

At the level of micro-analysis, few researchers either have the resources available or the inescapable need to conduct evaluation studies on the scale of those involved in a meta-level review. The potential benefits of testing systems on as many users as possible are not questioned. However, large-scale studies may not represent the best exploitation of evaluation resources, as they do not represent the best means of arriving at reliable conclusions about CBL effectiveness. Some aspects of educational effectiveness are relatively easy to measure, e.g.

- exam results;
- time on task;
- levels of user engagement and acceptance;
- subjective and objective data on usability issues.

Various suitable methods have been developed, tested and made widely available. For such objectives, it is a relatively simple matter to define which available tools best fit the particular task and context. The argument here is that only performing this level of evaluation is failing to measure and therefore influence other major contributory factors to effective courseware design. The less tangible aspects of learning will require specific measurement, and in pursuing the objective of promoting deep level rather than surface style learning, (Marton and Säljö, 1976), it is necessary to identify a methodology for measuring that such learning has in fact occurred. This requires use of performance indicators such as demonstration of the ability to transfer knowledge to appropriate novel contexts and drawing of analogies based on domain principles. Such measures represent valid means of showing that the important principles and concepts involved in a subject domain, and the context within which they exist, have been properly understood. An approach concentrating more on depth than breadth of coverage is implied, though the opposite is currently the norm.

In reality, evaluative research is usually constrained by lack of adequate resources to conduct ideal studies. The scope of CBL and the situations it may be used in vary so widely that an equally wide range of evaluative research methods is appropriate. The degrees of reliability, generality and usefulness of the different methods available vary considerably. A process can be used to define the best practicable methodology in the context of any particular product and set of circumstances in which it will be used.

Possible methods include case studies, surveys, observation and some evolving ways of measuring critical thinking and transferable skill development (e.g. MENO Thinking Skills Materials). These latter aspects represent some of the hardest developments to measure, i.e. the subjective, intangible elements of skill in learning, understanding and mental processing. Such aspects of learning are not easily revealed by results of traditional forms of testing, such as exams and practicals. It appears that a combination of before and after testing, attitude measurement and longer term academic success offer the best options. The literature suggests that effects may best be measured months, or even years after the treatment has been given. No less complex is establishment of some mechanism by which to relate the measured effects of these intangible aspects of learning effectively to the different media used for delivery.

Effective use of Computers in Education

Increasingly it is being recognized that augmentation of data delivery in conventional instruction, e.g. via hypermedia systems, is not the most effective use of computers in education (e.g. Dede, Fontana and White, 1993; Jonassen, 1993). On the problems encountered with this approach, Jonassen states :

> At least two reasons for the lack of efficacy exist. First the level of engagement and purpose among learners in most hypermedia systems does not require meaningful processing of the content. Second, effectively using hypermedia entails the use of learning and meta-learning strategies that learners are not skilled in. The assumptions about the ways that learners would use hypermedia and process the information in it have not been empirically supported . . . the most effective hypermedia applications are based on constructivist learning models.

Although Jonassen's remarks were specifically directed at hypermedia systems, the continuing trend towards inclusion of different media with flexible navigation capabilities in various CBL systems adds weight to their general relevance. Similar findings are reported by White and Horowitz (1988), who claim most notable successes in the field of CBL are where systems are based on a constructivist instructional strategy and where the learning model was designed to imitate the evolution of expert knowledge in a domain. In further support of this premise is the following comment :

> Intuition, experience and cognitive psychology suggest that new, interactive multimedia learning environments provide a closer match with the way in which humans store and retrieve information in memory than do conventional linear, single-mode formats that have dominated educational materials for decades (e.g. films and books) Polin (1990).

The implication is that problems encountered are not inherent in the introduction of technology to the classroom. On the contrary, computers have potential to offer infinitely better and more natural learning environments in many domains. Rather the problems may be inherent in the adoption of a conventional instructional approach as the basis for CBL design. The proposed solution lies in the designers' ability to understand and imitate the natural way semantic networks develop as learner understanding of a domain matures.

The main benefits of technology in the classroom are now being identified as the ability to foster higher order thinking skills through knowledge construction and based on development of formal enquiry skills in learners. This approach requires a new model of teaching and learning which integrates the capabilities of technology with HCI practice, an increasing body of knowledge from cognitive psychology and contemporary developments in the study of effective learning.

A Design Framework for Effective CBL: an overview

The requirements of various aspects of software design must be met in order to meet the objective of designing CBL for educational effectiveness. The impact of all influential factors should be assessed during the formative stages of design and implementation and adequate standards ensured. Otherwise it may be an impossible task in summative evaluations, to attribute cause and effect to any particular combination of factors. The following sections elaborate on some of these crucial aspects, outline their significance to the design model and suggest means of ensuring their positive contribution to the finished CBL system.

Psychology of learning research

A shift in emphasis in the field of learning psychology has evolved over the last twenty or so years. The move has been from research based on formal or mechanical models embodying chains of causality, to more qualitative study of student experiences. It was prompted by empirical evidence demonstrating the inadequacy of previously employed methodologies (Marton, Hounsell and Entwistle, 1984). Current research methodology is based on the following assumptions :

Students' approach to learning is significantly affected by the way academic tasks are presented to them, and by the powerful demands of assessment procedures. It is therefore important to consider the content and context of learning related to current thinking in the field of learning psychology in order to decide what action or decision is implied.

A number of published works are available on the subject of learning psychology related to computer-based instructional design, e.g. Laurillard (1993), West, Farmer and Wolff (1991), Ramsden (1988). The factors relevant to the proposed evaluation model are discussed in the following sections.

Understanding the Users

Two methodologies are proposed as offering useful contributions to understanding of the learning process and the different perspectives students might bring to the educational setting in focus. The ability to realistically anticipate learner characteristics has important implications for design of educational material. Empirically supported works by Ference Marton in Sweden and William Perry in the US have provided a basis for extensive research and development in the area of understanding learning in the context of instructional design. Both methodologies are proposed as theoretical support for the formative aspects of the model for design and evaluation of effective CBL. Finally, a model of the teaching learning process recently published by Diana Laurillard (1993), offers a useful view of the process from the learner's perspective.

MARTON AND PHENOMENOGRAPHY

Marton (1981), coined the term 'phenomenography' to describe research that systematically focuses on the second order perspective of how different people interpret significant aspects of reality. This kind of research aims at description, analysis and understanding of experiences. The fundamental difference between first- and second-order perspectives is important to the methodology. First-order perspective aims to describe various aspects of the world, whereas second-order perspective describes people's experiences of various aspects of the world. The ideology is made explicit in the following extract:

> Conceptions and ways of understanding are not seen as individual qualities. Conceptions of reality are considered rather as categories of description to be used in facilitating the grasp of concrete cases of human functioning. Since the same categories of description appear in different situations, the set of categories are thus stable and generalizable between the situations even if individuals move from one category to another on different occasions. The totality of such categories of description denotes a kind of collective intellect as an evolutionary tool in continual development (Marton 1981)

The important aspects of this approach to learning are that it recognizes that individuals may view the same educational experience from very different perspectives, thus resulting in different learning experiences and outcomes. While this may at first suggest that designers can have no general guidelines on which to base courseware development, further research identified a relatively limited number of commonly occurring perspectives which were then subject to classification (e.g. Marton 1981, Marton and Säljö, 1976). A rationale for these perspectives was developed and is referred to as categories of description.

Conceptions of reality are considered as categories of description to be used in facilitating the grasp of concrete cases of human functioning. Since the same categories of description appear in different situations, the set of categories is thus stable and generalizable between situations even if individuals move from one category to another on different occasions (Marton, 1981).

Design decisions can thus be made to incorporate a finite range of possible perspectives. The result should be more generally successful courseware than where design is based on one specific perspective. If outcomes are expected to vary among individuals, there will naturally be corresponding differences in the processes of learning that produce them.

Earlier research by Wertheimer (1945), demonstrated what may now seem fairly obvious, that teaching the principles underlying a problem and the processes required to reach a solution is a more effective means of promoting understanding and retention than by simply teaching the solution without the means of reaching it. In simplified terms, this relates to identification by Marton and Säljö (1976), of two levels of processing for learning, deep and surface, which correspond to the different aspects of the learning material that the learner focuses on. However, it is not a simple case of every learner falling neatly into one of the two categories. In fact, individuals tend to display different styles in response to varying situations and times. The important principle for courseware designers to recognize is that degrees of difference exist. Some characteristics of each level of processing are shown in Table 1.

Table 1

Deep level	understanding intention, comprehending principles, ability to transfer, interpretation of meaning
Surface level	learning to repeat, memorizing, rote learning, precise reproduction of content

The implications of this is clearly that deep-level processing of learning material must be promoted through the materials themselves if effective understanding is to be the outcome.

PERRY'S MODEL OF COGNITIVE DEVELOPMENT

If Marton and Säljö's work sought to observe and to classify different processes of learning and their corresponding outcomes. Perry's 'Model of Cognitive Development in Learners' (1988), which is summarized in Table 2, offered insight into why learners might adopt any particular approach. There has been well-founded criticism of the belief in clearly definable stages of development in learning ability such as those advocated most notably by Piaget, but also by Perry. It is argued that Perry's classification of developmental stages offers useful input to the design model, though not in the form of an definitive statement of how learners' cognitive processing functions develop through age and education. The value is rather in knowing that individuals do go through stages of cognitive development although progress in any domain is also heavily dependent on content and contextual factors. Perry's work has been accepted as a classification model and theoretical basis by many researchers in the field. Empirical evidence based on application of the model in various studies supports its validity (e.g. Battaglini and Schenkat, 1987). Perry's work can offer valuable input on the following aspects of courseware design :

* allowing realistic prediction of typical user conceptions and abilities;
* targeting of courseware to particular ways of thinking and levels of cognitive development;
* provision of appropriate scaffolding for preliminary and transitional phases.

It remains doubtful however, that the ability to transfer knowledge across domains will automatically result from a generic learning environment which uses Perry's classification system as a starting point. More specific effort must be directed at solving the transfer problem. While there is no empirical evidence to disprove the possibility of problem solving, critical thinking and metacognitive skills being developed as executive processes that successfully transfer across all domains, the prospect may be viewed as an issue for serious research and potential development.

ASSESSING LEARNING OUTCOMES

Despite some well directed research and curriculum development initiatives over the past forty or so years, current practice of assessing students principally on examination results still does not, in many cases, give any indication of what levels of cognitive development have been achieved or whether deep- or surface-level learning has produced the results. Perry's chosen methodology involved open-ended interviews and collection of subjective data in such quantities that conclusions could be drawn from frequency of occurrence. However, the method is too time-consuming and labour-intensive to be practical in most contemporary CBL evaluation studies.

Table 2 Perry's model of cognitive development in learners

Learner type	Characteristics
Dualistic	See the world as a place of absolutes, such as right and wrong, true or false. Knowledge is seen as existing absolutely. Tend to think of their own role as learning the 'right answers' and the teacher as the provider of these answers. Likely to present judgements as if they were self-evident without the need for substantiation
Multiplistic	Recognize that there are multiple perspectives to problems. However, they are unable to evaluate each perspective adequately. A typical multiplistic response might be 'We're all entitled to our own opinions'. Argumentation ends, or is avoided, with the multiplistic attitude.
Relativistic	See knowledge as relative to particular frames of reference. They show a capacity for detachment; they look for the 'big picture', think about their own thinking and evaluate their own ideas as well as those of others. Frequently, by seeing alternative perspectives, they have difficulty making a decision. Authorities are seen as people who can and should be questioned.

Quality control for educational software

An established standard for controlling the quality of software presentation would contribute greatly to the design/evaluation model. This aspect of quality can represent a major confounding factor in studies of different delivery media, comparison of different implementations as well as measurement of educational effectiveness. If badly designed educational courseware is presented to students, the most likely outcome is that they will not engage in an effective learning experience, though the blame cannot fairly be attributed to use of the computer as a delivery platform. Recent work in the domain of HCI has gone a long way to promoting software quality assurance but principles are not yet universally accepted and applied. In fact, most courseware development projects have to rely on formative data from studies with small numbers of users and interested experts to ensure the quality of courseware before it goes out to larger scale user testing. There are now enough useful guidelines and reference works available to render this approach adequate in most cases.

QUALITY OF PRESENTATION – OVERVIEW

Relevant and logically presented content material is a crucial element in designing effective CBL. This aspect draws on knowledge of what is effective with traditional media and teaching, how appropriate aspects can be successfully incorporated into CBL and what the 'added value' component of the computer-based system may be that justifies investment of the necessary resources. Relevant areas of research cover educational psychology, cognitive science, HCI and studies of the use of multiple media in educational settings. The area of educational psychology has been in focus for a number of years and there is a wealth of literature and experience to draw on. Relevant aspects are discussed elsewhere in this report. Cognitive science literature also has a useful contribution to offer (e.g. Paivio, 1990). Studies of HCI and use of multimedia in education are more recent developments which consequently leave a lot more unanswered questions and untested theories. There is however, a growing body of literature which provides useful guidelines on the successes and failures experienced by practitioners to date, e.g. Feldman (1991), Nix and Spiro (1990), Hodges and Sasnett (1992), Jonassen (1993).

EFFECTIVE USE OF MULTIMEDIA

Research into the uses of multimedia in education is currently a very topical area. Results of many studies offer suggestions of which media combinations provide the most effective delivery methods for particular types of subject material, e.g. Hulley, Holland and Ward (1993), Hodges and Sasnett, (1993). Although studies of different media combinations in CBL are still at the stage of discovering and explaining phenomena, results may be accepted as a basis for further hypothesis testing with specific contexts and implementations. The domain of cognitive psychology offers valuable input with its analysis of optimal combinations of media for cerebral processing and memory capabilities, e.g. Kintsch (1974), Paivio (1990).

QUALITY OF CONTENT

There are a number of components which may be included to a greater or lesser extent, dependent on the type of CBL system being designed. For example, a knowledge based system would have greater requirements in terms of domain knowledge than would a content free framework. This concept is illustrated in Figure 1.

The various system components are illustrated in Figure 2 and described in the following sections. The metaphor of objects and attributes has been adopted to help develop this description, with components referred to as objects and characteristics as their attributes.

Domain knowledge: how far this element extends will be a function of the degree of intelligence or more simply, the required information component of any system. It may be closely related to a specific domain, as in e.g. an instructional system for third-year mathematics students, or more general in coverage, e.g. a framework for developing effective learning and study skills for students entering higher education. A system cannot teach or aid learning effectively if the subject material it is based on is inadequate, incomplete, inaccurate or otherwise flawed.

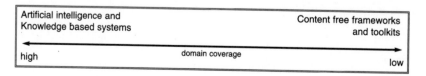

Figure 1 : Continuum of CBL system knowledge requirements

Didactic element: Inclusion of this component, as with domain knowledge, depends to a great extent on what type of system is being developed and what its objectives are. Where included, the didactic or teaching element of any system should ideally be based on proven instructional strategy and material relevant to the particular subject domain. Allowance should be made for the existence of different perceptions, learning styles, levels of prior knowledge and possible objectives of students using the system.

Communication component: This aspect of a system is concerned with how well the material is presented to students and how meaningful the context of presentation makes it appear. An important design consideration here is recognition of the different objectives and perceptions of the subject domain a student might bring to the task as this will determine how the design should be targeted for perceived relevance. This component is important to the success of any type of system as it will influence what may be the two most important extrinsic factors contributing to educational effectiveness, i.e. user motivation and acceptance.

Student knowledge model: This is a variable factor which is often hard to define. If the target user group is very specific and homogeneous, e.g. masters degree students in computer science, the model may be reasonably easy to quantify. With many systems however, the plotting must be done at any point on a scale that extends from no assumed knowledge of the topic to expert knowledge in the domain. Realistic assessment of user knowledge is important to effective design. Perry's Model of Cognitive Development provides a widely accepted basis for defining the general characteristics of the student knowledge model and is equally applicable to the various types of CBL system.

Control mechanism: This refers to the behaviour and performance of the system in reaction to user actions. It should be as intuitive and as relevant as possible. The major importance of this factor is in the ability of the system to provide meaningful feedback. It does not require a great deal of intelligence built into a system to apply a few simple rules for assessment of user performance and generation of personalized feedback. Control in this sense is the relationship between the learner, the interface and the underlying functionality. As such it should be subject to strong influence by HCI design principles and attention to usability factors, as well as psychological considerations. Important factors such as user motivation and acceptance of a CBL system are influenced by the control mechanism, so its careful specification cannot be underplayed.

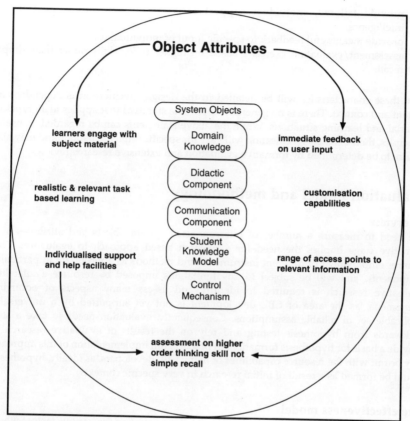

Figure2 : CBL system model

CONTENT CHARACTERISTICS

If the elements described above are equated to system objects then the characteristics of those objects may be referred to as object attributes. A system including the correct balance of components, requires an appropriately weighted combination of the following attributes to ensure effectiveness.

- learners actively engaging with subject material to reach clearly defined goals;
- guide/support learners in defining relevant mental or visual representations of knowledge structures;
- provide realistic and relevant task scenarios as a basis for learning;
- provide a wide range of access styles to relevant information, e.g. simulations, reference sections, question/answer sessions;
- permit individual preferences in representational styles through customization features;

- provide tailored, individual support facilities through simple or complex intelligence;
- provide meaningful feedback to specific input of individual users;
- assessment/evaluation exercises based on higher order skills rather than simple recall.

How these characteristics will be detailed in the design specification is dependent on content and context. There is no generally applicable standard that applies to all types of material and learning situations. While the above statements can be regarded as useful principles, their detailed specification will vary for specific implementations and may also require to be determined by formative evaluation and extensive research reviews.

Evaluation model and methodology

Overview
The need to measure a number of interconnected system objects and attributes at a formative stage implies the need for a research based approach to evaluation. This requires employment of different instruments and methods as appropriate to particular components, and will be subject to any limitations imposed by resource availability. Evaluative research is required to identify and assess many aspects of occurring phenomena, as the area of CBL development is not yet supported by a universally applicable set of reliable assumptions. Consequently, evaluation needs to take a step backwards from hypothesis testing and rely on the results of evaluative research to provide a basis for hypothesis formation. In practice, full implementation of this approach may be out with the resource capabilities of many CBL developers, as ideally, hypotheses would be formed as a result of initial research in very specific contexts.

The effectiveness model
Figure 3 shows the proposed evaluation model, demonstrating the various factors which interact to determine success or failure of CBL systems. Each component must be assessed for its effects on overall outcomes before any conclusions about educational effectiveness per se can successfully be reached.

Implementing the model: Some general considerations
An ideal evaluation technique would provide both the certainty of a formal analysis and the detail meaningful for in depth analysis of a complex system. Whether such techniques can be developed and what they would involve are challenging topics for future research

(Mark and Greer, 1993).

The effectiveness of this model depends largely on the successful choice of tools and methods for assessing each component of the system. The following sections discuss some useful options.

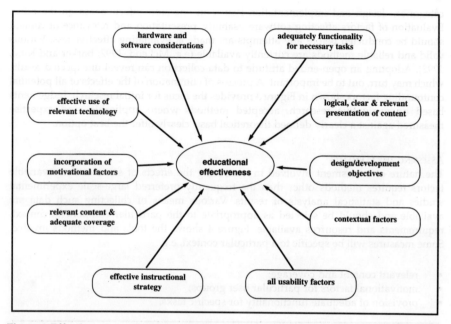

Figure 3 Effectiveness evaluation model

EVALUATIVE RESEARCH AS A STARTING POINT
Accepting the fact that evaluative research methods may produce data that is less reliable and less accurate than results of large-scale studies using statistical data analysis does not mean it is any less valuable. Only that it must be treated with caution and consideration of all influential factors as well as the degrees of reliability likely to be achieved. Bates (1981) defined a set of general questions which apply to design of evaluative research. These questions represent a useful starting point for considering what evaluation strategy and methods to use in any given situation. They can equally be applied to each element included in the system design model.

- reliability – is the total user population represented?
- accuracy – have the full range of effects been identified and measured?
- discrimination – do results indicate the conditions which cause different outcomes?
- explanation – do results explain phenomena observed and give possible alternatives?
- usefulness – is the information gained really new and useful to specific purposes?
- heuristic quality – does it help to build a theory on which predictions can be based?
- contextual detail – does the research take due account of specific situational factors

Working with the best information possible in any given situation should be the aim of the CBL evaluator. This information will fall into two distinct though inter-dependent categories, design and implementation issues on one side, effectiveness on the other. Evaluation of factors affecting software usability, presentation and relevance of content should be conducted before any attempts are made at evaluating effectiveness. Various valid and reliable methods are currently available (e.g. McLeod, 1992; Barker and King, 1993). Adopting an open-ended attitude to data collection can reveal unexpected results which may turn out to be important. A process of elimination of the effects of all potential confounding factors shown in Figure 3 provides the focus for initial research. Judgements based on evaluative research, accepted methods where applicable, and expertise measured against a clearly defined theoretical basis clearly offer the best option.

ASSESSING THE ELEMENTS

The nature of assessment involved in measuring the effects of some of these variable factors requires methods other than the frequently preferred large-scale experimental studies and statistical analysis of results. Various means of collecting such data are available and should be selected as appropriate to the particular component, context, requirements and resources available. Figure 4 shows the tools and methods involve. Some measures will be specific to a particular context, e.g.

- relevant content and coverage;
- motivational factors for particular user groups;
- provision of adequate functionality for specific tasks.

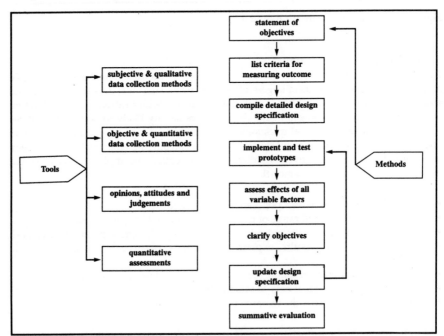

Figure 4: Evaluation framework, tools and methods

Others are more generalizable and therefore more likely to be available 'off the shelf', from existing sources, e.g.

- suitable instructional strategy;
- inclusion of motivational factors;
- effective use of technology;
- interface design/usability issues;
- hardware and software considerations.

A choice of method/s specifically geared to each component offers the best application of this evaluation model. Suitable methodologies may be borrowed from other disciplines for these purposes though strict attention should be paid to their relevance to the task.

There are now a number of useful tools and instruments available that have been specifically designed for evaluating different aspects of computer-based learning environments, e.g.

- Software Usability Measurement Inventory (SUMI, University College of Cork)
- Motivational Aspects Assessment Instrument (McAleese and Gunn, Heriot Watt University)
- Metrics for Usability Standards in Computing (MUSIC, The National Physical Laboratory)
- Subjective Mental Effort Questionnaire (SMEQ, Delft University of Technology)

Some components and attributes present a problem of applying systematic measurement and may therefore require less formal, investigative methods which cannot be expected to produce statistically significant or generalizable results. It must be remembered, however, that some valuable research findings have resulted from unsystematic research based evaluation. An excellent example of this is Perry's work on cognitive development modelling discussed in an earlier section of this chapter. The outcome of Perry's research could never have been arrived at using formal systematic methods, and yet it has provided a relevant theoretical basis for significant further research. The following sections discuss some suitable methods for use with elements of the evaluation model.

EXPERIMENTS IN REAL SITUATIONS

It is desirable, where practical, to conduct experiments involving testing of concepts, components or finished products with target users in authentic educational contexts. Selection of appropriate methods and tools for recording and interpreting of data is required. This type of evaluation is most relevant where prototypes are being used to define the full requirements specification, instructional strategies require testing or final products are being tested. More accurate data is likely to be achieved from studies in authentic settings than artificial experimental conditions. It is also more relevant to user requirements, indicative of actual performance and less resource intensive to set up.

SUBJECTIVE DATA COLLECTION METHODS: ATTITUDES, OPINIONS AND JUDGEMENTS

These include interviews, questionnaires, checklists, etc. and are useful methods where target users provide the best source of evaluation data. However, each instrument has its own limitations which should be identified and considered when a choice of methods is made. Inclusion of large numbers of users from different target groups may be used to provide fairly general information or smaller numbers involved for in depth study of specific issues. The type of information best suited to collection by these methods is initial requirements capture, opinion on existing products and ideas about how users perceive and perform tasks.

Expert evaluation

One perhaps underrated method with an important contribution to make is expert evaluation and reference to professional opinion. Alone it does not provide an adequate basis for judging educational effectiveness as it examines only the teacher/expert perspective. However, it can offer valuable input to formative evaluation as well as useful indicators in summative measures of effectiveness and interpretation of evaluation results. Experts in the subject domain and teaching profession have a significant contribution to make in e.g. providing guidelines on what successful methods are currently applied using traditional media and other experience based input. Such experiential factors provide a sound basis for further study to determine if factors perceived as contributing to success can :

1 be identified and

2 provide a workable basis for software design in terms of e.g. content, style of delivery and coverage.

The value of expert opinion extends through requirements analysis and prototype testing to summative evaluation. In the latter case, comment on whether the introduction of CBL coincided with improved overall results may be useful. Pass rates, attendance levels and interest in CBL where other materials are available may indicate effects worthy of further investigation. However, a problem to avoid is that of experts no longer being able to put themselves in the place of novices and making wrong assumptions about prior knowledge, how tasks are approached and what factors affect progress in learning.

OBJECTIVE DATA COLLECTION METHODS

These include video or observer recording of software in use, though it is arguable that in interpreting such data, the researcher is making it subjective, and that the presence of observers or cameras introduce an artificial element to the study. Interaction data logging, literature searches and other 'off-the-shelf' information sources are other appropriate instruments. Relevant areas of application for such methods include identification of instructional strategy, usability issues, hardware/software considerations and factors relating to the effective use of technology in education. It is often the case that objective data collection methods are useful in identifying areas of focus for subsequent in depth subjective studies. This approach reflects the findings of early research in the field of CBL evaluation which relied heavily on scientific experimental methods borrowed from other domains (Kulik and Kulik, 1991).

An Empirical Trial of the Effectiveness Model

The evaluation model described above has been applied to components of a CBL system currently being developed under TLTP (Teaching and Learning Technology Program). The CLASS (Courseware for Learning and Study Skills), project aims to produce a set of generic computer based tools that promote effective learning through structured inquiry, knowledge mapping, frequent reflection and self-assessment. There are two distinct components included in the courseware, the tools themselves and a set of subject based tutorials. The tools include writing, knowledge mapping, reading, hypermedia authoring and other generic study aids. The tutorials are designed to provide students with real tasks that demonstrate and require use of the generic tools in different subject areas. The implicit intention is to develop cognitive and metacognitive skill, in the forms of knowledge processing, organizing, critical thinking and executive techniques, that will be helpful in all areas of study. The underlying assumption that generic skills for learning do exist and can be taught is supported by e.g. Nisbet (1993).

Evaluating an innovation

The evolution of an effective evaluation strategy was considered crucial to the success of the finished product. The areas of learning addressed by CLASS courseware are not scientific in nature, nor are they currently (or easily) taught and measured. Consequently there are few existing guidelines to follow, and detailed design specification relied heavily on formative evaluation data. Given the innovative nature of the objectives and the consequent importance of gathering accurate data, much effort was devoted to developing an appropriate, innovative evaluation methodology. The model is proposed as being generalizable across different domains and types of CBL systems, though at this preliminary stage, no empirical support for such a proposal is claimed.

An innovative CBL environment

The CLASS project provides an excellent example of the need for the specific and contextually relevant measures outlined in this chapter. Study of a tool-based system, which aims to offer maximum flexibility to users and facilitate a wide variety of learning styles and objectives, must examine the details of how the different components of the system are actually used, by whom and for what purposes. Implementation of a novel pedagogic approach implies the need for tailoring of evaluations to the specific product and educational context it is designed to function within. Availability of existing computer based tools which are not widely used suggests the need for further study to ascertain if the problems are inherent in the conceptual design or presentation related. The assumption that such tools have been successfully used as learning aids is accepted. This is supported by e.g. de Vries and Kommers (1993), Kommers, Mayes and Jonassen (1991), Heeren and Collis (1993), Reader and Hammond (1993). A detailed design specification with theoretical foundations for CLASS software can be found in Gunn, Granum and McAleese, (1993).

Demonstrating the need for evaluative research

The innovative learning environment in focus underlined the need for an open-ended, research-based methodology where unpredictable results are not ignored. A classical experimental researcher set out with a fixed hypothesis which would either be proved or disproved. Any significant data arising from a study would normally be ignored if considered out with the scope of the tightly controlled investigation. One CLASS study revealed such unexpected results in the form of positive expert and user attitudes towards what was initially designed as a throw-away prototype. The prototype was developed to provide an interface level and guided introductory exercise to using the computer-based concept mapping tool, with the main objective of evaluating usability aspects. The outcome of the evaluation suggested that the prototype should be further developed as an introductory tutorial as both users and experts found it a useful means of developing aspects of study skills. Suggestions were made for additions and improvements to the material and the way it should be presented. Had recognition of significant data been restricted to that relating to the main purpose of the study, i.e. usability and functionality of the concept mapping tool, these significant findings would have been missed.

CLASS Report

In context of the CLASS software environment and its stated objectives, initial evidence supports the underlying assumptions, though further testing will be conducted to support the following claims :

- the generic 'knowledge processing' tools approach detailed in the CLASS specification succeeds in demonstrating and promoting the ability to transfer skills across contexts and subject domains, as in Salomon & Globerstone (1987);
- the pre-constructivist and constructivist instructional strategies adopted for development of the introductory and tutorial elements are properly implemented and successfully achieve the specified learning outcomes;
- generic knowledge processing tools such as those developed are really useful across a wide variety of subject domains.

Conclusions

The focus of suitable methods for evaluating CBL has definitely moved away from those defined by the classical experimental approach. Such methods have proved inadequate to the requirements of developers of innovative CBL programs. The need for a novel approach has become increasingly apparent and recent research has already provided the beginnings of a framework for effective evaluation. However, many studies have stopped at the level of measuring what is easily measured e.g. usability, or simply tried to make comparisons of unlike systems. One contemporary need is for a definition of quality assurance which will remove the possibility of aspects of poor software design acting as confounding variables. The model outlined in this chapter suggests an approach to design and evaluation that addresses many of the problems encountered with traditionally adopted methods. One specific application of the model provides initial support for its relevance and usefulness. It is now necessary for the model to be applied to other types of CBL systems in different domains to empirically assess the degree of generality it offers.

References

Barker, P. and King. T. (1993). Evaluating interactive multimedia courseware, *Computer Education*, **21**(4) 307–19.

Bates, T. (1981). Towards a better research framework for evaluating the effectiveness of educational media. *British Journal of Educational Technology*, **12**(3), 215–33.

Battaglini, D.J. and Schenkat, R.J. (1987). *Fostering Cognitive Development in College Students : The Perry and Toulmin Models*, ERIC Digest ED284272.

Cronbach, L.J. and Snow, R.E. (1977). *Aptitudes and Instructional Methods*, John Wiley & Sons, London.

Dede, C., Fontana, L. and White, C. (1993). Multimedia, constructivism and higher order thinking skills. In H. Maurer (ed.) *Ed Media Proceedings*.

de Vries, S. and Kommers, P. (1993). Concept mapping as a mind tool for exploratory learning. In H. Maurer (ed.) *Proceedings of Ed Media '93*. AACE Publications.

Draper, S. et al. (1994). *Observing and Measuring the Performance of Educational Technology*, Glasgow University TILT Project Report.

Feldman, T. (1991). *Multimedia in the 1990s*, British National Library Research Fund Report 54.

Gunn, C., Granum, G. and McAleese, R. (1993). *Concept Mapping Tool Evaluation Study*, CLASS Internal Report, ICBL, Heriot-Watt University.

Heeren, E. and Collis, B. (1993). Design considerations for telecommunications - supported cooperative learning environments : concept mapping as a telecooperation support tool, *Journal of Multimedia and Hypermedia*, **4**(2), 107–27.

Hodges, M.E. and Sasnett, R.M. (1992). *Multimedia Computing : Case Studies from the MIT Athena Project*, Addison-Wesley.

Hulley, A.J., Holland, C.A. and Ward, P.S. (1993). *An Evaluation of Comprehension and Memory for Information Presented in a Book or in a Computer Based Hypermedia System*, University of Leeds Psychology Department.

Jonassen, D.H. (1993). The future of hypermedia based learning environments : problems, prospects and entailments. In H. Maurer (ed.) *Ed Media Proceedings*. AACE Publications.

Keller, J. (1993). Motivational design of instruction. In C.M. Reigeluth (ed.) *Instructional Design Theories and Models*, Lawrence Erlbaum Associates.

Kintsch, W. (1974). *The Representation of Meaning in Memory*, Lawrence Erlbaum Associates.

Kommers, P.A.M., Jonassen, D.H. and Mayes, J.T. (eds) (1991). *Cognitive Tools for Learning*. Springer-Verlag.

Kulik, C. and Kulik, J. (1986). *Effectiveness of computer based education in colleges*, AEDS Journal, 19, 81–108.

Kulik, C. and Kulik, J. (1991). Effectiveness of computer based instruction : an updated analysis. *Computers in Human Behaviour,* **7**(1–2), 75–95.

Laurillard, D. (1993). *Rethinking University Teaching, a Framework for the Effective Use of Educational Technology.* Routledge.

McAleese, R. and Gunn, C. (1994). *Assessing Motivation in Courseware.* Workshop paper and Assessment Instrument, Heriot-Watt University.

McLeod, M. (1992). *An Introduction to Usability Evaluation.* National Physical Laboratory.

Mark, M.A. and Greer, J.E. (1993). *Evaluation Methodologies for Intelligent Tutoring Systems,* Aries Laboratory, University of Saskatchewan.

Marton, F. (1981). Phenomenography – describing conceptions of the world around us. *Instructional Science,* **10**, 177–200, Elsevier.

Marton, F., Hounsell, D. and Entwistle, N. (1984). *The Experience of Learning.* Scottish Academic Press.

Marton, F. and Säljö, R. (1976). On qualitative differences in learning: outcome and process. *British Journal of Educational Psychology,* **46**(4–11).

Nisbet, J. (1993). The thinking curriculum. *Educational Psychology,* **13**(3 and 4), 281–90.

Nix, D. and Spiro, R. (1990). *Cognition, Education and Multimedia. Exploring Ideas in High Technology.* Lawrence Erlbaum Associates.

Paivio,A. (1990). *Mental Representations : A Dual Coding Approach.* Oxford University Press.

Perry, W.G. (1988). Different worlds in the same classroom. In P. Ramsden (ed.) *Improving Learning: New Perspectives.* Kogan Page, London,145–61.

Polin, L. (1990). Research Windows. *Computing Teacher,* **17**(7), 6–8.

Ramsden, P. (ed) (1988). *Improving Learning: New Perspectives.* Kogan Page Ltd, London.

Reader, W. and Hammond, N. (1993). *Computer Based Tools to Support Learning from Hypertext: Concept Mapping Tools and Beyond.* York University.

Salomon, G. and Globerstone, T. (1987). Skills may not be enough: the role of mindfulness in learning and transfer. *International Journal of Educational Research,* **11**, 623–38.

Säljö, R. (1988). Learning in educational settings : methods of inquiry. In P. Ramsden (ed.), *Improving Learning: New Perspectives.* Kogan Page, London, 32–48.

Schramm, W. (1977). *Big Media Little Media,* Sage, London.

Wertheimer, M. (1945). *Productive Thinking,* Harper, New York.

West, C.K., Farmer, J.A. and Wolff, P.M. (1991). *Instructional Design, Implications from Cognitive Science.* Allyn & Bacon.

White, B. and Horowitz, P. (1988). Computer microworlds and conceptual change: a new approach to science education. In P. Ramsden (ed.), *Improving Learning: New Perspectives.* Kogan Page, London.

14

Teaching and learning on three undergraduate courses: meeting students' perceived needs and preferences: a preliminary analysis of some of the findings of work in progress

Linda Evans and Ian Abbott (University of Warwick)

Introduction

The British Government has made explicit its intention to maintain and enhance the quality of higher education and has identified a need for greater emphasis on student needs and, in particular, on teaching quality (DES, 1991). The effect of this has been to bring to centre stage discussion about what constitutes and characterises effective teaching and how it may best be achieved (see for example, Barnett, 1992; The Committee of Scottish University Principals, 1992; Ramsden, 1992; Stubbs and Maddison, 1992).

There is no shortage of prescriptive literature identifying criteria for and characteristics of teaching which is considered effective in maximizing student learning and achievement, but the extent to which this has drawn upon pertinent research is not always made explicit.

This chapter presents preliminary analysis of some of the findings of a one-year pilot study, described below, which aims to identify and examine students' perceptions of their own learning needs and of the extent to which these are met on their degree courses. One of the main objectives of the study is to provide an empirical basis upon which prescriptions for appropriate course content and teaching may be made. The study, which is still in progress at the time of writing, constitutes an evaluation of student learning and the findings inform discussion of how student learning may be improved.

The Pilot Study : a brief outline

The findings which are presented and discussed in this paper relate to what is, effectively, only a half of the entire study being carried out. In its entirety, the research focuses on both students' and higher education lecturers' perceptions.[1] More specifically, in the present climate of expansion in higher education and the implications for staff/student ratios, and of increasing emphasis on accountability, relating to both teaching and research quality, the study seeks to identify the perceived needs, requirements and preferences of students and lecturers and to investigate the extent to which their courses and the ways in which these are delivered may be made more effective in meeting both parties' needs and

---

[1] We use the term 'lecturer' to include lecturers, senior lecturers, readers and professors

requirements and satisfying their preferences. The idea for the research emanated from our identifying a need, on the part of university lecturers, to adopt teaching methods which are cost-effective in terms of time, allowing for sufficient time to be freed up for research, but which are acceptable to students and effective in meeting their perceived needs. This influenced our sampling, and we have chosen, for this pilot study, to focus on one university with a strong research ethos and a good research record, where lecturers are likely to experience pressure to carry out research and to publish. Clearly, there is much scope for follow-up studies to make comparisons with universities which, traditionally, have stronger teaching, than research, reputations.

We feel that it is important to clarify the precise scope of study, in order to avoid unwarranted criticism. Our intention has been to investigate lecturers' and students' perceptions of the extent to which their courses are effective in meeting their respective needs and satisfying their preferences. In particular, we wished to examine the extent to which particular teaching methods are cost-effective in terms of lecturers' time , as we have explained above, and to explore the feasibility and practical implications of identifying organizational strategies which fulfil this specific interpretation of effectiveness. It is this narrow, very specific, interpretation of effectiveness that we wish to emphasize. It has never been our intention, in this study, to investigate anything beyond the extent to which individuals perceive their needs and preferences as being met. University teaching's effectiveness in terms of, for example, achieving academic success, course aims and objectives, or employment, has only featured in our research if it has been identified by research subjects. This is not because we consider such issues unimportant, but because the resources and time available for our study necessitated a narrower scope, focusing on the immediacy of predominantly pragmatic issues.

The conceptual basis of the study is that of individuals' personal needs' fulfilment as a crucial determinant of their perceptions, attitudes and behaviour. In the case of students, their perceptions of the teaching which they receive will be influenced by individual personal needs, reflecting values held and incorporating consideration of issues such as course requirements, their own expectations, future career ambitions and interpersonal relations. Some students, for example, will be assessment-driven, some will give social intercourse higher priority than studying, some may wish to strike a balance between maintaining an active social life and achieving academic success.

Similarly, in the case of university lecturers, the organizational strategies which they apply to their teaching are devised and selected with a view to fulfilling their personal, job-related needs. These needs, in turn, reflect values held and will, therefore, as with students, vary from individual to individual but they will incorporate perspectives on issues such as students' needs, course requirements, institutional/departmental requirements, career ambitions, role conflict and ambiguity. These may be constraining or enabling in terms of personal needs' fulfilment. Moreover, in relation to both lecturers and students, individuals' personal needs may not remain static but will alter as their priorities change and as different constraints present themselves, are dealt with, or are overcome.

The key to identifying university teaching which is effective in meeting both lecturers' and students' perceived needs lies in exploring the degree of congruence between the different lecturer and the different student perceptions. When the study is completed and further data analysis undertaken, it is possible that typologies may emerge, through analysis of case studies. We anticipate developing various formulae for achieving match, or appropriate compromise. For example, research-focused lecturers may need to employ teaching methods which place the onus of responsibility for studying onto students. Such methods may satisfy intrinsically -motivated students, but not those who give studying lower priority. In so far as they relate to the student perspectives half of the study, we discuss these issues in a later section of this chapter.

Arising out the conceptual framework, described above, we identified six specific research questions:

1 What are (a) students' and (b) lecturers' perceptions of students' needs, requirements and preferences in relation to their course and how effectively do they consider that these are being met/satisfied?

2 What are (a) students' and (b) lecturers' perceptions of the implications of perceived course effectiveness and what, if any, remedial measures do they suggest?

3 What range of organizational strategies in relation to their teaching do lecturers employ; (a) to what extent do these enable or constrain them in their work, and (b) how does this affect their job satisfaction and morale?

4 What degree of congruence exists between students' and lecturers' perceptions of effective teaching?

5 In relation to 1), 2), 3), and 4), what differences, if any, are identifiable between (a) subject departments, (b) the student sample, (c) the lecturer sample, and what factors account for these differences?

6 Is it possible to identify factors which contribute towards making teaching effective in meeting the needs both of students and of lecturers?

In order to address these research questions we have sought lecturers' and students' perceptions by qualitative data collection; semi-structured interviews with a sample of second year students registered on four different degree courses at one university and a sample of lecturers teaching on these courses. The findings which we present in this chapter relate to the interviews with students on three of the degree courses; LLB Law, BA English and American Literature and B.Sc Physics. Student sample sizes are:

LLB Law – 10
BA English and American Literature – 6
B.Sc Physics – 9

Sample sizes are proportional to the number of second year students registered on each course.

The Findings

Study-related needs

Our research findings have revealed basic study-related needs which, amongst our sample, are common to all students. These basic needs which we have identified are hierarchical in the sense that they form a progression, which we illustrate in Figure 1. We do not imply that the progression reflects an increase in educational value associated with the different needs, merely that it represents increasing proximity to the gaining of a degree. At this early stage in our analysis of our data we have identified five needs, each on a different level, demonstrating the cumulative, or incremental, nature of the composite picture of student learning-related needs. We consider these to be core needs, and have chosen to end our model, in the context of the issues addressed in this particular chapter, with the need to gain a degree. Clearly, though, the picture does not end there, and our students varied in the extent to which, and the clarity with which, they identified more far-reaching needs. Some failed to identify needs which went beyond gaining a degree.

Figure 1 : Draft model of students' perceived basic study-related needs

Figure 3: Study-related needs and preferences and course-related influences on their satisfaction

TO ENHANCE SELF-ESTEEM AS A STUDENT

STUDY-RELATED PREFERENCES (illustrative examples)	STUDY-RELATED NEEDS	COURSE-RELATED INFLUENCES ON THE SATISFACTION OF STUDY-RELATED NEEDS AND PREFERENCES (illustrative examples)
to gain a class 1 degree / to feel 'well educated' / to be well equipped for a specific job or activity	To gain a degree	course content/assessment requirements / availability and quality of tutorial advice / departmental structure and coherence / inter-departmental structure and coherence
to satisfy minimum course requirements / to gain high marks / to apply own high standards (e.g. perfectionism) / to be interested / to enjoy the work	To successfully complete course assessment	course content/assessment requirements / availability and quality of tutorial help with preparation / availability and quality of feedback on progress / availability of resources / quality of resources
to contribute own ideas / to be able to seek approval/verification / to be interested / to understand / to be challenged / to avoid involvement in oral exchanges of information	To utilise knowledge, skills, experience in their participation in course components	course content/assessment requirements / lecturers' availability/approachability / teaching group sizes / lecture/seminar structure / quality of help with preparation
to be interested / to participate actively / to be able to seek clarification / to understand / to be able to apply / to be challenged	To acquire specific knowledge, skills, experience	course content / availability of lecturers, lab. demonstrators, technicians, etc... / teaching group sizes / lecture/seminar structure / availability of resources
to be interested / to participate actively / to be able to seek clarification / to understand	To receive appropriate information	lecturers' knowledge and expertise / lecturers' availability/approachability / lecture structure / lecture delivery / availability of resources

Figure 1: Draft model of students' perceived study-related needs

Figure 2: Study-related needs and associated study-related preferences

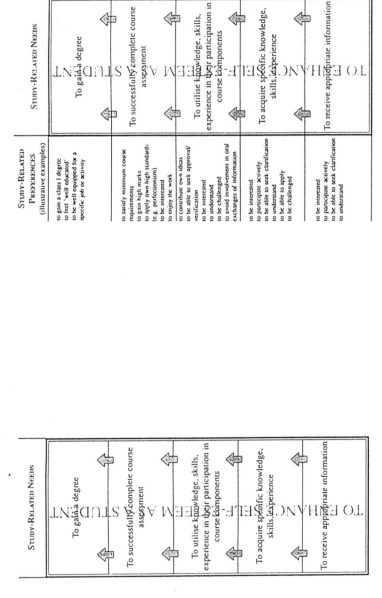

Figure 1: Draft model of students' perceived basic study-related needs

STUDY-RELATED NEEDS

TO ENHANCE SELF-ESTEEM AS A STUDENT

- To gain a degree
- To successfully complete course assessment
- To utilise knowledge, skills, experience in their participation in course components
- To acquire specific knowledge, skills, experience
- To receive appropriate information

Figure 2: Study-related needs and associated study-related preferences

STUDY-RELATED PREFERENCES (illustrative examples)	STUDY-RELATED NEEDS
to gain a class 1 degree to feel 'well educated' to be well equipped for a specific job or activity	To gain a degree
to satisfy minimum course requirements to gain high marks to apply own high standards (e.g. perfectionism) to be interested to enjoy the work	To successfully complete course assessment
to contribute own ideas to be able to seek approval/ verification to be interested to understand to be challenged to avoid involvement in oral exchanges of information	To utilise knowledge, skills, experience in their participation in course components
to be interested to participate actively to be able to seek clarification to understand to be able to apply to be challenged	To acquire specific knowledge, skills, experience
to be interested to participate actively to be able to seek clarification to understand	To receive appropriate information

TO ENHANCE SELF-ESTEEM AS A STUDENT

At this rudimentary stage in its development, our model of students' perceived study-related needs identifies the need to receive appropriate information as the most basic of the five, and at the first level, progressively leading to the second-level need to acquire specific knowledge, skills and experience; the third-level need to utilize knowledge, skills and experience in the participation in course components; the fourth-level need to successfully complete course assessment, and the fifth-level need to gain a degree. Throughout all of these needs we have identified a pervasive need to enhance self-esteem as a student. We emphasize, however, that this model, being based on preliminary data analysis, constitutes a first draft only and may be modified in the light of further analysis.

Study-related preferences

Supplementing students' study-related needs are study-related preferences, which, while they are related to needs, are distinct from them in that they reflect what students would, ideally, like, but which, unlike needs, are not perceived as absolute necessities. Another distinction is that preferences vary from individual to individual, whereas all of the core needs which we have identified above are common to all of our students. We have been able to associate specific preferences with specific levels of needs, and illustrate this in Figure 2. As Figure 2 indicates, some preferences may be applicable to more than one level of need. It should also be noted that the preferences which we list represent only an illustrative sample and that, since they do not all apply to all students, some of the preferences listed within one level may be mutually exclusive or contradictory.

Figure 2 : Study-related needs and associated study-related preferences

Satisfying needs and preferences

To varying degrees, aspect of different course elements; content, organization, delivery and resources, were identified by our students as being influential upon the extent to which their study-related needs and preferences were being met, or satisfied. Specific factors relate to specific needs and preferences, though not necessarily exclusively to one level, and we provide illustrative examples in Figure 3. We have, in this chapter, confined our analysis to involving only course-related factors, although, clearly, there are other kinds of factors, relating, for example, to students' personal circumstances and personality traits, which would also influence the extent to which study-related needs and preferences are satisfied.

Figure 3 : Study-related needs and preferences and course-related influences on their satisfaction

Illustrating the model: students talking

In this section we present examples from the qualitative research evidence upon which we have based our draft model. These examples will serve both to elucidate how we were able to draw out commonalties and identify the patterns and generalisations which underpin the model, and to illustrate its applicability.

Study-related Needs

Particularly noticeable was the universal identification, amongst our students, of the basic need for pertinent information. Some students identified this need more explicitly than did others, but reference to it was included, sometimes repeatedly, in some form or other, in all students' interviews. It was clear that the need for information was, fundamentally, assessment-driven:

> The bottom line has got to be the information because, at the end of the day, that's what you're going to be tested on. (Law student)

> The whole purpose of going to lecturers is to get information, which you need to pass the exam. (Physics student)

> You need a solid basis from the course to do the exam and do the course work well. (Law student)

> I just try to have a full set of notes so that, when it comes to the exam, I've got something to revise from. (Physics student)

Some students' comments illustrate how the need for information is considered so fundamental that it supersedes other needs and, in some cases, influences students' choices of which components of their courses to participate in:

> I go for the information which will help me in the exam. I don't go for the 'extras'. (Law student)

> I haven't been to any examples classes. I've got enough information for passing the exam in my lecture notes. Besides, you can buy the model answers to the examples at the end of the course. (Physics student)

While identification of the need for information was universal, there was disparity, with respect to degree subject, in the emphasis placed upon information and in the number of references to it. The need was emphasized the most by the physics students, less so by the law students, and least of all by the English and American literature students.

We suggest that this disparity emanates from differences in course design and content, which, in turn, influence assessment requirements. The physics students commented frequently on the important role, within their course, of the transmission of information:

> The purpose of lectures is merely to pass information across – simply to write down the information.

> I think a lecture should be for the lecturer to convey all the information to us.

A typical lecture is fifty minutes of lecturing and making notes on the blackboard, or using OHPs and, basically, we just take down notes and, sort of, fill in gaps if he's talking about something, but not writing it down. And you ... sort of, leave gaps for looking stuff up later in books ... occasionally there's a lecturer that likes to ask questions and does expect an answer from someone.

They're lecturing to us and we have to copy it straight down, and maybe it's difficult ... and there's no time to think about it all ... just copy it down. And unless you read it over in the next ten minutes after the lecture, then ... well, you've basically forgotten it really.

I've been to so many lectures now, on so many courses, and there's so much information to digest, I don't believe I'd remember any particular lecture.

All it is, really, is working through methods, theories ... and lecturers will do that on the board at the front, and it's just, sort of, copied into notebooks and, depending on the lecturer – some will just, sort of, stand at the front and write out boards and boards full of notes and stuff that no one, at the time, really understands ...

Indeed, one physics student suggested that, because of what he perceived as the course's emphasis on rote learning and regurgitation of information, at the expense of understanding and application, it would be conceivable for non-physics specialists to pass a physics examination, having digested the appropriate information.

Relevant experience, understanding, knowledge and application evidently featured much more prominently in the other two courses and this was reflected by the needs identified, explicitly and implicitly, by students on these courses:

We are going to be Lawyers – most of us – well, personally, I will. And I need to step into someone else's shoes and see the argument from their point of view, for example. (Law student)

What I need, on the academic level, is an overview of literature, focusing on particular areas, as with the American course, knowing what American literature is, knowing what poetry is, in another sense, and how history fits into it ... er, and getting some form of critical experience. (English and American literature student)

It's not enough to just work and to get it from books. You can't get by with that. You've got to have the thing that makes – I don't know ... the empathy with English, or something. (English and American literature student)

I think if you have done the work and you go to the seminars, the seminars are a lot more valuable because you're interacting with the lecturer that's just previously been lecturing at you, and it just helps you understand so much better and you can just bring up your queries and everything. I think we would run into great problems if we didn't have seminars. (Law student)

The lecturers tend to take it in turns ... and have different ideas, and contradict each other. But, I mean, as long as you've got your head screwed on, you can – you learn, by the second year, you learn to just follow your own ideas and other people's ideas are either interesting, or they're not. But you don't really base your ideas on theirs, by the second year ... It's quite interesting, seeing both sides of the input. Also, we're encouraged to look at criticism, which is also conflicting opinions, and you learn to just pick out the best bits of each one, and make it your own ... At school we were spoon-fed opinions on literature. We were told what to think. And when I came here in the first year I was, kind of, waiting for an opinion to write down and we were given, maybe, two or three, maybe one. And, for the first six months, I was just completely baffled ... and then I started to learn to develop my own opinions. (English and American literature student)

The third level need in our model (see Figure 1), the need to utilize knowledge, skill and/or experience in their participation in course components, was common to all of our students, since this represents completion of course assignments and sitting examinations. For some students, however, this particular need was more acute and was manifested by their perceived need, in order to enhance their self-esteem as students, to contribute to seminar discussion. In such cases, this was quite clearly a real need which far exceeded the intensity of mere preference. Several students fell into this category, but the most extreme case was as English and American literature student:

In my American South seminar I was interested right from the beginning, and was speaking, and felt at ease speaking. But, in seminars where I find it harder to settle in, to find out what kind of things we have to know and talk about, er ... I feel that I get myself into the role of the quiet one. And it makes it such a big deal if I would speak, that everyone would think, 'Wow! She's said something after two terms' that, even if I did have something to say, by that point, I don't. I keep it to myself ... The very first American South seminar we had, the tutor went around to each person – she just asked them what their pre-conceptions were about the American South, which forced everyone to speak first of all and it, kind of, broke the ice. Also, there were third years in the group as well and I didn't know anyone and I didn't feel that ... er ... I wasn't really bothered what people thought about me saying something, because I didn't know them and I wouldn't really see them outside the seminar ... So I just said whatever came into my head ... But then, once I'd done it ... For people who are really confident and talk all the time, it sounds silly, but for people who find it so difficult to talk, ... to have said something, and everyone's listened ... and, maybe, even writing it down – is just an amazing feeling! ... At the beginning I tended to talk a lot of rubbish – and everyone did – but then, when I started really getting interested and researching on my own, then, to have an intelligent conversation about literature, in front of everybody, with the tutor, was just ... amazing!

Interviewer: Did you feel it raised your self-esteem?

Yeah, definitely! ... But, then, by the same token, when I don't speak in the other seminars, I come out feeling like a nobody ... feeling, kind of, useless ... Sometimes peoples say things. Sometimes, in a seminar where I haven't spoken and the tutor asks a question, and, in my head, I know the answer, and then my heart starts thumping and I start panicking and wait for someone else to come up with it. And then when they say it, I think, 'Well, there's nothing to it, I could've done that.' But, at the time, it's just ... panic. ... Every time I see my personal tutor I say, 'I wish I could speak. I wish I could get the guts to do it'. ... Last week only four people turned up for a seminar and I spoke for the first time. But then, this week, the other fifteen turned up and I was the quiet one again.

The five levels of study-related needs which we have identified (see Figure 1) related directly to the course requirements of degree students and, therefore, any variation in the magnitude with which students experienced specific needs is attributable to the variations of different degree course requirements, or, more accurately, to students' perceptions of their course requirements. Thus, variations in individual needs' intensity are most likely to occur between subject groups, as in the case of our students. The clearest illustration of this, in our findings, is the variation in the extent to which each of the three subject sub-samples perceived the need for appropriate information. However, with respect to the pervasive student-related self-esteem needs, variations are attributable much more to individuals' characteristics and personality traits than to subject group and course requirements, although subject-specific requirements will play some part in determining self-esteem in terms of meeting the requirements of, and behaving according to, accepted, and valued, student peer groups norms of their courses.

Study-Related Preferences

Study-related preferences relate to one or more study-related needs, as we illustrate in Figure 2, since they reflect students' preferred way(s) of attempting to meet that, or those, need(s). In Figure 2 we present an illustrative selection of the specific preferences identified by our students. In the previous section we included an English and American literature student's frank and illuminating account of how her reticence in seminars resulted in lowering her self-esteem. Following on from that evidence, in this section we illustrate the range and diversity of students' preferences in relation to different aspects of the wide issue of students' active participation in course delivery.

Physics students' discussions about their course revealed that, of all the degree courses upon which our study focuses, the physics one offered the least opportunity for student interaction in the non-practical components. Opportunities for students to engage in oral exchange would occur in what were referred to as 'examples classes' but these were reported to be so badly and infrequently attended that they were, to all intents and purposes, redundant. Most of our sub-sample of physics students reported never having attended these sessions, and knowing of no other students who attended them, during their second year, and the rest reported having attended only one or two sessions. None of the reasons given for non-attendance included reference to unwillingness to participate in oral exchange with the tutor and/or other students. One student commented that the classes are 'useful if your want to ask a question about something that you don't understand', although he admitted to having attended none of them. On the other hand, it is clear that any preferences which these physics students may have for active participation of the kind available through these classes are insufficiently strong to override the practical consideration which influenced their decisions not to attend them.

The picture that emerged of the other non-practical component of the physics degree course, the lectures, was that, for the most part, they represent didacticism which is only very occasionally, and only in some cases, interspersed with opportunities for student participation, as when lecturers ask questions of the student audience. The majority of the physics students reported preferences for such opportunities for student participation, as the following comments illustrate:

Some lecturers ask questions in the lectures, which, I think, is a better way to do it because it gets us all thinking instead of just copying down and not thinking what we're doing. ... I don't think enough of the lecturers do that, though.

The smaller classes, I find, are a lot better. There's one lecture that we had last term, and there were only about six of us in the group. That was really good because the lecturer was asking questions and individuals were answering back.

> There was one course where the guy would throw the odd question into the crowd. I preferred that, I preferred the interaction ... It makes you think about it. I enjoyed it. I just thought the questions he'd thrown, you know, you could ... you'd think about it and you could give him a valid response – if you got it right, that is.

One student, however, indicated a preference for non-participation, suggesting that the purpose of physics lectures should be simply to impart information, rather than to ask questions:

> Occasionally there's a lecturer that likes to ask questions ... but most people don't really feel able to, like, respond, even if they do know the answer, in front of so many other students in the lecture theatre. So, quite often, there's, say, a couple of minutes wasted while the lecturer's waiting for someone to come up with the answer – 'cos he knows that some one knows, but, of course, no one will say anything. I think a lecture should be for the lecturer to convey all the information to us ... question and answer sessions should be for, sort of, seminars or examples classes.

With this one exception, it seems to be the case amongst our physics students that, while they preferred lectures to involve lecturer–student interaction, on the grounds that this encouraged students to think, rather than to be passive recipients of information, they accepted that, for the most part, this would not occur. Many attributed this to the nature of the subject, making comments such as, 'I don't know how else they can do it', and suggesting that some courses within the physics degree course as a whole did not lend themselves to participation of the kind which they preferred. They accepted didacticism as, for the most part, par for the course and, based on their perceptions of the nature, content and requirements of the physics degree course, did not consider it an impediment to their meeting their study-related needs.

Both of the other two courses provided considerably more scope for student participation in seminar discussions, but the students whom we interviewed varied in their enthusiasm for participating. Some manifested a definite preference for active, rather then passive, participation. The clearest example was a law student who has ambitions to be come a barrister:

> When I come to a seminar group I've always prepared my work – I always like to prepare so I can answer questions. I'm one of these – you may have gathered – quite a loud mouth in seminar groups. I tend to take over sometimes. I just, you know, run rampant with my mouth. (Law student)

Other students reported feeling comfortable contributing to seminar discussions, but several others commented on how intimidatory seminars could be:

> You have to have a lot of nerve, in some seminars, to say anything. (Law students)

> I think it's variable, depending on who's in the group and how you interact with each other, if you're going to ... if you've got one shy person in a group of people who are very confident, then you, personally, aren't going to get much out of it. You can scribble down everything that everybody else says, but you don't necessarily understand it. And that's

where I put myself. But, in other seminars, where I feel more comfortable with people, you're prepared to talk and so you get more out of it ... When I'm put on the spot and have to argue the case for something, I fall to pieces and can't do it. ... The facilities are all there for me. The seminars could work. It's just – you're your own worst enemy. (English and American literature student)

Unlike the physics students, the law and the English and American literature students accepted student active participation as a feature of their courses and they all valued the discursive-oriented activities as integral to their education. Amongst the law students, oral exchanges were regarded as useful vocational training for those who intended to practise law and, in particular, to become barristers. Amongst English and American literature students, exchanging views was considered valuable preparation for undertaking literary criticism. Nevertheless, students' preferences in relation to their own involvement varied quite considerably. A particularly worrying issue, though, is that, since students accepted and valued, in principle, the role which student participations plays in their courses, those who failed to participate as frequently and as effectively as they would like, suffered anxiety and damaged self-esteem. In several cases, contributing to seminar discussion was seen as a daunting challenge to be faced up to three or four times every week.

Factors influencing the satisfaction of study-related needs and preferences

In Figure 3 we list examples of the various course-related factors which our students identified as potential influences, either positive or negative, on the satisfaction of their study-related needs and preferences. In this section we elaborate, providing illustrative examples of students' perceptions of how one specific aspect of the delivery of their courses, lecture presentation, constrained or enabled them.

All of our students consider the quality of lectures; their organization, structure, delivery and content, to be important since this determined the quantity and quality of information which they received, their understanding of the information, and their interest in and enthusiasm for the topic. We asked all students to identify the features of a good lecture and those of a bad lecture. In the case of physics, there seemed to be little to distinguish the two, although students clearly favoured lectures where they were able to record as much as possible of the relevant information. They were constrained by badly structured lectures, which confused them, insufficient or unclear information being conveyed, inadequate explanation, and information presented too quickly:

Some lecturers come in, and they start lecturing, and it's all in one voice and they're just continually writing on the board – they don't stop for a break or anything, and I think some of them need to break it up a bit – maybe just stop, turn around, and explain the notes they're going to write next, rather than just write it on the board. ... A bad one comes in, writes their notes on the board, and goes out again. A good one gets the students contributing a bit. (Physics student)

Some of the lectures – the lecturers like to explain things to you, and some of them – they don't really explain it and, basically, you're just copying down what's on the board, and just hoping you can understand it when you come to read it through. Whereas some lecturers will actually take time to explain things to you, so you can actually understand it.

Some of them will speak too quickly and rush past all the important points. (Physics student)

The lecturer, he tends to ... well, last week, for instance, there was a time when he couldn't get anything right at all. There were about three or four equations which he tried to do, and he couldn't – he just knew the final answer. He had an off day! (laughs). And, sometimes, he starts drawing a circuit diagram on the board, and then we're drawing it in our notes reasonably large ... and there's so much information that he keeps putting in, and in ... and in ... and, eventually, his writing gets so small that it's only about an inch high on the board, and the board's quite a long way away, so, sometimes it's hard to read. (Physics student)

What makes a good lecture? ... a clear structure ... progression. (Physics student)

Some lecturers are better in the way that they tell you, sort of, side notes to keep you interested ... sort of, tell you applications of the theory they're working through. (Physics student)

I think it depends very much on the lecturer's style. For example, some subjects that I thought I'd take as an option, 'cos they'd be interesting, have been made, in my opinion, quite boring by the way they're presented by the lecturer, whereas something else that, maybe, hasn't interested me as much is made much more interesting by the way the lecturer presents it ... It's a bit picky, probably, but it's sometimes just got to do with little habits the lecturer's got ... like, er, some don't seem to be able to write down a whole sentence without stopping half-way through it to explain something, whereas I'd rather they'd, like, finish the sentence and then explain it ... I don't really know what the difference is between whether the lecturer makes it interesting or boring. It's just their own, sort of, personal style, I think. (Physics student)

The law students' assessment of the quality of their lectures were also based upon considerations such as structure, coherence, clarity and delivery style:

One person who lectures, he knows what he's talking about ... He can start off saying one thing, and you're dutifully writing it down, and listening, and he'll break off, mid-sentence, or reverse himself, or go to another point, and then come back to the bit's he's done. So you're all over the page, and you've arrows showing how this bit goes here, and this bit, there ... and, like, it's just silly! And everyone ... people just look at each other, throw down their pens and just sit back, and, like, just try and take in what he's saying, rather than waste time writing it down. Because, if they write it down they know that it's just going to go over their head because they're just spending so much time trying to concentrate on putting the right stuff in the right place. And, in the end, things just go from bad to worse and you end up just sitting there, and then you mind wanders and then it's all over for the day.... And there are two or three who are like that ... The better lecturers are the ones who give out lecture sheets, just outlining what they're going to do in that lecture. Because, then, it's very easy to follow and, also, they're not going to lose themselves, because they can see what they're supposed to be talking about and you get the point. (Law student)

[The lecturer] is up there in the clouds somewhere! And although everything he's saying is right, everything he's saying is fabulous ... for somebody who knows very little about the subject ... and trying to make notes is almost impossible! I mean, I've been to so many of his lectures and I've just started my notes, and I've put my pen down half-way through and just ... given up. (Law student)

Lectures are really good – some of them are **really** good. Some of the lecturers give us guidelines. They say, you know, 'This is the structure I'm following during the lecture'. So, you know, it's easy to follow the lecture and that gives us time to take some notes.... But some of the lecturers, because of the amount of work they have to cover, they're very quick during the lecture – they don't even give any structure or anything – and they expect you to sit down there and to understand what they're talking about and take down some notes, which is quite difficult, in a way. .... Now, coming from Cyprus into this system, it took me quite a long time to get used to taking notes during the lecturers without someone giving me guidelines. I've got used to it, but I still find some lectures very difficult to follow. ... It doesn't matter how hard it is – if he's structured and if he's expressing himself well and then you can understand what he's talking about – that's it. It doesn't have to be easy. And I think that's what makes a good lecture. (Law student)

I think the constitutional and administrative law course is very good. ... Both lecturers give very structured lectures. You often get a hand-out at the beginning so you follow it through and you know what's happening. (Law student)

I think it's very good when they give you outlays, and that sort of thing – they actually give you something on paper that you can work from, and some of the lecturers give you a hand-out which they'll base their lecture around. And they'll stick to it, which is very good, so you know where you're at. But you get other lecturers that'll not give you anything. They'll start the lecture – sometimes they won't even say what they're talking about and will just go straight into it. And that's very difficult, especially for revision, to come back to it and say, 'Oh, yes, this is about this.' (Law students)

There's a lot of the fact that they know what they're talking about and sometimes it's difficult for them to know what level everybody's at. I mean, there are people in the group who understand everything, and there's people like me who'll only understand half of it. (Law student)

I like it when they give you a printed sheet and it's very carefully structured – I think that's really important. Because I don't think there's any point in just scribbling down everything they say, I think there needs to be a structure. (Law student)

As these examples of students' comments clearly illustrate, there are many commonalties between physics students' and law students' perceptions of good and bad lectures. In both groups' cases, the key feature of a good lecture is evidently the transmission of appropriate (in terms of both quality and quantity) information in a way which effectively allows that information to be transferred from lecturer to students. What students perceived as effective transference of information generally constituted their having full, accurate, written records of it. The transfer process was, therefore, most effective, in the opinion of students, if sufficient time were allowed for copious note-taking during lectures, and/or if lecture handouts were provided. On these issues, physics and law students were, generally, in agreement. Our evidence suggests, though, a slight distinction, **in general**, between the sub-samples' preferences for rather more explicatory-oriented lectures. There seems to be a tendency amongst our physics students to be satisfied with the effective transference of information during lectures, whereas law students tended to want the 'extra' of understanding the information which is transferred. The clearest evidence of this may be seen in some law students' accounts of how, when faced with a confusing array of information being conveyed during a lecture which lacks structure and coherence, they abandon note-taking in the interests of gaining a clearer understanding by simply listening. In contrast, physics students facing similar confusion persevere with recording, rather than trying to understand, the information. Evidently, the content and nature of their course is such that physics students perceive a greater need for information than for understanding. As many of them suggested by the comments they made, if they have records of the information they can try to understand it at a later date, when such understanding may be required. Law students, on the other hand, considered understanding to be a much more on-going process, and vital for the requirements of their course.

If law students want a little more out of lectures, in general, than do physics students, our evidence suggests that the English and American literature students want more still. A good lecture, according to these students, involves supplementary, background information which helps present a more complete picture of the topic in question; it involves various devices for developing appreciation and encouraging and sustaining interest. That lectures would convey basic information satisfactorily and that students would understand that information seemed to be taken for granted, for the most part. What makes a lecture particularly good seems to be its entertainment potential, which may take various forms:

A good lecture is where the lecturer gives you the background of ... er, the novel, or the poet, or whatever, and ... er, maybe some historical context and ... er, tells you what happens in it, or some of the major themes. ... A bad one is where he just tells you what different people have thought of the novel. (English and American literature student)

Some lecturers, what they write is very good – very interesting – but the way they deliver it! I mean, there's one who sits at a desk, looking down, reading off a sheet of paper, and it just doesn't hold your attention after ten minutes. There was a lecturer we had in the first year, who was a really funny guy. He acted out parts of the stories himself and was, kind of, a one-man theatre company. And he had jokes, and stories from his own experience, but, then, he always brought it back to work at the end of the day. He taught mediaeval studies and he turned it round into a modern perspective, and then you felt you'd really learned something at the end of it. Some perform in the lecture, and hold your interest, and others are just reading off a sheet ... like, they're delivering a paper – and that's a lecture! (English and American literature student)

Humour is always something to wake everybody up. You can make the material interesting ... you can pick out some funny bits ... er, some tutors include biographical details that get you interested. Some lecturers, as well, set out at the beginning what they're going to go through, so you've got a set of points you can follow and know what direction you're going in. The worst kind of lectures are where there's so much material squashed in, you're not really given the time to think about each one. Some lecturers, as well, forget that you haven't read as much as they have, and they draw examples and parallels from books that aren't on the course, and they assume you're widely read, when ... I mean, at 20, you can't have read as much as a 50 year old, and so you tend to lose the point of what they were saying. (English and American literature student)

Despite the slight variations, which we have illustrated above, between the three sub-samples' general assessments of what makes their courses' lectures helpful or unhelpful, our evidence revealed several specific features which were considered by all our students to contribute towards meeting many of their perceived study-related needs and satisfying many of their preferences. Based on this evidence we were able to identify the key components of a student-satisfying lecture as: structure, coherence, explication, relevance and clarity. The basic requirement is that a lecture should convey pertinent information effectively. After this comes a supplementary requirement that it increases students' understanding and, added to this, a third; that it interests students.

Improving Student Learning by Accommodating Their Needs and Preferences

The symposium at which this chapter was presented as a paper focused on improving student learning. Our study, in part, is about contributing towards meeting students' study-related needs and preferences, which is not necessarily the same as improving their learning. We are well aware of, and accept, the notion that students, not least because they are undergoing learning processes, are not always the best judges of what will improve their learning. Improving student learning involves a much more far-reaching, and wider, vision than that which sees immediate, day-to-day issues as those which require attention, and students themselves seldom have such a vision. Nevertheless, it is not unreasonable to establish a positive link between meeting study-related needs and preferences and improving student learning. We suggest that accommodating their needs and preferences is likely to reduce students' dissatisfaction, which will lead to increased satisfaction with their courses and, in turn, improve learning. We are aware that this is a rather simplistic reasoning which neglects consideration of the possibility that, if needs are met, they are replaced by other, generally higher order, needs, so that dissatisfaction is not removed, or reduced, it is simply displaced. We are also aware that careful analysis of the concept of learning, and definition of the term, ideally need to be undertaken if learning is to be linked with, or distinguished from, studying, or academic achievement, for example. Putting these issues, aside, however, as being beyond the scope of this chapter, we believe that the findings presented provide a valuable source of information which includes consideration of how the delivery of courses may take account of factors which influence student learning, by addressing and accommodating their needs and preferences.

We have identified a range of our students' perceived study-related needs and preferences and course-related factors which, to varying degrees, facilitate or impede satisfaction of these needs and preferences. These are listed in Figure 3. In this last section of our chapter we focus more sharply on consideration of some of the practicalities involved in accommodating one specific study-related need and/or preference; that of students' needs/preferences in relation to their own active participation in group discussions. This has been given particular attention in previous sections. Based on our students' comments about what they find helpful or unhelpful, we suggest organizational strategies which are likely to accommodate these needs and preferences.

The issue of students' participation in group discussions is not an easy one to tackle, in practical terms. Put simply, some students are perfectly comfortable expressing their views to an audience of any size within the limits of normal seminar group size, and some are not. Indeed, some even seem to thrive on the experience, as in the case of our law student who admitted to 'running rampant' with his mouth. Many students, however, are uncomfortable speaking in front of groups of more than about four or five, and a few even experience severe symptoms of stress at the prospect of having to speak. In many cases, students' anxiety is increased, and the problem exacerbated, by their actually **wanting** to speak, but finding themselves incapable of it.

By those students who find speaking out in groups traumatic, either, or both, of two factors were identified as significant; group size and group composition. Group composition involves factors such as level of friendship, or acquaintance, with other group members, the inclusion of individuals perceived as intimidating, the inclusion of particularly loquacious individuals, and gender balance. Group size is a more straightforward issue; it simply involves students' having a threshold of acceptability (which may vary subject to other factors, such as group composition) in relation to how many others they are prepared to speak out in front of.

Most of our students, irrespective of whether they describe themselves as reticent or loquacious, felt group sizes should be reduced, to allow for greater student–tutor interaction. Clearly, though, this is not a viable proposition. But what can be done, within teaching groups which are larger than most students would, ideally, like, is to incorporate facilities for allowing small group discussions to occur. The most obvious suggestion is a strategy which is probably already quite widely used; organizing discussion groups of three or four, initially, and then a plenary session where the outcomes of initial discussions may be reported. There are several variations to this strategy, all of which provide reticent students with the opportunity to participate in group discussions which are less intimidating than more conventially-run seminars, where discussion is aimed at the whole group. Yet our students' comments provide clear evidence that, certainly in **their** departments, less conventional ways of organising seminars were not particularly widely used in the university upon which our research focused.

But just how far towards meeting students' different preferences and needs do the less conventional organizational strategies go? As we have illustrated in the extracts from transcripts of interviews with students, in the case of some particularly reticent students, high self-esteem may be dependent upon their capacity for speaking articulately in front of a fairly large group of their peers, and in front of, or to, the seminar tutor. It is quite possible that both of these ideals may never be realized if such students are confined to small group discussion. Even if students find themselves able to participate in groups of three and four, they still may be unable to take the next step, that of speaking in front of the entire seminar group, which is necessary if they are to avoid, as one of our students commented, 'feeling a nobody'.

If university lecturers are to take seriously the business of trying to raise teaching quality and of meeting students' needs and satisfying their preferences – and we are aware that many do not take it seriously – then it is important that they do not neglect those needs which are less obvious because they may be obscured by students' successes in course assessment tasks. What is needed, if students are to develop in areas which are essential to their realizing their potential; areas such as communication skills and building up self-confidence, is a greater concerted effort on the part of those who teach them to provide facilities for such development to occur. We suggest a few specific strategies for organizing seminars, which aim to provide opportunities for students to develop confidence in communicating their views. These strategies are based upon the premise that the fundamental reason why students are reluctant to speak out in front of others is that they fear disapproval or contradiction. They are frightened of appearing stupid. Most of the strategies therefore incorporate facilities for providing peer, or tutor, approval:

- Build into the seminar structure a system of constructive peer evaluation. Establish guidelines which will ensure that this evaluation always includes praise. For example, short prepared presentations from students, either individually or in groups, could be followed by peer evaluation which must follow the format: **praise, question, polish**. Refer to this as PQ. evaluation.[2]
- Where students are discussing in small groups, the tutor could take on an active role of joining in, or listening in on some groups, purposefully praising valuable contributions from students who are normally reticent in large group discussions.
- In plenary sessions, make examples of valuable contributions which quieter students made in earlier small group discussions.
- Build in a structure for ensuring that students are not confined to discussing in one small group. For example, ten minutes' discussion in groups of 3 and 4 could be followed by rearrangement into different groups of 3 and 4, with each student reporting the main points of the first discussion to members of their second group. This way, students interact with a wider range of people.
- Allow opportunities, from time to time, for one-to-one discussions between students and tutor. Either arrange individual tutorials to replace seminars, or conduct a few minutes' discussion with individuals, during seminars, when the rest of the group are engaged on other tasks.

These practical suggestions are examples of ways in which lecturers can undertake to meet the needs and preferences of students in one specific area. The findings which we have presented in this chapter identify, in more general terms, other areas of student needs and preferences, and students' perceptions of the extent to which these are being accommodated within their courses. The draft model which we present (see Figures 1, 2 and 3) provides a blueprint for developing strategies within course design, organization, delivery and resourcing, which may contribute towards improving student learning by accommodating some of the study-related needs and preferences identified. What is now required is for university teaching to continue to investigate and incorporate a variety of methods which will improve student learning. At one level this is the responsibility of individual lecturers but, ultimately, successful implementation of new approaches to student learning will depend upon the support and co-operation of senior management within higher education.

---

[2]*We wish to extend our thanks to Joyce Simpson, University of Northern Iowa, who passed on to us the idea of the PQP guidelines for student peer evaluation.*

References

Barnett, R. (1992). The idea of quality: voicing the educational. *Higher Education Quarterly*, **46**(1), Winter.

Committee of Scottish University Principals (1992). *Teaching and Learning in an Expanding Higher Education System*, Edinburgh, CSUP.

Department of Education and Science (1991). *Higher Education: A New Framework*,. London, HMSO.

Ramsden, P. (1992). *Learning to Teach in Higher Education*. London, Routledge.

Stubbs and Maddison (1991). Improving teaching quality in Higher Education. *Education Today*, **41**(1).

15 Using a student experience questionnaire for improving teaching and learning

R. D. Gregory, Dr G. Harland and L. Thorley (University of Hertfordshire)

Synopsis

This chapter describes the use made of a Student Experience Questionnaire in the School of Engineering at the University of Hertfordshire over the past two years in attempting to improve the quality of the student educational experience. The results of a survey conducted in 1993, already reported, and a new 1994 survey are compared. The process of investigation of the results involving both students and staff is described. Conclusions are drawn on the schemes of study surveyed and the usefulness of such questionnaires in assisting to improve the student learning is discussed.

Background

This chapter describes the process which has evolved in the School of Engineering at the University of Hertfordshire in attempting to use the results from the Ramsden Student Experience Questionnaire (Ramsden, 1990) to improve the learning experience of students. The questionnaire identifies five elements of the learning experience which are scored on a scale of 1–5 (ie Good Teaching, Clear Goals and Standards, Appropriate Workload, Appropriate Assessment and Student Independence). It has been used in surveys by the school over the past two years.

The first survey was carried out in May 1993 and reported in September 1993 (Gregory et al., 1993). A number of trends were identified for further investigation and the report concluded that priority should be given to investigating the apparent high student workload.

The trends and conclusion were generally consistent with anecdotal evidence and were ·supported by the students. The survey results were also used by each Scheme Tutor as part of their annual monitoring and evaluation report to the School Academic Committee. The report on the questionnaire results was considered in the autumn 1993 term and the School Academic Committee agreed that:

1 the survey should be repeated in the spring term of 1994;

2 the reasons for the poor scores for Appropriate Workload should be investigated by the Scheme Tutors;

3 the results and recommendations for further action should be reported back;

4 the Scheme Committees should consider the implications of all the results and discussions.

The second survey was carried out at a similar time of the year as the first; there were more schemes involved and the whole process took longer (i.e. most of the 1994 spring term). The survey this time covered the majority of the schemes of study in the school; more than in the first exercise. In the 1994 survey a total of 917 replies were received from 36 'cohorts' (eg first-year Civil Engineering BEng) representing a total 1512 students.

Joint Student–Staff Seminar

Student involvement is seen as a key to real improvements in teaching and learning. The students are currently involved in School Committees through elected representatives for each year of each scheme. These representatives serve on Scheme Committees and form the School Student Council. The Chair of the Council works closely with the Dean of School and the School's Learning Development Tutor. The findings of the 1993 questionnaire and the recommendations of the School Academic Committee were discussed by the Scheme Committees and the School Council. It was agreed to involve the students in the further investigation by organizing a joint student–staff seminar.

The seminar was conducted in two parts. First the students and staff met separately for a discussion; second the students presented the result of their discussions. The students were asked to prepare a presentation based on a framework for discussion which included comments on the results of the questionnaire, comments on the strengths and weaknesses of their overall learning experience and suggestions for improvement.

Twenty student representatives attended the first part of the seminar and five went on to present their conclusions to the staff. The students responded with a confirmation that high workload was a significant problem and needed to be addressed. They identified the major problem not as being too much content but that scheduling and planning was either not carried out or not adhered to by staff.

Other issues of a more detailed nature were reported back to the staff or relevant Scheme Committees for action. The students had two other major concerns; the poor quality of a minority of lectures and the feeling that consultations with students were not being followed through by actions. It was agreed that these two points could be dealt with outside the meeting in different ways; the former by the new university-wide questionnaire which asked students opinions of individual lecturers which is then processed through the staff self-appraisal system; the latter by the Dean of School attending the next meeting the School Council and explaining the actions to be taken. This would be supported by further consultations with students to monitor the changes resulting from the seminar.

The seminar then focused on the issue of student workload. The student presentation was followed by a joint discussion in which staff gave various reasons for the low scores for Appropriate Workload. These included:

- students with lower entry grades taking longer to do the work;
- the quantity of material in the courses;
- group work demanding more time than individual work;
- the 'bunching' of coursework at certain times of the year;
- the lack of clarity in the standard required for high marks for coursework;
- insufficient feedback to staff on how long students are spending on coursework.

The meeting agreed that more information on student workload was required and that many of the issues raised needed to be addressed in detail by Scheme Committees. It was also agreed that all undergraduate Scheme Tutors should obtain more evidence from staff and students concerning the extent to which staff plan the coursework loading (timing and number of hours for completion), the schedules produced and how well they are both kept to.

Scheme Tutors' Investigations

Results for the 1994 survey were not available at the time of the student – staff seminar or in time for the Scheme Tutors' investigations. They will, however, be used as part of the next monitoring and evaluation reports to the Academic Committee. The Scheme Tutors each produced a single-page report based on their investigations. A number of issues were identified.

- There are large variations in the extent and practice of scheduling and planning.
- Good practice was evident which could be extended.
- Scheme Tutors often experience considerable difficulty in obtaining the required information from some staff and ensuring that schedules and plans are kept to.
- Evidence from student discussions indicated that the Appropriate Workload scores are sensitive to the time in the course when the survey takes place.
- Staff reported students spending too much time on coursework and identified the need for more coaching and information on how students should use their time effectively.
- Assessment procedures and practice need to reflect the time expected to be spent on a piece of coursework more accurately.

Two Schemes of study were identified as already making progress in addressing many of the above issues by using the concept of 'student learning hours'. A standard proforma is used for course planning which requires the specification of topics expected to be taught each week and the exercises, projects and tests that are to be set with all relevant dates. The 'student learning hours' are estimated and quoted for their guidance. After completion of the project/exercise the students feed back to their tutors the actual time spent.

The 'learning hours' quota for the courses is derived from the university's definition of a module as 90 hours of student effort for a 'good honours student'. This is used as the average 'learning hours' per module (a student takes ten 'modules worth' of courses per year).

A final report is now being compiled for the Academic Committee which will summarize the Scheme Tutors' investigations. It will recommend that the School adopt a common policy based on the good practice in scheduling and planning described above. It will also recommend that the number of 'learning hours' per module be reviewed and brought into line with a more realistic value in the region of 120 hours per module (i.e. 1200 hours per year).

The 1994 Survey

Table 1 shows the average element scores, their range and standard deviation, the number of 'cohorts' surveyed and student numbers involved for the 1993 and the 1994 surveys. Table 1 also shows the correlation coefficients for the 1993 and 1994 scores where a direct comparison can be made (18 'cohorts'). The element scores can range between 1 and 5; a high score representing a good performance in that element. The results from Ramsden's work for engineering in Australian colleges are also included in the table for comparison (Ramsden, 1990).

Table 1: 1993 and 1994 Average element scores

Elements	Average Element Scores 1993			Average Element Scores 1994			93 vs 94	Ramsden Results (ref 1)
	average	standard deviation	maximum to maximum	average	standard deviation	maximum to maximum	correlation coefficient	average for engineering
good teaching	3.11	0.30	3.83 2.58	3.14	0.24	3.54 2.73	0.18	2.79
clear aims & standard	3.04	0.25	3.53 2.39	3.12	0.23	3.42 2.62	0.48	3.18
appropriate workload	2.62	0.44	3.24 1.80	2.55	0.41	3.06 1.71	0.57	2.86
appropriate assessment	3.13	0.18	3.65 2.57	3.06	0.17	3.46 2.83	0.24	3.05
student independence	2.50	0.27	3.15 1.79	2.50	0.24	2.94 1.98	0.43	2.56
total score	14.40	1.01	16.77 12.38	14.37	1.04	16.42 11.33	0.46	14.41
number of cohorts	36			24			18	–
number of students	1512			1230			–	
number of replies	917			756			–	–

The second survey generally supported the trends of the first. Poor scores are again seen in student workload and independence compared to other disciplines surveyed in Ramsden's work (Ramsden, 1990). The average element scores for the 1993 and the 1994 show remarkable consistency but there is less correlation between individual scores comparing 1993 to 1994 for particular 'cohorts'. The correlation coefficients for these 'cohorts', in Table 1, are in the region of 0.5 for three of the elements with Appropriate Workload being the highest at 0.57. It appears that these three individual elements have some degree of repeatability and could be used for monitoring purposes. The correlation coefficients for Student Independence and Good Teaching elements are, however, much lower and need to be treated with great caution on an individual year by year basis. The reasons for these variations in individual element scores is not known and little can be deduced from only two years of data. It appears that some elements are more sensitive than others to interference by other factors which change from year to year.

The stability of the average element scores, their agreement with Ramsden work for engineering, the difference in scores compared to disciplines such as humanities (Ramsden, 1990) and the engineering students seeming acceptance of the current quantity of material in their courses may suggest that the overall scores reflect a 'paradigm view' of engineering education. If this is true, then significant improvements would not just require minor changes in course design and management but a radical shift in the way the engineering profession perceives education. This will only be revealed by further work over a longer time scale.

Comments on the Process

It is interesting to note that the highest correlation coefficient came from the Appropriate Workload element which had the some of the lowest individual scores strongly supported by anecdotal evidence. It seems that in this element, where the feelings were stronger and more easily identified, the results were more stable. A detailed analysis of two cohorts with particularly low Appropriate Workload scores indicates that changes made, as a direct result of the survey, to assessments and scheduling appear to have contributed to improvements in these scores. This process needs, however, to continue since it has not yet made an impression on the much more reliable average element scores.

The original aim of using the questionnaire was to improve the student learning experience by providing an indication of the priority for investigation and change. The process has so far consisted of two school-wide questionnaires, a report to the Academic Committee of the school, a student-staff seminar and a detailed investigation and report on the workload issue by the Scheme Tutors. The outcomes so far have been involvement of the students in the evaluation process, a raised awareness of workload and a discussion by Scheme Tutors and Scheme Committees of the likely causes of the problem. The school has now issued standard procedures for course scheduling and planning including the specification of student workload in terms of 'learning hours'. The student representatives will be involved in monitoring the effectiveness of the changes and give feedback to the school's various committees.

The process has highlighted a number of issues in using the questionnaire as a development instrument. Change is slow and hence it is difficult to rigorously monitor since many other variables change with time. The element scores will always remain only indicative and a stimulation for investigation.

The evolving process has underlined the value and limitations of using questionnaire surveys actually to improve teaching and learning. It is easy, as happened during the discussions of these results, to take issue with the questionnaire itself and the questions used and miss the developmental aspects of the process. There are many interpretations of the same data. For example, the poor scores for final year cohorts were attributed by some staff to 'the student experience becoming worse' and by others to 'the students becoming more discerning' (i.e. success!).

Conclusions

The questionnaire has proved to be a very useful instrument in identifying overall areas of weakness which motivated further investigation. It can initiate the process of research and change which is at the heart of improvements in teaching and learning. It has resulted in significant 'awareness raising' and the formulation of procedures to improve and further monitor the situation. It is unlikely that this would have occurred on such a wide scale and action undertaken at school level without the stimulation of such a tool.

The questionnaire results appear to reflect the 'overall learning experience' of the school's students but are much less reliable when applied to individual 'cohorts'. The average element scores appear to have the potential of being sufficiently stable to identify improvements over a number of years on a school wide basis. The elements used are easily related to the teaching activity and hence of immediate relevance to practitioners. Student workload, an important element of teaching and learning, has been addressed and the process of improvement initiated and modelled. Students and staff have worked together on the problem with a mix of quantitative data, consultation, 'awareness raising' and formal directive procedures.

It is not yet clear whether the process described in this chapter will produce significant changes in teaching and learning in the engineering schemes or whether more radical changes are necessary. The problems, particularly seen with student workload and independence, may relate to the relative unpopularity of engineering schemes for undergraduate study. If true, this have important implications for scheme design and for the nature of engineering education which need to be addressed by schools/faculties and by the engineering profession and its institutions.

References

Ramsden, P. (1990). *Report to the Higher Education Performance Indicators Project on the Course Experience Questionnaire Trial* ,NSW. Centre for Technology and Social Change.

Gregory, R. D., Harland, G. and Thorley, L. (1993). Using a standard student experience questionnaire with engineering students – initial results. *Improving Students Learning Conference*, University of Warwick.

16   Learning styles and student progress

Angela Packwood and Anne Sinclair Taylor (University Of Warwick)

Introduction

The Department for Education (DFE) statistical bulletin 18/92 for August shows that 237-000 mature students and 232-000 school leavers entered United Kingdom Higher Education (HE) in 1990 (these figures exclude the Open University). The increase in mature students was 77per cent compared with 1980 figures. This implies that the student body of the future will be more heterogeneous in character due to new policies that afford entry to increasingly modularized flexible degree structures through a diversity of access routes. Institutions will therefore be faced with classes which may consist of a wide age range, diverse previous experiences and reasons for being in HE. There will also be an increase in the potential numbers of international students. By the end of the decade total student numbers should rise by over 50per cent from today's figures. This raises many issues including how institutions encompass expansion while at the same time taking account of:

- the steadily increasing staff / student ratio;
- the increasing emphasis on accountability in relation to student learning experiences;
- the acknowledgement that undergraduates who arrive straight from sixth form as well as mature entrants may not necessarily possess the skills for independent study at HE level.

The *Charter for Higher Education* (1993) published by the DFE makes the issue of accountability at HE level explicit. It engages in a market discourse urging universities and colleges to 'deliver high quality services, responding to the needs and demands of customers' (DFE, 1993, p.1). The charter specifies that students 'should receive a high standard of teaching, guidance and counselling' (DFE, 1993, p.3) and that the university should explain the teaching and learning facilities available including library, IT, and other resources (DFE, 1993, p.13). It also outlines actions students should take if they are not satisfied with the service they have received (DFE, 1993, p.18–19).

The Higher Education Funding Council for England (HEFCE), established in 1992 under the Further and Higher Education Act 1992, is required to 'Secure that provision is made for assessing the quality of education in institutions for whose activity they provide ... financial support' (Section 70 (1) (a)). This to ensure that all education which receives funding from the HEFCE is of a satisfactory quality or better. The HEFCE is committed to the principle that institutions should be judged against their own standards, i.e. the objectives they set themselves. Responsibility for enhancing and maintaining quality lies with the providers.

Policy about teaching and learning at personal, institutional, regional and national levels must take account of and reflect these major changes. Learning as a commodity is to be measured and weighed in an unprecedented way at HE level. What these documents fail to do is to analyse what is meant by learning. There is however an underlying agenda which interprets it as something which is transmitted/delivered to people rather than a process over which they themselves have responsibility. In adopting a commercial market model of learning it would be appropriate to look at what is delivered – the inputs – and what comes out at the end – the outputs. This reductionist approach fails to look qualitatively at the intervening process, i.e. the 'critical intervening activities of teaching and learning which link objectives and outcomes' (Coffield, 1994).

Teaching and learning are part of a complex and interactive system, influenced by the way the learning environment provided by an institution and its courses interacts with the individual characteristics and competencies of students. This will include teaching and learning styles, relationships between staff and students and the hidden curriculum of learning in HE. With greater competition for students and greater heterogeneity in students abilities due to expansion in HE the issue of effective learning strategies will become of increasing importance.

It is the effective and efficient support of the **learning process** which is the key to maintaining high quality. In turn this will result in the containment of costs in any successful expansion of higher education as a proportion of non-applications as well as 'wastage' within the current system is caused by failure to take sufficient account of differences in the readiness of entrants to study effectively.

There are certain distinctive features which characterize the learning process at HE level. Students are required not only to acquire an extensive technical knowledge of their subject area but also the associated skills involved in applying that knowledge within a profession or an academic discipline. This knowledge goes well beyond the acquisition of detailed factual knowledge; it involves the development of conceptual understanding and critical independent thinking about the subject matter which can only take place through active and flexible approaches to learning and teaching. This paper explores the use of learning styles as a strategy for understanding and enhancing the learning process and experience for students.

Conceptual Framework

Personal individual differences are reflected in **all** aspects of education. Learning style is the composite of characteristic cognitive, affective and physiological factors that serve as relatively stable indicators of how a learner perceives, interacts with and responds to the learning environment. Unique individual programming involves sensations and perceptions; knowledge is created through the organization and transformation of those sensations through action, most particularly, internalized thoughts.

Learning style is concerned with:

* cognition: people perceive and gain knowledge differently;
* conceptualization: people form ideas and think differently;
* affect: people feel and form values differently;
* behaviour: people act differently.

Research on style as a distinctive and characteristic trait has long been a concern of psychologists (Jung, 1921; Myers and Briggs, 1943; Allport, 1961, Myers, 1962; and Tyler, 1965); however until relatively recently it has not held much appeal for educators who have been more concerned to focus on the **content** of the learning programme and the **method** of delivery rather than the way individuals learn.

There has been increasing interest in the relevance of learning styles and their applicability in the teaching/learning situation. This interest has given rise to a number of research studies, developing a range of models of style and producing a variety of instruments for assessing learning style (Gregorc, 1982; Kolb, 1984; McCarthy, 1980; 1987; Honey and Mumford, 1986).

Our work intends to evaluate a selection of these style models of learning styles and the instruments developed from them in relation to their usefulness at HE level. We intend to develop a composite model and learning styles instrument for use in HE and also to develop and test strategies which will enable students to enhance their own learning style and to become more flexible in adapting to teaching styles which may not match their preferred style of learning.

Stage 1

This has been the pilot project for this research. Using a cohort of 84 BA (QTS) students, 42 first-year and 42 second-year, we have trialled one of the models and its learning styles questionnaire. This model was chosen because it was aimed not at school-age children, but rather at management trainees and therefore we felt would be more sophisticated in its approach and, so we hoped, would elicit a more ready response from our students.

The model upon which this instrument is based is that of the learning cycle developed by Kolb (1984) based on the work of Lewin (1936). The learning cycle is shown in Figure 1.

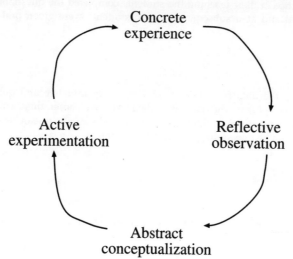

Figure 1 Learning cycle

It can be **entered** at any point but it must be followed **in sequence**. Kolb extended Lewin's work by recognising that not all individuals are equally well equipped to handle each stage of the learning cycle. Kolb developed an inventory through which it was possible to identify which individual had a preference for a particular stage of the cycle (Kolb, 1984). The model and questionnaire which we used is a further development of Kolb's work by Honey and Mumford (1986). They built on Kolb's model and inventory in order to develop their Learning Styles Questionnaire (LSQ). This is designed to access four learning styles which can be differentiated in both principle and practice. The four styles equate with the four stages in the cycle:

- Activists involve themselves fully and without bias in new experiences (Concrete experience).
- Reflectors like to stand back and ponder experiences and observe them from many different perspectives (Reflective observation).
- Theorists adapt and integrate observations into complex but logically sound theories (Abstract conceptualization).
- Pragmatists are keen on trying out ideas, theories and techniques to see if they work in practice (Active experimentation).

Data

We used the LSQ with the groups of students we taught and we also applied the cycle to the course materials and the assessment tasks. This work was **embedded** in the students' Education course. They were introduced to the importance of the theory and practice of models of learning and learning styles in the context both of their own learning **and** that of their pupils. After the theoretical introduction and discussion of how the theory could be put into practice in their teaching the students completed the questionnaires. These were then scored and at a subsequent session students were given oral and written feedback.

Analysis

We are analysing the data from two perspectives – quantitative and qualitative. The following is an excerpt from the qualitative data. We have chosen this particular session because of the issues it raised, both for the students and for us as researchers who believe that research should be done **with** people, not **on** them.

Qualitative Data

Session 19.5.94 Giving feedback on the Honey and Mumford Questionnaire

Issues surrounding the labelling and categorization of student learning styles in a university culture

University student culture is hierarchical and competitive; labels convey status. Cultural capital is predominantly linked to intellectual and academic ability. Any form of assessment taking place within this climate has the potential for presenting difficulties.

The labels which the Honey and Mumford model use – Theorist, Activist, Reflector and Pragmatist – might be described as essentially contested concepts in that they convey descriptive and evaluative messages. As such, students perceived these labels as hierarchical, with Theorist carrying the highest status and Pragmatist the lowest.

This was understandable given the cultural capital referred to earlier; however it was also ironic given the frequency with which BA(QTS) students criticize courses as being 'too theoretical', that what they appreciated and respected was work with a practical application.

This session which focussed on students receiving feedback on the results of the questionnaire was interesting, challenging and a learning experience – for us. While the majority of the group showed positive interest, they also questioned generally the appropriateness and applicability of such an activity. As the majority of the group were identified as Activists, it occured that this open questioning and lively debate actually linked to their learning style.

The following account is included to illuminate the personal perspectives of three students, Sam, Anne and Dan. Issues arising from their views will then be discussed.

SAM

Sam was identified as being a Reflector, personified as cautious, preferring to consider as many perspectives of a problem as possible and tending to contribute only when they have a good sense of others' opinions. At the end of the session he made it clear that he thought – he was a theorist. That is, someone whose philosophy was based on rationality and logic. Who was keen on analysis and synthesis of principles, theories, models and systems of thinking. Theorists according to Honey and Mumford like to maximize certainty by systematic problem-solving, shun subjectivity and seek objectivity wherever possible.

Sam was very critical of this exercise. About five minutes before the end of the session he became angry. He talked about the limits of such an exercise. Questioned how widely it had been trialled and asked about the validity and reliability, he thought the assessment was 'rubbish' because testing was 'rubbish'. 'Putting people in boxes is appalling. Aren't we all here on this course to do the opposite?' This last comment was because the course he was on was called 'Equal Opportunities and Differentiation'.

He raised the issue of testing again.

'What about IQ testing? I was tested loads of times in school and always came out in the 90s – it shows what a waste of time all this testing is.'

He then went on to insist on completing the questionnaire again. The result was the same. I returned the second questionnaire to him via internal mail and he did not come to our final session although his attendance had been excellent throughout the year. A subsequent conversation with him revealed that he saw his role at university as being that of someone who had a job to do and he had adopted a professional approach.

ANNE

Anne was identified as being an Activist. She immediately spoke up and expressed her concern at this label. Activists are described as involving themselves fully and without bias in new experiences. They are gregarious and inclined to centre activities around themselves. Anne felt that this label implied a 'selfishness' which she 'just did not have'.

It clearly troubled her to see herself in this light. In her own eyes she was giving and helpful to others and selfishness was an attribute she shunned.

Anne's label of Activist, from my perspective as her tutor, did reflect much of her learning style. She was vivacious, amusing and very enthusiastic about new ideas: but frequently failed to follow through. She was used to the attention and amusement she created in others: but felt vulnerable about being seen as someone who liked the limelight.

DAN

Dan was identified as being an Activist but felt a more accurate description would have been Reflector. She did not see herself as proactive but rather passive. Dan had changed enormously throughout the year. She had grown in stature and confidence and had been to me on behalf of friends in order to get materials to help with their work. She had a very successful teaching practice and the school had written a glowing report. When she expressed her reservations about being an Activist we spoke about these achievements and she concluded that she was stronger and more confident of late. She acknowledged that her family and friends had remarked on how she had changed. She went away thinking that the label Activist did indeed suit her.

What is revealed through this qualitative data?

1 Labels carry emotive messages. No matter how confidently you try to frame the notion that no one style subordinates the others, status and personal perspectives of worth are involved. A system which removes labels altogether may help with this as well as re-working some of the descriptors into more positive definitions.

2 Looking closely at an individual's personal attributes may cause them to react emotionally. You are probing, what are for some, sensitive areas and subsequent discussions need to be carefully managed:

(a) by giving feedback individually and confidentially if necessary;

(b) by being prepared to self-disclose.

3 Contextualisation may be important:

(a) being clear about the evidence on which assessment is based;

(b) discussing the validity and reliability of materials;

(c) sharing any reservation you may have;

(d) setting clear goals about how the activities will benefit students; leaving them with clear ideas/strategies for capitalizing on this new information;

(e) at all costs avoiding a 'pop psychology' approach – justification of methodology is important.

4 To avoid 'pigeon-holing' and negative labelling effects students must engage in this activity voluntarily and be free to disengage at any stage in the process. Those with negative experiences of 'testing' may find it threatening personally, emotionally and intellectually.

Above all students must have confidence in you and the process. They must see the relevance of the exercise and confidently be respected if required.

Discussion

The model upon which the LSQ is predicated is not sufficiently sophisticated. It needs to be extended so that there are more descriptors in each category; or there are more categories; or there is a further instrument to define between two categories when a student shows an equal preference for both. We feel that there needs to be both more descriptors and more categories in order to reflect more accurately the complexity of learning style.

The learning descriptors need to be re-defined in terms of the type of learning which takes place at HE level. The descriptors were useful to give a general picture of how that broad type of learner operated, but the examples used did not match sufficiently closely with the experience of student learning at HE level. This prevented the students from making the transfer from the model to their own experiences.

The affective domain of learning styles is vitally important, and we feel has been neglected. A corollary of our qualitative findings was that students did not seem able to approach this exercise from a professional perspective. They saw it only in terms of the personal. Evidence shows that teaching is a profession where it is very difficult to separate the personal from the professional (Ball and Goodson, 1985; Nias, 1989); indeed teachers predicate their professional identity upon personal characteristics (Evans *et al*, 1994; Packwood, 1994). There may be an issue hidden within the qualitative responses to the LSQ which is that student teachers do not see themselves as professionals and need to be helped to develop a professional perspective and philosophy of teaching.

The low and very low preferences were for the pragmatist stage and style of learning. On the face of it this would appear to be a paradox for in course evaluations students repeatedly tell us that it is this style of learning they want and which we do not offer them. This is a constant cause of concern to us as tutors for we know that it is this point in the cycle that the other three stages are put into operation. It is at this point that the reflective practitioner becomes operational. This apparent paradox is one which we intend to make a focus of the next stage of the research.

There is also a question raised by those students who evidence only moderate or low preferences for a particular style of learning. At this point we have three tentative explanations for this:

1 The instrument is not sufficiently sensitive to clearly identify or define their dominant learning style.

2 They are very flexible learners who have no dominant learning style.

3 They are not engaging with the learning process as it is being offered to them at HE level.

This issue is also one which we intend to make a focus in the next stage of the work.

The data also raise questions about the correlation between subject preference and dominant/preferred learning style. In order to identify possible correlations we intend to test a larger sample across discipline boundaries.

With regard to the nature of the learning experiences offered to the students, in terms of course content and delivery there is an obvious bias towards the theoretical and reflective stages of the cycle. We have to point out that the learning experiences which students undergo in seminars is very much dependent upon the individual tutor. This data was drawn from groups which **we** teach and as both of us are strongly activist in our learning styles we believe that this has a direct impact upon our teaching styles. Therefore our seminars fall into the activist/pragmatist sectors of the cycle. For students in other groups their seminar work might well have fallen into the reflective or theoretical stages. The connection between teaching styles and preferred learning styles is one which we intend to explore by correlating our work on learning with that of our colleagues in the Teacher Development Unit who are exploring styles of teaching at HE level.

There are some examples of mismatch in the course documentation between aims, content and delivery. The most striking of these is in the area of assessment where in theory the aim is to assess the theorist stage in the cycle, but the nature of the tasks set actually fall into the reflective sector. This mismatch highlights the issue of balance as revealed by the patterns emerging from these data. If different students have different preferences in learning style and if each stage of the learning cycle is of equal importance then two issues need to be addressed. Firstly students need to be offered a range of experiences, activities and styles of assessment which cover all stages in the learning cycle in order that some students are not disadvantaged. Secondly for successful learning to take place courses need to be structured so that each stage is covered.

McCarthy (1987) argues that education at school level is biased towards the theorist stage of the cycle and those whose preferred learning style is that of theorist are advantaged in the deduction system. Our pilot study is leading us to question which stage of the learning cycle is most advantaged at HE level. In terms of course aims the bias would seem to be towards the theorist stage, but actual content and delivery falls into the reflector category. We hope, through our work, to produce material designed to redress the balance.

References

Allport, G. W. (1937, 1961). *Pattern and Growth in Personality*. NY, Holt, Rinehart and Winston.

Ball, S. J. and Goodson, I. F. (1985). *Teachers' Lives and Careers*. Lewes, Falmer.

Coffield, F. (1992. Training and Enterprise Councils: The last Throw of Voluntarism? *Policy Studies*, **13**, (4), 11 – 32.

DFE (1993. *The Charter for Higher Education*. London, HMSO.

DFE (August). *Circular 18/92*. (London, HMSO).

Evans, L., Packwood, A., Neill, S .R. St. J. and Campbell, R. J. (1994). *The Meaning of Infant Teachers' Work*. London, Routledge.

Gregorc, A. (1982). *An Adult's Guide to Style*. Mass,Gabriel Systems Inc..

Honey, P. and Mumford, A. (1986). *A Manual of Learning Styles*. London, Honey.

Jung, C. G. (1921, 1971). *Psychological Types*. N. J., Princeton University Press.

Kolb, D. (1984). *Experiential Learning*. N. J.,Prentice-Hall.

Lewin, K. (1936). *The Principles of Topological Psychology*. McGraw-Hill.

McCarthy, B. (1980 1987). *The 4Mat System,Teaching to Learning Styles with Right/Left Mode Techniques*. lll,Excel Inc..

Myers, I. B. (1962). *Introduction to Type*. Calif., Consulting Psychologists Press Inc..

Myers, I. B. and Briggs, K.C. (1943, 1976) *Myers-Briggs Type Indicator*, (Calif., Consulting Psychologists Press inc.).

Nias, J. (1989). *Primary Teachers Talking*. London, Routledge.

Packwood, A. (1994). *Voice and Narrative, Realities, Reasoning and Research through Metaphor*. Unpublished PhD. thesis, University of Warwick.

Tyler, L. (1965). *The Psychology of Human Differences*. N.Y. Appleton-Century-Crofts.

17   The co-operation with students in course planning and development

Ulrich Peter Ritter (Department of Economics and Business Administration J. W. Goethe-University, Frankfurt am Main, Germany)

Why Student Participation?

Starting hypothesis

Teaching and learning can become more relevant and effective by involving students in course development and planning.

No matter, what we may say or think, our socialization as professors leads us to the belief that it is we who are qualified best for making decisions on what and how students should learn. This belief is also generally found in society, and the making of these decisions is generally considered to be not only one of our foremost tasks and responsibilities but also one of our foremost sacred rights. Under the name of *Wissenschaftsfreiheit*, i.e. the freedom of the sciences, and *Lehrfreiheit*, i.e. the freedom of teaching, it is even guaranteed in the German constitution. (The *Grundgesetz*, the German constitution essays in articles 5.3.1: 'Arts and Science, research and teaching are free.')

This constitutional right is a good thing and I most certainly do not want to bicker with it. However, in my experience this belief can also become a stumbling block to a true improvement of teaching and learning, because it excludes the students from all considerations about the designing of the process of teaching and learning. This is a mistake. As much as we may consider ourselves experts in our fields of research and teaching, the expertise and the experience of learning rests to a large degree with the students.

From this the following principles may be deduced:

- Learning can only be done by the students; therefore it should be left to their authority and responsibility.
- The authority of the professor should be limited to providing the conditions for learning (information, orientation, guidance) and to the functions of feedback, boundary definitions (such as hours, requirements and grades) and certification.

Since the early 1970s, these two principles have motivated many of my activities in the didactics of higher education. They developed indirectly out of earlier endeavours inspired by a contradicting paradigm of education: the improvement of teaching and learning through programmed instruction, computer-assisted instruction, and television. (Ritter, 1970; 1072(a); 1072(b)). That paradigm – admittedly one of particular appeal to the economist – ultimately in practice, brought about a complete alienation of the learning process. The personal element, i. e., the relationship between the teacher and the student as individual persons in the learning process was removed: What was called personalized or individualized construction was in reality impersonalized, if not dehumanized, instruction. Experiences with this approach taught me the importance of the personal aspect of teaching and learning and of such factors as caring and respect. Learning is not just a question of knowledge acquisition. It is also deeply intertwined with the development and growth of persons.

This outcome had a major impact on my teaching philosophy. I started to make the student – teacher relationship itself an important element in my teaching by accepting students both as partners and as a resource in the planning and development of courses. Since that time, I developed and worked with two models and now I am embarking on a third. Each successive model was built on the experiences of the previous one.

The First Two Models – a brief sketch

Students as experts in the field and partners in teaching: the development of the orientation course for beginning students of economics and business administrations 1972 – present.[1]

The first model, developed during the early 1970s, formed part of a larger movement of university reform. In this model students and I participated as equal partners in the planning, the running and the evaluation of the orientation course in economics and business administration. In this course students were not only experts on the question of learning, but also on the question of course content. They were the ones who best understood the problems beginning students have and what they needed to know to get along better. The professor was the expert on what the faculty expected and required from beginning students. This course was highly successful. Not only did the model spread to many faculties of economics and business administration in Germany, Austria and Switzerland but it was also adapted to the needs of other disciplines and faculties. Offered first during the winter semester 1972/73 at the university of Göttingen, it is still being offered every semester for all beginners there. When I moved to Frankfurt in 1975 it was redeveloped here and is still being offered in a modified form.

---

[1] *There is quite alot of literature on courses of this type. To cite only the publications referring to this particular course, see Ritter 1976 (a), (b); 1977; 1980; and W. Reik 1982; 1983.*

1st Day	2nd Day	3rd Day
Introduction and orientation. Formation of group and warming up. Motivation to study ec. and bus. ad.	Information about the study of economics and business administration. Counseling: Individual sessions and group.	Graduates in society: Roles, functions, fields of work, pay and career.

4th Day	5th Day
The student in the political structure of the university: Institutional framework, conflicts and problems	Introduction to the object, methods and issues of economics. Planning for the work of the rest of the semester.

Figure 1: Content of the orientation course

The difference of approach between students and professors became very obvious to me during the preparation of this course. This refers to the selection of problems as well as the course objectives and goals and the design of learning situations. Thus I had in mind such things as information about the requirements of study, the course catalogue, study techniques and information on how to use the library. Students attached more importance to such questions as the motivation to study, problems of gender, job possibilities etc. Also, the way we arrived at course content was different: we interviewed first-year students, students in their last year of grammar school and job counsellors. And instead of lecture and discussion classes we had debates, interviews, projects and games.

Qualifying students to become partners: course graduates as tutors and designers in the course on macroeconomics, 1982 –85[2]

Since the model was so sucessful the question thus posed itself: how could a similar situation be reached with a course other than that of freshman orientation, like for instance, macroeconomics? How could we get students with enough knowledge in that field to participate in the planning and development of such a course? The answer to this question was to have course graduates serve as tutors and designers.

During the summer of 1982 I hired six tutors and started to plan a new course in

---

[2] *For a more detailed description see U.P. Ritter, M Karl Col and M Seebach 1984 and U.P. Ritter 1987*

macroeconomis for the fourthcoming semester. Although the basic principles of the operation of the orientation course were maintained just as the basic content of the macroeconomic course, we introduced several innovations:

1 Course content was presented in a new order and form. Instead of going through the material step by step in a linear fashion, the first six classes gave an overview of the whole field and explained the necessary terminology and basic model and equations. Subsequent classes were dedicated to in-depth discussions of important topics and their political implications.

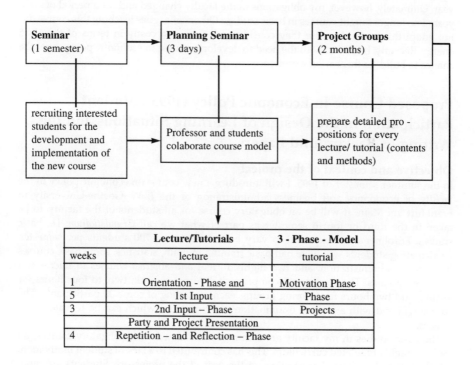

Figure 2: Participative lecture on macro-economics

2 The role of the tutors changed. During the first five weeks, they fulfilled their traditional role of clarifying the content of the lecture and doing exercises. Then, however, students formed groups of five in which they did statistical, library, or praxis research projects. Here the tutors became advisers, who were responsible for different types of projects. In the third phase, with the tutors serving as consultants, students formed working groups in which they prepared for the examination at the end of the course.

As to other results of students' participation the quality of the learning, the motivation of the students, and the overall effectiveness of the course were greatly superior to other courses in basic studies. Thus, while at the beginning of the course 60 students left to attend a parallel course, because it looked like too much work to them, one-third through the course 75 students wanted to join because of what they had heard about it from fellow students. Fifty-six project groups presented satisfying to excellent results. Also, the drop-out rate, usually quite high in such courses (30 to 70 per cent), was almost 0 and 95 per cent of the students passed the final examination versus only 50 to 75 per cent in other basic study courses.

All in all it was a very successful course. Not surprisingly, I repeated it the following year. Ultimately, however, my obligations in the faculty changed and for a period of eight years I no longer taught courses in basic studies. Other colleagues teaching this course did not adopt this model because they considered it to be too costly in terms of time and energy. Recently, however, with the need to develop a course in economic policy, I got the chance to build on this earlier experience.

Proposed Course in Economic Policy (1995): Student Participation in the Design of Learning Situations and the Writing of Background Papers

Objective and context of the project

In the summer semester of 1995, I will introduce a new course on economic policy in the faculty of economics and business administration of the J. W. Goethe-University in Frankfurt am Main. It will be an obligatory course for all students of the faculty, to be taken in the third or fourth semester as part of what we call *Grundstudium*, i.e. basic studies. Enrolments are expected to vary between 300 and 700 students per semester. Participating students will have had basic training in math, statistics, some basic courses in business administration, and two highly formal and abstract courses in micro- and macro economics. The course will comprise six hours per week: two, to four hours for lecture, and two hours for tutoring groups, each consisting of some 30 participants. The course will end with a written examination of 90 minutes, which can be repeated only ounces.

The basic studies in my faculty are commonly associated with obligatory courses, all part of a highly regulated curriculum. This has contributed to a lack of student motivation, which in turn has created frustration on the part of the professors. Students are more concerned about passing exams than understanding the material. Professors, meanwhile, are overly focused on how to cover the course content and too little on learning. This situation is aggravated by the fact that there is a hidden curriculum. The function of the basic studies curriculums not only to provide students with the fundamental knowledge considered necessary for their later studies, but also to separate the wheat from the chaff, i.e. to discourage and flunk those students considered unfit for the field.

There are, of course, exceptions to the rule. Some students are not satisfied with the minimalist approach to their studies; they take reading lists seriously and study on their own. And there are quite a few colleagues who look at the unfavourable conditions as a challenge and produce some outstanding teaching. Occasionally professors even go beyond the status quo and try to provide meaningful learning experiences for a high proportion of their students. The model for a new course in economic policy described below is one such endeavour.

The model

According to this model, third or fourth-year students participate in a seminar on economic policy in which particular emphasis is put on effective learning and the design of interesting learning situations. The best students from this seminar then become members of the 'project team', which actually prepares one part of the new course, i.e. the reading material and the design of the learning situations in the tutorials.

The first phase of implementation: the preliminary seminar

During the summer semester of 1994, I offered a preliminary seminar on the theme: 'Foundations of economic policy and its application to the problem of an aging population'. Forty-five students were admitted. During the first half of the seminar which was devoted to the 'foundations of economic policy' each student wrote a paper of up to 12 pages on one of 8 topics, so that we had about four papers for each topic.

In the third week of the summer semester my two assistants and I spent three days with the participants in a youth hostel in the old imperial city of Worms. One week in advance, each student had received one paper on each of the eight topics. Students were expected to read these papers beforehand so that the time during the seminar itself could be reserved for fruitful discussion and learning. The first morning after arriving in Worms was dedicated to orientation, clarification and planning as well as group-building activities. This was extremely important for setting the tone for our future work. Much time was invested in establishing norms, clarifying values and procedures, and in establishing a good working climate. This proved to be a good investment, and the next two days went by smoothly with stimulating presentations and discussions. Following the morning orientation, and with the exception of the final afternoon, the rest of the time was divided into 1 and 1/2 and 2 hour sessions for a discussion of the papers. The four authors in each group of the eight groups were responsible for the session on their topic. Each group had complete freedom to run its session as it chose, with two restrictions:

- the students were not to read their papers;
- each group of four authors was to get the other students interested and involved in their topics.

The last afternoon was used for the introduction of the theme for the second part of the seminar, 'policies for an aging population', and for the formation of project groups. Students interested in the same topic for this second theme would write a background paper for one seminar session of 1 and 1/2 hours. This would be distributed to all participants of the seminar a week in advance, allowing time for reflection on the potential questions, problems and arguments the topic raised.

The second task of each group was the design of the seminar session they were responsible for. My two assistants and I provided a list of possible approaches, including simulations, cases, role plays, debate etc., but they were encouraged to make use of their creativity to find ways of designing other approaches to learning situations that would at the same time be adequate to the topic and stimulating for participants. They also were informed that they as a group would get two grades for this part of the seminar: one for the background paper and one for the design and running of the session, each counting 50 per cent of the total group grade or 25 per cent of the total grade of each participant.

Figure 3: Development of the course in economic policy

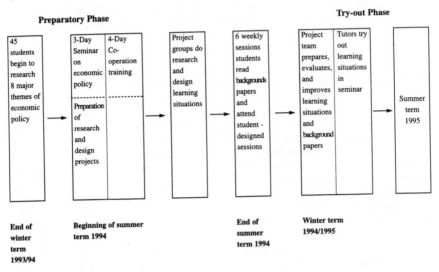

Following the Worms discussions, each group then had six weeks before the seminar met again for weekly sessions, two of 1 1/2 hours and four of three hours, two groups then running their sessions thus taking care of the total of eight groups. During the interval project group members were invited to take part in a group training programme of four sessions, six participants making use of this offer. Ute Schädler (Chapter 38) gives more information on this part of the project.

Today we can say that this part of the project was highly successful. Seldom have I experienced such a lively and interesting seminar with such dedicated students.two-thirds of the papers and one-third of the sessions were way above average and hardly any of the students ever missed a session. And what was even more impressive: three or four of the background papers and the same number of designs the students had prepared for this seminar were of such excellent quality that we will consider them for use in the next semesters; also we had twelve candidates we considered qualified to be invited to participate in the next phase of the project when we had expected five at most.

Phase 2 of the project: a trial run and then the real thing

While up to here past events could be related, from here on only plans can be reported. During the summer break the new project group will be formed. It will consist of the three members of the original project group, i.e. my two assistants and myself, plus the students accepting our invitation to participate. This group then will discuss the themes for background papers and the designs of the seminar sessions for the coming winter semester. Also these students will be invited to participate in a five-day workshop on the moderation of learning situations which I will offer at the beginning of the winter semester – a workshop I offer regularly once a year.

The next winter semester will serve as a try-out phase for the coming summer semester 1995. I will offer a course of two hours per week on economic policy for students who have finished their basic studies plus a seminar on economic policy. For the course I expect 150 – 300 students. For the seminar 55 students were assigned to me. The course as well as the seminar will be basically similar to the one I will offer in the summer with the difference that instead of seminar sessions in 1995 we will have tutorials and the number of participants will increase dramatically.

In the seminar students choose one of the ten topics we will run tutorials on in the summer semester of 1995. Thus there will be around five students writing a background paper on each topic. They will be available in the library one week in advance of each weekly seminar session for reading and xeroxing, one of the five being recommended by us. Students were told that these papers should not be written to impress me but rather to prepare fellow students for the seminar session. It is hoped that some of these papers will be of such quality that they can be used in the next semester.

In the tutorials we will use the learning situations the project group will have prepared for the winter semester and background papers which the students must read before each tutorial. These background papers will be selected from the papers the students have prepared in the seminar.

In the summer semester 1995 student members of the project group will in addition be tutors. Their task as the project group will be the continuous evaluation and improvement of the course, of the individual designs for each session, and of the background papers. At the end of the project this material will be made available to my colleagues.

Teaching, Student Learning and Student Participation: some Theoretical Reflections

There are many models for having more student participation within learning situations and even in planning and running courses and seminars. Besides the approaches described here, I have personally worked with many forms of group and project work, whenever this was possible, i.e. in smaller classes and seminars. Coming back to the initial hypothesis I shall now discuss the third model, trying to give some answers to the following three questions:

- What reasons can be given for such efforts?
- What are the particular features of the models presented in this paper?
- Where do we go from here?

What reasons can be given for such efforts?

I suppose the dream of every professor interested both in his subject and also in the object of his teaching, i.e. his students is of teaching classes with students truly interested in the course: we wish for students who ask questions, who enquire, critique, enter into dialogue and discussions, and who study, if possible not only their assignments but also do reading and research on their own in the quest for deeper learning and truth; in other words we yearn for students who really are willing and able to get involved. But how can we go about creating learning situations in which such a climate can materialize?

Too often the external enemy is held responsible for our giving up on such efforts: if we only had fewer and more qualified students in our classes and if other conditions were more favourable, teaching and learning could really be fun. There would be not the alienation and fragmentation of learning experienced by today's students. Dullness and monotony would be replaced by excitement and variety, passivity and consumptive attitudes by active involvement.

But is it really just the external conditions, which prevent us from teaching in a way, which becomes truly meaningful and relevant to students and thus produces the kind of motivated students we all long for? Could we allow ourselves the experience described in the famous quote of Pogo: 'I have met the enemy. It is us!'?

Be that as it may, the models described here aspire to the positive goals implied in our dreams. They take the bad conditions under which we work as an unchangeable given and as a challenge. They do not pretend to succeed in every one of these goals for every student. However, they have proved successful to such an extent as to make the additional effort and investment of energy and time more than justified.

What are the particular features of the models presented in this chapter?
The peculiarity of the models presented in this chapter is contextual: while many other models refer to small or relatively small groups, classes and seminars often in a rather loose curricular context, these models were developed for and implemented in the context of mass education and a very tightly regulated and controlled curriculum: classes range in size from 200 – 750 or more; the curriculum is stiff, leaving almost no choices, and consequences for not passing the final exam at the end of the course are severe.

The models presented in this chapter were designed with the purpose of swimming against the stream and achieving what is generally believed to be impossible: have students become active, automous and motivated learners and engage in interaction, discussion and small group work in courses of study and learning environments more favourable to passivity, anonymity and disengaged and extrinsically motivated learning.

Where do we go from here?
This question has two aspects. One refers to what I and the team with which I work might do in the future and the other refers to the more general potential of these models.

As to my own ideas I envision a second run more similar to the second model of the course on economic policy, i.e. the course on macroeconomics. I will invite students who have successfully gone through the summer semester of 1995 to plan with us the course for the summer semester of 1997. If I succeed, I foresee major structural changes, which will make this course even more exciting and more effective.

As far as the potential of this model for other applications is concerned I see it mostly in similar contexts, i.e. 'mass education'. Maybe it could even be of help in other forms of teaching such as distance education or computer assisted instruction. It seems plausible that this could be a method to achieve a movement away from expert towards learner-oriented teaching.

On the other hand even in the context of smaller classes with a highly regulated course of study this model (as well as the second model of the course in macroeonomics) could probably bring about interesting changes and improvements.

Afterthoughts: Some Reflections on the Cost-Effectiveness and Innovative Potential of the Models

In discussion following my presentation two sceptical views were prominent: one questioned the timeliness of the described efforts. Were they not outdated in times of cost-saving, lean production and mass phenomena in higher education? Quite to the contrary, is my answer. Japanese management models draw in part on the same sources as the models presented here: the motivation and innovative potential of the production workers are mobilized through participation. Also these models help to minimize waste and increase productivity of education substantially. Besides, the cost-effectiveness ratio seems favourable, particularly when one looks at the results and the quality of the learning achieved.

The second view questioned the innovative potential of this approach in view of the fact that the second model was considered to be too costly in time and energy by my Frankfurt colleagues. It is true, compared with traditional methods of teaching, that these models require more time and effort on the part of the professor and the institution. Thus the use of these models can only then become more common when the benefits and sanctions in the system become more oriented towards rewarding good learning results, i.e. when also the benefits of good teaching gain more weight vis-a-vis teaching costs.

Bibliography

Ritter, U. P. (1979). Universitätsfernsehen in den USA – Fehlschläge und Erfolge, *Mitteilungen des Arbeitskreises fur Hochschuldidaktik*, **19**, 272 – 6.

Ritter, U. P. (1972b). Translation and edition of the 2nd ed. of: Keith G. Lumsden, Richard Attiyeh, and George Leland Bach, *Programmierte Einführung in die Volkswirtschaftslehre* (in cooperation with Dr Peter Rhmann). Teil 1: Mikro^konomie, Teil 2: Makro^konomie Frankfurt - Z,rich, Harri Deutsch.

Ritter, U. P. (1972b). *Entwicklung und Verwendung von programmierten Texten* in den *Wirtschaftswissenschaften-Ergebnisse der Begleituntersuchungen zu dem volkswirtschaftlichen Lehrprogramm von Lumsden, Attiyeh und Bach*, Jahrbücher für Nationalökonomie und Statistik, Stuttgart, Vol. 186, Heft 3: 254 – 62.

Ritter, U. P. (1976a). *Orientierungsphase: Einführung in das Studium der Wirtschaftswissenschaften*, Berichte zur Hochschuldidaktik der Wirtschaftswissenschaften, Vol. 1, Göttingen 1973, 3rd, Frankfurt.

Ritter, U. P. (1976b). *Gruppenarbeit in Studium und Ausbildung*, (together with J. Ritter) in: P. Diepold und J. Ritter,Gruppenarbeit und Tutorenausbildung in den Wirtschafts wissenschaften, Berichte zur Hochschuldidaktik der Wirtschaftswissenschaften, Bd. 8, G^ttingen 1975, 2nd ed. as Vol. 38, Blickpunkt Hochschuldidaktik, Hamburg: 1 – 8.

Ritter, U. P. (1977). *Good-bye Mr. Skinner or the Art of Student Participation in Course Development.* Paper presented to the Congress of the European Association for Research and Development in Higher Education, Louvain-la-Neuve, Belgium, 30 August. 1976. In: A. Bonboir (ed.), *Proceedings, Vol. 1, Instructional Design in Higher Education. Innovations in Curricula and Teaching*, Louvain: 333 – 48.

Rieck, W. (1982). *Orientierungsveranstaltungen zum Studienbeginn – eine hochschuldidaktische Analyse*, Hamburg, AHD – Blickpunkt 68.

Rieck, W. (1983). Orientierungsveranstaltungen. In: L. Huber (ed.) *Enzyklopädie Erziehungswissenschaft*, Band X 'Hochschule', Stuttgart.

Ritter, U. P. (1984). together with Michael Kerkloh und Michael Seebach, *Studentische Partizipation in einer Hauptveranstaltung des Grundstudiums. Ein Arbeitsbericht.* Frankfurt, Diskussionspapiere, Professur für Hochschuldidaktik der Wirtschaftswissenschaften, 17.

Ritter, U. P. (1987). Die Beteiligung von Studenten als Lernexperten an der Grundstudiumsveranstaltung 'Makroökonomie'. In: B. Berendt (ed.) *Massenveranstaltungen - Probleme und Lösungsansätze*, AHD bei Beltz, Blickpunkt Hochschuldidaktik 81, Weinheim, Basel: 196 – 232.

18   A multi-faceted approach to the evaluation of student learning

Dr John Mallatratt, (Department of Computing, University of Central Lancashire)

Introduction

This chapter reports on the approach to evaluation adopted when the Department of Computing at the University of Central Lancashire decided to introduce an innovation to improve student learning. The innovation concerned was a formalized system of peer tutoring.

The scheme was designed to make peer tutor support available to students on the first years of the HND Computing and the HND Software Engineering courses, both of which had higher than average wastage rates. In particular, it was intended that students would be given extra help, through the provision of a 'peer' tutor, to study for a course unit (Principles of Computer Systems) which appeared consistently to cause difficulties. Peer tutors were volunteer students from the Department's degree programmes. By opting to become a tutor, these students were enrolled on to a course unit (Computing Peer Tutors' Unit) upon which they were assessed and for which, provided they passed, they were given credit.

Although the tutoring scheme *per se* has some interesting features which tend to distinguish it from similar schemes known to operate in the higher education sector, discussion of these characteristics can be found elsewhere (Mallatratt, 1994). In this paper, it is the scheme's evaluation strategy which provides the focus. In particular, consideration is given to the rationale for the strategy that was adopted and this is followed by discussion of its appropriateness.

Approaches to Educational Evaluation

Evaluation is a term that has been defined by many authors. Its essence is probably best captured by Kemmis (Kemmis, 1982):

> Evaluation is the process of marshalling information and arguments which enable interested individuals and groups to participate in the critical debate about a specific programme.

Here we can see that stress is laid upon the utility of evaluation findings to interested parties. It has not been the concern in the study described in this chapter to generate universal theory regarding the application of peer tutoring. Others have already sought, via meta-analysis, to do this (e.g. see Cohen, Kulik and Kulik, 1982). Instead, the primary purpose of the evaluation has been to give feedback to those most directly concerned with the innovation and its context. If, as a by-product, it is possible to make the findings and methodology of the evaluation accessible to others so that they can contribute to discussion of either then this is a useful additional outcome.

The simplicity of the definition of evaluation given above belies the complexity of the task of conducting an evaluation, particularly when the context is education.

[Educational] programmes are unstable, politicised consequence-laden and value-laden arenas of social action. Discovering the nature and dynamics of such social settings calls for field investigation of a particularly sensitive and evocative kind in order to construct knowledge in forms usable by a wide range of people and to do this in a way which is not in principle prejudicial to any particular interest. (MacDonald and Stronach, 1989).

The burden of designing and implementing an evaluation strategy which can operate effectively within such a complex environment is significant. Apparently elemental tasks are revealed, upon scrutiny, to require compound, and potentially iterative, processes to be undertaken. For instance, the task of defining the objectives of the evaluation might be perceived as merely requiring reference to be made to the objectives espoused by the sponsor, or initiator, of the evaluation. However, this would deny the opportunity of other stakeholders to add items to the objectives list or to input alternative perspectives to those already identified. Instead, a process should be effected by which all concerned can contribute to objective setting. The extent of this process will be influenced by the nature of the time and resource constraints applying to the evaluation, but omission of this stage would significantly impair the value of findings.

Clearly the nature of the objectives of the evaluation will have a direct bearing upon the choice of the items that will be measured. According to Stake (Stake, 1979), educational evaluations which concentrate exclusively upon student results are ill-founded:

The worth of an educational program is seldom indicated by the achievement of students . . . the worth of a program is dependent on its relevance to other courses and programs, on its effect on teacher morale, on its compatibility with community ideology, etc. No evaluation study can examine all the nuances of worth, but the study that ignores them to concentrate on objective measures of achievement is potentially irresponsible.

It is implicit in this statement that qualitative as well as quantitative methods will be required. However, those pursuing predominantly qualitative methods have, in the past, been the target for substantial criticism concerning the subjectivity of their approach. Without opening up the debate between positivist and ethnographic approaches (and all the shades in between) which has been well addressed by others (e.g. see Chalmers, 1982), it is perhaps appropriate at this stage to tackle the question of the perceived validity of results acquired through qualitative methods. Just like the results acquired through quantitative methods, such observations are susceptible to threats to validity. One source of advice (Hutchison *et al.*, 1988) gives a list of eight measures which can be followed in order to minimise threats. Although several of these items are truisms (e.g. 'Be alert to threats to validity'), the recommendations to be catholic in the use of data sources and to triangulate are well made.

Finally in this section, reference must be made to the threat to data subjects implicit in undertaking any evaluation in the social domain. Where staff are scrutinizing one particular subset of students, the latter are bound to be concerned about what will be done with the findings. Although it is possible to minimize anxieties by making the objectives for the investigation well known (and properly negotiated – see above) and by ensuring the anonymity of the data subjects wherever possible, there is no guarantee that concerns can be eradicated. In such instances, there are two choices: either continue with the evaluation design as planned or modify it to be less intrusive. Taking the second option might make it impossible to elicit the information that was sought to test a hypothesis, while taking the former could result in whatever data is collected being invalid. Clearly the decision that is taken will be influenced by the culture of the environment.

Expected Benefits of Peer Tutoring

The institution of a peer tutoring system within the Department of Computing was motivated by an expectation that benefits would accrue. Literature from the US (Martin, 1991) suggested that recipients of Supplemental Instruction (SI), a scheme upon which the intervention was loosely based, gained higher mean grades than non-participants. In the UK, findings from a study in the Computing domain undertaken at Brunel University (McDonnell, 1992) indicated that peer tutoring had helped tutees to assess their own work, and to improve both their research skills and the way they presented their work. To some extent, tutees also felt that tutoring had helped their software design skills. The findings about study skills have been supported by the work of Falchikov (Falchikov, 1990) who discovered that tutees regarded the benefit to their personal and study skills to be the best feature of their tutoring scheme. In the same paper, it is suggested that the benefits to accrue from the use of peer tutoring in the higher education sector may be similar to those observed from the use of cross-age tutoring in the schools sector. In this latter sector, it has been reported (Fitz-Gibbon, 1988) that tutoring was the most effective and cost-effective intervention out of four (the other three being reducing class size, increasing instructional time, and computer assisted instruction).

However, although it might be reasonable to have an expectation of some benefits given the extent of evidence, it has to be remembered that the nature of tutoring schemes is so diverse that there can be no guarantee that findings derived in one context will be replicable within another. It is for this reason that it was felt to be of paramount importance that an evaluation strategy for the Department of Computing scheme was designed and implemented. This would provide the opportunity for judgements about that scheme to be made in the context of what was felt to be important by its stakeholders.

Design of Evaluation

One of the main conclusions to be derived from study of the evaluation literature was that it was unlikely to be practicable to investigate all the areas of interest. (Another lesson learned was that even when a subset of areas had been chosen, the tasks of collecting and analysing data about these aspects were likely to prove problematic!) Accordingly, in this section consideration will be given to how the items for exploration, and the methodology for investigation, were selected. Although the issues that were considered are presented as a list in the ensuing sections, it should be made clear that this is not intended to imply a sequential approach to the design of the evaluation strategy; the process was iterative, with early decisions being reviewed in the context of the constraints and opportunities governing implementation.

Objectives

The primary point that needs to be made about the identification of objectives is that there is a need to disaggregate the objectives of the scheme from the objectives of the stakeholders involved in the scheme, since an evaluation strategy needs to give consideration to both. The scheme's objectives were comparatively well defined having recently been drawn up by the development team. They included objectives for the Department, the recipient students and the peer tutors:

- to reduce drop out rates on the Department's courses;
- to reduce failure rates on (a) course unit(s) which traditionally caused students problems;
- to provide extra support to students;
- to promote the tutors' deep learning of the material being tutored;
- to develop the skill of providing learning support to others.

However, the derivation of the objectives of the stakeholders was a less precise process, which was also less susceptible to being time bound. For example, consider the tutees. As a consequence of the way in which it was decided to implement the tutoring scheme, ie as a facility that prospective tutees could take up as and when they wanted, it was not possible to establish at the outset what objectives tutees had for making use of the scheme. Indeed this could only be established *post hoc* (and then be used later to inform new evaluations).

Some objectives for the evaluation appeared more accessible at the outset. For example, at least one of the scheme's progenitors was concerned that the evaluation should provide evidence to justify, if appropriate, the scheme's continuation. Although this could be done by focusing solely upon the scheme's objectives, such an approach might lead to the exclusion of significant evidence and thereby fail to provide sufficient information for making modifications or refinements to the scheme. But since it was not felt to be possible to determine at the outset what extra information would be relevant to the scheme's future operation, the data collection techniques employed were designed to be sufficiently 'open' to allow for unpredicted information to be reported. A logical extension to this approach is that the evaluation design itself should be flexible enough to be able to accommodate some 'following' of the data. This principle has been termed emergent evaluation design and is more fully discussed elsewhere (Sadler, 1984). In the context of the present study, some semblance of the approach was manifest in the way that the tutee questionnaire was compiled. This was prepared about eight weeks after the scheme's implementation had begun and in such a way as to allow for early insights of the peer tutors, and the member of staff responsible for the implementation of the scheme, to be incorporated.

The final point to be made about objectives here is that there should clearly be a relationship between the objectives that are selected and the evaluators' domain of competence. In the case of this innovation, there was potentially an opportunity for a study to be conducted into how students learn within peer relationships. However, as neither of the two members of staff concerned with the evaluation felt that they had sufficient expertise in this area, and that the inclusion of extra evaluators would be intrusive, the opportunity was not pursued.

Criteria and mechanisms

We now come to discussion of the evaluation criteria that were selected. A fundamental requirement for each criterion was that it showed at least some potential of being measurable. A refinement of the requirement was that it should be practicable to measure the criterion reliably within the known context of resource constraints and practical difficulties. This led to selection of the following tentative groupings of criteria.

BENEFITS TO THE TUTEE
- reduced failure rates;
- greater comfort with course unit;
- greater comfort with overall course;
- improved feeling towards department.

BENEFITS TO THE TUTORS
- deeper understanding of the material tutored;
- more developed tutoring skill.

BENEFITS TO THE DEPARTMENT
- reduction in drop out rate;
- better learning environment for students.

Even this relatively limited set of criteria presented a considerable challenge to evaluate, especially since it was the intention to triangulate findings wherever possible. Below, consideration is given to criteria which were (relatively) successfully measured; criteria that weren't specifically measured but about which some impressionistic/anecdotal data was acquired; and criteria for which no claim of measurement can be made.

It might be assumed (and was by the author) that the collation of past and present cohort statistics in order to identify drop-out and pass rates would be a relatively unproblematic process. However, two factors contrived to make this task one that consumed more energy than originally envisaged. Firstly, in the period for which statistics were sought (three years was chosen), the department in which the courses were located was the subject of two faculty re-organizations. During transitions, departmental student records had been misplaced, making it necessary to access central university records in order to effect the evaluation. The second complication concerned the format in which the results lists were generated. Results for all students taking the targeted course unit were shown together, regardless of the fact that some were studying at the university (where peer tutor support was provided) and some at franchised colleges (where it was not).

In spite of these two complications, this part of the evaluation was conducted relatively successfully. The drop-out data for the current cohort was even triangulated to some extent. *Inter alia* tutees were asked, via a questionnaire (see more below), to declare whether peer tutoring had had any effect upon whether or not they continued with the course – 10 per cent of them indicated it had been the factor that had prevented them from leaving.

Other parts of the evaluation which could be judged to be at least a partial success were the assessment of tutees' comfort with the course unit and course, and of their feelings towards the department. Testing of the three items was incorporated within the same anonymous questionnaire referred to above. This was completed by all students (70 in total) who had had the opportunity to attend peer tutor sessions. Although the responses given in some instances might have been those that the tutees believed that staff wanted to hear, support for the positive results obtained on the first two items did come through a slightly different source. This occurred when student representatives attending a course committee meeting gave unsolicited praise to the scheme and cited its effectiveness in reducing student anxieties.

Reasonably detailed consideration was also given to evaluation of one of the criteria affecting the peer tutors. Three different approaches were adopted to the assessment of their tutoring skills. These included evaluation by the tutors themselves (who made a critical appraisa' of each 'class' and discussed it in their weekly support sessions), evaluation by the tutees (who graded several aspects of their tutor's performance on the questionnaire) and, to a much lesser extent, classroom observation by the member of staff leading the scheme. This last method was used only once. Although the student tutor observed claimed that it was very helpful, the member of staff felt that tutees might have reservations about the process. Since the latter had been promised that their attendance at peer tutoring sessions would not be recorded, a staff member's presence in a tutoring session could be perceived as a breach of trust.

One criterion was less rigorously evaluated. This concerned the deep learning of tutors. It had been intended to administer a pre-test and post-test to tutors to assess whether their understanding of the material for which they were giving support had developed during the scheme's operation. However, time constraints prevented this from happening although some impressionistic and anecdotal data was recorded. For instance, all four tutors declared that they had had to read up material and understand more about it than when they themselves had been taught. In addition, one of the tutors who was re-taking a unit on the degree programme which had a similar curriculum, managed to achieve a 2:1 grade on the re-sit. She attributed the change in grade to her involvement as a peer tutor.

Finally in this section, attention should be given to the criterion for which no evaluation was made, namely whether a 'better learning environment' had been created. The task of measuring this criterion appeared insurmountable when subjected to scrutiny. Principally, this arose because the concept of a better learning environment was ill-defined. For example, it could have been construed to equate to the provision of better access to learning resources. In this case, the evaluation strategy would have focussed upon how access had changed as a result of the introduction of the innovation. However, an alternative perspective on 'better learning environment' would be one that saw it as being concerned with being more caring towards students. This would lead to a different approach to evaluation.

Whichever view had been adopted, there would have been inherent difficulties in conducting a reliable evaluation. These arise because there are potentially harmful, as well as beneficial, changes to the learning environment resulting from the introduction of peer tutoring. If access to learning resources is considered, there are ways in which this could have diminished as well as increased. For example, staff tutors could have made themselves less accessible as a result of the introduction of the scheme. If the caring environment approach was evaluated, it would have been necessary to attempt to identify the extent to which informal networks of peers supporting (i.e. caring for) each other were affected by the introduction of a formal scheme. Would the scheme represent the institution of a credit for caring culture whereby one student would only help another if there was an extrinsic reward? If this was suspected, then how could it be measured? Resource constraints prevented these complex issues from being given due consideration.

Conclusion

In this brief chapter an attempt has been made, through the presentation of a case study, to highlight some of the issues arising from the design and implementation of educational evaluation. It is the author's view that the process of evaluation is complex and requires a set of skills that many educators cannot be expected to possess. Whereas lecturers may be able to engage the support of others who have these skills, and thereby also enhance the objectivity of an evaluation, people so recruited will need to have the sensitivity to handle the task in a way that is not prejudicial to any of the stakeholders. Evaluation conducted by people without the necessary skills is likely to show a pre-disposition to focus upon 'objective' measures and ignore much of the rich data about an environment which could be of greater significance.

Finally, the case study is intended to illustrate that in matters of evaluation there is a role for pragmatics. The 'ideal' design of an evaluation may be impractical to implement. Judgements therefore need to be made about how maximum reliability can be delivered within the known constraints. These decisions should not be arbitrary but should be well grounded in evaluation theory.

References

Chalmers, A.F. (1982). *What is This Thing Called Science?* Open University Press.

Cohen, P.A., Kulik, J.A. and Kulik, C.L. (1982). Educational outcomes of tutoring: a meta-analysis of findings. *American Educational Research Journal*, **19**, 237–48

Falchikov, N. (1990). An experiment in same-age peer tutoring in higher education: some observations concerning the repeated experience of tutoring or being tutored. In Goodlad, S. and Hirst, B. (eds) *Explorations in Peer Tutoring*. Blackwell.

Fitz-Gibbon, C.T. (1988). Peer tutoring as a teaching strategy. *Educational Management and Administration* **16**, 217–29.

Hutchison, B., Hopkins, D. and Howard, J. (1988). The problem of validity in the qualitative evaluation of categorically funded curriculum development projects *Educational Research*, **30**(1), 54–64.

Kemmis, S. (1982). Seven principles for programme evaluation in curriculum development and innovation. *Journal of Curriculum Studies*, **14**(3), 221–40.

MacDonald, B. and Stronach, I. (1989). The independent policy evaluation. *Journal of Computer Assisted Learning*, **5**, 51–64.

Mallatratt, J. (1995). A study of the effects of a peer tutoring scheme. In Hart, J. (ed.) *Innovations in the Teaching of Computing*, SEDA.

Martin, D.C. (1991). *Effectiveness of Supplemental Instruction for Enhancing Student Success.* Report, University of Missouri, Kansas City.

McDonnell, J.T. (1992). Peer tutoring: a pilot scheme among computer science undergraduates. In *Proceedings of Conference on Developments in the Teaching of Computer Science*, University of Kent.

Sadler, D.R. (1984). Follow-up evaluation of an in-service programme based on action research: some methodological issues. *Journal of Education for Teaching*, **100**, 209–18.

Stake, R.E. (1979). Should educational evaluation be more objective or more subjective - more subjective. *Educational Evaluation and Policy Analysis*, **1**(6) 45–7.

19 Student Project Work in Relation to a Meaning Oriented Approach to Learning

Katherine Cuthbert (Manchester Metropolitan University)

Introduction

This chapter will investigate student approaches to learning within the context of a degree programme in which students complete a major project during their final year. The degree is the BA in Applied Social Studies (by Independent Study) at the Crewe+Alsager Faculty of Manchester Metropolitan University. It is a modular, multi-disciplinary degree based in the social sciences. The first two years of the degree are relatively conventional in character and have the objective of providing students with an understanding of core content in the disciplines that they are studying.

During their second year, students are required to develop a proposal for a project that they will then complete during their final year. This project will constitute between 40% and 80% of a student's final year programme and will now be up to 30,000 words in length. Projects are composed of inter-related component essays. They are quite likely to be interdisciplinary in character and will frequently have an applied problem orientation. They are likely to include practical work, for example, questionnaires, case studies, correlational investigations and placements. Projects must obviously develop out of the discipline areas which students have studied in the first two years of the degree. Although original work at the level expected in a post-graduate research degree cannot be required, it is nevertheless expected that the project will be more than a straightforward text-book summary. Frequently, a degree of originality will derive from the way in which a student draws upon personal experience, or investigates a local example to examine a particular issue or problem area.

Although project work is increasingly a part of many degree programmes, it is still unusual for it to have quite such a prominent role as is possible within the BA in Applied Social Studies. To what extent, and on what basis, is this central role justified? The original rationale for the degree, which was initially validated in 1981, was derived from a number of sources. A central concern was to help students to 'learn how to learn' and to provide them with an opportunity to commit themselves to work that was personally meaningful, with the expectation that this would lead to increased motivation (e.g. Decci, 1975; Rogers, 1969).

More recent developments in psychological theory and research and a much extended understanding of the student learning process have enabled us to develop and extend this rationale (Cuthbert, in press). This present chapter derives from the work on student learning which is central to this symposium on Improving Student Learning (e.g. Marton and Saljo, 1976; Entwistle and Ramsden, 1983; Biggs, 1987; Entwistle and Tait, 1990; Gibbs, 1992). The central theme of this work is that it is desirable for students within higher education to be adopting a meaning oriented approach to their learning. However, it is also recognized that it is deceptively easy to encourage a reproducing or surface approach, and there is even some suggestion that a surface approach can increase as students progress through higher education (Gow and Kember, 1990).

The work of Entwistle and Ramsden (1983), Biggs (1989) and Gibbs (1992) has helped to identify some of the characteristics of the learning environment that are conducive to the development of a meaning oriented approach to learning. Such strategies may be summarized as follows:

- freedom in learning, that is students having some discretion in the choice and organization of their academic work;
- a workload that is not overwhelming;
- encouraging motivation through personal involvement in learning;
- promoting independent learning and using project work;
- making use of problem-based learning;
- emphasizing reflective processes;
- promoting active and experientially based learning;
- developing student learning skills;
- emphasizing a well-structured and discipline-based knowledge structure.

Many of these characteristics either specify, or are compatible with student project work. These findings are important for the BA in Applied Social Studies (by Independent Study) in two ways. Firstly, they contribute towards support for the degree rationale. Secondly, they contribute towards the development of appropriate teaching strategies, particularly in relation to the provision of appropriate support for students during the project planning process (see details in Cuthbert, 1994).

However, whether these strategies are conducive to the development of a meaning oriented approach to learning within the context of the BA in Applied Social Studies must be a matter of empirical investigation. Empirical evidence can help us to identify positive outcomes, but less supportive findings can also be of eventual value through the stimulation of ideas for alternative practice.

Hypotheses and Focus of Investigation

The purpose of this study is to investigate student perceptions of the BA in Applied Social Studies and their approaches to studying within the degree. The overall hypothesis is that perceptions and approaches will change as students progress through the degree programme and especially as they move into the final year. The expectation is that students will develop a stronger meaning oriented approach to learning and that there will be a decrease in reproducing approach.

Design of Study

The study has both a cross-sectional and longitudinal component. In the cross-sectional part of the study, students who were then in the first, second and final year of their degree were tested between May and July 1992. Students completed the approaches to Studying Inventory and the Course Perceptions Questionnaire (Entwistle and Ramsden, 1983).

First- and second-year students completed the questionnaires within class sessions. Final-year students were contacted by post after graduation.

In the longitudinal part of the study, the 1991/92 cohort of students was followed through to their graduation this year. They completed the Approaches to Studying Inventory at the beginning of May, just prior to handing in completed independent projects and prior to final examinations. The Approaches to Studying Inventory was completed at the end of a scheduled session. Students took away a copy of the Course Perceptions Questionnaire to complete in their own time, but insufficient of these were returned for a useful analysis.

Questionnaire Measures

Course Perceptions Questionnaire

The Course Perceptions Questionnaire developed by Entwistle and Ramsden (1983) was used in this study. Thus the sub scales being measured were formal teaching methods, clear goals and standards, workload, vocational relevance, good teaching, freedom in learning, openness to students and social climate.

Specific hypotheses in relation to the Course Perceptions Questionnaire are of decreased scores on formal teaching from year one to year three, and increased scores on freedom to learn, and possibly openness to students. Entwistle and Ramsden (1983) also specified that good teaching and (low) workload are conducive to the development of a meaning oriented approach. However, there would seem to be no particular *a priori* reason for hypothesizing a change in these between years one and three.

Approaches to Studying Inventory

Richardson's shortened version of the Approaches to Studying Inventory was used in this investigation (Richardson 1990). This was chosen over Entwistle's original version partly for the pragmatic reason of it being easier to prevail upon students to complete a shorter questionnaire, but primarily because the main interest was in meaning and reproducing approaches to learning, rather than in achieving orientation and styles and pathologies of learning for which scales are included in the original questionnaire. Richardson's version was also preferred over Gibbs' even shorter version because of its lack of adequate sub-scales and problems with its factor structure (Richardson, 1992). Richardson's version, based on Entwistle's original inventory and analysis, assesses meaning orientation in terms of four sub scales. These are deep approach, comprehension learning, relating ideas and use of evidence. It measures the reproducing orientation in terms of the sub-scales surface approach, improvidence, fear of failure and syllabus boundness.

Specific hypotheses in relation to this questionnaire are that there will be an increase in scores on each of the meaning orientation scales from years one to three in relation to both the cross-sectional and longitudinal data, and a corresponding decrease in scores on the reproducing orientation scales.

Sample and Response Rate

First- and second-year students were tested within scheduled class sessions in an attempt to get response rates as high as possible. However, attendance at these sessions was not compulsory and so, of course, there was some degree of absenteeism. A few of the questionnaires were not fully completed and so had to be excluded from the analysis. This was particularly so for the Course Perceptions Questionnaire where some students failed to turn onto the final page of the questionnaire despite being reminded to do so. This led to the lowest response rate for the study for the second-year group of 57.1per cent.

Third-year students, who were part of the longitudinal follow up group, were also contacted within a scheduled class session and absentees were followed up on one further occasion. The third-year group in the cross-sectional study were contacted by post and follow up requests were sent to those who did not reply on the first occasion.

For the longitudinal study, there was the additional problem of maintaining the sample over the two administrations of the questionnaires. Almost inevitably sample size was reduced because some students who completed questionnaires in the first year didn't do so in the third year and vice versa. It was still possible to maintain the overall percentage response rate for the longitudinal group at a reasonably acceptable 64.4per cent. Full percentage response rates for all groups are provided in the results tables.

Results and Analysis

Means and standard deviations were obtained for each of the variables, for each year group, for both the cross-sectional and longitudinal data. The cross-sectional results for the Course Perceptions Questionnaire are presented in Table 1. The cross-sectional results for the Approaches to Studying dimensions are in Table 2, while the longitudinal results for the 1991/92 cohort are to be found in Table 3. For each of these sets of data, tests were performed to investigate differences between first- and third-year performance on the various measures.

Results in relation to the Course Perceptions Questionnaire

Taking the results for the Course Perceptions Questionnaire first, it is evident that the predictions made above have been upheld. The cross-sectional data show that third-year students perceived teaching to be less formal in character than did first-year students. Third-year students, who have chosen their own project area, as expected perceived that they had greater freedom to learn in comparison with first-year students. It is also worth noting that in comparison with wider norms for psychology students, derived from Entwistle and Ramsden (1983), even first -year students were rating themselves as having quite a high degree of freedom to learn, whereas the mean for final year students was well above the highest mean recorded in Entwistle and Ramsden's sample.

Table 1 - Cross-sectional data in relation to course perceptions: scores on the Course Perception Questionnaire for students on the BA in Applied Studies (by Independent Study) for the Academic Year 1991/92

Course Perception Dimensions	Year One Students		Year Two Students		Year Three Students		Norms for Students Psychology+
	Mean	*SD*	*Mean*	*SD*	*Mean*	*SD*	*Mean* / *Range*
Formal teaching	6.930		6.313		4.800**		6.7
		2.840		1.887		2.145	3.8-9.1
Clear goals	10.837		10.938		10.933		8.6
		3.047		4.041		3.411	5.6-11.9
Work load	8.000		9.063		8.600		9.0
		4.140		3.376		3.355	5.3-12.6
Vocational relevance	9.023		9.125		8.467		6.5
		3.158		3.181		3.067	4.7-8.4
Good teaching	12.837		13.250		15.733**		11.8
		3.873		3.924		1.580	9.2-14.0
Freedom to learn	12.163		10.625		15.933**		9.7
		4.776		4.145		3.731	7.9-12.6
Openness to students	10.070		9.688		12.800*		9.9
		4.636		3.497		3.155	7.4-12.8
Social Climate	12.00		10.313		10.200		11.5
		4.298		3.754		4.459	10.5-13.5
Sample size	43		16		15		
% response rate	69.4%		57.1%		68.2%		

+From Entwistle and Ramsden (1983)

* Indicates a significant difference at the .05 level between first- and third-year students.

** Indicates a significant difference at the .01 level between first- and third-year students.

Although this was not predicted, it is interesting to note that third-year students judged there to be higher levels of good teaching than did first year students, although even the first year mean was higher than the overall mean reported by Entwistle and Ramsden (1983). There was also a difference between the two groups, at the .05 level of significance, in relation to the openness to students variable. This may derive from the one to one, supervisor–student relationship in the final year, although it should also be noted that the third-year students in the cross-sectional study have been part of a much smaller year group throughout their degree course.

These results suggest that at least two of the variables identified by Entwistle and Ramsden (1983) as being conducive to the support of a meaning oriented approach, i.e. freedom to learn and good teaching, are perceived by students to be a part of their experience of the degree course. However, the third variable referred to by Entwistle and Ramsden – that of workload level – is perceived to be at a fairly constant level over the three year groups. In the final year it is fairly close to the average for the samples of psychology students investigated by Entwistle and Ramsden (1983).

Table 2 Cross-sectional data in relation to approach to studying: scores on the Approaches to Studying Inventory for students on the BA in Applied Studies (by Independent Study) for the Academic Year 1991/92

Approach to Students Dimensions	Year One Students		Year Two Students		Year Three Students		Norms for Psychology+ Students	
	Mean	SD	Mean	SD	Mean	SD	Mean	Range
Deep approach	10.896		11.316		11.337		10.8	
		2.408		2.668		3.016		9.9-12.4
Comprehensive learning	9.979		8.842		7.933		9.0	
		3.265		3.304		4.008		7.9-10.1
Relating ideas	11.208		12.105		13.733**		10.9	
		3.059		2.492		2.658		10.1-12.0
Use of evidence	9.021		9.789		10.333		9.6	
		3.145		2.616		2.690		8.5-11.0
Suface approach	14.708		13.842		12.200**		12.8	
		4.332		3.563		1.580		11.7-14.1
Improvidence	8.417		8.211		8.133		7.4	
		3.143		3.780		3.335		6.2-8.7
Fear of failure	6.938		6.263		5.333		5.9	
		3.284		3.160		2.895		4.8-7.0
Syllabus bound	8.021		7.316		7.733		7.7	
		2.365		3.757		2.520		6.4-8.6
Sample size	48		19		15			
% response rate	77.4%		67.9%		68.2%			

+From Entwistle and Ramsden (1983).
* Indicates a significant difference at the .05 level between first- and third-year students.
** Indicates a significant difference at the .01 level between first- and third-year students.

Results in relation to the Approaches to Studying Inventory

These results have been rather more mixed in relation to the support offered for the initial hypotheses. Although almost all the differences between first- and third-year responses (excepting those of comprehension learning) have been in the predicted direction, by no means all have approached statistical significance. However, there is a pattern here in that there is reasonably clear support for a reduction in reproducing approach but less evidence for a significant increase in meaning approach.

Table 3 - Longitudinal data in relation to approach to studying: scores on the Approaches to Studying Inventory for students on the BA in Applied Studies (by Independent Study) for the Academic Year 1991/92

Approach to studying dimensions	Year one Students		Year three Students		Norms for Students Psychology+	
	Mean	SD	Mean	SD	Mean	Range
Deep approach	11.172	2.564	11.586	2.529	10.8	9.9-12.4
Comprehensive learning	9.931	3.116	9.793	3.256	9.0	7.9-10.1
Relating ideas	11.000	3.047	11.966	2.442	10.9	10.1-12.0
Use of evidence	8.862	3.593	9.103	3.342	9.6	8.5-11.0
Surface approach	15.310	4.368	13.241*	5.249	12.8	11.7-14.1
Improvidence	8.690	3.253	8.241	3.192	7.4	6.2-8.7
Fear of failure	7552	3.007	6.759	2.734	5.9	4.8-7.0
Syllabus bound	8.414	2.130	6.862**	2.961	7.7	6.4-8.6
Sample size	29		29			
% response rate	64.4%		64.4%			

+From Entwistle and Ramsden (1983).
*   Indicates a significant difference at the .05 level between first- and third-year students.
**   Indicates a significant difference at the .01 level between first- and third-year students.

Looking in more detail at the changes in reproducing orientation, it can be seen that there is significant reduction (at the .05 level) in surface approach for both the cross-sectional and longitudinal data. It should be noted though that first-year students are particularly high in surface approach in comparison with the norms available from Entwistle and Ramsden's data.

For the longitudinal results there is also a reduction in levels of syllabus boundness between the first and third year. The mean level in the third year is close to the lower end of the range found in Entwistle and Ramsden's samples. In the cross-sectional data, third-year students have lower scores on fear of failure (significant at the .05 level) and the difference between students in their first and third year is also approaching significance in the longitudinal part of the study.

As indicated briefly above, changes in meaning orientation are less clear and consistent. It is only on the dimension of relating ideas that there is evidence of a significant difference between first- and third-year students. This occurs at the .01 level of significance for the cross-sectional data, but is only approaching significance for the longitudinal results.

Discussion of Findings

These results provide some, but not complete support for the initial hypotheses of this investigation. Results deriving from the Course Perceptions Questionnaire suggest that from the students' perspective some of the conditions which could be expected to increase meaning orientation and decrease reproducing orientation are present. This supports the *a priori* account of the teaching/learning context derived from the relevant literature.

Results from the Approaches to Studying Inventory demonstrate quite considerable evidence for a reduction in reproducing orientation. Findings from the cross-sectional and longitudinal parts of the study are supportive of each other. These results are encouraging in the contrast provided with earlier research (Gow and Kember, 1990) which demonstrated that surface approach can all too easily increase during the years of higher education. The results obtained in this current investigation provide further support for the research reported in Gibbs (1992) suggesting that teaching approaches can make a difference.

Disappointingly, evidence to support an increase in meaning orientation between the first- and-third year of the degree has been more limited. There is some initial evidence from other research that it might be more difficult to produce this kind of change than a reduction in reproducing approach (see Norton and Dickins, Chapter 35 of this volume, and some of the research reported in Gibbs 1992). It might be that the influencing factors are more complex. The remainder of this discussion section will be used to review some of the factors which might be operating within the particular context of the BA in Applied Social Studies (by Independent Study) with the expectation that such issues will also be of wider interest.

Workload influences

Entwistle and Ramsden (1983) identified high workload as being counter-productive in supporting the development of a meaning oriented approach. But what exactly constitutes a high workload? There are probably different kinds of ways in which a work load can be appropriately described as being high. Traditionally, one would probably identify a high lecture loading, strong examination pressures, and many (often conflicting deadlines) for course work. Final-year students on the BA in Applied Social Studies probably suffer less than many students on traditional degrees from these pressures. However, they would (and do!) complain that they are under different kinds of pressure, in having to complete a lengthy project report by a specified date. (Failure to hand in the project on the due date is treated as would absence from a final examination.) The pressure of 'having to keep up with the word production' throughout the year, in order to have a chance of finishing on time, **may** be counter-productive in terms of supporting a meaning oriented approach. As a result of these kinds of concerns, and external examiner comments on student performance, the demands placed upon students are being currently re-assessed.

Meaning orientation and effective self-management

There is, though perhaps an alternative way of viewing this issue of work load. It can be argued, quite reasonably, that the kind of pressure faced by students in the final year of the BA in Applied Social Studies is similar to that present in many job situations. This is the requirement to take personal responsibility for managing a complex set of ongoing demands. Learning to manage demands of this kind is almost certainly an important transferable skill in the current world. Of course, the most able and the most successful students will be able to both search for meaning and effectively manage their own learning when under pressure. However, for the less outstanding it may be that the skills of effective self management may be won at some cost to in-depth, meaning oriented understanding. (A much fuller discussion of the support of self -regulation processes within the BA in Applied Social Studies is provided in Cuthbert, 1995.)

When is project work best placed within the degree programme?

During the development of the BA in applied Social Studies degree programme, in the beginning of the 1980s, considerable emphasis was placed on the importance of establishing strong foundations in relevant discipline areas **before** students embarked on independent project work. This strategy is in agreement with current emphases upon the importance of a well-structured knowledge base as a foundation for the development of a meaning orientation (Biggs, 1989, Candy, 1991). However, this approach to organizing independent study was in some opposition to the pre-existing Independent Studies degree at the then North East London Polytechnic where students embarked on independent project work from the onset of their degree studies. This issue of the best placement of project work (of any kind) within a degree programme is raised again by the recent research of Gibbs (1992). He has emphasized the importance of using teaching strategies, including project work of one kind or another, from early on in a student's career in Higher Education. Once a student has become used to using reproducing strategies it may be difficult to alter these. Within the BA in Applied Social Studies there has always been a concern to provide a base for project work within the first two years of the degree course (see Cuthbert, 1994). It is possible that we still haven't got the balance quite right, but perhaps there is some inevitable tension between the requirement to provide a structured knowledge base, and to provide a context within which students can engage in meaning-oriented, and to some extent independent, exploration of a topic area?

To what extent is project work conducive to the development of a meaning orientation?

As indicated in the introduction to this paper there **is** reason and evidence to suppose that project work is likely to be conducive to the development of a meaning-oriented approach to learning. This evidence has been used to inform teaching and project planning strategies used within the BA in Applied Social Studies (see Cuthbert, 1994) and also underlies the hypotheses proposed in this investigation. However, it is perhaps too easy to assume that project work, **necessarily**, by its very nature, engenders a meaning-oriented approach in students. The reality is almost certainly much more complicated. It is probably necessary to accept that project work **can** be reproductive as well as meaning-oriented in character. The challenge of encouraging students to take a meaning-oriented approach within this kind of context continues, as it does within the more traditional teaching context.

Conclusion and Future Developments

The hypotheses underlying this research have been partly supported. Results from the Course Perceptions Questionnaire were largely in agreement with initial hypotheses. Data from the Approaches to Studying Inventory provided evidence to support a decrease in reproducing approach between year one and final-year students, but without much evidence of an increase in meaning approach. As discussed above it may be that it is more difficult to encourage and produce this latter kind of change. Currently within the BA in Applied Social Studies (by Independent Study) we are designing a new first-year compulsory course unit which is intended to have relevance to the promotion of a meaning approach. The unit will be experiential in character, will use discussion rather than being primarily didactic, and will encourage students to reflect upon their own approaches to studying and learning. Future research will evaluate the success (or otherwise) of this new unit.

References

Biggs, J. (1989). Approaches to the enhancement of tertiary teaching. *Higher Education Research and Development*, **8**, 7–25.

Candy, P.C. (1991). *Self Direction for Lifelong Learning*. San Francisco: Jossey Bass.

Cuthbert, K. (1994). Individual project work in relation to meaning and reproducing orientations within an applied social studies degree. In G. Gibbs (ed.), *Improving Student Learning: Theory and Practice*. Oxford: The Oxford Centre for Staff Development.

Cuthbert, K. (1995). Project planning and the promotion of self-regulated learning: *From Theory to Practice*. *Studies in Higher Education*, 20, 3.

Cuthbert, K. (in press). An innovative approach to teaching undergraduate psychology: Rationale for a major final year project. To be published in *Psychology Teaching Review*.

Decci, E.L. (1975). *Intrinsic Motivation*. New York: Plenum.

Entwistle, N. and Ramsden, P. (1983). *Understanding Student Learning*. London: Croom Helm.

Entwistle, N. and Tait, H. (1990). Approaches to learning, evaluations of teaching, and preferences for contrasting academic environments. *Higher Education*, **19**, 169–94.

Gibbs, G. (1992). *Improving the Quality of Student Learning*. Bristol: Technical and Educational Services Ltd.

Gow, L and Kember, D. (1990). *Does Higher Education Promote Independent Learning?* Higher Education., 19, 307-322

Marton, F. and Saljo, R. (1976). On quality differences in learning: I Outcomes and processes. *British Journal of Educational Psychology*, **46**, 4–11.

Rogers, C. (1969). *Freedom to Learn*. Columbus, Ohio: Merrill.

Richardson, J. T. E. (1990). Reliability and replicability of the Approaches to Studying Questionnaire. *Studies in Higher Education*, **15**, 155–68.

Richardson, J. T. E. (1992). A critical evaluation of a short form of the Approaches to Studying Inventory. *Psychology Teaching Review*, **1**(1), 34–45.

20

Should we always be aiming to promote deep approaches to learning? An evaluation of the ISL questionnaire in practice.

Stephen Blundell, (University of Central England)

Introduction

In *Improving Student Learning* (Gibbs, 1992) fostering 'deep approaches' appears the crucial objective. Is this relevant or reasonable for all subjects, or categories of student? Does fostering deep approaches conflict or complement objectives in art education? For post-experience students can this clarify or confuse their dual roles as 'recipient-student' and 'instigator-teacher'?

This chapter unravels some of the assumptions behind the questionnaire when applied to post-experience students of art. The results suggest we should be wary of fostering deep approaches in art education or for professional development.

Leslie Perry has noted that

policies and practices for In-service Education and Training (InSET) remain an accretion rather than a system[1]

In an article otherwise devoted to describing how problematic systematizing education really is this solitary comment about InSET appears suspiciously flawed, suggesting accretion to system should be an objective for InSET as well! But how can we describe InSET and how can we recognize the characteristics of this accretion? InSET has been typified, singularly or in combination, as:

a system -driven cafeteria of short, insular offerings lacking in nutrition,

related more to the interests of university staff [deliverers] than to teachers' needs [and/or]

workplace-based provision . . . hierarchical and paternalistic.[2]

---

[1] *Perry, L. (1993). Theoretical Comments, Journal of Art and Design Education 12(3) p.343–55. Perry does acknowledge that domination on initial training has been at the expense of 'inset training . . . that should be continuous after a brief initial training phase' p. 350.*

[2] *.O'Donoghue, T., Brooker, R.and Aspland, T. (1993). Professional Development: A Queensland Initiative , British Journal of In-Service Studies, 19(2), p 14-21*

InSET has been fairly immune from government interference that has so cripplingly systematized initial teacher training (ITT) and the curriculum of compulsory general education. This lack of interference is an important characteristic of InSET and has ensured that change, remains haphazard – organic might more accurately follow Perry's imagery. Not surprisingly, as InSETs remains peripheral to political intervention, it also remains a low-priority area for educational research.[3]

This chapter aims to redress this deficiency before, perhaps, the inevitable systematization of InSET occurs. By bringing together one InSET subject specific course :the DPSE course at Birmingham Institute of Art and Design: and some recent national studies into students' learning: that undertaken by Biggs, Gibbs and Ramsden for CNAA and Oxford Centre for Staff Development, I hope to demonstrate some of the strengths that manifest themselves through accretion.

What follows is a description of the Approaches to Learning Questionnaire arising out of the Oxford CSD study (Section1), an outline of the DPSE course (Section 2), results of pilot questionnaires completed by DPSE students (Section 3), and a section summarizing the issues raised and exploring implications for InSET in Art and Design, and on Professional Development of Teachers(Section 4) and some concluding remarks(Section 5).

The CNAA/ Oxford Centre for Staff Development Research Improving Student Learning

The OCSD study

During March 1992 the CNAA and Oxford Polytechnic circulated a report entitled 'Improving Student Learning', summarizing a national study which set out to identify

whether students' take a surface or a deep approach to learning

and to locate how

crucial this differentiation was for determining the quality of learning outcomes.[4]

Ten case studies were described, representing a range of undergraduate subject disciplines, revealing that if fostering 'deep' approaches is desirable, as was assumed, then four key features are essential,

• motivational context;
• learner activity;

---

[3] *A cursory glance at Journal of Art and Design Education shows InSET poorly represented where predominant concerns have been National Curriculum and the general education phase. The British Journal of InService Education and Training may purport to be international in flavour, is heavily consumed by quantifiable methodologists, with a smattering of participant observer articles. No specific art and design education articles appeared in recent years.*

[4] *CNAA & Oxford Centre for Staff Development (1992). Improving Student Learning. Quoted from below as OCSD. (Published as Gibbs, G. (1992). Improving the Quality of Student Learning Bristol:Technical and Educational Services.)*

- interaction with others; and
- a well structured knowledge base.[5]

It was claimed that strategies for course team design, careful monitoring and fine tuning devices, were likely to be as important for improving student learning, as concern for classroom practice or teaching skills; and that students' conservative reproductive learning approaches, and assessment systems not oriented closely to students' efforts, were just as likely to obstruct improvements.[6]

The Oxford study appeared to offer a useful model for investigating the relationship between teaching procedures, learning activities and learning outcomes. The subjects– art and education – and the student categories – InSET or post-experience – hardly featured in the case studies.[7] Was the model presented only relevant therefore to full-time undergraduate students, or could it be constructively applied, or amended elsewhere? In particular,

1 was the DPSE developing in students 'deep approaches to learning'?

2 was the promotion of 'deep approaches ' relevant, constructive or desirable for DPSE student?; and

3 were there lessons for INSET in Art or structuring professional development in general?

Fostering deep approaches

The distinction between surface and deep approaches to learning was first promoted by Marton and Saljo in 1976 [8] revealing that most Higher Education teaching required regurgitation by students, where the examination form, content and practice determined the motivation, strategy and method of study.[9] The distinction between deep and surface approaches is now a part of the conceptual framework of student learning researchers,

although there are distinct differences in methodologies and basic frameworks.[10]

Contemporary researchers tend to follow one of two lines of enquiry. Both utilize factor analysis of questionnaires, some 'loyal' to the original Marton and Säljö sense of

---

[5] *Ibid., p.1*

[6] *Ibid., p. 1. The Teaching and Learning strategies enumerated are: independent learning; problem-solving learning; reflection; independent group work; learning by doing; project-work;development of the individual and fine tuning.*

[7] *Ibid., p.2–4 A case study of one part-time course was included, a BA in Business Studies for mature students, with evening-only attendance. Very formal in teaching styles, with consequent poor staff–student, and student–student interaction prompted participation in research project.*

[8] *Marton, F. and Säljö, R. (1976). On qualitative differences in learning :1 outcomes and process. British Journal of Educational Psychology, 46, 4–11.*

[9] *Oxford Centre for Staff Development (OCSD) instigated research as a result of HMI report into English Polytechnics 1988: claiming identical grounds for concern as twenty years earlier. What does this say about learning research and its impact?*

[10] *Biggs, J. (1990). Teaching Design for Learning. Paper delivered Higher Education Research and Development Society of Australasia Conference, p. 5.*

approaches as descriptions of an immediate engagement with a specific task [11]

others, as Biggs would claim himself to be, concerned

with yielding approaches in a presage sense...as a fairly stable characteristic of the student.[12]

The Oxford study inclines towards the latter 'presage' model, building up, through separate case studies, various relationships between the variants. Changes in course design, often precipitated by student dissatisfaction, poor staff– student interaction, or, alternatively through staff initiative or experimentation, are recorded where the learning emphases shift from 'surface' to 'deep' . The changes recorded are by no means always 'successful', but overall methods employed offer a potentially useful tool for any course team. The following definitions, used in the Oxford study, distinguish deep from surface approaches :

- **Deep** Students focus their attention on the overall meaning or message in a lecture, text or situation. [13] They attempt to relate ideas together and construct their own meaning, possibly in relation to their own experience.
- **Surface** Students focus their attention on the details and information in a lecture or text. They are trying to memorize these individual details in a form they appear in the lecture or text or to list the features of the situation.[14]

Three orientations provide the framework for the questionnaire: achieving, reproducing and meaning. The claim is that returns can alert student and tutor to individual and group orientations to learning, draw comparison with national norms, and assist course planning, by indicating features likely to encourage deep approaches, and those teaching and learning strategies that may need accommodating.[6]

Before looking at these orientations and their application in detail a brief description of the DPSE course will provide a clear context to the study.

---

[11] *Ibid., p. 5.*

[12] *Ibid., p. 5.*

[13] *The term 'situation' is the catch all presumably for any other learning style. Does this ignorance of the design studio, the art workshop demonstrate ignorance of the essential means through which art and design activity is conveyed: and by implication, is art and design therefore excluded from the impact of this research? It was bought to my attention following the symposium that there have been alternative versions of the 'standard' ISL questionnaire designed for subject specific students, and art and design is no exception. Refer to 'The Learning Methods Unit', UCE.*

[14] *OCSD, ibid, Questionnaire, p. 2.*

The course: The Diploma in Professional Studies in Education (Art and Design Technology) (DPSE)

The DPSE [15]

Forming one of three validated and well-established courses in the School of Art and Design Education devoted to the initial training, and subsequent professional development, of teachers and lecturers in art and design, the School is located, alongside the School of Fine Art, uniquely within the Department of Art, of an Institute of Art and Design.[16] Close proximity to art and design practitioners has affected course philosophy which claims school-based practice and professional development are best enhanced through 'personal subject development in art and design' . The course aims to

> provide a framework within which teachers . . . can engage in and reflect upon their personal and professional experience in art and design, and education and develop new knowledge, skills and understanding as Art and Design educators [17]

Students are encouraged to gain:

(a) a deeper involvement in the practices associated with Art and Design ,

(b) a critical engagement with contemporary issues affecting Art and Design educational practices, and

(c) a clear understanding and appreciation of the factors which inform their own professional context [18]

within a learning context that recognises

> these factors are inter-related throughout the course and the listing or sequence here does not imply emphasis or structure.[19]

According to the most recent external examiner's report these aims are clearly achieved for:

> there is *abundant evidence* of a variety and range of teaching styles being adopted appropriate to the diversity of teaching contexts and backgrounds of the students and the various expectations each has of the course.[20] [emphasis in original]

That factors inter-relate may appear clear from this source, but how this relationship

---

[15] *The title of the course reflects the changes in National Curriculum in recent years. The course is centred around Art: and thus addresses the NC subject Art and also Arts' contribution to NC Design and Technology. The shorthand for Art is used throughout.*

[16] *The three courses in the School of Art and Design Education are PGCE (Art and Design), MA (Masters of Art Education) and DPSE; in addition there are higher degree and research provision in the School.*

[17] *UCE DPSE Student Handbook (1993) p. 4*

[18] *Ibid., p. 5.*

[19] *Ibid., p. 5.*

[20] *Taylor ,R. (1993). External Examiners' Report, para. 3.*

develops for each student remains infuriatingly opaque, often for the student as much as for the tutor. Perhaps the ALQ would reveal some helpful indicators.

Factors affecting teaching and learning

Factors affecting learning are conditioned by the climate for learning, students' needs, opportunities and motivations, the quality, relevance and delivery of teaching, a supportive environment for learning, and fair and appropriate mechanisms for assessment.

Sustaining InSET has never been a political, or indeed, educational priority. Only through teachers' determination has any profile for INSET been maintained, accompanied all too often by an increasing need for self-funding. This is a sorry state of affairs and not surprisingly has led to provision declining as institutional targets become more and more difficult to meet: a vicious circle that severely limits the range and opportunities available. Justifying and engaging in InSET remains very much an optional extra for the teaching profession.

Untypically this DPSE actively encourages applicants with diverse interests, experiences and knowledge of art and design, and aims to accommodate their differing expectations on the course. These differences complement students' common experiences as teachers and the inevitable degree to which students inform each others' learning on the course.[21]

Teaching and learning styles do include formal lectures, educational visits, and individual tutorials, but the tutor-led taught programme is dominated by experiential learning, through practical-based enquiries; individual and small group work; reflection on past and current practices; and speculation on future implications. These characteristics mirror those features claimed to be essential to promote deep approaches to learning, namely: ensuring a motivational context, learner-based activities, structuring interaction with peers and others and a clearly organized knowledge base. This mirroring here is co-incidental and these features are the result of years of art educational experience in a post-experience context. So there have arisen, been refined and developed to satisfy students' very much in a subject specific context only: a process, you could accurately describe as an accretion rather than a system.

Learning, in such a context, become an acceptable 'imbalance' of achievements, replications and meaning making.[22] Success or failure is determined by course-dictated factors, issues affecting students' responsiveness, and the inter-actionalist capacities affecting each session. Tutors have to allow for the stresses of each working day that inevitably accompanies part-time student attendance, as much as the determination of students to share and reflect on common educational experiences.

---

[21] *A typical cohort may contain a primary deputy or head-teacher, an infants' teacher, a primary teacher responsible for technology, a primary teacher qualified in HE and relatively new to the profession, a middle-school art teacher of extensive teaching experience, two other primary teachers, a head of faculty of art and technology in a secondary school, a head of department of art in a secondary school, a part-art, part-science teacher in a secondary school, a textiles teacher in secondary, a part-time secondary teacher with experience as a professional potter, a teacher from special school, from the prison service or further education.*

[22] *The term 'imbalance' is used analogously as the constant state of alertness, endemic to life, in a biological sense. This might well be an over-optimistic view to take of our awareness of our own learning!*

Course characteristics

The course provides a suitable and flexible framework where sharing and discussion of individual contexts is an established component. This is visibly reflected in delivery, which can be in students' schools, a local teachers' centre or a UCE base; through a structure which comprises taught, and directed, programmes; through content which enables individual interests and priorities to be sifted, studied and acted upon; and through an assessment strategy which enables evidence from school-based and/or home-based studies to be negotiated and exhibited.

Advancing professional development, as the DPSE claims, is characterized by provision of a climate for experience, analysis and development; one where the emphasis is on creating a flexible and supportive climate for student learning rather than simply on staff teaching. Assignments, in the form of small exhibitions or illustrated reports, conclude each terms' module, and reflect self-knowledge, classroom knowledge, or 'action knowledge', as Barnes might term it.[23] The DPSE qualification is seen increasingly as a means of rewarding learning, of rewarding studies, not defining them. How will deep or surface approaches support or supplant these objectives?

The Questionnaire: DPSE Returns

Distribution and returns

Two sets of identical questionnaires were circulated separately to whole year groups early in a spring term. The questionnaire comprised the standard 18 separate questions, confined to one side of A4.[24] A straightforward request was made, in each case, for participants to give 'quick responses' by circling a number that corresponded to an appropriate response code. It was explained that responses could indicate students' differing approaches to studying. No additional explanation was provided. The resulting scores were tabulated and results posted.

The timing of the questionnaires' circulation was random. Year-one students were awaiting the results of assignment one and preparing for module 2, the beginning of term 2: year-two students, having completed four termly assignments, were entering their fifth and final term.

There were 100 per cent returns- year 1 =10 returns, year 2 =7. The scores were tabulated following instructions on page 2 of Appendix 1. Description of the returns together with analysis of scores were based upon accompanying category definitions provided on the same page.

Definitions and orientations

THE ORIENTATIONS
The ISL orientations were described as follows:

The Achieving Orientation – 'A' Scale Score

---

[23] *Barnes (1977). From Communication to Curriculum. Harmondsworth.*
[24] *See appendix for example of material used.*

This indicates competitiveness, [25] well organised study methods, and hope for success. Students who score high on this scale are orientated towards doing well, whatever this involves. They tend to do well.

The Reproducing Orientation – 'B' Scale Score

This indicates a surface approach to learning. Students who score high on this scale attempt to memorise subject matter and are not interested in studying a subject for its own sake but only out of a concern to pass or gain qualifications. They keep narrowly to the syllabus as laid down in course descriptions and do not follow up interests of their own (if they have any). Despite their concern to pass they tend to do badly.

The Meaning [26] Orientation – 'C' Scale Score.

This indicates a deep approach to learning: the intention to make sense of the subject, an interest in the subject itself, and a desire to learn. Students who score high on this scale follow up their own interests even if outside those parts of the course which are assessed. They tend to do well.

All orientation scores are out of 24.

SOME OBSERVATIONS ON THE ORIENTATIONS

These orientations and their definitions invite comment. In particular: what messages do we send students and colleagues by using them?

On the three orientations

It is claimed that the three orientations are not mutually exclusive. [27] How is this to be interpreted and to what extent are they inclusive of each other? How, therefore, do we measure segregation and inclusivity through their scorings? Indeed how were the three initially selected, and how appropriate are they deemed to be in providing quantitative evidence? These are questions that I do not feel competent to judge in the context of questionnaire design and analysis, but I can make assumptions about the implied separateness of the orientations and attempt to focus upon the essential differences between them.

Meaning, for instance, can derive quite legitimately from the activities of achieving or reproducing. The meaning orientation can not easily be segregated from the other two orientations. But there is the strong implication that it can be so isolated and that only a particular sort of meaning making is appropriate in the context of this questionnaire. In art meaning is a notoriously complex affair and I am sure that this is also the case for other disciplines. So I am uneasy with the status of the meaning orientation per se: there is insufficient distinction between it and the other two orientations and there appears to be a range of 'correct' meanings implicitly ascribed to it in this context.

---

[25] *Perry, in a letter of 20/9/94 to the author, questions the meaning of competitiveness. His observation is taken up in the section : 'On the definitions provided for each orientation', p. 265.*
[26] *Meaning, in particular problems of its exclusivity role, is touched in the section 'On the three orientations'. p. 264.*
[27] *This was a strong assertion during the discussions that followed session delivery.*

On the definitions provided for each orientation

In reality students and tutors will utilize the definitions provided under each orientation to explicate a particular score. The meanings attributed to each orientation become of paramount importance therefore and the interpretation and nuances provided can be the lynch-pin of the entire process. So how do the meanings given relate to the experience of students and tutors in utilizing them?

Competitiveness, for instance seen within the 'achievement orientation', presents a fairly typical problem. What is the role of competitiveness within this orientation, how does competing differ from achieving, is competing subsumed within achieving or vice versa, is there a causal connection between the two? Clearly how we interpret this element requires considerable sensitivity before we jump to any conclusions. Given the definitions in this form I, and more importantly my students, have found it impossible to avoid ambiguity and confusion.

Undoubtedly the definitions require considerable fleshing out, not only if we are to act to interpret data, but also if we are to become rather more convinced of the structure, division and definition of these basic orientations to learning.[28]

Such subtleties may appear pedantic but they are nevertheless important in revealing some of the underlying assumptions about the design and function of the questionnaire itself. To be wary of the results of any questionnaire must, in my view, be a pre-requisite for utilizing them.

PUBLISHED NORMS

Norms have been published for the questionnaire reflecting differing subject categories and the standard deviation for all three orientations. Evidence of 'deep' approaches to learning will appear above averages for achieving and meaning, and below average for reproducing scales.

Table 1 Published norms

	Achieving	Reproducing	Meaning
Arts norms	12.5	11.9	15.1
Social Science norms	12.7	13.6	14.2
Science norms[28]	13.0	14.2	13.9
Overall norms	12.8	13.5	14.3
Standard deviation	4.2	4.4	4.5

The tables below sequence student returns and through from the individual to the group, the particular to the general :

---

[28] *A further response of staff and students was the organization of the questionnaire itself. Two orientations, 'achieving' and 'meaning', act posnce of a 'surface' approach. I am unsure whether this is 'only' an aesthetic issue, but the discomfort of balancing levels, depths and polarities can perceptually be very disorientating: they do not 'hang' well together. The whole issue of questionnaire design, by whom, for whom, and to what extent they can be changed was only briefly explored during symposium. The central question here is what can I change to suit my circumstances while retaining the integrity of the original questionnaire.*

- individual student profiles;
- individual student patterns;
- distribution of results; and
- results overall compared to norms.

Individual student profiles

In order to maintain anonymity each student was asked to identify him/her self by means of a number code, in the case of year 1, and a letter code, for year 2.

Figure 1 – year 1 students

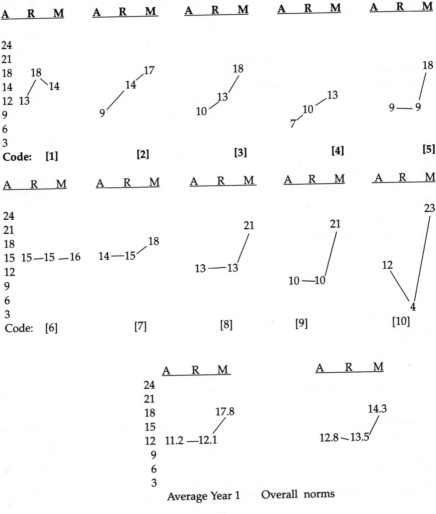

Average Year 1   Overall norms

266

YEAR 1 STUDENTS

Year 1 profiles show individual variation across all three orientations, most dramatic when comparing students [1] and [10]. The former offers strong 'surface' approaches on reproducing and meaning scales. The latter extends averages and overall norms to an extreme position, showing exceptional 'deep' learning approaches for each orientation. The remainder demonstrate a typical, normal' profile, albeit, with some consistently high meaning scores compared to overall norms.

YEAR 2 STUDENTS

Figure 2 year 2 students

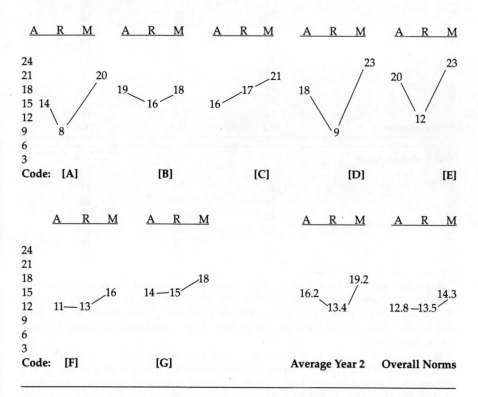

Code: [A] [B] [C] [D] [E]

Code: [F] [G] Average Year 2 Overall Norms

Profiles show significant variation for year 2 students although not as dramatic as for year 1s. Year 2 profiles fall into two categories, those loosely grouped together – [B],[C], [F], and [G], and those offering exaggerated profiles – [A],[D], and [E]. The former group exhibits some high achieving and reproducing scores, with consistently high meaning scores, indicating some evidence of deep approaches but also significant surface symptoms. The latter group shows fairly high achieving and much lower reproducing scores, with consistently higher meaning scores: indicating deep approaches across all three orientations.

Individual student patterns

Scores below are bold and underlined when signifying 'deep' approaches to learning. These will appear above averages for achieving and meaning, and below average for reproducing. Overall norms have been used as the 'norm' figures.

Table 2

	Achieving	*Reproducing*	*Meaning*
Overall norms	*12.8*	*13.5*	*14.3*
Year 1 students code			
1	**<u>13</u>**	18	14
2	9	14	**<u>17</u>**
3	10	**<u>13</u>**	**<u>18</u>**
4	7	**<u>10</u>**	13
5	9	**<u>9</u>**	**<u>18</u>**
6	**<u>15</u>**	15	**<u>16</u>**
7	**<u>14</u>**	15	**<u>16</u>**
8	**<u>13</u>**	**<u>13</u>**	**<u>21</u>**
9	10	**<u>10</u>**	**<u>21</u>**
10	12	**<u>4</u>**	**<u>23</u>**
Overall norms	*12.8*	*13.5*	*14.3*
Year 2 students code			
A	**<u>14</u>**	**<u>8</u>**	**<u>20</u>**
B	**<u>19</u>**	16	**<u>18</u>**
C	**<u>16</u>**	17	**<u>21</u>**
D	**<u>18</u>**	**<u>9</u>**	**<u>23</u>**
E	**<u>20</u>**	**<u>12</u>**	**<u>23</u>**
F	11	**<u>13</u>**	**<u>16</u>**
G	**<u>14</u>**	15	**<u>18</u>**

Comparing year 1 to year 2 scores shows increasing evidence of 'deep' approaches: individual patterns increase representation from 40% to 84% on the achieving scale and 80% to 100% on the meaning scale, whereas the reproducing scale reduces slightly from 60% to 56%. This represents a marked increase in deep approaches overall year 1 to year 2 from 60% to 80%.

The individual profiles themselves show further evidence of 'deep' approaches, for those that are 100% underlined across all three orientation scales, show a solitary year 1 student [8] – 10% of student body – with a marked increase to three year 2 students [A],[D], and [E] – 42% of student body.

The low-achieving scores of year 1 students [2],[3],[4],[5], and [9] compare with only one year 2 student [F]: thus 50% of year 1 reduces dramatically to 14% for year 2. This may indicate a low period of self-esteem for the year 1 students, slow growth in confidence, tendency to over-criticize their own abilities; all tendencies one would expect to see reduce significantly by their second year.

Evidence of deep approaches to learning appear to be progressively and comprehensively demonstrated by these individual students scores.

Distribution of results

Table 3   shows the scored returns distribution pattern, year by year.

Table 3	Achieving		Reproducing		MEANING	
Score	Yr1	Yr2	Yr1	Yr2	Yr1	Yr2
Averages: For year= underlining.						
24					1	
23						2
22						2
21						1
20	1					1
19	1					19.2
					[18.9]	
18	1		1		2	2
17				1	17.6	
	16.2					
16	1			1	2	1
15	1		2	1		
14	1	2	1		1	
	[13.7]			13.6		
13	2		2	1	1	
			[12.8]			
12	1		12.1	1		
11	11.2	1				
10	2		2			
9	2		1	1		
8				1		
7	1					
6						
5						
4			1			
3						
2						
1	Achieving		Reproducing		Meaning	

Comparing distribution of year 1 to year 2 scores, the achieving scale, retains an even distribution but shifts the average substantially in the direction of 'deeper' approaches. The reproducing scale narrows the distribution by 50% (the year 1 scores idiosyncratically across 14 points, using 60% of the available scale), while raising the average slightly against the flow of 'deeper' approaches.

Similarly the meaning scale reduces the distribution, by 40%, as the average increases in excess of the standard deviation figure using two of the three norms (see Table 1 taking standard deviation as 4.5 for meaning arts norm = 19.6; social science norm = 18.7 and overall norms = 18.8).

Results overall compared to norms

ARTS NORMS

Table 4 Arts norms

	Achieving	Reproducing	Meaning
Yr1 overall	11.2	12.1	7.8
Yr2 overall	16.2	13.4	19.2
Arts norms	12.5	11.9	15.1
Social Science norms	12.7	13.6	14.2
Science	13.0	14.2	13.9
Overall	12.8	13.5	14.3
Standard deviation	4.2	4.4	4.5

The achieving score for year 2 supports 'deep' approaches, as does the meaning scores for both years. The reproducing scores for both years are above average, therefore indicating shallower 'surface' approaches. Noticeably year 2 reproducing score increases, rather than reduces, the likelihood of 'shallower' approaches – shift from year 1 to year 2 that one might not anticipate.

Compared to national 'overall norms' and 'arts norms', high meaning scores clearly indicate 'deep approaches': implying strong interest in the subject, desire to understand, and willingness to initiate developments. Conversely, or perversely, a shift from year 1 to year 2 increases 'surface' approaches as well: implying concern to do well, to pass, limited subject focus and restricted syllabus interests. Let us consider briefly two issues, that may illuminate these inconsistencies: the 'concern' factor, and the 'comparable norm' factor.

THE 'CONCERN' FACTOR

How does the 'concern' factor affect both yr 1 and yr 2 students? Year 1 students, in the early stages of their course, wait to gauge the level of achievement for their first module assignment. Likewise yr 2 students near completion of studies are uncertain as to expectations for the external examination. In both cases degrees of anxiety or uncertainty, could be understandable. How much are these concerns 'watersheds'; how much necessary, normal, course considerations? How much do these considerations form part of the normal healthy concerns of all students: are they as Biggs may claim part of the 'stable characteristics of students', or are they, in the context of art, and InSET not only unstabling elements but also unstabling concerns for all students?

THE 'COMPARABLE NORM' FACTOR?

The second factor centres on the high 'reproducing' scores compared to arts norms. Broad differentiation into arts/social science and science norms beg many questions; not least differences in learning methods as a condition of norm segregation. [29] This does raise complications for the DPSE. We could accept, as the course aims suggest, that art – 'the principal discipline' – would normally entertain comparison with norms in the arts category. Yet as the course concerns art and education, and also factors professionally relevant to each student, could social science norms alternatively or additionally apply? The implication here is that, among other factors, learning methods affects norms gradings. A brief comparison with other discipline norms would appear sensible.

Table 5 Compatible norms

	Achieving	*Reproducing*	*Meaning*
Yr1 overall	**11.2**	**2.1**	**17.8**
Yr2 overall	**16.2**	**13.4**	**19.2**
Arts norms	12.5	11.9	15.1
Social Science norms	**12.7**	**13.6**	**14.2**
Science	13.0	14.2	13.9
Overall	12.8	13.5	14.3
Standard deviation	4.2	4.4	4.5

The achieving score for year 1 remains beneath the average, as the year 2 score appears above the norm; both years demonstrate below average scores on the reproducing scale; and the meaning scores consistently supports 'deep' approaches.

Students' 'concerns', and ' identifying comparable norms' may not be as significant as claimed. I may be merely bending the rules to accommodate the figures. However the spread demonstrated by the differing norms show significant changes and it is vital to utilize correct and accurate comparisons otherwise any credibility is dissipated, and perhaps false assumptions made about learning methods as a consequence.

---

[29] *For instance, how do we log what our students do, in what category do we place Art Education students, and how do we therefore apportion norms and arrive at standard deviations?*

Summaries

Is the DPSE developing 'deep' approaches to learning? Is this desirable or relevant?What are the implications for DPSE and for InSET students?

AN ACCEPTABLE LEARNING PROFILE FOR DPSE STUDENTS?

Post experience students are often highly motivated and DPSE students are no exception: they want to learn and they want to take advantage of educational provision. This despite having to fund themselves, undertake study in addition to full-time employment and frequently with family commitments. The DPSE is an investment for them as individuals not just as educators. So what they require needs to relate to them and enable them to reflect on past experiences, extend their knowledge base and prepare for futures. These are high expectations.

Given this context we could be forgiven for expecting a narrowing of learning approaches as students progress through their course: one that offers a clear uni-directional orientation from surface to deep. A narrowing does occur and deep approaches are in evident. But this does not necessarily present a clear or conclusive picture and this admittedly modest experiment should caution us not to make false assumptions about an 'acceptable profile' for DPSE students.

EVIDENCE OF A 'DEEP' AND 'SURFACE' DUALISM

The shifts from year 1 to year 2, across all scores, show a range of approaches, from deep to surface. These, unfortunately can be rather clumsy terms and I frequently sought more subtle terminologies. Evidence of 'deep' approaches is, however, clear and consistent, but surprisingly so is evidence of 'surface' approaches. What lies behind this?

One possible explanation for this dualism in approaches is that levels of negotiable learning become more available to DPSE students as they progress through their studies: these are opportunities to share in and shape the development, pace and content of their own learning. This, of course, not only increases the potential for 'deepening' learning it also increases the risk of 'shallowing' learning as opportunities become risky or threatening. The 'concern' factor thus increases by introducing precisely those strategies that herald 'deeper' approaches.

It could be argued, as it was in discussions at the symposium, that we should not so much view the approaches to learning as a dualism (despite the clear visual thread implied by the terms deep and surface) but as a range of interacting approaches that incorporates a 'strategic' dimension as well as 'deep' and surface' approaches. [30]

INTRODUCTION TO QUESTIONNAIRE DESIGN AND DELIVERY

Clearly to utilize this questionnaire introduces insights into data analysis, questionnaire design and application, learning theories, and differentiates subject specific issues from

---

[30] *The 'strategic' dimension as an additional orientation, to accompany 'deep' and 'surface' , was raised and debated following my presentation. I was convinced that a greater understanding of how 'deep' and 'surface' were interpreted was essential before introducing another category, although I would accept the potential for differentiating between 'tactical' approaches to learning (that could encompass both 'deep' and 'surface' approaches) from, more longer term, 'strategic' intentions. This seems to be an area for fruitful enquiry and will be one of the issues I will be pursuing with my students during this academic year.*

general educational ones . It also addresses perceptions on students' learning and could be a useful tool if subsumed as an integral part of the educational experiences of students.

DPSE/InSET STUDENTS AS BOTH 'RECIPIENTS' AND 'INSTIGATORS'

One factor that distinguishes InSET and DPSE students from other types of students is that they are both 'recipients' and 'instigators' in the education field, particularly acute if studying on a part-time basis, which is currently the most common mode. This dichotomy often puts conflicting pressures on 'students'; pressures we could infer from the high meaning and reproducing returns. Generally the more experience of and knowledge about differing approaches to learning a teacher, as student, experiences (and by implication, evidence of application), the greater confidence to select, apply and discern learning approaches for their children and students.

MARKING THE INDIVIDUAL ACCRETION OF LEARNING FOR InSET?

Introduction of this research could be carefully integrated into the taught programme, as part of the practically based enquiries that characterize the DPSE. Introducing ISL has the potential to mark for an individual their accreting learning. There is evidence, from individual tutorials with DPSE students, that suggests that it could indicate areas for speculation, offer a direction for self-reflection: that at best it may illustrate 'a passage for my own learning and not confine it'. Could this be construed as the sort of accretion of learning, of which Perry speaks? [31]

AN ADDITIONAL DIALOGUE FOR POST-EXPERIENCE STUDENTS?

For all students there are constructive degrees of tensions implicit in courses of higher education. In the context of post-experience study, pairings of 'the personal with the professional', and 'teaching with learning', offer two important model dialogues. DPSE students are no exception to these needs and the introduction of approaches to learning, with its emphases on 'deep or surface approaches', add, not another model for action but another opportunity for dialogue.

HOW CHARACTERISTIC ARE THESE ORIENTATIONAL SHIFTS?

How much these orientational shifts are characteristic of InSET students, of all adult , continuing students, how much the subject disciplines affect these shifts, how 'normal' these features are remains, unfortunately, beyond the scope of this enquiry. There was little opportunity to carry out the post-questionnaire interviews that so clearly informed the original Oxford case studies and it was also regretted that no trace was made to gauge the developing levels of individual orientation as students moved from year 1 to year 2. [32]

---

[31] Perry, *op. cit.*, suggests that there are *'serious variables'* in the learning process . . . and *'it may be . . . that "accretion" is a way of describing an accumulated mass of theory . . . [and practices], that lies mainly undisturbed'*. This may be one way to differentiate the individual accretion of learning as opposed to *'a'* system for learning.

[32] During this current year post-questionnaire interviews will form an integral part of the individual student tutorials, as will some attempt to compare and contrast the individual student profiles with success rates on the course.

IMPLICATIONS FOR UTILIZING THE ISL QUESTIONNAIRE

While it appears that there are a number of gains to be made in utilizing the ISL questionnaire there have also been sufficient uncertainties raised to question the wisdom of anticipating any acceptable profile that relies upon 'deep' rather than 'surface' approaches as the guiding objective. Confidence through individual discrimination by students is surely what we are encouraging: in this subject area no less than in other disciplines.

There are fundamental issues being raised here and I am uncertain whether I have the competence to delineate them. Some questions however can be put forward: is anything intrinsic to art education being revealed: can we begin to clarify the complexities of post-experience students educational experiences; how does the design of the questionnaire influence any resulting returns; what relationships are endemic between the three orientations; what value do post experience students attribute to 'deep' or 'surface' approaches; how can one proceed to uncover the individual connections between teaching and learning strategies, questionnaire returns and levels of students satisfaction; and what are the perception of students themselves of such investigations? Perry wisely reminds us to take an even wider view, when asking, could the professional artist's role in learning be 'worthy of much more investigation'? [33]

Concluding Remarks

At least two hidden issues have emerged throughout this enquiry: what do we understand by the terms 'professional' and 'development', in the context of art and education? These are briefly outlined below as preludes to my final cautionary note.

What do I mean by the term 'professional'?

The term 'professional' remains obscure, used on occasions to infer, rather than to evidence, quality, and to separate hierarchically from notions of 'amateur'. All 'professions' retain their often idiosyncratic understanding of what constitutes professionalism, and consequently erect mechanisms to quantify the expected competencies expected of members. It is assumed that to be a member or to form a profession is inherently a good thing, and that resultant professionalism, as sanctioned by guiding spirits, will reap benefits not only for members but also for those outside the profession, whether the ubiquitous 'general public', or the direct recipients of the 'professionals' attention; in the case of education, teachers, children, parents and society. The role of a professional is frequently bounded by non-professional, leading to severe lack of professional confidence of members. Systematizing InSET, any more than it is already, can only add to this decrease in confidence of professionals.

So anything that encourages learning about learning, empowering the learner, as ISL questionnaire suggests it might, in however limited a way, can make a contribution to increasing self-confidence for InSET professionals.

---

[33] *The artist as model for the art educator was predominant during the nineteenth century, usurped by the child as model, and the subject as model during this century. So Perry re-introduces a dimension for the learner that is very much currently 'out of favour'.*

What do I mean by 'development' in the context of 'professional development'?

Lack of development, 'un-' or 'under-' development, implies unrealized potential, a wasteful, almost extravagant luxury hardly affordable. We might consider development the antithesis of deprivation, the withdrawal, the restriction of potential. Higher education would claim development as one of its key purposes, but in so doing it is likely to manage development in ways that encourage deprivation. One example of this might be to consider claiming always to promote deep approaches to learning. Not only is this unattainable, but more importantly it is likely to be impractical, inappropriate or potentially damaging, by setting too high, irrelevant or unrealistic standards. Bower describes development as a human characteristic where the motives to understand and to commune with people are paramount [defining development as] a process of differentiation without loss. [34]

Pursuing professional development and the impact of ISL?

It is likely that developing a framework for competencies for InSET will be a logical extension of the further centralizing of the present educational system.Whether this becomes a condition of teaching as a profession, as is happening in initial teacher training, or whether pluralist perspectives on professionalism will prevail for professional development, to be 'the further, continuing, and extending, differentiation without loss' to paraphrase Bower, remains to be seen.

Patterns for post-experience professional development change dependent upon a series of complicated criteria, including: level and maintenance of interest, type and form of stimulus, perceived purpose, and degrees of satisfaction, as well as organisational, financial and social factors. If the ISL is utilized to condition a system for InSET, to present prepared objective profiles for differing students and differing discipline applications, there will (or 'should' – I should not be so optimistic) be strong resistance; if it can be utilised as one of a number of factors to assist students and staff together in empowering the learner then it could have some significant benefits.

A cautionary note

Biggs was not the first to claim that it is time for research into tertiary teaching and learning to be

> less a search for 'best' methods of teaching [more] encouraging staff awareness of the relationship between teaching procedures, learning activities and learning outcomes. [35]

Studies by Abercrombie, and Mason, during the 1970s similarly directed attention to the quality of students' learning in higher education, emphasizing not so much what the teacher did, or what the teacher had to say, as to what the learner interpreted. They both, separately, devised mechanisms to

---

[34] *Bower, T. (1979). Human Development. Wiley, London, p. 430.*
[35] *Biggs, op. cit., p. 2.*

gauge the effectiveness of the teaching programme [36]

by, for instance, involving students and tutors in discussions about the qualities of learning. That staff at University College, London wanted little to do with such contentious issues did not stop Abercrombie striving to gather meaningful information rather than mere speculation from students and staff: she was into accretion, not system (perhaps not co-incidentally she was originally trained as a biologist if I recall, so accretion would have had a special import). Perhaps the ISL questionnaire may promote a similar stance particularly with regard to InSET, and provide a vehicle for instigator and recipient alike.

I could become complacent on the strength of these questionnaire returns. They do proffer evidence of deep approaches to learning. But I am not going to be lulled into any false sense of security that this was necessarily intended or the results beneficial for my students. I was not entirely surprised, therefore, at the symposium to find the title of my paper and my session delivery were regarded as 'rebel' contributions. I make no apology for asking what might appear to be simple questions, and I expect to be able to question assumptions about the design, application and interpretation of the ISL research, as I saw it affect my students. However cursory my own knowledge of the research is, there is no denying the importance of the issues I feel need raising for Art and for Education, and for more communal issues of professionalism and the development of learning.

In addressing 'approaches' to learning the ISL research has undoubtedly been provocative and raised important issues about motivation, intentionality, purposefulness, reflection, and the making of meaning that require considerable and sensitive delineation. If my rebellious (artistic?) nature flies in the face of acknowledged wisdom, I do so with the intention of empowering students, not constraining them.

Finally there are times when we need to have a surface approach to things, perhaps to learn to recite texts by heart, perhaps to ingest pre-formed knowledge, or to become reluctantly, almost casually, engaged, or to be restrained and to keep our emotions unruffled. There are important times in art education, in InSET, in higher education and life in general when these learning approaches are essential. My purpose in this chapter is to ask that we remember that.

---

[36] Abercrombie, J. (1972). *Gauging the Effectiveness of the First Year Teaching programme. University College London, School of Architecture.*
Mason, E. (1978). *Evaluating Student Learning. Both authors were convinced of the need to engage students, right from the first 'taught' session, in the learning about learning process, and both were immensely skilled in enabling students to want to know about their own learning. I was privileged to have worked for both of them in a small capacity.*

Appendix

THE LANCASTER APPROACHES TO STUDYING QUESTIONAIRE

Please answer every item quickly by giving your immediate response. Circle the appropriate code number to show your general approach to studying modules

4	(++)	means Definitely agree
3	(+)	means Agree with reservations
2	(?)	is only to be used if the item doesn't apply to you or if you find it impossible to give a definite answer
1	(-)	means Disagree with reservations
0	(--)	means Definitely disagree

		++	+	?	-	–	Scale
1	I find it easy to organise my study time effectively.	4	3	2	1	0	(A)
2	I like to be told precisely what to do in essays or other set work.	4	3	2	1	0	(B)
3	It's important to me to do really well in the course here.	4	3	2	1	0	(A)
4	I usually set out to understand thoroughly the meaning of what I am asked to read.	4	3	2	1	0	(C)
5	When I'm reading I try to memorise important facts which may come in useful later.	4	3	2	1	0	(B)
6	When I'm doing a piece of work, I try to bear in mind exactly what that particular lecturer seems to want.	4	3	2	1	0	(A)
7	My main reason for being here is so that I can learn more about the subjects which really interest me.	4	3	2	1	0	(C)
8	I suppose I'm more interested in the qualifications I'll get than in the courses I'm taking.	4	3	2	1	0	(B)
9	I'm usually prompt in starting work in the evenings.	4	3	2	1	0	(A)
10	I generally put a lot of effort into trying to understand things which initially seem difficult.	4	3	2	1	0	(C)
11	Often I find I have to read things without having a chance to really understand them.	4	3	2	1	0	(B)
12	If conditions aren't right for me to study, I generally manage to do something to change them.	4	3	2	1	0	(A)
13	I often find myself questioning things that I hear in lessons or read in books.	4	3	2	1	0	(C)
14.	I tend to read very little beyond what's required for completing assignments.	4	3	2	1	0	(B)
15	It is important to me to do things better than my friend, if I possibly can.	4	3	2	1	0	(A)
16	I spend a good deal of my spare time in finding out more about interesting topics which have been discussed in class.	4	3	2	1	0	(C)
17	I find academic topics so interesting, I should like to continue with them after I finish this course.	4	3	2	1	0	(C)
18	I find I have to concentrate on memorising a good deal of what we have to learn.	4	3	2	1	0	(B)

SCORE SHEET

The 18 questions above are selected from the Lancaster Approaches to Studying Questionnaire. Score your questionnaire by writing down the numbers circled for questions A, B and D.

A	B	D

Totals

'A' scale score
This is a score out of 24 on '*Achieving* orientation'. This indicates competitiveness, well organised study methods, and hope for success. Students who score high on this scale are oriented towards doing well, whatever this involves. They tend to do well.

'B' scale score
This is a score out of 24 on '*Reproducing* orientation'. This indicates a surface approach to learning. Students who score high on this scale attempt to memorise subject matter and are not interested in studying a subject for its own sake but only out of a concern to pass or gain qualification. They keep narrowly to the syllabus as laid down in course descriptions and do not follow up interests of their own (if they have any). Despite their concern to pass they tend to do badly.

'C' scale score
This is a score out of 24 on '*Meaning* orientation'. This indicates a deep approach to learning: the intention to make sense of the subject, an interest in the subject itself, and a desire to learn. Students who score high on this scale follow up their own interests even if these are outside those parts of the course which are assessed. They tend to do well.

Norms are available from large-scale national studies of how students learn, so you can compare your scores with national averages.

Scale	Arts	Social Science	Science	Overall	Standard deviation
(A) Achieving	12.50	12.73	13.08	12.82	4.26
(B) Reproducing	11.98	13.65	14.26	13.51	4.40
(C) Meaning	15.17	14.21	13.93	14.31	4.51

Deep and Surface definitions

Deep   Students focus their attention on the overall meaning or message in a lecture, text or situation. They attempt to relate ideas together and construct their own meaning, possibly in relation to their own experience.

Surface   Students focus their attention on the details and information in a lecture or text. They are trying to memorise these individual details in the form they appear in the lecture or text or to list the features of the situation.

Deep and Surface examples

A   *I don't like having to take notes in lectures. I would prefer to concentrate on understanding. I like to be able to listen so I can understand what the problem is.* (Law)

B   *I learn Law by cases: listing cases and listing principles. I have a good short term memory and I can memorise enough to get through exams.* (Law)

C   *I read it, I read it very slowly, trying to concentrate on what it means, what the actual passage means. Obviously I've read the quotations a few times and I've got it in my mind, what they mean. I really try to read it slowly. There is a lot of meaning behind it. You have to really think 'Well what does this mean?' You mustn't regurgitate what David is saying because that's not the idea of the exercise, so I suppose it's really original ideas in this one, kind of getting it all together.* (Geography)

D   *When you use the word learning in relation to this course, what do you mean?*

       Getting enough facts so that you can write something relevant in the exam. You've got enough information so you can write an essay on it. What I normally do is learn certain headings. I'll write a question down, about four, five different headings, which in an exam I can go: 'Introduction' and I'll look at the next heading and I know what I've got to write about without really thinking about it really. I know the facts about it. I go to the next heading and regurgitate. (Computing)

21

Improving Student Learning by collaborative action research by human sciences undergraduates in evaluative inquiry: evaluating seminar practice[1]

Tom Wengraf (Higher Education Action Research and Design Unit Middlesex University)

A . . . system that does not engage in experiential self-study can neither produce nor collect valid data because of the unexamined incongruities within its experience. Such a system will both deliberately and unintentionally distort data and will resist processing feedback which identifies incongruities. A primary index of the capacity of a social system to produce valid data becomes the degree to which confrontation and exploration of possible incongruities is initiated and welcomed . . . The acting system must cultivate an 'attention span' which embraces the translations back and forth among intuitive purposes, theoretical strategies, behavioural methodologies, and external effects, rather than being captured by any one of those qualities at a given time . . . Each social actor can gain increasingly valid knowledge of social situations only as other actors collaborate in inquiry, disclosing their being, testing their knowledge, discovering shared purposes, and producing preferred outcomes. (Torbert, 1981: pp. 146–50).

Introduction

Valid and cost-effective methods of enquiring into student experience of the curriculum

The government is constantly reducing the unit of resource per student – thereby decreasing the likelihood of mass quality outcomes – while at the same time multiplying quality-assurance and quality-assessment procedures. In large part this is just a public-relations management of appearances. In some part, this is a genuine attempt to reduce the damage they know their policies will increasingly cause.

Pressure for quality assurance and quality assessment increases our need to find cost-effective and valid ways of monitoring the quality of the student learning experience.

How? Most administrators, faced with this need, multiply survey questionnaires to students. They can face a barrage of multiple-choice questionnaires which can start to feel very much like additional (don't bother-to take-home, but put-in-the-bin) optional examinations. The rate of return of student survey questionnaires is low (10–20 per cent). Filling them in does not seem like a rewarding experience. Any percolation of the 'results'

[1] This is an enlarged and revised version of my earlier 'Undergraduate students as action researchers into student learning' submitted for publication in Sally Brown (ed) (1995) Research Learning and Education (Kogan Page) after a conference of the Staff and Educational Association (SEDA, November 1993).

back from the centre is very slow, partial, and not that interesting either. Neither administrators nor most staff nor most students take much interest in their results, except defensively. The process and the results are not very much 'owned' by staff and students. In Torbert's terms, as quoted above, such research is fairly uninformative and pretty uneducational.

What other (perhaps alternative, perhaps complementary) ways are there?

Preparing students for lifelong relearning

As modes of production and social relations both globally and locally continue to change, student experience of the curriculum should increasingly prepare them for lifelong relearning. Relearning and research are connected.

If students after graduation eventually stay in 'one job for life', there will be constant relearning on the job, as the context of the enterprise and the opportunities within the enterprise change. More likely, they will not have 'one job for life' but a multiplicity of 'jobs' in sequence and at certain times probably simultaneously. In each of these sequential jobs, for each of these evolving tasks, they will need to research their context and re-examine their fundamental assumptions, so as to apply them afresh to new particular circumstances.

How can students best be prepared for such at least intermittent and probably continuous lifelong relearning?

One response to this has been the attempt to increase student reflexivity about learning as such. Students learn particular things at a given moment, but they basically need to improve their learning about how to learn. Undergraduate students are professional learners who need **institutionalized** support from academic staff to enable them to be 'professionally reflective' (Schon,1987) about their practice as students.[2]

This practice of reflexivity by self-evaluation and contextual evaluation can properly be described as research. Students who have not learnt the principles and practices of such reflexive research while at university can be said to be unprepared for lifelong relearning.

Our slogan should be: **Every student is a researcher into their microenvironment and their (relearning) practice within it, as a preparation for the same lifelong activity when they leave the university or college**. How can this be fostered?

Collaborative Action Research as part of a solution to both problems?

According to Zuber-Skerrit (1992), p. 1.

action research . . . may be defined as collaborative, critical inquiry by the academics themselves (rather than expert educational researchers) into their own teaching practice, into problems of student learning and into curriculum problems. It is professional development through academic course development, group reflection, action, evaluation and improved practice.

---

[2] *They need this support from academic staff in the support of 'institutionalized self-research' precisely to the extent that worsening SSRS and mass modularization mean that staff's informal grasp of the conditions of student learning can no longer be relied on to substitute for student self-knowledge achieved through institutionally-supported and required collective self-research.*

The principle is right, but this definition is unnecessarily restrictive. 'Collaborative critical enquiry' supporting institutional self-evaluation and student self-evaluative reflexivity can be undertaken by undergraduate students themselves (rather than just by Zuber-Skerrit's 'academics themselves'). In this chapter, I show how undergraduate students can undertake such 'collaborative critical enquiry' inquiry into a field that might best be reformulated – another modification to Zuber-Skerritt – as 'the students' own **learning practice** and into the problems of **teachers teaching**'.

As far as possible, we should **institutionalize undergraduate student evaluative action research as part of ordinary coursework**.

In this chapter, I first give an example of what could be characterized as a start in this direction, and describe how it evolved. I report on some of the evaluative material. I then identify what I take to be the distinguishing features which enabled it to be reasonably successful. I then conclude with a brief discussion of where, in a typical university or college, similar activities could be developed and a final question.

First Year Student Self-Research at Middlesex – The Initial Project

Aims and design

Students on a human sciences research methods module[3] at Middlesex in 1991–1992 were asked in their first-year to do semi-structured interviews for a coursework report. The topic of the report was a determinedly evaluation-oriented one: 'What could be done to improve module X?' The students had a free choice of module and of informants, subject to the restriction that the informants should ideally be two other students and a tutor involved in module X. They then had to produce their report to a given format (described below).

What were my original aims in designing this piece of coursework?

1 To deliver a coded message to the students: your reflection on student experience and

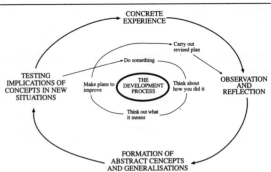

3 *At the time, roughly one-half of the undergraduate programmes at Middlesex had been 'modularized' and 'semesterized': for full-time students, three modules in each semester, two semesters per year.*
4 *This was in line with the useful Kolb Learning Cycle above -- as identified, for example, from K.B. Everard (1993; 32) though of course the student reports went as far as suggesting 'implications of concepts in new situations' but did not in fact do such testing.*

suggestions for improvement are important and worthy of study and reporting[4].

2 To send a clear message to the students as human-science researchers: if you cannot apply the concepts and methods of social research that you are learning to your own experiences, then you have not yet learned anything you are able to use.

3 To motivate me as their tutor (by choosing a subject of sufficient interest to me as a practising tutor) to work through their coursework material properly and to give them good feedback

4 To motivate both interviewers and interviewees for their first exercise in semi-structured interviewing. This is a research method in the human sciences which can typically foster the discovery of subject-centred perspectives.

I thought that the topic 'What could be done to improve module X?' would be of great relevance to first-year students and to the staff with whom they came in contact. It would help them to think more explicitly about varying criteria for their evaluations. It would enable them to use their full intelligence as natural participators in using the concepts and methods they were being trained to acquire.

HOW DID THE INITIAL PROJECT DEVELOP?
The student researchers were in the second semester of their first year. In respect of interviewing method, they were given about 12 hours (lecture + workshop training) before going out to do their interviews plus a short manual devised by myself. They were given a broad interviewing brief. They had freedom to design a question-schedule for their interviews, which might identify 'improvement areas' in advance or might leave the definition of 'improvement areas' to the interviewees. Semi-structured interviews typically operate with relatively open-ended questions, and this was important to the success of the project.

For their coursework assessment, they had to produce 5000 word reports to a designed four-section structure.

1 In their 'Introduction', they were asked to describe and justify their choice of informants and to give the question-schedule(s) to be used with students and staff.

2 In the next section, they were asked to provide a transcript of one of the three interviews they undertook, being free to choose either a staff or a student interview for this purpose.

3 The main section which followed was that of 'Interpretation', where they were asked to describe (using chunky quotations) compare and evaluate the results of all three interviews as a basis for their recommendations about how to improve module X.

4 A final section required them to reflect upon and evaluate the project process as a whole, including the writing up of their report.

Outcome
In all, some 25 staff and 122 fellow-students were interviewed for an average of 10–30 minutes each. Some 49 reports were produced and assessed as coursework.
Virtually all the students became very committed to their 'What can be done to improve

module X?' activity and put in a great amount of energy into doing the research and writing up the reports.

Not only were they more motivated to do the interviews and reports, they produced data of a higher quality and of greater interest than I had anticipated.This method of student-designed and student-conducted semi-structured interviews provided a much deeper vein of evaluative feedback than the more frequently found standard multiple-choice survey questionnaire.

Given the deliberate focus on problems to be remedied and my deliberate decision not to specify any system of random sampling, the results did not provide an overall evaluation of first-year modules. What the students did was to illuminate curriculum questions by identifying student perceptions of what students and/or staff involved in a module experienced as bad or confusing practice by themselves or others[5]. In the act of what we may call 'evaluation-oriented descriptions and recommendations', students revealed much about their own, their peers' and their tutors' pedagogic ideologies.

It should not be thought that the students at this level can achieve 'objectivity' and that their recommendations about improvement can be simply acted upon.

1. Very frequently, the contrast between (a) the transcript and (b) the interpretation supposedly based on it enabled me to identify the researching student's 'pedagogic ideology' by discovering how they systematically misinterpreted their own data. But even when they had described the situation adequately, another problem typically arose as follows.

2. Very frequently, students thought of the educational process as having one function only to perform. They thus failed to come to grips with the complex struggle to balance different values off against each other that is inherent in the difficult craft of education. Such weaknesses were themselves revealing and were reported back to the students by me in my feedback on their reports. The next section of this chapter identifies some pedagogic ideologies as they emerged in a particularly revealing arena of 'struggle and cross-purposes': the 'seminar'.

Deciphering the Pedagogic Ideologies in the Evaluative Descriptions Given by Student Interviewees

The small-group seminar (10–25 students) I found to be an area in which the struggle of recommendations and evaluations was strongest.

Four normative models of what should happen in seminars

I think I went to two seminars and the first one of that was with Tutor A and that was like being back in an 'O-level' classroom . . . Tutor A was too severe, you knew she was right and you were wrong and she'd ask a question and there'd only be one answer and she was too severe, too brutal, it was sort of 'Rubbish, what nonsense, wherever did you get that

---

[5] *Similarly, I understand, at the former Birmingham Polytechnic, it was focus groups composed of students who decided each year what the themes should be for the 'student satisfaction survey' that year. What themes students select, what questions they think are most appropriate. . . these are all themselves data for staff reflection and understanding.*

idea from?' . That's Tutor A's approach . . . she'd have a list of questions in her head and she'd expect the right answer and then move on . . . a lot of people left that group.

Then I switched to Tutor C who was too relaxed . . . it just ended up being a chat about anything.. nothing to do with the subject (Interviewer Jane Finden-Crofts)

Students, as well as staff, seemed typically to be torn between quite different expectations of what should be happening in seminars: expectations which were neither fully-conscious or minimally coherent. Often, quite contradictory expectations were voiced in two parts of the same sentence. As a result, what students (and staff) do, and what they resent other people for doing or not doing, varied.

On the basis of the reports, I suggest four different models to try to sum up some major variations. Two can be grouped as being about Data-transmission, the other two as being about Viewpoint-articulation.

Data-transmission: Transmission of Facts model

This most traditional model of education in general and the seminar in particular is one in which data are to be transmitted from the notes of the lecturer to the notes of the student[6]. The seminar can then become the place where the lecturer clarifies the original data-transmission in the lecture and is asked to give further tailor-made, client-requested, mini-lectures or data-transmissions by the students. The seminar becomes a further mini-lecture or set of mini-lectures. Many students expect this to happen and are angry when it doesn't. Some staff expect themselves to do this, and are uncertain if this does not fully meet student expectations.

Basically it's for the lecturer to give us information if we needed it. . . In the lectures they were giving us condensed information and, um, for you to understand it at, um, a greater level you had to attend the seminars in order to get information from the lecturer and also through private study all round . . . I think the teachers could contribute more to the seminars. It's quite obvious they know the subject really well but . . . it's they're very dependent on the student and I think the students they probably don't read up enough of the work so that when they come into the class they've got no questions to ask them and they don't really know what it's all about . . . **the seminar tutor should be prepared to put more into it . . . be ready to just talk, not even discuss, just give you more information** (Interviewer Julie Dexter)

It is one in which, most typically, the 'data' to be transmitted are 'the facts', facts conceived as pieces of knowledge about reality. If education is about accumulating 'facts', then seminar tutors are there to provide 'more facts' and make sure they are 'put down in your brain':

Do you think there were clear aims in the seminars you attended, what were the purposes of the seminars?

There has been a specific aim for each one, that is, you have got to rehash all the stuff that's been given in the lecture, and the aims are actually that reinforce the things in your mind . . . , cos they're going to give you the points that you need because the idea is to pass this

---

[6] *The traditional joke continues, "without passing through the brains of either party"*

degree . . . They give the key points to pass . . .

How do you see seminars as concerning passing your degree?

I don't know. I took seminar . . . to be literally to reinforce the ideas that were put forward in the lecture, to reinforce and to make sure that it's put down in your brain . . .
Generalities are O.K. but . . . you're not going to want to do too much if it starts blotting out the the basic information that you're going to need . . . they're literally superfluous to what you are going to need.

What is this basic material needed for?

Basic facts and guidelines for those facts (Interviewer Alan Dixon).

Data-transmission: Framework-for-Facts Transmission model

This is the second model oriented to data-transmission and is implied perhaps by the vague notion of 'guidelines for those facts' in the previous quotation. These Frameworks may be seen as 'bodies of articulable Theory' (as, for example, in the hard-natural and soft-social sciences). The Frameworks may be seen as only transmissible in a non-articulated way as 'deeper understandings' (e.g. in the Humanities) and 'more profound practical graspings' (as in pro-professional practical courses). They may be seen as requiring elements of both in different proportions. In any case, in this second model, the transmission of listable facts is seen as a less important function than the transmission of a sophisticated and adequate Framework for the handling of whatever the facts turn out to be.

Both data-transmission models – whether it is transmission of facts or transmission of frameworks for facts – however, make it varyingly probable that the Seminar Tutor is expected to continue unilateral transmission within the seminar-time.

Viewpoint-articulation

This model is one in which the function of the Seminar is not to continue the transmission of knowledge with which the lecture may properly have been concerned. It is a model in which there are a plurality of viewpoints, of perspectives, on a topic, a problem, an experience, a reality, and the task of the seminar is the development of the such plurality of viewpoints as may be represented and representable within the seminar group. This Viewpoint-articulation model is also to be found in a primary and in a more sophisticated version among staff and students.

Viewpoint- articulation: Viewpoint-Ventilation model

In this 'democratic' version, every person in the seminar has 'a viewpoint' and has an equal right to express or 'ventilate' it. The lecturer has already 'ventilated' their viewpoint in the lecture, and so should not normally take up more than the minimum necessary of further time in the seminar as well. Students gain maximum benefit by ventilating their own viewpoint, and some degree of benefit by hearing the expressed viewpoints of others. The role of the lecturer here is limited to that of regulator of the access of all students to the public space so that their viewpoints can be ventilated. He or she is predominantly or exclusively to act as procedural chairperson in a parliament of views.

I was fighting to get a word in and I couldn't just get to say it . . . there just wasn't time for everyone to get their point of view across, it was the same people speaking every time, it should have been that everyone got a chance to speak (Interviewer Angela Acharia).

Our tutor didn't seem to mind or do anything about it being the same people speaking out each week . . . He didn't say 'Let's hear somebody else's view' or ' Would anyone else like to add to that?. . . I think some of the younger students were even afraid to speak because they felt so intimidated . . . He was only too happy to let the mature students take over . . . I felt totally ignored and inadequate. My tutor seemed so much into the maturer students that he took no notice of us, and so didn't notice or do anything about our not contributing.

Sometimes the process is better, and there is a clear consensus about what happens. One student remarked:

I enjoy a tutorial far better than a lecture because you're getting everybody's point of view . . . Everyone's different opinion should count . . .

The way in which the [University] teaches is very different to the way I've been taught and I think it's a lot better as well, and it's more thought-provoking than just learning by rules and parrot-fashion, being tested constantly, and you're actually required to use your brain so you think about it and the thing I do like is that your opinion counts . . .

The other student said:

The teaching is done in the form of one to one and a half hour lectures a week from a specialist in the field, followed by a two-hour class seminar of around approximately 10 students together with the **seminar tutor acting as a chairman. It's really designed for students to argue their views on the subject and bring their own feelings out into the open and discuss the issues,** that's how it teaches (Interviewer Suzanne Nash).

This is the advanced version of the viewpoint-articulation approach.

Viewpoint-articulation: Viewpoint-Improvement model

In this model, it is important **for the seminar not to stay stuck in the process of going round-and-round expressing viewpoints**. The seminar needs to work in order to find the 'best viewpoints' and to 'improve them' by criticizing and rectifying their weaknesses and so developing their strengths. Consequently, rather than be left to the laissez-faire of the reiterative expression of the greatest number of viewpoints that can be found, not all viewpoints have to be treated as equals. The seminar needs to be organized around the critique, rectification and improvement of a small number of viewpoints and the development of 'better thinking about' viewpoints and expressed views.

The following extract gives an idea of the distinction between 'discussion-debate' as in Viewpoint-Ventilation and the notion of 'a proper intellectual argument' as would be needed for a systematic Viewpoint-Improvement process. To me, the student seems to be struggling to articulate such a difference:

What made that a really good lecture? I think it must have been a very concise lecture, he told us exactly what was going on . . . And his ideas were really weird and whacky and I really liked them and, um, I got the chance to disprove them. I like disproving ideas cos the only way you can move forward in knowledge is to disprove old ideas – like good old Einstein turned physics on its head by disproving things – and the only way you can move forward in life is by disproving . . .

Did you find that in the seminars you were able to challenge and disprove things?

No, I used to drop to sleep in seminars, the guy that took us used to rabbit on, terribly boring, for hours . . .

Was there discussion?

There was discussion . . . there was discussion, but it's not like an argument. People, I found people couldn't say "maybe if that happened, something would happen". They couldn't grasp the concept of **maybe**. Therefore, if you said something, that was what you thought . . . They couldn't juggle things in the mind, which I thought was very disturbing really. A lot of people were very young, about my age 19, 18.. There were some older ones there but they were a bit quiet . . . and the young people were loudmouthed and they had all these high ideals, they couldn't juggle in their minds, kind of saying 'Well if that happened, what would be the consequence of that, and then what would be the consequence of that?'. . . which did kind of stop any proper intellectual discussion I think (Interviewer Gay Schreim).

Both Viewpoint-Articulation models require a varying degree of self-suppression of the unilateral-transmitting function of the Lecturer...who **should not** give the mini-lectures under these latter two Viewpoint models that he or she **ought** to be giving under the former two Data-Transmission models.

Many of the transcripts and the student report 'interpretations and recommendations' show students on the same module and staff also sharply divided by different expectations as to what should or should not be happening in the seminars, clashes of expectations which can be seen as expressing one or more of the above four models. Very often, the same informant will express two or more of these models and their contradictory demands in the same interview, even in the same sentence.

Final note: the problem is the non-explicit undiscussed holding of these four mental models

Reading the transcripts and the interpretations, I feel clear that an efficient working of seminars requires both staff and students at any given time in a given seminar to be in agreement about which of these four normative models ought to be operating. It may be the case that all four 'functions' need to be satisfied to varying extents at various times, and that a well-structured seminar might address itself to different functions at different well-structured moments during its life-cycle.

What seems clear from the transcripts and interpretations is that normative models about what should be happening in seminars in general or at particular structured moments in seminars **are not shared or properly discussed or negotiated** between staff and students and between students and other students Consequently, much of the time there is deep concern that 'what should be happening' (according to one normative model) is not happening and something else (comprehensible and desirable only according to another model) is happening instead.

A very explicit discussion of the types of expectations that it is legitimate or illegitimate to have in different seminar situations and over the course of a given seminar would have enabled staff and students could identify confusions about legitimate purpose and practice.

At the moment, though the staff and students involved seemed to have no explicit vocabulary for such meta-discussions, and so cannot recognize the problems well, let alone discuss them across the staff/student boundary.

First-year Student Self-Research at Middlesex: the Meta-Analysis Project

Although as far as I could tell none of the students doing the research nor their interviewees nor myself at the time took into account the conceptual distinction of 'deep' and 'surface' approaches to learning, it is clear that the material in the evaluative descriptions given by student interviewees is readily comprehensible in terms of such distinctions.

In addition to the value of the student reports in themselves, standing alone, I decided that it would be possible, due to the structure of the 49 individual reports, to write a second-tier meta-analysis[7]. I had been informed by reading the results of their research reports. On the basis of those individual research reports, I was then in a position to re-synthesize.

This did not mean simply summarizing or generalizing their accounts (as one might summarize the results of 49 questionnaires) but rather re-evaluating the meaning of each student report in the light of information they revealed separately and together about ideologies, perspectives and perceptions.

'Triangulation' was made easier by two features: one, that each report contained some information from three informants, sifted by a fourth, together with one interview transcript with one of the informants; two, that, though just over one-half of the modules had only one report written about them, seven of the modules had between two and ten student reports written about them. In addition, most of the issues raised (for example, seminars, tutor availability, feeling intimidated) were common to many of the modules.

My meta-analysis was written for circulation primarily to University teachers[8]. It was therefore straightforwardly written to illustrate for teaching staff:

1. a range and pattern of aspects that were significant to the student researchers, and to a lesser extent the staff and student interviewees

2. a range and pattern of responses to those aspects by the staff and student interviewees.

In particular, my eventual meta-report with its large proportion of direct quotes from students and staff talking to students provides **a less censored source of feedback on student's perceptions** than is normally available to staff.

---

[7] *See Noblit and Hare (1988) for a brief discussion of this type of operation.*

[8] *Now, three years later, I would think it as important certainly to produce a version that would be of use to my primary research collaborators: the students involved.*

Because the researchers are fellow students – typically fellow-students on the same module – the interviews with fellow students are likely to be less stilted and more realistic than any conducted by 'outside' researchers. As a way of clarifying student perspectives, ideology, interpretations and misinterpretations, the method yields a rich pattern of information. As a way of clarifying staff perspectives when interviewed not by 'academic peers' but by their student subordinates or customers, the method is equally rich.

"Deciphering the pedagogic ideologies in the evaluative descriptions given by student interviewees" of this chapter is – with the exception of the first paragraph, and some minor changes – a simple reprint of a section of my meta-report and an example of such triangulation-based work. I used material from a number of different student-interviewers, and developed a 'grounded descriptive theory' – I prefer to call this 'emergent theory' – using concepts – for example, **data-transmission** and **viewpoint-articulation** – none of which was to be found in that form in the first tier of student interview reports.

The concepts and argument of this chapter and the meta-report as a whole emerged as a Torbert-style 'collaboration' – in this case unexpected on both the students' parts and on my part – between these first-year undergraduate students, the staff who let themselves be interviewed, and myself. A project for 1994–95 will be more self-consciously collaborative from the start.

Distinguishing Features of the Project Contributing Towards its Relative Success

On reflection, the following features seem to have been important in determining the relative success of the project.

Student 'free hand 'in designing the question-schedule within a broad brief

The students were given the brief of interviewing about 'What could be done to improve the experience of a particular module?', plus the injunction to interview three people – including if possible a member of academic staff teaching on the module. The brief was deliberately unspecific to ensure that any further decisions about focus and questions and angle came from the student's own experience. It was the first-year student who had to decide which first-year module might be worth improving, how far to identify issues in advance, and what questions to ask their student and staff informants.

The student as interviewer: confidential peer evaluative interviewing for validity

Given that students were doing the interviewing and could guarantee effective anonymity to their peers, the chances are that 'fewer punches were pulled' by peers in terms of identifying sources of dissatisfaction than might have been the case had the interviewers been staff or other 'outsiders' to the student community.

In addition, my impression from talking to students was that the 'What can be done to improve module X' evaluative focus was very important in motivating both the enquirers and the respondents to discuss matters . . . for the tape-recorder record and eventually to me as a perceived-as-influential member of staff who might 'do something' about the information and the recommendations.

The student as interviewer: problems of interviewing staff 'from below'

My impression was that those teachers who agreed to be interviewed by one of 'their' students typically were much more 'defensive' than they would have been had they been interviewed by another member of staff or by an 'outsider'. This very widespread 'defensive strategy' even on the part of the minority of staff who freely gave of their time to be interviewed suggests the difficulty that all staff have in having a 'free and frank exchange of views' with students about how their module or their teaching could be improved.

What relations of power/knowledge (in Michel Foucault's terms) block the staff's capacity to learn how to learn from students?

Student analysing and reporting: three interviews modify the initial perspective of the student

Each student had to interview three interviewees: preferably two other students and a member of staff. All 49 students interviewed three people. Half managed to obtain an interview with a member of the teaching staff; the other half interviewed three students.

They then had to cope with the usually quite different perspectives of their three interviewees and bring them into a coherent whole. The 49 student reports in the main showed that the task of attempting to grapple with these perspectives was a source of considerable creative strain, in which the student reporter-interviewer typically modified – though to varying degrees – his or her own perception as a result of the enquiry and reporting process. There was a clear self-educational value to the process.

Meta-analysis of full student interpretation plus sample transcript

In order to know what weight to give to the three-interview 'interpretation' section of each report, it was crucial for me as tutor to have a full transcript of (at least) one of the interviews. This made it possible to evaluate the probable strengths and weaknesses, biases and accuracy of the' student interpretation' on the basis of a direct contact with an interview transcript. It also made it possible for me to use material from the transcript that the student had not used at all in his or her own interpretation section.

Staff learning from grappling with the material from the 49 student reports

The full range of aspects selected by the interviewees and the interviewer was impressive, and the relative frequency of certain issues was informative. Similarly the variety of very different responses documented in the student reports to the same issues was also an

---

[9] *Given the student researcher/informant's freedom to focus on any topic, it was interesting to discover that most perplexity and dissatisfaction seemed to crystallize around the topic of 'seminars'. Students and staff typically had very contradictory views of its functions and typically never seemed to communicate effectively to each other what those views were. It is perhaps not surprisingly that ambiguities of power and purpose are perhaps greatest in this area.*

invaluable source of insight.[9] I learnt a lot from doing the meta-analysis.

My distribution of the meta-report and excerpts from it led to largely but not entirely favourable reception.

The material was later used in the University's *Learning Action Bulletin* (distributed to all teaching staff) in order to sensitize staff to some of the issues involved.

One colleague who berated me (especially given my other role as Chair of NATFHE) strongly for collecting and above all distributing such 'unbalanced accounts' of student perceptions on the grounds that 'it would give management a stick to beat us with' (under certain conditions, this might have been and may well be a serious problem which researchers need to think about, but not under current management conditions at Middlesex) later conceded that 'the student material had made her think a lot' and she was revising her handbook for students as a result.

Uses of the Information

Such information from students researching into student learning can then be used, and has to some extent been used:

- for the development of checklists with which those in charge of modules and programmes can consider the quality and mechanisms of their delivery;
- as a basis for staff discussion and staff development training;
- as a basis for student discussion and student development training;
- as a basis for staff-student discussion in the functional equivalent of 'quality circles';
- for the development of institution-wide research, e.g. questionnaire surveys;
- for the development or enrichment of 'grounded theory' research into student learning.

I did not, unfortunately, do a formal survey to tap the responses of student researchers to the experience of having engaged in such student action research. My impression from informal talking to them was that a very significant majority felt, as a result of doing the research, much more **conscious** of their educational practice and those of other students and their teachers.

Carrying Out Such Student Research Exercises as a Part of Ordinary Coursework Learning?

Social and cultural 'research methodology' courses

My experience suggests that 'human sciences' methodology courses can provide a suitable base in which such work can be carried out as part of the student's ordinary programme, and that semi-structured interviewing is a user-friendly point from which even first-year students can start.

The types of disciplinary programmes with such activity would include psychology, writing, humanities (e.g. oral history), cultural studies, communication studies, management training, trade union studies, community studies, nursing and other service-industry vocational training where 'programme evaluation' and 'organization analysis' is relevant.

Research method strategies other than semi-structured interviewing

These include:

- 'focus group discussions' in themselves or (like the University of Central England in Birmingham) for the designing of a student satisfaction survey;
- the production and analysis of individual or collective 'personal autobiographical documents' as part of mini-projects in first-year methodology introductory courses, expanded versions of Records of Achievement, Personal Resource Statements (often developed for mature students), and Student Logs/Diaries are all suitable material for research (see for example, Ribbens, 1993).

Non-methodology courses

Substantive courses might well include similar activities: e.g. in Sociology, modules in the sociology of education, of work and organization, of deviance, etc. might all include such 'students as researchers into student learning' work as part of developing the substantive knowledge-base of the student.

A Final Question

Why are undergraduate students in higher education not brought as a matter of course – and possibly of coursework too – to study the literature on undergraduate students in higher education?

There is a considerable knowledge-base developing about student learning in mass higher education, but it is my impression that the number of undergraduate courses on which such material is systematically disseminated as an object of formal study to students is relatively small.

The number of courses in which undergraduate students are enrolled as **contributing and collaborative researchers** to that knowledge-base is probably even fewer.

Given the importance currently being given to help students learn to learn more effectively, it is striking that, as far as I am aware – and I would welcome disproof and knowledge of exceptions – in the main,

1 we fail to teach undergraduates systematically about current research findings and debates about undergraduate learning; and

2 we fail to use them as contributing collaborative researchers into those research findings and those research programmes.[10]

If 'action research' is defined as research in which the peer actors explore the consequences of different ways of changing the actions they engage in, then undergraduate students are only engaging completely in action research to the extent to which they

---

[10] *No administration is spontaneously keen to empower its potential 'insider critics'. Only the most advanced 'learning organizations' take the step. Conversely, to take that step is to make a large movement towards being a very advanced 'learning organizations' take that step. Conversely, to take that step is to make a large movement towards being a very advanced 'learning organization' as described by Senge (1990)*

1 collectively contribute towards, write, and discuss reports on their research;

2 have the power to change aspects of the module design and the delivery of the curriculum and their own practice in relation to the curriculum, and explore the repercussions of such changes on their own experience.

Will not full implementation of a policy of promoting learning through student action research depend on tutors engaged in some form of power-sharing?

Despite the questions identified above, I hope that this chapter has suggested the potential value – for the students themselves, for staff, for research – of enrolling undergraduates as (action) researchers oriented towards evaluative questions into student learning and the experience of the curriculum.[11]

---

[11] *My thanks to Dr. Chloe Stallibrass for comments on an earlier draft of this chapter.*

References

Elden, M. (1981). Sharing the research work: participative research and its role demands. In Peter Reason and John Rowan (eds.) *Human Inquiry: A Sourcebook of New Paradigm Research.* John Wiley.

Everard, K. B. (1993). Development training. In Norman Graves (ed.) *Learner-Managed Learning.* Higher Education for Capability.

Gregory, M. (1993). Accrediting professional development at Masters level through action research and action learning: a model for empowerment. Paper presented to the Staff and Educational Development Association's conference on *Research and Teaching in Higher Education*, Nov 93 at Cardiff, UK.

Noblit, G. W. and Hare, R. D. (1988). *Meta-Ethnography: Synthesising Qualitative Studies.* Sage.

Ribbens, J. (1993). Facts or fictions: aspects of the use of autobiographical writing in undergraduate sociology. *Sociology,* Feb.

Schon, D. (1987). *Educating the Reflective Practitioner.* Jossey-Bass.

Senge, P. (1990). *The Fifth Discipline: The Art and Practice of the Learning Organisation.* Doubleday.

Torbert, W. (1981). Why educational research has been so uneducational: the case for a new model of social science based on collaborative inquiry. In Peter Reason and John Rowan (eds) *Human Inquiry: A Sourcebook of New Paradigm Research.* John Wiley.

Wengraf, T. (1990). Documenting domestic culture by ethnographic interview. In Tim Putnam and Charles Newton (eds) *Household Choices.* Futures Publication.

Wengraf, T. (1992). *Some Reflection on Quality-Control and Customer-Satisfaction Issues Implied by First Year Student Interviews with First-Year MDS Students and Staff.* Higher Education Action Research and Design Unit, Middlesex University.

Wengraf, T. (forthcoming). *Semi-Structured Depth Interviewing: A Conceptual and Practical Guide.* Sage.

Zuber-Skerritt, O. (1992). *Action Research in Higher Education: Examples and Reflections.* Kogan Page.

22

An exploration of the association between students' approaches to learning and their perceived locus of control

P. Rossouw (School of Teacher Education, Cape Technikon) and Philip G. Parsons (Teaching Development Unit, Cape Technikon)

Abstract

A number of instruments for determining students' locus of control, from different theoretical perspectives, were compared and analysed to determine their suitability for use in the context of higher education. Subsequently a composite instrument was used to explore the association between two theoretical perspectives of locus of control and to establish whether the composite instrument illuminated the posited theoretical associations between students' approaches to learning, using the External Approaches to Studying Inventory (EASI), and academic locus of control. Insights gained from the research could be applied to improve student learning by providing a basis for intervention programmes and by informing teaching practice.

Introduction

Against the background of increasing demands on our human resources, the problem of success or failure at tertiary level, especially in the first year of study, is particularly significant as is evident from the increased interest in and research undertaken into the factors and determinants involved. Two variables that have received considerable attention in recent studies are **approaches to learning** and **locus of control**. These variables have been investigated as independent factors and also as part of a cluster of factors (Van Overwalle, 1989a; Watkins, 1987), but the relationship between these two variables has not received extensive attention, and as yet this has not been explored within the technikon context.

The aim of this pilot study was to investigate and compare two different theoretical perspectives of (academic) locus of control as they applied to higher education. Subsequently, using existing instrumentation, the relationship between students' approaches to studying and their perceived academic locus of control was investigated.

Locus of Control

According to Van Overwalle (1989a), locus of control can be seen as either a personality disposition (Rotter, 1966) or a **generalized causal expectancy** (Brown, 1990). Rotter (1966), who initially proposed the concept, perceived locus of control as a single dimension in which an individual could be located between internal and external poles. Hyman (Hyman *et al.*, 1991) is of the opinion that many researchers have since proposed that the concept of locus of control should be seen, rather, as a multidimensional construct.

Rotter (1966) defines locus of control as the manner in which a person feels that he himself (internal control) or factors in the situation (external control) determine his behaviour. Brown (1990) p. 337 on the other hand defines locus of control as an individual's expectancy that 'events in their environment are contingent upon their behaviour'. Thus internal control is equated with a belief that individual actions are instrumental in producing results, whereas external control is equated with a belief that events are determined by fate, chance or luck.

Levenson (in Brown, 1990) p. 377 feels that the concept of external control, as defined above, is too broad and should be divided into two dimensions of fate, chance or luck and a dimension referred to as 'powerful other'. The rationale for his argument is that people who perceive the world as unordered will behave differently from those who perceive some form of social order, and therefore perceive some powerful other to be in control.

It follows that two theoretical perspectives can be identified in relation to the locus of control construct (Butler and Orion, 1990) p. 63. The first is based mainly on the **social learning theory** and specifically on Rotter's (1966) ideas.

This perspective has been primarily concerned with the identification of individual or dispositional tendencies in perceptions of control and also with investigating the relationships between such tendencies and broad outcomes such as school achievements. The other perspective is based on **attribution theory** (Kelly, 1972; Weiner, 1974), and focuses on the identification of those situation-specific variables which produce reliable differences in causal perceptions across subjects, and with relating these differences to specific outcomes such as expectancy of, or affective responses to, success and failure (Butler and Orion, 1990 p. 63).

Thus social learning theory suggests that locus of control is an expectancy, whereas attributional theory suggests that locus of control is but one of a more specific set of attributions.

A number of studies have investigated the relationship between different measurements (based on different theoretical perspective) of locus of control (see, for example, Hyman, *et al.*, 1991; Goodman and Walters, 1987). Hyman *et al.*, (1991, p. 409) concluded that problems associated with the measurements of locus of control derived from the attribution perspective could be ascribed to the application of an inadequate two-dimensional model, as proposed by Weiner (1974), instead of a three-dimensional model as Weiner later proposed (1986).

Early attributional scales were based on a two-dimensional model, with stability as one dimension and the other a locus of control. More recently Weiner (1986) and Hyman *et al.*, (1991) have proposed that the theoretical model should be modified to define a third dimension. Weiner (1986) proposes controllability as this third dimension, where causal beliefs can be classified on a controllable – uncontrollable continuum. This suggests that the initial single locus of control dimension should be divided into two dimensions of locus (the 'location' of causality – internal versus external) and control (the associated 'processes of control' resulting from the particular locus – controllable versus uncontrollable factors).

As stated earlier a number of researchers have since proposed that locus of control should be seen as a multidimensional construct. This implies that there are unique qualities associated with the different domains with the global locus of control construct and that these domains should be studied separately. Lefcourt (Lefcourt *et al.*, 1979) started to move in this direction with his goal-specific rather than generalized measures, although his instrument incorporates both achievement and affiliation measures. For the purposes of this pilot study the authors proposed that this could be refined further to focus only on the academic domain, thereby producing an academic or achievement scale, and that this academic (or achievement) locus of control should first be investigated as a substantive domain on its own.

Locus of Control – The Development of an Academic Locus of Control Scale

In terms of the aims of the project, a number of instruments for determining students' locus of control were analysed and compared for their suitability in the context of academic achievement in higher education. These instruments were the **Multidimensional Multiattributional Causality Scale** (MMMCS) (Lefcourt *et al.*, 1979), the **Multidimensional Measure of Children's Perceptions of Control** (MMCPC) (Connell,1985), the **Academic Locus of Control Scale** (ALC) (Trice, 1985) and the **Internal Control Index** (ICI) (Duttweiler, 1984).

These instruments were analysed according to specific predetermined criteria. Firstly, the items of the instrument should be specific to achievement in higher education. The instrument itself should address the issue in terms which relate to perceptions of the educational context and should include perceptions of both success and failure. In addition, the different subscales should have reliable and effective discriminatory value and these results should be consistent over time and different discriminatory tertiary settings. Finally, and most importantly in terms of the longer-term aims of the project, the results should be able to inform intervention. None of the existing instruments met all the criteria, and therefore a composite instrument was developed, based on selected items derived from the original instruments.

The revised academic locus of control instrument combines the two theoretical perspectives of attribution and social learning theory in relation to the domain of academic locus of control. This had a two-fold purpose: to test a three-dimensional model that draws on two different theoretical approaches and to determine the conceptual association between these two theoretical perspectives.

The MMCS (Lefcourt *et al.*, 1979) consists of two subscales, achievement and affiliation. Each of the two subscales includes items that measure attributions for success and failure experiences in relation to the four attributions of ability, effort, contextual characteristics and fortuitous events (luck). The MMCPC consists of four cognitive, social, physical and general subscales. Each of the four subscales is divided into the different sources of control (internal, powerful others and unknown) in relation to success and failure experiences. In the composite instrument the attributional perspective is represented by the **achievement domain** of the MMCS and the social learning perspective by the **cognitive domain** of the MMCPC.

Connell (1985) uses a conceptually different approach, based to an extent on social learning perspectives, although he acknowledges the role of attributional theorists.

Connell's model is based on the perceived control children attribute to their experience of educational success or failure, and to an extent on a partial merging or combination of attributional and social learning perspectives. The MMCPC corresponds largely, in terms of the subscale structure and terminology (except in terms of the unknown control dimension), to other measurement scales based on the social learning theory (see Levenson, 1981).

The difference between Connell (1985) and the perspectives described so far is that he focuses mainly on the **perceived control of children** in relation to educational success or failure, whereas other instruments have focused on **perceived locus of control** in relation to educational success or failure of **higher education students**. This distinction is supported by the suggestions of Butler and Orion (1990) and Skinner and Chapman (1984) that researchers should distinguish between perceptions of causality (ie. people's understanding of the relationships between causes and outcomes) and perceptions of control (i.e. the degree to which people feel that they can influence their outcomes).

Connell (1985) thus includes a control dimension which reflects the unknown control children associate with educational success or failure. Connell's (1985) unknown control dimension therefore represents a measurement of the controllability dimension that could help to define academic locus of control more adequately – which is in line with the proposals of Hyman (Hyman *et al.*, 1991) and Weiner (1986) mentioned earlier.

It was necessary for the authors to change the formulation of the items of the MMCPC to make it applicable to the context of higher education. The motivation for the reformulation of items from an instrument that focused on children's perceived control to similar items applicable to a higher education context lies in the perceived need to address a fundamental assumption on which higher education is based. It is generally assumed that students in higher education are aware of the factors which control their academic achievement. Connell's (1985) three-dimensional model pioneered an assessment of not only what children **know** about these attributes which control their success or failure ('internal' and 'powerful others' perceptions) but also how much they **don't know** about why they succeed and fail ('unknown' perspectives of control). The current investigation aimed to explore the authors' contention that the above model applies not only to education on a pre-tertiary level but also to a large extent to higher education. The specific academic locus of control instrument thus attempts to provide a combined theoretical and conceptual formulation of the academic locus of control construct, by combining different theoretical approaches and through this formulating a three-dimensional model to improve the previous two-dimensional model, and thus our understanding of this construct (Hyman *et al.*, 1991; Weiner, 1986).

The composite instrument consists of the following subscales: attributions in terms of ability for success (ABS) and failure (ABF), effort for success (EFS) and effort for failure (EFF), context for success (COS) and context for failure (COF), luck for success (LUS) and luck for failure (LUF), internal control for success (ICS) and internal control for failure (ICF), powerful others control for success (POCS) and powerful others control for failure (POCF) and unknown control for success (UCS) and unknown control for failure (UCF). (See appendix for the list of items and subscales contained in the composite instrument.)

Approaches to Studying

In terms of students' approaches to studying there are at least two important theoretical perspectives. One perspective (Marton and Säljö, 1976a, 1976b; Biggs, 1978; Entwistle and Ramsden, 1983) focuses on qualitative differences between the different categories of approaches to studying exhibited by groups of students. In terms of this sub-groups of students may be considered to be exhibiting a reproducing/surface, a meaning/deep or an achieving/strategic approach. Approaches to learning are thus viewed from the perspective of qualitative categorical differences.

The basic premises upon which this is based are:

Students who use a **reproducing** (or surface) approach are characterized by an intention to reproduce the material to be learnt, avoiding failure by focusing on specific details and using rote learning strategies.

Students with a **meaning** (or deep) approach are characterized by an intention to understand the material to be learnt, and strategies such as reading widely, using a variety of resources, relating ideas, reflection and appropriate study habits.

Although having much in common with the above perspective, an alternative perspective has developed which may be termed the qualitative individual differences model (Meyer, Parsons and Dunne, 1990). This emphasizes the qualitative individual differences in terms of students' approaches to learning. This model defines the concept of study orchestration as the contextualised study approach that individual students adopt (Meyer, 1991). The term orchestration captures the unique nature of individual approaches to studying viewed as a qualitative responsive approach to a qualitatively perceived educational context.

It was the intention to explore the association between approaches to studying and academic locus of control using the composite locus of control instrument and the Extended Approaches to Studying Inventory (EASI) which has proved so successful in exploring qualitative differences in approaches to studying at both the individual and the group level (see Meyer, 1991).

Results of the Empirical Investigation

In order to investigate firstly the empirical structure of the composite locus of control instrument and then its association with students approaches to studying, the two instruments was administered to two groups of mainly male students in the subject Electronics in the course Electrical Engineering at the Cape Technikon.

The first aim of the investigation was to determine if the composite locus of control instrument could provide a more adequate conceptualization (specifically of academics locus of control) than the existing instruments. For this purpose the results obtained from the administration of the instruments to the two groups analysed firstly by determining the internal consistency of the different subscales. All subscales were deemed to be satisfactors with Cronbach Alpha values between 0.79 and 0.81. A factor analysis using oblique (Promax) rotation was then conducted. The results of this analysis are given in Table 1.

If the factor structure of Table 1 is examined, it is apparent that factor 1 constitutes a theoretical external dimension which comprises external locus attributions of context, powerful other and luck (for success and failure in all three cases), as well as unknown control factors (for success and failure). Surprisingly, ability (for failure) also loads on this factor, although in terms of the theoretical structure of the MMCS it constitutes a part of the internal dimension. Factor 2 constitutes a theoretical internal dimension comprising internal locus and effort (both for success and failure) as well as perceived control (evidenced by the absence of unknown control for success and failure loading on this factor). Significantly ability does not load on the internal dimension.

Table 1 **Oblique factor pattern for locus of control subscales ($\underline{n}$ = 131)**

	F1	F2	F3	F4
COF	**70**	-27	38	.
COS	**69**	.	47	.
POCF	**64**	-37	35	.
LUF	**64**	.	41	32
ICF	.	**85**	-38	.
EFF	.	**81**	-35	.
ICS	-27	**60**	.	.
UCS	31	-28	**69**	.
UCF	48	-47	**70**	.
POCS	50	-33	**67**	.
LUS	**67**	-30	73	.
EFS	.	**48**	-46	52
ABS	.	.	.	49
ABF	45	.	38	26
F1		-28	57	9
F2			-42	18
F3				-4
F4				

Notes
1. The theoretical external dimension is printed in bold italics; the theoretical internal dimension is printed in bold; the theoretical control dimension is printed in italics.
2. Decimal point and loading less than 0.25 have been omitted.

Factor is a variation of factor 1 defined by the control dimension of unknown control with higher negative loading for subscales associated with the internal dimension. Factor 4 brings together the association between ability and effort (for success) which is not apparent in the other three factors.

Table 1 appears to lend support to the theoretical division of locus into two dimensions of perceived control, namely internal and external, and for including subscales from both attributional and social learning theories to provide a more comprehensive representation of students' academic locus of control. The introduction of the concept of controllability and its empirical associations in the factor pattern are consistent with the posited theoretical relationships between perceived control and locus.

The second part of the project sought to explore the association between students' approaches to studying and their [academic locus of control. For this purpose the subscales of the two instruments (the EASI and the composite academic locus of control) were subjected to factor analysis using oblique (Promax) rotation. The results of this analysis are given in Table 2.]

Table 2   Oblique factor pattern for EASI and academic locus of control
             (n = 131)

	F1	F2	F3	F4	F5
BD	**75**	.	.	**28**	.
DA	**64**	.	.	.	.
RI	**67**	.	.	.	.
CS	**64**	.	.	.	.
LS	**59**	.	**27**	.	.
RD	**63**	.	.	**30**	.
IN	**60**	.	**-32**	.	.
ST	**62**	.	.	**39**	.
UE	**62**	.	**-39**	.	.
LD	**47**	.	.	.	.
AD	**64**	**-39**	.	**37**	**-35**
OL	**53**	.	**35**	.	**-33**
RE	**46**	.	.	**33**	.
DS	**-44**	**42**	**50**	.	**44**
LUF	.	*77*	.	.	.
LUS	.	*73*	.	.	*39*
COF	.	*68*	.	.	.
COS	.	*68*	*34*	.	*27*
POCF	.	*61*	.	.	.
POCS	*-33*	*66*	*27*	.	*32*
ABF	.	*56*	*36*	.	.
UCF	.	*61*	*29*	*-46*	.
EN	.	**50**	**47**	.	.
IP	.	**26**	**73**	.	.
NA	.	**25**	**69**	.	.
SB	.	.	**68**	.	.
FF	.	**42**	**70**	.	.
WL	.	**32**	**61**	.	.
FA	**-43**	**36**	**61**	.	.
RS	.	.	**53**	**26**	.
ICF	.	.	.	*84*	.
EFF	*25*	.	.	*85*	.
ICS	*27*	.	.	*67*	.
EFS	*35*	.	.	*70*	*-49*
AN	**31**	.	.	**36**	.
CL	.	.	.	.	*70*
GL	.	*26*	*47*	.	*62*
UCS	.	*48*	.	*-42*	*49*
ABS	*27*	.	.	*42*	*-49*

Interfactor correlations	F1	F2	F3	F4	F5
F1	•	-16	-7	29	-14
F2		•	36	-19	22
F3			•	7	13
F4				•	-11
F5					•

Notes
1.   EASI subscales are printed in bold; academic locus of control are printed in italics.
2.   Decimal point and loading less then 0.25 have been omitted.

In Table 2 there is a clear **meaning/deep** dimension which loads on factor 1 and which is weakly linked to attributions for **failure** in terms of lack of effort (EFF) and for **success** in terms of internal control (ICS), effort(EFS) and ability (ABS). Factor 2 represents an **external** locus dimension (luck, context, powerful other, ability for failure and unknown control) associated with a **reproducing** dimension which is characterized by the absence of the loading of syllabus-boundness on this factor. Factor 2 correlates positively with factor 3, which represents a conceptually more clearly defined **reproducing** dimension (with the addition of syllabus-boundness, operation learning and surface relationships). Locus subscales which load on factor 3 are external factors of context (for success), powerful others (for success), ability (for failure) and unknown factors (for failure). The loading of ability (for failure) as an externally perceived dimension is consistent with the factor pattern shown in Table 1.

Factor 4 could be considered to be a **strategic** dimension (defined by strategic approach and achievement motivative) supported by attributions of internal control, effort and ability (for success), which is a theoretically consistent association. However, the evidence for this factor must be viewed as highly tentative at this stage. The same is true of factor 5 which is an intriguing association of comprehension learning and globetrotting, disorganized study methods and attributions for success of luck, powerful other, context and unknown factors. In addition there are negative loading for ability and effort (for success). It might be that this factor indicates the presence of a learning style which seeks global understanding unsupported by effective study methods, and which (possibly as a consequence) attributes success to external rather than internal focus.

Discussion

The results of the factor analyses of the academic locus of control subscales, and the EASI together with the composite locus of control instrument are very encouraging. In Table 1 there is tentative support for a three-dimensional model of academic locus of control which confirms the suggestions made by Hyman (Hyman *et al.*, 1991) and Weiner (1986). The support is tentative at this stage because of the exploratory nature of the current research project, together with the possible influence of contextual factors linked to the educational setting involved (Electrical Engineering at the Cape Technikon), the relatively small number of students involved and the predominance of male students in the sample.

An interesting observation from Table 18.1 is that ability for failure attribution, which in the theoretical structure of the MMCS should indicate internal control, is perceived as an external dimension. This finding supports similar findings by Hyman *et al.* (1991) p. 409 who suggests that the constructs of effort and ability are relatively independent dimensions of internality on the achievement of the MMCS.

The negative loading of unknown control on the internal dimension in Table 1 supports Connell's (1985) contention that the unknown control dimension can be perceived as the uncontrollable part of Weiner's (1986) controllability dimension. Unknown control implies a lack of knowledge regarding the locus (internal versus external) of the sufficient cause. it is thus logical that students would perceive this lack as 'outside' their control and therefore inversely associated with an internal dimension.

This project found that students associate **control** with success due to perceived effort or failure due to perceived lack of effort. This implies that when students acknowledge responsibility for the amount of effort they excert in terms of a learning task, they perceive and accept control for the outcome of that learning engagement. This could be of value for intervention and teaching strategies. Students that appear to be academically 'at risk' due to a theoretical less desirable approach to studying could be encouraged through intervention to qualitatively improve the effort they excert in terms of a learning task. This means that such students should be taught how to improve the effectiveness, efficiency and validity of their efforts when engaging learning tasks.

All students could benefit from qualitatively improving the effort they excert. Here the teaching practice that teachers adopt could be improved so that a climate is created where students are encouraged (irrespective of they being conceptually at risk or not) to develop a more efficient and effective (in terms of learning outcome) engagement of learning tasks. This supports what de Bono (1985), p. 44) identifies as one of the characteristics of successful people: their achievement of success usually involves hard work!

In summary, it may be stated that the broad findings described above lend support to two conclusions: firstly, tertiary students do not necessarily know what factors control their academic outcome and secondly (as put forward by Weiner, 1986) that the two-dimensional attributional perspective of locus of control (stability and locus of control) should be extended to a three-dimensional model (an internal dimension, an external dimension and a control dimension).

Table 2, which describes the underlying dimensions of the EASI together with the locus instrument, also provides potentially interesting results. This simultaneous analysis retained the three-dimensions of locus of control indicated in Table 1. The factor structure of the EASI approximates well to the pattern found in previous studies (see, for example, Meyer and Parsons, 1989; Meyer, 1991). The exploration of the association between students' approaches to studying and perceived locus of control suggests that the specific academic locus of control instrument used in this study might result in a more conceptually comprehensive and support model. This might be ascribed to the fact that the three-dimensional model significantly improves associated measurements and the conceptual descriptions of academic locus of control, but such a conclusion must, at this stage, remain tentative. Further investigation and research to confirm (or modify) these findings in other educational settings is clearly needed.

There are two tentative implications from this study for educational practice and for the design of intervention. The first is that this study supports the contention that students in higher education do not necessarily know what constitutes a theoretically desirable approach to studying. The second conclusion is that students perceive the factors that they believe are influential in determining their academic achievement in terms which are fundamentally different over a number of dimensions. Qualitatively different approaches to studying are (logically) associated with different perceptions of the locus of control and the **degree of control** that they exert over both internal and external factors.

In the past intervention was mainly directed at changing students' approaches to studying, with limited success. In terms of informing intervention aimed at enhancing students' ability to employ theoretically desirable approaches to studying, the results suggest that the dimension of unknown control is significant in describing students' perceived academic locus of control since it is empirically associated with an external dimension and a reproducing approach. This could indicate additional relevant areas in which intervention could be focused. Perry and Penner (1990) p. 264 propose that by increasing the perceived control (through, for example,attributional retaining – see Van

Overwalle, 1989b) of students, their achievement could be improved. Other recent studies (Perry and Penner, 1990; Dart and Clarke, 1991; Butler and Orion, 1990) provide evidence to suggest that by concentrating rather on improving students' perceived locus of control, associated qualitative improvements in students' approaches to studying could be achieved.

The results described in this project tentatively suggest that intervention should not only focus on addressing the needs of students with theoretically undesirable approaches to studying (as has traditionally been the case), but that the qualitative performance of many apparently successful students' might be enhanced by addressing more explicitly some of the underlying assumptions regarding the factors that influence learning quality and learning outcome in the context of higher education. Successful students in higher education may indeed fall into two distinct groups: those who succeed and know the determinants involved, and those who succeed yet do not understand the determinants for their success. A similar distinction could also exist for failing students. This is clearly an area in which considerable further research needs to be undertaken.

In conclusion, the results reported in this chapter provide a clearer understanding as to the conceptual basis of factors which might contribute to success or failure in higher education. Further research needs to be undertaken to confirm the results and conclusions drawn and to explore their integration into the form of intervention and the practice of higher education. The relationship between these aspects and measures of academic performance also needs to be investigated. It is hoped that the insights gained can be applied to improve the academic outcome of tertiary students through improved intervention and teaching practice.

Acknowledgement

The financial assistance of the Centre for Science Development towards this research is hereby acknowledged. Opinions expressed in this chapter, and the conclusions arrived at, are those of the authors and are not necessarily to be attributed to the Centre for Science development.

References

Brown, R. (1990). The construct and concurrent validity of the social dimension of the Brown locus of control scale. *Educational and Psychological Measurement*, **50**, 377–91.

Biggs, J. B. (1978). Individual and group differences in study processes. *British Journal of Educational Psychology*, **48**, 266–79.

Butler, R. and Orion, R. (1990). When pupils do not understand the determinants of their success and failure in school: relations between internal, teacher and unknown perceptions of control and school achievement. *British Journal of Educational Psychology*, **60**, 63–75.

Connell, J. P. (1985). A new multidimensional measure of children's perceptions of control. *Child Development*, **56**, 1018–41.

Dart, B. C. and Clarke, J. A. (1991). Helping students become better learners: a case study in teacher education. *Higher Education*, **22**, 317–35.

De Bono, E. (1985). *Tactics, the art and Science of Success*. London: Fontana.

Duttweiler, P. C. (1984). The internal control index: a newly developed measure of locus of control. *Educational and Psychological Measurement*, **44**, 209–21.

Entwistle, N. and Ramsdon, P. (1983). *Understanding Student Learning*. London: Croom Helm.

Goodman, S. H. and Walters, L. K. (1987). Convergent validity of locus of control scales. *Educational and Psychological Measurement*, **47**, 743–7.

Hyman, G. J., Stanley, R. and Burrows, G. D. (1991). The relationship between three multidimensional locus of control scales. *Educational and Psychological Measurement*, **51**, 403–11.

Kelly, H. H. (1972). *Attribution: Perceiving the Causes of Behaviour*. Morristown, N.Y.: General Learning Press.

Lefcourt, H. M., Von Baeyer, C. L., Ware, E. E. and Cox, D. C. (1979). The Multidimensional-Multiattributional Causality Scale: the development of a goal specific locus of control scale. *Canadian Journal of Behavioural Science*, **II**(4), 287–04.

Levenson, H. (1981). Differentiating among internality, powerful others, and chance. In Lefcourt, H. (ed.), *Research with the Locus of Control Construct: Vol 1. Assessment Methods.* New York: Academic Press, pp.15–63.

Marton, F. and Säljö, R. (1976a). On qualitative differences in learning. I – Outcome and process. *British Journal of Educational Psychology*, **46**, 4–11.

Marton, F. and Säjlö, R. (1976b). On qualitative differences in learning. II – Outcome as a function of the learner's conception of the task. *British Journal of Educational Psychology*, **46**, 115–27.

Meyer, J. H. F. (1991). Study Orchestration: the manifestation, interpretation and consequences of contextualised approaches to studying. *Higher Education*, **22**, 297–316.

Meyer, J. H. F. and Parsons, P. (1989). Approaches to studying and course perceptions using the Lancaster Inventory – a comparative study. *Studies in Higher Education*, **14**, 137–53.

Meyer, J. H. F., Parsons, P. G. and Dunne, T. T. (1990). Study orchestration and learning outcome. *Higher Education*, **20**(1), 67–89.

Perry, R. P. and Penner, K. S. (1990). Enhancing academic achievement in college students through attributional retaining and instruction. *Journal of Educational Psychology*, **82**(2), 262–71.

Rotter, J. B. (1966). Generalised expectancies .for internal versus external control of reinforcement. *Psychological Monographs*, **80**(1), 1–28.

Skinner, E. A. and Chapman, M. (1984). Control beliefs in an action perspective. *Human Development*, **27**, 129–32.

Trice, A. D. (1985). An academic locus of control scale for college students. *Perceptual and Motor Skills*, **61**, 1003–46.

Van Overwalle, F. (1989a). Success and failure of freshman at university: a search for determinants. *Higher Education*, **18**, 287–308.

Van Overwalle, F. (1989b). Improving performance of freshman through attributional testimonies from fellow students. *British Journal of Educational Psychology*, **59**, 75–85.

Weiner, B. (1974). *Achievement Motivation and Attribution Theory*. Morristown, N. J.: General Learning Press.

Weiner, B. (1986). *An Attributional Theory of Motivation and Emotion*. New York: Springer-Verlag.

Watkins, D. (1987). Academic locus of control: a relevant variable at tertiary level? *Higher Education*, **16**, 211–29.

Appendix: Composite Locus of Control Instrument

Achievement (MMCS)

ABILITY

(Success)

The most important ingredient in getting high marks is my academic ability.
I feel that my high marks reflect directly on my academic ability.
When I get high marks it is because of my academic competence.

(Failure)

If I were to receive low marks it would cause me to question my academic ability.
If I were to fail a subject it would probably be because I lacked skill in that area.
If I were to get low marks I would assume that I lacked ability to succeed in that subject or subjects.

EFFORT

(Success)

In my case the high marks I receive are always the direct result of my efforts.
Whenever I receive high marks, it is always because I studied hard for that subject.
I can overcome most obstacles in the path of academic success if I work hard enough.

(Failure)

When I receive a low mark, I usually feel that the main reason is that I haven't studied hard enough for that subject.
When I fail to do as well as expected academically, it is often due to lack of effort on my part.
Low marks indicate to me that I haven't worked hard enough.

CONTEXT

(Success)

In general, when I have received a high mark in a subject, it was due to the teacher's easy marking scheme.
My high marks may simply reflect that these were easier subjects that others.
I get high marks only because the subject material was easy to learn.

(Failure)

In my experience, once a teacher gets the idea you're a poor student, your work is likely to receive low marks than if someone else handed it in.
Often my lower marks are obtained in subjects that the teacher has failed to make interesting.
The low marks I've received seem to me to reflect the fact that some teachers are just stingy with marks.

LUCK

(Success)

My success on exams depends on some luck.
I feel that my high marks depend to a considerable extent on chance factors, such as having the right questions show up on an exam.
I feel that I have to consider myself lucky for the high marks I get.

(Failure)

My lower marks have seemed to be partially due to unfortunate circumstances.
My academic failures make me think I was just unlucky.

My low marks may have been a function of bad luck, being in the wrong course at the wrong time.

Cognitive domain (MMCPC)

INTERNAL CONTROL
(Success)
If I want to do well academically, it's up to me to do it.
It's up to me to get high marks in tests or exams.
(Failure)
If I get low marks in the exams, it's my own fault.
It's my own fault if I don't do well academically.

Powerful others control
(Success)
When I do well academically, it's because the teacher likes me.
The best way for me to get high marks in a test or exam is to get the teacher to like me.
(Failure)
I won't do well in my subject if I have a bad teacher.
If I don't have a good teacher, I won't do well in that subject.

UNKNOWN CONTROL
(Success)
When I get a high mark on a test or exam, I usually don't know why I did so well.
When I do well academically, I usually can't figure out why.
(Failure)
When I don't do well on tests or exams, I usually can't figure out why.
If I get a low mark on a test or exam, I usually don't understand why I got it.

23

Researchers of our own teaching: theory into practice in the evolution of a teaching and learning strategy for an interdisciplinary environmental studies degree

Jennifer Blumhof, Andrew Honeybone, Debbie Pearlman and Keith Pinn (Division of Environmental Sciences, University of Hertfordshire)

Introduction

At the University of Hertfordshire, staff within the Division of Environmental Sciences have come together to establish the Environmental Education Action Research Group (EEARG). This group is using action research for the rigorous development, testing and evaluation of educational innovations which form part of the experiential learning approach within environmental courses at the university.

This chapter will explain the rationale for an action research approach which seeks to bring together research, teaching and staff development. Teachers become researchers of their own teaching and, through successive cycles of action research, bring about their own staff development and the development of the curriculum which in turn helps to improve student learning. The difficulties involved in implementing this approach will be discussed. The ways in which academics, who are subject specialists rather than educational researchers, can break into the 'deep' learning research literature will be considered. Appropriate applications of the research findings in a subject specific context will be outlined, including a discussion of the particular merits of interdisciplinary study as a means of achieving the 'deep' learning outcomes associated with the higher levels of SOLO taxonomy. Case studies will be used to clarify the approach and their contribution to the evolution of an overall teaching and learning strategy and curriculum design will be assessed.

The chapter will conclude by relating our work to the current concern with quality assessment and consider the merits of this internally generated form of quality evaluation compared with externally determined quality assessment exercises. The importance of this action research approach to improving student learning will be stressed.

The Divisional Context

The University of Hertfordshire, formerly Hatfield Polytechnic, established its first environmental course, the BSc Environmental Studies Sandwich Degree, in 1976. This degree was designed as a broadly based and applied programme of study which aimed to give students a scientific understanding of environmental issues but with that understanding set firmly in its social, economic and political context. Thus interdisciplinarity lay at the heart of the degree and students were encouraged to develop their interdisciplinary understanding as a means of formulating their own solutions to environmental problems.These broad aims continue to form the basis of the approach to environmental education adopted by the Division of Environmental Sciences at the University of Hertfordshire even though the original degree programme has gone through many modifications and the range of environmental courses has been greatly expanded.

Formerly, in common with most areas of higher education, few environmental lecturers had any background in educational ideas or teacher training. With years of experience they may have picked up many fragments which may make useful contributions to their knowing- in-action (Schon, 1983). Educational staff development opportunities were few. Lecturers were primarily subject specialists who had developed broader interests in the solution of environmental problems. Now explicit attention is being given to the theoretical underpinnings of the approach to learning and teaching within environmental courses. The critical development has been the establishment of the Environmental Education Action Research Group (EEARG) at the University of Hertfordshire.

The Rationale for Establishing the Environmental Education Action Research Group (EEARG)

As reported elsewhere (Blumhof and Honeybone, 1993), the origins of EEARG can be found in the concerns of a group of staff teaching principally on the BSc Environmental Studies Degree at the University of Hertfordshire. Those concerns stemmed from a variety of factors both internal and external to the university. Internally, the growth in student numbers on the long established environmental courses led to a less than commensurate increase in staff numbers but nevertheless a rise that was sufficient to lead to the establishment of a separate Division of Environmental Sciences. In these changed circumstances, with an intake on the main degree scheme expanding from about 40 to nearly 100 and the student/staff ratio rising from 12:1 to 20:1, there was the opportunity, as well as the pressure, to move from a largely intuitive approach to teaching and learning to one that articulated more clearly the theoretical underpinnings of student learning and teaching practice. Without such an underpinning it was difficult to determine which changes in teaching and learning strategy were consistent with the stated educational objectives and which were not.

To begin with, hardly any environmental lecturers had any background or real knowledge in educational ideas or formal teacher training. Educational staff development opportunities were few. Lecturers were primarily single-subject specialists who had developed broader interests in the solution of environmental problems. As far as their teaching was concerned, they based their approach on the intuitive notion that students would develop a greater understanding of the environment if they came into contact with it. Where direct contact was not possible, various devices, including case studies and role plays were used. Courses required the active involvement of students but this was not articulated in terms of 'student centred learning', 'experiential learning' or any other formal theoretical ideas about the learning and teaching process.

External influences added considerable weight to the internal motivation and pressure for change. The national move towards mass higher education, coupled with a declining unit of resource, led to similar pressures nationally as had been experienced internally. The Polytechnics and Colleges Funding Council *Teaching More Students* project (Gibbs, 1992b) provided one link between theory and practice. That was developed further in the Council for National Academic Awards *Improving the Quality of Student Learning* project (Gibbs, 1992a). The Enterprise in Higher Education initiative provided another stimulus to change. In the case of the University of Hertfordshire, these three projects became interlinked and provided a source of funding for teaching and learning innovations with members of staff from the Division of Environmental Sciences being successful in gaining a number of awards. A change arising from the ending of the binary divide then provided a further stimulus to the developing staff interests in teaching and learning. The participation of the University of Hertfordshire in the research selectivity exercise for the first time led to the Division being awarded a rating of 2 with environmental education action research being identified, alongside two areas of substantive environmental research, as a priority research area.

In these circumstances early in 1993, a group of subject specialists with a particular interest in teaching and learning (but only one of whom had a formal teaching qualification) came together and formed the Environmental Education Action Research Group (EEARG). We considered that our work would best be co-ordinated and structured within a clearly defined group conferring an internal structure and external profile. Though all members of the teaching staff have been encouraged to join EEARG in fact there has been a core group of activists who have been attending conferences and workshops, experimenting with fresh approaches in their teaching and more recently giving papers themselves. EEARG is also active in disseminating ideas to divisional and other university teaching staff and facilitating teaching and learning innovations. EEARG brings together research, teaching and professional development and through this, enhances the quality of the learning environment for staff and students alike. It is providing a focus for the co-ordinated programme of action research, encouraging collaboration and experimentation based on mutual and shared expertise. The overall research strategy will be discussed later but first it is necessary to discuss our research approach, action research.

Action Research

The name (EEARG) arises out of the theoretical approach we have been adopting (maybe, at the outset, without quite knowing it), namely action research. This approach was the one adopted in the CNAA *Improving the Quality of Student Learning Project* (Gibbs, 1992a) and it has recently been defined as

> collaborative, critical enquiry by the academics themselves (rather than expert educational researchers) into their own teaching practice, into problems of student learning and into curriculum problems. It is professional development through academic course development, group reflection, action, evaluation and improved practice. (Zuber-Skerritt, 1992, pp. 1–2).

Teachers become the researchers of their own teaching and, through successive cycles of action research, bring about their own staff development. We plan our educational 'experiments', we act on them, we observe and reflect on the results, rigorously evaluating them before we move on to a new cycle of action research building on our experience from the previous cycle. Of course, this action research cycle is essentially the Lewin/Kolb experiential learning cycle (Kolb, 1984, p. 21) used for a particular purpose, in this case for the rigorous development, testing and evaluation of educational innovations which are themselves part of the student experiential learning approach within environmental courses at the University of Hertfordshire.

Within the Division of Environmental Sciences at the University, environmental education action research has been identified as one of the three foci of research as the division strives to increase its research rating at the next research assessment exercise. Although action research has gained quite wide acceptance and academic credibility, its inclusion alongside two areas of more conventional subject based research is, perhaps, not uncontroversial (Ball, 1993; Kingman, 1993). Rigorous action research focused on learning and teaching in higher education could be one significant means of meeting what the MacFarlane Report sees as the greatest challenge in higher education today, namely 'to persuade a majority of those involved in higher education to see teaching as their prime activity, and one posing intellectual challenges and offering rewards comparable to those of standard research'. (Committee of Scottish University Principals, 1992, p. ix).

Environmental Science, Action Research and the 'Deep' Approach

The underlying premise of EEARG' s work is that through action research we can improve the quality of student learning outcomes by identifying more clearly the type of learning situation and teaching role which will encourage students to see learning as 'making sense' (adopting the 'deep' approach) rather than as purely 'reproducing' ('surface' approach). The reasons why students in higher education should adopt this orientation in their studies are now well documented (see for example Gibbs, 1992a, pp. 2–11 and Committee of Scottish University Principals, 1992, pp. 52–62), the aim being to create a learning environment which encourages students to adopt a 'deep' rather than a 'surface' approach to learning, aided by teachers who adopt a facilitating rather than a didactic role (Her Majesty's Inspectorate, 1989, p. 10).

Before considering in more detail EEARG's research strategy it would be useful to discuss briefly some ideas about the particular merits of interdisciplinary study as a means of achieving the deep learning outcomes. This belief has encouraged us to pursue our pedagogic aims despite the considerable challenges of working in an area which encompasses aspects of both natural and social sciences. To extend Becher's metaphor (Becher, 1969) environmental sciences/studies can be seen as a battleground between academic tribes defending their territories. Our aim is to try and form a more unified 'state' which offers a more holistic view of environmental issues. However, the 'hard science' – 'soft science' debate ebbs and flows through curriculum design, teaching and learning strategies and research methodology. We are ever vigilant of the problem that Passmore describes as being 'forced to slosh about in that primordial ooze known as inter-disciplinary studies' (Passmore, 1974).

Despite these concerns we would argue that interdisciplinary environmental studies have particular qualities in relation to the development of a 'deep' understanding. We have argued in an earlier paper that the deep approach is a *sine qua non* of environmental education (Blumhof and Honeybone, 1993). We base this claim on the view that environmental studies are essentially concerned with examining environmental issues not simply from a variety of disciplinary perspectives (multidisciplinarity) but with making connections between those perspectives, continually striving for a more structured, integrated and holistic understanding, that is an interdisciplinary understanding. Thus the concept of interconnectedness is central to environmental studies as it is to Level 4 (relational) and Level 5 (extended abstract) of the Structures Of Learning Outcomes (SOLO) taxonomy (Ramsden, 1992, p. 55). Research indicates that those levels can only be achieved by students who adopt a 'deep' approach (Gibbs, 1992a): hence there appears to be a vital link between environmental studies and the 'deep' approach.

We would also advance the view that interdisciplinary environmental studies, because it is not wedded to the established patterns of thinking of any one discipline, provide a context which can help students to achieve another of the key aims of higher education, namely the adoption of an independent critical stance. Indeed, if it is accepted that "... disciplines call for rules of engagement to be mastered and kept" (Barnett, 1990, p. 177), environmental studies by being problem focused rather than subject focused provides a continual challenge to established disciplinary ways of thinking. Those ways of thinking are continually exposed to different paradigms and remain valid (for environmental studies) not because they satisfy some internal logic of a particular discipline but only if they help to clarify a particular environmental problem. Furthermore, as Barnett has argued (1990, p. 176), "... the problems of the world do not come in simple disciplinary containers.... In the end, all knowledge is connected, and anything we do in our educational transactions to convey a different picture is damaging."

Aware of the challenge of interdisciplinarity but keen to construct an action research programme with the aim of enhancing the learning environment, we decided to adopt a two pronged strategy.

EEARG's Research Strategy: Framework and Specific Projects

EEARG's research strategy consists of **framework** and **specific** projects. Framework projects are intended to increase understanding of the overall learning environment within which the environmental courses were operating whereas specific projects investigated at a more detailed level some particular aspect of the course programme. One example of a framework project will be used to demonstrate how the action research approach is being used to try and bring theory and practice together.

A 'framework' action research project: Approaches to Learning

The framework project that will now be described is the approaches to learning project. The background to the project was that, prior to the establishment of EEARG, a number of investigations had been undertaken that were evaluated by a variety of means such as student feedback questionnaires (Honeybone, 1993). However, there was no firm evidence that more students were being encouraged to adopt a 'deep' approach (Gibbs, 1992a) by these projects or that higher level outcomes (Biggs, 1991) were being achieved more frequently. Student preparation and performance in assessment might suggest that motivation and understanding had been increased but no well-grounded claims could be made that the innovations in teaching and learning had facilitated 'deep' approaches to learning. Therefore the approaches to learning project was set up to provide some evidence on that point.

The project is divided into two phases (Blumhof and Honeybone, 1994). The main phase seeks to obtain clearer evidence on whether or not teaching and learning strategies are being successful in encouraging students to adopt deeper approaches to learning. This will be done by using one of the approaches to studying questionnaires (Gibbs, 1992a), by in-depth interviews with students (Entwistle and Entwistle, 1992) and possibly by use of Ramsden's student experience questionnaire (Ramsden, 1992) . However, before embarking on the main phase of the research, it was considered to be particularly important in an interdisciplinary subject area like environmental studies to include a preliminary phase which sought to clarify the attitudes and perceptions of staff towards the learning process. The reasoning behind this was that if students are given conflicting signals by different members of staff coming maybe from different academic backgrounds, this might lessen the positive effects of individual changes in curriculum design which in themselves might be valid ways of fostering a deep approach. On the one hand, in environmental studies there may be the potential for staff, coming from a variety of academic 'tribes' with their possible predispositions for different learning styles (Kolb, 1984; Becher, 1989), to offer a stimulatingly wide range of learning opportunities to students while on the other hand, the establishment of a coherent teaching and learning strategy may be made more difficult by the self same variety if staff have very different expectations of students in terms of the aims of higher education and the importance of a 'deep' approach.

Therefore, as a first stage in testing the former possibility, a small pilot survey of all academic staff in the Division of Environmental Sciences was conducted using the Kolb/McCarthy Learning Style Inventory (Kolb, 1984). In the case of the latter possibility, differences in staff expectations were tested by asking all staff to complete the Gibbs' Approaches to Studying Questionnaire as if they were an ideal student (Gibbs, 1992a). While the results of this preliminary phase are not of direct relevance to this chapter, it can be noted, with some reservations about the smallness of the numbers involved, that there did seem to be some variation in learning style associated with disciplinary background. Also, the results from the approaches to study questionnaire did indicate quite clearly that staff in environmental sciences had very similar views on the desirability of students adopting a deep approach to their learning. Whether there is the same virtual unanimity concerning the means of encouraging deep approaches has still to be investigated.

A 'specific' action research project: the Mediterranean Case Study

A useful example of one of the 'specific' action research projects that we have embarked upon is the Mediterranean Case Study.This Case Study highlights the many benefits of our action research strategy in that through our becoming 'researchers of our own teaching' we have discovered research evidence to move us from 'knowing what' rather than 'knowing how', (Ryle, 1949 quoted in Downie, 1990) – that is understanding the processes. Because we now have a deeper understanding of the processes we are able to confidently support the somewhat complex structure to fellow professionals and students alike .

The background to the project was as follows. In order to integrate personal transferable skills into the subject curriculum of an Environmental Sciences four-year sandwich degree the Integrative Project was initiated in 1991 (Blumhof, Broom and Stallibrass, 1994). The impetus for the redesign of first-year and second-year courses came from the growing recognition of the importance of skills development in Higher education and the realization that skills development in 'stand-alone' or 'bolt-on' courses was ineffectual. This is particularly emphasized in the Mediterranean Case Study. In this work we have tried to integrate skills development with academic content using the assessment process as the catalyst for change. We have evaluated this work in a range of ways and over the three years that it has run monitored progress and instituted modifications.Through embarking on the project we investigated the research in the area of skills development and hopefully have contributed to the body of that knowledge.

The Mediterranean Case Study, forms part of the second-year compulsory Environmental Issues module, the subject aims of increasing student understanding of environmental problems in the Mediterranean Region are integrated with the aim of developing transferable skill considered to be of particular use to second-year students prior to their placement year (Blumhof, Honeybone, Pearlman, Pinn, 1994). The case study seeks to achieve these aims by providing students with introductory lectures as a basic framework around which they can build their own detailed study of a selected environmental problem in the Mediterranean Region.The assessment is a group exercise where students are asked to produce a poster which should analyse and suggest solutions to a specific environmental problem in the Mediterranean Region. Apart from the 'content' lectures there are workshops which provide students with time for group discussion of selected specific environmental problem and the opportunity for structured skills development sessions.

At the start of the Mediterranean exercise students are issued with a chart setting out the assessment criteria for the posters. The decision to do this was based on the notion that assessments should be 'front-ended' with clear and explicit criteria being communicated to students right from the beginning of the exercise (Gibbs, 1992b). In the present case, the attempt has been made to relate the specific criteria for the assessment of the presentation and content of the posters to the overall qualities of honours degree level work. By means of the explicit statement of criteria, linked with discussion in class, it is hoped that students will be encouraged to see learning as 'making sense' rather than as 'reproducing' and thus be more likely to achieve a 'deep' rather than a 'surface' outcome to their learning (Gibbs, 1992a).

As a further means of stimulating student reflection, an element of peer group assessment is incorporated in the case study (see Blumhof and Stallibrass, 1992). Marking is undertaken in groups with each student group marking all the other posters. Students assess the posters during the presentation session by looking at all the posters in turn and discussing in their groups how each poster performed in relation to the assessment criteria. Using the assessment sheet, they agree which box to tick for each criteria. Students are advised to use the distribution of ticks as a guide, rather than mechanistically, and they then agree their marks for presentation and content. At the same time a group of staff assess all the posters and agree marks in the same way. The student and staff marks are then combined into a single mark for each group in the 60: 40 proportions previously agreed. As a means of getting students to consider how well they had used their individual skills in completing the group task, they are asked to decide on how the group mark should be divided up between the individual members of the group. In cases where groups are unable to agree, a member of staff may be called in to adjudicate but only as a last resort as the purpose of adopting this form of mark allocation is to improve students' abilities of self-criticism and self-evaluation. This year a further assessment element will be added that will aid self-evaluation. This will be marked on the basis of 'done/not done' as the point is to encourage self-awareness not to try and mark it.

An important feature of the case study is that it promotes, particularly through the workshops, a continuing dialogue between students and staff, a dialogue covering both the development of the environmental content of the posters and the use of transferable skills. Thus feedback is being continually obtained and detailed adjustments can be made to the case study programme while it is in progress, giving additional emphasis to points which are causing student (or staff) concern. Over the three years EEARG activists have encouraged other members of staff to participate in the project, sharing experience and expertise.

The method of assessment also facilitates rapid feedback to students. The posters for over 80 students were marked on a Wednesday and assessment sheets returned to them during a workshop two days later. During that workshop, apart from additional comments being made on individual posters, a general review is undertaken of what factors contributed to the production of good and bad posters. Another feature of the same final workshop is that students are asked to complete an evaluation questionnaire. The questionnaire provides students with the opportunity to reflect and comment on how well they felt that the environmental and skill related aims of the case study have been achieved.

The comments made by some students indicate, not surprisingly perhaps, that some students are resistant to the notion of the lecturer as a facilitator rather than a disseminator of information. Some students expressed a strong preference for more 'factual content' lectures and a return to traditional forms of assessment such as essays or reports. The type of non-traditional assessment used in this case study would appear to require more careful and explicit structuring and context setting than have normally been provided for more conventional assignments. The very fact that aims and assessment criteria are made more explicit would seem to evoke greater student criticism, both positive and negative. Indeed, that is part of the purpose of the exercise, to encourage students to adopt a more critical stance.We are now more explicit about driving our students around the Lewin/Kolb experiential learning cycle, which , as we noted earlier, is essentially the action research cycle, or more accurately, spiral.

Some Concluding Comments on the Evolution of a Teaching and Learning Strategy for an Interdisciplinary Environmental Studies Degree

In summary we consider that the establishment of EEARG has helped us towards our pedagogic goals by :

- building rationally on the foundations we have laid so far;
- developing a more clearly articulated theoretical framework;
- providing a supportive framework for our collaborative activities which harnesses and focuses the enthusiasm and dynamism of the teaching staff (innovation and experimentation can be a risky and stressful business particularly when undertaken in isolation);
- improving contact with one another and other academics and organizations to ensure that we are not reinventing the wheel;
- stimulating other staff to become involved;
- encouraging us to disseminate and publish results;
- enhancing our external profile.

In conclusion what comments might be made about the value of the action research approach we have adopted in the Division of Environmental Sciences, University of Hertfordshire and the obstacles we are having to overcome.

Firstly, the effort required by the core group of EEARG activists to familiarize themselves with the educational research literature was considerable. In striving to develop their role as professional teachers through action research, it proved very difficult to maintain their subject expertise at preexisting levels. Thus while action research and the notion of the researcher/teacher may be one appropriate means of developing greater professionalism in teachers in higher education, it probably could not be seen as a principal activity of all staff. A majority of staff might participate in action research projects from time to time as participants alongside core members of the action research group. Nevertheless, that form of participation, although more limited in terms of time, could be a means of clarifying the teacher's conception of the learning process and of the teacher's role in that process. Core members of the action research group would be taking on a facilitating role in relation to staff development within their own department.

In contrast, the second point arising from the EEARG experience highlights that there are dangers as well as advantages in teachers attempting to become researchers of their own teaching. Subject specialists coming into the action research/educational development lack the extensive experience and familiarity with the literature that one would expect from experts in the field. Take the example of the EEARG approaches to learning project. The decision was taken to use the Gibbs version of the approaches to study questionnaire but this was done, not on the basis of a thorough review of all the alternatives available but because that particular questionnaire was readily available. There was an awareness that some 'health warnings' had been issued about the use of such questionnaires (Richardson, 1993) but it cannot be claimed that a rigorous review of the alternatives was undertaken. If that had been done, given the limited time available, a better planned study with a stronger theoretical underpinning might have been formulated but there would not have been time to carry it out. An alternative approach, thought to be consistent with the experiential learning model (Kolb, 1984), was adopted: take the plunge, start the investigation and then progressively refine the theoretical basis through successive cycles of planning, acting, observing and reflecting. Otherwise the ideal state of preparedness might never be reached and teachers would never start to become researchers of their own teaching. But the degree of nerve needed to take the plunge should not be underestimated! We were also faced with the particular issues of interdisciplinarity which as we have argued can be considered the *sine qua non* of a deep approach but can also instigate tribal warfare.

A third point may provide a way of minimizing some of the dangers identified in the previous paragraph. EEARG was not established in a vacuum. As already mentioned, staff had been extensively involved in the staff development activities brought together under the Enterprise in Higher Education banner. Thus a continuing two-way exchange took place with professional staff developers and, as interest developed, contact was also made with educational researchers. In this way, action research may help to break down any 'them' and 'us' feelings between academics, staff developers and educational researchers and enable academics to take responsibility for their own learning (about teaching and learning) in the same way that they might wish their own students to take responsibility.

A fourth and final point follows from the value of action research in the participants own learning. Part of this learning would be a greater self-awareness of the strengths and weaknesses of one's own teaching. This might be a step towards the self-critical communities (Carr and Kemmis, 1986) or, as Brown (1992) puts it, one way of ensuring that institutions 'operate at a more self conscious level'. In this way action research could be seen as a means of internal quality assessment. External assessment such as that carried out by the Higher Education Funding Councils may be a necessary stimulus to change (Elton, 1993) but unless the responsibility for quality is internalized by a more surely established teaching profession engaging in reflective practice and action research, the effects of external assessment may be short lived.

References

Ball, C. (1993). Modern miracles by SORT code'. *Times Higher Education Supplement*, **1079**, 16.

Barnett, R. (1990). *The Idea of Higher Education*. Buckingham, The Society for Research into Higher Education and Open University Press.

Becher, T. (1989). *Academic Tribes and Territories:Intellectual Enquiry and the Cultures of Disciplines*. Buckingham, The Society for Research into Higher Education and the Open University Press.

Biggs, J. B. (ed.) (1991). *Teaching for Learning. The View from Cognitive Psychology*. Hawthorn, Australian Council for Educational Research.

Blumhof, J. and Honeybone, A. (1993). 'Getting Going in Action Research: A Practical Approach'. *Staff and Educational Development Association Conference – Research and Teaching in Higher Education*, Cardiff, 29–30 Nov 1993.

Blumhof, J.and Stallibrass, C.(1993). *Peer Assessment:A Pragmatic Approach*. Higher Education for Capability.

Blumhof, J., Broom, C. and Stallibrass, C. (1994). Integrating transferable skills into the subject curriculum: A case history. In Bridges, D. (ed) *Transferable Skills in Higher Education*. University of East Anglia.

Blumhof, J., Honeybone, A., Pearlman, D, and Pinn, K. (1994). Assessing assessment practices in environmental studies. *Staff Educational and Development Association. Conference Assessment for Learning in HE*.Telford16–18 May 1994.

Brown, H. (1992). Staff development in higher education – towards the learning organisation. *Higher Education Quarterly*, **46**(2), 174–190.

Carr, W. and Kemmis, S. (1986). *Becoming Critical: Education, Knowledge and Action Research*. Lewes, Falmer Press.

Committee of Scottish University Principals (1992). *Teaching and learning in an Expanding Higher Education system* (the MacFarlane Report).

Downie R.S. (1990). *Professions and Professionalism* Journal of Philosphy of Education. Volume 24 no 2 pages 147-159.

Elton, L. (1993). University teaching: a professional model for quality. In Ellis, Roger (ed.) *Quality Assurance for University Teaching*. Buckingham, The Society for Research into Higher Education and Open University Press.

Entwistle, A. and Entwistle, N. (1992). Experiences of understanding in revising for degree examinations. *Learning and Instruction*, **2**(1), 1–22.

Gibbs, G. (1992a). *Improving the Quality of Student Learning*. Bristol, Technical and Education Services Ltd.

Gibbs, G. (1992b).*Teaching More Students: 1. Problems and Course Design Strategies*. Oxford Polytechnic/PCFC.

Gibbs, G. (1993).Lecture research into student learning. *Staff and Educational Development Association – Research and Teaching in Higher Education Conference.* Cardiff, 29–30 Nov 1993.

Her Majesty's Inspectorate, Department of Education and Science (1989) *Quality in Higher Education.* A Report on the HMI Invitation Conference. London, HMSO.

Her Majesty's Inspectorate, Department of Education and Science (1990) *Higher Education in the Polytechnics and Colleges.* London, HMSO.

Honey, P. and Mumford, A. (1986). *The Manual of Learning Styles.* Peter Honey.

Honeybone, A. (1993). Integrating the assessment of subject content with skills development in an environmental case study. *Higher Education for Capability Conference - Using Assessment to Develop Capability,* Institute of Education, University of London, 16 July 1993.

Honeybone, A. (1994). *Understanding Environments. Some Reflections on an Environment for Learning in Learning about the Environment.* Unpublished dissertation for MA Higher and Professional Education, Institute of Education, University of London.

Kember, D. (1994). Action research into the quality of student learning: a paradigm for academic staff development. *Innovations Conference on Curriculum and Professional Development for Larger Numbers in Higher Education,* University of Wales, Bangor.

Kemmis, S. (1985). Action research and the politics of reflection. In Boud, David, Keogh, Rosemary and Walker, David (eds.) (1985). Reflection: *Turning Reflection into Learning.* London, Kogan Page.

Kingman, J. (1993). 'The pursuit of truth'. *Times Higher Education Supplement,* **1076**, 15.

Kolb, D. A. (1984). *Experiential Learning. Experience as the Source of Learning and Development.* Englewood Cliffs, New Jersey,Prentice Hall.

Passmore, J. (1974). *Man's Responsibility for Nature.* London, Duckworth.

Polytechnic and Colleges Funding Council (1990). *Teaching Quality.* Report of the Committee of Enquiry Appointed by the Council (the Warnock Report). London, PCFC.

Ramsden, P. (1992). *Learning to teach in Higher Education.* London, Routledge.

Richardson, J. T. E. (1993). Using questionnaires to evaluate student learning: some health warnings, *Improving Student Learning Symposium,* University of Warwick, 13–14 Sept.

Ryle, G. (1949). *Concept of mind.* London, Hutchinson.

Schon, D. A. (1983). *The Reflective Practioner. How Professionals Think in Action.* New York. Basic Books. Education and Open University Press.

Zuber-Skerritt, O. (1992). *Action Research in Higher Education. Examples and Reflections.* London, Kogan Page.

24 Identifying and advising students with deficient study skills and strategies

Hilary Tait, Carol Speth and Noel Entwistle (Centre for Research on Learning and Instruction, University of Edinburgh)

Introduction

The Higher Education Funding Council's **Teaching and Learning Technology Programme** was set up in 1992 with the broad aim of making 'teaching and learning more productive and efficient by harnessing modern technology' (UFC, 1992). The project reported in this chapter was funded under this scheme to develop computer software to identify and advise students who are at academic risk due to deficient study skills and strategies. Unlike the work of Meyer and Parsons (1993), the project has not aimed to develop a model of student learning to which individual students are subsequently compared, but rather uses the substantial research on student learning firstly to identify students who appear to be using study skills and strategies which are unlikely to lead to academic success, and secondly to develop principled advice to deliver to students.

The Importance of Study Skills

In recent years, most higher education institutions have expanded their student numbers and in some cases in doing so have had to accept less well-qualified students than previously. The level at which the course begins though tends to remain the same as before, and weaker students start at a disadvantage, often subsequently experiencing difficulty in getting help because of the increased demands on teaching staff. Student diversity has grown too, and institutions are seeing increased numbers of overseas students, mature students and other non-traditional entrants. It has thus become important to discard the notion of an homogeneous first-year class, and instead to take stock and respond to the diversity of needs which does exist.

For students to perform well in higher education, they need to come to grips with a considerable quantity of complex material and be able to demonstrate their knowledge and understanding of it. To do so, they also need to develop appropriate study skills and strategies and previous research has shown that, in addition to entry qualifications and motivation, study habits are closely associated with academic performance (Entwistle and Wilson, 1977).

This importance of study skills training in higher education is often undermined by the assumption that entrance selectivity itself guarantees that students are adequately prepared for what lies ahead. But, selection is most often based on grades obtained in examinations taken at school, and the nature and complexity of the tasks demanded by higher education can be very different (Wall *et al.*, 1991). Many students for example, will enter higher education seldom having written an essay of more than a few hundred words, yet essays of one or two thousand words are commonplace in many first-year courses. Few students will have had experience of taking lecture notes, or of having so much unstructured study time. Many fail to realize that they must now take on the responsibility for their own studying: fewer people, if indeed anyone at all, will be 'checking up' on them. Some students seem able to pass first year yet still have study skill weaknesses. But as the complexity of material and tasks increases in later years of the course, it becomes more important to have appropriate study skills to cope with the course requirements. The study skills required in higher education are **not** the same as those needed at school, so some initial help and advice plus support for students who continue to struggle seems essential.

Study Strategies and Approaches to Studying

Over the past twenty or so years, research into student learning that has sought to describe study behaviour has followed a number of different theoretical perspectives. Yet, there is broad agreement that at least two clearly defined approaches to studying are readily identifiable. These have been called **deep approach** and **surface approach** to relate to the ideas of Craik and Lockhart (1972) and later, Marton and Säljö (1976, 1984). Deep approach students set out to understand course material by interacting closely with it, elaborating and transforming it, and ultimately making it their own. Surface approach students, on the other hand, intend to pass the course, but with very little active engagement with the course material. Rote learning and memorization are common, and students often fail to see connections between parts of their courses.

In everyday learning environments, a third approach, called **strategic approach** (Entwistle and Ramsden, 1983), is generally also identifiable. Strategic students aim to gain the highest possible grades using whatever strategies or approaches seem appropriate. They are generally well-organized, have good study habits and manage their time effectively.

These approaches are more usefully seen as conceptual categories than as descriptions of individual students, and the importance of them to different disciplines varies to some extent. High deep and strategic approaches are generally associated with good performance, while high surface approaches are less likely to be so. However, in science-based subjects in particular, high surface approach combined with high deep or high strategic approaches is commonly seen in successful students because of the nature of the discipline they are studying (Tait, 1992).

There are exceptions to this pattern of relationships between approaches and academic achievement, particularly where departments use methods of assessment which do not encourage students to seek to understand what they are learning. Some multiple-choice or short-note examinations, for example, contain low-level questions which require little more of students than rote-learning of isolated facts.

The broad goal of higher education is that students should develop a conceptual understanding of the discipline they are studying, and be able to demonstrate this in assignments and examinations. It therefore seems justifiable to expect departments to teach in a way which promotes deep and strategic approaches, and to label low deep approach combined with low strategic approach and high surface approach as a 'risky strategy'.

The Project

There are many reasons why some students fail to do well in higher education, particularly in their first year. Some students find they are unable to devote the time and energy required by their studies because of financial worries, personal relationships, family commitments, travel problems or stress (to name but a few). Some have significant problems with the course content and others have difficulties getting to grips with the study skills required of them in their course.

The remit of the project reported in this chapter is restricted to study skills and approaches. Because it is acknowledged that there are many other factors affecting a student's performance, and because individual courses and institutions define failure differently, no attempts have been made directly at any stage to identify those students who are likely to fail or perform badly. Rather, the initial concern is with identifying students who appear to have weaknesses or deficiencies in their study skills and approaches, and, following this, the aim is to make the nature and extent of these difficulties explicit to teaching staff, and to offer help and advice to the students themselves.

Three pieces of software have been developed, the shells of which are built on HyperCard so run on Macintosh computers. The software will be described below.

Identifying Weaknesses in Study Skills and Strategies

A questionnaire for students has been developed and revised during the course of the project to gather information about their study skills and approaches, with a view to identifying weaknesses or deficiencies. The core of the questionnaire is based on the **Approaches to Studying Inventory** (ASI) developed in Lancaster in the late 1970s (Entwistle *et al.*, 1979; Entwistle and Ramsden, 1983). The revision was undertaken to take account of recent research findings in student learning, and to redirect the inventory's use towards identifying weak students who would benefit from help and advice in study skills and strategies. Recent research had suggested that Pask's learning styles and pathologies (Pask, 1976) could be subsumed within other scales, that additional scales to support strategic approach could usefully be added (following the work of Weinstein, *et al.*, 1987 and Janssen, 1992), and that a scale measuring academic self-confidence would be beneficial to serve as a proxy for ability (Janssen, 1992).

The revised inventory of 60 items was administered to some 1500 students in the first year of the project and repeated analyses with various subgroups suggested that a reduction in the inventory's length would be possible without adversely affecting its conceptual coherence. This reduction was sought because a new section focusing on study skills had to be added to the surrounding questionnaire, so that deficiencies in study skills as well as strategies or approaches could be identified. The resulting self-report questionnaire contains four main sections.

The first asks for background details including level of preparation for higher education in terms of entry qualification, ability to study independently, study skills and prior knowledge. The second section is the revised and shortened **Approaches to Studying Inventory**, the third asks students about their study skills in nine main areas – lectures and lecture notes, discussion classes, practicals, reading, asking for help, writing essays, tackling set problems, organizing studying, and revision. The fourth and final section asks to what extent other factors such as travelling time, health and stress, and financial problems affect the student's ability to study. Further details about the development of the revised inventory can be found in Entwistle and Tait (1993) and Entwistle *et al.* (1994).

Once the revised inventory and surrounding questionnaire had been 'finalized', an interactive computer-based version was developed using HyperCard (Odor, 1994a). Questions are displayed one at a time on the screen, and students indicate their desired response by pointing and clicking with the mouse. When a response has been given, the next question appears automatically, though students have the facility to move backwards or forwards manually using directional arrows if they wish to change the response to a question. A horizontal bar at the bottom of the screen fills up as the questionnaire is completed. Completion takes between 15 and 20 minutes in total. Figure 1 shows an example of one card from the interactive questionnaire.

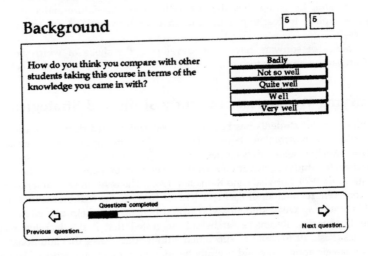

Figure 1

After the questionnaire has been completed, a 'profile' is saved for the student. This computes scores for the three main approaches to studying measured by the inventory (deep, surface and strategic) and stores other information such as those study skills with which the student has indicated he or she has difficulty. It is not anticipated that the student would look at, or interpret, this profile alone: it is used by the other two pieces of software described below.

Providing Information to Departments about their Students

Although a number of learning strategies questionnaires has existed for some time now, teaching staff are often unsure how to analyse data, interpret results and make use of the information they collect. It was therefore decided that a piece of software could usefully be developed to help in this process, and in the context of this project, **StudentView** was designed with two purposes in mind. Firstly, it aims to inform teaching staff about the difficulties the students in their classes experience, and the ways in which their students are going about learning and studying. Secondly, it can act as a filter for determining which students would benefit from help and advice on study skills and strategies, and can indicate the particular advice that would be appropriate for each student.

StudentView takes the responses to the questionnaire from all students within a class and displays them in a three-dimensional interactive plot which has deep approach, surface approach and strategic approach as its axes (Odor, 1994b). Students are positioned as points within this plot by considering their scores on the three approaches to be co-ordinates. Because the three-dimensional plot can be somewhat difficult to interpret when the class size is large, the corresponding three two-dimensional views are also available.

Although factor analysis of the Approaches to Studying Inventory indicates that the deep, surface and strategic dimensions are not orthogonal, it was decided nevertheless to orientate the axes at 90°. This is because StudentView is intended to be a simple visualization tool, and is consequently not sufficiently sophisticated to calculate the precise relationships between the dimensions for a particular class of students or to orientate the axes accordingly. Accompanying documentation will make it clear that this 90° orientation of axes is not intended to have any conceptual or empirical basis, but is for display purposes only.

Conceptually, students located in the region within this plot characterized by low deep and strategic approaches and high surface approaches could be said to be employing approaches to studying which are incompatible with what is required by higher education. They could therefore be said to be employing inappropriate, or perhaps even deficient, approaches to studying, or at least those which would not be particularly likely to lead to ultimate academic success. A pull-down menu in StudentView contains the study skills and other study influences from the questionnaire, and any of these skills or influences can be individually mapped on to the plot. A scrolling bar at the side presents a list of all students from the class for whom the selected skill was problematic, and, because the plot is interactive, any of these students can then be selected and their position within the plot identified. Alternatively, a point within the plot can be chosen, and the identity of the student revealed. A comments box can also be requested which summarizes all the study skills with which a particular student has reported having difficulty, and suggests from where students might obtain advice. There is also a variety of ways in which teaching itself can promote deeper approaches to learning (Entwistle, 1992), and relatively simple ways in which teaching staff can enhance various study skills in their students, and a short document will be written to accompany StudentView which will suggest some possibilities. Figure 2 shows examples of both a three- and a two-dimensional StudentView plot.

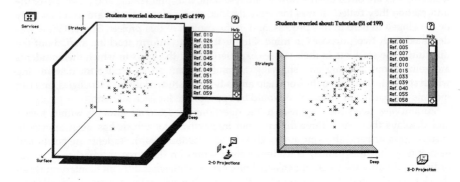

Figure 2

To superimpose study skills problems on a three-dimensional plot that has study strategies as its axes, might invite speculation as to the empirical relationship between the two. Clearly it is possible for a student to have problems with specific study skills and yet be using appropriate study strategies, and conversely to be employing study strategies which seem unlikely to lead to ultimate academic success yet have no study skills difficulties. When StudentView was being designed at the outset of the project, little besides a conceptual relationship was hypothesized, whereby the likelihood of a student failing to perform adequately in his or her courses increased as the number of study skills difficulties rose, or when problems with study skills coincided with weaknesses in approach. Evidence has however been produced from the small number of departments that participated in the development stages of the questionnaire to indicate that there are statistically significant negative correlations between the number of skills which a student finds problematic, and scores on both deep and strategic approaches, and that a positive correlation exists between number of problematic skills and scores on a scale measuring lack of direction in studying.

Providing Help and Advice to Students

When StudentView was developed to working prototype, teaching staff in a small number of departments were asked to comment on its usefulness. Most felt it would help them to understand better the problems their students were facing, but some commented that although specific students in difficulty would now be known to them (and perhaps relatively early on in the year), they were still not in any better a position to offer help, support or advice to these students. As a result, it was decided that a third piece of software, **StudyAdvisor**, would be developed (Odor, 1993) to provide help and advice directly to students, and with the capacity of delivering advice only in relation to each particular student's needs.

Thus StudyAdvisor is designed to be profile-driven. Students can import their own profiles created by questionnaire completion, and will then find that only information on study skills which they were reporting finding problematic will be revealed to them. This then cuts down considerably the amount of reading required of a student. Information concerning students' study approach scores is also imported and embedded into the text to personalize it.

In writing advice chunks for StudyAdvisor, a rationale was drawn up to try to ensure that many of the criticisms levelled at traditional study skills advice would be avoided (Nisbet, 1979). The advice written emphasizes developing metacognitive awareness and a deep/strategic approach to studying, and aims not to make use of out-of-date ideas from cognitive psychology or to suggest practices which are unreasonably demanding of time or resources. Care has been taken to develop an appropriate writing style which is neither patronizing nor overly 'academic', and yet which does not trivialize a serious subject. The advice is also written to cater for a range of abilities and stages. This is achieved by having a bottom track or level of advice which gives helpful tips and handy hints. By selecting emboldened words in the text, greater detail can then be accessed. The text also contains underlined words which act as 'pop-ups': clicking on a pop-up using the mouse reveals a comment made by a student relating to the issue being discussed currently. Where appropriate, the advice suggests a number of different ways of doing or thinking about tasks, to illustrate that there is no single 'right' approach. This range of possibilities is also intended to encourage students to reflect more on their current practices and to evaluate their appropriateness and effectiveness relative to alternatives. Figure 3 shows examples of cards from the 'Revising for exams' branch in StudyAdvisor.

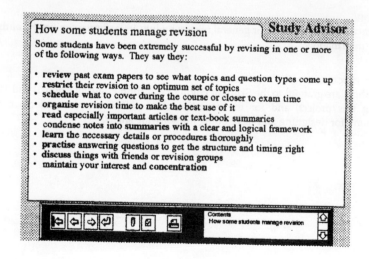

Figure 3

Students are able to create a personal study skills booklet for themselves by 'marking' cards of interest to them, and then printing them out later. If students have imported their own profile to guide them through the most personally useful advice in StudyAdvisor, but they then feel there is additional information of potential interest or use, they can simply start again, this time without importing a profile.

Summary and Conclusion

Most students would benefit from some study skills help and advice, particularly when they first come into higher education. The software described in this chapter is designed to be used as an integrated package by departments to identify students with study skills or strategies deficiencies, to provide help and advice to these students, and to help staff gain an overview of the nature and extent of problems experienced by their students. However, it can also be used by individual students who could complete the questionnaire then go on to use StudyAdvisor, or could use StudyAdvisor by itself as a 'free browser'. The questionnaire could also be used just with StudentView by a department, particularly if a well-developed study skills programme already existed. The questionnaire could even be used as a pedagogical device in isolation from the other two packages, if appropriate support were available. It is thus believed that the package is flexible and will cater for a number of different departmental needs. Trials carried out to date have indicated that students recognize a need for study skills help, that they find StudyAdvisor easy and enjoyable to use, and that they find the content valuable and interesting.

FOOTNOTE
Software is due to be ready for general release by July 1995. Please contact the authors for further information.

ACKNOWLEDGEMENTS
The authors are grateful to the **Scottish Higher Education Funding Council** and TLTP for funding this project, and for the expertise of Mr J.P. Odor, the project's computer consultant, for designing and developing the software shells.

References

Craik, F.I.M. and Lockhart, R.S. (1972). Levels of processing: a framework for memory research. *Journal of Verbal Learning and Verbal Behaviour*, **11**, 671–84.

Entwistle, N.J. (1992). *The Impact of Teaching on Learning Outcomes in Higher Education*, Sheffield: CVCP Universities' Staff Development and Training Unit.

Entwistle, N.J., Hanley, M. and Hounsell, D. (1979). Identifying distinctive approaches to studying. *Higher Education*, **8**, 365–80.

Entwistle, N.J. and Ramsden, P. (1983). *Understanding Student Learning*. London: Croom Helm.

Entwistle, N.J. and Tait, H. (1993). *Identifying Students at Risk through Ineffective Study Strategies*. Paper presented at the 5th EARLI Conference, Aix-en-Provence, France.

Entwistle, N.J., Tait, H. and Speth, C.A. (1994). *Identifying and Advising Students at Risk from Deficient Study Skills: A Computer-based Package for Departments*. Progress report. University of Edinburgh: Centre for Research on Learning and Instruction.

Entwistle, N.J. and Wilson, J. (1977). *Degrees of Excellence: the Academic Achievement Game*. London: Hodder and Stoughton.

Janssen, P.J. (1992). On the construct and nomological validity of student descriptions of studying and lecturing by means of Likert-type questionnaires: a 3 x 3 matrix of nine common 'primary' factors. In M. Carretero, M. Pope, R-J Simons, and J. I. Pozo (eds.) *Learning and Instruction: European Research in an International Perspective*. Vol 3, Oxford: Pergamon Press.

Marton, F. and Säljö, R. (1976). On qualitative differences in learning : 1 – Outcome and process. *British Journal of Educational Psychology*, **46**, 4–11.

Marton, F. and Säljö, R. (1984). Approaches to learning. In F. Marton, D. Hounsell and N.J Entwistle (eds). *The Experience of Learning*, Edinburgh : Scottish Academic Press.

Meyer, J.H.F. and Parsons, P.G (1993). Conceptually at risk students: diagnostic and intervention strategies based on individual differences. Paper presented at the 1st *Improving Student Learning Symposium*, University of Warwick.

Nisbet, J.D. (1979). Beyond the study skills manual. In P.J. Hills (ed.) *Study Courses and Counselling*. London: SRHE.

Odor, J.P. (1993). *Study Advisor Editor. Author Handbook Draft Release 3*. University of Edinburgh: Centre for Research on Learning and Instruction.

Odor, J.P. (1994a). *Questionnaire – an Interactive System for Administering Student Questionnaires. Student and Administrator Handbook version 1.2* University of Edinburgh: Centre for Research on Learning and Instruction.

Odor, J.P. (1994b). *StudentView II – an Interactive Graphical System for Analysing and Exploring Student Questionnaire Data. User Handbook version B2.1*. University of Edinburgh: Centre for Research on Learning and Instruction.

Pask, G. (1976). Styles and strategies of learning. *British Journal of Educational Psychology*, **46**, 128–48.

Tait, H. (1992). *Students' Perceptions of Teaching in Relation to their Approaches to Studying*. Unpublished PhD thesis. University of Edinburgh: Department of Education.

UFC (Universities Funding Council) (1992). The aims of the Teaching and Learning Technology Programme. Letter 8/92.

Wall, D., Macaulay, C., Tait, H., Entwistle, D. and Entwistle, N. (1991). *The Transition from School to Higher Education in Scotland*. Final report to the Scottish Office Education Department. University of Edinburgh: Centre for Research on Learning and Instruction.

Weinstein, C.E., Schulte, A. and Palmer, D. (1987). *Learning and Study Strategies Inventory* (LASSI). Clearwater, Flor.: H & H Publications.

25   Motivating students: relation to the world of work

Lewis Elton (University of Surrey)

Introduction

Until comparatively recently the perception of student motivation for learning held by academics was that motivation to pass examinations was bad because it interfered in a harmful way with motivation due to interest in the subject studied. More recently this has been replaced by a recognition that it is effectively impossible for students to ignore that they will be examined on what they have learned and that any strategy which aims to motivate students in a desirable way must take this fact into consideration. This chapter will consider parallels between motivation at work, on which there is a large literature, and motivation for learning in order to clarify the question of strategies designed to motivate students in their learning.

Background

In an earlier paper (Elton, 1988) I argued that the traditional view (see e.g. Paulsen 1908) that examinations unfortunately but inevitably favour those students that put the passing of examinations higher than their interest in the subject of study depended on the equally traditional and unfortunate but not inevitable divergence between the learning objectives that were examined and the learning objectives that were considered desirable, so that the problem of students being wrongly motivated would largely disappear, if the two sets of objectives were the same. This admittedly was not easy, because it required a very different attitude towards student assessment from that prevalent in traditional university examinations, but it was certainly possible. I also, in order to provide a theoretical basis to the whole question of student motivation, related the latter to Herzberg's theory of motivation to work. This chapter will be concerned in the main with two matters (a) an analysis of the validity of Herzberg's theory, which is important in view of the doubts that have been cast on it, and (b) the lessons concerning motivation that can be learned by considering both the world of work and that of learning.

Herzberg Revisited

The fundamental principle of Herzberg's theory (see e.g. Herzberg, 1968) is that the factors which affect job attitudes are of two kinds: those whose presence can lead to extreme satisfaction, which he calls motivator factors, and those whose presence can lead to extreme dissatisfaction, which he calls hygiene factors. The essential point of the theory is that each works over only half the motivational scale; i.e. the removal of bad hygiene factors cannot lead to extreme satisfaction, neither can the absence of motivator factors lead to extreme dissatisfaction. In all this, the theory fits in with Maslow's hierarchy of needs (Maslow, 1954), according to which humans are not concerned about satisfying their higher needs – corresponding closely to those covered by Herzberg's motivator factors – until their lower needs – corresponding closely to Herzberg's hygiene factors – have been met. What this amounts to in the case of students is that they cannot be expected to be interested in learning for learning's sake until they are satisfied that their needs to learn in order to pass their examinations have been met.

A persistent criticism of Herzberg's theory has been its implication that, although workers valued success, they were indifferent to failure (see e.g. Locke, 1969). Another very valid criticism, to which I shall return later, is that of Shamir (1990) who criticises motivation theories in general for being concerned too much with the individual and not enough with collective work efforts. More recently, Herzberg appears to have been forgotten. Thus Coates (1994) argues, without any reference to Herzberg, for a more humanistic and less behavioural approach, which in fact appears to be similar to what Herzberg calls 'job enrichment'. However, following Locke, the suggestion most immediately relevant within the Herzberg canon (Nias, 1981) is that while hygiene factors may work over only half the motivational scale, motivator factors work over the whole scale. This leads Nias to distinguish between motivator factors that could be both positive and negative – e.g. in line with Locke, achievement, which was one of Herzberg's motivators, could become negative when there was an absence of achievement – and dissatisfiers which worked over only the negative half of the motivation scale – e.g. work conditions. When Herzberg's results are reanalysed in terms of this distinction between negative satisfiers and dissatisfiers, it is actually found that his original data fit the theory better, as can be seen from Figure 21.1. There the motivator factors have quite sizeable negative components, but with one exception the hygiene factors do not have sizeable positive components. The exception is 'salary' which is evenly balanced and which will be discussed later. (It is important to realize that what Herzberg has plotted is the frequency with which a given factor occurs in his findings and not the motivational strength of that factor.)

Herzberg's main concern was to provide advice to employers to create high motivation in their work force and he therefore concentrated on the positive satisfiers. For students, and indeed not only for students, the role of negative satisfiers and of dissatisfiers, and the distinction between them is crucially important. Students' most important dissatisfier is undoubtedly 'failure on the part of teachers to prepare students adequately for their examinations', while their most important negative satisfier is probably 'lack of personal achievement'. In terms of Maslow's hierarchy, the former is concerned with satisfying a low level need, that of safety, while the latter is concerned with satisfying a high level need, that of personal satisfaction. Hence, to think of motivation as a variable that can be measured along one linear scale is wrong; the limited motivation that can be produced by making students feel safe is qualitatively quite different from the limited motivation that can be obtained through moderate personal achievement. That the same will apply to motivation at work is indicated by Nias's analysis, where the sources she finds of job dissatisfaction fit neatly into one or other of the two categories that I have identified.

The situation gets even more complicated, when students get conflicting messages, as to what is considered important, as was indicated earlier. In that situation, the measures which make students feel safe are in direct conflict with those that make them feel satisfied. I shall return to this point below.

Cryer's Reconceptualisation and Extension of Herzberg's Theory

Cryer (1988, see also Cryer and Elton, 1990) reconceptualized Herzberg's two factors in a two-dimensional diagram, which is very much easier to handle than Herzberg's one-dimensional one. She also used the more neutral terms 'intrinsic' and 'extrinsic' for the two factors, with the added caution that what may be extrinsic for one, such as salary, could be intrinsic for another. More generally, a factor might be extrinsic for an employer, but intrinsic for an employee, so that an employer's action that was designed merely to remove a dissatisfier (in Herzberg's terms) may actually act as a satisfier for the employee. Cryer's method of conceptualizing the factors also makes it possible to add a third dimension, which shows the resulting level of motivation explicitly. Here again Cryer uses a different word, i.e. 'commitment', which describes an outcome and hence is a much clearer descriptor than motivation, which could describe a process or an outcome. I shall however use both Herzberg's and Cryer's terminology, whichever appears more appropriate to me.

Cryer's diagram is plotted in Figure 2 (see Appendix), but rather than complicating it by drawing the third dimension to describe the level of commitment, I have indicated these levels through descriptors for the four different areas of the diagram. This also brings out the essential difference between the two different forms of commitment which fall short of high commitment and which arise respectively from unfavourable intrinsic and unfavourable extrinsic factors. The former is appropriately labelled 'low commitment', in line with Herzberg's finding and Nias's conclusion that the extrinsic factor works over only half the scale, i.e. that a favourable extrinsic factor cannot by itself produce high commitment. The latter, which Cryer was the first to identify explicitly, is labelled 'rebellion' and is psychologically quite different from that of low commitment. It corresponds to the situation where workers (or students) perceive a conflict between their own high intrinsic motivation and their employers' (or teachers') failure to provide positive extrinsic motivation. Herzberg *et al.* (1959, p. 40) actually experimentally identified such a state, and characterize it as one of 'extreme tension with a very deleterious effect on morale concurrent with a high degree of positive emotional involvement in the job', but do not pursue the matter further, because they explicitly exclude from their considerations cases in which workers did not feel either exceptionally good or exceptionally bad. Altogether, the motivational literature has concentrated on the transition from low to high commitment through making the intrinsic factors more favourable; a procedure which would actually increase the rebelliousness of those in the rebellion state, who require more favourable extrinsic factors. Finally, the 'withdrawal' state is one, where an employee has lost all commitment and is probably looking for another job.

Cryer incorporated her diagram within an approach based on Catastrophe Theory. This enabled her to show that, once a rebellion state has been reached, the transition to high commitment through making the extrinsic factors more favourable is exceptionally difficult and requires the extrinsic factors to be far more favourable than would have been necessary if, starting from a state of no commitment, these factors had been made more favourable before any attempt had been made to make the intrinsic factors more favourable. (This phenomenon is sometimes called the Waterloo syndrome after the apocryphal response to an enquirer 'if you want to get to Waterloo, I wouldn't start from here'.) Conversely, it is exceptionally difficult to reach the rebellion state from that of high commitment, although this could be very desirable in instances where enthusiasm keeps a programme going long after logic would indicate a radical change of direction. This too has a nickname, the Concorde syndrome, since the building of Concorde was pursued long after it was known that the plane could never be commercially viable.

What Advice can one give to Employers?

Herzberg's prescription to employers is essentially to concentrate on the improvement of factors which cause intrinsic motivation, but not only may this be a counsel of perfection, since employers often have more control over what employees perceive to be extrinsic factors than over what they perceive to be intrinsic factors, it also ignores the possibility of extrinsic and intrinsic factors giving conflicting signals, which is recognized in Cryer's rebellion state. Herzberg further assumes, as Cryer does not, that the perception as to what employees perceive as hygiene and what as motivators is the same for the average employer and employee and we have already discussed the question of salary from this point of view. Another important example where this may not be so is 'interpersonal relations' which Herzberg classifies as hygiene. That may well be true for most employers, but there are many employees who get intense satisfaction from co-operating with others, i.e. from good interpersonal relationships and whose work is motivated by that rather than by, say, personal achievement which is a more competitive concept (see e.g. Shamir, 1990). As regards salary, Herzberg's own results show that different people treat it as hygiene and as motivator.

It is also clearly important to distinguish between strategies that move people from low to high commitment and strategies that move them from rebellion to high commitment. Since the state of rebellion only occurs where people feel deeply about their work and often affects some of the best workers, it ought to be avoided at all costs. Hence one of Cryer's important contributions was to show that in moving from withdrawal to high commitment it is important to improve extrinsic factors before the intrinsic ones.

The situation of rebellion was experimentally noticed, before it was theoretically identified, also for students. Some of the most able of the students at MIT dropped out in disgust, when they found that perversely they could best earn good grades through pursuing assessment objectives which neither they nor their teachers considered desirable (Snyder, 1972). One might think that this is a situation that is not common in the world of work, but this may not be so. While in the private sector it might rapidly lead to bankruptcy, the situation has become increasingly common in the public services and has led to a loss of morale, which goes beyond what is usually thought of as a loss of motivation (Evans, 1992). Nurses for instance may now be rewarded more readily for the excellence of their paper work than for that of their treatment of patients; school teachers are rewarded more for their assessment of student learning than for their teaching; and academics find that their ability to raise large sums for research is more important than their ability to do research. Perhaps this is a case where the world of work can learn from education, for nowhere is this discrepancy between desirable objectives and those that are rewarded more common than there.

What Advice can one give to Teachers?

At its simplest, one may postulate, as Becker (1968) did and as we implicitly did above, that 'grades are the currency of campus', i.e. that they replace what for the rest of us is financial reward. There is little doubt that this is so, but this does not mean that all students work just for grades. One of the consistent lessons coming out of the Enterprise in Higher Education Initiative (see e.g. Elton, 1991) with its stress on the acquisition of transferable skills is that students are mostly keen to develop these, but want there to be some recognition for their achievements, preferably as part of their degree assessment. This does not of course mean that they work only for grades; what it does mean is that they are unlikely to work hard without there being a recognition through grades. This by now well-established conclusion (Elton and Laurillard, 1979) gives grades or, more generally, the existence of assessment a trigger role, but it is no more than that. It is also in line with Maslow's hierarchy that lower level needs have to be met before people perceive their higher level needs, and Herzberg's findings that a strongly favourable extrinsic factor can by itself not lead to high commitment. This is not to deny that for some students success through high grades is their prime motivator, i.e. for them grades constitute an intrinsic factor, just as financial rewards can for some employees.

This is not, however, how it is seen by those who have investigated student motivation. Entwistle (1981, p. 102) for instance considers that students who are motivated by the need for qualifications will employ a strategy which 'limits activities to those demanded and learn by rote'. This statement has to be seen against the learning objectives which the students have to meet and the extent to which these are imposed on them. The more students have a say in their learning objectives, the less meaningful is the word 'demanded'. Such students may for instance learn much about management and leadership through student union work, but although universities by and large consider such work valuable, they mostly refuse to incorporate it in their degree assessment schemes. Similarly, students will not learn by rote, unless they find that this pays off in terms of good grades (Laurillard, 1979). It would therefore appear that in many instances the reason that academics devalue this kind of motivation is because they either may be unduly restrictive in what they recognize as valuable or – much worse – because there is this divergence, already referred to, between learning and assessment objectives. Indeed, the bad effect of assessment on students is far less than the bad effect of assessment on curricula (Ramsden, 1992, p. 67), for which teachers and not students are responsible. This has been expressed exceptionally well by a student, quoted by Booth (1993):

> Course structure focused on exams means I have not been allowed to fully develop. Exams have been drilled into me since I was 13; two terms of enlightenment and one of exam cramming and question spotting. What is the function of exams? I study a topic for hours, involve myself in research and then have to answer a question on it in 45 minutes or an hour (if you're lucky). I feel that I am not allowed to show what I have learnt; exams place a student under great pressure but for historical study I do not think they are appropriate.

Similar considerations apply to another of Entwistle's categories, that of achievement motivation. In academia it is what Entwistle calls 'interest in what is being learned' and not achievement that is the most respectable motivator. In addition academics have a propensity to make students feel failures, which makes achievement a negative satisfier. In contrast, the world of work considers achievement one of the most important positive satisfiers. On top of that, to expect the majority of students to be primarily motivated by interest in what they are learning may actually be unfair, since the majority will not pursue their studies beyond the first degree and will then go on to work that is quite unconnected with their degree work.

We appear to have reached two conclusions. Firstly, the academic respectability of different forms of motivation is closely related to the respectability of certain learning objectives as judged by academics, so that academics have a hierarchy of motivations which may differ considerably from that of their students. Secondly, as long as academics are unable to reconcile learning objectives with assessment objectives they should mend their own ways before criticizing students for theirs. All this would of course be very different, if students were normally allowed to negotiate their own learning objectives and be assessed in terms of them. That such an approach frequently leads to enthusiastic and creative learning can be observed every year in the results of the few degree courses that allow for negotiation of this kind, such as the Independent Studies degree at Lancaster University, for which I have at present the privilege of acting as external examiner. But there are not many such courses.

So how should students be treated in more normal courses? The most important measure to be taken is surely the removal of the discrepancies between learning and assessment objectives, since as long as these persist, students cannot be blamed for being either not committed or revolting. This is not the place to discuss this matter in detail (see e.g. Boud, 1990 and Atkins *et al.* 1993), but what is clear is that it is likely to involve a much more sophisticated approach to assessment than is common today and should lead to replacing the classified honours degree by profiling (Winter, 1993). Beyond that, we should allow students to develop their personalities and personal commitments within the overall framework within which they live and move and have their being, as would any good employer. They will then be motivated by what they consider important and what enthuses them, which is unlikely to be so very different from what their teachers would like it to be. For the majority of students, the need for grades would then become the extrinsic trigger factor that it ought to be.

At this point it is appropriate to return to Shamir's concern about collectivity. Academia has always placed a lower value than the world of work on team skills, largely because it has been difficult to find ways of assessing the contribution of individuals to teams, another sacrifice to the demands of the classified honours degree and a difficulty that would largely disappear if students were given profiles instead of simply grades.

And so Back to the World of Work

And this brings me finally back to what the current world of work can learn from the world of students. If, as is increasingly the case in the public sector, people are rewarded for what they despise and are not rewarded for what their professional consciences tells them they ought to be rewarded for, then they will finish up either unmotivated or rebellious. In the first case this leads employers and government to the mistaken conclusion that public servants are lazy, in the second it leads to control and repression. Herzberg thou shouldst be living at this hour: England has need of thee.

References

Atkins, M. J., Beattie, J. and Dockrell, W. B. (1993). *Assessment Issues in Higher Education*. Department of Employment.

Booth, A. (1993). Learning history in university: student views on teaching and assessment. *Studies in Higher Education*, **18**, 227–36.

Boud, D. (1990). Assessment and the promotion of academic values. *Studies in Higher Education*, **15**, 101–12.

Coates, G. (1994). Motivation theories' lacklustre performance: identity at work as explanation for expended effort. *ETTI*, **31**, 26–30.

Cryer, P. (1988). Insights into participants' behaviour in educational games, simulations and workshops: a Catastrophe Theory application to motivation. *Simulation/Games for Learning*, **18**, 161–76.

Cryer, P. and Elton, L. (1990). Catastrophe theory: a unified model for educational change. *Studies in Higher Education*, **15**, 75–96.

Elton, L. (1988). Student motivation and achievement. *Studies in Higher Education*, **13**, 215–21.

Elton, L. (1991). Enterprise in higher education: work in progress. *Education + Training*, **33**(2), 5–9.

Elton, L. and Laurillard, D. (1979). Trends in research on student learning. *Studies in Higher Education*, **4**, 87–102.

Entwistle, N. (1981). *Styles of Learning and Teaching*. Chichester: Wiley.

Evans, L. (1992). Teacher morale: an individual perspective. *Educational Studies*, **18**, 161–71.

Herzberg, F. (1968). One more time: How do you motivate employees? *Harvard Business Review*, **46**, January/February, 53–62.

Herzberg, F., Mausner, B. and Snyderman, B. B. (1959). *The Motivation to Work*. New York: Wiley.

Laurillard, D. (1978). The process of student learning. *Higher Education*, **9**, 395–409.

Locke, E. A. (1969). What is job satisfaction? *Organizational Behaviour and Human Performance*, **4**, 309–36.

Paulsen, F. (1908). *The German Universities and University Study*. London: Longmans.

Maslow, A. H. (1954). *Motivation and Personality*. New York: Harper and Row.

Nias, J. (1981). Teacher satisfaction and dissatisfaction: Herzberg's 'two-factor' hypothesis revisited. *British Journal of Sociology of Education*, **2**, 235–46.

Ramsden, P. (1992). *Learning to Teach in Higher Education*. London: Routledge.

Shamir, B. (1990). Calculations, values and identities: the sources of collectivistic work motivation. *Human Relations*, **43**, 313–32.

Snyder, B. R. (1973). *The Hidden Curriculum*. Boston: MIT Press.

Winter, R. (1993). Education or grading? Arguments for a non-subdivided honours degree. *Studies in Higher Education*, **18**, 363–78.

Appendix

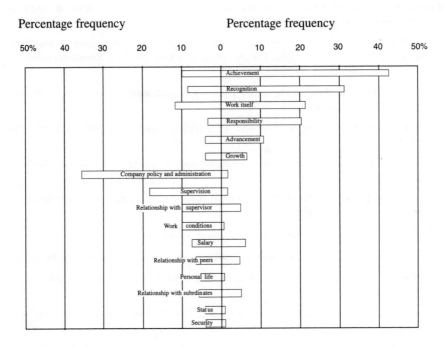

Percentage frequency   Percentage frequency

Fig. 1 Factors affecting job attitudes, reprinted from Herzberg (1968)

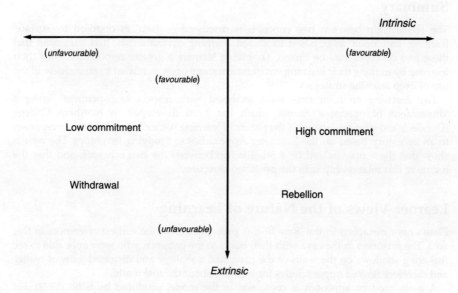

Intrinsic

(*unfavourable*)   (*favourable*)

(*favourable*)

Low commitment   High commitment

Withdrawal

Rebellion

(*unfavourable*)

Extrinsic

Fig. 2 The effect of different extrinsic and intrinsic factors on levels of commitment

26   Learning environments and students' perceptions of learning

Wyllie Fyfe (Northern College Dundee)

Summary

The relationship between two concepts is discussed – 'deep' as opposed to 'surface' learning, and 'open' as opposed to 'closed' learning environments. It is suggested that these two concepts may be linked, i.e. giving learners a greater responsibility for their learning by making their learning environment more open, is related to an increase in the use of deep learning strategies.

Two learning environments were analysed with respect to 'openness' using a 'dimensions of openness' model which has been developed in Northern College (Dundee), and students' views of the nature of learning were elicited from their responses to an inventory based on the Lancaster Approaches to Studying Inventory. The results show that there may indeed be a relationship between the two concepts, and that the nature of this relationship is in the predicted direction.

Learner Views of the Nature of Learning

Plato's cave metaphor in the 'Republic' is probably one of the earliest references in this area. The prisoners in the cave with their backs to the entrance, who were only able to see flickering shadows on the walls of the cave, had a shallow and distorted view of reality and therefore limited opportunities for learning about the real world.

A more modern approach is contained in the model produced by Säljö (1979). He suggested that learners' perceptions of the nature of learning ranged from a belief that it was to do with 'a quantitative increase in knowledge' through three intermediate levels to the highest point where learning was held to be 'an interpretative process aimed at the understanding of reality'. Conceptions that learning was to do with memorizing were described as 'surface learning' approaches (Plato's shadows?), whereas those which emphasized meaning were classified as 'deep learning' approaches (Plato's real world?).

Van Rossum and Schenk (1984) took Säljö's work a stage further and found that there was a close correlation between students' views of the nature of learning, i.e. whether it was surface or deep, and the actual learning strategies they employed when faced with a task.

Gibbs (1992) argued that the learning environment was a major factor which influenced learners' views of learning. A particularly striking example in support of this conclusion was a student, who had gained an upper second class honours degree, following two different strategies of learning, a deep approach in Geography and a surface approach in Computing.

How can a learner have two different views of learning? It could be argued that a course which gives the impression that deep learning strategies are valued is more likely to produce learners who perceive learning as a deep process than another course which stresses rote memorization. One of the major influences is likely to be the messages given by the summative assessment used in the course. The presence of higher order objectives in the rhetoric of the course design, which might stress 'critical thinking', for example, is likely to be outweighed by final assessments which suggest that a reproducing strategy would be successful. The influence of assessment on students' perceptions of learning is well documented (Entwistle (1987), Ramsden (1984), (1988), Entwistle and Ramsden (1983), Laurillard (1984), Wilson (1981))

Classifying Learning Environments

The 1980s and 1990s have seen a trend at most levels of education and training towards courses which give learners greater responsibility over decision-making in the learning process. (SOED, 1982; Temple, 1991; Boud, 1988; Robbins, 1988; Paine, 1988; McColl, 1991; MacFarlane, 1993; SOED, 1993).

Courses, where the learning decisions are in the hands of the institution, can be described as inflexible, or 'closed'; those, which involve a great deal of learner choice, can be regarded as flexible or 'open'.

In one particular model of open learning, which has been developed in Northern College, as many as twelve dimensions of openness are identified (Fyfe, 1993). These are:

- course population (age and ability);
- start and end points of courses;
- where a course is delivered;
- when a course is delivered, e.g. time of day, day in week;
- course objectives;
- course content;
- course methods;
- sequence of topics;
- pace of learning;
- choice of tutor support;
- timing of tutor support;
- assessment (content, timing, criteria for marking and the process of grading).

Each of these represents a dimension along which a course may be classified from closed to open. In two cases, the first and the last, there are also sub-dimensions in the most recent revision of the model (see above and Appendix 2).

At the closed end of each of the dimensions, all decisions are made by the tutor, the institution or an outside body; at the open end, all decisions are made by the learner. For example, in the case of the 'place of study' dimension, at the closed end study is restricted to particular rooms or buildings prescribed by the institution; an intermediate position on this dimension may be represented by a requirement to attend at a defined place for only part of the time; at the open extreme the learners may choose to study anywhere they wish.

It is possible to classify any course, or learning experience, along each of the twelve dimensions so that different patterns of openness in different courses can be revealed. The model also shows that the question 'is this an open learning course?' is not an easy one to st, since the model is based on continua, there are no obvious cut-off points. is possible for course A to be relatively open on, say, four or five of the as and course B to be equally open on a different set, but which course is more open.

Two themes underlie this model. One is concerned with the amount of personal meaning the learner wishes, or is able, to ascribe to the learning. This may be described as **ownership** of learning. The second relates to the presence or absence of barriers to the learning and may be summed up as **access** to learning.

For some dimensions, e.g. 'where a course is delivered', it could be argued that the predominant theme is access, i.e. if learners can study anywhere they wish, then distance from the institution is removed as a barrier to learning. For other dimensions, e.g. 'course content', the principal concern appears to be ownership, ie if learners choose what they want to study, then they are more likely to own that learning. Often both aspects feature in a single dimension, e.g. 'course objectives' seems to be predominantly about ownership, but it could be argued that allowing the learners to choose or devise their objectives also allows them to gain access to the particular learning they want.

This model may be help to clarify the distinction between distance and open learning which are two terms which are often confused (Carr, 1989; O'Reilly, 1991). Openness in the place of study, the major characteristic which differentiates distance learning courses from those which take place in traditional institutions, refers simply to **one** of the dimensions of openness which may be used to analyse courses. So if an institution provides distance learning courses, this may guarantee only a limited amount of openness, i.e. the learner may only have responsibility for the place of learning. However removing the place requirement usually allows other dimensions to be opened up, e.g. when the learning takes place, and the pace of learning.

Open learning Environments and Deep Learning

It can be hypothesized that courses which allow the learner a greater responsibility for decision-making about the learning, ie courses which tend towards the open end on many dimensions, are more likely to provide contexts in which learners will see learning as a deep process. However it would seem reasonable to assume that some dimensions might have more effect than others, e.g. it could be argued that openness on the dimensions which are more related to ownership of learning is more likely to lead to views of learning as a deep process, than openness on dimensions which are primarily to do with access.

The Northern College Second Year B.Ed Mathematics Course

Northern College is based on two campuses in Aberdeen and Dundee and runs a number of courses which operate on both campuses. One such course is the B.Ed for students who are intending to become primary teachers. The B.Ed contains a number of elements, one of which is mathematics in the primary school. The focus of the mathematics course is on teaching and learning strategies in mathematics rather than on the content of the subject. This topic runs through the first three years of the B.Ed.

The mathematics course tutors on one of the campuses began to question the didactic approach they had been using. Given that they were trying to encourage their students to become teachers who would make use of more active methods with **their** learners, a lecture-based approach seemed to be somewhat inappropriate. They decided therefore to make a number of changes in the second year part of the course which would make it more open. These were as follows.

1 The students were given more opportunities to work at their own pace. Typically, after a short introductory lecture, they were given a set of tasks, not all of which required to be completed in the weekly two hour workshop period. Although the students were given the option of completing the tasks during their 'free' time, they did not have to complete all of them.

   The course therefore appeared to move towards the open end on four of the dimensions in the open learning model, i.e. 'pace', 'course content', 'where the course was delivered' and 'when the course was delivered'. However, as will be seen later, the only substantial change related to the first.

2 The tutors employed a system of team-teaching, ie instead of dealing with his/her own class, each tutor had responsibility for all of the students for part of the time, and the students were encouraged to seek assistance from any member of the team at times out with the normal timetable.

These changes suggested moves towards the open end on two other dimensions, i.e. 'choice of tutor support' and 'timing of tutor support'.

The author had no direct control over the setting up of the new approach but he, and one of his colleagues, supplied advice on the design of the course and the materials which formed the basis of the tasks. However, although there was some outside influence on the course design, the decision to conduct the research was made some time after the course started, i.e. the research was opportunistic rather than planned.

Meanwhile the mathematics staff on the other campus continued to deliver the course in the old didactic way.

For brevity the version of the mathematics course which appeared to have been modified in an open direction was referred to as the 'open course' and the one which continued to be delivered in the old way was described as the 'closed course'. Despite the earlier discussion regarding the difficulties associated with a complex classification process, the decision to label the courses in these ways could be defended on the grounds that the open course appeared to be no nearer to the closed end on any of the dimensions and it was more open on six. (The detailed justification for these classifications will be discussed later.)

The Research Questions

This study attempted to answer three questions:

1 Did the students in the two courses have different perceptions of the nature of learning in mathematics as measured by a questionnaire?

2 What were the staff perceptions of the differences between the learning environments in the two courses in terms of degrees of openness?

3. Was there a relationship between the students' perceptions and the descriptions of the learning environments

Method of Enquiry

Although the course team carried out an evaluation of the course, most of this article is based on an investigation conducted by the author. However reference will be made later to one of the course team's major findings since it will throw some light on the results of the research.

A questionnaire on approaches to studying was administered to both groups of students, i.e. those taking the closed and the open courses. This questionnaire was based on The Approaches to Studying Inventory developed at Lancaster University in the late 1970s (Entwistle and Ramsden, 1983) and modified at Oxford Polytechnic in 1984 (Gibbs, 1992).

Since the focus of both of these questionnaires was on the total learning experience of students, and the current study was looking at the mathematics part of the B.Ed only, each of the statements was modified to reflect the narrower context which was being investigated. Thus the statement 'I find it easy to organize my study time effectively' was changed to 'I find it easy to organize my maths studying time effectively' (see Appendix 1). These changes were made by the author and were checked by a member of the course team.

The Lancaster questionnaire produces three scales concerned with:

A Strategic Orientation, i.e. extrinsic motivation, strategic approach and achievement orientation;

B Reproducing orientation, i.e. surface approach, syllabus-boundness, fear of failure, improvidence;

C Meaning orientation, i.e. deep approach, use of evidence, relating ideas, intrinsic motivation;

All three of these scales were present in the modified mathematics questionnaire.

The course leaders on both campuses were both interviewed using a set of questions which reflected the twelve dimensions model of open learning referred to above (See Appendix 2.) Their answers to these questions were then coded by the author using the current version of the twelve dimensions model (see Appendix 3).

Analysis of the Results

The learners' views of learning

The mean scores of the two groups for each of the scales in the questionnaire are shown in Table 1

Table 1

	n	Strategic Orientation	Reproducing Orientation	Meaning Orientation
Open course	52	m = 13.42 (sd = 3.28)	m = 14.37 (sd = 3.11)	m = 13.83 (sd = 3.37)
Closed course	119	m = 13.65 (sd = 2.72)	m = 15.45 (sd = 2.82)	m = 12.88 (sd = 3.67)

For the purposes of the investigation, Scales B and C were of most relevance. However the fact that, the groups were very close as far as scale A is concerned, was interesting ($t169 = 0.451$, $p > 0.05$). Whatever else had happened, a move in a more open direction appeared not to have been accompanied by a change in strategic orientation, i.e. the students in both courses appeared to be equally concerned about such things as extrinsic motivation and achievement.

The open course students had a significantly lower score on the Reproducing Orientation scale ($t169 = 1.964$, $p < 0.05$) and a higher one on the Meaning Orientation scale, although this latter difference was not significant ($t169 = 1.484$, $p > 0.05$). However both of these differences were in the predicted direction.

An additional score was calculated for each student by subtracting his/her scale C score from his/her B scale score. This was referred to as the scale D score. .

Table 2

	Scale D mean scores
Open course	m = 0.53 (sd = 6.26)
Closed course	m = 2.57 (sd = 5.25)

When the two groups were compared using the above scores, a significant difference was found ($t169 = 2.200$, $p < 0.05$). In other words if the Reproducing Orientation scores were used as a base-line, then there was a significantly greater drop in the Meaning Orientation score for the closed course students.

Taking both sets of results together there was evidence that the open course students views on studying were different from those in the closed course. The open course group were less likely to agree with statements about studying which reflected a reproducing orientation, and their meaning scores were relatively higher than those in the closed course.

The course environments

As was explained above, the description of the courses vis-a-vis the dimensions of openness was based on interviews of the course leaders. Table 3 shows the classification of the two courses for each of the dimensions of openness.

Table 3

	Dimension	Closed course	Open course	Highest point on the scale
A1	course population (age range)	2*	2	3
A2	course population (ability range)	2	2	3
B	start and end points of course	1	1	4
C	where course was delivered	1	2	5
D	when course was delivered	2	3	5
E	course objectives	2	2	5
F	course content	2	2	5
G	course methods	1	1	5
H	sequence of topics	1	2	5
I	pace of learning	1	3/4	5
J	choice of tutor support	1	3	5
K	timing of tutor support	1/2	3	5
L1	assessment content	N/A	N/A	5
L2	timing of assessment	N/A	N/A	5
L3	assessment criteria	N/A	N/A	5
L4	assessment grading	N/A	N/A	5

* A low number indicates a course which is closed on a particular dimension. A high number indicates a course which is open.

N/A Not applicable since the summative assessment in year 2 of B.Ed Mathematics was not related to this part of the course.

There were no differences between the courses on six of the dimensions, i.e. course population, start and end points of the course, and learner responsibility for course objectives, course content, course methods, and assessment. However it should be noted that, although the learners in the open course had no greater responsibility for the methods used than their colleagues on the closed course, there was a lesser emphasis on lectures and a greater emphasis on workshops in the open course.

On three of the dimensions there were small differences. In each case the open course was nearer to the open end of the dimension than the closed course. These were where the course was delivered, when the course was delivered, and sequence of topics.

The largest differences were in the three remaining dimensions, choice of tutor support, timing of tutor support, and pace of learning, with the greatest difference, in terms of scale points, being on the last of these dimensions.

The key decision in the design of the open course, which determined most of the differences in these classifications, was the one which moved the emphasis from lectures to the use of learning materials in a workshop. This permitted a greater learner responsibility for the pace of learning, as well as where and when it took place, and gave the learners a greater amount of access to a range of tutors at times which were more suitable to them.

Discussion

This study was based on the learners' views of their learning style as reported in the questionnaire. It did not **observe** the techniques used by the learners. However if Van Rossum and Schenk (1984) are correct, the learners' reported preferences could be used as indicators of their probable learning practices. It could therefore be argued that the open course students were more likely to use deep approaches than their closed course colleagues.

Although this study appears to show a relationship between an open learning environment and deep learning, it would be quite wrong to state that the results indicated that an open learning course was likely to lead to learners who used deep learning, particularly since there was no collection of data about the students' views before they began the mathematics courses.

However at least two potential causes can be eliminated.

1. A major student view expressed in the mathematics tutors' own evaluation of the open course was a desire to return to the safe haven of the didactic approach which they had experienced in year 1 of the course. Thus it could not be argued that the open group's feelings of security had made them more positive towards aspects of it, i.e. there was no major sign of any halo effect. If anything it was the reverse.

2. It is difficult to argue that the open course students were giving the answers they thought the college wanted since the course made no explicit claims about the value of deep learning for the students as individuals.

Although a higher level of recognition of learning as a deep process in the open course group before the course started cannot be ruled out, equally there was no evidence that it **was** differentially present at that point in time. In addition the fact that there was no difference between the group scores for factor A in the Approaches to Studying Questionnaire, ie strategic orientation, was interesting. If the hypothesis that the learning environment has some effect on the deep/surface learning orientation is tenable, then it is likely that it would also have predicted that there would have been no differences between the group scores in the strategic orientation factor since this factor appears to be somewhat independent.

It should also be noted that the learning environments experienced by the two groups were similar for the dimensions which might appear to be most concerned with ownership of learning, e.g. the course objectives, the course content and the assessment. If the two groups had indeed started with similar views about learning, it would appear that a relatively minor move in an open direction was related to changes in learners' views about the nature of learning. The study therefore suggested that courses which give learners more responsibility for learning in key dimensions might be associated with even greater changes.

Conclusion

This investigation was based on a fortuitous set of events but it has shown that the relationship between the degrees of openness in courses and the learners' views of the nature of learning is an area worth pursuing in a more tightly controlled study. Particular features of such a study would be an attempt to gain a measure of the learners' views at an early point in the course, and a focus on the potentially more powerful dimensions of openness.

References

Boud, D. (ed.) (1988). *Developing Student Autonomy in Learning*, 2nd edn. London: Kogan Page

Carr, R. (1989). Open learning – an imprecise term. *Times Educational Supplement (Scotland)* 8 Sept.

Entwistle, N.J. (1987). *Understanding Classroom Learning*. London: Hodder & Stoughton

Entwistle, N.J. and Ramsden, P. (1983). *Understanding Student Learning*. Beckenham: Croom Helm.

Fyfe, W. (1993). *The Nature of Open Learning: Unit 1 What is Open Learning?* Dundee: Northern College.

Gibbs, G. (1992). *Improving the Quality of Student Learning*. Bristol: Technical and Education Services Ltd.

Laurillard, D. (1984). Learning from problem-solving. In F Marton, D. Hounsell and N.J. Entwistle (eds) *The Experience of Learning*. Edinburgh: Scottish Academic Press.

McColl, H. (1991). *Flexible Learning – A framework for Education and Training in a Skills Decade*. Dundee: Training Agency and Tayside Region Education Department.

MacFarlane, A.G.J. (1993). *Teaching and Learning in an Expanding Higher Education System: Report of a Working Party of Scottish University Principals*. Edinburgh: CSUP

O'Reilly, D. (1991). Developing opportunities for independent learners. *Open Learning*, 6(3), 3–13.

Paine, N. (1988). *Supported Self Study in Scotland*. Glasgow: SCET 1988.

Ramsden, P. (1984). The context of learning. In F. Marton, D. Hounsell and N.J. Entwistle (eds) *The Experience of Learning*. Edinburgh: Scottish Academic Press.

Ramsden, P. (ed.) (1988). *Improving Student Learning: New Perspectives*. London: Kogan Page.

Robbins, D. (1988). *The Rise of Independent Study*. Milton Keynes: Open University Press

Säljö, R. (1979). Learning in the learner's perspective. I Some common-sense conceptions. Reports from the Department of Education, University of Goteborg, 1979, 76.

SOED (1982). *Distance No Object: Examples of Open Learning in Scotland*. HMSO.

SOED (1993). *Curriculum and Assessment in Scotland: National Guidelines: The Structure and Balance of the Curriculum*, 5–14.

Temple, H. (1991). *Open Learning in Industry*. Harlow: Longman

Van Rossum, E.J. and Schenk, S.M. (1984). The relationship between learning conception, study strategy and learning outcome. *British Journal of Educational Psychology*, **54**, 73–83.

Wilson, J.D. (1981). *Student Learning in Higher Education*. London: Croom Helm

Appendix 1: Northern College Research on Approaches to Studying (Maths)

The purposes of this research are to find out:

1 the approaches to studying used by students in the B.Ed;

2 if there is any relationship between the approaches used and the learning experiences provided by the course.

I would be most grateful if you would complete the attached questionnaire on Approaches to Studying in Second Year Maths.

I guarantee that I will not pass information relating to a named individual to staff teaching on the course.

I need your name in case it is decided to do some follow-up work, with a sample of students from your year.

Questionnaire on Approaches to Studying in Second Year Mathematics

Name ....

Section ....

Campus Aberdeen / Dundee (please circle as appropriate)

Please respond quickly to each of the following 18 statements.

Circle the appropriate code number to show your approach to studying in the B.Ed second year maths course so far.

4   (++)   means you definitely agree with the statement
3   (+)   means you agree with the statement but have reservations
2   (?)   is only to be used if the item doesn't apply to you or if you find it impossible to give a definite answer
1   (-)   means you disagree with the statement but have reservations
0   (--)   means you definitely disagree with the statement.

          ++   +   ?   -   --

1   I find it easy to organise my maths studying time effectively.
                            4   3   2   1   0

2   I like to be told precisely what to do in maths assignments and other set work in maths.

                4   3   2   1   0

3   It is important to me to do really well in the maths course.

                4   3   2   1   0

4   I usually set out to understand thoroughly the meaning of what I am asked to do in maths.

                4   3   2   1   0

5   When I am doing a piece of work in maths, I try to memorise important facts which might come in useful later.

                4   3   2   1   0

6   When I am doing a piece of work in maths, I try to bear in mind exactly what the particular lecturer seems to want.

                4   3   2   1   0

7   An important reason for studying maths is that I find it interesting.

                4   3   2   1   0

8   I suppose I am more interested in the qualifications I'll get than in the maths course.

                4   3   2   1   0

9   When studying maths in my own time, I am usually prompt in starting work.

                4   3   2   1   0

10   I generate a lot of effort into trying to understand things in maths which initially seem difficult.

                4   3   2   1   0

11   Often I find I have to do things in maths without having a chance to really understand them.

                4   3   2   1   0

12   If conditions aren't right for me to study in maths, I generally manage to do something to change them.

                4   3   2   1   0

13   I often find myself questioning things I hear in maths or read in maths books.

                4   3   2   1   0

14   When completing a maths assignment, I tend to read very little beyond what is required.

                4   3   2   1   0

15   It is important to me to do things in maths better than my friends, if I possibly can.

                4   3   2   1   0

16   I spend a good deal of my spare time finding out more about interesting topics in maths which have been discussed in class.

                4   3   2   1   0

17   I find maths topics so interesting that I'd like to continue with them after
      I finish the course in BEd2.   4   3   2   1   0

18   I find I have to concentrate on memorising a good deal of what we have
      to learn in maths.   4   3   2   1   0

Thank you for your assistance.

Appendix 2: Questions for programme leaders B.Ed 2 Maths

Context: the B.Ed 2 Maths course provided for the second year in 1991–2

1   What is the timetabled length of the B.Ed 2 Maths course?

2   To what extent is the pace of learning the responsibility of the learner?

3   How much choice does the learner have over where the learning takes place?

4   How much choice does the learner have over when the learning takes place.

5   Are the start and end points of the B.Ed 2 Maths course fixed? If not, what control
      does the learner have over these?

6   To what extent are the objectives of the course determined by the learner?

7   To what extent does the learner have responsibility/choice re the methods of
      learning used?

8   What is the extent of learner responsibility for the choice of content?

9   To what extent is the learner able to vary the sequence of his/her learning?

10   How is summative assessment handled? Does the learner have the responsibility
      for the content, timing, criteria and/or grading of summative assessment?

·11   How flexible is tutorial support/formative assessment? Is it supplied at fixed times
      only, e.g. during timetabled class meetings? If it is within that time, is its timing
      controlled by the tutor?

12   Does the learner have a choice of tutor support, ie is more than one tutor available?

13   Are there any other features of flexibility in the B.Ed 2 Maths course not covered by
      the previous questions?

14   Are there any other features of the B.Ed 2 Maths course which may affect the
      learner's view of the nature of learning?

Appendix 3: Rating scales for dimensions of openness in a course

A1. Course population – age range

1   Narrow age range, e.g. pupils in one school year, adults with an age range less than ten years.
2   Moderate age range, e.g. pupils in more than one school year, adults with an age range greater than 10 years.
3   Wide age range, e.g. school pupils and adults.

A2. Course population – ability range

1   Narrow ability range, e.g. one Standard Grade level in a school (i.e. F, G or C), an adult basic literacy course, students who have to achieve an entry qualification which is well in excess of the minimum entry standard for higher education.
2   Moderate ability range, e.g. a class in a school which covers two Standard Grade levels, students who have achieved the minimum entry standard for higher education.
3   Wide ability range, e.g. a common course class in a school, an adult course with no entry standards.

B. Start and end points of the course

1   The course has fixed beginning and end points.
2   The course has a fixed beginning point with an end point which is the learner's responsibility within limits laid down by others, or it has a fixed end point, eg a date of an exam diet, with a flexible start point within limits laid down by others.
3   The course has beginning and end points which are the learner's responsibility within limits laid down by others.
4   The course has beginning and end points which are the learner's responsibility.

Individual Learning Responsibility

		nil	minor	50/50	major	total
C	Where course is delivered					
D	When course is delivered*					
E	Course objectives					
F	Course content					
G	Course methods					
H	Sequence of topics					
I	Pace of learning					
J	Choice of tutor support					
K	Timing of tutor support					
L1	Assessment content/method					
L2	Timing of assessment					
L3	Assessment criteria					
L4	Allocation of assessment grades					

* i.e. hour in day, day in week, week in year when course takes place.

27 Coming out of the corner: teaching masters students to manage their thesis

Adele Graham (The University of Auckland)

Overview

In this chapter a week-long induction programme for postgraduate research students is outlined. At one level, the programme was intended to give students an overview of the thesis process, get them launched, and develop skills that would help them during their study. At another, it attempted to subvert some aspects of existing postgraduate culture – a culture in which power relations between students and supervisors can affect progress in unproductive ways.

An evaluation conducted immediately after the course suggested that some of the management tools we taught the students, including those that were aimed at repositioning them in relation to their supervisors, were effective. Being aware that over time not only can good intentions fade but personal, interpersonal and structural factors can get in the way of change, I surveyed some of the students six months later to find out about their progress and whether the learning they had previously identified had been maintained. The results from the survey are also reported in this chapter.

The induction programme described in this chapter was jointly planned and facilitated with my colleague Barbara Grant who works with both HERO and the Student Learning Centre (SLC) – hence the reference throughout the chapter to 'we'; I conducted the follow-up interviews.

Background

Current discussion in the postgraduate education literature shows that, internationally, there is a concern about completion times and completion percentages (Blume and Amsterdamska, 1987; Holdaway, Deblois and Winchester, 1994; Moses, 1992; Rudd, 1985). In checking the figures here at the University of Auckland, it appears that the rates of non-completion and lengthy completion are at a similar level to those reported in other universities that have similarly structured degrees. According to Cullen and Pearson (1993), solutions to addressing current postgraduate education concerns include improving supervision, and introducing coursework and graduate schools.

Prior to 1990, HERO had run an annual three-hour course for supervisors. The rationale was to improve supervision skills and, in so doing, influence completion times and percentages. Then, in 1990, the Faculty of Arts requested we offer some workshops for MA students. In response to issues that were raised in these workshops, along with the negative reaction we had from some supervisors when we floated the notion of a postgraduate supervision contract at a supervisors' workshop, HERO decided to re-examine its commitment to this area. Barbara Grant and I assumed responsibility for this and since then we have developed a comprehensive programme for both postgraduate students and supervisors (Grant and Graham, 1992a) under the umbrella of both HERO and the SLC.

In recognizing that supervisors are not compelled to engage in professional development activities and that many are resistant to the very thought, much of our energy and effort has been directed into working with students – in particular those who are about to enrol or have newly enrolled as research students. Inducting them into the process of postgraduate research through a structured programme is, we believe, a viable strategy for improving the chances of successful completion.

Induction Programmes for Research Students

The need for postgraduate students to participate in introductory courses is frequently suggested in the literature (Phillips and Pugh, 1987; Rudd, 1985; Salmon, 1992) but the specific contents are rarely made explicit. However a number of directions do emerge: students need introductory courses about research methodology; there needs to be emphasis on process issues (expectations, the supervisory relationship, planning etc.); it helps when students see the relevance of the course content.

It might be asked why experienced students should need an induction programme? From the work we are engaged in, we know that many postgraduate research students come unprepared to this role. Up until this point, life – particularly at undergraduate level – has been dominated by lectures, imposed assignments with their consequent deadlines, term tests and final exams. Oppressive teacher authority (Heron, 1993) is the norm and relationships with academic staff are often formal, if not distant. Moreover, the process of engaging in an extended piece of research is a new experience for most students because, as Jones (1992) notes, undergraduate programmes '[r]arely, if ever, ... offer an introduction to what research is really like' (p. 61). In short, previous experience in the academy is rarely a preparation for being a research student where survival is based on such characteristics as independence, self-motivation, and the ability to 'self-learn' (Bowden, 1988).

Within our own institution, the provisions for inducting research students into the process are very uneven; while a few departments make a creditable effort, others leave students entirely to their own devices. Knowing this to be the case, over the last three years we have included a one-day workshop, 'Managing Your Masters Thesis', in the programme we offer to postgraduate students. This particular workshop runs either at the beginning or the end of the long vacation when students have completed their papers but have not yet enrolled in their thesis. Demand for places has always been high – each year around 150 students have enrolled so the workshops have been repeated four or five times. However it soon became evident that a single day was not enough to induct students into the process, so at the end of last year, we offered a week-long induction 'mini-conference' to students who were intending to enrol as research students in 1994. With only minimum advertising, enrolments outstripped available places, and what was to be a workshop for 30 was extended to accommodate the first 50 applicants. The students came from 17 departments (six faculties) across campus. Because of its extended time frame, this event offered us the opportunity to prepare students more thoroughly for what lay ahead and has provided us with the experience upon which to propose the following model.

A Model for Inducting New Research Students

The programme: our theoretical position

As teachers, we are committed to an emancipatory model of education (Freire, 1972; Gibson, 1986; Grant, 1993a). Working within a critical theoretical paradigm, we see the university as a hegemonic agent which acts in part to reproduce existing social inequalities. The interactions which dominate teaching in many universities influenced by the British tradition of higher education, including our own institution, are underpinned by profoundly unequal power relationships between teachers and students. As Paludi (1990) has commented:

> [t]he bottom line of the relationship between faculty members and students is POWER. The faculty member has it and the student does not. All power lies with the faculty member . . . (p. 145)

From the cases that come to our attention, we know that abuse of power in one form or another is not uncommon in the supervisor/student relationship. Instances range enormously in seriousness – from sexual or academic harassment by supervisors, to supervisors simply being unavailable, providing inadequate feedback about specific work and general progress, not facilitating access to resources and so on. Some of these are flagrant and can arise from supervisors protecting their position of privilege but many are unintentional – supervisors unthinkingly misuse their power and may be completely unaware of the powerlessness students can feel in relation to them.

Along with Salmon (1992), we believe that real problems are created for students because 'academic power is seldom made explicit' and '[p]olitical considerations are seldom recognised in the discussion of academic life, where the discourse of scholarship and rationality tends to preclude the acknowledgement of power dynamics' (p. 93). It seems to us that students, in the main, enter supervision arrangements without any due consideration of the power imbalance and the way it can impact on their progress. However we do not accept the university culture as an irresistible force against which students and teacher have no power – rather we are constantly looking for ways in which we can empower students and teachers to behave in ways other than the 'commonsense' ones they have taken on through their lived experience in the academy. The mini-conference was no exception. Our goal was to place students in a better position to manage their own learning and complete their degrees. Phillip's and Pugh's (1987) message '[u]nder your own management' (p.2) was extended to 'you are in the driving seat', and this became the theme for the week.

The programme: intentions and content

The programme is described in some detail here to address a gap in the existing literature on postgraduate supervision. Our key intentions were as follows:

1 TO GIVE STUDENTS A GENERAL OVERVIEW OF THE PROCESS OF CONDUCTING AN EXTENDED PIECE OF RESEARCH

We spent time focusing on what is involved in this process because, for the majority of students, it is unknown terrain. While supervisors' own experiences as research students might provide some idea of what to expect, we have not heard of many supervisors sharing these.

Being conscious that there is no one truth about writing a thesis, we wanted to expose the students to some of the different realities. To do this we used several different strategies. We invited along former students who had recently graduated to talk about their experiences. We frankly discussed our own fairly recent thesis writing experiences: the pains, the pleasures; the successes, the mistakes. Further, we alerted students to the potential pitfalls we were privy to through our positions as staff and student developers – information-broking, so to speak. In effect, we were providing the students with a vicarious experience of thesis writing.

Alongside this, we introduced students to the **Process Model of a One Year Thesis** (Grant, 1993).[1] This model formed the foundation for discussions about the processes involved in doing a thesis, the different stages through which students can expect to pass, the importance of working to deadlines, the continuous nature of writing and the emotional dimension of thesis research and production. In discussing the emotional states (boredom, dwindling motivation, disenchantment, despair, self-doubt, frustration, loneliness) that are known to affect students who are engaged in thesis research (Phillips and Pugh, 1987; Rudd, 1985; Salmon, 1992) it was our intention to 'normalise' these emotions – not to protect the students from them. Forewarning, we believed, was forearming.

2 TO FAMILIARIZE THE STUDENTS WITH THE DIFFERENT ELEMENTS OF, AND EXPECTATIONS
   AROUND, 'THE PRODUCT'

From our work with students, particularly those who are experiencing problems, we know that important questions can go undiscussed: ' ... what is a thesis?; ... what should be covered in a literature review?; ... is writing in the first person permissible?; ... how long should the finished document be?; ... what bibliographic convention should I use?; ... do the chapters have to follow a given format?; ... do all theses have to have some statistical analyses?' Students hesitate to ask such questions for fear of looking foolish; staff fail to check students' understandings of these points because they often presume that postgraduate students are independent and self-motivated and if they have questions then surely they will ask them.

In preparing students to find out about 'thesis as product' we furnished them with some questions they might put to their supervisors [see later discussion on the document we have developed, *Postgraduate Supervision: Guidelines for Discussion* (1993)]. We introduced them to panels of academic staff who came and discussed their various perspectives on topics including the meaning of 'thesis'; the criteria by which theses may be judged; what 'reviewing the literature' might mean. We also sent them to the library to look at some theses. We provided information that would enable them to identify those theses that had received a high pass; we got them to take note of structure and style. Our explicit intention here was to emphasize to students that even within departments there are different opinions and it is imperative to talk through these matters with their own supervisors – especially if they are the markers!

---

1 *You can get a copy of this model by writing to the Barbara Grant, HERO, The University of Auckland, Private Bag, Auckland, New Zealand*

3 TO INFORM THE STUDENTS OF THE RESOURCE PEOPLE AND THE PHYSICAL RESOURCES ON CAMPUS

To provide a basis of information which might be useful in the upcoming year we introduced students to a variety of resource people: the reference librarian, the secretary of the Human Subjects Ethics Committee, and the University Mediator. We also told them about the support that was available to them through the Student Learning Centre and the Student Counselling Service. Wherever possible, we tried to set up meetings within the students' own departments so that they knew what facilities and services were available to them.

We also encouraged the participants to see their peers as a resource and provided information about setting up Peer Support Groups and the different functions these might serve: from providing academic support to counteracting the loneliness and isolation that is associated with postgraduate research work. By structuring group-work so that students had opportunities to work with students from both their own and other departments and faculties, we hoped to lay the foundations for informal networking and more formal support groups.

4 TO REVIEW SOME STUDY AND PERSONAL MANAGEMENT SKILLS THAT WE KNOW TO BE USEFUL

In suggesting to academic staff that skill development might be a legitimate area of supervisor responsibility, we have, on occasions, been met with accusations of 'spoon-feeding'. However, our contact with postgraduate students who are experiencing progress problems convinces us that supervisors, in general, have a more rosy view of postgraduates' skills than do the students themselves. In the programme we included sessions on: goal setting; time management; information management; skills for writing and getting over writing blocks; and journal writing as a tool for both monitoring progress and integrating work and ideas.

The sessions were participatory and interactive and so the students learned not only from us, but from each other and, where possible, we provided opportunities to practise new skills.

5 TO DEVELOP SKILLS THAT WOULD HELP STUDENTS MANAGE THE SUPERVISION RELATIONSHIP

We do not deny that many supervision relationships are productive (there are many good theses to substantiate this) and collegial (some students and supervisors form lasting friendships). Nevertheless, our experience has been that it is a problematic terrain and, along with others (Brown and Atkins, 1988; Moses, 1985; Rudd, 1985); we further believe that poor supervision can contribute to completion problems.

In telling students what they might reasonably expect from their supervisors and providing them with some supervision management tools, we hoped to increase their chances of getting useful support and guidance.

In order to help the students become more powerful participants in the supervision process we first alerted them to the literature findings which address lengthy/non-completion. Alongside this we got students to actively consider what factors they might take into consideration when finding a supervisor.

Second, we introduced the *Postgraduate Supervision: Guidelines for Discussion*[2] – a document we recommend for use at the outset of a supervision as a basis for open discussion between supervisor and student. The document, set out like a workbook, comprises explicit questions that are grouped into three categories: supervisor/student understandings, departmental expectations and resources, and university requirements. While it is not constructed from one point of view – either students or supervisors can suggest its use – we are acutely aware that when we suggest to students that they take it to their supervisors, they are generally reluctant. For many students the notion of putting the document down for discussion is inappropriate and risky, even when they know that supervisors are familiar with it. [3]

Third, to encourage and prepare the students to use the *Guidelines*, we spent time talking about the benefits and exploring their resistance. We then prepared them to initiate discussion with their supervisors by trying out opening lines on each other and role-playing such interactions in the larger group.

Fourth, we worked through a process for managing meetings (the same process we use for training supervisors) which we had adapted from Brown and Atkins (1988). The point of this was to ensure that students go to meetings with a clear agenda and know how to maximize the use of this time. We also suggested that it was their responsibility to keep a record of meetings, giving a copy to their supervisor. In doing this we recognized that not all supervisors have meeting management skills and students often leave meetings frustrated and unclear.

Fifth, we developed skills for getting feedback. While the need for supervisors to give students constructive criticism and written appraisal of their work is included in the University's guidelines relating to the supervision of theses, our own research (Graham and Grant, 1992b) has shown that there is considerable variation in the feedback skills of different supervisors. Again, we provided students with the same information we give to supervisors but approached this from a 'getting feedback' rather than a 'giving feedback' tack. We emphasized that feedback is needed not only about written work, but also about ideas, experimental work and overall progress; we talked about using cover sheets to alert supervisors to the status of the work (e.g. first draft) and to direct them to where feedback might particularly be required; we got them to devise and practise strategies for changing the behaviour of supervisors who only give negative or unconstructive feedback.

Finally, we stressed the importance of, and suggested ways that students might contribute to maintaining, a productive supervisory relationship.

In teaching them new ways of engaging with their supervisors we are actively encouraging the students to reposition themselves in relation to their supervisors. In doing so there is a risk attached – some supervisors do not like students who resist the power imbalance and students need to be warned of this. But in the long term, we believe that students who learn to act more powerfully will better serve themselves and the wider academic community.

Overall, we believed we had put together a comprehensive programme. But how effective was it?

---

[2] *A copy of this document is available by writing to the author.*

[3] *We promote the document, Postgraduate Supervision: Guidelines for Discussion, whenever we can. At draft stage it was sent to all academics on campus for their comments; we distribute it to staff and students at relevant workshops; we send it to the supervisors of students who attend workshops.*

Programme Evaluation

Immediately after the course

At the final session we conducted an evaluation. The open-ended comments were overwhelmingly positive about the usefulness of the course. Most students reported multiple gains which indicated that we had achieved our aims:

> It's got me thinking early about the things that are required just to get going e.g. supervision, organisation. The things that were most useful were hearing from the students who have just graduated about their experience and advice; hearing from the panel of staff what they considered a good thesis to be and expectations around reviewing the literature; discussing what could be expected from each party in the supervision relationship and possible ways of approaching the relationship and things to be discussed; how to keep a journal, organising a timeline and managing meetings.

And further, the comments indicated that what we had wanted to emphasize had been taken up by the students. In particular we were heartened by what they had to say about the supervision relationship. The tentativeness we had observed at the beginning of the week was absent – students were much clearer about their own role and the role of supervisors in the research process. Moreover, for at least some of the students who had already established supervision there had been some repositioning in relation to their supervisors:

> I feel much more confident in my dealings with my supervisors, especially the one who normally intimidates me and is really negatively critical. I have had one meeting with them both yesterday where I'd – following your advice – got my act together and had a list of things I wanted to say instead of cowering in the corner being criticized.

There were other outcomes, the strength of which we had not anticipated:

> [What I gained from the course was] Motivation. Since Monday [now Friday] I've decided on a thesis topic, had a group meeting with my supervisor and established further meetings for all the students under that supervisor and had an individual meeting which wasn't nearly as scary as it could have been.

> [What I gained from the course was] encouragement to begin on a thesis! I now feel capable of actually producing a thesis. Before the course I felt fearful of the unknown ... I now have lots of concrete ideas to follow-up on – how to manage my supervisor, what to do if things go wrong in that relationship, people to contact ...

Knowing the limitations of evaluations which are conducted immediately a course finishes, I surveyed the students six months later to check on their progress. In particular, I wanted to gauge the effects of the mini-conference on their progress and supervision.

Six months later

Twenty-two students were telephoned at random and invited to participate in an interview – 20 were available. The interview consisted of a number of open-ended questions which were aimed at getting the students to identify what they had learned at the conference. The questions were used as points of departure from which conversations would develop – not a script to be followed. Such an approach is consistent with my view of the researcher/participant relationship: the participant has had experiences that I have not been party to therefore I cannot be definitive in the questions I ask. This model also has the advantage of incorporating elements of reciprocity: the participant provides the researcher with information; the researcher can allow spaces for the participants' problems and questions to be addressed. In this light, the interview can be seen as serving an emancipatory function.

The two students who were not available to be interviewed, along with 22 others who completed the course (six students had 'dropped out' by the beginning of the third day), were sent questionnaires asking the same questions as those that were used in the interviews: nine replied. However, only the interview data is used in this chapter. The questionnaire data is not directly incorporated but it was used as one of a number of validity measures that I put into place (Lincoln and Guba, 1985).

LEARNINGS ABOUT THESIS AS 'PROCESS' AND 'PRODUCT'

The students' stories showed clearly that most of the students had come to the mini-conference with little idea of what lay ahead:

[Before I came to the mini-conference] I knew nothing really about the process of doing a thesis. I knew who I wanted to supervise me but he was overseas at the time ... I hadn't thought about methodology – that wasn't a word that was in my vocabulary; I hadn't thought about ethics; I hadn't thought about the process at all except that at the end of the year I had to produce this 60,000 word document.

[Before I came to the mini-conference] ... I didn't even know what the thesis had to look like; I wasn't so thoroughly aware that I had to have a thesis; I didn't know what was involved psychologically; I didn't know what was involved practically; I didn't know how to tackle the supervisor relationship.

Generally it seems that the students have become more aware of 'thesis as product'. Looking at some theses and hearing academic staff talk about literature reviews and what they looked for in a thesis was regarded as helpful:

The best thing for me was looking at the theses .... Prior to that I didn't have a clue.

I had been working on my thesis for some months when I came along but there were lots of things that I didn't know about until the mini-conference .... The literature review thing was really useful .... I still didn't have any idea about thesis structure as far as writing it and neither of my supervisors had given me any indication as to what was expected in a thesis. They had told me about my research but not the process of writing the thing.

For some students what they learned at the mini-conference shifted the task of doing a thesis from the arcane to the achievable:

I had this image of a thesis being this huge thing, but essentially what the course did for me was to bring it to a manageable thing . . .

I think the conference was good in the fact that it addressed a lot of simple questions .... It made it much less daunting than I thought it would be .... You see all these thesis students running around and they are totally stressed out, and you're thinking, 'oh my god, I've got to do this next year'. And the conference brought it down to earth.

Over half the students commented that hearing about the emotional dimension of doing a thesis had been useful:

[Before I came to the mini-conference] I didn't really think about the whole emotional thing that was involved. And having someone who has just finished sit up there and say, 'it's horrible, and you'll hate it, but it will be worth it at the end' – that's something I hadn't thought about.

It was helpful just knowing that it's natural to get depressed and so on occasionally and that emotional ups and downs are part of the process. And knowing what I might expect to happen so that if it does happen I don't think, 'gosh, what's wrong with me that I am feeling this way'.

In one way or another, most students had made use of the information that had been presented in this section.

THE UTILIZATION OF RESOURCES

Apart from three students who said that they found the information about the Human Subjects Ethics Committee helpful, nothing was said about the relevance (or indeed the irrelevance) of the other information we provided.

Some students continued to use us and our services and this was discussed, e.g. two students had consulted me when they had supervision problems and we had successfully worked through strategies for solving these; and about one third of the students had gone on to enrol in the on-going writing workshops that Barbara Grant offered through the Student Learning Centre.

Our goal of laying foundations for informal networking and more formal support groups was not achieved. There was no doubt that students enjoyed the camaraderie of being with people in 'the same position' who they could 'identify with',but once the mini-conference had finished these across-campus links were not maintained. And while several students belonged to support groups set up by their departments no-one had initiated a support group as a result of attending the mini-conference (although one student said she was about to do so). Several students commented that support groups did not 'get off the ground' at the mini-conference because specific time was not allocated for these to be formalized.

STUDY AND PERSONAL MANAGEMENT SKILLS

All the students identified one or more skills that they were using as a result of attending the mini-conference. They had made use of the ideas we presented and adapted them to their own situations.

The notion of journal keeping had been taken up with enthusiasm. All but three students had started journals. For some students the journal was used purely for organizational matters, e.g. recording meetings, but most students used them more organically:

I also [in addition to organizational matters] use my journal for writing how frustrated and mental and panicked I am.

I do keep a journal. That's been very helpful – it's sort of an advocate in a way. I write down, in quite [a lot of] detail, what I'm feeling and what I'm doing; where I feel I need to go – what I need to look at. It shows you've changed but it also shows you've achieved things as well ....

And nearly as many students said they had successfully adopted new approaches to writing and notetaking:

I started free-writing quite furiously everyday – phone off the hook and everything. And I found that really helpful, as for a while there I had my thesis ideas and it was all unformed and it was all revolving around and doing nothing. It helps focus on certain ideas.

I'm using her [Barbara Grant's] 'not taking notes as much as reading and writing' approach and that is excellent. It was hard at the beginning as I had to throw out all my old undergraduate techniques of taking copious notes and then turning them into an essay.

Goal-setting, using the *Process Model of a One Year Thesis* as a starting point, was embraced by three-quarters of the students. Some used the model for forward planning, adapting it to how they thought their own projects would pan out; others used it, as it was, to monitor their progress:

The timeline [process model] was helpful. I started it in class, fiddled with it that afternoon and finished it the day after. It was a really good discussion tool that I took to speak with a woman friend of mine who was working in a similar area. So, with her, I could project the reality of my research.

The best thing I got out of it [the mini-conference] was the process model .... I've blown it up and it is on my wall .... For the sort of research I am doing it is great.

The time management skills were only commented on as being useful by five students who said they had resurrected the information when they had encountered progress problems:

When things were really going bad – I was really flaking and I felt really depressed – I remembered we talked about the management of time so I dragged back out that information .... I started a timetable for each week and each day and I put down what I wanted to have done. And I didn't worry if I didn't stick to it, but it helped me get more motivated.

Less than half of the students commented that they had implemented, to good effect, some of the information management systems that had been discussed.

Overall, the students appeared to have made good use of what we had taught them. Relatively few students talked of experiencing problems with writing, time management, procrastination, and those who did had strategies in mind for addressing these.

IMPACT ON THE SUPERVISION RELATIONSHIP

Overall, we were pleased at the number of students who said they had put to use some of the supervision management tools we taught them, i.e. *Guidelines for Discussion*, strategies for managing meetings and getting feedback. However, assessing the impact of the mini-conference on supervisory relationships was a much more difficult task than assessing how effective we had been in the other areas that I have described. And given the unique nature of every supervision relationship, this is not surprising. But fragments of the stories illustrate certain dimensions.

Five students told me how they no trouble bringing the skills and tools they learned at the mini-conference into the supervision. In each of these cases there was one vital ingredient: the supervisors were receptive and, it seems, thought about supervision in a way that was complementary to what we had taught the students:

> The mini-conference definitely had an impact on how I am now with my supervisor .... I don't feel ... from any stage, that she used her power over me and that I had to do this and that, and that her way was the only way. It was always negotiation. It was helped by the fact that she had done your course .... If I didn't agree with her, I could talk to her about it – straight out. We had in the document [Guidelines for Discussion] that we would be upfront with each other – she asked me – 'you don't want to pussyfoot around do you?' And I said that I wanted her to tell me if my work was rubbish .... The Guidelines for Discussion were really useful. We went through the questions quite thoroughly – everything on that document. I wrote notes, later put it onto the document and gave her a copy.

> I meet with them both once a week ... Each meeting varies from one to two hours – I had to learn to run them in the beginning ... The conference helped me a great deal here. Just how to go in prepared and clear about what I wanted in a meeting – just a matter of planning everything well before I went in ... When I leave I've usually got two or three tasks that I'm following through from there.

In sharp contrast, three students said they had used the management tools we had taught them but they did so in the face of supervisor resistance. Two of these students reported positive outcomes:

> After the mini-conference I just felt more in control. I'm much more assertive. He is really critical and I gave him the opportunity to criticise me pretty easily by not presenting work that I do in a very positive manner. It used to be [in apologetic voice] 'oh, I did this and it didn't really work very well'. Whereas now I tend to – I guess I approach him much better. Whenever I am now dealing with him I always just try and be really really assertive so that I don't get into a situation where I'm vulnerable.

> They really wanted me to do a topic that I didn't want to do .... And that is where the mini-conference helped. Without it, I wouldn't have been as sure of myself when I went to see [my supervisor] .... It helped having practised what I was going to say – that's something you and Barbara told me to do – and it was useful having rehearsed the whole thing with you so it was very clear in my own mind. It meant I didn't fumble with words. I could be very direct and carry on arguing and it showed that I was convinced. If I had been uncertain they may have tried to push me more. [My supervisor] was quite taken that I actually looked him in the face and argued ...

But the third student was not able to negotiate with her supervisor at all. His reluctance to work in a mutual way was apparent at the beginning when she asked if they could use the *Guidelines for Discussion* and this continued for five months until she decided to seek alternative supervision:

> If I hadn't been to the mini-conference I wouldn't have known that the power relationship was so unbalanced. I learned there that it does happen and ways to counteract it, but I couldn't with him because he intimidated me so much. It was getting really bad – I couldn't get regular meetings, every time I approached him I felt I was a nuisance, I had no control over the direction of my work, I was given the impression that none of my ideas were worthwhile . . . I wrote to him with my concerns and when he refused to meet with me to talk about the problems, I realised it just wasn't going to work . . . so I am now looking for a new supervisor. It's all quite uncertain and it is a bit scary.

Nine other students said they had applied the skills they learned, and in the main, supervision was going 'well'. But at the same time it was clear that they were cautious rather than confident when negotiating with their supervisors:

> My supervisor told me to come and knock on her door when I wanted to discuss an idea. But that hasn't happened yet because she is never there when I want her. I'm going to take up my courage ... and I'm going to go and book some appointments on a regular basis.

> I originally started drip-feeding [my supervisor] these questions [from the Guidelines for Discussion] without letting on where they came from. And then when [he] got the document in the internal mail, he actually asked me about it so I knew it was okay ...

The remaining students, while acknowledging that the mini-conference helped them in forming an understanding of mutual responsibilities and obligations, said they had not applied any of the supervision management skills they had learned. Some lacked confidence and the other decided it was too risky:

> I haven't put into practice some of the things you said because I am too scared. It would be counterproductive to put some of those things into practice.

> I find it difficult to be assertive. .... Like, I asked him about handing in some work to him the other day. And he said that with good students he just expects them to hand in one draft and he'll go through it, hand it back, and that will be it. I'd possibly like to hand it in twice. You can still get things wrong the second time around.

Working from these diverse stories it is difficult to draw any conclusions, but some themes emerge. Perhaps the most significant in terms of understanding how the structured power equality impacts on the supervision relationship is the evidence that, in many cases, it is up to the supervisor whether or not students are able to put into practice the management tools we teach them. Many students buy into this because they see power relations as uneven and relatively fixed, and there is risk involved when challenging this power.

Yet, on the other hand, it is evident that some students operated more powerfully than others in terms of getting what they wanted from the supervision relationship. In this way we can see that the issue of power is not a simple one of the supervisor having it all and the student having none – there is a power relationship that is susceptible to change. What factors might make change more or less likely would bear further exploration.

Conclusion

From what the students said overall, we had achieved much of what we had set out to do. Most of the students got launched early and were productively working towards the target date they had set themselves. Those who were behind schedule were actively addressing this. These outcomes indicate that induction programmes are a viable strategy for improving research students' chances of successful completion. Because of this we will provide another mini-conference in 1994, but at the same time we do not believe our work replaces the need for departments or faculties to set up their own introductory programmes and on-going support for research students. Cross–disciplinary programmes have some value, but there are specific aspects that would be better handled in-house.

Another outcome is that, as student developers, we have become a little more realistic about what we might achieve in a one-week course in terms of interrupting non-productive supervision practices. Not all students will be prepared to 'come out of the corner' – and not all supervisors will let them! And so we will continue to work with staff, departments, faculties as well as students – as this multi-directional approach offers more opportunities to change practices than does an "attack" from one quarter.

References

Bowden, J. (1988). Achieving change in teaching practices. In P. Ramsden, (ed.), *Improving Learning: New Perspectives.* London: Kogan Page.

Blume, S., and Amsterdamska, O. (1987). *Postgraduate Education in the 1980s.* Paris: OECD.

Brown, G. and Atkins, M. (1988). *Effective Teaching in Higher Education.* London: Routledge.

Cullen, D. and Pearson, M. (1993, July). Structuring supervision. Paper presented at the conference: *Improving Supervisory Practice in Research Degree Education,* La Trobe University.

Freire, P. (1972). *Pedagogy of the Oppressed.* Middlesex: Penguin.

Gibson, R. (1986). *Critical Theory and Education.* London: Hodder & Stoughton.

Grant, B. (1993a). *Making University Students: The Construction of Student Subjectivities.* Unpublished Masters thesis, The University of Auckland, NZ.

Grant, B. and Graham, A. (1992a). Naming the game: Reconstructing the supervision process at Masters level. In M.S. Parer (ed.), *Proceedings of the 18th Annual Conference of the Higher Education Research Society of Australasia,* **15**, 392–9.

Graham, A. and Grant, B. (1992b). *A Survey of Students Writing Theses for Postgraduate Degrees.* Auckland: The University of Auckland.

Heron, J. (1993). *Group Facilitation: Theories and Models for Practice.* London: Kogan Page.

Holdaway, E., Deblois, C. and Winchester, I. (1994). Practices and opinions reported by coordinators of graduate programs. *Interchange,* **25** (1),. 65–86.

Jones, J. (1992). Undergraduate students and research. In O. Zuber-Skerrit (ed.), *Starting Research: Supervision and Training.* (pp. 50–68). Brisbane: The Tertiary Education Institute, University of Queensland.

Lincoln, Y. S. and Guba, E.G. (1985). *Naturalistic Inquiry.* Beverly Hills, California: Sage Publications.

Moses, I. (1985). *Supervising Postgraduates.* Green Guide No.3. Higher Education Research and Development Society of Australasia, University of New South Wales.

Moses, I. (1992). Research training in Australian universities – undergraduate and graduate studies. In O. Zuber-Skerrit (ed.), *Starting Research: Supervision and Training.* (pp. 3–24). Brisbane: The Tertiary Education Institute, University of Queensland.

Paludi, M. A. (1990). *Ivory Power: Sexual Harassment on Campus* (2nd edn), Albany: State University of New York.

Phillips, E.M. and Pugh, D.S. (1987). *How to Get a Ph.D.* Milton Keynes: Open University Press.

Rudd, E. (1985). *A New Look at Postgraduate Failure.* University of Surrey: The Society for Research into Higher Education & NFER-Nelson.

Salmon, P. (1992). *Achieving a PhD.* Stoke-on-Trent: Trentham Books.

28 Can students learn to change their approach to study?

Ian Solomonides and Malcolm Swannell (The Nottingham Trent University)

Abstract

Attempts have been made in the Department of Mechanical Engineering to alter the learning strategies and skills of students at the start of their chosen engineering degree courses. With this aim in mind two interventions were developed; (1) a computer based, interactive 'course map' and study guide, helping students orientate themselves with the course, and (2) a series of seminars run by the authors, based on the work of Gibbs (1981,1992) and others, aimed at making explicit the approach and orientation students have in regard to undergraduate learning.

Supporting the rationale for these interventions are Student Approach to Study or Approach to Learning theories (for example: Biggs, 1979; Entwistle, 1981). Qualitative and quantitative research was undertaken in an attempt to identify the Approach to Study of students before and after the interventions. No conclusive statistical evidence of an 'improvement' was found, although some students initially identified as 'at risk of failing' have progressed into subsequent years of the course following the personal interventions of one of the authors. The majority of the students moved away from a predominant meaning orientation and towards reproducing and achieving orientations. This chapter reports the design and delivery of the interventions, discusses the research outcomes and suggests reasons for the shifts in approach that were identified.

Introduction

Within British universities, 'Approach to Study' is becoming one of the principle genre by which student learning can be studied and explained. We are assuming at this stage that the reader is familiar with the Approach to Study theories as described for example by Biggs (1979) and Entwistle (1981), and so only a brief outline will be described here. Essentially Approach to Study is concerned with describing how students interact with the learning tasks they are presented with or that they select for themselves. The student is seen to have a series of motivations, intentions and processes related to learning (Entwistle, 1988) as well as learning predispositions which when influencing strategy or style of learning will lead to consequent qualities of learning outcome. This seemingly reactive process has been previously and subsequently described as an 'orientation to study' (Biggs, 1987) and as 'study orchestration' Meyer (1991).

Approach to Study is a description of what a student intends to do with a given learning task. There is some consensus that Approach to Study is a very complex mechanism involving both the cognitive and affective systems. These personal systems are constantly under pressure from the immediate environment to produce distinguishable learning approaches, orientations and outcomes. Biggs (1993) describes the systematic nature of these interplays using a presage-process-product model where presage factors such as student perception of the learning context affect and effect subsequent task processing and consequent outcomes. Solomonides and Button (1994) have similarly described learning as operating within a system as in Figure 1.

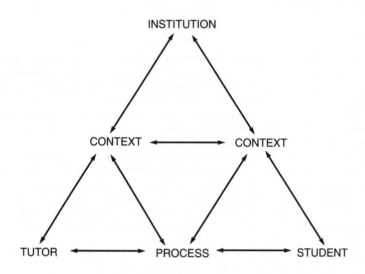

Figure 1 Interacting elements of the learning and teaching system

In figure 1, the Institution, the Tutors and the Student act as a mutually dependent triad, each responding to the others. Between them lie the content, context and process of learning which are all viewed uniquely by each member of the triad. The central elements of content, context and process represent the interrelated affective and cognitive elements of learning. It is this system that students perceive prior to its affecting behaviour (Schmeck, 1988). This notion of system is very important as (1) students will perceive implicitly or explicitly the state of the system respective to their expectations of that system, (2) students will make assumptions based on their perception about what the system or sub-systems requires of them, and (3) desired changes to any of the elements will have repercussions throughout the system or will be ineffective as they respond to pressure from the other elements.

Descriptions of such a system of learning begin to describe how the student's perception of the teaching he or she is confronted with will affect and effect his or her quality of engagement. We have acknowledged the function of perception in our own model described in Figure 2.

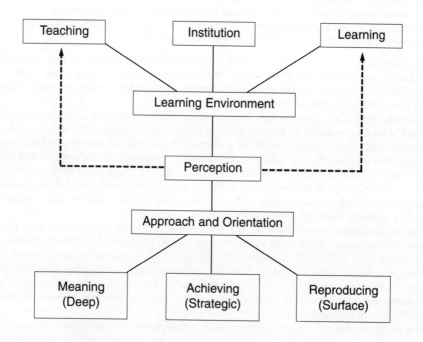

Figure 2 Perceived elements of teaching and learning

Here in Figure 2, the elements of the learning environment are perceived and subsequently responded to by the learner to produce a characteristic response, an approach and orientation to study. The elements of the learning environment include the personal and social characteristics of any individual members of the institution and might at one level be described as the learning culture. The perceptually affected response, the approach, is the description of the student's activities mediated and moderated by his or her perception of the learning environment. That environment may be as formal as a grand lecture presented by an eminent practitioner or as deceptively simple as fleeting conversation in a corridor with a student. Everything is included and perceived at a conscious or unconscious level by the learner and when combined with his or her predispositions, conceptions of learning, feelings and beliefs will produce a distinguishable Approach to Study.

We are compelled to respect this notion of perception and what it means for our students and their learning behaviour. All learning needs to be interpreted from the position of the learner (Meyer and Kaschula (forthcoming)) and so it is our responsibility to explore this notion of perception and to discover the ways in which the perception of our students is either helping or hindering their learning abilities. As Meyer and Kaschula put it:

... we attempt to engage the objects of our intellectual curiosity (our students) not as we see them, and not how we think others see them, but as they see themselves. We thus seek to derive our understandings of educational transactions from the perceptions of the participants ... The appropriateness or otherwise of how students engage learning can only be fully appreciated from their own internal perspective.

In our model, perception is at the heart of the student learning experience both in terms of what the students do and also in terms of what tutors do according to their 'view' of their students. Likewise, we believe that perception a pivotal factor when it comes to the adoption of differing Approaches to Study.

The descriptions of approach and orientation are well documented at conceptual and empirical levels elsewhere to varying degrees of consensus (Biggs, 1985; Entwistle and Ramsden, 1983; Meyer, 1991). The Meaning orientation describes a context bound learning strategy that involves the assimilation of information for personal development and the furthering of understanding. It involves a Deep Approach to Study. Deep study implies a deep level of conceptual understanding as the intrinsic motivational goal. Information is examined to identify the underlying concepts and meanings. The Achieving orientation is a highly strategic mode. It involves the Strategic Approach to Study. This involves an achieving motivation where the student is determined to do well regardless of what that takes. The mercenary application of effort respective to the implied desires of lecturers and assessments will result in success. The Reproducing orientation is instrumental in character; it involves the superficial collection of knowledge; i.e. a Surface Approach to Study. Surface study is shallow in nature and implies the use of rote and routine as a substitute for understanding. The motive is the gain of extrinsic reward by the reproduction of facts and ideas.

For purposes that will become apparent later in this chapter we must spend a moment contemplating the nature of one of these orientations and approaches, namely the Achieving orientation and Strategic Approach. Biggs, (1993) makes a claim that the achieving and surface strategies are institutional creations promoted by the offer of reward and sanctions. The same text suggests that a deep-achieving orientation and structure is the most adaptive as the process of learning is such that the student achieves optimal outcomes within the context available. This infers, along with statements made by other researchers, that the Deep Approach and Meaning orientation are the natural learning approaches and that higher education should endeavour to promote meaning via the Deep Approach on the part of its students.

To conclude this section we declare our beliefs about the learning environment and its effect on the learning of students. We work from a model of student learning that acknowledges the descriptions given above. The student operates and has the opportunity to display certain learning outcomes within the institutional system he or she subscribes to. This system has political, social, cultural and ethical characteristics.

The Activities at Nottingham

There are two major research activities we explore. Firstly a series of 'learning to learn' seminars supported by a computer-based interactive package. Secondly, the development of our own research into student learning and the effect of our interventions. These activities support and promote discussion between all members of the university on the quality of teaching and learning in our department, faculty and institution.

Interventions with students aimed at promoting effective learning are not new. What is new and innovative was the appointment of a 'Learning Skills Facilitator' (Ian Solomonides) to the Department of Mechanical Engineering who was originally employed to 'improve the learning skills and time-management of students'. To facilitate this study the Integrated Engineering Degree Programme (IEDP) was selected as a course within which a pilot study could be conducted in order to develop techniques and materials that support the learning skills and strategies of students. One of the reasons for this selection was that the course was lead by an engineer (Malcolm Swannell) with an interest in educational theories, concepts and practices, having recently gained a PhD in Engineering Education.

During 1992/93 two interventions were developed and trialed and these have subsequently been refined and re-presented in 1993/94. The first of these interventions is a series of tutor-led interactive seminars or workshops. They became known as 'Learning Strategies for Students' and contained the kind of activities found in Gibbs (1981, 1992) and in Entwistle and Tait (1992). The scheme of work departs from the traditional methods of teaching students to become more efficient and critical learners by concentrating on the development of study strategies rather than skills. After critical review and development, they were included within the Communication and Organisation modules of four degree courses in the Faculty of Engineering and Computing. They have also been adapted in various forms to suit undergraduate and post-graduate students on other courses within the institution.

The overall goal of the workshops is to facilitate the development of students as effective and flexible learners within an engineering education context. This is seen as a result of promoting:

* appropriate educational orientations of students;
* appropriate concepts of learning; and
* appropriate study strategies.

The objectives are tightly linked to the three aims above:

* to promote appropriate educational orientation by:
  enabling students to become more aware of their values and
  attitudes in relation to higher education;

* to promote appropriate concepts of learning by:
  making explicit the types of learning available to students so as to create an
  understanding of what effective learning is;

* to promote appropriate study strategies by:
  describing differential approaches to study and explaining them in terms of
  educational orientation and concepts of learning.

The workshops are organized so as to maximize active and experiential learning, a session typically involving students in discussion with each other, feedback through plenary and the provision of supporting theory. Students are encouraged to interact with the tutor and to raise any issues of concern. In this format it is found that students are encouraged to develop a 'voice' and to be active rather than to be passive. They are encouraged to become pro-active in the assimilation of skills and understanding rather than re-active as a result of a particular directive. This supports an implied need for students to generate appropriate enthusiasm and motivation before a particular learning event can take place. This has obvious implications for the ability to self-direct and update any learning they may attempt within their own discipline. This scheme models reflection and self-awareness so that students may be more inclined to use these strategies in the future. Any skill, transferable or not, is effectively useless unless it can be applied appropriately with meaning and integrity. These qualities are only developed and improved through honest reflection.

The second intervention involves an interactive computer-based package written using Assymetrix Toolbook for Windows. This runs on our locally networked IBM compatible PCs. The package addresses the same kind of issues generated in the workshops and has been described by Meyer (1994) as being 'too low-level in content to help students with real problems', but it is precisely because the individual differences between students are so extensive and variant that the procedures we employ for intervention are relatively simple. There is no possible way that a package such as the one we present can firstly identify these differences and then offer systematic advice to suit the attentions of students. To attempt to do so also subscribes to the belief that computer-based packages are a neat bolt-on cure-all to fundamental teaching and learning difficulties. There are packages being developed (Entwistle, Tait and Speth, 1994) which aim to identify and inform student study behaviour. While these are conceptually appealing there are questions that must be asked about the effectiveness of the study advice they proffer, not necessarily regarding the content, but more so the volume and pace at which information is presented.

The package we present to our students is somewhat different. It contains first and foremost information regarding the construction of the course our students are undertaking. The aims and objectives as well as the philosophy of the course are made explicit in the hope that this will fuel and support the notions of motivation and intent deemed so important by Entwistle and Ramsden (1983). The study 'skills' side of the package is reduced in stature to about twenty minutes of student time, is renamed Study Strategies and aims to promote some gentle introspection rather than explicitly promoting certain skills. The computer-based package is never seen as a replacement for human intervention into what is effectively individual human potential development. In our experience the package does offer students the impetus to go and see a real person for some 'real' advice.

Concurrent Research Activities and Outcomes

Earlier research by the authors into the learning strategies and styles of undergraduates revealed some of the relationships between student learning strategies, learning styles and performance over a variety of assessments. The research focused on the use of Biggs' Study Process Questionnaire (SPQ)(1987) and Honey and Mumford's Learning Styles Inventory (LSI)(1986). In regard to Approach to Study, the intention was to focus on learning strategies and motives while the LSI was used to identify learning styles appropriately suited to learning in engineering. The research showed that there was no strong correlation between deep learning and student assessment performance. This may reflect the assessment procedures used in engineering rather than the absolute effectiveness and value of this deep approach.

With regard to learning styles it is proposed by Swannell (1992) that students should develop a wide range of learning styles to suit differing learning situations and that engineering courses (and others) should be designed to reflect this. The research does however show that Theorists are most likely to be successful in engineering degree courses at The Nottingham Trent University. It is thought that this is associated with students' predispositions developed at GCE 'A' Level studies in analytical subjects such as mathematics and physics. The work also highlighted other issues that need to be addressed such as the need to examine the effect of heavy workload and assessment techniques in determining the Approach to Study of students.

Following the work of Swannell (1992) we are currently completing research into 'The Effect of Learning to Learn Material on the Approach to Study of First Year Engineering Undergraduates'. While the title is specific, we believe there is generic benefit and worth in the study of how students engage with their learning context and how that might be modified.

We are currently using the Revised Approach to Study Inventory (RASI)(Entwistle and Tait, 1992) within a research methodology that aims to tackle a series of five hypotheses. This paper is concerned with the first hypothesis which states that:

Learning to learn workshops or similar material will have a positive effect on student Approach to Study.

The 1992 first-year Integrated Engineering students were asked to complete the RASI. These students were exposed to the 'Learning to Learn' workshops during the course of teaching in 1992/93. The students were asked to complete the RASI again at the start of their second year of studies. Essentially therefore a direct comparison is available by testing the hypothesis in relation to two dependent means.

Table 1 presents the results from paired sample t-tests for each of the main scales tested. The main scale means are indicated, followed by their standard deviations (STD DEV), the difference between the two means (DIF) and then the probability level (p). Suffix 'pre' indicates data taken prior to the 'learning to learn' workshops; 'post' was taken after the workshops.

Table 1 Summaries of paired t-test results: pre/post workshops

Variable	Mean	STD DEV	DIF	(p)
Deep pre	61.6	8.5		
Deep post	57.5	8.8	-4.1	.000
Surface pre	46.5	8.2		
Surface post	49.9	8.4	3.4	.005
Strategic pre	51.3	6.9		
Strategic post	52.9	10.3	1.6	.124
Apathetic pre	15.9	4.8		
Apathetic post	17.7	6.0	1.8	.030

$\underline{n} = 41$

As can be seen, there are statistically significant differences (p <.05) between the student profiles taken before and after the 'learning to learn' workshops with a decrease in Deep Approach and increases in Surface and Apathetic Approaches. The Strategic results indicate an increase, but at p = 0.124 cannot be described as statistically significant.

Notably though, there has been an increase in the standard deviation of both the Strategic and the Apathetic scales. This indicates increasing diversity in the cohort in terms of these two approaches and therefore suggests that there are extremes of Strategic and Apathetic scale scores present in the sample.

Using methodologies set out by Biggs (1987) and local norms from our background data of 531 cases it was possible to establish low, moderate and high categories of each approach representing the lower 30 per cent, middle 40 per cent and upper 30 per cent of the population respectively. Checking the low, moderate or high categories both before (pre) and after (post) the workshops revealed that following the workshops there was a decrease in Deep Approach frequency of 13 per cent, a decrease of 5 per cent for Surface Approach, an increase of 12 per cent for Strategic and a decrease of 10 per cent for Apathetic. This seems to support the t-test outcomes for Deep and Strategic shown in Table 1, but contradicts the Surface and Apathetic outcomes. An explanation for this could be that while there has been an overall global increase in Surface, Strategic and Apathetic, and a decrease in Deep as indicated by the means, there may have been a significant change within individual students. The question asked is, how has the distribution of students within the cohort changed in terms of Approach level profile?

Table 2, reports the changes of Approach distribution between the Low, Moderate and High Approach groups. Each column therefore describes the number of students moving from one group to another. For example, the column marked H > M refers to students moving from a High to a Moderate Approach; M > L indicates Moderate to Low and so on. The table is split so as to show the relative difference between net decreases and net increases in the numbers of students changing form one band to another.

Table 2 Summaries of changes in approach distribution.

CATEGORY	H>M	M>L	L>M	H>M	M>L
DEEP	6	6	1	0	2
SURFACE	3	7	3	1	8
STRATEGIC	1	3	7	0	5
APATHETIC	3	5	3	2	7

Various interpretations could be applied to this table but the most obvious is that there has been a distinct drop in Deep Approach and a distinct increase in Strategic Approach. It could be argued that Surface and Apathetic do not have clear shifts in Approach, but we would suggest that there has been a net increase in Surface and Apathetic Approaches. This effect is compounded in that most of the increase has been within the moderate to high categories of the Surface, Strategic and Apathetic Approaches, while the decrease is in the high to moderate and moderate to low categories of the Deep Approach.

To deduce whether or not there really was a shift in these Approaches, difference between individual Approach means before and after the workshops was calculated. This revealed that 34 out of the 41 students (83%) displayed a decrease in Deep Approach; 28 (68%) were showing an increase in Surface Approach; 28 (68%) were showing an increase in Strategic Approach, and 26 (63%) an increase in Apathetic Approach. It appeared that contrary evidence to this obvious shift (see Table 1) was caused by extreme shifts in means across a handful of cases. These cases in turn may provide an interesting sub-group which might now be observed for their future academic performance. Likewise the profiles of students withdrawing from the course in the first year might now be looked at retrospectively for clues as to their reasons for failure.

Overall there does seem to be a general decrease in Deep Approach and general increases in Surface, Strategic and Apathetic Approaches. Taking the paired t-test results alone there is a difference between the samples at a very significant level with the exception of Strategic where there is a positive shift, but at a lower p value. Taking the rest of the data into account it would appear that this initial analysis is correct and it has to be assumed that the student sample in general has adopted more Surface, Strategic and Apathetic strategies, while reducing the Deep strategy. From this evidence it has to be concluded that the hypothesis: learning to learn workshops or similar material will have a positive effect on student Approach to Study, is open to question assuming that a move toward the Deep Approach is the desired positive effect.

Subsequent local work has served to confirm these results. It has been found that there are significant differences between the factor structures of student populations either failing or succeeding on our courses. It seems that students who fail have assessment outcomes (marks) correlated with the Apathetic Scales of the RASI, and that students who pass have assessment outcomes correlated with the Strategic Scales.

Further, qualitative analysis of essays that reflected on Approach to Study written by students at the end of the workshops shows that those students who then failed made absolutely no reference to either the Strategic or Deep Approaches to Study. It was if as these students were conceptually unaware of these Approaches even though they had just completed at least six hours of workshops specifically designed to raise awareness of them. It would seem that the presence of the Surface or Apathetic Approaches does not directly correlate with failure. It is more likely that it is the absence of the Deep and Strategic Approaches that will result in failure.

These two outcomes alone would suggest that anyone considering the inclusion of Approaches to Study or other descriptions of Learning Styles within a 'Learning to Learn' scheme of work should be sure of the logic involved. It is currently popular to believe that the Deep Approach to Study is the Approach that all our students should be adopting in order to succeed. Indeed some inventories of Approach to Study only include two major scales: Deep and Surface. While these are central to the level of understanding attained, it seems that the Strategic Approach is as its name implies the controlling factor and a misplaced or underdeveloped Strategic Approach will inevitably lead to failure. Methods and techniques must therefore be sought so that the development of this Approach is central to any 'Learning to Learn' innovation.

Discussion

> In other courses the undergraduate is expected to think; in engineering staying level with coursework is regarded as the sign of achievement.

Could this description by Ince (1990) be reflected by the data reported above? The workshops were aimed at evoking a deeper level of learning in students and specifically at restricting their tendency to be instrumental. And yet, one academic year after the 'Learning to Learn' workshops, these students have clearly begun to drop their tendency to adopt Deep Approaches and are moving toward more Surface/Strategic Approaches. It would seem therefore, that either the workshops do not meet their aims and may even have a negative effect, or, there is something about the context of learning that is affecting the way in which these students operate.

The context dependence of Approaches to Study and is consistently supported by the likes of Meyer (1991) and Entwistle and Tait (in preparation), who write:

> Other evidence does confirm that the nature of the learning environment affects the approaches to learning of most students, but subsequent work has indicated that students' individual reactions depends on their own purposes in studying, their approaches to learning and learning styles.

It was with these predispositions in mind that the authors' 'Learning to Learn' workshops were designed with the explicit aim of getting students to review these very characteristics. It was hoped that encouraging students to reflect on and review their purposes, approaches and styles would put them in a better position to deal effectively with the learning environment, an environment that profoundly affects what students do:

The case for the influence of the learning environment being indirect – mediated by the students' own perceptions – has been argued most persuasively by Meyer (op cit.). The relationship between approaches to learning and preferences for different kinds of teaching and assessment has proved to be remarkably close. The conclusion must be, therefore, that approaches to learning are to some extent consistent, but are also affected by the specific task and by the learning context. Entwistle and Tait (ibid).

These conclusions about student learning were also covered in the workshops; effectively, the workshops required students to examine both their functional learning predispositions as well as their perception of the immediate environment they found themselves in. As can be seen, such a syllabus would have taken into account the factors most likely to have influence on the quality of learning engaged in. Indeed, students commented on the value of the workshops in evoking this self-examination during qualitative feedback sessions and in self-evaluative essays. So why should students report positive changes in their disposition towards learning quality and then go on to produce profiles suggesting a rapid shift towards more superficial Approaches to Study?

Between the start and end of the 1992/93 academic year over 60 per cent of the students moved toward a more Surface/Strategic/Apathetic orientation, and over 80 per cent moved away from Deeper orientations. Most alarmingly, a statistically significant ($p > .05$) shift was detected towards Surface and Apathetic – results that contradict the aims of the workshops and self reporting by the students. Two possible explanations for this may be as follows.

1. Students report their willingness to take a Deep Approach following the realization that this is the conceptually 'best' approach. In reality they cannot change from an established instrumental approach; they are so affected by their learning experiences prior to higher education that they cannot without great effort, improve their learning disposition.

2. The context of the course and the learning environment in general, despite an initial willingness by the students to perceive them in a way conducive to high quality learning, are forcing the students into more instrumental attitudes and methods and therefore away from the Deep Approach and meaning orientations.

To only support the first supposition it might reasonably be argued that a predominant style mediates the Approach to Study taken by the student, in other words the student has a preferred method of processing information. It is argued therefore, that unless the learner arrives into higher education with a predisposed effective style, he or she is unlikely to take the stance needed for the active examination of ideas associated with Deeper Approaches to Study.

To support the second supposition while neglecting the first, implies that it is the student's perception of the course that will become the determinants of his or her Approach to Study, and that style is just that – only a preferred method of assimilating information. Thus a student will consciously or unconsciously perceive course task requirements, atmosphere and ethos in a way that leads to a reaction on his or her part – a decision by the student to adopt a learning strategy based on the perceived demands of the course. Thus if the student perceives the course to have excessively high workloads, to be over-burdened with content, he or she is likely to adopt a Surface Approach as a strategy and process for coping with meeting deadlines. A perceived lack of 'space' to think about information being presented may force the student into a memorization strategy, thereby unable to examine ideas and evidence presented before him or her. The assumption in terms of improving this situation is that the course must be designed with the contextual reactions of students in mind, and that overloading students may well result in Surface, 'coping' strategies. Further, because the way in which the student views the context of the course is mediated via his or her perception, there will be a range of reactions to the same context displayed by individual students . . . they will all look at the course in different ways.

In our opinion, there is no comfortable demarcation between one conclusion and the other. Some students are arriving into degree courses with the expectation of the instrumental styles of learning and the perception that the learning context is requiring the simple assimilation of factual detail. Clearly this is partly a reaction associated with established style, and partly a reaction to course provision and the context of the learning environment in general. However, the interrelation does not end there. It could be argued that instrumental styles are certainly qualitatively, and possibly developmentally inferior to versatile, in depth learnin. In other words, some of the data reported above is very likely to have come from some students who simply do not have the potential (either as a function of experience, or of ability, or of both) to reach a Deep Approach to Study.

The student in the situation above might be described as having an incomplete concept of deep level learning and as such is unable to recognize either the conditions that lead to in-depth processing, or the functions of the mind that are associated with it. If this is the case, it is unlikely that workshops of the type we have developed will move the student toward a Deep Approach to Study, even though the workshops contain explicit descriptions of the motivations, intentions, learning processes and outcomes that Deep learners have:

> It is as if they are unable to comprehend that other forms of orchestration are actually possible. In interviews with (first year) students manifesting disintegrated orchestrations, it has been concluded that some individuals are unable to reflect on intrinsically satisfying learning experiences at all; it would appear that they have never experienced deep-level learning and there is no referential basis on which to build. Meyer (1991)

Some students may well have the conceptual ability to appreciate the Deep Approach, but are then denied the opportunity to enter into it by deleterious contexts and are consequently forced into more instrumental approaches. We suggest to the reader that this is likely to be the case for most of the students reported above as indicated by the shift from an initial Deeper, more meaning orientation, to a more instrumental Strategic or Surface orientation. However, there are likely to be some students who are quite prepared to be only predominantly Surface or Strategic. The possibility of this type of student existing is theoretically valid, but the identification of such is at this point beyond the remit of the current research.

Summary

The data extracted so far indicates a broad move by the students surveyed towards Surface/Strategic Approaches and away from Deep Approaches to Study. This is despite the 'Learning to Learn' workshops. In this respect the hypothesis stated at the beginning of this section can be reasoned as being untrue. However, there seem to have been some success at an individual level, and in this respect perhaps the workshops serve as a useful mechanism for raising students' awareness of learning issues, which can then be followed up at a personal level in the case of those at risk of failing.

It seems likely that there are a number of factors militating against the adoption of Deep Approaches to Study, and that these are tightly linked to the overall course design, structure, aims and ethos as well as the predispositions of the learners. These predispositions may be natural, inherent abilities, or rooted in the experiences of the learner, or both. Either way, there does seem to be some theoretical support for the idea that some students, even though they may perceive correctly what is required to interact at a Deep level, do not have the conceptual or cognitive tools required. Others have the tools but are simply unable to use them within the constraints of the course as a whole.

Can Students Learn to Change their Approach to Study?

Quite clearly some students do change their approaches after they enter courses in this institution. The question is can they learn to adopt more favourable approaches following our interventions? It appears from the evidence available that the objectives related to developing a Deep Approach are not met and the answer in this specific case has to be no.

However, there is emerging evidence to be reported fully elsewhere, that our students are quite capable of identifying appropriate approaches for dealing with their immediate context. We are beginning to question the validity of attempting to explicitly teach our students via 'Learning to Learn' activities to take a Deep Approach when in fact it is the Strategic Approach that is emerging as the Approach for dealing with the complexities, intricacies and constructs of engineering knowledge. It may just be that the Strategic Approach and engineering practice are mutually supportive and compatible.

While the empirical evidence available here contradicts the hypothesis, we are aware of individual students who have derived enormous benefits from partaking in the Learning Strategies workshops. At this moment in time we are prepared to accept that we cannot directly effect the Deep Approach taken by a group of students, but we can give students the language register, forum and confidence in which they can discuss their learning. At its best this has had the effect of giving students a focal point for their concerns, and it is believed that there are students still on our courses who otherwise would have retired at or before the first-year examinations. Likewise, the influences of the Learning Skills Facilitator allied to other internal and external factors are such that there is an emerging interest in teaching and learning issues throughout the department, and that this in the long-run may truly effect the desire for improved quality of learning.

References

Biggs, J.B. (1979). Individual differences in study processes and the quality of learning outcomes. *Higher Education*, 8, 381–94.

Biggs, J.B. (1985). The role of metalearning in study processes. *British Journal of Educational Psychology*, 55, 185–212.

Biggs, J.B. (1987). The SPQ *Manual*. Victoria, Australian Council for Educational Research.

Biggs, J.B. (1993). What do inventories of students learning processes really measure? A theoretical review and clarification. British Journal of Educational Psychology (1993) 63 pp. 3-19Council for National Academic Awards (CNAA)(1992). See Gibbs (1992).

Entwistle, N. (1981). *Styles of Learning and Teaching*. Wiley.

Entwistle, N. (1988). Motivational factors in students' approaches to learning. In Schmeck, R.R. (ed.) *Strategies and Styles of Learning*. Plenum Press.

Entwistle, N. and Ramsden, P. (1983). *Understanding Student Learning*. Croom Helm.

Entwistle, N. and Tait, H. (1992). Learning actively on one's own. *Effective Teaching and Learning in Higher Education*. CVCP Module 8 part 1

Entwistle, N., Tait, H. and Speth, C. (1994). *Identifying and Advising Students at Risk From Deficient Study Skills: A Computer Based Package for Departments*. University of Edinburgh, Centre for Research on Learning and Instruction.

Entwistle, N. and Tait, H. (in preparation). *Identifying Contrasting Study Strategies Through a Revised Approaches to Study Inventory*. CROLI, University of Edinburgh

Gibbs, G. (1981). *Teaching Students to Learn*. Open University Press, Milton Keynes.

Gibbs, G. (1992). *Improving the Quality of Student Learning*. TES, Bristol.

Honey, P. and Mumford, A. (1986). *The Manual of Learning Styles*.

Ince, M. (1990). A lot of learning is a dangerous thing. *The Engineer*, 18.

Meyer, J.H.F. (1991). Study orchestration: the manifestation, interpretation and consequences of contextualised approaches to studying. *Higher Education*, 22, 297–316.

Meyer, J.H.F. (1994). Personal communication with the author (IS).

Meyer. J.H.F. and Kaschula, W. (forthcoming). *Helping Engineering Students to Learn Better: The Concept and Creation of a Learning 'Hot Seat'*. University of Cape Town.

Parsons, P.G. and Meyer, J.H.F. (1990). The academically at risk student: a pilot intervention programme and its observed effects on learning outcome. *Higher Education*, 20, 323–34.

Piaget, J. (1950). *The Psychology of Intelligence*. Harcourt and Brace

Schmeak, R.R. (1988). (ed) Strategies and styles of learning. Plenum Press.

Solomonides, I. and Button, B.L. (1994). Improving the quality of student learning: a systems approach. *Engineering Science and Education Journal*. June, 131–7, IEE.

Swannell, M.J. (1992). An Investigation into the Learning Strategies and Styles of Engineering Undergraduates. Unpublished PhD Thesis. The Nottingham Trent University.

29 Improving students' thinking and learning skills through Supplemental Instruction

Chris Rust and Margaret Price (Oxford Brookes University)

Background

In 1992/93 Oxford Brookes University piloted an SI scheme in the School of Business. The pilot was funded through the University's Staff Release Scheme which aims to promote innovation in teaching and learning. The scheme provided us with the hours we needed to run and monitor the scheme. In 1993/94 we received additional funds from the HEFCE as part of a research bid from a consortium of ten institutions, which we have used to continue the pilot and research its effectiveness.

What is SI?

Supplemental Instruction (SI) was developed in the mid-1970s at the University of Missouri Kansas City (UMKC) to address a number of problems, most importantly: a high failure or drop-out rate on certain courses, and the fact that traditional student support services are seen as remedial, and are generally turned to too late, if at all. SI is different in that it is aimed at what are described as high-risk or traditionally difficult courses, and offers optional SI sessions from the very beginning to all students on that course interested in improving their performance. These sessions are taken by trained SI leaders who are students who have already successfully taken and passed the particular course.

Theory of SI

The most important characteristic of SI is that it is not didactic teaching; SI leaders are trained as facilitators, to organize and enable the students attending their session to find the answer for themselves. It is an axiom of SI that the answer to the students' problems should be in their collective notes and/or heads. If the answer cannot however be found the SI leader should redirect them to their lecturer. Another key aspect of SI is that many of the students' problems are to do with study skills and SI is intended to help them to address these problems in relation and with relevance to the subject being studied, rather than in isolation as on study skills courses.

US claims for SI

After a rigorous review process in 1981, the SI Program became one of the few post-secondary programmes to be designated by the US Department of Education as an 'exemplary educational program'. The National Diffusion Network, the national dissemination agency for the US Department of Education, has provided federal funds for dissemination of SI, and it can now be found in over 30per cent of American institutions of higher education.

The three claims of SI's effectiveness, validated by the US Dept of Education are:

- Students participating in SI within the targeted high risk courses earn higher mean final course grades than students who do not participate in SI. This is still true when differences are analysed, despite ethnicity and prior educational achievement.
- Despite ethnicity and prior academic achievement, students participating in SI within targeted high-risk courses succeed at a higher rate (withdraw at a lower rate and receive a lower percentage of D or F final course grades) than those who do not participate in SI.
- Students participating in SI persist at the institution (re-enrolling and graduating) at higher rates than students who do not participate in SI.

Why SI for Oxford Brookes?

We knew that SI schemes are intended to be run on programmes that are considered 'difficult' but at Oxford Brookes we decided to run it for our business programme in the modular course. Generally business is not seen as traditionally difficult and does not have a high failure or high drop out rate. We chose to run it because of the large student numbers. The flexibility of our modular programme allows first-year student to take several modules from outside their chosen field. Many of them choose to take the business modules, the result being that these modules run with between 400 and 500 students each term. Despite its original purpose SI seemed to be a mechanism whereby students could be helped to come to terms with the sheer scale of the operation and thereby support their learning.

The Course Context

The three stage I modules which offered SI were the compulsories for the Business Administration and Management course. This course must be combined with another course from the modular programme and leads to a joint honours degree. For full-time students Stage I is equivalent to the first year and they must pass nine modules including the compulsories to progress to Stage II. This is an important factor to consider as there is no incentive to do better than pass apart from the fact that a better grounding in the subject should benefit them later in the course. The wish to do well per se comes from the motivation of the student rather than the instrumental gain of a higher degree classification.

The BA&M course has approximately 80 students in Stage I (60% UK, 40% Overseas), the remaining students taking the modules (approx. 400) come from other courses within the modular framework. For some of these students the Business modules may have been adopted as compulsories for their courses within the School of Business, e.g. Marketing Management, Retail Management, use one or two of these modules. Other courses may recommend the modules to their students while the remaining students have chosen the module out of personal interest. Therefore the students who were offered SI had a wide variety of backgrounds, knowledge and motivation. They could not by any stretch of the imagination be considered an amorphous group.

One of the business compulsories runs each term, *Introduction to Business* in Autumn term, *Management Concepts* in Spring term and *Changing Environment of Business* in Summer term. They each adopt a similar format for delivery but use different assessment methods. Each module has nine teaching weeks and each week there is a one-hour lecture followed by a two-hour seminar with students in groups of 18–20. The lecture is delivered twice in order to accommodate the large numbers of students and any student with timetable clashes. An effort is made to group the students on the same course in seminars, especially the BA&M students to whom these modules 'belong'. The lecture each week is delivered by a subject specialist and the seminar activities are designed to check students' understanding of lecture material and develop their learning. Consequently seminar activities vary week by week and include the use of case studies, role plays, presentations etc. At the start of the module each student is provided with a workbook which contains an outline of the course, a week by week breakdown of the reading, lecture review questions and seminar material and the assessed coursework tasks.

On the first two modules the assessment was 50per cent coursework: 50per cent exam and on the third module it was 100per cent coursework. The coursework tasks included a major project to examine the operations and performance of real business, investigation of the work of a manager including conducting an interview, making a group presentation on the topic of training and mapping the environment of a particular industry. The examinations used multiple-choice questions to cover the whole spectrum of material covered.

SI Attendance (1992–93)

In Autumn term, with eight trained SI leaders (two working together), we offered seven one-hour sessions at different times in the week totally unsure how many 1st-year students would attend any one. In fact we were so concerned that the sessions could be overwhelmed that we only offered them to half the students taking the module *Introduction to Business* i.e. those attending one of the lecture slots. In the event the attendance was a little disappointing. Out of 265 students who could have attended, 50 (19%) chose to attend at least one session in the term. We are still not sure why more did not attend; one possible reason could of course be that the lectures and seminars were doing a good enough job for the majority of students. Out of the 50 who did attend however, 54per cent attended more than once during the term and 40per cent attended more than twice, which would seem to suggest that for those students SI was meeting a need.

In the Spring term we offered SI to all the students on *Management Concepts* in the hope that this would increase attendance at individual session and thereby utilize the SI leaders we had to the maximum. The attendance was 16.5per cent at least once with 49per cent of those attending more than once and 40per cent more than twice.

The Summer module, *Changing Environment of Business*, attracts fewer students than those in the Autumn and Spring terms, but SI attendance was 21per cent at least once with 63per cent of them attending more than once and 35per cent attending more than twice.

Research Intentions

There were at least four:

- Although the improvement of results apparently achieved by SI are well documented for the US there is very limited data for the UK or in non-traditional SI subject areas such as Business Studies. We wanted to see whether SI did improve the students' results.
- If SI is beneficial, we wanted to know in what ways.
- We wanted to see whether students who attended SI had any particular characteristics and find out why they attended.
- We wanted to see whether any improvements gained through SI were sustained and transferred into later courses.

Research Methodologies

We have gained both quantitative and qualitative data, as follows:

- A database has been created of the 563 students who attended one or more of the three consecutively run Stage I business modules in 92/93 on which SI was offered, which has been subjected to statistical analysis. The database includes performance data from three Stage 2 modules in the 1993/94 year of those students who attended SI the previous year
- A questionnaire was issued (see Appendix) to students on the Introduction to Business module in the 1993/94 cohort, which has been analysed.
- Face-to-face interviews with students on the Introduction to Business module in the 1993/94 cohort who attended SI more than twice

The Results

Statistical analysis of the database reveals:

- no correlation between entry qualifications and performance on the modules;
- high correlation between performance on these modules and other Stage I modules; i.e. these are not atypical modules in terms of difficulty;
- no correlation between SI attendance and entry qualifications;
- no correlation between SI attendance and average Stage I mark i.e. SI attenders would appear to be typical students in that they are not weaker or more able;
- no correlation between SI attendance and age but a significant difference in mean age:
attenders 23.5, non-attenders 22.1
($t = 2.95$; $df = 563$; $p < 0.005$)
- significant difference in gender between SI attenders and non-attenders:
attenders 73.5% females, total cohort 57.4% female
($X2$ with Yates' correction = 7.25; $df = 1$; $p < 0.01$)
- no correlation between SI attendance and ethnic background;

- no correlation between SI attendance and first language;
- no correlation between amount of SI attendance and results, but a significant difference between attenders and non-attenders:

Module 7001
Introduction to Business

SI attenders* 60.8, non-attenders 56
(t = 2.62; df = 429; p < 0.01) *attended at least once

SI attenders*61.4, non-attenders 56.2
(t = 2.18; df = 429; p < 0.05) *attended at least twice

Module 7002
Managing Concepts

SI attenders #58.5, non-attenders 54.7
(t = 2.13; df = 398; p < 0.05)
#attended at least once on either 7001 and 7002

SI attenders#60.7, non-attenders 54.6
(t = 3.01; df = 398; p < 0.005)
#attended twice on either 7001 or 7002

Module 7003
Changing Environment of
Business

SI attenders§ 56.6, non-attenders 45.2
(t = 4.04; df = 189; p < 0.0001)
§attended at least one SI session on one of the modules

SI attenders§59.6, non-attenders 46.4
(t[separate variances] = 6.2; df = 126.2; p < 0.0001)
§attended at least two SI sessions in one of the modules

The questionnaires show very similar results with regard to the characteristics of attenders and non-attenders [NB 350 were distributed after a lecture in week 9 and 177 were returned – a 51% response. Over a third of the respondents (36.7%) had attended SI at least once]:

- no significant difference in age, race or the student's first language between SI attenders and non-attenders;
- significant difference in gender between SI attenders and non-attenders: attenders 73.8% female, all responders 65.5% female.

Of the respondents who had attended SI, 36 (57%) had attended more than twice. Their judgment on their reasons for attending is shown in Table 1.

Table 1.

REASONS FOR ATTENDING MORE THAN TWICE:(*36 respondents*)	NOT TRUE N	----- N	----- N	VERY TRUE N
MEET OTHER STUDENTS	5	12	9	3
IMPROVE STUDY SKILLS	0	7	14 ◄— **67%** —► 10	
IMPROVE KNOWLEDGE/ UNDERSTANDING	0	4	18 ◄— **78%** —► 10	
HELPED WITH LANGUAGE OF SUBJECT	2	14	11	4
INCREASED CONFIDENCE	3	10	13 ◄— **53%** —►	6
HELPED ME UNDERSTAND COURSEWORK	2	14	◄— **81%** —► 11	4
WANTED TO IMPROVE FINAL GROVE	2	3	◄— **72%** —► 10	16
LIKED SI LEADER	2	8	16	5
LIKED GROUP	1	16	9	3
OTHER REASONS: (*only 1 response*): "Helped broaden and examine business in depth."				

(% are of all respondents)

Asked whether SI had helped with other modules, 21 (40%) said Yes, against 31 who said No. Their judgment of how it had helped are shown in Table 2.

Although numbers are too small to attach any statistical confidence to the percentages, it is nevertheless interesting to note that information gathering and the approach taken to coursework are the two areas where most feel they have gained some transferable benefit.

Table 2

HELPED IN OTHER MODULES – 21 RESPONDENTS	NOT TRUE N	----- N	----- N	VERY TRUE N
IMPROVED NOTE TAKING	6	1	4	0
IMPROVEDSTUDY SKILLS GATHERING	2	0	7 *(62%)*	6
IMPROVED APPROACH TO COURSEWORK	1	3	9 *(71%)*	6
IMPROVED EXAM PREPARATION	4	6	3	2
IMPROVED GROUPWORK SKILLS	3	4	3	2
IMPROVED CONFIDENCE	2	3	7 *(43%)*	2
OTHER	2	14	11	4

(% are of all respondents)

Research in Progress

There are three strands of the research still in progress:

- the face-to-face interviews with those who attended SI more than twice are still being transcribed;
- further analysis of the data to see if there is any significant difference between coursework results and examination results in the results of SI attenders;
- the data entry and analysis of three second-stage modules to consider the current performance of previous SI attenders.

Problems with the Results

We are aware that there is a problem in demonstrating a direct causal link between SI attendance and better results, and there is always the possible accusation that both are due to motivation. In fact, having provided so many opportunities to attend SI during the week, one could almost argue that SI attenders must be more motivated because, apart from lack of motivation, there was little else to stop them (except perhaps a belief that they did not need it, the reason given by 26.3% in the questionnaire) which makes the fact that 59% did give inconvenient times as their reason for non-attendance in the questionnaire very difficult to believe.

Even if SI attenders are more motivated, there is however the fact that, assuming their motivation levels with regard to learning have remained constant, their extra motivation has not resulted in the past in better examination results than those of the presumed less motivated non-attenders. In the States they have also done some research into this area which attempts to isolate motivation as a factor and claims to have shown that it is insufficient to explain the success of SI attenders (Martin *et al.*, *Supplemental Instruction: Improving First-Year Student Success in High Risk Courses*, Freshman Year Experience Monograph Series, No 7, 1992).

When it comes to exactly how SI may have benefited attenders, we must be cautious of the results for two reasons – the fact that the numbers involved become quite small, and the fact that we are dealing primarily with perceptions.

Conclusions

- The data strongly suggests that there is a significant connection between SI attendance and better results on these modules, whoever the student is, but it is attendance at some SI rather than the amount of SI which appears to be most important.
- SI appeals more to female students, and students who are, on average, slightly older.

ACKNOWLEDGEMENT

We would like to acknowledge our great debt to Roger Lindsay, and thank him for all his help and invaluable advice.

Appendix   Please return to: Chris Rust EMU   **Educational Methods Unit**

Supplemental Instruction (S.1.) Evaluation and Feedback Module	**OXFORD** **BROOKES** UNIVERSITY

Please tick boxes as appropriate

Are you	Male ☐	Female ☐
Is English your first language	Yes ☐	No ☐
Are you a mature student (over 21)	Yes ☐	No ☐
Are you	Caucasian p	Not Caucasian p

[One reason for offering S.I. is that it may assist people from different cultural and linguistic backgrounds to adjust to H.E. The reason for the data above is to help us to see if this is true]

1   Did you attend S.I. Sessions   Yes ☐   No☐
     (If 'Yes', go to Section B)

Section A: Non-Attenders

2   Why did you not attend S.I.?
     Reasons(s)
     Didn't know about S.I.   ☐
     Didn't need S.I.   ☐
     Inconvenient times   ☐
     Other reasons(s)   ☐
     Please state below

....
....

Thank you for your help in completing and returning this form

Section B: S.I. Attenders

3   How often did you attend an S.I. session?
                        Once or twice ☐ More than twice ☐
     (If 'More than twice', Go to question 5)

4   Why did you stop attending after the first or second session?
     Reason(s)
     S.I. Leader not competent   ☐
     Didn't like the group   ☐
     Process unhelpful   ☐
     Problems solved   ☐
     Other reason(s)   ☐
     Please state below

....
....

(Go to Question 6)

5   If you attended more than twice, please rate the statements below as reasons for your attendance:

Reason(s)	Not True 0	1	Very True 2	3
It enabled me to meet other students	❐	❐	❐	❐
It improved my study skills	❐	❐	❐	❐
It improved my knowledge/understanding	❐	❐	❐	❐
It helped me with the language of the subject	❐	❐	❐	❐
It increased my confidence	❐	❐	❐	❐
It helped me understand the coursework	❐	❐	❐	❐
I wanted to improve my final grade	❐	❐	❐	❐
I liked the S.I. Leader	❐	❐	❐	❐
I liked the group	❐	❐	❐	❐
Other reason(s)	❐	❐	❐	❐

Please state below

....

....

6   Has attending S.I. helped your work in other modules?   Yes ❐   No ❐
     If 'Yes', can you indicate in which of the following ways:

Reason(s)	Not True 0	1	Very True 2	3
It improved my note-taking skills	❐	❐	❐	❐
It improved my information gathering skills	❐	❐	❐	❐
It gave me a better idea of how to approach coursework	❐	❐	❐	❐
It improved my exam preparation	❐	❐	❐	❐
it improved my group-work skills	❐	❐	❐	❐
It improved my confidence	❐	❐	❐	❐
Other reason(s)	❐	❐	❐	❐

Please state below

....

....

30 Developing critical understanding: the effects of course design changes on a first-year Sociology course in South Africa

Michael Drewett (Rhodes University)

Introduction

There has been a gradual transformation in Academic Development Programme (ADP) practice over the past few years towards a more holistic and integrated approach to student learning, in which the emphasis is on universities and departments to change, in order to provide for more effective forms of instruction.

The need for such changes are crucial for a number of reasons:

1   the effects of schooling under apartheid;

2   increasing student numbers;

3   broadening access to university;

4   increased staff rationalization:

    •   in mainstream departments;

    •   in ADP.

ADPS (especially the Rhodes University ADP) have never received much financial support from the universities in which they operate, but given the relatively large amounts of external funds available to them in the past, ADPs – like the one on the Rhodes University campus – have been able to provide quite widespread student support both from a central ADP office as well as from within many of the larger departments. So for example, the Rhodes University Sociology Department has had an academic development staff member assigned to it for the past eight years (initially in a part-time capacity, and recently as a full-time member of staff). But due to a rapid drying-up of funds, and limited university funding, this particular post as well as a number of other posts will not be continued next year.

The repercussions of this situation for the Sociology Department and especially its students are potentially severe. Whether or not the department is able to provide effective student development without an academic development post depends very much on the extent to which structured changes within the department's teaching have been implemented during the years in which this post has operated. This chapter considers the role of the academic development specialist in the Sociology Department in the past, and examines the moves towards improved student learning which have arisen as a result of the adoption of a 'critical integration' approach to student learning. In particular it considers course design changes that have transpired within one section of a first-year course in the Rhodes University Sociology Department.

In general, the process of critical integration is based on Jurgen Habermas' theory of communicative action (Habermas, 1979), in which the department needs to strive towards a situation of rational discourse in which all interested parties are given an equal chance to influence events and practices within the department (see Drewett, 1993). On a specific level, a policy of course design change has been implemented in order to attempt an approach to learning which both student independence and interaction are fostered so as to promote participation and understanding.

From Remedial to Integral: Changes in Approach to Student Learning

Towards the end of the 1980s it became clear that the most effective way of dealing with student difficulties was to teach academic skills to students in a manner which is integrated with course content (see for example Zuber–Skerritt, 1987). This led to ADP staff being situated within departments, where they were able to focus on discipline–specific student learning difficulties. In this sense the first of two `faces' of integration can be seen to have been realized – that is, the integration of skills and content in ADP workshops. But this instruction nevertheless occurred in a peripheral manner, whereby students attended ADP sessions in their own time in addition to course requirements. Some staff members within ADP began to realize that academic development instruction needed to be more holistic, and as a result of such thinking, a second 'face' of integration can seen to have been recognized: a form of integration in which the traditional ADP role becomes integrated with departmental teaching and course design. This is the path which the Sociology Department took at the beginning of 1993 when they were first allocated a full–time academic development specialist.

Course Design Changes in a Section of a First-year Sociology Course

It is within this context that the focus of this chapter is situated. The most significant changes which have been initiated have been in a section of the first-year course entitled `Social Institutions' which the Sociology academic development specialist lectured. But before considering the changes in this particular section of the course it is worth considering the context of the first-year course as a whole. ADP sessions would run concurrently with this term's work. An average term programme would offer academic skills sessions in a number of areas, for example:

- essay writing;

- examination preparation;

- library skills;

- focused supplementary discussion on important areas of the content.

Students would attend ADP sessions in an area where they felt they needed additional support.

Course Design Changes in 1993 and 1994

It became clear that the type of academic support referred to above was not able to deal with the range of difficulties which first year Sociology students' experience. The gap between school and university is, for many students, too severe to bridge by simply attending a number of ADP workshops in their extra time. Not only does such an approach disadvantage students who attend ADP (having to attend extra sessions), but it also attempts to deal with issues outside of the mainstream course, without tackling problems which very often are caused by the mainstream teaching and course design itself.

Many problems which lead to student difficulties with courses stem from poor course design and problematic instruction practices. As Graham Gibbs (1992b; p. 8) has noted, formal lectures are usually able to achieve the transmission of knowledge and comprehension, but they are unlikely to achieve application, analysis, synthesis and evaluation. Yet it is these last few goals which are most often expected of students in essays and examinations. If they are not receiving practice in these areas in lectures, then they have to rely on tutorials and written work. But tutorials are often spent discussing vague topics in an unstructured way while students only have the opportunity to write three formal essays during the year. While most students do improve from essay to essay, this improvement is often paralleled by increasing standards and in any case, is not adequate preparation for examinations which constitute the bulk of the year mark. As a result, many students drop–out, fail or pass with borderline grades.

For this reason it became clear that changes within department teaching and course design were necessary if students were to experience effective academic development within the first-year course. Given a certain amount of scepticism among some staff, the initial strategy adopted was one in which some changes would take place in various sections of the course in general (where possible) but that the 'Social Institutions' section of the course, which is lectured by the academic specialist in the department, would be the focus of lecturing and course design change in the department. Once the changes had proven effective within this course, they could be applied more effectively and with greater co–operation in the other areas of the first-year course. It is on changes within this section of the first-year course that this chapter now concentrates.

A Case Study in Curriculum and Course Design Changes: the 'Social Institutions' Section of the Sociology 1 Course at Rhodes University.

Part 1: Theoretical rationale

As has been noted, changes in the 'Social Institution' section of the Sociology 1 course are based on the perceived need for 'critical integration' within university courses. Critical integration is based on Habermas's notion of communicative discourse whereby the goal of effective student learning depends on the participants in the process developing an 'emancipatory interest'. This emancipatory interest 'can be realised only in a social context in which self–understanding is attained through dialogue with others who are striving for the same kind of understanding' (Howard, 1991, p. 83). In other words, it is argued that improved student learning and academic development more generally can only be achieved effectively if all those concerned are involved in the process in a co–operative way. This means that academic development specialists, department staff and students all have an important contributions to make, and all need to participate if progress is to be made.

It is important that the process take on this participatory format because the outcome aimed for is a participatory one, which ought not to be enforced on any of the participants. But what exactly is the desired outcome?

Unfortunately it is not a straightforward and overtly predictable situation. 'Any programme geared towards academic development should involve an inherent flexibility which allows for cooperative achievements to prevail, regardless of their outcome' (Drewett, 1993, p. 209). Habermas (in Pusey, 1987, p. 121) emphasizes this point in arguing that: 'Every intervention in complex social structures has such unforeseeable consequences that processes of reform can only be defended as scrupulous processes of trial and error, under the careful control of those who have to bear the consequences."

This is not to say that there is no desired outcome, but rather that the final outcome of any curriculum and course design changes can never be entirely predictable. Academic development practitioners do have experience and knowledge which needs to be utilized, but not in a bungled manner which ignores the interests and experiences of the others involved in the process. Indeed, a crucial aspect of communicative discourse is that, decisions be made 'on the basis of the force of the better argument' (Howard, 1991, p. 112). In this sense academic staff do play a more powerful and determining role because of the experience and knowledge which they possess. But they do need to provide justifications for the types of instruction which they suggest if communicative discourse is to occur.

The form of course design and curriculum development process which has been used in the ensuing case study is referred to by Veronica McKay and Norma Romm (1992, p. 139,140) as the negotiated curriculum. The two fundamental characteristics of the negotiated curriculum are, firstly, that all participants need to be viewed as intellectuals who are co–creators of knowledge and, secondly, that the process or method of learning takes priority over content. Through the negotiated curriculum students therefore co-operate with academic staff on what is taught as well as how it taught.

The role of the lecturer thus becomes one in which s/he facilitates a learning situation in which students play a part in determining their education. They are given the opportunity to decide:

'what they want to know about a particular theme/topic ... [and] ... are invited to implement plans on how to find out more after negotiation with peers and teachers, and also to evaluate the success of their enquiries by reflecting on what they have learned in the light of their initial aims and plans' (McKay and Romm, 1992, p. 140).

The negotiated curriculum has been used as a theoretical basis for the changes which have taken place in the 'Social Institutions' section of the Sociology 1 course over the past two years.

Part 2: The negotiated curriculum in practice

We need to bear in mind that the changes being discussed here are motivated by academic development needs rather than other considerations (for example the needs of the workplace and so on). The negotiated curriculum is regarded as the most appropriate form of curriculum development in terms of the general goals of academic development. And as has been noted, the negotiated curriculum affects both the content and process of courses. The discussion which takes place here focuses on both of these aspects. It will deal with different areas in turn. These include: evaluation, course content, course design and assessment.

STUDENT EVALUATION

Given that within the negotiated curriculum strategy student participation is crucial, it is appropriate to begin with changes in mechanisms for student feedback.

Firstly, regular and detailed course evaluations are conducted at the end of each term. These include both closed-ended rating questions and open-ended questions. These provide general tendencies (once analysed) on issues such as course structure, interest in the course, pace and volume of lectures and so on. They also provide comments on aspects of the course which could be dropped, areas where improvements could be made and aspects of the course which were especially good. An end of year report is compiled and an intensive meeting is held in which problems and strengths are discussed and changes implemented. Recently venue and timetable changes have been organized to deal with some of the issues raised by students. Some parts of each section have been dropped and others added, and different teaching techniques have been tried on the basis of these forms.

Secondly, and more in line with communicative discourse is an innovation which came into effect this year. The class representative system was not working very well. Many students didn't know who the two class representatives were, and even if they did, they didn't use them much, preferring to keep quiet about any grievances or ideas they might have. This year a tutorial representative system was introduced. After a few tutorials had been held and students had begun to get to know each other in their tutorial groups, each of the 20 tutorial groups (of no more than ten members each) was asked to elect an accountable tutorial representative. Tutorial representatives are regularly provided with the opportunity to determine the opinions of their tutorial groups during the term, and then meet with staff members (although not necessarily with the one lecturing them) in what have turned out to be very productive meetings in which both students and staff can put forward their arguments, ideas, responses and so on. The form of feedback received here has been far more direct and useful then other forms of feedback used, and this new forum will play an important role in determining future change in the Sociology 1 course. It is a very representative system, and is in tune with the idea of communicative discourse: not only are opinions expressed, but answers have to be given, and debate can take place.

Thirdly, a process which is presently getting under way is an experiment which is going to be tried out in a two-week section on 'mass communication' at the end of the fourth term, in which interested students will meet with the lecturer a while before the course begins to decide what issues they would like to cover in lectures and how best they think they should be taught and assessed.

COURSE CONTENT

The area of course content will be divided into two areas: firstly, content which falls under the traditional category of sociological content, and secondly, content which has traditionally been taught as academic skills or learning strategies and so on.

Sociological knowledge

- The overall **conception** of the Sociology course as it stands at present has taken place over the last few years. The 'social institutions' section is taught in the third term, following from a term spent on a general introduction to Sociology and a term which focuses on 'social inequalities'. Students thus begin this section of the course with a general understanding of what sociology is and what sociological thinking entails, as well as with an understanding of broad social inequalities along the lines of class, sex and race. The 'social institutions' section of the course continues from this point and considers the areas of society in which social inequalities occur (social institutions) and examines some issues with relation to each social institution. The aim of the course being to introduce students to four central areas of society by dealing with issues pertaining to each as well as by considering the strong inter–relationship between the different institutions. The actual topics chosen within the study of each institution are chosen on the basis of relevance to students living in South African society, as well as on the basis of interest and relevance. The topics covered within the course are by no means absolute and are selected as a means to an end – of taking students through a process in which they learn to think about the world in a sociological manner.

- At the start of each new topic a major attempt has been made to consider the existing **backgrounds** of the students in the class. Open class discussion is used, as well as written submissions (done in lectures) to get a feel of what students know about a particular topic. Lectures then take as a starting point the area of ignorance or confusion. Most of the time there is an imbalance between the background knowledge of different students, but context–provision can be interesting even to those students who do have adequate background knowledge on a topic by incorporating them in the lecture – through using a questioning technique and so on.

- Also included under content is the issue of **sources** to which students can turn in order to research areas of work. In the past the prescribed text book was used as the basis for most sections (the South African one excluded). Now there has been a change in emphasis. Although there still is a prescribed text book (a British one) the readings for the Social Institutions course come from a variety of sources. The course outline is very structured, so that there is at least one recommended reading listed for each lecture. This allows for a more varied course with which students can keep in touch through a wider range of reading than simply the text book – recommended readings are placed in the short loan section of the library or in the departments' own resource centre. Access to books is thus rarely a problem for students.

Academic skills knowledge

While in the past lectures on various academic skills have generally not been successful, it became clear that there was a need to include lectures on **critical thinking** as a subject in itself if students are to properly grasp this important aspect of thinking sociologically (see Drewett, 1994). For this reason the first week of the section on 'social institutions' in this year's course was set aside for participatory lectures on critical thinking. With this background students would then be able to attempt different types of critical thinking within a variety of contexts – such as tutorials, lectures, essays and so on.

COURSE DESIGN CHANGES

It has been stressed that the negotiated curriculum depends very much on the participation of students in impacting on their own education. This participation develops both student independence and interaction. Participation simultaneously fosters understanding because students are involved in the process, and thus experience the education process in a far more integral manner then more passive alternatives.

John Biggs (1989) argues that a deep approach is fostered through a learning process in which they are provided with:

1 A **motivational context** in which the student is attracted to the learning context by his/her need to find out more about something;

2 There needs to be some form of **learner activity** in which the student is actively involved in the process of discovering knowledge and in applying it to their already existing understanding of society.

3 **Interaction between students** facilitates understanding through mutual processes such as planning, conceptualizing, discussing, arguing and execution of plans.

4 New knowledge needs to be introduced within the context of a **well–structured knowledge base**, so that students are taught new information in relation to their existing understanding, so that new information adds to their existing knowledge, rather than being viewed as something taught in a manner which is abstracted from previous knowledge.

Because these various elements of learning actively involve and interest the student in his/her education, they facilitate understanding rather than superficial memorization of facts. The learning process becomes real, so students understand what is going on and are able to apply that understanding to different situations and contexts. When the process is passive, students have no other recourse than to rely on rote–learning to remember the ideas/knowledge with which they have come into contact.

The course design changes which were introduced in this year's section on 'social institutions' attempted to put into practice the framework provided by Biggs. While at the same time it is important to remember that any measures taken to improve participation also increase students' ability to involve themselves in a process of negotiated curriculum. An active approach to learning thus challenges traditional passive conceptions, and empowers students in their ability to impact upon their own education. This in turn encourages further participation and so on.

A number of innovations were introduced in order to provide for an active an varied learning experience, which put Biggs' framework into practice in diverse ways. These are as follows.

• Content was selected on the basis of interest and relevance.

- A large volume of content from previous years' courses was dropped in favour of process. Content thus becomes a means to an end, rather than an end in itself. It is not sufficient to simply teach sociology. It is more important to teach students valuable processes involved in thinking sociologically and so on.

- In designing the course a combination of control and independence strategies (Gibbs, 1992a) was incorporated. On the one hand students were supplied with a well-structured course outline and were expected to attend lectures and tutorials, while on the other hand they were given tasks and exercises to do which relied on their own freedom and independence. For example, a group task was set in which groups were left to decide on an issue entirely on their own.

- Fragmented lectures were introduced. Based on Adam Morton's (1994) notion of fragmented lectures, lecture content was conveyed to students, who then had to discuss it amongst themselves in relation to certain problems which they had to solve. Large group discussion then followed before the lecture continued.

- A portfolio approach to assignments was introduced. This is based on the knowledge that different students appreciate different forms of assessment. By offering a fairly wide range of assessment formats, students have a number of chances to prove themselves. Those who do badly in one area might well excel in others. In this instance students were expected to complete six separate assignments, four of which (when combined) would count as their term mark.

- Class debates were introduced in which students prepare for participation in debate, as an alternative to a traditional lecture.

- Problem–based learning was introduced in which each tutorial group had to confront an assignment task which required a participatory approach to learning. In this instance they had to relate Ralph Miliband's theory of legitimation (which includes a focus on advertising) to their particular task – which was to create an advertisement. The problem–solving task for them was to create an advertisement which emphasized an aspect of Miliband's theory. There were a wide variety of advertisements ranging from video and radio advertisements to posters and pamphlets. Issues covered ranged from AIDS, abortion and euthanasia to drug use, wife beating and slimming. Most impressive were the reports which accompanied the advertisements. Students had a much stronger grasp of the theory then students from previous classes.

- The use of dialogue writing as a means to characterizing and personalizing theory. Students were set the task of writing a dialogue in which two theories are represented by two characters who engage in an argument. While this was ostensively an exercise in critical thinking, it also allowed for students to apply theory to practice in a creative and innovative way.

- Videos were also used to facilitate discussion. In a variant of the fragmented lecture, a 15- minute lecture explaining a video would be followed by the video (a short piece – even a music video – to create interest) and then small-group discussion (in pairs or threes) and then a broader group report back discussion which is rounded off by the lecturer.

- Small group discussion within lectures (in pairs or in threes) is a good break from large group discussion, which Mark Weinstein (1994) refers to as a small group discussion with a large audience.

- Developing essay and examination questions so that they provide students with a clear presentation of the requirements of the question (both in terms of structure and content).

While it is still too early to assess the overall effect of these changes, the student feedback and enthusiasm throughout the course has reflected a far more positive view towards the course than in previous years. Written work has, on average, been of a considerably higher standard. Here are a few of the comments received from students in their course evaluations:

I enjoyed the varied assignments which made the subject more interesting. For example, the advertisement, dialogue and the debate in class. Thank you.

The course has been interesting and done a great deal towards expanding the sociological knowledge we already have.

It was a well-structured course and the lecturer made it as interesting as possible which was great!

I really appreciated the lecturer's efforts to make this an exciting and fun course. I missed far fewer lectures this term than in the previous two!

[The lecturer's] approach is splendid! There's more student participation. Students feel a part of what's happening in the lecture.

I really enjoyed being lectured by (the lecturer) and I hope he takes us next term.

Course structure and lecture outlines were excellent. We had a sense of direction. The videos, quotes and readings were interesting and made a change. I enjoyed the course.

I really enjoyed the visuals – the videos etc. ... – I felt they made me enthusiastic and I could relate well to them.

I liked [the lecturer's] style. His interest and energy in the students and course provided incentive to work. The course was enjoyable.

There was however, a strong opposition to the week on critical thinking.It was common to find strong attacks on the critical thinking section by the same students who passed favourable comments about other aspects of the course. And there were a few complaints about the additional workload which this course entailed. As one student commented: 'I feel the course has improved tremendously since last term, however, there was so much to be done – I enjoyed it – however there are other subjects which I need to pay attention to.'

ASSESSMENT

Assessment can be divided into two areas: term assessment and end-of-year assessment in the form of the final examination.

A major contradiction exists between teaching for understanding and a system which relies on a final examination in which 70per cent of the student's mark is decided in one three-hour examination. Rhodes University is not very flexible in this regard, and the Sociology Department has been reluctant to force this issue much at all. As a result this course, in its attempt to assess understanding rather than memory, operates according to a dual assessment structure.

Firstly, as has been mentioned, a portfolio type system is employed to determine the term mark. There are six components to this, divided into three sections.

Category A: Written assignments

1 An essay of approximately 1000 words. Questions were set in relation to practical examples with the structure of the required answers set out in the questions. This made for more structured answers which were related to the given examples – students generally found it easier to understand theory in this manner.

Example: A usual essay question in Sociology would take on the following sort of form:

Critically compare and contrast Ralph Miliband's notion of legitimation and Antonio Gramsci's concept of dual consciousness, indicating with reasons, your support for one or the other theory.

In this course the question was worded as follows:

Fred, in every respect a working class man, has recently been retrenched by South African Breweries (S.A.B.), who, in trying to maximise profits, have laid-off 500 workers. Fred's life has become increasingly depressing and frustrating. One evening, having received his monthly unemployment benefit, he and two of his friends who were also retrenched by S.A.B. when he was, walk down to the local pub and each order a Castle Lager. Caught in a spirit of comraderie and escapism they lift their glasses in the air and raise a toast to Charles Glass (in Castle Lager advertisements Charles Glass is reputed to be the founder of Castle Lager). Note: Fred and his friends' behaviour is not to be interpreted as an act of sarcasm – they are genuine in their toast. This clearly is a contradictory act, given their recent retrenchment. If Ralph Miliband were to explain this contradiction he would do so in terms of his notion of **legitimation**, but Antonio Gramsci would disagree, arguing instead that a more accurate explanation of the retrenched workers' behaviour would be derived through his concept of **dual consciousness**.

Write an essay in which you:

(a) briefly outline Miliband and Gramsci's arguments;

(b) explain clearly the point of disagreement between the two; and

(c) present a well–structured argument in which you justify your support of one or the other of the above mentioned two theories.

2 A dialogue of at least 750 words. Dialogues have been mentioned previously, but the main purpose in this style of writing is to encourage students to consider in a practical manner two sides of a debate, disagreement or discussion. The dialogue can take the form of a play, a straightforward dialogue, a court case, a short story and so on. It allows for creativity and exploration in a less academic format which nevertheless is able to gauge student's understanding of content and process.

Category B: Comprehension class tests

These are tests which attempt to break away from conventional styles of testing. Two were held during the term, and thus provided students with feedback on their progress during the course. In these tests pieces of writing were included and questions were asked about each piece of writing. For example a poem about education was included, and students were asked questions in which they related the poem to theory. Ability to memorize is not important whereas ability to think about concepts and apply them to practical situations becomes the essence of the assignment.

Category C: Tutorial assignments

Here the aforementioned advertisement assignment as well as an individual 'take home' critical thinking assignment were included. In future this section of the assessment system will be based solely on problem–solving tasks done co–operatively an small groups. Feedback on the problem–solving task was very favourable.

One last means of assessment which hasn't been mentioned in this section was the class debate. Here volunteers were asked to present arguments for or against the idea that 'education is a necessary evil'. Those who participated could do so instead of submitting an essay, and they were marked on their ability to present a particular theory in terms of the topic of the debate. There was a very good response (nine students in the two classes–the students were demographically varied in terms of race and sex – which was obviously encouraging). Students were given a written assessment on their performance.

Secondly, in terms of assessment, there is a final examination which constitutes 70per cent of the final mark. As has been mentioned the end of year examination is not a good test of understanding and a deep approach to learning. And given the rigid stance of the university administration at present, a compromise situation has had to be sought. The questions on this section of the course will thus be reflective in nature. In other words, students will be asked to reflect on tasks undertaken during the course (for example the group project and the dialogue), and analyse the process in terms of questions asked. For example they could be asked to explain what their group did in their advertisement, and how this relates to the theory which they were supposed to be representing. In this manner understanding is a crucial part of answering the question. Even though students still need to have grasped the content, they have to internalize it in relation to practice.

Conclusion

What has become clear in the exercise of curriculum and course design development which has been outlined here is that it is a very multi-faceted task which impinges on all areas of the learning process. Each aspect which has been referred to could have been discussed in more detail, in order to provide a more analytically detailed account of the processes undertaken.

The positive aspect of the changes which have taken place is that the response from the students has been far more positive than ever before. Their written work has improved, their enthusiasm towards their work has increased, their involvement in lectures has become more relaxed and widespread, and their ability and willingness to offer criticism has developed tremendously. Through the aforementioned changes the course is much improved, but at the same time there is a lot of room for improvement.

The immediate path ahead is to provide further changes which will transform the 'social institutions' section of the course even further, while it is also important to apply these changes to the entire first-year course. From an academic development perspective in particular, these changes have gone a long way in making the course more accessible to all students in the class, and while there are still failures, these are decreasing year by year. One of the main purposes of these changes was to close the performance gap between students from varying educational backgrounds, and this indeed appears to be taking shape.

Through the process of communicative discourse in the form of the negotiated curriculum it is clear that course design and curriculum changes can bring about the sort of academic development which critical theorists insist is necessary, if students are indeed to develop a learning approach which will encourage them to become 'thinkers–and–actors' (McKay and Romm, 1992, p. 156) in a university which itself can be transformed into 'a vital and critical part of society (which encourages and facilitates)...free and open communication' (Howard, 1991, p. 118).

References

Biggs, J. (1989). Does learning about learning help teachers with teaching? Psychology and the tertiary teacher. *The Gazette*, **26**(1). University of Hong Kong.

Drewett, M. (1993). *The Integration of Academic Skills/Support Programmes into University Department Structures: a Case Study in the Sociology of Education.* Masters thesis. Grahamstown: Rhodes University.

Drewett, M. (1994). Oh dear not another critical thought!: An analysis of student critical thinking difficulties. Paper presented at the *Second British Conference on Critical Thinking and Education,* University of East Anglia, Norwich. 6–8 Apr.

Gibbs, G. (1992a). *Problems and Course Design Strategies. Teaching More Students. No.1,* Oxford: Oxford Centre for Staff Development.

Gibbs, G. (1992b). *Lecturing to More Students. Teaching More Students. No.2.* Oxford: Oxford Centre for Staff Development.

Habermas, J. (1979). *Communication and the Evolution of Society.* London:Heinemann.

Howard, C. (1991). *Theories of General Education.* London: Macmillan.

McKay, V. and Romm, N. (1992). *People's Education in Theoretical Perspective.* Cape Town: Maskew Miller Longman.

Morton, A (1994). Teaching philosophy: some new tricks. *Cogito.* **8**(1).

Pusey, M. (1987). *Jurgen Habermas.* London: Tavistock Publications.

Weinstein, M. (1994). Critical thinking and academic disciplines: expanding the relationship. Paper presented at the *Second British Conference on Critical Thinking and Education,* University of East Anglia, Norwich. 6–8 Apr.

Zuber–Skerritt, O. (1987). The integration of university student learning programmes. *Programmed Learning and Educational Technology.* **24**(1).

31   The impact of learning and teaching styles in vocational preparation

Philippa Ashton (University of Central Lancashire)

Aims

- Explore the relevance of learning and teaching styles.
- Show the results of a learning styles questionnaire completed by design students.
- Pose some questions for educators.

The purpose of this chapter is to consider learning styles and in particular how they are acquired and their relevance to the way we think, behave and approach new situations. Many of the ideas in this chapter are illustrated with examples from design education. One of the aims of the research on which the chapter was based was to understand more fully why designers and 'managers' are different and how these differences can lead to conflict and misunderstanding in the workplace.

Finally, there will be an examination of new data indicating the preferred learning styles of undergraduate design students and the implications of these results for their vocational preparation.

Delegates to the workshop/presentation will have an opportunity to determine the learning style profile of their own courses

> If manager and designers have different aims, different education, different ways of communicating and to cap it all, different styles of thought, how can they possibly deal with each other? (Walker (1990). Two tribes at War? In Mark Oakley (ed.), *Design Management Handbook*.)

The research on which this chapter is based attempts to add to the debate about why managers and designers are 'different' and how these differences occur. It is often said in design management literature that these differences are one of the major sources of conflict between design and other functions in an organization, often leading to the production of uncompetitive products.

It is not suggested of course that all managers and all designers are the same, but from observation designers generally appear to exhibit a particular way of thinking and working. There are three main areas where design and other functions exhibit differences. These are in thinking, skills and methods.

Designers tend to adopt a lateral approach to thinking, progressing in a random and often unpredictable way. They are divergent thinkers, able to freely generate ideas and go off at a tangent.

In their working methodology, designers will tend to want to bring together many strand, often in innovative ways instead of breaking problems down into logical elements then re-building in an equally logical manner. They often prefer to work holistically, that is approaching the whole problem in an unstructured way, starting first perhaps, at the part that appeals most. This is in contrast to the managerial approach which can be described as serialistic-tackling stage one before moving on to stage two and so on.

Many of these behaviours and ways of thinking all reemerge later in this chapter when the characteristics which define the different styles of learners are explored.

The quote from *Design Management Handbook* above sums up the differences just outlined. It also raises the question of the role of education in creating and reinforcing these polarities. While there can be many factors which shape people's ways of looking at the world, our education, often at a time when we are younger and more impressionable, will play an important part in developing personal schema.

Higher Education in Great Britain at least, has been ascribed three main purposes. In 1988 in his paper 'The Goals of Universities' Allen describes these as preparation for employment, both general and specific, personal development and learning to learn.

These aims imply that universities should achieve more than providing the skills and knowledge required to do a particular job, but that they should also develop the students' ability to think, reason and problem solve and establish patterns of learning which will extend beyond education.

Higher Education is therefore concerned with shaping cognitive abilities both in terms of knowledge, thinking and learning. Designers are obviously trained to develop and apply different and unique skills – visual and three dimensional rather than verbal and mathematical but these are not the full extent of the uniqueness of designers. What role does Higher Education play in shaping these other 'skills'?

What are Learning Styles?

... a description of the attitudes and behaviours which determine an individual's preferred way of learning. (P. Honey and A. Mumford (1992). *The Manual of Learning Styles.*)

Learning is a very individual process. Personal learning styles obviously have an impact on the ability to succeed in education but they also appear to have an impact on our professional lives too.

Goals and needs will effect individual approaches to learning as does the degree to which we posses appropriate learning skills. However, the extensive research of Honey and Mumford indicates that learning styles have a direct relationship to behaviour outside the learning environment. Our preferred learning styles will reflect our characteristics as employees, employers and outside the world of work. As we are in life, so we will be in learning.

Because learning is so individual, people with particular preferences will learn more from some situations than others.

The person who is inclined towards experimentation may learn little merely from observing others. Another may enjoy hours of assimilating facts and figures or getting to grips with underlying theories while others will need to test ideas in practice before learning takes place.

Why are Learning Styles Important?

Today's highly successful managers are distinguish not so much by any single set of knowledge or skills but by their ability to adapt to and master the changing demands o their job and career, i.e. by their ability to learn. (Kolb, Rubin, McIntyre (1979). *Organizational Psychology.*)

David Kolb's theories about learning will probably be familiar to delegates conference. He believes that learning involves thinking, reasoning and problem and that our approaches to learning are directly as a result of the way that w reason and problem solve. He also believes that learning is not just confi.ae classroom and thinks that the style of learning offers an insight into how ur tackle new situations and improve their effectiveness.

Honey and Mumford describe learning as the most important life skills par a dynamic work culture where change is rapid and unpredictable.

Throughout our working lives we are confronted with the new. It would ble to respond quickly if each new challenge was tackled from scratch. It is ne, ply what we have learnt from our previous experiences.

How are they 'Learnt'?

• culture
• education
• work environment

There are several factors which can encourage the development of partic alar learning preferences.

The culture in which we are bought up has an important impact. Textile designer Charles Grey argues compellingly that the influence of Zen and Buddhism equips the Eastern Asian with a particular approach to life. Zen teaches that to understand anything fully it is necessary to experience it. Contemplation and reflection are encouraged and furthermore Buddhist society has few if any taboos which means that they are invariably open minded and can see things from many perspectives.

There is some evidence to suggest that styles of thinking can be established as more familiar in childhood depending on the balance of 'exercise' to either the right or left side of the brain. In secondary school students will tend to gravitate towards subjects where they use their preferred learning styles and avoid teaching strategies they do not feel comfortable with. This practice continues into higher education and so through the better part of education the students uses repeatedly, limited approaches to thinking and learning and where they have already established a preference for this style, it is rewarded and reinforced.

It is possible to change learning styles to a certain extent. A person moving from a bureaucratic to a more dynamic organization where risk and intense activity are rewarded, will develop tendencies in this direction. It is not possible to change dramatically however, and a change of job is more likely than a complete reversal of style! To this extent organizations can also be said to have a 'learning' style. Change is also possible if we are aware of our preferences and determine to alter our behaviour.

Types of Learning Style

activist	accommodator
reflector	diverter
theorist	assimilator
pragmatist	converger
Honey and Mumford	*Kolb*

The two key research projects which have sought to identify learning style types are represented here. Although different words are used to describe the categories Honey and Mumford and Kolb's meanings are broadly similar. These categories may be familiar to delegates at this conference, but it is worthwhile nevertheless to outline their meanings briefly.

The activist or accommodator enjoys new experiences and experimentation, they tend to be risk-takers and be impatient and pushy. They thrive on being the centre of attention and like to draw on the abilities of others to help solve problems.

Reflectors or diverter can view things from many perspectives and like to think things through carefully before coming to a conclusion – if they ever do! They are often imaginative and emotional but prefer to keep out of the limelight.

Theorists or assimilators will enjoy constructing theoretical models in a logical and serialist manner. It is more important that the theory is sound than that it works in practice.

However pragmatists are much more concerned with how things work in practice. They tend to be down-to-earth types who dislike the abstract and who will act quickly to come to very practical solutions to problems.

It is often true that people will have two quite strongly held preferences, but some people appear to be balanced across the four areas and can therefore learn something from most situations.

The categories identified by Kolb and Honey and Mumford both represent stages in the learning process. Effective learning requires the completion of the whole process. However, learning styles will have strengths and weakness and those with a strong preference representing one part of the cycle may put more emphasis on this stage to the detriment of others, thus distorting the process.

Learning Styles and Jobs

- activist – sales, marketing
- reflector – personnel
- theorist – finance, R&D
- pragmatist – engineering, production

Both Kolb and Honey and Mumford have recognized particular learning styles to be prevalent in certain professions. These are some examples from Honey and Mumford's research.

I think we would all recognize the 'types' identified, although it may surprise you to know that Honey and Mumford have found policemen to be thoughtful and reflective while bank managers are quite strongly practical!

Although there are no right or wrong styles, they assert that an individual with a strong preference in one direction may find it difficult to work with someone who has a different, strongly held preference. Others, like Kirton, believe that different styles of thinking and approach create a necessary balance, particularly in team work. It is important however that individuals understand their own styles and the impact they have on others in order that conflict does not occur.

In the belief that learning styles appear to be a significant factor in the vocational preparation of students, I set out to found out what learning styles design students preferred. The results of the study allow us to understand the impact of teaching strategies within design education and to understand their role in preparing students for work.

The Learning Styles Questionnaire

The Honey and Mumford Learning Styles Questionnaire has been extensively used. It is simple to apply and has been used on sixth Form students, I felt it would therefore be appropriate for students in higher education.

There are existing norms for the population at large and, as seen in the previous slides comparisons for different kinds of profession.

One hundred and forty six second and final year students on seven courses in the Faculty of Design and technology at the University of Central Lancashire completed and returned their questionnaire.

The respondents answered 80 questions based on their behaviour, not in a learning situation, but in everyday life. It was not necessary for students to have any perception themselves of how they learnt. The students analysed and retained their own scores, giving them a little insight into their own learning styles. In general they were interested to find out how they scored agreed with the results.

Where sufficient students from one course returned completed questionnaires it was possible to compare the mean scores with the norm for design students as a whole.

Key Findings

* strong activist preferences
* low theorist and pragmatist preferences
* some differences between design subjects

The results of this survey show significant differences between the norms for design students and those established by Honey and Mumford. The students appear to have a stronger tendency towards activist preferences and lower preferences for theoretical and pragmatic approaches. (see, figure 1 + Table 1 + 2.)

It is not yet known if design students have similar learning styles to designers. However, the characteristics of the activist learner with a low preference for the theoretical and pragmatic reflect quite closely the descriptions of the approaches of designer as identified by walker and others.

The results also confirm the differences between design students and arguably therefore designers, and other organizational functions, notably finance and R&D. There are also marked differences between people in design and marketing. Although Honey and Mumford have found marketing and sales managers, who often work closely with designers, to have strong activist preferences they are also strongly pragmatic which sets them apart from designers.

Cynics might say that these results show design students to be quick to act without thinking of the consequences and slow to arrive at practical solutions. Others might say however that they indicate the positive abilities of designers to be proactive in producing innovative ideas. It could be that an activist approach is necessary to work effectively as a designer. Perhaps there can be no such thing as a theoretically orientated designer.

The Nature of Design Teaching

- emphasizes experimentation
- low on theory
- interaction within the peer group
- many possibly solutions, few conclusions

If we now look at the learning and teaching strategies employed in design education it is easy to see why design students might feel comfortable in this environment.

The atelier or studio system traditionally used to teach design, emphasizes experimentation, an holistic approach to problem-solving and the importance of the approval and interaction with the peer group. All these are characteristics of activist learning. The use of project-based learning reinforces experimentation without the constraints of theory and often practicality too with an emphasis on the process rather than the appropriateness of the final product.

Perhaps the only time design students encounter theoretical and practically orientated learning is in business and contextual studies, now a feature of the majority of design courses in Great Britain. It is little wonder that they do not enjoy and learn as much from this kind of teaching as they do from studio-based learning.

The characteristics of the studio system attempt to mirror the working environment of designers. Similarly, business studies students use learning methodologies which mirror the working practices of managers. It also appears that the teaching strategies applied to design education also require the students to think and problem solve in the same way that designers do!

Questions for Educators

- strengths and weakness of teaching and learning strategies
- harnessing learning styles
- developing balanced learners

An understanding of learning styles, how they are developed and the role they play in the working lives of individuals is a key factor in the way we prepare students for work, this study of learning preferences poses a number of questions for educators.

The study of learning styles can contribute to several debates currently taking place in Higher Education today. In all areas of education in Great Britain, there is a major threat to the unit funding for each. The studio system of teaching design is relatively expensive and it is necessary to know what is critical within the educational experience in order to allocate what funding there is effectively. Despite changes to course curricula in recent years there is still a perceived gap between the skills of graduates and the needs of industry. In order to bridge the divide between the two it may be more important to concentrate on how students think and learn rather than what they know about businesses.

How do we cope with the apparent dilemma that to be a designer (or manager) a certain style of thinking and learning is the norm but this very style may make interaction with colleagues in other functions more difficult? Is there not a good case for encouraging students to become more balanced learners and exhibit or at least be sympathetic to, the characteristics of others. In the case of designers, it is undoubtedly important that they produce innovative ideas but it must be possibly in an industrial context, to turn these ideas into practical solutions. Students may acquire this skill if the teaching strategies they encounter are more pragmatically orientated.

It would be possible to alter the balance of students' learning and problem-solving styles by introducing a variety of teaching and assessment strategies which stress particular styles and stages of the learning cyclen (see figure 2). In this way students will have the opportunity to practise their reflective and theoretical skills and even to learn techniques to assist learning in these areas. It is interesting to note that Honey and Mumford believe that teaching strategies are chosen to suit the teachers styles rather than the learner. If this is the case, there are considerable staff development implications to the introduction of a wider range of teaching strategies.

Finally, educators need to understand how to harness learning styles to achieve effective learning across the curriculum. Design students apparently learn most and best in the studio environment. Should we not then be teaching business studies – traditionally an unpopular subject – within this environment? It is certainly necessary for students to understand their own learning preferences in order that they can take full advantages of their time at university and can understand their impact on others both in this environment and at work.

This research has shown that thinking and learning styles have a strong and enduring influence on the individual, and have as much impact on professional abilities as what we know or can do. It is possible that here lies the key to the differences and conflicts between designers and others and to the further development of design education.

Above all what seems to be important for education in general is a varied diet of teaching and learning strategies, providing an opportunity for students to acquire skills in all stages of the learning process. In this way we will be more likely to produce balanced lifelong learners.

Analysis of Results of Questionnaire

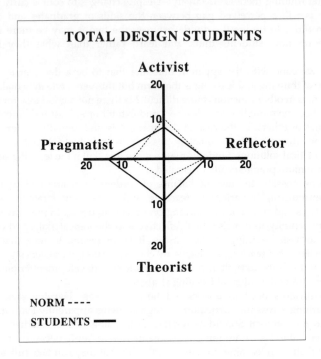

Figure 1 Total design students

The results of the questionnaire analysis were plotted on the arms of an axis
The solid line indicates the Honey and Mumford's mean scores based on a population of 3500 respondents. They have found over many years of applying this questionnaire that the profile remains remarkably accurate.
The dashed lines shows the profile of the mean scores based on the 146 design students questioned.
The key differences are the stronger activist tendencies and the relatively low pragmatist and theorist scores. The average activist score for the students was 11.17 while the Honey and Mumford's norm is 9.3. Their norm for pragmatist preferences is 13.7 while the design students scored 9.80.
The scores for theorist preferences were 8.18 for the design students and 12.5 for Honey and Mumford's norm.
The students' reflector preferences score was the close to the norm of 13.6.

Table 1 Distribution of activist preferences (total students)

	Very strong	*Strong*	*Moderate*	*Low*	*Very low*
Students	38%	21%	27%	13%	6%
Norm	10%	20%	40%	20%	10%

This is confirmed when we look at the distribution of responses within activist preferences (Table 1). 59% of design students had strong or very strong activist learning preferences, against Honey and Mumford's norm of 30%.

Table 2 Distribution of pragmatist preferences (total students)

	Very strong	*Strong*	*Moderate*	*Low*	*Very low*
Students	3%	8%	18%	29%	41%
Norm	10%	20%	40%	20%	10%

The distribution within pragmatist preferences indicates that 70% of students have low to very low preferences in this area whilst the norm is 30% (Table 2).

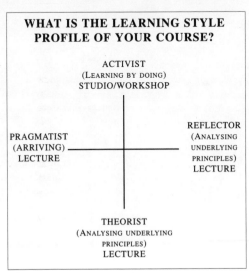

WHAT IS THE LEARNING STYLE PROFILE OF YOUR COURSE?

ACTIVIST
(LEARNING BY DOING)
STUDIO/WORKSHOP

REFLECTOR
(ANALYSING UNDERLYING PRINCIPLES)
LECTURE

PRAGMATIST
(ARRIVING)
LECTURE

THEORIST
(ANALYSING UNDERLYING PRINCIPLES)
LECTURE

Figure 2 Course Learning Style Profile.

Figure 2 has teaching methods against each of the learning styles. These are suggested and not definitive, and teachers may wish to define each of the teaching methods used on their course under one of the four learning style categories.

The purpose of the axis is to allow teachers to plot the time students need to spend using learning styles in each of the four areas. This profile might be then compared with a learning styles profile of the students. The profile might suggest that there is an imbalance of styles represented on the course.

32   The impact of knowledge about aspects of personal learning style on team effectiveness.

Pauline Hunt and Liz Beaty (University of Brighton)

Introduction.

There are a great many different descriptions of individual learning styles, (Mumford, 1986) and individual style of working within groups (Belbin, 1981). These descriptions are seen primarily as traits of the individual where their particular style will influence their approach to group tasks. Other descriptions refer more to an intentional aspect of study such as Orientation (Beaty, 1983) which is more context-dependent and implies some control by the learner. These differences are also shown to influence the outcome of learning.

This study is concerned with how awareness of these learning constructs impact on teamwork. Firstly, we wanted to test whether an awareness of learning constructs improved teamworking. Secondly, we were interested to discover how far raising students awareness of their own orientations and styles, as identified by inventories etc., would influence their learning about teamwork. Thirdly, we wondered which constructs about learning would be most useful to students in understanding teamwork.

The aim of the case study was therefore twofold; to identify how to create favourable conditions for effective working teams and concurrently to identify the impact of raising awareness of learning constructs on learning about teamworking.

Research Approach

Improving student learning in groups is a complex task and one that does not sit easily with the intention to advance our knowledge about how students learn. Advances in knowledge about how students learn must take account of complex contextual issues. Theoretical descriptions of styles of learning do not in themselves imply a use. How does a teacher use a knowledge of learning differences to enable students to learn most effectively? Should we test for learning styles and then offer carefully tailored teaching events to match? Should we only take students who have similar learning styles and approaches to our own or our preferred ones? Should we offer so much choice in our teaching and learning environment so that students can opt for that which is consistent with their style? This last suggestion is getting closer to our position and yet it assumes students are able to make appropriate choices and that we have the resources to make it available.

Raising student's awareness is, in our view, fundamental to enhanced learning. When students are aware of their own tendencies and their preferred approaches; when they are clear about their needs and wishes for learning, they are likely to make better strategic choices within the opportunities that are offered to them (Boud, 1988).

In relation to teamwork, awareness of different styles may be important in learning about how teams work. In addition, learning about their own individual learning through these constructs may enhance their learning about how they individually work within teams. Reflection is an important part of learning from experience (Boud, *et al.*,1985; Warner Weil and McGill, 1989) and awareness is key to this reflection. In addition to awareness raising through reflection on what happened is an awareness based on ideas. This conceptual awareness, we argue, enhances effective reflection leading to learning: we need to reflect on what happened and then be able to thematize what happened with the aid of concepts and models. It is possible for concepts and models of learning to be generated by the group, generalizing from their own learning experience. We believe, however, that conceptual frameworks already existing in the literature are useful as catalysts for effective learning.

We have taken an approach to the case study which could be seen as action research. This approach to educational research has been recommended by Gibbs (1992) and Zuber-Skerritt (1992) as a way of improving teaching while generating knowledge about how students learn. As such it is an approach consistent with our needs to focus primarily on these particular students and their learning while learning from it to enhance and improve our future teaching. The results remain tentative rather than clearly conclusive. This report aims at a rich description which allows understanding of the complex situation. Teachers may learn from it in so far as they can empathize with it. Researchers may learn from it as far as it provides a case study of use of concepts within a particular setting. As usual with research this report will raise more questions than it answers.

Background to the Study

In the construction industry many activities are carried out in project teams. Hence, the MSc course in Construction Management, run at the University of Brighton, actively encourages student group learning and team development.

This chapter examines a group of 16 part-time MSc Construction Management students who currently work full time for the same large construction company. They were commencing their first year of study, on a two-year course. In the first two months of the course they attended two five-day residentials, at a local hotel. The first residential was an introduction to study skills and personal development, and their second was concerned with people management. The case study was carried out by one of us (Pauline Hunt) who is a member of the MSc staff course team.

The aim of this part of the course was to create favourable conditions for effective learning teams, so that they would accomplish far more than the sum of the efforts of individuals. I believed that considerable educational benefit could be derived by deliberately making students aware of their own Belbin preferred team roles, and their Kolb preferred approaches to learning and their Orientation to study. I expected that the students heightened awareness of themselves and others would lead to more effective support of one another and create more efficient team process working.

The First Residential

During the first residential I welcomed the students onto the course and ran an informal workshop on student learning expectations. This workshop gave the students an opportunity to discuss with one another the reasons why they had chosen to study for the MSc in Construction Management, and the various hopes they had concerning what they each wanted to get out of the course. During this workshop Beaty's orientation typology (1983) was completed by each student. The results of this typology were not made known to the students at this stage.

During a later seminar session with the students I discussed the various approaches to learning that students could adopt. I asked them to complete a Kolb's learning style inventory (1984). After they had completed the inventory we discussed their results and what implications these may have on their approaches to learning and studying. The students seemed to enjoy discovering what their preferred learning style was and comparing it to their colleagues. It emerged that some of the participants had completed a Kolb's inventory before, on an in-house course, but on that occasion they had not been informed about what each style meant! They had merely been given the label without any discussion about the significance. Those participants were particularly interested to see any shifts in their learning style.

A training manager from the company joined the course team on the third day of the residential. He was writing a PhD on 'Effective Teams in the Construction Industry', and was therefore very keen to lead a seminar and workshop on team-building skills. He encouraged the students to participate in brainstorming sessions to discover what they thought a group and a team was. They were then asked to discuss the differences between groups and teams, and to debate, with reference to their own work experience, what they considered was an effective team. This session worked well, as these students really appreciated the opportunity to participate fully, and in some ways 'drive' the workshop session.

After lunch, we shared the seminar session, which aimed to develop the students' awareness of themselves as team players and also to develop their awareness of others within the team. The seminar focused on team processes and development. After these discussions, students were asked to complete Belbin's self- awareness inventory (1981) to discover their preferred team roles.

The students spent some time analysing the results of their own Belbin preferred team role. Some students seemed to take on board their type description wholeheartedly, others seemed to doubt the reliability of the inventory, and a few seemed disappointed, and would rather have been identified as another type. An example of this was where one student was classified as a Teamworker, but really she wanted to be a Chair, this desired type was her lowest score! This is an interesting phenomenon. It suggests another dimension along which learners can be affected by a raised awareness of concepts about learning.

The students were then asked to arrange themselves into three groups for a fairly simple negotiation exercise. Interestingly, they choose to group themselves according to their Belbin types. Despite a few cynics, the students in general seemed to accept that teams with a balanced diversity of Belbin types would be more effective.

The First Team Exercise.

A fairly straightforward negotiation exercise was distributed to the three student groups. Each group was instructed to have an observer to record the team's process of working on this exercise. They were given one hour and a half to work together, before the full class re-assembled to hear the individual groups comment on their progress, and their observers comments.

The observers' comments on the group processes were quite enlightening. For example, Group 1's observer commented that the whole group was a good mix of people with no one dominant personality. He stressed that everyone chipped in and that they were all very conscious of process and behaviour. The group members commented that the Belbin types were useful for discussion, to get to know team members' strengths and weaknesses. This information was used actively in the negotiation exercise, when one opposing team member addressed a group one member and said 'What's your offer?' This question was posed very early on in the negotiation exercise, and when the group discovered that the questioner was a Shaper, the group then decided to take a recess and discuss 'What's really the question?'

Group 2's observer commented that the group deliberately considered who was best suited for the negotiation roles. They decided that the Chair should adopt a listener, questioner, non-aggressive role, and the rest of the team should be more aggressive. The team members thought that it was a useful exercise to look at styles, because they then had the benefit of choosing the right person for the lead and for summarizing and for closing the deal at each stage of the negotiation process.

They concluded that knowing your own role is important – but knowing who you are negotiating with is even more important: if you know your adversary you can match the best person to meet and negotiate with them. They observed that it is best to select a team member who could respond to the weaknesses of the style of management over the table. For example, 'If you were facing an aggressive shaper, you need to use someone with good listening skills, who is patient and will not short fuse and throw petrol over the situation, but at the same time, still stand their ground' (Group 2 team member)

Group 3's observer remarked on the importance of knowing the person you are working with, and suggested that if the relationship was already good it makes all the difference. The team expressed the view that high performing teams do not happen overnight – Belbin and self-awareness more generally can speed up the learning stage, but high-performing teams need maturity.

This last sentiment is interesting, because as well as improving thinking and learning skills, the course team believed that deliberately making students aware of aspects of their learning, and in particular their Belbin preferred team role, would increase the effectiveness of team development. If we consider the development of the team process as being composed of the stages of: forming, storming, norming and performing, we believed that the teams may be facilitated into the norming stage almost immediately. This has the effect of reducing the sometimes painful storming phase, and shortens the time necessary to get the teams to perform effectively.

In general all the teams reported that the tangible result, i.e. the deal they reached with each other in the final negotiation stage, had been an acceptable one, and the exercise was seen to have been a useful learning experience.

The Second Team Exercise

In the second residential concerning people management, the course team wanted to develop further effective student team working. A rather complex strategic management brief, relating to a large construction company, was distributed to the same three team groupings of students. The students were asked to work together, in their separate teams, during set working periods over three days. Their task was to put together a convincing verbal presentation, to the company's Board of Directors. This presentation was to cover the devising of an appropriate strategic plan for the Directors to consider. All three groups were given identical briefs, and asked not just to concentrate on the project tasks, demanded of the groups, but also to pay attention to the process of team working.

As well as working on the project brief, students were expected to attend some complementary workshops on management theory and team building. During this time they were reminded of their Belbin's preferred team roles, and Kolb's preferred styles of learning. I also asked them all to complete another Beaty's orientation typology. This time I fully discussed what the results of this typology meant, and the students were interested to discover any changes that may have occurred since they last completed the typology, one month previously.

During the time that the three groups were given to work together on their project brief, the course team periodically visited each group. On these facilitating visits, the staff actively encouraged each group to develop their process aims, as distinct from satisfying the brief's content aims. It was noticeable that there was a developing of diverse relationships within every group. Students in all groups tended to be choosing what they wanted out of the learning experience. Some groups were voluntarily putting in a 16-hour working day, often working until after midnight to prepare for the next day.

When asked for assistance by individual groups, I acted as a facilitator, questioning and reflecting back what I observed or heard. I later thought that the students would benefit from actually seeing themselves working together in groups. Following discussions with the students, it was agreed that each group would be videotaped for approximately two hours while working on the brief, and all three final presentations would also be videotaped.

From watching the videotapes and observing groups in action, I could detect that there were critical incidents within each of the groups, which, although they were completely different, seemed to help move the group to the performing stage of their development. For example, Group 1 successfully managed a very aggressive situation, involving two individuals of different workplace rank. Essentially, an aggrieved middle manager was criticizing a senior manager for completely monopolizing the group discussions. This situation was highly emotional, but managed fairly successfully by the group. The group members persuaded the two not to come to physical blows. A lengthy discussion then followed which increased self-awareness and identified new choices of behaviour for the group members concerned. This resolution of conflict meant that the group was moved on to the performing stage.

In this critical event, other individuals within the group took responsibility for helping those two dissenting members to adapt in order to successfully execute the set task, i.e. the management project. Despite obvious difficulties the aggrieved member and the senior manager began to attempt to see the situation through each other's eyes, in order to resolve issues and reach a new understanding. A wonderful throwaway line came from one of the members in the group: 'Goodness John, I did not know you were such an Activist.' This incident did, however, enable the group to undertake the project successfully, and incidentally score the highest mark!

The Debrief

A couple of weeks passed before I was able to give students a debriefing session. This was held at the very beginning of their third residential concerning procurement procedures. My input was to provide feedback from my observations of the videotapes taken of each group working together and giving their presentations.

I made it clear from the outset that my own view of what was happening was just that, an interpretation. I informed the students that I was also interested in their own individual perceptions of what it was like working together in a group. In particular, I was interested in whether they believed that my deliberately increasing their awareness of their Belbin team roles, Kolb's preferred learning styles and Beaty's orientation types, had influenced the way they worked together on the management brief.

Following my very general feedback, I asked the group members to complete individually a detailed questionnaire (see Appendix 2). This questionnaire asked students to comment upon the degree of impact/influence they thought their awareness of each individual learning construct had over their group process.

The groups seemed energized by my feedback and were keen to complete the questionnaire, which formed the basis for subsequent discussions. The responses to the questionnaire questions were very diverse. For example, a member from Group 3 commenting on his awareness of his learning style, stated:

'I do not think I have worked as I should have done, mainly because I had trouble motivating myself during the session. I believe that later on my style was reflected.'

This answer clearly demonstrates the importance of other influences on the learning process, notably lack of motivation. On the other hand, in the same group an individual comments, 'I am a theorist and made a point of studying the text we had to work with – I knew I had to be the role of reader.'

The subsequent discussion with Group 3 revealed far more about the group process. It reinforced my impression that the learning process is also shaped by an array of emotional processes, including anger, frustration, impatience, confusion, anxiety and occasional satisfaction!

One individual from Group 3 actively took advantage of the debrief session, to speak about his discomfort with the relationship he had with the other individuals in this group. He was very aggressive towards the group members, suggesting that he was made to feel isolated because he was the only 'personal intrinsic' member in the group. In his opinion the other group members orientation – all being 'vocationally extrinsic' – was the major reason why he was prevented from being able to make a successful contribution to the group process. His general remark on his questionnaire read: 'You have observed aggression in the debrief as I have particularly tried to illustrate it.'

The individuals he was criticizing responded to his attack and were clearly quite upset that they had ignored his frustration and annoyance with them throughout the management exercise. They all expressed regret at not listening or paying attention to his contributions, and felt that they had probably all missed out as a group for not doing so. One of these members added that it was only now, at this debrief, that he felt 'real learning' had taken place. The aggrieved member later privately requested to the course team, never to be placed in this grouping again. He added that he felt more at peace following the debrief, and stated that he felt that this was his most powerful learning experience on the course so far.

However, I am clear that some individuals did leave the debrief session with some unresolved issues. For example, in Group 1, a member stated that the debrief session 'made me realise I can be pushy and susceptible to criticism, I did not like it. I always thought I was easy-going, which I suppose I am not. Does that mean I am an actor?'

More positively, a contradiction for another member in Group 1 was resolved. Here the group member was wrongly informed by another (on video!), 'You should be acting like a Plant!' When his Belbin type was actually a Shaper/Chair! This contradiction was evident by his responses on his questionnaire, for example 'I tried to behave as a "Plant" but found it very difficult to restrain myself from being more assertive in my contribution', and again he wrote, 'As a Plant – I think I was restrained forcibly.'

His confusion was lifted when I explained the misunderstanding, and he was able to justify his feelings of frustration and conflict.

In Group 2, there was general dissatisfaction that the group did not score high marks on the presentation. It was revealed by the group members that they had been acting to safeguard members in their group from failing the residential assessment. The situation was that there were three members of that group that had not delivered presentations successfully, and needed to do so if they were to be allowed to remain on the course. As one member responded on his questionnaire, 'all our self-awareness concerning team roles and learning styles went out of the window . . . the over-riding factor was of ensuring three team members were helped to make presentations', and another statement from another group member stated that – for the betterment of the team – 'I decided to withdraw and let others (the three concerned) take on tasks that they did not usually get on with.'

When the assessment evaluation placed this team in second place, they felt cheated. Group 2 felt that they should have been the 'favourites' to score the highest marks on the presentation. They had the most senior manager in their group, and had regularly worked until after midnight on their project. It seemed fairly clear that following this debrief they would modify their behaviour in another team setting. However, working through their frustrations, resolved many issues for the members, particularly the guilt felt by the three presenters who felt they owed their 'stay on the course' due to the sacrifice of the other group member's overall marks. A couple of group members stated that this debrief session had made the sacrifice worthwhile, and on reflection felt that they had gained the most insights into their group processes at this debriefing session. The three presenters offered to buy me a drink!

Discussion

The major observation is that students appear to be able to learn from reviewing and reflecting on their own experiences, particularly through the relative safety of a debriefing session. The MSc students were invited to reflect on their team working experience, prompted by my evaluation of the team work recorded on video. This session encouraged discussion and the completion of a questionnaire, where groups relived parts of their experience in a private supportive environment.

Most students seemed fairly at ease, giving and receiving feedback in an informal discussion setting. It was here where all of them felt they had benefited the most from the group exercises. It was recognized that just to experience team working was not enough, the students were so deeply involved in the experience itself that they were unable to step back and reflect upon what they were doing. The debriefing session gave them the opportunity to do just that. It addressed the fundamental questions of – what happened? How did you feel? How important was your awareness of your learning style etc. In particular the discussion revolved around the 'there and then' and I feel seemed far less risky to the students than would have been the case, if the discussion was focused on the 'here and now'.

The debriefing session seemed more powerful because I was reflecting back from a position of involvement, I felt part of the discovery process. I was not commenting from a position of detachment, or speaking with 'expert judgement'. It seemed very important to allow time for students to be able to integrate their learning experiences. The feedback I was offering was in the service of the learner, each student felt able to accept or reject the information, and this became the basis for subsequent discussion, which was felt to be fruitful for all concerned.

However, within the feedback session, it became apparent that individual group members had differing perceptions of events, particularly over causes of conflict and progress within the group working experience. It is worth remembering that facilitator and student accounts of what happened are only perceptions of reality, and these have obviously strong subjective dimensions.

Many students were unsure about whether my deliberate attempts to increase their awareness of different aspects of their learning, actually influenced their behaviour or group process, although most stated that the preferred Belbin team role was the most important influence on their group role/behaviour. However, by discussing the outcomes of process, the awareness of different aspects of their learning actually served to engage the students in the process of analysing and evaluating their individual and group learning processes. Many claimed to be thinking about how they learn, in the debriefing session, for the first time in their lives!! My role was therefore transformed into helping students make sense out of their learning experiences.

This case study proved to be a process of experiential learning for me as well as for the students. My interaction with the students was fairly intensive and most felt that the powerful learning experience of the debrief occurred because of the interactions between group members and myself. The students commented that during the debrief, they were able to make more sense of the differences in individual perceptions concerning group processes, among group members. The students stated that they felt they had all realized a common understanding of the learning process, and this was the main source of satisfaction for them all.

Conclusion.

It is inappropriate to suggest prescriptive generalizations from a specific case study experience. However, we feel able to offer a set of suggestions for how to improve student learning awareness about process. They are:

1 It is important to use the constructs in forming groups. It would not be sufficient just to inform participants of the information, they need to be able to see it in action. This is probably why most students reported that the Belbin preferred team role had the most influence on their behaviour.

2 It is advisable to use a rich array of learning constructs, as this gives more self-awareness and peer awareness than just using one at a time. The study shows how individuals chose to focus on one construct rather than another, and this may change over time. Facilitators should impart information in the service of learners, it is then up to them whether they believe, or use it. An array of constructs provides the information that can enhance the learning experience.

3 Feedback from facilitators, and observers in groups, during the group work tasks, seems to be very important. This needs to be given sufficient time slots in the course programme for students. It can become the focus for discussion, and may serve to legitimise group participants own observations in a relatively 'safe environment'. In this case study it promoted healthy debate and discussion among students.

4 An appropriately timed debrief session is an essential learning experience for all participants. It is important for a debrief session to be divorced from the task. It is also useful to debrief students after any assessment has taken place.

Once an assessment has taken place (in this case the residential assessment had already been completed, some two weeks earlier) participants are able to speak more freely, as they feel they have less to lose. Also, by allowing some time to pass before the debrief session, it seems safer for the participants to discuss the 'there and then', and how they may do things differently in the 'here and now'! It also serves to heighten the students' critical awareness and judgement.

The fundamental conclusion about the debrief session is that this session gives the students the opportunity to reflect, discuss and write about their learning experience and, arguably, this is where real learning occurs. Students are able to relive the experience and form their own individual and group understanding that is personal and relevant.

Suggestions 3 and 4 really hinge on the ability of the facilitator to identify and develop the necessary interventions to help individuals learn and change. Facilitators need to have the necessary temperament and intuition to apply feedback and debriefing sessions successfully, and at appropriate times. These sessions may generate controversy, and/or uncertainty, so it is essential that the facilitator plans carefully the nature and frequency of interventions in the learning process.

Research Conclusions

The case study was carried out with the aim of deliberately increasing the awareness of aspects of student learning. The question underlying the case study was asking which aspect would be more useful for the students to learn and understand about group processes. This case study has demonstrated that this is the wrong question to ask. It is not so much the information you make available to the student to increase their awareness, but what they choose to use. Individuals differ as to what they find useful. It is the reflection time and the debrief where many students realize, sometimes for the first time, that they have gained significantly out of being aware of their individual learning constructs and participating in the group exercises. This is because they are using their learning processes as the focus of reflection and critical debate. This is the point at which the students move beyond reflection on what happened to reflection about what it signified; a thematic learning outcome. This could be seen as a 'deep approach' to reflection in Marton and Säljö's terms (1984).

Important research questions are raised by this case study, which merit further investigation. For example, arising from the use of the learning constructs: what is the importance of student acceptance, rejection (or disappointment) of the categories in which they find themselves? In essence, does it matter whether the results of the instruments are accurate? A further concern may be whether the student by continually reflecting on say, the Belbin team role construct, ends up fulfilling the expectations of this team role? If there is a danger of a 'self-fulfilling prophecy', how can we use the learning constructs to mitigate against this occurrence happening? Finally, how far do already existing conceptual frameworks enhance learning from reflection, more than self-generated ones?

We are left with further questions about the nature of the link between experiential learning, reflection and knowledge about learning. In particular, this case study (in its current stage) cannot answer the question about the longevity or transferability of the students' learning. The students worked very intensively throughout the residentials. Our concern is whether the speed at which their learning takes place lessens its potential lasting effect. In addition, the artificial conditions present in the residential environment raise doubts about whether the students will be able to transfer their learning to their workplace.

It would be interesting to follow the individuals and the group into further activities involving teams to find out more about what they have learnt about teamwork, about themselves as learners and about themselves within teams and how this affects their development of skill within teams. It would also be interesting to examine whether the students feel that they have been able to use their learning in their day-to-day working environment.

References

Beaty, E. (1983). Orientations to Study. Unpublished PhD thesis, University of Surrey.

Belbin, M. (1981). *Management Teams: Why They Succeed or Fail.* Heinemann.

Boud, D. (ed.)(1988). *Developing Student Autonomy in Learning.* Kogan Page.

Boud, D., Keogh, R. and Walker, D. (eds)(1985). *Reflection: Turning Experience into Learning,* Kogan Page.

Bligh, D. (ed.)(1986). *Teach Thinking by Discussion.* SRHE and NFER, Nelson.

Clark, N. (1991). *Managing Personal Learning and Change.* McGraw-Hill.

Gibbs, G. (1992). *Improving the Quality of Student Learning.* TES.

Jacques, D. (1984). *Learning in Groups.* Croom Helm.

Kolb, D. (1984). *Experiential Learning.* Englewood Cliffs, NJ, Prentice Hall.

Marton, F. and Säljö, R. (1984). Approaches to Learning. In Marton, F., Hounsell, D., and Entwistle, N. (eds) *The Experience of Learning.* Scottish Academic Press.

Morgan, A. (1993). *Improving your Students' Learning, Reflections of the Experience of Study.* Kogan Page.

Mumford, A. (ed.)(1986). *Handbook of Management Development.* Gower.

Warner Weil, S. and McGill, I. (ed.)(1989). *Making Sense of Experiential Learning; Diversity in Theory and Practice.* SRHE and OUP.

Zuber-Skerritt, O. (1992). *Action Research in Higher Education – Examples and Reflections.* Kogan Page.

APPENDICES

APPENDIX 1

STUDENT ORIENTATIONS QUESTIONNAIRE

Please allocate a TOTAL of 10 points across the Aims displayed in the table below.

STUDENT ORIENTATIONS EXPLANATORY TABLE

Aims	Concerns
Training	Relevance of course to future career
Qualification	Recognition of worth of qualification
Following intellectual interest	Room to choose stimulating lectures
Educational progression	Grades, academic progress
Broadening or self-improvement	Challenge, interesting material
Compensation or proof of capability	Passing course, feedback
Having a good time	Facilities for sport and social activities

This table represents a very simplified version of the categorisation of orientational types which was originally developed from a longitudinal interview study over three years. The most reliable to gain an understanding of a students orientation is, in our view through an in-depth individual interview. In this case however a number of different ideas were being used with students to raise their awareness of aspects of their learning. This version of the description of types of orientations was therefore developed for this particular context.

While orientation types themselves may seem fairly obvious, the distinction between intrinsic interest and extrinsic interest variants of the orientation is crucial. This distinction refers to whether the course content is directly involved in the students gaining what they want from study or not. So that for students who are vocationally orientated some are interested in the content of the course (intrinsic interest) while others mainly interested in the outcome qualification (extrinsic interest). In this latter case their interest in the content is spurious or coincidental. The difference between intrinsic and extrinsic interest therefore greatly affects their wish to engage with the subjects of study and alters the nature of their concerns in giving feedback on their experience of learning.

Orientation	Interest	Aim	Concerns
Vocational	Intrinsic	Training	Relevance of course to future career
	Extrinsic	Qualification	Recognition of worth of qualification
Academic	Intrinsic	Following	Room to choose intellectual interest stimulating lectures
	Extrinsic	Educational	Grades, academic progression progress
Personal	Intrinsic	Broadening or self-improvement	Challenge, interesting material
	Extrinsic	Compensation or proof of capability	Passing course, feedback
Social	Extrinsic	Having a good time	Facilities for sport and social activities

APPENDIX 2

INDIVIDUAL FEEDBACK QUESTIONNAIRE

Name: ....

Learning Style: ....

Belbin: ....

Orientation: ....

Please answer the questions below relating to the Group project experience, try to answer each question as fully as possible:

1. General Introductory Question

    Reflecting back on Group xxx group process; what impact/influence do you think the seminars concerning effective groups and teams had upon Group xxx decision-making processes?

2. Learning Style Question

    What effect do you think that your awareness of your own learning style affected the way in which YOU worked in the group?

3. Learning Style Question

    What effect do you think that your awareness of your own learning style affected the working of the group as a whole?

4.   Belbin Group Role Question

Reflecting on the group processes again, what effect do you think that your awareness of your Belbin team type role affected the way YOU worked in the Group?

5.   Belbin Group Role Question

What effect do you think that your awareness of your Belbin team type role affected the working of the group as a whole?

6.   Student Orientations Question

On reflection, what impact did the knowledge of your own learning orientation have on the way YOU worked in the group?

7.   Student Orientation Question

What impact did the knowledge of your own learning orientation affect the working of the group as a whole?

8.   Priority Question

Out of the three aspects of learning you are aware of - Learning Style, Belbin Team

Type Role and Learning Orientations - which do you think had the most impact on the group process?

9.   Evaluation Question

Did these three aspects of learning - Learning Style, Belbin Team Type Role and Learning Orientation - reinforce one another, or were there contradictions?

Was your learning style interfering with the team role prescribed by the Belbin test?

Was your learning orientation at odds with your Belbin team role?

Please write any other comments about your group working experience which you consider to be important.

33

Enhancing lecturer involvement in their students' learning skills development

Roger Catchpole (University of Plymouth) and David Acres (College of St. Mark and St. John)

Introduction

This chapter is based on a workshop run at the symposium by David Acres (College of St Mark and St John, Plymouth) and Roger Catchpole (University of Plymouth). The aims of the workshop were to give a progress report on the development of an Action Booklet for lecturers and to involve participants in the evaluation of this development.

Background

Our experience as learning skills counsellors / advisers has led us to see that good learning skills provision can help students become more effective as learners. In these roles, though, we are often helping individual students who come to us with learning skills problems. We also both run learning skills workshops for groups of students. While these may meet some generic learning skill needs they are bolt-on and are difficult to relate to the students' real learning context. While we try to 'infect' course staff by involving them in discussion of student need and in the planning process, it seems that little transfer takes place from this process into the teaching and learning provision. Awareness raising is probably the only certain outcome.

In addition, we have shared our experience and expertise to produce a range of learning skills support materials using a range of media. We have completed a new set of learning skills leaflets which are made available to students through induction programmes, course handbooks and libraries. As students and colleagues have been involved in their development, we hope they do meet user needs. Again, though, they are generic and students are left to apply the techniques, methods and approaches to the real world of their studies.

We became aware that the impact of the range of provision described above has been limited. The main cause for this is in our view the lack of integration into course provision. The closest to integration has been when tutors have used learning skills materials with their groups and when one faculty not only targeted learning skills as a part of its induction provision but also started to build both generic and course specific learning skills development into their course programmes. One of us worked with a lecturer as he attempted to follow up an induction session on effective note making by setting tasks requiring application of Mind Mapping (Buzan, 1987) techniques and enabling his students to share their mind maps and their ideas for improvements and application.

Lecturers and tutors have many materials which exhort them to introduce new teaching and learning methodology to help their students become more effective as learners ('500 ways to . . .'). We and other staff development colleagues promote the use of these materials but wonder how many lecturers find it easy to pick out an idea, try it out, evaluate its effectiveness and if of value build it in to their teaching and learning practice. If this is happening around our institutions, then it is probably true that the stories of these developmental experiences are not recorded and shared.

Development of an Action Booklet

Reflecting together on the various elements of the scenario above, we decided that there was a need for a tool which would combine a range of the most practical ideas for lecturers and tutors to try out, references to learning skills materials for students and staff to use and a mechanism for supporting them in their efforts to develop learning skills in their teaching / students.

At the outset of our work to develop such a tool we fell into the trap of making yet another list for lecturers / tutors to try out. Perhaps this was an inevitable first step. This list did include ideas which colleagues felt would be valuable for most students. The second step involved our realization that many colleagues would not need just ideas but also an aid which would help them in their efforts to apply one of the ideas through their teaching. They would also probably benefit from sharing their experience with colleagues attempting similar innovatory work. Our response to these reflections was the **action booklet** concept – to produce a booklet which included not only lists of good, practical ideas but also encouraged recording of the story of what happened when the idea was tried out, a story which could then possibly be shared with others going through the same process to provide a collective story of the experiences. We could now see three possible levels for the use of our Action Booklet. This is how these levels are described in the latest version.

Using this Action Booklet

You can use this Action Booklet at three different levels:

- Level 1
  As a source of ideas. A wide range of ideas are included. Try out one or more which you feel might help meet the needs of you teaching and learning situation. You need go no further then that.
- Level 2
  You may find that it would be helpful to you, as you try out a particular idea, to jot down notes which will act as a record of how things develop. At the back of the booklet you will find blanks which you can use for this purpose. Other pages give you examples of how two colleagues made use of two of the ideas and how they used a sheet for recording. The particular examples are written to explain to others the process that occurred: you may prefer to use these sheets, once duplicated, simple to record jottings – notes to yourself. As a guideline the sort of things you might want to record are listed at the top of each blank. The notes you write are first and foremost to facilitate reflection and to aid the development of the process.

- Level Three
  At a certain point you may have a sheet of jottings which record developments you feel would be worth sharing with colleagues. At this point we hope that you would be prepared to photocopy the particular sheet and send it to either David Acres or Roger Catchpole. We will build a collection of these contributions and, when we have enough, come back to the contributors to discuss how we could share the material more widely with colleagues.

This version is now 25 pages long. After an introduction explaining the reasons for an Action Booklet and a section explaining the three levels for use, it presents 27 ideas grouped into three areas: 'Ideas for Group Tutorials', 'Ideas for Lecturers', 'Ideas for a Course Team/Course Colleagues'.

An example of an idea in the Lectures section:

- Give students time to compare the notes they are taking and to exchange ideas about the effectiveness of the techniques an approaches they are using. They could report back to you and to the group as a whole, highlighting positive aspects and problem they are still facing.

An example from Group Tutorials is:

- Case studies. Use case studies to stimulate discussion on issues such as time management and organization. This will be particularly valuable in early tutorials when a group are probably not so forthcoming with their views or with sharing experiences.

At the back of the Action Booklet there are lists of resource materials for lecturers/tutors and for students to use (see Appendix 1 for an abbreviated version). The description of Level 2 above refers the user to blanks at the back which they can use to keep jottings recording the story of the implementations of the idea with the students (see Appendix 2). The user can refer to four examples of how the story could be recorded.

The Workshop

The Action Booklet has evolved to its fifth version through a continuous process of peer evaluation. Our symposium workshop enabled us to get evaluative feedback from the participants, colleagues from 17 other institutions. After a brief introduction from us we asked them to imagine that they were picking the booklet up for the first time (each had a copy) and were considering using it. We asked them to record their initial impressions putting positive comments, ideas for improvements and their concerns/negative comments on separate post-its. At the end of the session they pinned these on a separate sheet for each type of response. The level and amount of comment was amazing. In all, we were given 32 separate comments. An example of the 12 positive comments was,

> This booklet is the equivalent of jump-leads or a kick-start! Anyone wary of 'new' approaches will find it reassuring, jargon-free and genuinely facilitating of reflection on practice. As someone who uses these sorts of methods more or less routinely, I especially

found the levels 2 and 3 interesting and potentially enriching. It is good not to have **too many** ideas on methods and I liked the fact that you kept this part at the minimum necessary to stimulate change.

One of the 13 ideas for improvement was:

Include common pitfalls/constructive advice associated with your suggested approaches. Handy hints e.g. size of group suited for/not.

A concern was:

Currently reinforces a particular approach to curriculum delivery, i.e. lectures and tutorials – this bothers me.

All of the comments both positive and negative will be taken into account when we produce Version 6. We are most grateful to our 17 workshop participants for giving so much in such a short time. Several have asked that we keep them up to date with further developments. We will do that and will value feedback from any institution which uses the booklet.

Plans for the Future

We now have colleagues in our two institutions using Version 5. We aim to come together as a group, two or three times a year. We will be able to share the stories that are emerging as members of the group work with their students and colleagues to improve basic learning skills. Our role will be that of editors rather than authors and from now on we will have collective ownership of the process. We can continue to develop our Action Booklet and we can maybe publish a selection of the 'Action Stories', sharing them with a wider audience.

Appendix I:

Resource materials specifically for lecturers and tutors

Allen, A. (1992). *Open Teaching Toolkit: Writing Skills*. Milton Keynes: Open University.

Bournes, T. and Barlow, J. (1991). *The Student Induction Handbook*. London: Kogan Page.

Brandes, D. and Ginnis, P. (1986). *A Guide to Student-Centred Learning*. Hemel Hempstead: Simon & Schuster Education.

Cole, S. (1992). *Open Teaching Toolkit: Revision and Examinations*. Milton Keynes: Open University.

Cox, B. (1994). *Practical Pointers for University Teachers*. London: Kogan Page.

Evans, P. and Deehan, G. (1988). *The Keys to Creativity: Unlocking the Secrets of the Creative Mind*. London: Grafton books.

Gibbs, G. (1981). *Teaching Students to Learn: A Student Centred Approach*. Milton Keynes: Open University Press.

Gibbs, G. Habeshaw, S. and Habeshaw, T. (1984). *53 Interesting Things to Do in Your Lectures*. Bristol: Technical and Educational Services.

NB: All the 53 Interesting Ways to Teach series offer particular useful ideas relevant to the aims of this Action Booklet.

Resources for students materials

BOOKS

Acres, D. (1987). *How to Survive at College*. How To Books. A comprehensive guide to all aspects of coping with life in higher education.

Acres,D. (1994). *How to Pass Exams Without Anxiety*. How To Books. 3rd edition, Plymouth.

Ashman, S. and George, A. (1982). *Study and Learn*. London. Heinemann. A recommended study guide.

Bourner, T. and Race, P. (1990). *How to Win as a Part-Time Student*. Kogan Page. For those tackling study in what can be a very difficult way, a helpful book to guide you through.

Buzan, Tony (1987). *Use Your Head*. London. BBC Publications, Chapter by chapter of different memory approaches for different situations. Comprehensive and,generally, comprehensible.

Audio/video tapes and further help

Acres, David. David Acres answers your questions about 'How to Pass Exams Without Anxiety'. Audio Tapes and Guidance available from Marjon Learning Support, College of St Mark & St John, Derriford Road, Plymouth PL6 8BH.

Buzan, T. (1993). *Get Ahead: A Short Cut to Straight As*. Video and notes available from: Buzan Centres Ltd, Suites 2/3, Cardigan House, 37 Waterloo Road, Winton, Bournemouth, Dorset BH9 1BD.

Appendix 2:

A Record Sheet for Your Use

Name:	The idea you are working on:
Dept:	The setting (eg, in lectures):

Records you might want to make:

What are your/your students' needs?
What are your intentions in using the particular idea?
What are you and the students' doing?
What are the steps in the process?
What feedback about the process are you receiving from the students?
What reflections do you have on the process?
Where might this lead?

34   Improving the quality of the student learning experience on a modular semesterized degree programme

Neil Harris (Southampton Institute of Higher Education)

Introduction

This chapter explores attempts to develop effective student thinking and learning in the context of rapid growth at Southampton Institute during the period 1989–94. The transition to a modular semesterized study programme is analysed in terms of its impact on the quality of the student learning experience. The problems of measuring quality are also discussed. European Business is used as a case study of a typical module to evaluate any improvement of student thinking and learning skills against a theoretical model of cognitive learning. A future strategy for modular evolution, based on the Oxford Brookes experience, is suggested.

The Theoretical Basis for an Effective Student Learning Experience

The student learning experience is taken to be the totality of influences to which a student is exposed during the course of his/her programme of study. These occur both inside and outside the classroom. They include directed and independent learning; interaction with staff and fellow students; facilities such as library, IT suites and student union; study groups; student accommodation; sport, social and cultural activities etc. Figure 1 (*overleaf*) illustrates this.

This chapter takes as its theoretical basis the cognitive theories of student learning. These, argue Atkins, Beattie and Dockrell (1993), place the learner at the centre of the learning process, each student bringing to the task 'a unique set of prior experiences, prior knowledge, self and task perceptions . . . and genetically endowed abilities'.

A limited study of the first-year learning experience at Southampton Institute, undertaken by the author, reinforces the wide range of experiences, skills and knowledge that non-18-year-old entrants in particular bring with them. These include:

- spoken and written communication skills;
- team work and social skills from working in an organization;
- IT skills, both keyboard and detailed knowledge of computer packages, most typically word processing and spreadsheets;
- personal organizing skills including time management.

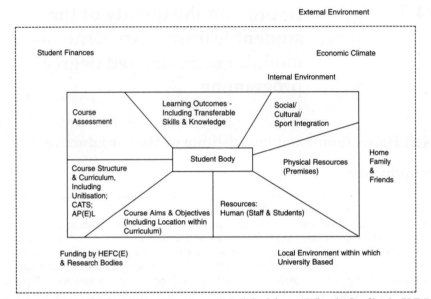

Figure 1. The Student Learning Experience (Modified from "What is Quality in H.E." Diana Green)

Interviewees have stressed that this has helped them significantly to relate learned theory to previous practice. Eighteen-year-old school-leavers cannot bring the same range of prior experiences, knowledge etc., although they do bring theoretical knowledge and some skills acquired in further education. By operating multi-mode courses, and by a deliberate policy of putting school-leavers and older students in the same tutorial groups, the former can share and learn from the experiences of their older peers. Of course mature students also learn from school-leavers.

What neither group brings, in many cases, is effective thinking and learning skills. Although no formal investigation has yet been undertaken at Southampton this has been demonstrated through observation in tutorials/seminars, assessment performance and student responses in end of semester module evaluation sheets.

The cognitive model appears, perhaps, the most realistic and effective to explain the student learning process. It consists of three stages of learning. Students use a selection of their prior experiences, knowledge etc, to relate to and explain new knowledge and stimuli. These in turn are placed in a structured form in long-term memory for future learning. Indeed the progression of intellectual development and abilities as a student moves through the three years of a degree course from knowledge at Level 1 to analysis, synthesis and evaluation at Level 3 (to paraphrase Bloom's taxonomy) would appear, at least partially, to support this.

This is further reinforced by the cognitive model's emphasis on knowledge as a unifying and integrating process which provides a framework, greater than the sum of the parts, on which subsequent learning may be built; a parallel in business theory would be the synergistic gains to two firms resulting from a merger, or to put it simply 2 + 2 = 5. Figure 2 presents the author's diagrammatic representation of the cognitive model of learning.

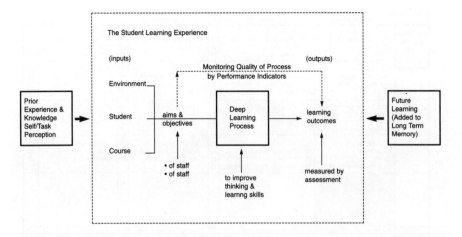

Figure 2 Cognitive Model of Student Learning

Ellis and Young (1988) argue that the areas of knowledge students acquire, and the skills used to process them as learning frameworks, are independent from discipline to discipline. Atkins *et al.* (1993) argue that this casts doubt on the cafeteria or modular type of degree with its unconstrained choice, precisely because the learning framework cannot be transferred from one discipline to another.

At Southampton Institute a modular (or unitized, as it is called) model of constrained choice within named degree routes is employed within the Business School Undergraduate Programme (BSUP), each offering a number of discrete pathways, rather than the unconstrained choice of a fully modular or pick and mix programme. This is one way to circumvent Ellis and Young's criticism since it brings together disciplines which are, at least partially, related by content.

As a case study the Level 2 module European Business is considered to be typical of the BSUP programme. In this chapter it is used to evaluate what is effective student thinking and learning and whether any improvement in these skills has occurred, against rapid background change. European Business is a core module on nearly all named degrees on the BSUP and accounts for one-sixth of the Level 2 programme of study. It has as its pre-requisite Level 1 Business Economics. For the BA (Hons) Business Studies and BA (Hons) Business Administration degrees it draws on the Level 1 modules Law, Accounting, and Organizational Behaviour, and the Level 2 modules Marketing and Work and Employment. It also feeds into Level 3 modules such as the core Strategic Management. The BSUP course structure is shown in Figure 3 (*overleaf*).

Since the Cognitive model identifies student learning as being informed by prior knowledge, experiences, self-perception etc. European Business has a particular advantage over a number of other modules. This applies whether the students are school-leavers or have previous work experience. As well as the knowledge and understanding of Business Economics, students also bring a wide variety of knowledge and experiences of Europe and the European Union, partly derived from holidays and television and

LEVEL	BUSINESS STUDIES		BUSINESS ADMINISTRATION		BUSINESS & LAW		ACCOUNTANCY & LAW	
ONE SEMESTER 1	Business Skills Quantitative Methods Accounting I Law	10 10 20 20	Business Skills Organizational Behaviour Economics Option	10 10 20 20	Business Skills Organizational Behaviour Economics Option	10 10 20 20	Business Skills Organizational Behaviour Economics Accounting I	10 10 20 20
SEMESTER 2	Economics Information Systems I Organizational Behaviour Option	20 10 10 20	Accounting I Information Systems I Quantitative Methods Law	20 10 10 20	Accounting I Information Systems I Quantitative Methods Law	20 10 10 20	Accounting II Information Systems Quantitative Methods Law	20 10 10 20
TWO SEMESTER 1	Work & Employment Financial & Legal Framework Option Business Research & Analysis	20 20 10 10	European Business Marketing Option	20 20 20	European Business Law (Option) Option	20 20 20	European Business Law (Option) Financial Accounting I	20 20 20
SEMESTER 2	European Business Marketing Option Business Systems Modelling	20 20 10 10	Work & Employment Financial & Legal Framework Option Business Systems Modelling	20 20 10 10	Work & Employment Financial & Legal Framework Law (Option)	20 20 20	Management Accounting I Option Law (Option)	20 20 20
	PLACEMENT							
THREE SEMESTER 1	Human Resource Management Project Option	20 20 20	Strategic Management Business Finance Option	20 20 20	Strategic Management Law(Option) Law(Option)	20 20 20	Law (Option) Financial Accounting II Option	20 20 20
SEMESTER 2	Strategic Management Business Finance Option	20 20 20	Human Resource Management Consultancy Assignment Option	20 20 20	Human Resource Management Option Option	20 20 20	Business Finance Law (Option) Option	20 20 20

Figure 2 Business School Degree Programme, Session 1992-93, Degree Course.

partly from contact with the increasing number of foreign students on Institute courses. They will also have knowledge of European businesses from newspapers and television, e.g. the Channel Tunnel, Euro Disney and the recent BMW takeover of Rover. Non-school-leavers may well have had involvement, directly or indirectly, with European businesses.

Entwhistle and Ramsden (1983) and Graham Gibbs (1992), among others, have developed and promoted the concepts of surface and deep learning. Perhaps the most effective identification of deep learning is Gibbs' image of students 'playing' with ideas. This reinforces the cognitive model of learning since the same processes which are undertaken as part of general learning are also those necessary for deep learning – in other words a system of reflection, conceptualization and integration.

Gibbs also argues that inappropriate course design, teaching methods and assessment can foster a surface approach and identifies the characteristics of a module/unit which foster a surface approach. These include 'a heavy workload; relatively high class contact hours; an excessive amount of course material; lack of opportunity to pursue subjects in depth; lack of choice over subjects and over the method of study; and a threatening and anxiety provoking assessment system'.

The European Business unit team has sought to promote deep learning as part of the process of improving student thinking and learning skills and hence enhancing the quality of the learning experience. Its approach is discussed in more detail below.

In summary then effective student thinking and learning has emphasized, through the cognitive model, the importance of relating new learning to previous student experience, knowledge, self-perception etc. This may be achieved by a seminar group, or sub-sets of it, sharing previous experiences and knowledge, as a reinforcement to the learning process. This new learning must be student centred and is likely to be substantially independent of the tutor and classroom. It must progressively develop thinking skills from the acquisition of knowledge to the ability to analyse, synthesize and critically evaluate. Most importantly it must be deep learning in that students create their own body of knowledge from their past and present experiences and learning.

Background Context

Difficulties students experience on modular semesterized degree courses

Semesters were introduced for the BSUP in 1992, and there is an Institute requirement that all courses be semesterized by September 1994. Each semester is currently of 15 weeks' duration, with 12 weeks' class contact and 3 weeks for assessment.

The introduction of modularization has run in parallel with semesterization, the standard model being 3 (or 2 + 2 halves) x 4 hour modules per semester of class contact, with each student being expected in total to undertake 150 hours of work per module (this includes formal class contact, directed and independent learning). For each module the four class contact hours are 1 lecture + 1 structured learning + 2 seminars/tutorials. Directed learning involves the use of Institute facilities, e.g. computers, library etc. in support of class-based work. Independent learning involves work off-site and includes assignment writing, revision etc. Additionally each student is required to undertake 10 hours per week study of a contextual nature.

Ashworth and Harvey (1994) argue that 50per cent – 75per cent of a student's time 'allocated to the promotion of learning is spent working independently of the teacher'. To make this independent learning most effective they argue the need for on-going help for students to develop and employ self-study skills and open access study areas and learning resources. Study skills at Southampton are introduced in the induction programme at the start of Level 1, and further reinforced by the provision of a Study Assistance Base which provides support to students for academic content, study skills and thinking and learning skills. This is of major importance since without the latter the development of deep learning at module level cannot be achieved. However there is certainly scope for further development at both Institute and module levels in terms of thinking and learning and assessment strategies to promote deep learning.

They also argue that a significant benefit of a modular scheme is that students can negotiate their own programmes of study; the modular scheme as employed at Southampton obviously offers reduced choice within that negotiation. Both full and constrained choice models enable students to undertake their programmes of study at their own pace however. Further, a modular programme of study offers 'a multidisciplinary dimension'. In the Southampton model negotiation involves a choice of pathways within named degree routes which has the benefit of promoting student ownership of study programmes. The common Level 1 further permits negotiation by enabling students to switch between routes before Level 2, while Business Studies students unable to secure a placement between Levels 2 and 3, or who wish to progress directly to Level 3, may switch to the Business Administration degree. Additionally a wide range of optional modules are available to students, subject to minimum numbers.

Institute related rapid growth

Tensions have been created by resource constraints due to rapid growth at Southampton Institute, particularly a lack of library space and classrooms for directed group work and independent study/group work. These problems are being alleviated in October 1994 with the completion of a new library extension and the conversion of a former department store in the centre of Southampton to further classrooms, offices etc.

Table 1 puts this growth into context. In particular the changing course portfolio from almost totally part-time professional to full-time degree is of major significance.

Many of the difficulties experienced by both students and staff in the last two years are in fact those identified by Gibbs and Jenkins (1992) in terms of the problems of teaching large numbers. This is a direct consequence of institute related rapid growth and hence government strategy rather than the adoption of semesters and modular programmes of study.

These difficulties include the problems of anonymity and passivity by students, particularly as they feel intimidated by being in groups with people they do not know. This has led to what one colleague has termed 'tutorial group drift' where students move from groups to which they have been assigned to groups where friends are, often without formal approval or notifying staff. This makes student tracking a significant problem with large class numbers. Interestingly where a group of friends rent a house this often tends to be the focal point of any self-study group rather than a tutorial group to which they have been assigned. Again from a staff viewpoint the problems have been those of not knowing the students they teach (or just establishing relationships by the end of the semester) and the stress of work overload.

Table 1: Growth indicators of Southampton Institute, 1989 –94

Growth indicator / Year	1989	1992	1994/95
Number of full-time students	1236	4400	8750
Number of part-time students	3805	3400	2900
Number of academic staff	500	349	405
			(+ 200.P/T)
Number of support/managerial staff	IN TOTAL	508	555
Number of first degrees	5	18	52
Number of higher degrees	0	2	8

Measuring the quality of the learning experience

Southampton Institute has had as its mission statement since its incorporation **Quality Academic Services Accessible to the Local Community**, where by quality is meant 'fitness for purpose'. Accessibility to the education provision of the Institute is particularly targeted at non-standard entrants such as mature students, those from access courses and under-represented ethnic minorities, as opposed to 18-year-olds with A-level points. Additionally the catchment area of Hampshire plays an important role with 52per cent coming from the county for 1993 entry. For students with A levels joining a Business

School degree course 10 points is the typical entry qualification.

In this context the mission statement defines the basis for assessing the quality of the student learning experience which Southampton Institute delivers. 'It is fitness for purpose which we judge and which defines the quality we expect and approve' (Perry, 1994). Emphasis has been placed on value added as a means of assessing the incremental quality of the learning experience. However since the first large cohorts are only now completing their courses then little progress has been made so far to measure the extent of value added between entry and exit. In summary one might take Pauline Perry's argument that 'The real quality of Higher Education must be measured in terms of what students know, understand and can do at the end of their higher education experience' i.e. the quality of the process and of the learning outcomes achieved.

Measurement of the quality of the student learning experience on modular semesterized courses and on individual modules has therefore been difficult at Southampton Institute, partly because there is little to compare against due to the short duration of the Institute's degree programmes. This applies to usual performance indicators such as degree classifications, both in absolute terms and relatively against other institutions, where by performance indicators is meant 'statistics, ratios and other quantitative information which indicate the way in which a programme of study or a college is operating' (Ashworth and Harvey, 1994). On a module basis it is, of course, possible to use performance indicators such as module mean marks and standard deviation as well as mark distribution. These are also analysed across named degree routes.

Course teams append to their annual course reports statistical data which include performance indicators of the quality of the course. These include withdrawals, whether because of failure to meet required academic standards or for more general reasons; awards (degree, HND etc.) and final classification.

Green (1994) has identified many disadvantages of performance indicators of which the most telling is the tendency to measure what is measurable rather than what needs to be measured. The difficulties of measuring the quality of the student learning experience demonstrate this clearly. She also raises an issue addressed by Graham Gibbs and summarised by Claire Sanders in a recent *Times Higher Education Supplement*, namely that performance indicators affect teaching staff behaviour through the pressures, for example, to secure high assessment pass rates. This encourages staff to lower standards to reduce student wastage.

So it might be concluded that performance indicators have limited use in determining the quality of the student learning experience, although they may be better for assessing the quality of teaching. Ashworth and Harvey also warn of the need for caution with the use of performance indicators, arguing validly that they 'should be used not as an end in themselves to draw definitive conclusions but to trigger areas of concern and provide a catalyst for further investigation'.

Quality grade descriptors, as discussed by Ashworth and Harvey, have been used at Southampton both via 'mock' HEFC(E) visits and as part of an Institute-wide classroom observation system which has been implemented this year. These are inevitably subjective but they are the basis of HEFC(E) assessments and so their use can be justified, if only on the grounds of realism.

There is a strong argument for developing exit interviews as a performance indicator of course quality and its impact on students (Lee, 1991); some course leaders do employ this process, with particular emphasis on Level 1 where wastage rates are likely to be higher. Southampton Institute is also establishing an alumni association and, as Lee argues, this forms another useful measure to be used in conjunction with exit interviews.

In addition to quantitative performance indicators other sources of information used by Southampton Institute course and unit leaders to monitor the quality of the learning experience are Institute and module questionnaires, given to all students and covering aspects of each module and course, and of Institute facilities and services. Regular feedback is also obtained through meetings of level tutors and student representatives, and through personal tutorials. The problem with these is that they seek to identify student satisfaction or dissatisfaction with a course or module. This may not necessarily equate with a quality learning experience nor, as part of it, the development of thinking and learning skills.

European Business: testing the Effectiveness of the Theoretical Model to the Learning Processes at Southampton Institute

So far this chapter has sought to explore what constitutes an effective learning experience against a background of very rapid growth of student numbers, and organizational change at Southampton Institute. It has also addressed the problems of measuring the quality of the learning experience both at module and course level. This section explores how, against this change, the European Business module team has sought to provide a quality student learning experience which improves thinking and learning skills and hence permits deep learning. This is tested against the cognitive model of learning.

One of the aims of the European Business module team has been to produce a curriculum which is both structured and coherent since it is important that students can clearly see the path they will follow. This sequencing of the curriculum has been a key feature to enable students to develop logical thinking and learning skills. Within the framework of the cognitive model of learning students are encouraged, during the module delivery, to share and apply their relevant prior experiences and knowledge. This enables them to move, in the module, from a comparative analysis of European economies to the European Union and its impact on business organizations. Then they explore how businesses behave in the European economy using book, video and newspaper based case studies as vehicles for the application of theories of business strategy to practice.

This use of chaining in the curriculum, where later subjects build on former, and where general principles lead to practical applications, has proved to be relatively successful in terms of developing student thinking and learning skills. This is demonstrated both in classes and assessments by student ability to build up knowledge and understanding by drawing on what has been learned previously, and by the ability to apply theory to practice, particularly through case studies. However as Ashworth and Harvey argue the overall most effective sequencing is that which optimizes student motivation, and that is a difficult variable to measure other than by student attendance.

The development of deep learning which integrates previous and new knowledge and enables its addition to long-term memory, to aid future learning, is perceived to be of major importance within the unit. This is because, quite obviously, in students' future careers the impact on them of the EU will be very substantial, starting probably with a single currency and also with many of them working elsewhere in the EU.

A number of key areas within the European Business unit are explored below in the context of this discussion. Specifically these are the learning process, independent learning and assessment. To address the problems of large numbers the teaching team has used a mixture of control and independent strategies. These are discussed in detail by Gibbs and Jenkins (1992) and are also explored more fully below.

The learning process

As noted previously the typical module at Southampton Institute involves 1 Lecture (typically 200 – 275 students) + 1 Structured Learning (40 students) + 2 Seminars / tutorials (20 – 25 students each). Lectures have sought to be interactive with student involvement via a variety of tasks such as mini group discussions, mini case studies and other involvement to develop the ability to analyse and critically evaluate. Students also buy learning packs which provide summary module content and learning tasks to be completed.

The structured learning sessions and seminars are, normally, a mix of control and independent strategies. Independence is emphasized through negotiated student involvement, student running of some classes, preparing material for discussion etc.; other classes are run by the tutor. A control strategy is employed for setting the overarching framework since modules are required currently to employ indicative content.

One example of structured learning sessions which seek to develop thinking and learning skills is the use of the lecture to present a framework of a topic and use of the structured learning to fill in the detail – with student interaction. This is particularly useful in providing exploration of a topic in depth. For example a lecture might consider the Single European Market. Separate structured learning sessions might look at particular examples of this, e.g. the single market for agriculture (the Common Agricultural Policy) and the single market for financial services. As well as prior knowledge, for example, of food mountains and wine lakes students will have been encouraged to undertake prior preliminary reading. To develop independent learning students have various support mechanisms such as tutor accounts on the student computer network and multiple copies of articles for short-term borrowing.

Student led seminars will subsequently reinforce this learning by specific case studies applying the theory to practice e.g. by considering the trans-national merger of two insurance companies as illustration of the single market in financial services. Running the seminar as a board room meeting of one of the companies with parties for and against the takeover enables students to bring in prior knowledge and experience of inter-personal skills and relationships, organizational behaviour, differing legal frameworks, cultural differences etc.

Other examples of the use of a structured learning session include:

1   students organizing a debate;

2   using a workbook/student learning pack to provide exercises – students are split into sub-groups to compete against each other, using a league table;

3   the class is split into groups and one group is seen (say) each three weeks – to provide 'quality time' learning/interaction – with the other students working on material to be developed in their next structured learning slot;

4   bringing in a guest speaker from outside the Institute, who can offer practical experience/knowledge;

5   developing scenarios which syndicates can work on, e.g. entering a European market; the tutor may provide detailed material or students are asked to gather it before tackling the tutor's problems;

6   asking students to summarize the conflicting arguments of two different people on a topic to provoke student involvement.

With seminars there is a tendency again to use a mixed control and independent strategy. One seminar tends to be student group presentations as noted above, with the requirement to produce a short paper for the rest the of group, OHPs, and manage the seminar. Students negotiate/choose their own topics within the constraints of the syllabus. Peer group marking using precise criteria is employed. The other seminar is more tutor led. Seminars and structured learning may both be used to run case studies, either book, video or newspaper based. Negotiation is important particularly when time needs to be freed up for new developments such as an exchange rate crisis.

In all these examples emphasis is placed on developing cumulative learning during the module and enabling students to relate it to the latest material inputted to the module. To encourage deep learning module content has been slimmed down several times over two years to free more time to explore issues in depth, as well as to accommodate the introduction of semesters.

Independent learning

The encouragement of student-centred independent learning is of major importance in developing thinking and learning skills. This is not just because of the diminishing resource base but also because it requires the student to take responsibility for his/her own learning. Since deep learning comes from the student's ability to 'play with ideas,' and since cognitive learning occurs when a student draws on past experiences to explain new knowledge then giving the student responsibility for their own learning, i.e. independence, is crucial for this to take place.

Ashworth and Harvey (1994) argue that, to be effective, independent learning needs 'the effective employment of self study skills by the student' and 'open access study areas and learning resources'. European Business has sought to develop the former, as have other tutors. As noted above open access study areas have been a problem in the past. Regarding learning resources the European Business module team provides support mechanisms which the student may draw on him/herself. These are perceived to give students confidence to take the first steps by themselves, without dependence on staff, and then to continue independent learning. These support mechanisms include:

- the use of a student learning pack with interactive materials;
- provision of comprehensive learning materials on the student computer network, which can be accessed or, until recently, downloaded if required; this has been particularly singled out by students as beneficial to their learning experience;
- key articles and videos on short and very short-term loan from library (the team is also exploring videoing classes for student borrowing) ;

- a Eurostat (European statistical service) database on the student computer network, with a range of facilities which students can use to explore data relationships within and across EU economies.

They also reinforce Institute facilities such as the study assistance base.

Obviously these are important tools for encouraging deep learning since the learning process becomes, to a greater extent, independent of teaching staff. Moreover the student learning pack specifically seeks to reinforce thinking and learning skills which promote analysis, synthesis etc. through the interactive tasks it provides.

Assessment

There is a desire by the module leader to move to continuous assessment but also there is a course obligation to give students a variety of assessment experiences across each level. This has provoked much debate at European Business module team level as to the desirability of formal examinations. A majority view, not shared by the author, is that a main justification for examinations is to ensure that students are assessed on their own efforts, i.e. cheating, which is a quality issue, is minimized. For next session, therefore, assessment will include an end of session examination. (Currently two short examinations have been used, one x 1 hour in week 7 and one x 1 hour in week 15; most students have identified this as a feature of the module which they particularly like.) Additionally students are assessed by the presentation of a paper to their tutorial group and by a 1500 word report/essay. As part of the Business school requirement structured assignment attachment forms are used which do provide valuable individual feedback.

Testing the module

The main performance indicators used by the European Business unit team have been discussed in detail above in the context of the Institute as a whole.

1 Assessment of student performance using criterion referencing is probably the most effective available measure of the quality of student learning although, as Gibbs and Jenkins (1992) have pointed out, students who surface learn can still perform very effectively and indeed may tactically adopt surface strategies depending on the subject being studied. In so far as the module team has sought to develop deep learning marks are as good as some modules' grades and better than many.

2 Module evaluation sheets obviously provide valuable feedback as to student satisfaction or dissatisfaction with the unit or aspects of it. Although there are at times criticisms of operational aspects or institute facilities students say they find the module stimulating and challenging. They also find the support mechanisms to be very useful in their learning. They also single out their ability to take responsibility for a part of their learning as important.

3 Student attendance is a useful measure of motivation although the increasing number of students with part-time jobs reduces the effectiveness of this. Monday mornings at times are not good but otherwise attendance is within acceptable levels and comparable with other modules. It is interesting to observe that in this context

Entwhistle and Ramsden's strategic approach to learning is likely to be even more relevant in the future. Because of significant time constraints through part-time working students will increasingly target only those areas of a module which they really need to study. Rather than reading around a subject study is likely to be focused on the minimum number of areas consistent with successful completion.

4 The quality of the assessments undertaken by students demonstrates to the team that the development of higher order intellectual skills such as analysis, synthesis and critical evaluation are being developed in the context of European Business by most students. What is interesting is that students specifically talk to the module team about the development of these skills and about the learning processes they employ. Discussing this in detail at the beginning of the module is seen to be of significant importance therefore.

5 External examiners' feedback is also perceived to be of importance yet there are criticisms with this model since, as has been noted elsewhere, the external is not fully involved with all aspects of the teaching and learning and assessment processes. Given this qualification the external has expressed satisfaction with the quality of the module and of the learning experience.

6 Testing the module against Gibbs' identification of the characteristics which foster a surface approach European Business compares well. The unit team has sought to pursue topics in depth which has involved progressive reductions of module content over two years. Assessment has not been perceived as threatening due to the establishment of a series of low hurdles rather than one high end of semester barrier. Students also have some ability to negotiate their areas of study and how they pursue them.

The Role of an Adaptive Model to Improve Quality Further

To pursue further how European Business might develop as a module it is necessary to return to a macro analysis of the Institute's development as a whole. This is because of the current constraints within which modules operate.

In many ways Southampton Institute is in the same position along the evolutionary path of developing student thinking and learning strategies that Oxford Brookes was in the mid 1980s. The process of adaption at Southampton has inevitably been accelerated by the very rapid short-term growth and change. Where problems still lie is that the module format developed three years ago for the BSUP needs greater flexibility. The current model of 1 lecture + 1 structured learning + 2 seminars/tutorials was extremely useful in 1991. It provided a framework for the development of the BSUP and a model for development in the rest of the Institute. Indeed courses which are moving from a term based to a unitized/semesterised base this year are largely employing this model (although some have dispensed with the structured learning for another lecture which, to the author, is a retrograde step). There are also strong organizational and economic arguments for retaining this standard model. There are also good educational and resource reasons for not doing so.

Many modules are also locked in an assessment model of a 2000 essay/written assignment (40% of marks) and a 3-hour end of semester examination (60% of marks). The teaching model and the assessment model are in fact difficult to break free from since the former have by convention become a standard for all validated and revalidated modules while the latter are strongly influenced by the Institute's Unitization Regulations.

What is needed fundamentally is to pursue a new strategy such as that employed by Frank Webster's sociology group at the then Oxford Polytechnic (Gibbs and Jenkins, 1992). A model based on learning outcomes with much greater student negotiation and flexibility is needed. This would be particularly useful for example in freeing up resources for Level 1 to provide more student support specifically to develop independent thinking and learning skills to facilitate deep learning. More of the Institute's scarce resources need to be devoted to this. This has implications for Level 1 retention rates and for achieving value added on which the quality of the Institute's mission is currently judged.

If therefore Southampton Institute has made very substantial progress in a short period of time, the next stage in terms of teaching and learning strategies is not one of consolidation, but one of a further leap forward, using the experience of universities like Oxford Brookes to make gains without the long learning curve other institutions have experienced.

There is lots of good practice already at Southampton Institute and a recent inspection noted that a number of classes were excellent. So there is much to build on but there is still some way to go.

Conclusion

This chapter has sought to explore the attempts by the European Business module team to improve the quality of student thinking and learning using a cognitive model of learning as a theoretical underpinning against which to test practice. Institutional developments have placed significant constraints upon the team and currently these need to be loosened to enable resources including time to be utilised more effectively. This is particularly important in the light of the Institute's mission statement. With further Government restrictions on funding it is vital that more flexible models of resource utilization are employed at the modular level. It is proposed to address these in the next session.

References

Ashworth, A. and Harvey, R. C. (1994). *Assessing Quality in Further and Higher Education.* Jessica Kingsley Publishers.

Atkins, M.J., Beattie, J. and Dockrell, W.B. (1993). *Assessment Issues in Higher Education.* Employment Department, Further and Higher Education Branch.

Ellis, A.W. and Young A.W. (1988) Human Cognitive Neuropsychology. Erlblaum

Entwhistle, N. and Ramsden, P. (1983). *Understanding Student Learning.* Croom Helm.

Green, D. (ed.) (1994). *What is Quality in Higher Education?* Society for Research into Higher Education & Open University Press

Gibbs. G. (1992), *Improving the Quality of Student Learning.* Technical and Education Service Ltd.

Gibbs, G. and Jenkins, A. (eds) (1992), *Teaching Large Classes in Higher Education: How to Maintain Quality with Reduced Resources.* Kogan Page.

Handy, C. (1989). *The Age of Unreason.* Arrow Books.

Lee, R.D. (1991). The use of exit interviews in Masters' programs of public affairs and administration. *American Review of Public Administration.* **21**(3), Sept., 183 – 95.

The Independent, 19 May 1994; 3 June 1994.

Miller, F., Chamberlain, D. and Seay, R. (1991). The current status of outcomes assessment in marketing education. *Journal of the Academy of Marketing Science.* **19**(4), Fall, 353 – 362.

Perry, P. (1994). Defining and measuring the quality of teaching. In D.Green, *What is Quality in Higher Education?* Society for Research into Higher Education and Open University Press.

Sanders, C. (1994). The Parts Assesors Can't Reach. Times Higher Education Supplement. 4 February 1994, P. 3.

Webster, F. (1992). Thinking strategically: a subject group's attempts to maintain quality with reduced resources. In: G. Gibbs, and A. Jenkins, (eds), *Teaching Large Classes in Higher Education: How to Maintain Quality with Reduced Resources.* Kogan Page.

ACKNOWLEDGEMENT

Thanks go to Professor Chris Hutchinson, Director of the Business School, and Jim Rumsey, Head of the Educational Development Service, for their comments on this chapter.

35   Do Approaches to Learning Courses improve students' learning strategies?

Linda S. Norton and Thomas E. Dickins (Liverpool Institute of Higher Education

Introduction

There appears to be a considerable amount of agreement in the literature about the benefits of taking a deep approach to studying (see Trigwell & Prosser,1991; Gibbs,1992; Joughlin,1992; Lublin & Prosser,1994) and increasing students' metacognitive awareness (see Biggs,1988; Wangerin, 1988; Wade & Reynolds, 1989). Researchers, however, are less in agreement about the benefits of courses designed to improve students' learning strategies.

Such interventions have taken one of two main approaches: the study skills programme and the learning to learn programme. Basically, the study skills programme teaches students to use particular study methods which they can then apply to their subject courses. Unfortunately, the study skills approach seems largely to have failed (see Leitch,1994 for a recent example). Wade & Reynolds (1989), amongst others, have argued that the reasons why traditional study skills methods do not work is that not only might they be interfering with what students are already doing effectively, but also they do not often include metacognitive knowledge about the usefulness of the study skill as well as about when and where to use it.

The learning to learn approach has been a development of the study skills approach with the emphasis being shifted much more directly on to how students perceive the learning task. This metacognitive element has meant that learning to learn programmes as opposed to traditional study skills programmes have been much more closely related to the content of the participating students' curriculum. Again though, the success of such courses appears to be limited.

An example is a study by Ramsden, Beswick and Bowden (1987) who reported on some experimental innovations consisting of small groups in which problems and approaches to learning were discussed. The emphasis was not so much on the right technique, but on being aware of the different techniques and selecting the one that was appropriate to the academic task. Somewhat surprisingly, these interventions showed an increase in surface approaches and no obvious academic advantantage for those students who took part.

Such a study is worrying for it suggests that courses designed to enhance the quality of student learning may have done exactly the opposite. Ramsden et al explain their findings by arguing that it is pedagogically naive to take a deficit model of student learning and assume that deficiencies in learning are an attribute of the student that can be remediated by teaching appropriate strategies. They argue that a more systemic approach needs to be taken whereby the focus switches away from students to that of teachers and how teachers can improve their teaching to enhance the quality of student learning.

This argument seems to be a fore-runner of the systemic approach , first put forward by Biggs (1994) and described by Lublin & Prosser (1994). Here the focus is on the whole context of learning from the perspective of the student and the perspective of the teacher, through to the environmental constraints of the department as a learning context and the institution itself as the overarching academic constraint. As Lublin & Prosser argue: "The way institutions structure the teaching and learning contexts of students has an important impact on what and how students learn." (p.1.)

It seems then that part of the failure of learning to learn courses might lie in them being designed in isolation and not as an integral part of the whole academic system. However, not all the research has been negative. A study by Martin & Ramsden (1987) compared a study skills course with a learning to learn course, both of which were designed to improve student learning in two British University History departments. Their findings indicated that while there were no advantages for the participants in the study skills course, there were some limited benefits for participants in the learning to learn course. Students who attended the learning to learn course did better than non-participants in their history assignments, but not in their examination performance. There was also evidence that students' metacognitive awareness had been raised by the learning to learn course.

The Research Study

This paper reports on an innovation in a psychology department of an Institute of Higher Education. The innovation was partly inspired by the Martin & Ramsden study. It involved the development of a course designed specifically for first year psycholgy undergraduates to raise their metacognitive awareness of their own learning strategies and to encourage them to take a deep, rather than a surface approach to their psychology studies. It was hoped that in this way, the course would improve their academic performance on essays and in examinations.

Rationale

Taking account of the suggestions from the research that a systemic rather than a deficit model might be more productive, this innovation has been designed to be more than just a learning to learn course for students. This has meant that as well as focussing on how psychology students might be encouraged to develop their learning strategies, tutors in the department too have been encouraged to reflect on how their assessment procedures might facilitate this development.

All this has not taken place overnight, rather it has been a gradual development taking place within the Institute over a number of years. The main thrust of this paper is to report on the last two years of this development, when the learning approaches course was first instituted.

Stage 1: The Workshop Programme

Designing the course

The first attempt at providing a learning to learn course for our psychology students involved designing a series of eight workshops which were primarily aimed at raising students' metacognitive awareness of their learning strategies. A subsidiary aim was to help them improve their study skills (particularly in essay writing and examination taking) specifically in relation to the psychology department's academic demands.

This workshop programmme was devised as part of the first year psychology timetable. It consisted of a general introductory session on the nature of study in higher education, a session on deep and surface processing, four sessions on essay writing and two sessions on examination taking. The whole emphasis of this programme was designed to help students reflect on their own learning and studying strategies and how effective they were in meeting the academic requirements of the psychology course.

Staff involvement

As well as taking note of the research findings about learning to learn courses being more effective than traditional study skills courses, it was also decided to actively enlist departmental support for the programme and to try and influence the assessment procedures in psychology to reflect a concern for deep processing. Researchers such as Sherman (1991) have argued that one of the reasons why learning to learn programmes may fail is because often there is insufficient support from other members of staff in the department to reinforce what students have been told in the programme. The other main reason appears to be the fairly robust research finding that assessment demands determine, more than any other factor, whether students will take a deep or a surface approach to their studies (see Boud, 1990).

In an attempt to gain support from the psychology tutors for the workshop programme, a detailed course outline, together with the aims and learning outcomes, was produced and circulated to all staff in the department. It was hoped that this might help change the quite commonly held view that the course was basically a remediation type of programme. By actually seeing what we were trying to achieve, it was thought that tutors might be made more aware of the developmental model underpinning the course and be in sympathy with our aims of helping students develop from novices to experts in learning.

The assessment question

ESSAYS

The assessment procedure was also tackled. In this case, because academic departments are usually conservative in these matters and quite resistant to change (probably due to the institutional constraints previously mentioned in relation to the systemic model of learning), there had to be an indirect 'attack'. Specifically, this involved holding a staff development session where tutors were asked to identify what given examples of essay titles were actually asking students to do. The aim of this exercise was to persuade staff to think much more deeply about the whole business of setting essay assignments. In particular, it was hoped to encourage them to set essays which demanded the deep approach skills of understanding, structuring an argument and evaluating evidence, rather than purely descriptive essays which asked for little more than a rehash of lecture notes and textbook material.

This exercise was moderately successful and reinforced workshop messages about deep processing because staff, when setting essay assignments, also produced student guides which gave an indication of what a deep approach to that particular essay titile would involve. It was also hoped that by focussing tutors' attention on deep processing in this way that they would positively reward evidence of this when they came to mark the essays.

THE EXAMINATION

The first year examination was not so readily changed. In the Psychology department, this has traditionally been a composite three hour paper made up of two sections, equally weighted. The first section asks students to write short, factual notes on a wide range of core topics covered in the psychology curriculum. The second section asks conventional essay questions. It has always been the first author's view that the short notes section encouraged nothing but rote repetition. There was, indeed, much anecdotal evidence to suggest that the only way our students felt they could prepare for such an exam was to memorise great chunks of the course textbook - a classic surface approach. However, for this year when the workshop programme was first instituted, this particular argument was lost and the examination remained the same.

Evaluating the workshop programme

Measures to evaluate the efficacy of the workshop programme included records of attendance, essay grades and examination marks as well as pre-course and post-course measures of conceptions of learning. These were derived from content analysing students' written responses to the question: "What do you actually mean by learning?" Using Saljo's (1979) model gave a framework of five categories into which students' answers could be assigned.

The five categories were:

1. Learning as the increase of knowledge.

2. Learning as memorising.

3. Learning as the acquisition of facts or procedures which can be retained and/or utilised in practice.

4. Learning as the abstraction of meaning.

5. Learning as an interpretative process aimed at the understanding of reality.

The first three categories have been clearly linked to a surface approach to studying whereas the last two reflect a deep approach (Gibbs,1992).

Results

An evaluation of this workshop programme has been reported in detail elsewhere (see Norton & Crowley, in press). Briefly, the main findings were that there did appear to be not only academic benefits to students who participated, but also there was evidence that their conceptions of learning had moved from an initially lower level to a higher level by the end of the programme. Looking at the 42 students who had attended a substantial number of the workshops, it was found that the percentage who started off with higher levels of conceptions was only 29%, but by the end of the programme this had risen to 60%. As far as academic performance was concerned, students who attended all four workshops on essay writing (N=32) obtained significantly higher essay marks than students who did not attend. Similarly, students who attended both the workshops on examination taking (N=56) obtained significantly higher examination marks than students who did not attend.

Conclusion

It was concluded from the success of this workshop programme that there is indeed evidence to support the notion that approaches to learning courses can and do improve students' learning in an objective and measurable way.

Such a success was seen as due to the fact that the intervention was naturalistic (ie not set up for experimental purposes) and was a course that was designed to relate specifically to our students' first year psychology curriculum. It was also considered to be an important factor that the messages being conveyed in the programme were being taken up by the departmental tutors in their teaching and, most importantly, in the way they set and offered guidelines for coursework essays.

Stage 2: The Approaches to Learning Course

Rationale

It was decided, therefore, to build on this initial success by developing a second learning to learn course for the next cohort of psychology undergraduates and to continue to discuss and develop tutors' views on student learning.

The first step in this process was to hold a staff development meeting to convey the results of evaluating the efficacy of the workshop programme and to ask for suggestions and support as to how we could most effectively go forward. This meeting had the effect of boosting staff support for the programme and initiating new staff members into the ethos of encouraging psychology students to take a deep approach to their studies.

Following discussion, it was decided to extend the original programme from eight to ten sessions and to rename it 'Approaches to Learning'. This was to get away from the study skills remediation image. It was also decided, to gradually phase out the study skills component and place a much heavier emphasis on developing students' metacognitive strategies. This would be done by relating the principles in the course quite specifically to current research findings in student learning. In this way, it was hoped that our students would see the course as an example of applied psychology with real benefits to them as developing, not deficient, learners.

Assessment Issues

A second step taken to capitalise on the degree of staff involvement and support for the principle of deep processing taught in the course, was to design a new essay feedback sheet which listed the criteria that tutors used when marking students' essays.

The criteria measuring deep processing were as follows:

Addresses the question throughout the essay;

Clearly organised with structure appropriate to question;

Quality and relevance of argument;

Synthesis of a range of material into a coherent whole;

Depth of understanding in relation to underlying psychological issues;

Evaluation of theoretical concepts and research evidence;

Originality.

The criteria measuring surface processing were as follows:

Presentation of references;

Academic style;

Grammar/spelling.

Using this feedback sheet, tutors could either give marks for each criterion (on a scale of 0-5) or written comments, or a combination of the two. The idea for giving such detailed feedback was to actually show our students what a deep approach to an essay is, and what is needed to turn an essay which reflects a surface approach into an essay that reflects a deep approach and thereby gain more marks.

To test the effectiveness of this innovation, a further staff development exercise was held whereby all tutors were asked to mark a photocopy of the same first year essay using the new feedback sheet. This was followed by a meeting to discuss each of the criteria and the amount of agreement or disagreement between individual tutors on their comments and marks. The main benefit to emerge in terms of the Approaches to Learning course and what it was trying to achieve was that staff were once again reminded of the necessity for care in devising essay titles, and to reward students for evidence of deep processing in their essays.

THE EXAMINATION

The final innovation that was put in place to support the learning course was to redesign the first year psychology examination. The short answer questions were finally abolished and the paper was constructed to consist of four essay questions. This was a major achievement and reflected the psychology staff's growing awareness of the importance of consistently encouraging students to take a deep approach in all aspects of their assessed work.

Thus, concerted efforts were made in this second year to involve staff more fully and actively seek to enlist their support for the venture. In addition, quite considerable changes were made to alter how the department assessed first year students, by changing both coursework essays and the format of the examination to positively encourage them to take a deep aproach to psychology.

Designing the course

The Approaches to Learning course itself consisted of the following sessions:

1 'Studying Psychology in Higher Education' - where the scene for the whole course was set. The emphasis was placed on research findings about the importance of metacognitive strategies and deep processing, instead of on traditional study skills advice.

2 'Deep and Surface Processing I' - the notion of deep processing was explored together with suggestions as to how this could be applied to note-taking in lectures, examination taking and seminar participation.

3 'Essays: style and structure' - research findings were used to point out to students the mismatch that exists between tutors and students in their perceptions of essay marking criteria (Norton, 1990). Students typically have a concern with surface processing whereas tutors are more concerned with deep processing. Guidelines were given regarding the psychology department's referencing requirements, and required essay style.

4 'Essays: analysis and argument' - being critical was explained as the basis for all scientific rationality and enquiry. Essentially this is what a deep approach is and the applications to writing psychology essays were made explicit.

5 'Essays: assessment demands' - students were given a practical exercise in which they were asked to assess three different essay introductions illustrating different levels of deep processing.

6 'Essays: acting on essay feedback' - the criteria on the essay feedback sheet were discussed with reference to students' own essays that had been marked.

7 'Deep and surface processing II' - a revision session to stress again the difference between deep and surface processing. Students were also given a practical exercise which involved reading an article and thinking how a surface approach would work as opposed to a deep approach.

8 'Active revision'- a session that stressed the importance of taking a deep approach to preparing for the psychology exam.

9 'Examination taking techniques' - mainly a study skills session but with the emphasis on answering examination questions using a deep approach.

10'Course evaluation' - an opportunity for students to reflect not only on the usefulness of the course, but also on their own development as learners during the first year of their undergraduate studies.

It can be seen that this course was substantially redesigned and developed from the original workshop programme. While there was some attention paid to traditional study skills, the whole emphasis of the course was heavily focussed on encouraging our students to develop a metacognitive awareness of their own learning strategies.

Evaluating the Approaches to Learning Course (APL)

In order to evaluate the effectiveness of the APL course, the following measures were used:

Records of attendance.

Pre- and post-course measures of conceptions of learning (using Säljö's (1979) categorisation as described previously in the section on evaluating the workshop programme.

Pre- and post-course measures of the Approaches to Studying Inventory (using the 32 item version described by Richardson,1990). The ASI has two main factors: Meaning Orientation, andReproducing Orientation. The meaning orientation factor is similar to the deep approach to learning and is made up of four subscales - deep approach, comprehension learning, relating ideas, and, use of evidence and logic. The reproducing orientation factor is similar to the surface approach to learning and is also made up of four subscales - surface approach, improvidence, fear of failure, and syllabus boundness.

Mean essay mark.

Mean examination mark.

Results

The findings from our evaluation will be presented in three main sections concerning; attendance, academic performance and metacognitive awareness.

Since the study was a naturalistic one (i.e. it was part of a real ongoing degree programme and not an experimental intervention) the numbers available for the different statistical analyses vary considerably.

ATTENDANCE

The percentage of students attending each session is shown in Table 1.

Table 1

Attendance at Approaches to Learning sessions

Session	Title of session	Percentage of students (N = 258)
1	Studying Psychology in Higher Education	83
2	Deep and Surface Processing I	65
3	Essays: Style and Structure	58
4	Essays: Analysis and Argument	47
5	Essays: Assessment Demands	33
6	Essays: Acting on Essay Feedback	22
7	Deep and Surface Processing II	17
8	Active Revision	21
9	Examination Taking Techniques	23
10	Course and Self Evaluation	7

This table shows a depressing picture with numbers steadily declining until only 7% of the entire year bothered to turn up for the last session which was designed to be both a course evaluation and an opportunity for students to evaluate their own development as learners. This was pretty much a repeat of the attendance pattern at the workshop programme in the previous year.

These figures are particularly discouraging since we thought we had solved the problem by firstly, moving away from a study skills orientation in this course, and, secondly, by asking tutors in the department to push the benefits of the course more forcefully to their students. It seems, however, that these efforts were to no avail!

In the year to come, we will be tackling this problem from two angles. Taking a purely practical approach, it is intended to present the course simply as one of the three compulsory courses that make up the first year curriculum in psychology. This represents a move away from our previous tactic of trying to persuade students how valuable this particular course is, thereby perhaps leading them to think that attendance is optional. Since there is no assessment linked to the APL course (for to do so would be contrary to what we are trying to achieve) students will be told not only that attendance is monitored, but also that tutors assess their coursework using principles that are to be explained in the course.

The second angle is to carry out some research and interview some of the non-attenders from the last two years to see if we can establish any consistent patterns in the reasons why they have not attended. It may be that at least some of these non-attenders are the very students who would have most to gain from such a course, especially if they are the type of students who never stand back from the degree curriculum to reflect on the learning process itself, or what type of learner they are.

ACADEMIC PERFORMANCE

Following on from the success of the workshop programme, we were predicting that students who had attended the APL course would do better on measures of academic performance than students who had not attended.

Looking firstly at the effect of attendance on essays, a comparison was made between students who had attended all four sessions on essay writing with students who had not attended any. Similarly with the examination mark, a similar comparison was made. In this instance it was a comparison between students who had attended both the examination related sessions and students who had attended neither. The results of both these comparisons are shown in Table 2.

Table 2

Effect of attendance at specific APL sessions on measures of academic performance

Essays	N	Mean mark	SD	t	p
Attenders (at all four sessions)	24	60.92	7.67		
Non-attenders (at none of sessions)	60	55.63	6.66	2.96	0.005

Examinations	N	Mean mark	SD	t	p
Attenders (at all both sessions)	22	58.86	5.52		
Non-attenders (at neither session)	148	49.94	12.54	3.28	0.005

As this table clearly shows, there were significantly higher marks for the attenders on both measures. It is perhaps worth pointing out that these sessions were not about essay writing and examination taking as study skills., they were focussed instead on the benefits of taking a deep approach.

METACOGNITIVE AWARENESS

In order to ascertain whether the APL course raised students' metacognitive awareness, two measures were used: i) students' conceptions of learning and

ii)students' scores on the Approaches to Studying Inventory. In both anbalyses, only those students who had attended more than half the APL sessions were used. It was hypothesised that students would move from an inchoate conception of learning (ie those at levels 1, 2, or 3) to a more developed conception by the end of the APL course (ie level 4 or 5). It was also hypothesised that the ASI scores would show a decrease on the reproducing orientation factor and an increase in the meaning orientation factor by the end of the course.

The first comparison was made between the number of students at the start and at the end of the course who held an inchoate as opposed to a developed conception of learning. The results of this analysis are presented in Table 3.

Table 3

Comparison of pre- and post- course

conceptions of learning

(N = 31)

Level of conception	Pre-course	Post-course
Inchoate (levels 1, 2 & 3)	25	20
Developed (levels 4 & 5)	6	11

As this contingency table shows, the numbers of students who shifted from an inchoate to a developed conception of learning was only 5, a difference that was not statistically significant using the McNemar test.

This was a surprising finding as it did not replicate the results of the previous year where there was a significant shift from inchoate to developed by the end of the course (see Norton & Crowley, in press). It does, however, replicate that study's finding in terms of the large percentage of first year undergraduates who started their degree with an undeveloped conception of learning In this study it was actually 81% of the 31 students who completed the task twice. In the Norton & Crowley study, it was 71% öf 42 students..

The second comparison involved looking at students' scores on the ASI at the start of the course and at the end of the course. The results of this comparison are shown in Table 4.

Table 4

Comparison of pre- and post-course scores

on the Approaches to Studying Inventory

(N = 37)

Meaning Orientation	Mean	SD	t	p
Pre-course	42.22	7.65		
Post-course	41.08	9.12	0.87	NS

Reproducing Orientation	Mean	SD	t	p
Pre-course	34.46	10.1		
Post-course	32.00	8.51	1.96	0.05

As can be seen, there was a significant decrease in the students' reproducing orientation scores, which was predicted, but there was no significant change in the meaning orientation scores. When we looked for differences in the subscales, the only significant finding was in the surface approach score which was a subscale of the reproducing orientation factor. This is shown in Table 5.

Table 5

Comparison of pre- and post-course scores

on the Surface Approach subscale of the ASI

(N = 37)

Surface Approach	Mean	SD	t	p
Pre-course	12.89	4.50		
Post-course	11.32	4.02	2.38	0.025

Here, we can see the same pattern of results as occurred in the reproducing orientation scores; namely that students showed significantly less of a surface approach by the end of the course. This, then adds further support to at least part of our hypothesis.

These findings show that while those students who attended more than half the sessions in the APL course did not appear to increase their meaning orientation strategies (they were apparently not taking more of a deep approach), they did significantly decrease their reproducing orientation scores overall and their surface approach strategies in particular (so they were taking less of a surface approach, by the end of the course).

Discussion

The results of this research indicate that for students who attended the APL course, there were significant academic benefits. This confirms the findings of the Norton & Crowley (in press) study. There does, therefore, appear to be fairly strong empirical evidence to suggest that approaches to learning courses may help students to perform better on academic measures, such as essay writing and examination performance.

What this study has not been able to unequivocally demonstrate is that the APL course helped students to raise their metacognitive awareness. While there was a shift to more students holding a developed as opposed to an inchoate conception of learning, it was not large enough to be statistically significant. One explanation may lie in the practicalities of the timing of the second task. It was shortly before their end of year examination (their first examination at degree level) when we asked students to complete again the task of writing an answer to the question "What do you actually mean by learning?" At the same time we also asked them to complete the ASI again. Perhaps then it was not surprising that so few students complied despite repeated attempts on the part of the authors. Those students who did comply, gave extremely brief answers to the conceptions of learning task - sometimes just a couple of sentences. This was in marked contrast to their first attempt where many students wrote a side or more. This may have meant that we were not getting a true reflection of students' conceptions this second time around.

The ASI findings were particularly interesting in showing a decrease in surface approach but no change in deep approach, by the end of the course. When these results were presented in a research seminar to both staff and students in the psychology department, one colleague suggested that this may be an indication of a transition stage. Students start the course with a surface approach and as the year progresses and they listen to the messages coming from the APL course they realise that such an approach is not desirable, consequently they reduce their surface strategies. At the same time, they realise that they are being encouraged to take a deep approach in psychology, but do not feel confident enough to take what appears to them a big risk. They know, if they stick to their usual way of doing things, they will be fairly safe and get marks in the 2.ii range. This would support Wade & Reynold's (1989) argument about some study skills interventions possibly interfering with students' already 'effective' strategies. If, however, they break away from their tried and tested formula, they may feel that they will fall flat on their faces and get a fail grade.

When this suggestion was put forward in the seminar, several students who had attended the APL course agreed this was exactly how they felt, and the ensuing exchange between these students and staff was illuminating. Tutors were quite surprised to hear that students were afraid of taking a deep approach in their essays and examinations, especially since the APL course stressed that that is what we are looking for, as do the essay feedback sheets. In spite of all this, students still feel it is too risky.

Another explanation as to why students did not show an increase in the meaning orientation factor may lie in the theory of skill learning put forward by Anderson (1982). His main proposition is that a major part of skill learning consists of changing what he calls declarative knowledge, (ie knowledge that is not specifically linked to the situation in which it can be used) into procedural knowledge (ie knowledge that is applied automatically and is particularly approriate to specific situations) by the process of practical application. Translated to a learning skills situation this basically means that for a student to develop a new method of completing an academic task (ie taking a deep approach) involves practice and a necessary decrease in performance standard until the new method has become fully integrated into the student's academic repertoire. Again, though this would mean psychology tutors actively rewarding students' attempts, however stumbling and unsophisticated, to incorporate more of a deep approach in their written assignments.

This is why we argue in this paper that the only way to encourage real change in our students is to take a systemic approach as advocated by Lublin & Prosser (1994) and.also to encourage staff to think about how assessment determines whether students take a deep or a surface approach. Only then, will courses, such as the Approaches to Learning course described here be effective in helping students to develop as learners.

Conclusions and Implications

The evidence seems to indicate at this stage of the research that learning to learn courses can be beneficial to students beginning a degree programme of study. The implications from this research and from the literature suggest that a number of factors ought to be considered if such courses are to succeed:

1 The course should be firmly embedded within the curriculum.

2 The course should be designed to focus mainly on raising students' metacognitive awareness of learning strategies which would involve some studying techniques.

3 The course should be predicated on the principle of a developmental and not a deficit model of learning.

4 The course should be seen as a central and integral part of the department's teaching activities and not some isolated "add-on" option.

5 The principles taught in the course should be strongly reinforced by the rest of the departmental staff in their teaching.

6 The principles taught in the course should be actively encouraged by the assessment procedures.

7 The course should be seen as a fundamental part of the systemic approach to learning where the importance of the total learning context is acknowledged and acted upon to improve both learning and teaching.

References

Anderson, J.R. (1982) Acquisition of cognitive skill. Psychological Review, 89, 396 - 406.

Biggs, J.B. (1988) The role of metacognition in enhancing learning. Australian Journal of Education, 32, 2, 127-138.BIGGS, J.B. (1994) Student learning research and theory. Where do we currently stand? In Gibbs, G. (ed) *Improving Student Learning. Theory and Practice*. Oxford: The Oxford Centre for Staff Development.

Boud, D. (1990) Assessment and the promotion of academic values. Studies in Higher Education, 15,1,101-110.

Gibbs, G. (1992) *Improving the Quality of Student Learning*. Bristol:Technical and Educational Services Ltd.

Joughlin, G. *et al* (1992) Distance Learners' Approaches to Studying : the nature of "Deep" and "Surface" Approaches reconsidered . Paper presented at the World Conference of the International Council for Distance Education. (16th, Bangkok, Thailand, November 8-13, 1992.)Leitch, A. (1994) Improving study skills: an experimental approach. In Gibbs, G. (ed) *Improving Student Learning*. Theory and Practice Oxford: The Oxford Centre for Staff Development.

Lublin, J. & Prosser, M. (1994) Implications of recent research on student learning for institutional practices of evaluation of teaching. In Gibbs, G (ed) *Improving Student Learning. Theory and Practice Oxford*: The Oxford Centre for Staff Development.

Martin, E. & Ramsden, P. (1987) Learning skills or skill in learning? In Richardson, J.T.E. , Eysenck, M.W. & Warren Piper, D. (eds) *Student Learning: Research into Education and Cognitive Psychology Milton Keynes*: Open University Press.

Norton, L.S. (1990) Essay-writing:what really counts? Higher Education, 20, 411-442.

Norton, L.S. & Crowley, C. M. (in press) Can students be helped to learn how to learn? An evaluation of an Approaches to Learning programme for first year degree students.

Ramsden, P., Beswick, D. & Bowden, J. (1987) Learning processes and learning skills In Richardson, J.T.E. , Eysenck, M.W. & Warren Piper, D. (eds) *Student Learning: Research into Education and Cognitive Psychology Milton Keynes*: Open University Press.

Richardson, J.T.E. (1990) Reliability and replicability of the Approaches to Studying Questionnaire. Studies in Higher Education, 15, 155 - 168.

Säljö, R. (1979) Learning in the learner's perspective I - some commonsense conceptions. Reports from the Institute of Education, University of Gothenburg, No. 77.

Sherman, T.M. (1991) Creating a disposition to learn:promoting enduring effects from learning improvement programs. Research and Teaching in Developmental Education, 8,1, 37-47.Trigwell, K. & Prosser, M. (1991) Improving the quality of student learning: the influence of learning context and student approaches to learning on learning outcomes. Higher Education, 22, 3, 251-266.

Wade, S. E. & Reynolds, R.E. (1989) Developing metacognitive awareness. Journal of Reading, **33**, 1, 6-14.

Wangerin, P. T. (1988) Learning strategies for law students. Albany Law Review, **52**, 2, 471-528.

Janet McGivern and Jane Thompson (University of Humberside)

Are you Sitting Comfortably?

Are you sitting comfortably, or as Calvino, anxious to engage with you, the reader, asks 'Well, what are you waiting for, stretch your legs, go ahead and put your feet on a cushion ... Take your shoes off first ...'[1]

This is the story of the redesigning of a foundation level course – People and Management. We tell of how a group of us worked together to question what might be taught, how and to whom. These questions are central to a continuing debate on the nature of management education. It is not our intention to enter that debate here but rather to describe our rationale for our own programme. We discuss our experiential approach to developing management skills, and our growing interest in using 'fiction' as management text.

Each member of the course development team brought different experiences to the designing of People and Management.

They will all have their own stories to tell. Here are ours:

1986 and all that

Jane: 'There was a fair bit of work around for sociologists in 1986. My part-time contract read "Jane Thompson, OB,PT, x 2". I began delivery of a unit entitled "organizational behaviour" to part-time mature students on the business studies degree programme at Humberside Polytechnic (now University of Humberside). The programme incorporated fairly traditional approaches to OB; a mixed diet of systems and action approaches at a fairly grand level of abstraction. A part from the odd "real-life" relief of, for example, work by Huw Benyon and Donald Roy, the material appeared divorced from students' experience of organizational life. It was typical of most O.B. programmes. I found it extremely hard to make much of it meaningful – to me or them – given its insistence on (explanatory?) meta-narrative. However, I struggled on in a peripheral sense, trying to deliver the programme as instructed ... 45 minute lecture-style format with a 5 minute slot to pick up any questions from the previous week's session; followed immediately by a seminar that was supposed to relate to the previous week's lecture. A glance at my watch ... nearly there – only another 25 minutes – and the hour and a half filled. The OHP provided the focus for the first half of session. Various theories of motivation, leadership, decision-making etc. were outlined, supported by such texts as Buchanan and Huczynski's *Organizational Behaviour*. Therefore followed a shuffling of papers while students tried to remember the topic of the previous session, and then a silence – interrupted by me – who, in what was becoming my familiar role of "rescuer", jumped at the opportunity to move onto the "seminar" part of the evening. This consisted of one or two as conflict, control etc., while the others looked on, heads slightly bowed, seemingly not understanding much? but aware that it would soon be their turn and thus treating the speakers' utterances with reverence. The last few minutes of the session were reserved to set the scene for the following week – for a repeat performance. What a relief at 7.30pm when we could go to the bar and give some "real" meaning to the session. I am pleased to say that now this happens in the actual session – while we still go to the bar it is more to continue our dialogue rather than to address something substantially new.'

Janet: 'My own route was quite different. Teaching first in a primary school and later in a comprehensive, in an era heavily influenced by the Bullock Report, [2] my early practices as a teacher were firmly grounded in a participative approach. I headed an English Department that was committed to student involvement; "language across the curriculum" was the buzz phrase. It was an enjoyable time.

Following a career break I joined the postgraduate management development programme at Humberside as a student in 1989. I was receptive to and excited by the experiential learning approaches employed by David and Judith Golding, and Nick Barclay. This was similar, but in many ways, different to my own teaching style. Student participation was central, but controlling the agenda, management of the seminars (and learning) were also the responsibility of individuals in the group.

Picking up some part-time undergraduate teaching, prior to my full-time appointment, it became apparent, to me, that these approaches had not filtered through to foundation units. I managed as best I could, corrupting the syllabus, startling sleepy students and keeping my head down. This was a time of discontent for many of my colleagues, who felt, as I did, that traditional programmes were not preparing students adequately for work. Over the past few years we have worked to dramatically revise the form and content of these units; a rewarding experience for all of us.'

Management Skills

Management Studies courses at Humberside bring together many disciplines, most notably, sociology, psychology, philosophy and literature. Drawing on the writings of Mike Pedler, [3] Gareth Morgan, [4] Carl Rogers, [5] RD Laing, [6] Erving Goffman, [7] Peter Anthony, [8] among others, and also a wide range of authors of fiction, we have designed units that attempt to reflect the paradox and complexity of managerial activity. In their preparation for seminars students sample a wide range of ideas through their reading. The message we give students at the onset is that there are no right answers but it is possible for them to think and manage their own way through the vast array of possibilities.

Our People and Management student handbook starts with the quote:

> Managing me is the first step for the self-developer – unless I take charge of myself, how can I contribute to creating order with others? Managing Me is the key of self-empowerment, and the empowerment of others.[3]

We offer students the possibility that they are **already** managers and that this unit could provide opportunity to develop further in this direction through an exploration of self and others.

What management skills are we hoping to develop? Iain Mangham's words set the scene for us quite aptly.

> Most of us, most of the time, in most circumstances, at home, work or play, perform without reflection. Even in circumstances where we are theoretically called upon to reflect plan meetings, interviews, decision points in our life and the like, most of us tend to enact our parts in well established scripts.[9]

We see developing the ability in students to think and reflect as fundamental to the work we do. We value John Burgoyne's writing in this area. He researched and identified attributes possessed by 'successful manager'.[10] With Mike Pedler [11] he lists eleven essential management skills (see Figure 1).

Figure 1 Eleven essential management skills

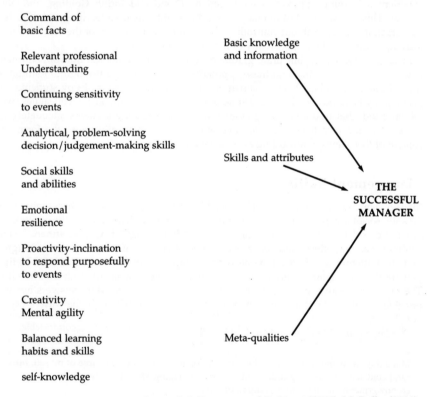

Source: J.G. Burgoyne and R. Stuart (1976); M. Pedler (1986).

These they divide into three broad categories, basic knowledge and information, skills and attributes and meta-qualities. In our management unit we aim essentially to develop the metaqualities of creativity, mental agility, balanced learning habits and skills, and self-knowledge. Metaqualities, Burgoyne discovered, are most successfully developed in experiential groups. Our findings support this. Students describe to us how they begin to listen to each other – **really** listen and hear; and so they start their development as 'reflective practitioners of management'. [12] In encouraging students to obtain management skills, we recognize the importance of placing the latter in a wider philosophical framework; therefore we draw from a range of paradigms, while questioning their implicit boundaries. Recent writings in organizational theory employ the notions of self-reflexivity, metaphor, ambiguity, contradiction and irrationality, which we use (fiction provides excellent material here) to enable students to gain greater understanding of individual difference and some insight into personal and political relationships in order for them to become adept at 'reading situations' with a view to action.

The Experiential Group

The focus of attention is the seminar group itself. These groups we suggest, **are** organizations, mirroring organizational processes. We avoid presenting management as something that is happening 'out there' in the business world but rather as something that is happening 'here', in the seminar group. '... the here and now learning tasks with which participants in groups grapple have an intellectual base, if being intellectual is defined as thinking through intricate problems of human behaviour. [13] By focusing on the dynamics of their own seminar group we encourage students to reflect on the social and political nature of their behaviour as it occurs. Leadership, domination, negotiating space to speak, creating trust, taking risks, giving feedback, feeding, collaboration and competition are identified and explored as managerial activities as they occur. Problematic issues such as, lack of preparation, non-attendance, silence, posturing are not ignored but raised as point for discussion. These processes, occurring naturally, provide students with opportunities to learn how to 'manage' using real problems but in a relatively safe environment, where the tutor's 'power' legitimizes this process. A student provides here an example of one such situation in an extract from her experiential diary:

We are trying to talk about power, and really struggling. I hadn't done the reading which didn't help. There were lots of silences, often these give me time to think but today I felt uncomfortable. Caroline was talking about the definitions of power in Morgan. [4] Then someone commented on how difficult it was to talk about something as nebulous as power. The tutor stood up and drew a circle on the board: 'This dot in the centre represents the power in this group now. Come and put your initials where you think you are in the circle.' Most people were fairly good-humoured about it. I became even more uncomfortable. I didn't want to put up my initials. I felt I was quite influential in the group but suppose I put myself near the middle and the others disagreed. How would I feel then? When it got to me I said I didn't want to take part. One or two people were quite angry about it. Matthew said he hadn't wanted to be involved but felt he had to do it. The tutor suggested we looked at the reasons why some people had felt obliged to go along with something they didn't want to do and how that related to power. That really got us talking! The interesting thing was – when I looked at the reading I should have done, our discussion was all there. We'd actually talked about Stephen Lukes' [14] third dimension of power without knowing anything about it.

An interesting example of how groups can create their own theories.

Through the work of R.D. Laing [6] and Gareth Morgan [4] we introduce students to the notion of 'reframing', always encouraging them to read situations in different way. We discuss the value or otherwise of adopting perspectives, the influence of modernism on our attempts to define the world and postmodernism on our desire to dissolve those boundaries. Management corner-stones such as rationality, linearity, predictability and accountability are challenged within this framework.

A Focus on Fiction

We are increasingly using fiction as way into exploring management issues. The following is a transcript of a dialogue recorded earlier in the year where we are attempting to clarify our thoughts on this.

11 February 1994

Dialogue: Jane Thompson, Janet McGivern

Jane: We have agreed to give a paper at the University of Hull Conference and what we thought might be useful is to try and identify some of our ideas as to why and how we actually use fiction in our management education programmes. Students often say to me when they get the reading list and they see authors such as Kafka, [15] John Fowles, [16] Alison Lurie [17] – they say 'Well, this looks very interesting but what has this to do with us, business studies students?' How do you address this, Janet?

Janet: I think that fiction is a very useful way of looking at the complexity of relationships in organizational life. Students are happy to use traditional management texts on business studies courses because a lot of education gears them to believe that they will find models, answers and ways of understanding in traditional texts. When they come to us a lot of students believe that we are going to provide them with some sort of magical formula, a 'tool kit' for managing people. What we are trying to put across to students is that it is not that easy – that we don't have any prescriptions and the way we use fiction demonstrates that there are no right answers. Traditional management texts only reflect the author's observations of 'good practice'. I have a problem with a lot of research in the area of business studies because what happens when research doesn't fit a model an author wants to use? I tend to feel information that doesn't fit a model is lost, whereas a novel does not attempt to tidy up ideas or tidy up relationships. I think Karen Legge alludes to this when she is looking at evaluation. In her book *Evaluating Planned Organizational Change* [18] she makes the point that management consultants are actually chosen on the basis of the fact they won't disrupt the status quo. We try to impress on students that there is no model that will fit every situation and novels actually illustrate and develop the idea that relationships are fluid, unpredictable, ambiguous, are untidy – none of these notions comes out in traditional management texts. Management texts give us the notion that things are fairly straightforward if you just know what you are doing.

Jane: Yes I think that it is important to recognize that the novel explores complexity, and does not give us any 'endings', or conclusions. Well, some novels do – but a lot of the novels that we have on our reading lists leave the reader to come to their opinion about what actually happens. I am thinking particularly of *The Magus*. [16] There are two editions of this novel and if I remember correctly Fowles provides two different endings – but neither of them are ending in the sense that we find, for example, in the Victorian novel when things are nicely tidied up – when the main characters got married or emigrated to Australia or whatever. But the kind of novels we are looking at focus on the uncertainty, paradox, ambiguity – the very essence of managerial life, we would suggest.

Janet: Yes the 'reality of life', and organizational life can be very frightening and perhaps students are able to face this fear of the unknown in the novel in a non-threatening way because they are happy to enjoy a story where all the untidy aspects of relationships are illustrated but it is no threat to them. I guess if the untidiness of say, group dynamics was portrayed in a management textbook, the management textbook would be failing to give the students the security that they want, so there is quite a dilemma there – I mean these texts can openly provide really the illusion of a safe and secure environment for the students – the reality is that the environment isn't safe and secure and the novel gives then that without threatening them.

Jane: Yes I understand that. I suppose one of the central philosophies of our management education programmes is the idea that management is a social and political activity – working life is full of ambiguity – and the management texts in general do not deal with these aspects. In a group recently a student asked me how we were actually going to use the novels on the reading list. She said at school when she read a novel she also had to read the critics' views of that novel, and so her interpretation of it became less important than the critics, and this spoiled her enjoyment of the novel. This I understood because that was my experience of literature at school. I now try to redress this by suggesting that we are not looking at critics' views on a particular novel but rather we are looking for their own views, their own understanding and we are looking for them to make links in fiction with what is happening in our seminars and what is happening in their worlds, and it is those links that are important.

Janet: I think the seminar group and the way we actually organize the teaching and learning is crucial here because that provides the experiential environment where students can make connections between what they have read and what their own experiences of working and being with other people are – so for instance if we asked them to read Donna Tarrt's *The Secret History* [19] we are not looking for a critique of what has gone on but instead they might make links between the ways individuals in groups manage and control others and they may relate to their own experiences of work so that it becomes part of the experiential process.

Jane: And what you are saying presumably is that the process that you see in that novel isn't evident in the management texts? We do not see that complexity of groups process – so really we have no choice in a sense other than to us fiction to explore complexity of relationships.

Janet: The other day a student was telling me that he had been trying to write an assignment about group dynamics and he asked me if I could recommend a text and I was able to do that but we discussed the dearth of good theoretical texts on group process. A lot of the text are written at a simplistic level – group dynamics seem fairly predictable and controllable and it occurred to me was that he could actually make better use of novels like *Lord of the Flies* [20] or the Donna Tarrt novel. [19]

Jane: Yes what else could we identify as being useful for understanding group process – perhaps I might refer to *Jonathan Livingston Seagull*.[21] Jonathan leaves the flock – he goes off because he wants to learn to fly rather than simply looking for food – he then returns to the flock, having developed some wonderful flying techniques – but he is seen as an outcast because he has left the flock in the first place – but that perhaps is not so much about intra-group conflict – or is it inter-? I can never remember – but more about how group members set norms and how easily you can be made to feel an outcast if you don't conform. The gull wanted to perfect his flying technique, which was not a group norm – it reminds me also of the story of Plato's Cave that Gareth Morgan makes accessible in *Images*. [4]

Janet: Yes its interesting that you mention that novel because the one that sprang to my mind was *The Handmaid's Tale* [22] which is again about a society of conforming and non-conforming but I wondered if somebody was writing a booklist and putting fiction on about group dynamics would they select this book because what occurred to me was that your interpretation of Bach's novel is different to mine, and this, of course is what we are trying to help students to see that there are many themes running through fiction and they will locate different themes at different times in accordance with what their particular interests are.

Jane: Yes and as importantly to recognize that those themes appear in their organizational lives.

Janet: Yes and that the themes occur and reoccur in fiction, and we can't categorize fiction – we can't say if you want to know something about control read this.

Jane: Right, and perhaps its important we don't try either because by categorizing, or by labelling – look, read these books because they are actually about inter-group conflict or whatever – we are actually shutting down other possible areas of interpretation. I suppose this is where I have welcomed ideas from postmodernism – important influences of postmodernism for me have been the breaking down of boundaries and recognizing commensurability between paradigms and that we can look to different disciplines and perspectives to get a wider picture. Having said that, though, of course, in postmodern discourse we are reminded that 'meaning' is constantly slipping and I think that it is important to recognize this, and thus avoid labels, which suggest a fixed position. So it is important for me not to categorize and say these novels are about group processed or whatever, because we are not only suggesting an interpretation but also it is inconsistent with our teaching practice – we are also preventing possible new ways of seeing for the student and depriving them of self-discovery.

A few last Words

Research in the 1980s into Management Education [23], [24], [25] underlined how inadequately managers were prepared for their work. Peter Anthony's work identified an over-concern in many educational institutions with quantifiable skills, at the expense of the academic rigor needed to develop critical analytical skills. He comments 'Much of management education is irrelevant and some of the rest naive'. [8]

Our courses have been developed against this backdrop. We have taken up the challenge to provide intellectual rigor, through an experiential self-developmental approach to learning where real managerial problems become vehicles for developing the 'metaqualities', required by today's managers.

References

1   Italo Calvino (1992). *If On a Winter's Night a Traveller.* Minerva.

2   Bullock Report (1975).

3   Mike Pedler (1990). *Self Development in Organizations.* McGraw Hill, p. 10.

4   Gareth Morgan (1986). *Images of Organization.* Sage.

5   Car Rogers (1989). *On Becoming a Person.* Constable.

6   R.D. Laing (1967). *Politics of Experience and the Birds of Paradise.* Penguin.

7   E. Goffman (1959). *Presentation of Self in Everyday Life.* Penguin.

8   P.D. Anthony (1986). *Foundation of Management.* London, Tavistock Publication.

9   I. Mangham (1988). *Effecting Organizational Change.* Blackwell.

10 J.G. Burgoyne and R. Stuart (1976). The naure, use and acquisition of managerial skills and other attributes. *Personal Review,* **5**(4).

11 Mike Pedler (1986). *A Managers Guide to Self Development.* McGraw Hill, ch.4.

12 Donald Schon(1991). *The Reflective Practitioner.* Aldershot, Avebury.

13 A. Blumberg and R. Goldenblenski, (1976). *Learning and Change in Groups.* Penguin, p. 24.

14 Steven Lukes(1974). *Power: A Radical View.* MacMillan.

15 F. Kafka (1957). *The Castle.* Penguin.

16 John Fowles (1977). *The Magus.* Picador.

17 Alison Lurie (1969). *Real People.* Abacus.

18 Karen Legge, (1984). *Evaluating Planned Organizational Change.* London, Academic Press.

19 Donna Tarrt,(1993). *The Secret History.* Penguin.

20 William Golding (1962). *Lord of the Flies.* Faber & Faber.

21 R. Bach(1972). *Jonathan Livingston Seagull.* Pan.

22 Margaret Attwood(19921). *The Handmaids Tale.* Virago.

23 Robinson A. Mumford, and D. Strading, (1987). *Developing Directors.* Manpower Services Commission.

24 J. Constable, and R. McCormick (1988). *The Making of British Managers.* BIM.

25 Charles Handy (1988). *The Making of British Managers.* BIM.

37   Foreign language learning and the improvement of thinking and learning skills

Marie-Madeleine Kenning (University of East Anglia)

Introduction

The learning of one or more foreign languages has long been recognized as having an important role to play in education. After forming part for many years of the curriculum for a significant proportion of pupils at secondary level, language study was included in 1988 among the 'foundation' subjects of the National Curriculum; language is offered by many higher education institutions under the umbrella of transferable or enterprise skills, and there have been a number of attempts to introduce it into primary schools (see, for example, Burstall *et al.*, 1974).

The case for foreign language learning has many aspects. There is little doubt that the extension of language study to all pupils is partly due to the force of economic and utilitarian factors. At a national level, the strengthening of ties and commercial links with the rest of Europe has made it imperative to increase the pool of linguistic expertise within Britain in an effort to ensure the country has enough people with the ability to understand, and use, a diverse range of languages effectively. Equally, the European Community now offers individuals prospects of jobs and mobility, which many find very appealing, but which require a minimum foreign language proficiency or at least some experience of learning a foreign language; hence a growth in demand for foreign language courses.

But the promotion and development of foreign language learning also rests on educational considerations, as described in the proposals of the Secretary of State for Education and Sciences and the Secretary of State for Wales (DES and Welsh Office, 1990). In addition to enabling learners to communicate with users of the target language, foreign language learning is intended to offer insights into the culture and civilization of other countries, and, through comparison, enhance learners' understanding and appreciation of their own cultural traditions. This should contribute to broadening horizons, fostering tolerance of differences and encouraging mutual respect.

At the same time, exposure to a different linguistic code is said by the proposals to develop an awareness of the nature of language and a better understanding of the mother tongue; it is seen as a source of intellectual stimulation, and, most importantly in the context of this conference, it is perceived to promote learning of skills of more general application (e.g. analysis, memorising, drawing inferences)' (DES and Welsh Office, 1990, p. 3)

As for other subjects, the fulfilment of the educational purposes of foreign language learning is crucially dependent on the type of pedagogy used. It is important to note therefore that major changes have taken place over the last 20 years. In the early 1970s, the inability of the methods of the previous two decades to produce learners who could express themselves in the target language prompted a shift to more eclectic approaches centred on the concept of language as communication, with the transmission of meaning as their prime concern. Unlike the methods of the 1950s and 1960s, so called 'communicative language teaching' devotes comparatively little time to the formal study of language features, favouring instead a more pragmatic approach with particular emphasis on the oral/aural mode and the use of techniques designed to encourage verbal interaction, such as role play and simulation. And there is little doubt that there has been a marked improvement in learners' oral skills, and that those going on to further language study are much more fluent and much more confident in their ability to speak the language than was the case 15 years ago.

But it has not been all gain. Written skills have suffered, and there is much concern in universities at students' poor knowledge of the grammatical system of the target language and their lack of familiarity with basic distinctions and terminology. Overall, and unsurprisingly, current school teaching methodology appears more suited to achieving certain aims than others. For instance, it seems likely to be fairly successful in bringing about greater knowledge of, and more sympathetic attitudes towards, other cultures; on the other hand, there are grounds for thinking that it is not particularly conducive to the development of thinking and learning skills. Indeed, some current practices may well be regarded as actually detrimental to thinking and learning. To give one example, it is not uncommon for courses to present verb forms in a somewhat piecemeal fashion without showing learners whole conjugation paradigms. The practice can represent a welcome means of shielding learners from too much data, but it has the disadvantage of giving little scope to their inductive abilities: incomplete, fragmented information makes it much harder to observe regularities and patterns, and form hypotheses; it hinders the building up of a mental representation of the language system, and can cause intense frustration to the learner (as when the forms for certain persons are deliberately missed out from verb tables).

Evidence shows that many advanced language students do not know how to learn or how to use resources and reference works effectively; they fail to capitalize on what they know, and they have difficulty in exercising such skills as predicting, selecting, comparing and interpreting information (see Béjoint, 1981, also Kenning and Guillot, forthcoming). Faced with terms such as *espoir* and *espérance* that cover overlapping semantic areas and have a single common English equivalent (*hope*), many undergraduates are unable to process dictionary definitions (Figure 1) (Rey, 1988) to gain access to the meaning differences between the two items. The approach described below aims to remedy such deficiencies and help students develop strategies that will enable them to move towards more autonomous forms of learning. It is illustrated here with materials focusing on vocabulary expansion but has been applied to other areas, notably listening and reading comprehension. It can be characterized as process – as opposed to product – oriented and is being piloted at the University of East Anglia.

espérance (esperas) n. f. 1. *L'espérance*, sentiment qui fait entrevoir comme probable la réalistion de ce que l'on désire. => confiance, croyance; espoir (plus cour.). / contr. désespérance / *Le vert, couleur de l'espérance.* 2. *Une espérance, l'espérance de (qqch.)*, ce sentiment appliqué à un object déterminé. *Entretenir, former des espérances. Avoir une espérance de guérir, de guérison. Il a l'espérance qu'tout ira bien.* — *Contre toute espérance, alors qu'il semblait impossible d'espérer.* => attente. — Au plur. *Cette femme a des espérances*, elle attend un enfant. 3. *Espérance de vie*, durée moyenne de la vie humaine, dans une société donnée, établie statistiquement. 4. Au plur, ESPERANCES : biens qu'on attend d'un héritage. *Ils ont des espérances.*

espoir (espwar) n. m. 1. *L'espoir de . . . un espoir*, le fait d'espérer, d'attendre (qqch.) avec confiance. => espérance. *J'ai le ferme espoir, j'ai bon espoir qu'il réussira.* => certitude, conviction. *J'étais venu dans (avec) l'espoir de vous voir. Je mets tout mon espoir, mes espoirs en vous. C'est sans espoir, c'est désespéré.*
— Personne sur laquelle on fonde un espoir. *Vous êtes notre seul espoir. C'est un espoir du ski*, on espère qu'il deviendra un champion. 2. *L'espoir*, sentiment qui porte a espérer. *Être plein d'espoir. Aimer sans espoir.* / contr. désespoir; appréhension, crainte / <= désespoir>

Figure 1

Source Rey (1988)

Theoretical Rationale

The framework underpinning the approach is cognitive theory. Unlike certain theories of language learning, cognitive theory,which derives from developments in contemporary psychology, focuses on the cognitive processes involved in language learning rather than on specifically linguistic issues such as the existence of predictable acquisitional sequences. It regards second language learning as the acquisition of a complex cognitive skill involving the automatization of sub-skills and the constant restructuring of internal representations. Both processes are said to occur throughout learning, but gains in automaticity are thought to be more characteristic of early stages and restructuring of later ones (McLaughlin, 1987).

Cognitive theory has some shortcomings: it is not a complete theory and needs complementing with a linguistic theory. But it has considerable significance for pedagogy. As McLaughlin points out (McLaughlin, 1987, p. 151),

> from a practical point of view, a fuller appreciation of the central processes of automaticity and restructuring has important implications for second-language teaching.

For instance, the recognition of differences between early and later stages supports the adoption of different methodologies at different points in time. Together with other factors, notably what is known of learning and processing variations between young and adult learners, these differences can be used to justify a change of approach of the kind advocated here. According to Widdowson (Widdowson, 1990, p. 97):

it seems on the face of it to be likely that with some learners a conscious awareness of how language works and the subjection of their experience to analysis should suit their cognitive style, increase motivation by giving added point to their activities, and so enhance learning. It would enable them to make comparisons between the language they are learning and their own language, and engage in the kind of rational enquiry which is encouraged in other subjects on the curriculum.

The adoption of an approach favouring analysis and reflection seems particularly appropriate in the case of higher education students, who have opted to pursue academic studies; even if it does not always correspond with their preferred – or customary – learning style (since on the whole they have had little exposure to this kind of teaching and may not be aware of the shortcomings of the methods they have experienced), it seems desirable that they should be encouraged in this direction.

In addition, cognitive theory has stimulated research in areas of direct relevance to teaching. Learner strategies, commonly divided into production, communication and learning strategies (see, for example, Ellis, 1985) have been the object of studies ranging from empirical investigations into their nature and role to enquiries focusing on the differences between beginning and advanced learners and between good and poor learners. This work has produced valuable empirical data and increased understanding of second language acquisition, but its main interest for educators lies in the provision of 'a mechanism for describing how language learning ability can be 'improved' (and of a foundation for])the development and use of learning strategies in second language instruction (O'Malley and Chamot, 1990, p. 19–20). That is to say, it has highlighted a number of cognitive aspects that are susceptible to training and guidance.

Lastly, the cognitive perspective has led to the development of a range of methodologies, typically involving introspection (Faerch and Kasper, 1987, O'Malley and Chamot, 1990), that can be used for studying both the use of strategies and the effectiveness of strategy training.

The choice of guided discovery learning as the instructional technique used for improving learners' strategies in the approach under discussion also derives from work on cognition. Guided discovery learning originates from the claim of cognitive scientists that to discover things on your own leads not only to the acquisition of knowledge, but also to the development of skills for utilizing what you know. In language learning, discovering a language rule is regarded as more challenging than simply being presented with a rule statement, and it is thought that it may facilitate recall. Discovery may, however, be difficult: 'certain types of guidance are often necessary, and a major goal of effective instruction ought to set the stage so that discoveries are more likely to be made' (Bransford, 1979, p. 243). Hence Hammerly's recommendation that guided discovery, which "accommodates both inductive and deductive learning styles" (Hammerly, 1985, p. 120) should be used whenever possible, for example by subdividing complex grammar rules into subrules associated with carefully selected examples.

The educational strategy illustrated below can be described as having long-, medium- and short-term objectives. The ultimate goal is student autonomy; medium-term aims are related to the acquisition of a range of core learning strategies (e.g. elaboration, self-monitoring, self-evaluation) which have been found to be applicable to a variety of learning tasks as well as characteristic of effective second language learners (O'Malley and Chamot, 1990, p. 197) and are necessary for the achievement of independence; finally, the immediate objective of the unit described is learner sensitization to meaning differences and to the complementarity of the various sources of information offered by dictionaries. The unit differs from traditional language exercises in seeking to foster metacognitive awareness and the acquisition of cognitive strategies rather than trying to teach a predetermined body of facts. The items used are not important in themselves and could easily be replaced with others; the primary function of the unit is to invite learners to undertake tasks of a heuristic and generic nature offering repeated opportunities to engage in hypothesis formation and hypothesis testing and discover and automatize certain techniques and skills.

Design Principles and Exemplification

The materials referred to in this chapter form part of a set developed by Marie-Noâlle Guillot with special funding from the University of East Anglia and intended to cater for both self and teacher-directed use. Although not directly inspired by writings on the 'experiential learning cycle', they can be seen to proceed from the same kind of philosophy and to apply a number of similar principles (e.g. progression round a cycle involving doing, followed by reflection, formation of principles and planning, Gibbs *et al.*, 1993, p. 9). Those quoted below are mostly drawn from a unit focusing on abstract vocabulary, a particularly thorny area for second language learners. They involve the use of the Robert Electronique (henceforth RE), which is the CD-ROM version of the Grand Robert in six volumes.

In common with other electronic resources, the RE lends itself particularly well to the exploration of language phenomena; it contains extended textual data, provides a wealth of information, including long lists of synonyms, antonyms, and a wide range of quotations, together with the kind of special search facilities (wildcards, etc.) associated with electronic media (for details, see Guillot and Kenning, 1994). For this reason, it may not always be possible to implement *verbatim* the activities mentioned below using a standard printed dictionary; but there is nothing in the approach itself that could not be applied to the kind of dictionary available in any institution.

As stated above, the unit aims to help learners come to grips with abstract vocabulary through the provision of guidelines for expressing, checking and refining their intuitions. But this is not its only objective: it is also designed to improve dictionary and information processing skills and to promote self-regulatory skills.

The materials have a number of distinctive design features. First and foremost is the use of a progressive and graded approach. At the level of the unit, this means beginning with a question or an exercise to be done **without** a dictionary, from existing knowledge about the language, the step-by-step integration of different sources of information, and some increase in complexity. A similar type of organization is to be found in the set as a whole, the first unit dealing with concrete terms, an area of vocabulary inherently more accessible than the abstract terms at the centre of the second unit. But it is within each section that gradation comes into its own, with first an opportunity for learners to make spontaneous observations, followed by the provision of increasingly focused support. This is illustrated below with an extract from a section on the processing of short definitions. As can be seen, the support offered moves from a gentle hint to consider differences and points of contact between the definitions of the terms (**bonheur, joie** and **bien-être**), through a more specific instruction to make a detailed comparison, to a list of pointers (note the terminology) showing the kind of analysis that can be engaged in. The aim is

- to give practice in fulfilling a given type of task;
- to provide opportunities for strategies to come into play without prompting;
- to foster the acquisition of appropriate strategies;
- to lay the basis for self-assessment.

Access the RE short definition of bonheur, joie and bien-être in turn, identify the relevant entry in each case and copy the corresponding definition in your document (to make comparison easier)

This will give:

bonheur   II. 1. Etat de la conscience pleinement satisfaite

joie   1. Emotion agréable et profonde, sentiment exaltant ressenti par toute la conscience humaine

bien-être 1. Sensation agréable procurée par la satisfaction de besoins physiques, l'absence de tensions psychologiques

Have a brief look at the copied definitions and make a note of your initial response (differences/points of contact between the meaning of these words?)

Now compare these definitions point by point, feature by feature; where this is not possible, study the impact of the presence/absence of particular features.

Here are a few [overlapping] pointers:

- what is the difference between état/émotion/sentiment/sensation?

- which is the least/most superficial? which is the least/most fleeting?

- emotion and sentiment [in the def. of 'joie'] and sensation [in the def. of 'bien-être'] are all qualified by adjectives; état [in the def. of 'bonheur' is not: does this make a difference? Implications for 'bonheur'?

   (. . .)

- in the definition of 'bien-être', sensation is defined as much by a positive feature [satisfaction de . . .] as by a negative feature [absence de . . .); does this affect the interpretation of the term? What is the prominence of besoins physiques in relation to tensions psychologiques?

A second major characteristic of the materials is the emphasis placed on self-assessment and self-monitoring. It was stated above that the procedure which has just been illustrated was intended to lay a basis for self-assessment. There are two reasons for making such a statement. On the one hand, while primarily intended to have an effect on the acquisition of cognitive skills, the process of going through the various steps can also have some impact on metacognition by inducing certain learners to compare their information processing strategies with those implied by the materials. This may lead to the identification of certain weaknesses and encourage reflection on practices and learning strategies. However, the procedure is liable to help self-awareness in another way, for what has so far remained an implicit invitation becomes an explicit request in the next sub-section, when the learner is told

> Compare the results of this enquiry with your initial responses: are your hypotheses Confirmed? If not, can you trace/explain the discrepancies?

Calls on learners to examine how their thinking has progressed are made at several points in the unit, notably at the end of sections, when they may be encouraged to make comparisons with other sections or units. This is viewed as fostering self-regulatory skills and as providing a sense of progress which should have a positive impact on motivation

Also worth stressing is the way in which explanations are presented as examples or possibilities rather than as model answers. Thus, where appropriate, statements are kept deliberately tentative, as in the following conclusion to an activity on the synonyms of **bien-être**:

> **bien-être:** 'bien-aise' (+physical, -absolute) seems close to 'bien-être'; so does 'quiétude', though it is more moral/psychological a sensation, 'felicité' and 'sérénité', on the other hand, seem closer to 'bonheur', and 'euphorie' to 'joie'.
>
> The list seems to pull in different directions (physical/moral, transience/permanence, superficial/deeply felt), which makes the word "bien-être" somewhat difficult to circumscribe, gives it fuzzy edges; and it may suggest that the word in fact refers to a vague, unspecified/unspecifiable feeling . . .

Since Boileau's famous statement, '*ce qui se conçoit bien, s'exprime clairement*' (what is well thought out, is clearly set out), it has been axiomatic in France that quality thinking and clarity of expression are inextricably linked. Whether or not one agrees that good logic has an intrinsic affinity with transparent language, that sound reasoning is easy to put into words, and that straightforward formulations testify to the correctness of the argumentation, there can be little doubt that the articulation of intuitions and the recording of observations can be hampered by lack of adequate terminology. Hence the introduction into the materials of some basic technical terms together with the presentation of semantic concepts and techniques for analysis, as illustrated by the following extract from the first unit in the set (see Channel, 1981 for a defence of this kind of approach):

> Prepare a table listing the examplificatory words [siège, banc, chaise, fauteuil, tabouret] horizontally on the top line, and all the differentiating features vertically in the margin
>
> Fill in the table: place a "+" symbol under each word for which a particular feature specified in the definition applies; leave a blank space when features are not specified in a particular word's definition

(See Table 1.)

Table 1

	siège	banc	chaise	fauteuil	tabouret
objet manufacturé	+	+	+	+	+
pour s'asseoir	+	+	+	+	+
long		+			
à dossier		(+)	+	+	
sans dossier		(+)			+
pour une personne			+	+	+
pour plusieurs pers		+			
côté à côte		+			
à bras				+	
sans bras		+	+		+
à trois pieds					(+)
à quatre pieds					(+)
	2	6	5	5	5

Then, after an invitation to consider what insights can be gained from building such a table, an activity conducive to incidental learning (e.g. use of **pied** where English has `legs'):

> The table, which is called a componential table, enables you to map out the differentiating features – here semantic [meaning-related] features – of the words considered; it gives you a visual display of relevant features which makes words easier to compare/contrast and facilitates analysis.

> What can be noticed in this case is that 'siège' is marked by only two features, which also apply to all the other words; all the other words can thus be defined as 'siège', but their meaning is narrowed down by additional features.

> 'Siège' – the most general term in the list – acts, then, as an umbrella term for the other words: it is a generic term, or superordinate, in relation to them (. . .)

But our review of design principles would not be complete without a mention of presentation and layout. Overall, presentation and layout have been the object of more modifications than other aspects. This is not to say that they were not paid any attention when the materials were first produced; but we have since evolved a house style which has not only improved the appearance of the text but has been elaborated with the aim of facilitating thinking and learning. In line with the advice given in books such as Race, 1989, and Lockwood, 1992, the density of the text has been reduced and most sections have been put in boxes. The use of different typefaces and other typographical devices to highlight differences in the function of the text has been extended and follow-up comments have been repositioned to reduce the chance of students reading the notes prior to forming their own hypotheses.

Evaluation

The original versions of the units were piloted with a small group of students in the Summer Term of 1993 prior to being used in a first year Honours course in Autumn 1993. Data collection methods comprised:

- student diaries;
- questionnaires;
- observation and audio-recording of two pairs of students working on the unit on abstract terms, followed by post-mortem discussions.

Of the issues investigated, those most relevant to the present paper were the effectiveness of the approach in sharpening learners' perception of words and their relationships, and the effect on the development of strategies. The evidence put forward in the rest of this chapter was mainly gathered via the third method: although necessarily limited and collected from volunteers, it is representative, and consistent with the feedback obtained from other students both during the trialling period and afterwards.

As far as improvement in thinking is concerned, there are clear signs in the recorded data of a progression from fairly vague intuitions to the discovery of important distinctions and relations, as corroborated by this extract from the follow-up discussion:

it makes you realise that [there are] various words that correspond to each situation.

Whether the impact extended to the longer term is not known but the insights developed by the participants in the project may have contributed to their slight superiority over a control group in the small test that took place at the end: the task, which involved new words, consisted in filling gaps in three short written texts, the deleted items being hyponyms of a superordinate provided as a clue in the opening sentence of each piece. Students who had taken part in the project were observed to have more immediate grasp of the nature of the task, as well as greater stamina, and their performance was marginally better.

But the small size of the samples, doubts as to their comparability, and the use of different dictionaries by the two sets (with the control group using a conventional dictionary instead of the RE) mean that the results need to be interpreted with utmost care.

Two factors appear to have been particularly important with respect to the evolution in the students' thinking noted above. One is the productivity of the pointers exemplified earlier, as indicated by remarks such as

absence de (with reference to the definition of **bien-être**) is not quite as positive . . . Is it? Do you reckon there's more emphasis on one of them, I reckon it's probably on the yeah physical things rather than the psychological, because it is actually the satisfaction of your physical needs whereas it's only just the absence of (psychological tensions).

The other is the opportunity to use each other as sounding boards:

(1) I think it's better doing, when you can do it together and discuss it; I've enjoyed that more than I did on Thursday when I did the concrete terms, that was just a question of really getting through it, it wasn't having someone there to say oh yeah you're doing this

right, or what do you think about this; because there are bits that you are not sure of, or you'd rather have someone's opinion. (2) yeah.

It should be pointed out here that students who used the unit on their own during the following term remarked that it would have been helpful to have a partner. Their opinion has been taken note of, and pair work is to be the methodology of study recommended to users of the materials.

The data collected during the evaluation also contains empirical evidence of a beneficial influence on learning strategies. Starting with direct evidence on cognitive strategies, one can cite the students' spontaneous use of the RE to clarify the meaning of unknown words and their willingness to apply the techniques to new areas, thereby multiplying opportunities for serendipity learning. Thus, in response to the suggestion made in the materials that they might like to look at antonyms in the same way as they had at synonyms:

(1) You want to do that one as well? (2) yeah because they should help you more understand the thing, shouldn't they. Yeah, see there (1) it's more passing emotion, they're just like joie aren't they? they are not states, well **tristesse** is but . . . what's the other one? **Bien-être**. Yeah, **pauvreté, souffrance**. Yeah, OK that helps quite a bit actually. (2) Yeah, that's a good idea.

Indirect evidence can be found in statements such as the following comment on the value of the preceding unit:

it gets you used to like looking at the different definitions and seeing the differences between them.

and the positive ratings given to the unit under discussion in terms of its usefulness in a survey carried out in the Autumn term.

Turning to the effect on metacognition, one finds instances of self-evaluation following requests to monitor progress:

(1) Yeah, well we've highlighted differences. (2) Yeah. (1) And we've got much more detailed definitions of the terms.

More interesting however, is the occurrence, in the follow-up discussion, of statements such as

(1) Well we learned more of the path of how to look something up if you're not sure of it, like before I wouldn't have looked at the quotations, if I was just using this. (2) Yeah and also if I was writing an essay and wanted to put **bonheur** or something in, then I think before, without all this, I would have just written **bonheur**, but now I might like look up some synonyms and try and find a better word

and of signs of an emerging realization that it is necessary to exploit different kinds of information for cumulative understanding, as in this discussion of definitions:

but you naturally go on to the detailed ones because there are so many short ones, you need to look at the full one to check it's the right one you need.

Conclusion

From the evidence available, the approach to language learning illustrated above would appear both practicable and reasonably successful at meeting immediate and medium-term objectives: as they go through the materials, students can be seen to acquire better dictionary skills, to become more aware of relations between words and to develop more effective learning strategies. It is too early to tell whether the improvements noted will be sustained. What is clear is that in order to be fully effective and make a real impact on students' ability to become autonomous language learners, the approach needs to be extended and integrated into a larger framework combining a wide choice of language resources with extensive and diversified guidance and ample opportunities for practice. The claim made here is that the building of such an environment will lead not only to increased linguistic competence but also to improvements in thinking and learning skills.

ACKNOWLEDGEMENT
I wish to thank Marie-Noëlle Guillot for her help and comments during the preparation of this paper.

References

Béjoint, H. (1981). The foreign student's use of monolingual English dictionaires: a study of language needs and reference skills, *Applied Linguistics*, **2**(3), 207–22.

Bransford, J. (1979). *Human Cognition: Learning, Understanding and Remembering*, Belmont, California, Wadsworth.

Burstall, C., Jamieson, M., Cohen, S. and Hargreaves, M. (1974). *Primary French in the Balance*, Berkshire, NFER

Channel, J. (1981). Applying sematic theory to vocabulary teaching. *English Language Teaching Journal*, **35**(2), 115–22.

DES and Welsh Office (1990). *Modern Foreign Languages for Ages 11 to 16*. HMSO.

Ellis, R. (1985). *Understanding Second Language Acquisition*, OUP.

Faerch, C. and Kasper, G. (eds) (1987). *Introspection in Second Language Research*, Clevedon, Multilingual Matters.

Gibbs, G., Rust, C., Jenkins, A. and Jaques, D. (1993). *Teaching Enterprise Skills*, Oxford Brookes University.

Guillot, M-N. and Kenning, M-M. (1994). Electronic dictionnaires as language learning aids – the Robert Electronique, *Computers and Education*, **23**(1/2), 63–73.

Hammerly, H. (1985). *An Integrated Theory of Language Teaching*, Blaine, Wash, Second language publications.

Kenning, M-M. and Guillot, M-N. (forthcoming). Adopting a process-oriented approach to vocabulary expansion, Cashiers AFLS

Lockwood, F. (1992). *Activities in Self-Instructional Texts*, London, Kogan Page.

McLaughlin, B. (1987).*Theories of Second-Language Learning*, London, Edward Arnold.

O'Malley, J.M. and Chamot, A.U. (1990). *Learning Strategies in Second Language Acquisition*, CUP

Race, P. (1989). *The Open Learning Handbook: Selecting, Designing and Supporting Open Learning Materials*, London Kogan Page.

Rey, A. (ed.) (1988). *Le Micro-Robert*, Paris, Dictionnaires Le Robert.

Widdowson, H.G. (1990). *Aspects of Language Teaching*, OUP.

38   Improving group work of students in seminars through team training

Ute Schädler (Department of Economics and Business Administration, Johann Wolfgang Goethe-Universitiy Frankfurt am Main, Germany)

Introduction

The reason for offering a team training as a supplement to the project groups [1] was our experience that students have little or no experience with group work. Group – or team work is not only a professional skill, but also a skill necessary for personal development. However, it is not recognized in the official curriculum of German universities. Also the students have little confidence in the outcome of group work. An example of this is the increasing number of extra curricular revision courses ('*Repetitorien*') students choose to prepare themselves for their exams, instead of studying in groups as used to be the case until a few years ago.

When we offer this supplementary team training we have to be aware that the openness and indeterminate nature of project groups give the students a feeling of uncertainty and instability in relation to the amount of work they have to do and the criteria of assessment which follows at the end. Also, the extra confidence they need for working with other students whom they don't know very well gives them a feeling of insecurity and anxiety. When we asked the students how they saw the difficulties involved in group work a common answer was the fear of freeloading and spending endless time with discussion without any result.

The background to team training was to give students the opportunity to focus on the group - and task process and learn from this experience. We know that this plays an important role in the work of their project groups and influences their results.

However, this means we need to find the link between the project groups and the team training.

Aims

The aim of the team training was to raise the capability of the participants not only to fulfil a given task but also to work as part of the group process. They had the opportunity to experience and reflect different levels of cooperation. Each session of the team training consisted of an exercise where students had the experience of teamwork and an equal period for reflection, evaluation and planning for improvements.

In helping students to complete the task, we focused on techniques such as goal-setting, planning, division of labour and time management. Another focus was the exploration of

---

1 By Ritter (*described in Chapter 16*)

and reflections on the student's own skills, which either support or inhibit this process.

Apart from the qualities students showed in the first part of the seminar, for example to reproduce theoretical contents and transfer to practical situations, they needed different skills or qualities for the project groups in the second part. It was evident that the students who presented good results in the first part of the seminar didn't always present good results in the second part.

Project groups demand skills from the students such as initiative, creativity and organizing skills. One idea of the team training was to focus on group skills, how to utilize these skills and to develop a different attitude in relation to the results, which means to develop confidence in student's own goal-setting and their self assessment.

Following the Coverdale-Method, we developed a four-session team training of 90 minutes. The task, the assessment, the motivation of the students and our roles have been very different from the project groups. I participated in the team training in the group process as observer and consultant. Students had the freedom to participate in the training or not without affecting their marks at the end. Once again in the team training we were more interested in the process than in the result-orientated project groups.

We assumed that participants who were aware of the group process would produce better results. This means that the project groups had to present a background paper, which included the important theoretical and practical details on the subject they worked on and the design and running of a seminar session related to their subject. This session had not only to be interesting but also had to use different didactical methods.

The Design of the Team Training

Each session of the team training consisted of an exercise which had to be solved. For this participants had 45 minutes. Another 45 minutes were dedicated to reflect the process and for discussion. At the end of each session I tried to find out what kind of difficulties they had in their project groups and then tried to integrate and work with these problems in the team training. Students didn't take advantage of this opportunity and told me there were no problems. This stands in contradiction to what we found out in questionnaire at the end of the work of the project groups.

The content of the training followed the seven-step-method, developed by Coverdale.

'Seven-step method'

1 What is the task? Do all participants have the same understanding of the task?

2 What is or what should be the goal?

- Why should we do this, for whom?
- What should the result look like?
- Which criteria would show that the work was a success?

3 Information: facts, ideas, resources, skills from the group members.

4 What has to be done?

5 Planning: who is making what, how, where, when. . . ?

6 Accomplishment

7 Evaluation (task- and process-orientated)

In the **first session** we focused on the sense and purpose of a task and the implication for the result. We encouraged students to ask themselves: why were they doing the task, for whom, which criteria would show them the success, what would the result look like?

The students could not present a result at the end of the first session and this had an enormous impact on the evaluation process, where I could easy develop together with them the priority of focusing on a task in group work. Already in this session the students explored the wish to get feedback about the roles they took and so develop the capability to act. This I found surprising so early in the process. One hypothesis for this could be that the narrow assessment, concentrated on analytical skills and reproduction of knowledge that students are used to at university, leads to enthusiasm for other forms of evaluation or feedback.

In the **second session** the main point was the planning of the task and decision-making. A group who wanted to get a good result had to make concrete decisions all the time. Decision-making influenced the kind of relationship group members built. In helping students to structure the planning and decision-making process we gave them the seven-step-method, as a handout.

I will now give you an example of one of the exercises we used.

We wanted them to build a mobile which would illustrate aspects of the participant's professional and social life. We stated that one measure of success from our point of view was that each participant should present at least one idea at the end of the work.

They started to work with the seven-step-method. After much too short a time they delegated these steps to different group members. Each member built his or her part of the mobile, there were no discussions about what they were drawing or writing. And again, without discussion, they quickly assembled the mobile within the time limit.

All but one of the group were happy with the result. His dissatisfaction fitted in the overall evaluation which highlighted the individualization and isolating nature of the group process. When participants realized what had happened they were surprised, and questions arose as to what group work meant and the benefit group work can have. Also we developed the different patterns and perceptions of what constituted individual work and what constituted group work. We also talked about students' anxiety and their distrust of group work. We also worked at the function and role of people who felt isolated in this context.

The **third session** started with brainstorming on the attitudes and attributes a good group member should have. This was followed by a personal feedback. The exercise we did was the well-known 'Building a tower' co-operation exercise.

This time participants worked on the group process as well as on the task. The evaluation showed that they had improved their ability to co-operate and that they had learned from their last experience. The whole group felt that this also had to do with the fact that some of the group members were not participating this time.

At the beginning of the **fourth session** the methods and factors which influence group work were reflected on and discussed. This time we gave them a task, where the participants had to design an exercise for the project groups from which participants came. This gave them the chance to transfer their experience from the project group to the team training. Our aim was that they should think about the kind of co-operation they had had in their project group and discuss their different experiences. To the end this was very creative and the result was surprising to us, since the students coped very well with the unusual amount of freedom they had. They discussed the contents of their project groups from a professional perspective rather than a group-work perspective and they felt that better co-operation would be the result of this particular type of professional discussion.

Part of the discussion focused on how to reach decision by consensus and how to integrate minority points of view in this process.

Results

Students who participated in the training were highly motivated. But although the participants told us in interviews that they had learned something about group work, they said that they found it difficult to transfer these ideas to the project groups. From our point of view perhaps the least satisfying aspect of their feedback, but never the less important to them, was the inability to transfer what they saw as having fun into real life situations. However, in saying this, given the short time and limited resources available, we felt that the outcome could not have been much better.

With regard to our original hypothesis that members who participated in the training will get better results in their project groups, we saw no direct relationship to the training, although the groups from which participants came got better marks. Our doubts as to the immediate practical relevance have been proven through interviews. We see a higher correlation between the participants involved in the team training getting good marks and their high motivation and the willingness to learn. Also, they felt that the highly motivating atmosphere within the project groups as a whole contributed to the good results.

Improved Design

Following our assessment that the team training had little to do with the skills they needed in their project groups I will suggest an improved design. As already stated, one of our main problems was the transfer of group work skills to the project groups and the integration of members who felt isolated by this process.

I suggest that the training would better be implemented within the framework and the context of the project groups. A more pragmatic approach would be the use of real experience of the project group as a basis for any exercises. These exercise would focus on particular problems relevant for the group at that moment. This would lead to more energy being used on evaluating and improving the work of the project group as a whole. However, we should be aware that learning from students' own experience is more important than imposing an additional model, which provides only extra experience. Starting from the point where students already are, can provide a base for their own development rather than merely asking them to fulfil our expectations of them. This demands a structure which provides both tasks centred and psychological support and supervision. This would give us a sociological link between what happens in the project groups and what happens in society.

A part of this new design could be a session, before the project groups starts, which informs students about project work where students can have their first experience of group work and its problems and prerequisites.

I know that not all project groups may wish to participate, but I feel that it is important that a group only joins when all members agree. I suggest that the different project groups should have the choice, and it is important to reflect their process and work within their structure instead of building a new team where the reality of their project group would get lost.

References

Antons, K. (1992). *Praxis der Gruppendynamik. Übungen und Techniken.* Pädagogische Psychologie.

Bailey, A. (1990). Personal transferable skills for employment: the role of higher education. In P.W.G. Wright. (ed), *Industry and Higher Education. Collaboration to Improve Students' Learning and Training.* The Society for Research into Higher Education and Open University Press, 68–75.

Gibbs, G. (1992). *Improving the Quality of Student Learning.* Technical and Educational Services Ltd.

Kunz, H.U. (1994). *Spitzenleistung im Team. Menschen erfolgreich führen, Aufgaben methodisch lösen.* Verlag Industrielle Organisation Zürich.

Meyer-Dohm, P. (1990). Graduates of higher education: what do employers expect in the 1990s? In P.W.G. Wright. (ed), *Industry and Higher Education. Collaboration to Improve Students' Learning and Training.* The Society for Research into Higher Education and Open University Press, 61–68.

39   Using questionnaires to evaluate student learning

John T. E. Richardson (Brunel University)

Introduction

During the last 25 years, a number of different questionnaires have been developed to evaluate student learning in higher education. Although originally intended as research tools, they potentially have an important role to play too in the assessment of the quality of education. In this chapter, I shall describe the development of three such questionnaires, and then go on to discuss their applications and limitations in research and practice in higher education.

Basic Concepts in Student Learning

First, I need to review some of the basic concepts in recent research into student learning. There is a general consensus in the literature that students in higher education exhibit a number of different approaches to learning. Some of the earliest research on this topic was carried out in Sweden by Marton (1975), who asked students to read and recall an academic text and then interviewed them about the way in which they had approached this task. To describe the individual differences that were apparent from their accounts, Marton referred to a suggestion made by Craik and Lockhart (1972), that remembering should be analysed in terms of the properties of the material on which the attention of different learners was focused, in terms of different 'levels of processing'. Craik and Lockhart argued that memory could be thought of as a hierarchical system of representations, in which the use of more abstract or 'deeper' levels of processing would tend to be associated with superior retention.

In the students' accounts, Marton duly identified two main levels of processing, and these were subsequently defined by Marton and Säljö (1976) in the following terms:

> In the case of surface-level processing the student directs his attention towards learning the text itself (the sign), i.e. he has a 'reproductive' conception of learning which means that he is more or less forced to keep to a rote-learning strategy. In the case of deep-level processing, on the other hand, the student is directed towards the intentional content of the learning material (what is signified), i.e. he is directed towards comprehending what the author wants to say about, for instance, a certain scientific problem or principle (pp. 7–8).

Marton also asked his students about their general academic studies. On the basis of their responses, he concluded that approaches to studying in higher education could be categorized in essentially the same terms, and this was confirmed in subsequent work. In particular, students tend to adopt a 'deep' approach insofar as they acknowledge the more abstract forms of learning that are demanded in higher education (Svensson, 1977) and are motivated by the relevance of the syllabus to their own personal needs and interests (Fransson, 1977); but they tend to adopt a 'surface' approach insofar as they encounter an overloaded curriculum and methods of assessment that emphasize the superficial properties of the material that is to be learned (Dahlgren and Marton, 1978).

The distinction between deep and surface approaches to learning was subsequently confirmed in other investigations using qualitative methods carried out in the United Kingdom (Hounsell, 1984; Laurillard, 1979, 1984; Morgan, Taylor and Gibbs, 1982; Ramsden, 1979, 1984), Australia (Watkins, 1983) and the Netherlands (van Rossum and Schenk, 1984). A study in Hong Kong found that the surface approach took the specific form of a 'narrow' approach that was 'characterised by a systematic, step-by-step, processing of information' (Kember and Gow, 1990, p. 356), and this suggests that the less desirable approaches to studying are subject to cultural influences. Nevertheless, the broad distinction between deep and surface approaches to learning appears to be essentially a universal feature of all systems of higher education (see Richardson, 1994a).

Ramsden (1979) identified a third approach based upon a particular category of students who had been described earlier by Miller and Parlett (1974) as 'cue-seekers'. These students

> buttonholed staff about the exam questions; sought them out over coffee; made a point of discovering who their oral examiner was, what his interests were and, most of all, deliberately attempted to make a good impression on staff. This for them seemed to constitute a very large part of what the exams were all about (p. 52).

Ramsden developed this notion of 'cue-consciousness' into the more general concept of a 'strategic' approach to assessment in higher education. The defining characteristics of the three different approaches to learning are summarized in Table 1. It should however be added that the existence of a strategic approach has typically not been confirmed in subsequent research using semi-structured interviews either in the United Kingdom or elsewhere (see Richardson, 1994a).

The interview-based methodology that gave rise to this categorization of approaches to studying has been variously described as 'experiential', 'introspective' and 'phenomenographic' (Bowden, 1986; Marton, 1979, 1981; Marton and Svensson, 1979). This has been claimed to be more sensitive to the different meanings that individuals ascribe to learning in particular academic situations, and yet the precise research procedures used in this work are typically not specified in any detail. Indeed, some researchers who follow this phenomenographic tradition are prepared to include 'chats at the foot of the stairs' with students as well as informal discussions 'over a beer' with their teachers (Eizenberg, 1986, p. 21)

Until recently, only one published piece of phenomenographic research contained reference to a formal methodology for analysing interview data. This study was carried out by Morgan *et al.* (1982) with students taking an introductory social-science course at the UK Open University. The authors began their report by asserting that Marton and Säljö's (1976) distinction between deep-level and surface-level approaches marked 'a crucial aspect of understanding how students handle learning materials' (p. 107). They then reported that transcripts of their interviews had revealed deep-level and surface-level approaches broadly similar to those described by Marton and Säljö (1976) when they were analysed using the procedures of 'grounded theory'. The latter is a methodology devised by Glaser and Strauss (1967) in which theoretical concepts and hypotheses are discovered in and refined against respondents' accounts. The 'grounding' of theory directly in data was supposed to replace an uncritical acceptance of existing theory and in particular of the forms of 'grand' theory then prevalent in sociology.

Table 1 Defining features of three approaches to learning

Deep approach

- Intention to understand
- Vigorous interaction with content
- Relate new ideas to previous knowledge
- Relate concepts to everyday experience
- Relate evidence to conclusion
- Examine the logic of the argument

Surface approach

- Intention to complete task requirements
- Memorize information needed for assessments
- Failure to distinguish principles from examples
- Treat task as an external imposition
- Focus on discrete elements without integration
- Unreflectiveness about purpose or strategies

Strategic approach

- Intention to obtain highest possible grades
- Organize time and distribute effort to greatest effect
- Ensure conditions and materials for studying appropriate
- Use previous exam papers to predict questions
- Be alert to cues about marking schemes

Source: adapted from Entwistle (1987, p. 16).

In the most radical version of grounded theory, specific themes are derived from the respondents' accounts without regard to the researcher's own preconceptions. For instance, Strauss and Corbin (1990) commented that in grounded-theory studies the researcher should not be 'constrained by having to adhere to a previously developed theory that may or may not apply to the area under investigation'. As a consequence, 'it makes no sense to start with "received" theories or variables (categories) because these are likely to inhibit or impede the development of new theoretical formulations'. Only after a category has emerged as pertinent should the researcher go back to the literature to determine whether the category is there (pp. 49–50). One of Glaser's students stated more bluntly that the grounded theorist 'enters the scene bereft of preformed theory', and that they should validate their theory by checking back with the informants and revealing the theory to them as it developed (Stern, 1994, pp. 215, 217). On this view, the analysis employed by Morgan et al. could be seen more as reading things into the facts than as grounded theory (Richardson, 1994b).

Glaser and Strauss (1967) had stated that it was quite appropriate to exploit insights from existing theory, provided that the latter was itself grounded in empirical data. Indeed, a researcher who used grounded theory could expect to cultivate a 'theoretical sensitivity' in which ideas from earlier work were applied to but not imposed on new data (pp. 6, 46, 255). Nevertheless, critics suggested that Glaser and Strauss had overemphasized the extent to which existing theory could be ignored, and that the fit and relevance of an existing theory could be tested against a new body of data regardless of whether that theory was itself grounded (e.g. Turner, 1981). This criticism was essentially accepted by Strauss and Corbin (1994), who acknowledged that grounded theory research might involve the generation of new theories from new data, the elaboration of existing grounded theories against new data, or the refinement of any relevant theory based upon the investigator's previous research, provided that in each case the matching of theory to data was rigorously carried out to ensure that the resulting theories were always traceable to the data that gave rise to them.

Indeed, Strauss and Corbin (1990) had recommended that the technical literature 'can be used to stimulate theoretical sensitivity by providing concepts and relationships that are checked out against actual data . . . You will look for evidence of whether or not the concepts and relationships apply to the situation that you are studying, and if so what form they take here' (pp. 50–51; see also p. 55). They saw this as a form of hypothesis testing in qualitative research (p. 148). In this case, it would still of course be good practice for researchers to disclose any prior theoretical commitments and render these permeable to new data by seeking out contrary instances and by validating their interpretations through peer debriefing (see Stiles, 1993). It is clear that the aim of Morgan et al. was to see whether the distinction between deep-level and surface-level approaches to studying constituted a useful framework for understanding learning in Open University students. Other reports by these investigators (e.g. Taylor, Gibbs and Morgan, 1981) confirm that this less radical version of grounded theory constituted the basis of their own research into student learning.

One recent example also endeavoured to spell out the specific process by which the theoretical categories used to describe student learning had been derived (Entwistle and Marton, 1994). This investigation adopted a phenomenological, experiential approach whose individualistic assumptions were somewhat at odds with earlier assertions of Marton and his colleagues to the effect that approaches to learning in higher education are cultural phenomena that are socially constructed (see e.g. Dahlgren, 1984; Marton, 1981; Säljö, 1984, 1987). This account also revealed an eclectic research strategy that combined elements of grounded theory, protocol analysis (see Ericsson and Simon, 1993) and discourse analysis (see Potter and Wetherell, 1987). Unfortunately, the origins of this research strategy were left unacknowledged, which makes it very difficult for other investigators to acquire the requisite skills to try to replicate and extend this study.

In seeking to collect information from large numbers of students, it is in any case unreasonable in practice to consider conducting one-to-one interviews. It would be feasible to administer open-ended questionnaires (cf. van Rossum and Schenk, 1984), but this would still leave the burden of analysing a substantial amount of qualitative data. Instead, teachers and researchers tend to use standardized questionnaires, and particularly those which generate quantitative scores on dimensions assumed to reflect the use of different approaches to learning in higher education. Three such instruments have been constructed for this purpose: the Approaches to Studying Inventory, the Study Processes Questionnaire and the Inventory of Learning Processes.

The Approaches to Studying Inventory

Possibly the most widely used questionnaire on student learning in higher education has been the Approaches to Studying Inventory (ASI), which was devised by Entwistle and his colleagues in the United Kingdom (Entwistle, Hanley and Hounsell, 1979; Entwistle and Ramsden, 1983; Ramsden and Entwistle, 1981). In its most widely used version, the ASI contains 64 items in 16 subscales, and these were published as an appendix to the book by Entwistle and Ramsden (1983, pp. 228–33). In each case, respondents are asked to indicate the extent of their agreement or disagreement with a particular statement along a five-point Likert-type scale from 'definitely agree', scoring 4, to 'definitely disagree', scoring 0. The 16 subscales are grouped in turn under four general headings, as shown in Table 2, and the responses to the relevant items are simply summed to obtain a score on each scale and each subscale. The subscales and their constituent items have a variety of origins (Entwistle and Waterston, 1988; Parsons, 1992).

Some subscales stem from earlier research into possible determinants of academic achievement. Entwistle and his colleagues (see Entwistle and Entwistle, 1970; Entwistle and Wilson, 1970; cf. also Entwistle, Nisbet, Entwistle and Cowell, 1971) had devised a Student Attitude Questionnaire (SAQ), which consisted of 91 items in four scales relating to motivation, study methods, extraversion and neuroticism. Motivation in studying was interpreted originally in terms of achievement motivation, but Entwistle, Thompson and Wilson (1974) argued that it was important to differentiate between intrinsic motivation or interest in the subject matter, extrinsic motivation or interest in the qualifications to be gained, and motivation that depended upon the maintenance of self-esteem or the fear of failure. Subsequently, Entwistle and Wilson (1977, pp. 38–43, 180–3) replaced the scales measuring extraversion and neuroticism with additional scales that were intended to measure syllabus-boundness and syllabus-freedom. These notions had been introduced by Hudson (1968, pp. 11–14) and Parlett (1970) in order to describe the extent to which different students seem to prefer direction as opposed to autonomy in their learning.

The study methods scale of the SAQ was concerned solely with whether students were organized or disorganized in their studying and with whether their general attitudes towards studying were positive or negative. The research carried out by Marton and his colleagues showed these dimensions to be inadequate as a way of characterizing individual differences among students in higher education. As a consequence, additional scales were devised to represent the deep and surface approaches described by Marton (1975) and the strategic approach described by Ramsden (1979). These were supplemented by two other subscales concerned with some of the cognitive processes that were presumed to be associated with a deep-level outcome of learning: the propensity for inter-relating ideas and the use of evidence and logic. More fundamentally, the distinction between deep, surface and strategic approaches to learning was subsumed within the broader framework of a 'meaning orientation', a 'reproducing orientation' and an 'achieving orientation' towards learning in higher education.

Table 2 Subscales contained in the Approaches to Studying inventory

Subscale	*Meaning*
Meaning orientation	
Deep approach	Active questioning in learning
Inter-relating ideas	Relating to other parts of the course
Use of evidence and logic	Relating evidence to conclusions
Intrinsic motivation	Interest in learning for learning's sake
Reproducing orientation	
Surface approach	Preoccupation with memorization
Syllabus-boundness	Relying on staff to define learning tasks
Fear of failure	Pessimism and anxiety about academic outcomes
Extrinsic motivation	Interest in courses for the qualifications they offer
Achieving orientation	
Strategic approach	Awareness of implications of academic demands made by staff
Disorganized study methods	Unable to work regularly and effectively
Negative attitudes to studying	Lack of interest and application
Achievement motivation	Competitive and confident
Styles and pathologies	
Comprehension learning	Readiness to map out subject area and think divergently
Globetrotting	Over-ready to jump to conclusions
Operation learning	Emphasis on facts and logical analysis
Improvidence	Over-cautious reliance on details

Source: Ramsden and Entwistle (1981, p. 371).

These three domains were supplemented by a fourth which represented particular styles and pathologies of learning that had been described by Pask. Pask and Scott (1972) had employed an interview-based approach in order to investigate the strategies adopted by experimental subjects when given artificial learning tasks. They had claimed that there were just two general categories of learning strategy: a 'serialist' approach and a 'holist' approach: 'Serialists learn, remember and recapitulate a body of information in terms of string-like cognitive structures where items are related by simple data links . . . Holists, on the other hand, learn, remember and recapitulate as a whole' (p. 218).

Nevertheless, Pask (1976) claimed that in academic situations 'some students are disposed to act "like holists" (comprehension learners) and others "like serialists" (operation learners), with more or less success' (p. 133). He suggested that comprehension learners were able to pick up an overall picture of their subject matter by using global 'description building operations', whereas operation learners picked up rules, methods and details by using relatively specific 'procedure building operations'. Comprehension learners were disposed to 'globetrotting' in their use of inappropriate speculations or analogies, whereas operation learners were disposed to 'improvidence' in their failure to exploit valid analogies and general principles. For Pask, truly effective learning was the result of a versatile approach that integrated description building and procedure building operations in an appropriate manner.

Unfortunately, research studies have consistently failed to reproduce the intended constituent structure of the ASI (for reviews, see Harper and Kember, 1989; Meyer and Parsons, 1989b; Richardson, 1994a). Studies which have carried out factor analyses upon students' scores on the 16 subscales have obtained clear evidence for two major factors:

1 a 'meaning orientation' factor indexed by the subscales concerned with deep approach, inter-relating ideas, the use of evidence and logic, intrinsic motivation and comprehension learning; and

2 a 'reproducing orientation' factor indexed by the subscales concerned with surface approach, syllabus-boundness, fear of failure, disorganized study methods, negative attitudes to studying, globetrotting and improvidence.

In addition, many studies (though by no means all; see e.g., Meyer, 1988; Meyer and Dunne, 1991; Morgan, Gibbs and Taylor, 1980) have produced some evidence for two additional factors:

3 a 'narrow orientation' factor indexed by the subscales concerned with operation learning and strategic approach; and

4 a 'goal orientation' factor indexed by the subscales concerned with extrinsic motivation and achievement motivation.

Moreover, several studies have carried out factor analyses upon students' responses to the 64 individual items, and these have typically failed to reproduce certain of the subscales, particularly those associated with an achieving orientation and with the styles and pathologies scale (Entwistle and Ramsden, 1983, pp. 50–2; Entwistle and Waterston, 1988; Meyer and Parsons, 1989a, 1989b; Schmeck, 1988; Speth and Brown, 1988).

Given the somewhat doubtful status of certain of the subscales of the full ASI, it might be thought useful to develop an abbreviated inventory that focused upon the more reliable study orientations. In his textbook on educational psychology, Entwistle (1981, pp. 57–60, 100–3) described a version of the ASI in which 30 items defined seven scales that included meaning orientation, reproducing orientation and achieving orientation. Although this was intended simply as an expository device, Entwistle and Ramsden (1983, pp. 53–5) referred to a pilot study in which it had been modified for use with sixth-form students. Subsequently, it was employed by researchers in Britain and Sweden to monitor approaches to studying in medical students (Chessell, 1986; Coles, 1985; Martenson, 1986). Gibbs, Habeshaw and Habeshaw (1988) presented a shorter version of the ASI that consisted of just the 18 items from Entwistle's inventory concerned with the different orientations to studying. This was commended for lecturers to use in evaluating their own teaching, and it was subsequently used to assess innovative forms of course design and delivery in several British institutions of higher education in a project sponsored by the Council for National Academic Awards on *Improving Student Learning* (Gibbs, 1992).

Watkins (1984) used the 30-item version of the ASI to monitor the approaches to studying of 445 secondary schoolchildren in the Philippines (see also Watkins, Hattie and Astilla, 1986). Their scale scores showed a meaningful pattern of correlations with their academic achievement, but the internal consistency of these scores was somewhat low. Watkins attributed this to the shortness of the individual scales, but in the absence of any comparable results from a British sample it is not clear whether Watkins' findings should be attributed to cultural differences in studying between British and Filipino students rather than to some inherent inadequacy in this version of the ASI. Indeed, Richardson (1992) found that the 18-item version recommended by Gibbs et al. (1988) had slightly better internal consistency and a satisfactory level of test–retest reliability when used with a sample of British university students (see also Newstead, 1992).

Nevertheless, Richardson (1992) carried out a factor analysis on the responses given by a sample of British students to the 18-item version of the ASI, and found that the three individual scales were measuring fairly specific aspects of study behaviour rather than more global orientations to studying. Although Newstead (1992) recommended this version of the ASI as one 'quick-and-easy' method of assessing individual differences in student learning, on close inspection his own results tend to confirm Richardson's interpretation. Thus, the 18-item version of the ASI does not seem to be useful for measuring the basic constructs that underlie studying in higher education. The same conclusion would presumably also apply to the 30-item version that was devised by Entwistle (1981), because this uses precisely the same items to measure meaning orientation, reproducing orientation and achieving orientation.

A more satisfactory approach to this problem is to focus on the items or subscales within the original 64-item ASI that define the constructs of meaning orientation and reproducing orientation. In order to evaluate the effectiveness of a course on learning skills at one Australian university, Ramsden, Beswick and Bowden (1986, 1987) assembled an inventory consisting mainly of items from the meaning orientation and reproducing orientation scales of the full ASI to produce measures of the use of deep and surface approaches to learning. This is not wholly satisfactory, however, because previous investigations have consistently failed to reproduce the intended structure of these two scales in terms of either the constituent subscales or the constituent items. For instance, 'extrinsic motivation' was one of the four subscales that was taken to define a reproducing orientation (see Table 2), and yet it consistently fails to load on the same factor as the three other subscales that supposedly define that orientation to studying (Harper and Kember, 1989; Meyer and Parsons, 1989b).

I have argued instead (Richardson, 1990) that it is more appropriate to abbreviate the original ASI by focusing upon the eight subscales which were empirically identified with meaning orientation and with reproducing orientation across the different academic disciplines studied by Entwistle and Ramsden (1983, p. 52) when they originally developed this instrument.

This yields an inventory of 32 items with the following structure:

Meaning orientation	*Reproducing orientation*
deep approach	surface approach
comprehension learning	improvidence
inter-relating ideas	fear of failure
use of evidence and logic	syllabus-boundness

The items in question can be found in an appendix to my published report, and I was able to show that both the eight subscales and the two principal study orientations could be successfully reproduced by factor analysis of the responses generated by a new sample of undergraduate students. This version of the ASI was also found to have levels of internal consistency and test–retest reliability that were satisfactory and superior to those of the 30-item ASI devised by Entwistle (1981). Thus, I would recommend this version of the ASI as a useful instrument for research and practice.

Nevertheless, it should also be mentioned that the ASI is currently undergoing fairly extensive revision. In 1992, a Revised Approaches to Studying Inventory (RASI) was developed which contained 60 items in 15 subscales that measured five major dimensions: deep approach, surface approach, strategic approach, apathetic approach and academic aptitude. In 1994, a reduced version of the RASI was produced; this contained 38 items in 14 subscales that also measured five dimensions: deep approach, surface approach, strategic approach, lack of direction and academic self-confidence. Neither of these versions has been formally published (although copies can be obtained from Noel Entwistle), and at the time of writing (September 1994) there is no published evidence concerning their psychometric properties. Because these instruments differ significantly from the established versions of the ASI, any research findings that may be obtained with them in the future are likely to be incommensurable with those contained in the established literature.

The Study Processes Questionnaire

Another early contribution to this line of inquiry was the Study Behaviour Questionnaire (SBQ) devised by Biggs (1970a, 1970b). Rather like the SAQ, this instrument sought to characterize students' approaches to learning as the product of a number of different enduring personality characteristics. The initial version of the SBQ was based upon 72 items, and an analysis of the responses given by 314 education students at an Australian university generated six orthogonal factors. Biggs (1973, 1976) developed the SBQ at a Canadian university, and the eventual version covered 10 scales measured by 80 items that were claimed to yield a useful classification of students in terms of their different patterns of study behaviour.

Subsequently, Biggs (1978) presented a revised instrument, the Study Processes Questionnaire (SPQ), in which some of the items in the SBQ were reclassified and the 10 scales were relabelled. He carried out separate factor analyses of the scale scores produced by 420 Canadian students and by two samples of 150 and 148 Australian students, and discovered that in each case the 10 scales could be subsumed under three second-order factors which he interpreted as representing the 'reproducing', 'internalizing' and 'organizing' dimensions of study processes. These encompassed the values, the motives and the cognitive strategies which were associated with different aspects of learning: in terms of students' motives, they reflected extrinsic, intrinsic and achievement-based motivation, while at the cognitive level they were considered to be broadly comparable with the 'surface', 'deep' and 'strategic' approaches which were defined in Table 1 (see also Biggs, 1979).

Entwistle (1988) took this to be convergent evidence for the general distinction between surface, deep and strategic approaches to learning in an Australian setting. Nevertheless, Watkins and Hattie (1980) were only partially successful in replicating Biggs's (1978) factor analyses in a study involving 562 Australian university students, and a more detailed statistical analysis suggested that the individual scales in this version of the SPQ were not homogeneous measures of aspects of study behaviour. In further research with Australian students, Biggs (1985, 1987) reduced the SPQ to just seven items in each of six subscales that reflected the respondents' motives and strategies on the three major dimensions, and he renamed these as 'surface', 'deep' and 'achieving' approaches to learning to bring his analysis into line with the usage of other researchers.

The items constituting the final version of the SPQ were published in an appendix to Biggs's book (1987, pp. 132–3). In each case respondents are asked to indicate the extent of their agreement or disagreement with a statement on a five-point Likert-type scale from 1 to 5, and the responses to the relevant items are summed to obtain a score on each scale and each subscale. Hattie and Watkins (1981) administered this version of the SPQ to 255 Australian students, and found that the internal consistency of the six subscales was wholly satisfactory. A factor analysis of the students' responses to the individual items produced a six-factor solution in which the subscales outlined by Biggs were said to have been 'clearly evident' (p. 243), and a further analysis of the students' scores on the subscales themselves generated three factors that could be identified with the three major approaches to studying. Unfortunately, this report did not provide any details of these extracted factor solutions.

However, subsequent attempts to reproduce the constituent structure of the 42-item SPQ have been less successful. Even in his own analyses of the subscale scores obtained by Australian students, Biggs (1987; Biggs and Rihn, 1984) consistently failed to retrieve the intended structure and found instead merely a generalized surface approach and a generalized deep approach to studying. Remarkably similar solutions have been obtained in studies conducted in Britain and Nigeria (O'Neil and Child, 1984; Watkins and Akande, 1992). In addition, in reports which have described factor analyses carried out upon students' responses to the 42 individual items, concern has been repeatedly expressed about the composition of some of the six subscales, especially those intended to measure a surface approach to studying (Christensen et al., 1991; Kember and Gow, 1990, 1991; O'Neil and Child, 1984; but cf. Biggs, 1993).

In short, while the SPQ has been widely used in investigating student learning in a variety of systems of higher education, serious doubts have been raised concerning the integrity of its subscales and the coherence of their constituent structure. The available research evidence implies that they do not provide distinctive, homogeneous and appropriate indicators of the theoretical constructs on which the SPQ is supposed to be based. (The same problem arises in the case of the 36-item version of the SPQ that was devised for use in secondary schools: see Biggs, 1987, p. 16; Watkins and Regmi, 1990; although cf. Andrews, Violato, Rabb and Hollingsworth, 1994.) It cannot be recommended as a useful instrument for research or practice.

The Inventory of Learning Processes

In the United States, Schmeck, Ribich and Ramanaiah (1977) developed the Inventory of Learning Processes (ILP) on the basis of contemporary ideas in experimental psychology concerning human learning and remembering. In particular, they referred to Craik and Lockhart's (1972) idea that memory performance would be dependent upon the 'depth' of processing, as well as a subsequent suggestion by Craik and Tulving (1975) that it would also be dependent upon the degree of elaboration or 'breadth' of processing.

The ILP contains 62 items in four scales, and these were published in Table 1 and Table 2 of the paper by Schmeck et al. (1977). In each case, respondents are asked to say simply whether a particular statement is true or false in terms of the way in which they generally learn rather than how they learn within any particular course or academic discipline. The four scales represent the common factors obtained from an analysis of responses given to a much larger set of 121 items. They were subsequently explained by Schmeck and Grove (1979) in the following manner:

> synthesis-analysis: assessing deep, as opposed to superficial, information processing;

> study methods: assessing repetitive, drill-and-practice habits of processing information;

> fact retention: assessing attention to details and specifics as opposed to generalities; and

> elaborative processing: assessing elaborative, as opposed to verbatim, information processing.

A score on each scale is obtained by counting the number of responses that are in accordance with the meaning of the corresponding scale. (To reduce the influence of response bias, some items demand the response 'true', but others demand the response 'false'.)

In the light of later developments in research into student learning, Schmeck (1983) relabelled the first two of the scales 'deep processing' and 'methodical study', respectively. Schmeck claimed that his notion of "deep processing" was distinct from that originally put forward by Marton and Säljö (1976), because it was concerned not with a student's intention or approach to a specific task but rather with the underlying cognitive processes. Nevertheless, both notions were explicitly derived from the 'levels-of-processing' framework for understanding human memory that had been proposed by Craik and Lockhart (1972; see Marton, 1975). Indeed, Schmeck and Geisler-Brenstein (1989) recently agreed that their own contrast between deep and surface processing was broadly equivalent to Marton's distinction between deep-level and surface-level processing and to Biggs's (1979) distinction between reproducing and internalizing, thus demonstrating the convergent validity of all of these constructs.

The ILP was extensively validated in research conducted at several institutions of higher education across the United States (Schmeck, 1983, 1988), but its use outside that country has been very limited. Watkins and Hattie (1981a) used the ILP in a comparison of students in Australia and in the Philippines. Some of the scales did not generate satisfactory measures of internal consistency, and factor analyses failed to replicate the ILP's intended constituent structure. Schmeck (1983) suggested that these discrepancies with his own results could be attributed to cultural and linguistic differences between the various populations, but a study by Speth and Brown (1988) in the United States using a shortened version of the ILP also failed to reproduce the ILP's original scale structure. This suggests that Watkins and Hattie's results may have been due to basic problems with the instrument itself rather than to cultural or linguistic factors.

Schmeck, Geisler-Brenstein and Cercy (1991) supplemented the original scales of the ILP with seven other scales that examined broader aspects of self-concept and personality, to produce a Revised Inventory of Learning Processes (ILP-R). In completing this instrument, respondents indicated the extent of their agreement or disagreement with each of 160 statements along a six-point Likert-type scale. Schmeck and Geisler-Brenstein (1989) had mentioned an unpublished study in which an early version of the ILP-R was administered to students in the United States and China. They stated that 'a similar factor structure was obtained for both groups' (p. 100), but, although they did not present any quantitative data, it is clear that the factorial solution which they obtained failed to replicate the scale structure of the original ILP.

Subsequently, Schmeck *et al.* (1991) reported the correlations among the scale scores produced by the American students in this study. While the scales of the original ILP had earlier been stated to be 'relatively independent' (Schmeck *et al.*, 1977, p. 420), the ILP-R showed substantial associations among the deep processing, fact retention and elaborative processing scales. Similar results were obtained from 89 students in the United States on the original ILP by Henson and Schmeck (1993). As with the SPQ, therefore, it would appear that the scales of the ILP no longer provide distinctive and homogeneous indicators of the constructs on which the instrument is supposed to be based, and accordingly the ILP cannot be recommended as a useful instrument for investigating student learning in higher education.

General Conclusions From Questionnaire-based Research

None of these established questionnaires appears to be wholly satisfactory for measuring students' approaches to learning in higher education. It is however reasonable to conclude that these quantitative instruments provide convergent evidence from a variety of national systems of higher education for two fundamental approaches to studying: first, an orientation towards comprehending the meaning of the materials to be learned; and, second, an orientation towards merely being able to reproduce those materials for the purpose of academic assessment (see Richardson, 1994a). In contrast, the evidence obtained with questionnaires provides very little support for any 'strategic' approach to academic assessment of the sort that was described by Ramsden (1979) nor equivalently for any 'achieving' orientation towards studying. There is in addition little unambiguous support for the various learning styles and pathologies that were described by Pask (1976), except as components of the two fundamental study orientations.

Unfortunately, this 'convergence' is at present apparent merely at an abstract level, since there is very little direct evidence that the three instruments are measuring the same underlying aspects of student learning. Schmeck (1988) described an unpublished investigation in which students at one North American university completed both the ASI and the ILP (see also Entwistle, 1988; Schmeck and Geisler-Brenstein, 1989). Their responses to the 126 items loaded on six clearly interpretable factors, but the latter did not unequivocally reflect the constituent scales of either instrument. This is also true of the results obtained in two studies using abbreviated versions of the ASI and the ILP in Scotland (Entwistle and Waterston, 1988; see also Entwistle, 1988) and the United States (Speth and Brown, 1988).

Of course, the fact that the responses given to formal questionnaires can be encoded and aggregated in a quantitative manner does not mean that they can be regarded as objective or unbiased measures of some underlying psychological reality. The respondents are to be sure highly constrained by the predetermined format of each questionnaire, and they are unable to calibrate their understanding of the individual items against the meaning intended by the person who originally devised the questionnaire or by the person who actually administers it to them. Nevertheless, as Strack and Schwarz (1992) demonstrated, responses to questionnaires are communicative and collaborative acts that are based upon the same principles of everyday conversation as responses to an interview. In the absence of any explicit feedback, the respondents will use cues that allow them to make pragmatic inferences about the questioner's intended meaning, such as the content of neighbouring items or the range of response categories available.

Accordingly, the responses given to formal questionnaires on student learning always stand in need of analysis and interpretation. As will be apparent from the preceding review, the most common analytic procedure is that of factor analysis, which endeavours to reduce the data generated by a large sample of individuals to a few coherent and consistent constructs. This procedure should always be carried out when employing a questionnaire in a situation different from that in which it was originally developed to check that its intended constituent structure can be reconstructed in this new context. Examples would include the use of a questionnaire originally devised to study conventional undergraduate students in research on Access students, disabled students, mature students, or postgraduate students, or the use of a questionnaire developed in Australia or the United States in research carried out in the United Kingdom.

Although the results of factor analyses carried out upon responses to questionnaires have been broadly consistent with those of interview-based studies in demonstrating two basic approaches or orientations to learning, they are discrepant in one fundamental respect. The accounts derived from interviews indicated the existence of two distinct categories or forms of understanding (see Entwistle and Marton, 1984; Marton, 1975; Marton and Säljö, 1984) or a single bipolar dimension along which individual students might vary (Marton, 1976). However, in standard questionnaires deep and surface approaches are typically operationalized as separate scales which turn out to be orthogonal to each other, so that an individual student might score high or low on both (Biggs, 1985; 1987, p. 16; Biggs and Rihn, 1984; O'Neil and Child, 1984; Trigwell and Prosser, 1991). As Trigwell and Prosser (1991) pointed out, this has the practical implication that interventions aimed at improving student learning should be concerned more with encouraging a deep approach than with necessarily discouraging a surface approach.

An explanation for this discrepancy between the results of interviews and questionnaires possibly lies in their intended level of generality or specificity. Interview-based research has often examined whether students actually do adopt a deep approach or a surface approach within particular course units or even within particular learning tasks and categorized them accordingly using a simple dichotomy of approaches to studying. However, questionnaire-based research tends to be more concerned with measuring the disposition of individual students to manifest a meaning orientation or a reproducing orientation across a range of academic situations, often with different course objectives, teaching styles and assessment requirements. In other words, the continuous measurements generated by questionnaires on approaches to studying reflect the result of aggregating a large series of bare dichotomies obtained from a variety of learning situations. It could therefore be claimed that they more faithfully reflect the constitutional factors that determine the adoption of different approaches to studying.

Factor analysis is based upon the aggregate data generated by a large sample of individuals, and it is possible that the features of a group do not adequately capture the range of features exhibited by its constituent members. Meyer and Muller (1990a, 1990b) advocated the application of multidimensional unfolding analysis to questionnaire responses because it allows one to make comparisons amongst the patterns of scores obtained by individual students. This procedure regards a score on a particular scale as a measure of the affinity of the student to the construct in question, and then represents both scales and students as specific locations within a multidimensional space. Using the ASI, Meyer and Muller found that most students produced a coherent pattern of associations or 'orchestration' in which the scales defining a meaning orientation were tightly clustered and clearly differentiated from the other scales.

However, this technique gives only an overall impression of the level of 'orchestration' shown by individual students and does not allow one to categorize individual students according to their approaches to studying. A different technique for analysing quantitative responses given by groups of students in reporting on how they engage with academic learning is that of cluster analysis. This procedure was employed by Entwistle and Brennan (1971) to analyse the scores from 875 students on 23 variables, including scales concerned with motivation, study methods and examination technique. This generated 12 discrete groups of students who differed qualitatively from each other in their aptitude, personality and attitudes to studying. I have recently shown that similar procedures can be applied to scores on the ASI to classify individual students in terms of a meaning orientation and a reproducing orientation (Richardson, in preparation).

Finally, it needs to be mentioned that in non-educational contexts the concept of 'learning styles' is commonly associated with the work of Kolb (1984; Kolb, Rubin and McIntyre, 1991). Kolb developed a Learning Style Inventory (LSI) to measure an individual person's orientation towards each of four learning modes. The LSI is however subject to a number of serious methodological criticisms despite having undergone extensive revision (see Veres, Sims and Locklear, 1991). At an empirical level, the LSI exhibits very little overlap with the other questionnaires discussed in this chapter (Cano-Garcia and Justicia-Justicia, in press; Ribich and Schmeck, 1979), and Newstead (1992) concluded from his own data that it was not a useful instrument for assessing individual differences in student learning.

Approaches to Studying and Academic Performance

A basic research question is whether scores on questionnaires concerning approaches to studying in higher education predict academic performance. In interview-based research, a deep approach or a strategic approach tend to be associated with good performance, but a surface approach tends to be associated with poor performance (Entwistle and Ramsden, 1983, pp. 176–8; Miller and Parlett, 1974, p. 55; Svensson, 1977).

There is only limited evidence concerning the relationships between students' approaches to studying and their qualifications on admission to higher education. Findings obtained using the ASI (Entwistle and Ramsden, 1983, p. 48) and the SBQ (Biggs, 1970b) suggests that these are unrelated. However, Schmeck and Grove (1979) found that the scores which students had obtained on the American College Testing examination were positively correlated with their scores on the synthesis-analysis, fact retention and elaborative processing scales of the ILP and negatively correlated with their scores on the study methods scale.

A number of studies have found that success in subsequent assessments can be predicted on the basis of scores on the subscales of the ASI. In particular, academic performance tends to be positively related to scores on deep approach, intrinsic motivation, and strategic approach, but negatively related to scores on surface approach, disorganized study methods, and negative attitudes to studying (Clarke, 1986; Entwistle, Hanley and Housell, 1979; Miller, Finley and McKinley, 1990; Ramsden and Entwistle, 1981; Watkins, 1982, 1983). Nevertheless, Kember and Harper (1987) found that the critical aspects of study behaviour depended on both the outcome being predicted (completion vs. final performance) and the mode of study (conventional learning vs. distance learning). Indeed, Trigwell and Prosser (1991) found evidence to suggest that even a surface approach could be associated with good assessment results if the teacher demonstrated the relevance of the subject matter, made opportunities for students to ask questions, and provided clear assessment criteria.

In developing the SBQ, Biggs (1970a) found a highly complex pattern of interrelationships between approaches to studying and performance that depended upon the students' gender and academic disciplines (arts versus science) (see also Biggs 1970b, 1976; Watkins and Hattie, 1981a). He took this as evidence against the assumption that there was a single dimension on which study habits could be characterized as good or bad, and against the notion that there was a determinate set of 'study skills' that somehow guaranteed effective academic performance. It followed that the value of study skills programmes was highly questionable. Nowadays, indeed, such ideas are commonplace in the literature on student learning (e.g. Cowan, 1989; Entwistle, 1992; Ford, 1980; Gibbs, 1981, chap. 4; Gibbs, Morgan and Taylor, 1980; Martin and Ramsden, 1987; Ramsden, Beswick and Bowden, 1986, 1987).

In developing the ILP, Schmeck and Grove (1979) found that students' current grade point average was positively correlated with their scores on the synthesis-analysis, fact retention and elaborative processing scales, though not on the study methods scale. Similar results were obtained by Miller, Alway and McKinley (1987), Miller et al. (1990), and Gadzella, Ginther and Williamson (1987) with American students and by Watkins and Hattie (1981a; Watkins, Hattie and Astilla, 1983) with Australian and Filipino students. However, Watkins and Hattie (1981a) found that magnitude of these correlations varied across different academic faculties, and Lockhart and Schmeck (1984) found that the pattern of relationships depended upon the demands of particular forms of academic assessment. Moreover, Moss (1982) found no positive correlations between ILP scale scores and grade point average in a sample of students who had been referred for remedial study skills tuition.

Thus, the relationship between approaches to studying and academic attainment is by no means a simple one. Indeed, several investigations in which subscale scores were obtained on different versions of the ASI have found that academically unsuccessful students do not simply show 'poorer' approaches to studying but fail to show any coherent approaches at all. This outcome was obtained in two studies that employed multidimensional unfolding analysis (Meyer, Parsons and Dunne, 1990a, 1990b) and two other studies that employed factor analysis (Entwistle, Meyer and Tait, 1991; Meyer and Dunne, 1991). In short, poor academic performance appears to be associated with a disintegration or fragmentation of the normal patterns of studying behaviour.

Using Questionnaires in Course Evaluation

The relevance of questionnaires on student learning to the evaluation of particular courses or programmes of study is fairly obvious. The notion of a meaning orientation or a deep approach to studying is more consistent with the avowed aims of higher education than a reproducing orientation or a surface approach to studying. It is therefore sensible to ask whether a particular course or programme of study succeeds in encouraging students to adopt a meaning orientation or a deep approach. In addition, nowadays it is often assumed that students' approaches to studying are determined principally by the content, the context and the demands of their learning tasks. It is therefore reasonable to ask how the curriculum, the setting and the assessment could be changed so as to increase the likelihood that students will adopt a meaning orientation or a deep approach to studying.

I want to provide just two concrete examples of the manner in which questionnaires on student learning can provide useful information in the context of course evaluation. The first arose from an observation in one of the case studies in the Council for National Academic Awards' project on *Improving Student Learning* that was mentioned earlier in this chapter (Gibbs, 1992, chap. 10). The case study was concerned with a unit on oceanography being studied by undergraduate students and also by students taking a postgraduate diploma. The effect of incorporating independent group fieldwork was evaluated by means of the 18-item version of the ASI. Both groups of students achieved high scores on meaning orientation, but the postgraduate students produced much higher scores on reproducing orientation, which was attributed to the heavier curriculum and the pressure of examinations on the diploma course.

This conclusion raises the question whether these factors are endemic to taught postgraduate courses or whether the findings are idiosyncratic to the particular unit being assessed in this case study. Discussions in my own department suggested that students on our taught Master's courses might also be subject to curriculum overload, and I therefore carried out a comparison of undergraduate and postgraduate students on four different course units using the 18-item version of the ASI. The scores obtained by 33 undergraduate students and 44 postgraduate students failed to replicate the pattern exhibited in the oceanography case study; indeed, if anything, the postgraduates produced slightly higher scores on meaning orientation and slightly lower scores on reproducing orientation. Consequently, there is no specific evidence that students on our taught postgraduate courses are induced to adopt a reproducing orientation by a heavy curriculum or the pressure of examinations.

The second example concerns an attempt to increase the effectiveness of student learning on a first-year course in discrete mathematics at my university by introducing a multimedia variant of the Keller personalized system of instruction. The course was taken by mathematics and computer science students, and was assessed using the 32-item version of the ASI. Four weeks later, the students were asked to complete the ASI once again with reference to a conventional, lecture-based course. The course that was delivered using the Keller PSI was found to induce much higher scores on meaning orientation than the conventional course, but paradoxically this was true only in the case of the students taking computer science.

This result is of general theoretical interest, because it seems to be the first time that significant changes in study behaviour have been produced within the same students as a result of specific interventions, though an investigation by Eley (1992) produced analogous findings using the SPQ by comparing pairs of courses that fortuitously appeared to differ in the extent to which they encouraged particular approaches to learning. However, it is also of considerable practical interest, not simply because it demonstrated the effectiveness of the intended intervention, but more important because it showed that the intervention failed to induce changes in the group of students for whom it might have been expected to be most effective (that is, those for whom mathematics was the main subject).

In short, although questionnaires concerning students' approaches to learning in higher education were devised as research instruments and have subsequently generated a substantial amount of data on particular issues, when the results are interpreted with care they can also provide valuable information in the context of evaluating courses or programmes of study.

ACKNOWLEDGEMENTS

I am grateful to Graham Gibbs, Karen Henwood and Alistair Morgan for their comments, advice and suggestions, and to Hilary Tait for information about the RASI.

References

Andrews, J., Violato, C., Rabb, K. and Hollingsworth, M. (1994). A validity study of Biggs' three-factor model of learning approaches: A confirmatory factor analysis employing a Canadian sample. *British Journal of Educational Psychology*, **64**, 179–85.

Biggs, J. B. (1970a). Faculty patterns in study behaviour. *Australian Journal of Psychology*, **22**, 161–74.

Biggs, J. B. (1970b). Personality correlates of certain dimensions of study behaviour. *Australian Journal of Psychology*, **22**, 287–97.

Biggs, J. B. (1973). Study behaviour and performance in objective and essay formats. *Australian Journal of Education*, **17**, 157–67.

Biggs, J. B. (1976). Dimensions of study behaviour: Another look at ATI. *British Journal of Educational Psychology*, **46**, 68–80.

Biggs, J. B. (1978). Individual and group differences in study processes. *British Journal of Educational Psychology*, **48**, 266–79.

Biggs, J. B. (1979). Individual differences in study processes and the quality of learning outcomes. *Higher Education*, **8**, 381–94.

Biggs, J. B. (1985). The role of metalearning in study processes. *British Journal of Educational Psychology*, **55**, 185–212.

Biggs, J. B. (1987). *Student Approaches to Learning and Studying*. Melbourne: Australian Council for Educational Research.

Biggs, J. (1993). What do inventories of students' learning processes really measure? A theoretical review and clarification. *British Journal of Educational Psychology*, **63**, 3–19.

Biggs, J. B. and Rihn, B. A. (1984). The effects of intervention on deep and surface approaches to learning. In J. R. Kirby (ed.), *Cognitive Strategies and Educational Performance* (pp. 279–93). Orlando, FL: Academic Press.

Bowden, J. A. (1986). Educational development and phenomenography. In J. A. Bowden (ed.), *Student Learning: Research into Practice. The Marysville Symposium* (pp. 3–18). Parkville: Centre for the Study of Higher Education, University of Melbourne.

Cano-Garcia, F.,and Justicia-Justicia, F. (in press). Learning strategies, styles and approaches: An analysis of their interrelationships. *Higher Education*.

Chessell, G. (1986). Learning styles in first year medical students. *Medical Teacher*, **8**, 125–35.

Christensen, C. A., Massey, D. R. and Isaacs, P. J. (1991). Cognitive strategies and study habits: An analysis of the measurement of tertiary students' learning. *British Journal of Educational Psychology*, **61**, 290–99.

Clarke, R. M. (1986). Students' approaches to learning in an innovative medical school: A cross-sectional study. *British Journal of Educational Psychology*, **56**, 309–21.

Coles, C. R. (1985). Differences between conventional and problem-based curricula in their students' approaches to studying. *Medical Education*, **19**, 308–9.

Cowan, J. (1989). Who needs study skills? *British Journal of Educational Technology*, **20**, 61–2.

Craik, F. I. M. and Lockhart, R. S. (1972). Levels of processing: A framework for memory research. *Journal of Verbal Learning and Verbal Behaviour*, **11**, 671–84.

Craik, F. I. M. and Tulving, E. (1975). Depth of processing and retention of words in episodic memory. *Journal of Experimental Psychology: General*, **104**, 268–94.

Dahlgren, L.-O. (1984). Outcomes of learning. In F. Marton, D. Hounsell, and N. Entwistle (eds), *The Experience of Learning* (pp. 19–35). Edinburgh: Scottish Academic Press.

Dahlgren, L. O. and Marton, F. (1978). Students' conceptions of subject matter: An aspect of learning and teaching in higher education. *Studies in Higher Education*, **3**, 25–35.

Eizenberg, N. (1986). Applying student learning research to practice. In J. A. Bowden (ed.), *Student Learning: Research into Practice*. The Marysville Symposium (pp. 21–60). Parkville: Centre for the Study of Higher Education, University of Melbourne.

Eley, M. G. (1992). Differential adoption of study approaches within individual students. *Higher Education*, **23**, 231–54.

Entwistle, N. (1981). *Styles of Learning and Teaching: An Integrated Outline of Educational Psychology for Students, Teachers, and Lecturers*. Chichester: Wiley.

Entwistle, N. (1987). A model of the teaching-learning process. In J. T. E. Richardson, M. W. Eysenck and D. Warren Piper (eds), *Student Learning: Research in Education and Cognitive Psychology* (pp. 13–28). Milton Keynes: SRHE and Open University Press.

Entwistle, N. (1988). Motivational factors in students' approaches to learning. In R. R. Schmeck (ed.), *Learning Strategies and Learning Styles* (pp. 21–51). New York: Plenum Press.

Entwistle, N. (1992). Student learning and study strategies. In B. R. Clark and G. R. Neave (eds), *The Encyclopedia of Higher Education: Vol. 3. Analytical Perspectives* (pp. 1730–40). Oxford: Pergamon.

Entwistle, N. J. and Brennan, T. (1971). The academic performance of students: 2. Types of successful students. *British Journal of Educational Psychology*, **41**, 268–76.

Entwistle, N. J. and Entwistle, D. (1970). The relationships between personality, study methods and academic performance. *British Journal of Educational Psychology*, **40**, 132–43.

Entwistle, N., Hanley, M. and Hounsell, D. (1979). Identifying distinctive approaches to studying. *Higher Education*, **8**, 365–80.

Entwistle, N. and Marton, F. (1984). Changing conceptions of learning and research. In F. Marton, D. Hounsell and N. Entwistle (eds), *The Experience of Learning* (pp. 211–36). Edinburgh: Scottish Academic Press.

Entwistle, N. and Marton, F. (1994). Knowledge objects: Understandings constituted through intensive academic study. *British Journal of Educational Psychology*, **64**, 161–78.

Entwistle, N. J., Meyer, J. H. F. and Tait. H. (1991). Student failure: Disintegrated perceptions of studying and the learning environment. *Higher Education*, **21**, 249–61.

Entwistle, N. J., Nisbet, J., Entwistle, D. and Cowell, M. D. (1971). The academic performance of students: 1. Prediction from scales of motivation and study methods. *British Journal of Educational Psychology*, **41**, 258–67.

Entwistle, N. J. and Ramsden, P. (1983). *Understanding Student Learning*. London: Croom Helm.

Entwistle, N. J., Thompson, J. and Wilson, J. D. (1974). Motivation and study habits. *Higher Education*, **3**, 379–95.

Entwistle, N. and Waterston, S. (1988). Approaches to studying and levels of processing in university students. *British Journal of Educational Psychology*, **58**, 258–65.

Entwistle, N. J. and Wilson, J. D. (1970). Personality, study methods and academic performance. *Universities Quarterly*, **24**, 147–56.

Entwistle, N. J. and Wilson, J. D. (1977). *Degrees of Excellence: The Academic Achievement Game*. London: Hodder and Stoughton.

Ericsson, K. A. and Simon, H. A. (1993). *Protocol Analysis: Verbal Reports as Data*, rev. ed. Cambridge, MA: MIT Press.

Fleming, W. G. (1986). The interview: a neglected issue in research on student learning. *Higher Education*, **15**, 547–63.

Ford, N. (1980). Teaching study skills to teachers: A reappraisal. *British Journal of Teacher Education*, **6**, 71–8.

Fransson, A. (1977). On qualitative differences in learning: IV. Effects of intrinsic motivation and extrinsic test anxiety on process and outcome. *British Journal of Educational Psychology*, **47**, 244–57.

Gadzella, B. M., Ginther, D. W. and Williamson, J. D. (1987). Study skills, learning processes and academic achievement. *Psychological Reports*, **61**, 167–72.

Gibbs, G. (1981). *Teaching Students to Learn: A Student-Centred Approach*. Milton Keynes: Open University Press.

Gibbs, G. (1992). *Improving the Quality of Student Learning*. Bristol: Technical and Educational Services.

Gibbs, G. , Habeshaw, S. and Habeshaw, T. (1988). *53 Interesting Ways to Appraise your Teaching*. Bristol: Technical and Educational Services.

Gibbs, G., Morgan, A. and Taylor, E. (1980). Why students don't learn. In *Institutional Research Review*, No. 1 (pp. 9–32). Milton Keynes: Open University.

Glaser, B. G. and Strauss, A. L. (1967). *The Discovery of Grounded Theory: Strategies for Qualitative Research*. Chicago, IL: Aldine.

Harper, G. and Kember. D. (1989). Interpretation of factor analyses from the Approaches to Studying Inventory. *British Journal of Educational Psychology*, **59**, 66–74.

Hattie, J. and Watkins, D. (1981). Australian and Filipino investigations of the internal structure of Biggs' new Study Process Questionnaire. *British Journal of Educational Psychology*, **51**, 241–4.

Henson, M. and Schmeck, R. R. (1993). Learning styles of community college versus university students. *Perceptual and Motor Skills*, **76**, 118.

Hounsell, D. (1984). Learning and essay-writing. In F. Marton, D. Hounsell and N. Entwistle (eds), *The Experience of Learning* (pp. 103–23). Edinburgh: Scottish Academic Press.

Hudson, L. (1968). *Frames of Mind: Ability, Perception and Self-Perception in the Arts and Sciences*. London: Methuen.

Kember, D. and Gow, L. (1990). Cultural specificity of approaches to study. *British Journal of Educational Psychology*, **60**, 356–63.

Kember, D. and Gow, L. (1991). A challenge to the anecdotal stereotype of the Asian student. *Studies in Higher Education*, **16**, 117–28.

Kember, D. and Harper, G. (1987). Implications for instruction arising from the relationship between approaches to studying and academic outcomes. *Instructional Science*, **16**, 35–46.

Kolb, D. A. (1984). *Experiential Learning: Experience as the Source of Learning and Development*. Englewood Cliffs, NJ: Prentice-Hall.

Kolb, D. A., Rubin, I. M. and McIntyre, J. M. (1991). *Organizational Psychology: An Experiential Approach*. Englewood Cliffs, NJ: Prentice Hall.

Laurillard, D. (1979). The processes of student learning. *Higher Education*, **8**, 395–409.

Laurillard, D. (1984). Learning from problem-solving. In F. Marton, D. Hounsell, and N. Entwistle (eds), *The Experience of Learning* (pp. 124–43). Edinburgh: Scottish Academic Press.

Lockhart, D. and Schmeck, R. R. (1984). Learning styles and classroom evaluation methods: Different strokes for different folks. *College Student Journal*, **17**, 94–100.

Martenson, D. F. (1986). Students' approaches to studying in four medical schools. *Medical Education*, **20**, 532–4.

Martin, E. and Ramsden, P. (1987). Learning skills, or skill in learning? In J. T. E. Richardson, M. W. Eysenck and D. Warren Piper (eds), *Student Learning: Research in Education and Cognitive Psychology* (pp. 155–67). Milton Keynes: SRHE and Open University Press.

Marton, F. (1975). On non-verbatim learning: I. Level of processing and level of outcome. *Scandinavian Journal of Psychology*, **16**, 273–9.

Marton, F. (1976). What does it take to learn? Some implications of an alternative view of learning. In N. Entwistle (ed.), *Strategies for Research and Development in Higher Education* (pp. 32–43). Amsterdam: Swets and Zeitlinger.

Marton, F. (1979). Skill as an aspect of knowledge. Journal of Higher Education, **50**, 602–14.

Marton, F. (1981). Phenomenography: describing conceptions of the world around us. *Instructional Science*, **10**, 177–200.

Marton, F. and Säljö. R. (1976). On qualitative differences in learning: I. Outcome and process. *British Journal of Educational Psychology*, **46**, 4–11.

Marton, F. and Säljö, R. (1984). Approaches to learning. In F. Marton, D. Hounsell, and N. Entwistle (eds), *The Experience of Learning* (pp. 36–55). Edinburgh: Scottish Academic Press.

Marton, F. and Svensson, L. (1979). Conceptions of research in student learning. *Higher Education*, **8**, 471–86.

Meyer, J. H. F. (1988). Student perceptions of learning context and approaches to studying. *South African Journal of Higher Education*, **2**, 73-82.

Meyer, J. H. F. and Dunne, T. T. (1991). Study approaches of nursing students: Effects of an extended clinical context. *Medical Education*, **25**, 497–516.

Meyer, J. H. F. and Muller, M. W. (1990a). An unfolding analysis of the association between perceptions of learning context and approaches to studying. *South African Journal of Higher Education*, **4**, 46–58.

Meyer, J. H. F. and Muller, M. W. (1990b). Evaluating the quality of student learning: I. An unfolding analysis of the association between perceptions of learning context and approaches to studying at an individual level. *Studies in Higher Education*, **15**, 131–54.

Meyer, J. H. F. and Parsons, P. (1989a). An empirical study of English- and Afrikaans-speaking students' approaches to studying. *South African Journal of Higher Education*, **3**, 109–14.

Meyer, J. H. F. and Parsons, P. (1989b). Approaches to studying and course perceptions using the Lancaster Inventory: A comparative study. *Studies in Higher Education*, **14**, 137–53.

Meyer, J. H. F., Parsons, P. and Dunne, T. T. (1990a). Individual study orchestrations and their association with learning outcome. *Higher Education*, **20**, 67–89.

Meyer, J. H. F., Parsons, P. and Dunne, T. T. (1990b). Study orchestration and learning outcome: Evidence of association over time among disadvantaged students. *Higher Education*, **20**, 245–69.

Miller, C. D., Alway, M. and McKinley, D. L. (1987). Effects of learning styles and strategies on academic success. *Journal of College Student Personnel*, **28**, 399–404.

Miller, C. D., Finley, J. and McKinley, D. L. (1990). Learning approaches and motives: Male and female differences and implications for learning assistance programs. *Journal of College Student Development*, **31**, 147–54.

Miller, C. M. L. and Parlett, M. (1974). *Up to the Mark: A Study of the Examination Game*. London: Society for Research into Higher Education.

Morgan, A., Gibbs, G. and Taylor, E. (1980). *Students' Approaches to Studying the Social Science and Technology Foundation Courses: Preliminary Studies* (Study Methods Group Report No. 4). Milton Keynes: Open University

Morgan, A., Taylor, E. and Gibbs, G. (1982). Variations in students' approaches to studying. *British Journal of Educational Technology*, **13**, 107–13.

Moss, C. J. (1982). Academic achievement and individual differences in the learning processes of basic skills students in the university. *Applied Psychological Measurement*, **6**, 291–96.

Newstead, S. (1992). A study of two 'quick-and-easy' methods of assessing individual differences in student learning. *British Journal of Educational Psychology*, **62**, 299–312.

O'Neil, M. J. and Child, D. (1984). Biggs' SPQ: A British study of its internal structure. *British Journal of Educational Psychology*, **54**, 228–34.

Parlett, M. R. (1970). The syllabus-bound student. In L. Hudson (ed.),*The Ecology of Human Intelligence* (pp. 272–83). Harmondsworth: Penguin Books.

Parsons, P. G. (1992). *An Investigation into the Association between Qualitatively Different Perceptions of the Learning Context and Students' Approaches to Studying.* Unpublished doctoral dissertation, University of Cape Town.

Pask, G. (1976). Styles and strategies of learning. *British Journal of Educational Psychology*, **46**, 128–48.

Pask, G. and Scott, B. C. E. (1972). Learning strategies and individual competence. *International Journal of Man-Machine Studies*, **4**, 217–53.

Potter, J. and Wetherell, M. (1987). *Discourse and Social Psychology: Beyond Attitudes and Behaviour.* London: Sage.

Ramsden, P. (1979). Student learning and perceptions of the academic environment. *Higher Education*, **8**, 411–27.

Ramsden, P. (1984). The context of learning. In F. Marton, D. Hounsell, and N. Entwistle (eds), *The Experience of Learning* (pp. 144–64). Edinburgh: Scottish Academic Press.

Ramsden, P., Beswick, D. G. and Bowden, J. A. (1986). Effects of learning skills interventions on first year university students' learning. *Human Learning*, **5**, 151–64.

Ramsden, P., Beswick, D. G. and Bowden, J. A. (1987). Learning processes and learning skills. In J. T. E. Richardson, M. W. Eysenck, and D. Warren Piper (eds), *Student Learning: Research in Education and Cognitive Psychology* (pp. 168–76). Milton Keynes: SRHE and Open University Press.

Ramsden, P. and Entwistle, N. J. (1981). Effects of academic departments on students' approaches to studying. *British Journal of Educational Psychology*, **51**, 368–83.

Ribich, F. D. and Schmeck, R. R. (1979). Multivariate relationships between measures of learning style and memory. *Journal of Research in Personality*, **13**, 515–29.

Richardson, J. T. E. (1990). Reliability and replicability of the Approaches to Studying Questionnaire. *Studies in Higher Education*, **15**, 155 - 168.

Richardson, J. T. E. (1992). A critical evaluation of a short form of the Approaches to Studying Inventory. *Psychology Teaching Review*, **1**, 34–45.

Richardson, J. T. E. (1994a). Cultural specificity of approaches to studying in higher education: A literature survey. *Higher Education*, **27**, 449–68.

Richardson, J. T. E. (1994b). Using questionnaires to evaluate student learning: Some health warnings. In G. Gibbs (ed.), *Improving Student Learning: Theory and Practice* (pp. 73–88). Oxford: Oxford Centre for Staff Development.

Richardson, J. T. E. (in preparation). Meaning orientation and reproducing orientation: A typology of approaches to studying in higher education?

Säljö, R. (1984). Learning from reading. In F. Marton, D. Hounsell, and N. Entwistle (eds), *The Experience of Learning* (pp. 71–89). Edinburgh: Scottish Academic Press.

Säljö, R. (1987). The educational construction of learning. In J. T. E. Richardson, M. W. Eysenck, and D. Warren Piper (eds), *Student Learning: Research in Education and Cognitive Psychology* (pp. 101–8). Milton Keynes: SRHE and Open University Press.

Schmeck, R. R. (1983). Learning styles of college students. In R. F. Dillon and R. R. Schmeck (eds), *Individual Differences in Cognition*, Vol. 1 (pp. 233–79). New York: Academic Press.

Schmeck, R. R. (1988). Individual differences and learning strategies. In C. E. Weinstein, E. T. Goetz and P. A. Alexander (eds), *Learning and Study Strategies: Issues in Assessment, Instruction, and Evaluation* (pp. 171–91). San Diego, CA: Academic Press.

Schmeck, R. R. and Geisler-Brenstein, E. (1989). Individual differences that affect the way students approach learning. *Learning and Individual Differences*, **1**, 85–124.

Schmeck, R. R., Geisler-Brenstein, E. and Cercy, S. P. (1991). Self-concept and learning: The Revised Inventory of Learning Processes. *Educational Psychology*, **11**, 343–62.

Schmeck, R. R. and Grove, E. (1979). Academic achievement and individual differences in learning processes. *Applied Psychological Measurement*, **3**, 43–9.

Schmeck, R. R., Ribich, F. and Ramanaiah, N. (1977). Development of a self-report inventory for assessing individual differences in learning processes. *Applied Psychological Measurement*, **1**, 413–31.

Speth, C. and Brown, R. (1988). Study approaches, processes and strategies: Are three perspectives better than one?. *British Journal of Educational Psychology*, **58**, 247–57.

Stern, P. N. (1994). Eroding grounded theory. In J. M. Morse (ed.), *Critical Issues in Qualitative Research Methods* (pp.212 - 223). Thousands Oaks, CA: Sage.

Stiles, W. B. (1993). Quality control in qualitative research. *Clinical Psychology Review*, **13**, 593–618.

Strack, F. and Schwarz, N. (1992). Communicative influences in standardized question situations: The case of implicit collaboration. In G. R. Semin and K. Fiedler (eds), *Language, Interaction and Social Cognition* (pp. 173–93). London: Sage.

Strauss, A. and Corbin, J. (1990). *Basics of Qualitative Research: Grounded Theory Procedures and Techniques.* Newbury Park, CA: Sage.

Strauss, A. and Corbin, J. (1994). Grounded theory methodology: An overview. In N. K. Denzin and Y. S. Lincoln (eds), *Handbook of Qualitative Research* (pp. 273–85). Thousand Oaks, CA: Sage.

Svensson, L. (1977). On qualitative differences in learning: III. Study skill and learning. *British Journal of Educational Psychology,* **47**, 233–43.

Taylor, E., Gibbs, G. and Morgan, A. (1981). *The Outcomes of Learning from the Social Science Foundation Course: Students' Understandings of Price Control, Power and Oligopoly* (Study Methods Group Report No. 9). Milton Keynes: Open University.

Trigwell, K. and Prosser, M. (1991). Improving the quality of student learning: the influence of learning context and student approaches to learning on learning outcomes. *Higher Education,* **22**, 251–66.

Turner, B. A. (1981). Some practical aspects of qualitative data analysis: One way of organizing the cognitive processes associated with the generation of grounded theory. *Quality and Quantity,* **15**, 225–47.

Van Rossum, E. J. and Schenk, S. M. (1984). The relationship between learning conception, study strategy and learning outcome. *British Journal of Educational Psychology,* **54**, 73–83.

Veres, J. G., III, Sims, R. R. and Locklear, T. S. (1991). Improving the reliability of Kolb's revised Learning Style Inventory. *Educational and Psychological Measurement,* **51**, 143–50.

Watkins, D. (1982). Identifying the study process dimensions of Australian university students. *Australian Journal of Education,* **26**, 76–85.

Watkins, D. (1983). Assessing tertiary study processes. *Human Learning,* **2**, 29–37.

Watkins, D. (1984). Student learning processes: An exploratory study in the Philippines. *Human Learning,* **3**, 33 - 42.

Watkins, D. and Akande, A. (1992). Assessing the approaches to learning of Nigerian students. *Assessment and Evaluation in Higher Education,* **17**, 11–20.

Watkins, D. and Hattie, J. (1980). An investigation of the internal structure of the Biggs Study Process Questionnaire. *Educational and Psychological Measurement,* **40**, 1125–30.

Watkins, D. and Hattie, J. (1981a). The internal structure and predictive validity of the Inventory of Learning Processes: Some Australian and Filipino data. *Educational and Psychological Measurement,* **41**, 511–14.

Watkins, D. and Hattie, J. (1981b). The learning processes of Australian university students: Investigations of contextual and personological factors. *British Journal of Educational Psychology,* **51**, 384–93.

Watkins, D., Hattie, J. and Astilla, E. (1983). The validity of the four subscales of the Inventory of Learning Processes for a sample of Filipino freshman college students. *Educational and Psychological Measurement,* **43**, 531–36.

Watkins, D., Hattie, J. and Astilla, E. (1986). Approaches to studying by Filipino students: A longitudinal investigation. *British Journal of Educational Psychology*, **56**, 357–62.

Watkins, D. and Regmi, M. (1990). An investigation of the approach to learning of Nepalese tertiary students. *Higher Education*, **20**, 459–69.

40   Methodography: the study of student learning as situated action

William G. Fleming (Soundings Research, Birmingham)

Introduction

For the past 20 years phenomenography (Marton, 1981) has been a major force in the study of, and our thinking about, student learning. These studies have helped us to understand the ways in which students approach a variety of study tasks, how they understand, or fail to understand, the key concepts in their disciplines, and how the characteristics of the educational settings in which they learn impinge on what they do and learn. More recently notions of **situated learning** (see Lave and Wenger, 1991; Brown and Duguid, 1993; and Chaiklin and Lave,1993) have begun to find a place in studies of activity in various settings and more specifically in work on student learning in school (see, for example, Säljö and Wyndhamn, 1990 and 1993).

The purpose of this chapter is to sharpen our focus on the examination of situated action as an approach to the study of student learning and to suggest ways in which such an approach, called methodography, might contribute to the enhancement and improvement of student learning.

Methodography: The Analysis of Student Learning as Situated Action

The notion of situated action directs our attention to the ways in which activities are accomplished through the ordinary, everyday, finely detailed methodic practices of participants to an activity in specific settings. Studies of conversationalists (Button and Lee, 1987), scientists (Latour and Woolgar, 1986; Lynch, 1985), politicians (Atkinson, 1984) and lawyers (Atkinson and Drew, 1979) have shown what some of these methodic practices are and the ways in which they are deployed in specific settings to accomplish particular conversational, scientific, political or legal tasks. Some research of this kind has been undertaken in school classrooms (see for example Mehan, 1979; Walkerdine, 1988; Edwards and Mercer, 1987). For example, Edwards and Mercer show how teachers and pupils develop a shared understanding of specific concepts through the use of particular discursive and interactional practices in classrooms. But little research has attended to the fine detail of the ways in which students accomplish particular learning tasks in higher education.

In previous work (Fleming, 1986 and 1987) I have addressed some of the issues which methodography might involve. The approach leans heavily on ethnomethodology (Garfinkel, 1967; Heritage, 1984) being concerned with the methodic practices people use to accomplish action in particular settings. Contemporary work of a related nature can be found in studies of human–computer interaction (Anderson et al. 1993), work on medical consultations and qualitative data (Silverman, 1987 and 1993) and discursive psychology (Edwards and Potter, 1992; Potter and Wetherell, 1987).

Learning a subject or discipline involves coming to be able to do it in particular academic and other settings, i.e. being able to participate appropriately in the settings (classrooms, laboratories, seminar rooms, etc.) where the subject or discipline is being done. Such participation involves deploying activity sequences appropriate to the subject or discipline and the setting.

In making students' situated activity sequences the focus of attention, methodography seeks to describe the ways in which student work is done in educational and other settings. Previously (Fleming, 1990) I have suggested that this would involve developing:

1 a structural anatomy of student activity;

2 a functional anatomy of student activity; and

3 an understanding of the 'machinery' by which such activity works.

A structural anatomy of student activity

A structural anatomy of activity sequences seeks to describe the ways such sequences are assembled and constructed in the specific settings in which they are used. For example, we might identify the discursive devices and procedures such as facts, descriptions, questions and versions of ideas that students deploy in furnishing an explanation of a particular concept in a tutorial. Examining the structural anatomy of activity sequences involves identifying the components of the activity which make it up. The components (methodic practices) are those which participants can be seen to be attending to in the ways in which they carry out the activity.

A functional anatomy of student activity

A functional anatomy of activity sequences seeks to describe the **use** to which methodic practices are put in the accomplishment of the activity on that occasion. For example, in examining the discursive devices deployed by students in giving explanations we might ask what these devices are used to **do** at various points in the development of the explanation. What part do specific descriptions, questions and statements of fact play in making this the type of explanation participants find it to be? How are the discursive devices 'situationally deployed' (Edwards and Potter, 1992, p. 89) in the versions of the explanation offered by students?

Understanding how student activity works

A search for the 'mechanisms' by which an activity sequence works goes beyond asking how the activity is constructed and what its constituent methodic practice do, to examine how the organization of these practices work together to accomplish the activity sequence as we see it. For example, in the explanation a student gives, how do the descriptions, facts, processes, work together to produce what the participants to the discussion recognize as an explanation of the phenomenon in question? Can we build explanatory machinery which shows how explaining is done? This would involve examining the ways in which such practices are organized and orchestrated to build the explanation in ways that are designed for the specific business in hand and to resist having the explanation challenged or undermined. In describing their Discursive Action Model, Edwards and Potter (1992) list a number of 'techniques of fact construction' which may be used to construct explanations. In doing so they make reference to the growing body of research which describes how these 'techniques' work.

In short, methodography directs our attention to what the components (methodic practices) of an activity sequence are, what each component is used for or does and how all the components work together to produce the activity we recognize.

In order to give a clearer view of what methodography might entail, I shall contrast it with phenomenography.

The Topics of Research Interest to Phenomenography and Methodography

Säljö (1988) provides an account of phenomenography which clearly indicates the ways in which the research topic is defined in that approach. The primary foci of interest are 'the conceptions of reality', the 'meanings people see and ascribe to what they perceive', 'people's conceptions of the world' (p. 37). Such an approach is described as a 'second-order perspective' (p. 36) in so far as it is concerned with describing people's perceptions of phenomena rather than with descriptions of the phenomena *per se*. The rationale for this interest is that people's actions are based on the various ways in which they construe and interpret the worlds they inhabit.

In contrast, methodography seeks to dissolve a distinction between perception/interpretation and action by treating perceiving, interpreting, conceptualizing and similar cognitive phenomena as actions in themselves and worthy of study as activities rather than precursors or preludes to action. Thus, when students talk or write about 'force' in physics, 'price' in economics or 'moles' in chemistry, they are doing conceptualizing and theorizing and their talk and writing can be examined to reveal the ways in which, on these specific occasions, such conceptualizing/theorizing work is accomplished. The primary focus for methodography is setting specific action. Thus knowledge itself is treated as an activity by asking and examining how knowing is done, as a sequentially organized activity, in specific situations. Know-how is taken as primary. Know-that, treated as a particular form of know-how, is constructed in ways designed to display knowledge as independent of the methods and practices which construct it.

While phenomenography seems to consider action as, in some ways, driven by interpretation, conceptions and meanings, methodography makes no such motivational attributions. Nevertheless, where students do allude, in their reflection on study tasks, to relationships between thought and action, the methodographic task would be to examine the discursive practices by which such relationships were established and maintained and ask what the use of such references enable students to achieve in the setting of their use, i.e. treat such distinctions as members' practices and therefore as appropriate topics for study.

How Variability and Versions of Reality are Treated by Phenomenography and Methodography

Phenomenography recognizes that concepts come in a variety of versions. For example, 'force' can be thought of in a number of ways. In analysing students' explanations the phenomenographic task is to reduce the versions to a 'limited number of categories (usually between three and five) that depict significant differences in ways of construing phenomena. The assumption is that conceptions of reality can be expressed in a large number of linguistic forms without necessarily changing the basic way in which the phenomenon is construed' (Säljö, 1988, p. 42).

For methodography, the fact that people use versions of phenomena is also significant, but in a rather different way. Variability in the ways students construct concepts is considered in the light of the action orientation methodography takes. Students use different versions, and a variety of linguistic forms to frame such versions, in ways which enable them to manage their contributions to classes, essays, projects, examinations and phenomenographic and other educational investigations. The task for methodography is to examine how such versions, constructed in the ways we find them to be, enable students to undertake such tasks. As conversational and discursive analyses have demonstrated, the fine detail in descriptions, explanations and other discursive events matters; the specific version deployed is used to do things. As Billig (1991) shows, when expressing strong views, i.e. doing perceptions and interpretations, one of the features of expressing strong views is the wide variety of versions of the phenomenon a person can draw on to make their case and refute and rebut challenges to their position. The account offered varies according to its function in the ongoing discourse. Thus a student may use a number of versions of 'force' in an explanation depending on what interactional purposes are being pursued at different times in the discourse. Rather than attempting to identify a version which 'really' underlies the linguistic forms the student deploys, methodography seeks to show how the variability in discourse is used to achieve particular interactional ends.

While the phenomenographic approach identifies a few conceptions of reality which can be found to underlie many linguistic forms, methodography treats such interpretations as actors' concerns. In discussions between students and tutors we sometimes find that the parties to the interaction are attending to the extent to which, and the ways in which, a variety of linguistic forms may or may not amount to the same thing, e.g. the various forms of words which formulate concepts such as price, force, life, etc. The task for methodography is to examine the ways in which different discursive practices, using subject matter material, are orchestrated to address this issue of variability on that occasion.

The ways in which Phenomenography and Methodography Handle Data

As has already been indicated, in searching interview transcripts and other accounts students give of their thinking in classes and on paper, phenomenography seeks to identify the conceptions, interpretations, approaches and perceptions which seem to underlie the statements students have made. This is a particular form of data reduction.

Elsewhere (Fleming, 1986) I have pointed out some of the difficulties with such an approach to interview material. Here I want to place greater emphasis on the ways in which methodography might handle such data.

In the first place, methodography treats the 'problem' the students face as setting specific, e.g. as an interview about 'force' with an education researcher. The task for the student is to construct, not just an explanation of the term 'force', not just an interview, but an explanation of 'force' in an interview, in collaboration with an education researcher. In doing so there are numerous things both participants must attend to if the interview is to be satisfactorily concluded, of which constructing an explanation of the term 'force' is but one. The interview is a collaborative construction where the conceptions which can be read into, or off, it are produced jointly through the interactive work of both student and interviewer. Where the interviewer reflects back words and phrases used by the student the agenda is being partly, and ongoingly, developed by the selective prompts the interviewer uses. (See, for example, Figure 1).

[Here an interviewer and student are exploring notions of evolutionary change]

Interviewer: What is the role of the environment do you think in that adaptation?

Calle: Well, in time you first have the changes in the environment and then the human adaptation to the environment.

Interviewer: And this adaptation ... how does it come about?

Calle: Well, it can be like this that when humans experience the environmental change, then well, to be able to survive something develops ... or it must depend on how they live in this here environment.

Interviewer: Is it the environment that starts this adaptation of the species?

Calle: Yes, I think it is ... it is the change in the environment that starts a process of adaptation of the species.

Interviewer: And this process of adaptation of the species, what could that be . . . what does it mean?

Calle: Well, it could be ... that humans in some way live in this new environment, that their way of living in some way can affect their hereditary factors or genes and so on, and that the hereditary factors change and that then, when new individuals are born then they get another appearance eventually ... gradually a different kind of individual appears.

(Säljö, 1988, pp. 39–40)

Figure 1

The interviewer picks up phrases, mostly towards the end of the student's turns at talk and repeats them, wrapped in a question. The student then constructs answers to the interviewer's requests for further explanation of the material in the question. For methodography the task is to examine the ways in which these question and answer sequences are sequentially constructed in the interview and draw on the versions of evolution in doing so. Phenomenographers suggest that Calle accomplishes the interview by drawing on Lamarchian conceptions of evolution.

Methodographers might agree, but would want to investigate exactly how Calle does this at each point in the interview using particular versions and partial constructions of the concept and how the work of the interviewer affects this accomplishment. Methodography would also want to examine the complete text of the interview to see whether, and how, alternative versions of evolution are deployed at other points in the interview to achieve particular interactional purposes. As Gilbert and Mulkay (1984) show, scientists can use quite different versions of science at different times in the same interview, depending on whether they are justifying their own results or indicating weaknesses in the work of colleagues and competitors. Rather than using forms of reduction (data implosion) to derive versions of reality from the data, methodography expands the data (data explosion) through a fine grained analysis of the ways versions are organized, constructed, used and deployed by those who produced them in accomplishing tasks at hand.

Situated Action

Phenomenography is engaged in one form of abstraction, identifying conceptions of reality which can be distilled from the observation of students at work or from interviews or written documents. Such analysis seeks to lift the phenomena of interest out of the settings in which they originated; to disengage them from the classrooms, essays and interview protocols in which they were originally embedded.

Methodography, in contrast, seeks a different form of description and takes a different view of the relationships between the setting of origin and the research findings. In the first place methodography is concerned with how the task at hand is carried out; with describing the methodic practices which participants use to accomplish the task and how these practices are deployed in making the task what it is. When analysing activity sequences in this way the setting is considered as that which is accomplished on that specific occasion. Thus, methodography asks how participants in a seminar construct that seminar, on that occasion, through the use of organized, methodic social practices, many of which are discursive. Hence the concern to examine the ways in which particular phenomenographic interviews are accomplished. For the participants, constructing the event as a phenomenographic interview is the task at hand, and one which they jointly achieve.

A key feature of the deployment of methodic practices is that they are 'recipient designed' (see Shone and Atkinson, 1983). That is, activity is finely tuned in ways which makes it recognizably appropriate and apt for the people and the occasion in which it takes place. Thus answers can be seen to be designed, not as answers in general, but as answers to specific questions, asked by specific people, on specific occasions. Methodography is concerned to understand how this is done, that is, to identify how actions are recipient designed in specific settings and on particular occasions. By describing actions and activity sequences as **situated**, methodography seeks to emphasize, and understand, the ways in which settings are methodically produced and reproduced in and through the orderly but ordinary, organized, recipient designed, practices of participants. The activities of students and lecturers produce a specific lecture as a sequentially organized, educational event using the architectural, technological and intellectual resources to hand. The question is, How is this done on specific occasions?

Situated learning is a theme which is addressed by a number of researchers; see for example, Lave (1988, 1992, 1993), Lave and Wenger (1991), Hennessy (1993), Brown, Collins and Duguid (1989), Brown and Duguid (1991 and 1993), Young (1993). In broad terms the notion of situated learning is treated by these writers in much the same ways as I have suggested methodography treats situated activity. By pointing to learning as a situated activity these writers focus on the setting specific nature of learning and its outcomes. Thus, in classrooms students learn the versions of their subjects and its practices appropriate to coping with life and tasks in those particular classrooms. They learn the forms of problem-solving and theorizing which enable them to display themselves as competently schooled. Students learn how to do studenting; how to produce and reproduce classroom knowledge. In presenting a similar view Becker (1972) seems to conclude that nothing of significance is learned from such experience, i.e. that learning to be schooled is not a valuable or valued educational goal. Yet as Atkinson (1983) points out, such experience does enable students to learn a version of their subject discipline. For teachers, and others concerned with the impact and effectiveness of education, such conclusions raise the issue of transferability of learning. Will students be able to use and adapt the versions learned in the academy to other settings in the world of work? While methodography does not take up this point, studies of student and other work can examine the uses to which such versions are put on particular occasions, in specific academic and other settings.

The differing ways in which phenomenography and methodography deal with situated activities, such as learning, can be further clarified by examining the ways in which Laurillard (1993) addresses the issues. Laurillard adopts a phenomenographic approach to developing a framework for the effective use of educational technology in higher education. The task of teaching is construed as 'seeking to persuade students to change the way they experience the world. It [teaching – WGF] has to create the environment that will enable students to learn from the descriptions of the world devised by others' (p. 28). In making her case, Laurillard considers the significance of the work of Brown *et al.* (1989) on **situated cognition**. Brown *et al.* argue that learning and cognition are situated in the sense that knowledge is produced through activity in settings and is as much defined by the setting as it is by the activity. Following Lave (1988), they suggest we should consider the unit of analysis, not as the person, or the activity, but the person-acting-in-setting.

Laurillard examines these arguments as a prelude to arguing for the phenomenographic approach. She takes Brown *et al.* to be making two significant points, firstly, that situated cognition implies that learning to do something is best accomplished when learning is situated in the setting in which the activity will be carried out, i.e. learning activities should be situated in the domain of knowledge use. For example, if we want students to be able to use Laplace transformations in specific projects then we need to design learning environments which involve students in learning such transformations while engaged in authentic projects. Secondly, situated cognition argues against the 'decontextualising of knowledge by teaching abstractions' (p. 19), but for providing students with a range of contexts out of which they can develop abstractions.

In providing a critique of situated cognition as it applies to academic learning, Laurillard starts from the premise that abstraction, i.e. symbolic representation, is what characterizes academic learning and is what enables learners to use knowledge in unfamiliar situations. 'The point of an academic education is that knowledge **has** to be abstracted, and represented formally, in order to become generalizable and therefore more generally useful' (p. 20). In making this case Laurillard argues that situated cognition is limited; that purely situated knowledge, i.e. knowledge developed in specific situations to deal with the practical task at hand, is not enough – it will not transfer. In pointing up the differences between academic learning and situated learning she uses a distinction between learning in a 'natural context', i.e. situated learning where 'the learning outcome is an aspect of the situation, an aspect of the relation between learner, activity and environment'; learning is therefore 'about the world and how it works' (p. 22). In contrast, academic learning, she suggests, does not, and cannot, involve such first hand experience of the world, but rather involves 'learning about descriptions of the world, about a particular way of looking at the world' (p. 22). Her argument goes on to build on this distinction between first-order and second-order phenomena – the foundation stone of phenomenography.

As has already been pointed out, methodography dissolves this distinction by considering both first-order knowing about the world and second-order knowing about descriptions of the world as situated activities. While phenomenography seems to be based on the notion that some activities are situated and some are not, methodography starts from the premise that all activity is situated, i.e. actions are located, occasioned, always involve the integration of person, activity and environment at particular times and places. Thus abstracting, generalizing and describing the world are themselves situated activities, the products of which are constituted through the local, ordinary, everyday methodic practices of participants to these activities.

A major concern of methodographic studies of science, e.g. Latour and Woolgar (1986), has been to show the ways in which scientific work is done in order to display its findings as disentangled and disengaged from its methodic practices. In the same ways, other academic work can be examined to show how describing, abstracting and generalizing are done in order to display its descriptions, abstractions and generalizations as independent of their situated production.

While phenomenography starts from a principled distinction between situated and non-situated activity, methodology takes such a distinction to be a concern of participants rather than a defining characteristic of academic learning. While Laurillard describes the problem of academic learning as addressing how learners are to engage with knowledge derived from someone else's experience, methodography considers this a problem which is ubiquitous in many everyday settings, including academe. In everyday conversation, participants often deal in descriptions of each other's experiences in a variety of ways, including challenge, disbelief, making requests for more detail and suggesting alternative interpretations. Such activities are not the sole preserve or defining feature of academic learning.

There are now a number of studies of student learning which acknowledge the analytical strength of the notion of situated action and activity, for example, Säljö and

Wyndhamn (1990 and 1993). In this work the authors examine the ways in which students, in the formal setting of school, solved the everyday problem of establishing the cost of sending a letter, given the table of postage rates of their national post office. Students were given a number of problem scenarios (one letter of particular weight, a series of letters) in a variety of settings (to solve as individuals, to solve in groups of three, in a mathematics class, in a social studies class). The findings reveal that there were significant tendencies for students to employ problem-solving strategies which were context sensitive and reflected the situations in which the problems were set. Students framed explanations of their actions in different terms, depending on the class (social studies or mathematics) in which they were asked to find the postage rate.

While these studies are based quite specifically on the principle of situated activity, they do not adopt the methodological approach outlined here, largely because they use some of the data reduction methods of phenomenography and do not apply the notion of situated activity to all aspects of the tasks the students undertake. For example, Säljö and Wyndhamn (1990) gave the postage 'problem' to 12 – 13 year olds in a mathematics class and required them to collaborate in groups of three to establish the postage rate for a letter using a letter-scale and the postage table. Säljö and Wyndhamn then examined the audio recordings of the group discussions at a number of levels, including; the time and number of conversational 'turns' taken to reach an answer; the number and types of suggested solutions made by the students; identification of the arithmetic strategies adopted in the groups; the extent to which these strategies draw on knowledge acquired in school; problem definition and problem-solving activities of the groups – in terms of whether or not first suggestions were accepted and dealt with. Extensive analysis of these data led to a set of conclusions which emphasize the situated nature of the students' task. 'Several of the modes of dealing with the problem can be read as attempts at reading some mathematics into it' (p. 253). In doing this the students tacitly recognize that apt problem-solving in a mathematics classroom should draw on particular types of intellectual and explanatory repertoires, i.e. of a mathematical kind, rather that strategies and tactics appropriate to the queue in the post office, such as asking a fellow citizen in the queue or putting on extra stamps 'just in case'.

S 231: Should we weigh it then?

S 232: 120

S233: Have you gotten anywhere?

S 232: 4 crowns

S 233: Me too

S 231: 4 crowns

S 232: 120 is between 100 and 250. It's closer to 100 that to 250. It's further from 250.

S233: Answer: 4 crowns

S 212: 7.50 (crowns) it is

S 211: Otherwise it should ... Maybe one should put on two stamps?

S 212: No, we are not!

S 211: One can get fooled too (looks at interviewer)

Source: Säljö and Wyndhamn, 1990, p. 249.

Figure 2

A methodological approach to this material would take the analytical framework of situated action equally seriously, might also generate some of the numerical data as Säljö and Wyndhamn have done, but would examine the fine grain of the group interaction in much more detail. A first question would be to ask to what do the students in their groups appear to attend in the work they do, i.e. what are they doing in their groups. From the data extracts Säljö and Wyndhamn include, see Figure 2, the group participants can be seen to attend to a number of things including: suggesting what to do next (p. 249, S2.31: *Should we weigh it then?*); requesting a progress report (p. 249, S233: *Have we gotten anywhere?*); agreeing a solution (p. 249, S233: *Answer: 4 crowns*); giving a reason (p. 249, S232: *120 is between 100 and 250. It's closer to 100 than to 250. It's further from 250*); the influence of outsiders (p. 249, S211: *One can get fooled too (looks at interviewer)*. The task for methodography is to show, through fine-grained sequential analysis of these things the students do, how they manage the activity as a local, occasioned accomplishment, involving managing the group, being observed and dealing with an out-of-school problem in a school mathematics classroom. Not only are they required to solve this (everyday) postage rate problem in this (mathematics classroom) setting, but they are required to do so through this (group) process while being watched by this (observing) interviewer – who may also have been responsible for setting the problem. Säljö and Wyndhamn address the first two aspects of the situation, but not the last two. Yet the last two are significant features of the setting, not only for analysts but primarily for the participating students. Their problem-solving work is done in and through their group work, in the presence of overhearing observer. The sequential organization of their discussions can be examined to find out how they do this, i.e. how their problem solution is arrived at through, and in, the details of the discursive practices of the group.

Table 1 summarizes the main differences between methodography and phenomenography.

Table 1 The difference between methodography and phenomenography

	Phenomenography	Methodography
Topic	How do students see things? Focus on perception.	How do students do things? Focus on action and know-how.
Versions and variability	Reducing discursive variability to a few underlying conceptions	Examining how discursive variability and versions are used to achieve study tasks.
Handling the data	Data reduction through rigorous qualitative analysis	Fine grained sequential analysis attending to how activities are constructed and how they function; with data available to public scrutiny.
Situated activity	Treats context, setting and situation as integral to how we make sense of reality	Treats activity as recipient designed in settings and reality (including situations) as constituted in and through methodic practices.

Methodographical Analysis: a rough guide

Examples used

All the examples used here are taken from a the transcript of a 'course evaluation' discussion with a group of General Medical Practitioners on a part-time, post-experience Masters course in Medical Science. The discussion took place in early December of the first term of the course which started at the beginning of October. The 'students' attended the university one day per week and had also attended a residential weekend at the start of the course. Appendix A includes the fragment of the transcript referred to here.

The following are some 'analytical levers' (Edwards and Potter, 1992) which can be used to identify methodic practices.

1 PAY ATTENTION TO THE DETAIL, IT MATTERS

Identify and examine the components of activity sequences. How is the sequence constructed? What is it made up of? What function is served by each component, i.e. what does it do? How does each component contribute to the activity sequence as a whole?

Example

In line 20 of the transcription Student 1 (S1) starts with 'I think' prior to making a comment on the difficulty of talking about expectations. This expression could easily be ignored in analysis, but we do not ignore it as listeners or readers of the transcript. It acts as an **opinion preface**, i.e. we hear what follows as an expression of the speaker's view rather than, say, a description of a factual state of affairs. But, in the context of this discussion 'I think' also carries some argumentative weight because it contributes to our hearing what follows as a challenge to the topic as suggested by the interviewer. As an opinion preface it is used to indicate the intended status of the assertion which follows, i.e.

hearers should take it as a personal view. Defining the assertion, that 'it's very difficult at this stage of the course to talk about expectations' as a personal view provides the statement with some protection from immediate challenge. An opinion preface draws on our common knowledge that in our culture people are 'entitled to their views', but within certain limits. We hear 'I think' as potentially being followable by a disagreement, partially protected by it being a personal view. In this example we have identified a component of the activity sequence. In this case the activity sequence is the disagreement or challenge made by S1 and the component is the opinion preface 'I think'. We have then asked and suggested what the component is doing there, i.e. what it accomplishes in this particular instance.

2 LOOK FOR THE WAYS IN WHICH SPEAKERS ATTEND TO THE LOCAL SETTINGS AND OCCASIONS OF
   THEIR ACTIVITIES, I.E. THE SITUATED NATURE OF WHAT THEY DO

Example

In line 24, Student 1 (S1) attends to the fact that he has made a statement on behalf of the group, 'I don't know about others, but this is the way I feel.' referring to the use of 'we' earlier ('we are in our initial stages', line 21). But to do so may be considered presumptuous. His comment deals with a potential challenge such as 'Speak for yourself.' In a group setting there may be some sensitivities concerning who speaks for whom and speakers may, therefore, seek to clarify this from time to time, either for themselves or for the group as a whole. The interviewer accepts this definition of individual responsibility for contributions by asking how others feel. The responses immediately following pick up this personal reference ('I see it ...', line 26 and 'I'm finding that ...' line 32).

3 LOOK FOR DIFFERENT VERSIONS OF EVENTS, ACTIVITIES, PEOPLE AND PLACES. THESE ARE
   PRINCIPAL WAYS IN WHICH DISCURSIVE ACTIONS ARE ACCOMPLISHED

Example

In line 20 Student 1 refers to 'this stage of the course' as 'our initial stages'. This version of the stage of the course is consistent with the activities he then goes on to link with it, i.e. 'just groping, sort of trying to find our way around'. His opening preface, 'I think' is also a version of such prefaces. In other places in the transcript we can find different versions of this stage of the course and different versions of opinion prefaces. Using these different versions provides for different implications to arise from what they say. We can examine how these versions are deployed and what such deployment achieves. 'Stage of course' is alluded to in other ways. In line 26 S2 talks of 'it so far'. In line 32–33 S3 talks of 'from the very first day'. Each of these versions of the stage of course is formulated in a way which is designed for the part it then plays in the discursive setting in which it is used. For example, 'our initial stages' (line 21) positions the students in a way which is consistent with the activities of that position, i.e. (line 21/22) 'just groping, sort of trying to find our way around'. The case against talking about expectations is strengthened by deploying a version of 'this stage of the course' and associated activities which are characterized by some confusion and a need to clarify 'things'. Equally, in line 20, other versions are used to make the challenge in a particular way. For example, he uses 'it's very difficult' rather than 'its very silly' or 'its inappropriate'. His usage takes some responsibility for the 'problem' rather than blaming the interviewer, thus lessening the likelihood of a return challenge on the grounds of personal attack.

4   LOOK FOR THE WAYS IN WHICH DESCRIPTIONS AND REPORTS ARE CONSTRUCTED TO BE MORE OR LESS FACTUAL

One way in which the 'factuality' or 'facticity' of statements can be strengthened is to place them appropriately on a 'hierarchy of modalisation' (see Edwards and Potter, 1992, p. 106):

> [. . .] – where the fact is assumed
> X
> X is a fact
> I know that X
> I claim that X
> I believe that X
> I hypothesise that X
> I think that X
> I guess that X
> X is possible

Example

There are a number of places in the transcript where statements are placed at particular points on this hierarchy and thus draw on the implications of having their descriptions displayed as more or less factual. Opinion prefaces, e.g. in lines 20, 26, 32, 52, 56, 71, mostly of the 'I think' variety, place assertions quite low on the hierarchy. In other places views are expressed by placing statements further up the hierarchy, without opinion prefaces or suffices, i.e. giving them greater 'factual' status. For instance, in line 37, S4 'It's quite difficult at this stage...' uses the 'X is a fact' level to assert a state of affairs as factual, independent of personal view, individual or group interest. Such factual statements gain their rhetorical strength from their reference to 'the way things are', but users of such discursive forms can be required to produce 'evidence' or show that such facts are not merely personal views or attributable to personal weaknesses or limitations, i.e. just the sort of people who would complain of difficulties. In this example, S4 goes on to provide supporting argument on the grounds of 'need' driven by the most laudable of educational aims 'to progress'. Thus the 'difficulties' are being shown to arise, not from what students want, nor from their lack of motivation or ability, but from their efforts to be model students, i.e. to do the reading, make progress and start their projects.

5   LOOK FOR THE WAYS IN WHICH SPEAKERS' REPORTS ETC. ARE CONSTRUCTED TO RESIST CHALLENGE AND UNDERMINE ALTERNATIVES.

Often a combination of factual reporting and specific versions are used to give persuasive, rhetorical force to what people say, as in point 4 above

6   IDENTIFY **ISSUES** TO WHICH SPEAKERS MAKE REFERENCE, I.E. MATTERS WHICH MAY BE SENSITIVE, CONTROVERSIAL OR ABOUT WHICH PEOPLE MIGHT BE EXPECTED TO DISAGREE

How are these matters being handled? How do speakers address issues through factual reports?

Example

As we have already found, Student 1, in lines 20–22, deals with the sensitive issue of challenging the topic as suggested by deploying a combination of discursive devices which include an opinion preface, a factual statement and a particular version of the 'stage of course' and its associated activities. The challenge works by attributing the 'problem' to the stage of the course and is justified by implying that talk about expectations is not what we would usually associate with 'our initial stages'.

7 HOW DO PEOPLE HANDLE ISSUES OF RESPONSIBILITY, AGENCY AND ACCOUNTABILITY IN WHAT THEY DO, BOTH IN REFERENCE TO THEMSELVES AND TO THE EVENTS, ETC., THEY DESCRIBE AND REPORT?

Whenever a person does or says something they lay themselves open to being evaluated as the sort of person who would do or say such things. How do the 'students' attend to their accountability in commenting on aspects of the course? How do they try to ensure that aspects of the course, rather than themselves, are the objects of evaluation, for example, by constructing their accounts of the course, and their activities within it, in ways which resist them being seen as 'poorly motivated', 'lacking ability' or 'whinging'? They also have to find ways of ensuring that course evaluation does not become a 'confessional'.

Example

S4, as discussed in point 4 is one illustration of this. S1 provides another example. Consensus reporting is used by Student 1, as we have seen. This also serves to avoid being held personally responsible. A second way in which Student 1 handles the issue of accountability is to acknowledge personal responsibility for the 'troubles' being reported, i.e. through the claim, 'this is the way I feel'. Any further attempt to 'blame' this student can easily be rebuffed by an assertion that a measure of personal responsibility has already been accepted.

8. HOW DO PEOPLE, IN ATTENDING TO ACCOUNTABILITY, ALSO ATTEND TO THE MORAL DIMENSIONS OF THEIR ACTIVITIES?

As suggested in point 6, when describing events people attend to their own accountability and that involving the events described. In doing so they tell 'moral tales', i.e. they draw on cultural norms which indicate obligations, duties and responsibilities associated with particular roles and activities. Many of these cultural norms pose common-sense dilemmas. For example, 'Look before you leap' contrasts with 'Nothing venture, nothing win'.

We have already seen how S4 draws on the activity of 'good students' in supporting a particular evaluation of the course 'so far'.

Conclusion

There are broadly two reasons for pursuing a methodographical approach to the study of student learning, one scientific and the other educational.

In the first place, we know from ethnomethodological studies of human interaction and work that the fine grain of action and activity matters. It is through the fine detail of our actions that we get things done. For example, Heath (1986) shows how a doctor's head movements during a consultation can have significant consequences for the patient and the contribution the patient makes. If we are to extend our understanding of student learning work we can do so by asking how such activities are sequentially constructed, what methodic practices are displayed and how these are orchestrated to achieve the effects we see them to have.

The educational reason for pursuing methodographic studies of student situated learning activity is to provide students and teachers with 'data' about activity which is an essential ingredient in development based on action research and reflective practice. Fine grained methodographic analysis will enable students and teachers to identify the practices students bring to particular educational tasks, to identify the practices required by particular educational tasks and more clearly identify what it is which students need to learn to do. In the example examined here the analysis has begun to show the ways in which course evaluations are accomplished in this setting. These discursive practices could be compared with the practices students use to do evaluation in seminars, essays and examinations.

By emphasizing student action, in this case discursive action, I am not advocating a return to the era of behavioural objectives. The action orientation of methodography is not a version of Skinnerian Operant Conditioning in disguise. The 'rules' which connect the actions we have been examining are fundamentally 'moral' not mechanistic. We provide answers to questions not because we are programmed to do so but because it is morally imperative that we do so if we are to continue to be considered to be reasonable and responsible people by our co-participants. It is in this sense that methodography provides details of the ways in which the moral rationality of action is accomplished on particular occasions. It is in this sense also that learning the discursive practices of a discipline is about developing the moral know-how, i.e. the fine-grained methodic practices, involved in displaying that discipline's knowledge in appropriate ways on specific occasions.

References

Anderson, R.J., Heath, C.C., Luff, P. and Moran, T.P. (1993). The social and the cognitive in human-computer interaction. *International Journal of Man-Machine Studies*, **38**, 999–1016.

Atkinson, M. and Drew, P. (1979). *Order in Court*. Macmillan, London.

Atkinson, M. (1984). *Our Masters' Voices: The Language and Body Language of Politics*. Methuen, London.

Atkinson, P. (1983). The reproduction of the professional community. In R. Dingwall and P. Lewis, (eds.), *The Sociology of the Professions*. Macmillan, London.

Becker, H.S. (1972). School is a lousy place to learn anything. In B. Geer, (ed.), *Learning to Work*. Sage, Beverly Hills.

Billig, M. (1991). *Ideology and Opinions*. Sage, London.

Brown, J.S., Collins, A. and Duguid, P. (1989). Situated cognition and the culture of learning. *Educational Researcher*, Jan–Feb, 32–42.

Brown, J.S. and Duguid, P. (1991). Organisational learning and communities of practice. *Organisational Science*, **2**, (1), 40–57.

Brown, J.S. and Duguid, P. (1993). Stolen knowledge. *Educational Technology*, March, 10–15.

Button, E and Lee, J. (1987). *Talk and Social Organisation*. Multiliqual Matterns Ltd, Clevedon.

Chaiklin, S. and Lave, J. (1993). (eds). Understanding Practice. Cambridge University Press, Cambridge.

Edwards, D. and Potter, J. (1992). *Discursive Psychology*. Sage, London.

Edwards, N. and Mercer, N. (1987). *Common Knowledge: The Development of Understanding in the Classroom*. Routledge, London.

Fleming, W.G. (1986). The interview: a neglected issue in research on student learning. *Higher Education*, **15**, 547–63.

Fleming, W.G. (1987). Student learning work: grounds for an in situ analysis. *Instructional Science*, **16**, 109–22.

Fleming, W.G. (1990). The observation of educational events. Medical Education Research Booklet No 5. *Medical Education*, **24**, 190–203.

Garfinkel, H. (1967). *Studies in Ethnomethodology*. Prentice Hall, Engleswood Cliff, N.J.

Gilbert, G.N. and Mulkay, M. (1984). *Opening Pandora's Box: A Sociological Analysis of Scientists' Discourse*. Cambridge University Press, Cambridge.

Heath, C. (1986). *Body Movement and Speech in Medical Interaction*. Cambridge University Press, Cambridge.

Hennessy, S. (1993). Situated cognition and cognitive apprenticeship: implications for classroom learning. *Studies in Science Education*, **22**, 1–41.

Heritage, J. (1984). *Garfinkel and Ethnomethodology*. Polity Press, Cambridge.

Latour, B. and Woolgar, S. (1986). *Laboratory Life: The Construction of Scientific Facts*. Princeton University Press, New Jersey.

Laurillard, D. (1993). *Rethinking University Teaching: A Framework for the Effective Use of Educational Technology*. Routledge, London.

Lave, J. (1988). *Cognition in Practice*. Cambridge University Press, Cambridge.

Lave, J. and Wenger, E. (1991). *Situated Learning: Legitimate Peripheral Participation*. Cambridge University Press, Cambridge.

Lave, J. (1992). Word problems: a microcosm of theories of learning. In P. Light and G. Butterworth, (eds.), *Context and Cognition*. Harvester Wheatsheaf, New York.

Lave, J. (1993). The practice of learning. In S. Chaiklin, and J. Lave, (eds.), *Understanding Practice*. Cambridge University Press, Cambridge.

Lynch, M. (1985). *Art and Artifact in Laboratory Science*. Routledge and Kegan Paul, London.

Marton, F. (1981). Phenomenography – describing conceptions of the world around us. *Instructional Science*, **10**, 177–200.

Mehan, H. (1979). *Learning Lessons: Social Organisation in the Classroom*. Harvard University Press, Cambridge, Mass.

Potter, J. and Wetherell, M. (1987). *Discourse and Social Psychology*. Sage, London.

Säljö, R. (1988). Learning in educational settings: methods of inquiry. In P. Ramsden, (ed.), *Improving Learning: New Perspectives*. Kogan Page, London.

Säljö, R. and Wyndhamn, J. (1990). Problem-solving, academic performance and situated reasoning. A study of joint cognitive activity in the formal setting. *British Journal of Educational Psychology*, **60**, 245–54.

Säljö, R. and Wyndhamn, J. (1993). Solving everyday problems in the formal setting: an empirical study of the school as context for thought. In S. Chaiklin, and J. Lave (eds.), *Understanding Practice*. Cambridge University Press, Cambridge.

Shone, D. and Atkinson, P. (1983). Ethnography and conversational analysis. In M. Hammersley (ed.), *The Ethnography of Schooling*. Nafferton Books, Humberside.

Silverman, D. (1987). *Communication and Medical Practice*. Sage, London.

Silverman. D. (1993). *Interpreting Qualitative Data*. Sage, London.

Walkerdine, V. (1988). *The Mastery of Reason: Cognitive Development and the Production of Rationality*. Routledge, London.

Young, M.F. (1993). Instructional design for situated learning. *Educational Technology Research and Development*, **41**(1), 43–58.

Appendix: Transcription

1	I	I'm going to (.) suggest some fairly broad themes for our discussion,
2		and I hope that eh all sorts of detail about different bits of the course
3		will come out eh under those headings. But there may well be lots of
4		things that don't come up that you'd like to talk about so please feel
5		free to raise any issue that you feel is of importance, em, something
6		that's cropped up during the course so far, something you (.) you want
7		to comment on. The broad themes that I'm going to raise with you are
8		your expectations, (.) in what sense do you feel your expectations are
9		being fulfilled on the course? What about the balance and mix of
10		things that you've done during this term, how have you found that?
11		What do you feel are, so far, (.) over the term, the strengths and
12		weaknesses of this course? Then, any comments on individual
13		subjects that have come up during the term that you'd like to make?
14		And then any perceptions of the future (.) of the course, what's going
15		to happen next, any comments you have on that. (.) And then in the
16		middle of all that, other things that you want to raise. (.) So we don't
17		need to agree. What we're trying to do is to get as wide a range of
18		views on the course as we can, give everybody who wants to
19		comment on an aspect of the course an opportunity to do so, (.) so do
20		(.) chip in as and when you feel you would like to. If I give you a very
21		broad question for starters like (.) eh to what extent do you feel that
22		your expectations are being met. Would anyone like to (.) start on that
23		theme?

S1   I think it's very difficult at this stage of the course to talk about expectations. I think we are still in our, eh, you know, initial stages, just groping, sort of trying to find our way around/

I   Right

S1   into the course. (.) I don't know about others, but this is the way I feel.(.)

I   How do others feel about that?

S2   I see it so far as being just a- a- sort of familiarising, (.) getting to know everybody else on the course, getting to know the tutors an' getting to know the structures of the course. I'm still not absolutely clear about where it's going or where we're expected (.) to be going.

I   Right, and how- how does- does that feel OK?

S2   It feels OK, Yes. (.)

S3   I'm finding that, eh, I'm trying to organise myself more and more, from the very first day I attended the course, to find time, and I can never find the time to do things, and I'm just getting more and more confused. I'm spending more time organising myself rather than doing anything.

Ss+I   Laughter

S4   It's- it's quite difficult at this stage in that, em, (.) there's a lot of sort of background reading we need to get under our belt, em, in order to progress, plus we also need to be starting our project and its difficult to find the time to do the two things, and you tend to spend little doing both, eh, it would be nice to get a lot of the reading out of the way and then start the project, e::m

I   How are you handling that (.) dilemma?

S4   Well, its difficult again because we're all in full-time practice, so there is little time, it obviously has to be at weekends or evenings or staying on on a Thursday, I mean, other people don't know, but I 'm at an advantage, I'm fairly near to the University, but other people may have difficulty getting to a library, which you have to do from the point of view of the project. Em::, we've got quite an extensive booklist that we've, em, had added to [gentle laughter] in more ways than one. It seems to be added to at every lecture. Em...

S5   It would have been helpful to have had the booklist somewhat earlier than we did because its a very big booklist, an::d had some guidance as to the level which we should (.) at the start point rather than eh, I think we started at ground level rather than, e::m perhaps been given some guidance as to (.) possibly the level of understanding of statistics and (.) epidemiology that was necessary for a start point. (.)

S6   Eh, well, I don't agree, eh, (.) if you don't mind me saying so. I thought we got the booklist fairly early on.

Ss   Yes, yes

S3   That's what I / / thought, in June or July.

S6   I must- must admit I chose not to (.) read it for two reasons, firstly em, it was over summer holidays and I hadn't really focussed on the start of the course, but secondly, I wasn't quite sure which were going to be the best books out of the long list to read.

S4   It's all taken on a new significance, the books, in that (.) to start with they were just names and now we know there's two or three key texts   that we do really need to read and em I think our eyes have sort of been opened about (.) general practice generally and we're sort of thinking in different directions, but I (.) to a certain extent, its difficult as I say, with the project as well, you just don't tend not to (.) you tend not   to do the reading. You feel you've got to (.) start your project and get that out of the way.

S6   I think, the present is very, I find fairly easy to deal with, I think. This term hasn't been too hard going once we've been able to (.) reasonably keep up to date. I mean the work has really consisted of perhaps reading up on the lectures. We've not been given any assignments. It's more p'rhaps the future that's uncertain. I still find it very difficult to predict actually how much time I'm going to have to put aside in the future. My view was that I wasn't going to start on the booklist until I started on the course. To me the course started at the beginning of October (.) and not before. And I'm not quite sure whether these books I'm going to read over t- (.) over the two years (.) or whether in fact by the end of the second term we're gonna have another (.) load of books, that eh, not that we have to read because it's up to us really how much we put in, but how far- (.) how many it would be useful to read in the next two terms.

I   M::m

S6   So its this idea of not really knowing how much pressure (.) there's going to be in the future and whether we should be (.) trying to organise our time now to cope with that pressure or whether its quite safe to sit and wait for that pressure to come, and then deal with it.

Transcription Symbols

a)   Double slashes (/ /) are used to indicate the point at which overlapping or simultaneous speech begins.

b)   A dot in round brackets (.) indicates an untimed pause. I have not timed any of the pauses in this transcription. Conventional transcripts would include pause lengths, to the nearest tenth of a second.

c)   A hyphen (-) indicates an abrupt stop.

d)   Colons (::) are used to indicate an elongation of the preceding sound.